Ius Municipale Magdeburgense in the Silesian-Małopolska Compilation

Medieval Law and Its Practice

Edited by

John Hudson (*University of St Andrews*)

VOLUME 44

FONTES IURIS POLONICI

SERIES MUNICIPAL LAW

VOLUME IX

The titles published in this series are listed at *brill.com/mlip*

Ius Municipale Magdeburgense in the Silesian-Małopolska Compilation

Latin Texts and English Translation

By

Maciej Mikuła

In cooperation with

Wiktor Dziemski
Anna Kijak

BRILL

LEIDEN | BOSTON

Proofreading and Open Access of this publication have been supported by a grant from the Priority Research Area Heritage under the Strategic Programme Excellence Initiative at Jagiellonian University.

Cover illustration: Jan Łaski presents a copy of the *Commune incliti Poloniae Regni privilegium, constitutionum et indultuum publicitus decretorum approbatorumque…* to the King Alexander I. Copy from the Jagiellonian Library, Shelfmark St. Dr. Cim. 8004. Public domain. https://jbc.bj.uj.edu.pl/dlibra/publication/383652/edition/365138/content Last accessed: 3 June 2025.

The Library of Congress Cataloging-in-Publication Data is available online at https://catalog.loc.gov

Typeface for the Latin, Greek, and Cyrillic scripts: “Brill”. See and download: brill.com/brill-typeface.

ISSN 1873-8176
ISBN 978-90-04-73012-0 (hardback)
ISBN 978-90-04-73503-3 (e-book)
DOI 10.1163/9789004735033

This book is printed on acid-free paper and produced in a sustainable manner.

Contents

Acknowledgments

I would like to express my sincere thanks to the persons whose advice, expertise and kindness have constantly accompanied me during the preparation of the edition.

Many thanks to Dr. Wiktor Dziemski for reviewing the Latin edition with the source base, as well as my translation of the Latin text. I am very grateful to Anna Kijak who peer-reviewed the introduction and the English translation of *Ius municipale Magdeburgense*. My sincere thanks go to Dr. Tomasz Kolowca, with whom I consulted the wordings of old Polish words. Thanks to them, I was able to avoid many errors, nevertheless I take full responsibility for any remaining defects and imperfections. I am very grateful to the staff of the archives and the libraries. Thanks to their kindness I was able to considerably speed up the examination of the copies of the *Commune incliti Poloniae Regni privilegium*. In particular, I would like to thank Wojciech Graś. His expert knowledge enabled me to identify about 20 copies of this early printed book.

I would like to thank Professors Krzysztof Fokt and Maciej Zdanek, with whom I was able to consult my doubts concerning the Latin texts.

Last but not least, I am deeply grateful to Professor Piotr S. Górecki for his friendly support, fruitful discussions and an incredible help in finalising the English translation.

Abbreviations

BJ 168	manuscript of High Court of German Law at the Royal Castle of Wawel in Cracow, in the Jagiellonian Library, Shelfmark 168 III
BJ 169	manuscript of the Cracow city council, in the Jagiellonian Library, Shelfmark 169 III
BJ 170a	manuscript in the Jagiellonian Library, Shelfmark 170a III
C1 (BN 12607)	manuscript in the National Library, Shelfmark 12607 III
C2 (Oss.)	manuscript in the Ossoliński National Institute in Wrocław, Shelfmark Oss. 832/I
C3 (II Q 4)	Żagań manuscript, in the Library of the University of Wrocław, Shelfmark II Q 4
Commune incliti	see Statute
Częstochowa manuscript	see K^{1} (AJG)
D.	*The Digest* of Justinian
Działyński codex I and IV	see S^{5} (Dział. I) and W^{1} (Dział. IV)
Florian manuscript	see K^{3} (Flor.)
II F 8	Henryków manuscript, known also as the Wrocław manuscript, in the Library of the University of Wrocław, Shelfmark II Q 8
JL	see Statute
K^{1} (AJG)	in the Archives of the Pauline Monastery in Częstochowa, Shelfmark AJG II-3
K^{2} (Kiel.)	manuscript in the Library of the Diocesan Seminary in Kielce, Shelfmark RK 45/28
K^{3} (Flor.)	manuscript in Sankt-Florian Abbey in Austria, Shelfmark 551/II
K^{4} (951b)	manuscript in the University Library in Leipzig, Shelfmark 951b
K^{5} (BN 3068)	manuscript in the National Library in Warsaw, Shelfmark 3068 III
Kielce manuscript	see K^{2} (Kiel.)
Leipzig manuscript	see K^{5} (951b)
Przemyśl manuscript	see S^{9} (Przem.)
S^{1} (Gn.)	manuscript in the Archdiocesan Archives at Gniezno, Shelfmark 104
S^{2} (F 143)	manuscript in the Library of the Russian Academy of Sciences in St. Petersburg, Shelfmark F 143

S^3 (Q II 157 (1))	the first text of the Weichbild in MS St.P. Lat. Q II 157 in the Russian National Library in St. Petersburg
S^4 (BN 12600)	manuscript in the National Library in Warsaw, Shelfmark 12600 III
S^5 (Q II 157 (2))	the second text of Weichbild in MS St.P. Lat. Q II 157 in the Russian National Library in St. Petersburg
S^6 (Dział. I)	manuscript in the Library of the Polish Academy of Sciences at Kórnik, Shelfmark 801
S^7 (Plesz.)	Witold Maisel, ed., "Prawo magdeburskie miasta Pleszewa" [The Magdeburg Lawbook of Pleszew], Studia i Materiały do Dziejów Wielkopolski i Pomorza 9/1 (1963)
S^8 (BJ 4405)	Żegota Pauli's manuscript in the Jagiellonian Library, Shelfmark 4405
S^9 (Przem.)	Liber legum, in the State Archive in Przemyśl, Archives of the City of Przemyśl, Shelfmark 428
S^{10} (BOZ)	manuscript in the National Library in Warsaw, Shelfmark BOZ 90
Statute	*Commune incliti Poloniae Regni privilegium, constitutionum et indultuum publicitus decretorum approbatorumque…*, ed. Jan Łaski (Cracoviae, MDVI)
SSp.	[Eike von Repkow], *Sachsenspiegel. Landrecht*, ed. Karl August Eckhart
W^1 (Dział. IV)	manuscript in the Library of the Polish Academy of Sciences at Kórnik, Shelfmark 800
W^2 (Warsz.)	manuscript in in the Library of the University of Warsaw, Shelfmark 5
Warsaw manuscript	see W^2 (Warsz.)
Wawel manuscript	see BJ 168
Żagań manuscript	see C^3 (II Q 4)
Żegota Pauli manuscript	see S^8 (BJ 4045)

The Magdeburg Weichbild in the Silesian-Małopolska Compilation

In the monograph on the Magdeburg *Weichbild* in the Kingdom of Poland (BRILL 2021), I have shown the evolution of the legal text from the emergence of the Silesian-Małopolska compilation in German to the official Latin text published by Jan Łaski (1456–1531) in *Commune incliti Poloniae Regni privilegium*. Although the appendix contains the text of the oldest surviving manuscript kept in the Archdiocesan Archive in Gniezno (manuscript no. 104)—it does not replace the critical edition. In the following section of the introduction, I explain in detail the basis on which the texts forming the present edition were selected and the method used. However, it is already worth mentioning that the main purpose of the present edition was to highlight the differences between the two main versions of the Silesian-Małopolska compilation, namely the Sandomierz version and the Cracow version. It was also necessary to present the official text compiled by Jan Łaski with an English translation. First of all, however, it is necessary to incorporate the main findings of my study on the Magdeburg *Weichbild* into the Silesian-Małopolska compilation, as well as the features of the text in the surviving manuscript transmissions.

The critical edition completes my study of the *Weichbild* in medieval Poland. This does not mean, however, that the work is finished. The texts of the so called *Weichbild* vulgate, both manuscripts and old prints in German, as well as the Latin translation by Mikołaj Jaskier of 1535, still await in depth study.

1 The Importance of the Magdeburg *Weichbild* among the Sources of Municipal Law

In his classic textbook on the history of Polish law sources Stanisław Kutrzeba wrote that the Magdeburg *Weichbild* (Magdeburg *Weichbildrecht, Ius municipale Magdeburgense*) was the most important medieval collection of German law for town and cities incorporated under the Magdeburg law in the Kingdom of Poland.[1] It was a collection of not only the provisions of Saxon customary law, but also judicial regulations in the form of *ortyle* (a Polish word

1 Stanisław Kutrzeba, *Historia źródeł dawnego prawa polskiego* [History of the Sources of Old Polish Law], 2 (Lwów–Warszawa–Kraków, [1926]), pp. 208–211.

 | DOI:10.1163/9789004735033_002

derived from the German *Urteile*—judgments; hereafter referred to as "judgments" or "Magdeburg judgments") of the Magdeburg bench court, dedicated to cities and towns.[2] In addition, it contained constitutional regulations relating to the powers of municipal authorities, as well as residual regulations regarding municipal commerce. A different view can be found in the Polish literature as well, pointing to the "Saxon Mirror" as the fundamental monument of Saxon-Magdeburg law in Poland. This is only partially correct, with regard to the period after 1535. It was then that an edition of the *Weichbild*, the Saxon Mirror and the *Promptuarium iuris Maideburgensis* (i.e., an alphabetical dictionary of subjects present in the two legal monuments in question) was published by Mikołaj Jaskier (1504–1539). In it the Cracow jurist included not only the main text, but also a gloss which was several times larger than the main text and which greatly expanded the content of the original substantive rule.[3] With the gloss the Saxon Mirror became more important than the *Weichbild*. Before that, however, when texts without a gloss were used in Poland, it was the *Weichbild* that contained the basic body of legal regulations. This primacy of the *Weichbild* was undoubtedly recognized by Jan Łaski (1456–1531). Łaski decided, following the example of the manuscripts with the Cracow version of the Weichbild, to label it "Liber primus", leaving the term "secundus" for the Saxon Mirror. Yet there is no doubt that both collections of laws—the *Weichbild* and the Mirror—played an important role as sources of law in Polish towns and cities.[4]

2 The literature on the subject is discussed in: Maciej Mikuła, *Municipal Magdeburg Law (Ius municipale Magdeburgense) in Late Medieval Poland. A Study on the Evolution and Adaptation of Law* (Leiden Boston: BRILL, 2021) [Series: Medieval Law and Its Practice, vol: 30]. See also: Maciej Mikuła, "Das sächsisch-magdeburgische Recht in den Manuskripten der Bibliothek des Priesterseminars in Kielce, Signatur RK 45/28—Ergänzung zu Deutsche Rechtsbücher des Mittelalters," *Zeitschrift der Savigny Stiftung für Rechtsgeschichte: Germanistische Abteilung* 137/1 (2020), pp. 505–510; Wieland Carls, "Rechtsquellen Sächsisch-magdeburgischen Rechts im Untersuchungsgebiet" in: *Sächsisch-magdeburgisches Recht in Tschechien und in der Slowakei. Untersuchungen zur Geschichte des Rechts und seiner Sprache* (Berlin, 2021) [(Ivs Saxonico–Maidebvrgense in Oriente, 5], pp. 113–116; the manuscripts in question, Pa 95 and BJ 168, do not include the Latin texts of the *Weichbild* (pp. 114–115). The research on Magdeburg law in Poland has been summarized by Danuta Janicka: "Wkład polskich historyków prawa w badania nad prawem magdeburskim w XX w. (1945–2010)", *Studia Iuridica Toruniensia* 10 (2013), pp. 46–75; eadem, "Neuere Rechtsgeschichte in Polen in den Jahren 2002–2014," *Zeitschrift für Neuere Rechtsgeschichte* 37 (2015), pp. 130–42.

3 See: Zygfryd Rymaszewski, *Łacińskie teksty Landrechtu Zwierciadła Saskiego w Polsce. Jaskier—tekst główny i noty marginesowe* [Latin texts of the Sachsenspiegel Landrecht in Poland: Jaskier—the main text and the marginal glosses] (Łódź, 1985).

4 Heiner Lück, "Die Verbreitung des Sachsenspiegels und des Magdeburger Rechts in Osteuropa", in: *Der sassen speyghel. Sachsenspiegel—Recht—Alltag*, Vol. 2: *Aus dem Leben gegrif-*

2 The Silesian-Małopolska Compilation

Two basic compilations of the Magdeburg *Weichbild* can be distinguished. The earlier literature on the subject designated them with the terms "Konrad of Opole's compilation" and "*Weichbild* vulgate". Following more recent findings, it is reasonable to use the term "Silesian-Małopolska compilation" instead of "Konrad of Opole's compilation", since we are not certain that the author of the compilation was indeed the translator of the Saxon Mirror from German into Latin, Konrad of Opole (13/14th century).[5] On the other hand, we know that the *Weichbild* compilation in question originated in German in Silesia and underwent modifications and translations into Latin in Małopolska (Lesser Poland). This version prevailed in Poland until the spread of a new Latin translation by Mikołaj Jaskier based on the *Weichbild* vulgate, which was very popular in east Germany, as well as in the Kingdom of Bohemia.[6]

---

fen—ein Rechtsbuch spiegelt seine Zeit. Beiträge u. Katalog zur Ausstellung 'Aus dem Leben gegriffen—ein Rechtsbuch spiegelt seine Zeit', ed. Mamoun Fansa, 2nd ed., (Oldenburg, 1996) [Archäologische Mitteilungen aus Nordwestdeutschland, 10], pp. 43–44; Heiner Lück, *Sachsenspiegel und Magdeburger Recht. Europäische Dimensionen zweier mitteldeutscher Rechtsquellen*, (Hamburg, 1998) [Adiuvat in itinere, 5], pp. 30, 37, 45, 48–49; Heiner Lück, "Prawo magdeburskie jako czynnik identyfikacji europejskiej rodziny miast," in: *Europejskie miasta prawa magdeburskiego: tradycja, dziedzictwo, identyfikacja. Sesja komparatystyczna Kraków, 13–15 października 2006. Materiały konferencyjne*, eds. Anna Biedrzycka and Agnieszka Kutylak-Hapanowicz (Kraków, 2007), p. 48; Heiner Lück, "Das sächsich-magdeburgische Recht als kulturelles Bindeglied zwischen den Rechtsordnungen Ost und Mitteleuropa," in: *Rechts und Sprachtransfer in Mittel- und Osteuropa. Sachsenspiegel und Magdeburger Recht. Internationale und interdisziplinäre Konferenz in Leipzig vom 31. Oktober bis 2. November 2003*, eds. Ernst Eichler, Heiner Lück, and Wieland Carls (Berlin, 2008) [Ivs Saxonico–Maidebvrgense in Oriente, 1], p. 12; Katalin Gönczi, "Städte des Magdeburger Rechts in Osteuropa," in: *Städtische Räume im Mittelalter*, eds. Susanne Ehrich and Jörg Oberste (Regensburg, 2009), pp. 185–186; Heiner Lück, "Sachsenspiegel und Magdeburger Recht. Grundlagen für Europa", *Denkströme. Journal der Sächsischen Akademie der Wissenschaften zu Leipzig* 4 (2010), pp. 81–104 (http://www.denkstroeme.de/heft 4/s_81 104_lueck, accessed 28 April 2023); Wieland Carls, "Rechtsquellen Sächsisch-magdeburgischen Rechts", in: Inge Bily, Wieland Carls, and Katalin Gönczi, *Sächsisch-magdeburgisches Recht in Polen. Untersuchungen zur Geschichte des Rechts und seiner Sprache* (Berlin, 2011) [Ivs Saxonico–Maidebvrgense in Oriente, 2], pp. 86–88.

5 Maciej Mikuła, "Das Magdeburger Weichbildrecht in seiner schlesisch-kleinpolnischen Fassung. Anmerkungen zur Autorschaft und Textevolution," in: *Kulturelle Vernetzung in Europa. Das Magdeburger Recht und seine Städte. Wissenschaftlicher Begleitband zur Ausstellung »Faszination Stadt«*, eds. Gabriele Köster, Christina Link, Heiner Lück (Sandstein Kommunikation, 2018), p. 147ff.

6 Wieland Carls, "Rechtsquellen Sächsisch-magdeburgischen Rechts im Untersuchungsgebiet" in: *Sächsisch magdeburgisches Recht in Tschechien und in der Slowakei*, p. 117.

Few German texts of the Silesian-Małopolska compilation have survived—these include a manuscript kept by the Cracow city council (1308, BJ 169), a Henrician (Wrocław) manuscript from the third quarter of the 14th century with a text from 1306 (II F 8), the *Weichbild* contained in the manuscript kept by the High Court of German Law at the Royal Castle Wawel (BJ 168), as well as two texts placed parallel to the Latin translation (manuscripts of the National Library 12607 III and at the University of Wrocław Library II Q 4). Texts based on the *Weichbild* of the Silesian-Małopolska compilation in German are also to be found in another manuscript from the Jagiellonian Library (BJ 170a).

As a result of comparative analyses of the surviving texts of the Silesian-Małopolska compilation, two versions of that compilation have been distinguished. The first the Sandomierz version, *versio Sandomiriensis*, specifically so named by historians—was written before 1359 by the fourteenth-century author Konrad of Sandomierz. Some manuscripts of this version directly provide information about the person of the translator. There are also surviving Latin texts which, when compared with those of the Sandomierz version, are characterized by differences in the selection of articles from the German base, their arrangement, the wording of the issues, as well as numerous additions incorporating the text of the Magdeburg judgments. These additional *ortyle* came from a collection that originated in Cracow. Hence the suggested name, *versio Cracoviensis*, for the second version of the Silesian-Małopolska compilation. This is not an entirely new translation: its author undoubtedly relied on the work of Konrad of Sandomierz. Nevertheless, the extent of the work he did (including translation of articles not included in the Sandomierz version and verification of Konrad of Sandomierz's translation) justify its being viewed as a new version. It is worth mentioning that Konrad of Sandomierz also prepared a Latin translation of the Saxon Mirror, referred to as *versio Sandomiriensis* as well. In 1975, Zygfryd Rymaszewski recognized that what was at that time known as the Sandomierz version varied intrnally, and suggested that there were two redactions, which he called *versio Sandomiriensis* I and II.[7] My further research revealed that in the case of the *Weichbild* the differences were so significant that it was not enough to indicate two redactions of one *versio Sandomiriensis*, and that two separate versions, Cracow and Sandomierz, had to be distinguished instead.

The Cracow version probably originated shortly after the Sandomierz version. A comparative analysis has shown that its features can be found already in

---

7 Zygfryd Rymaszewski, *Łacińskie teksty Landrechtu Zwierciadła Saskiego w Polsce. Versio Vratislaviensis, versio Sandomiriensis, Łaski* [Latin Texts of the Landrecht of the Sachsenspiegel in Poland: Versio Vratislaviensis, versio Sandomiriensis, Łaski] (Łódź, 1975), *passim*.

the second oldest surviving manuscript of the *Weichbild* from 1368, now stored in the Library of the Russian Academy of Sciences in St. Petersburg (F 143). There may have been at least two reasons for producing a new translation: to compensate for deviations from the German base and to correct the shortcomings of Konrad of Sandomierz's translation. The unknown author's intention was put into effect only partially—the correction of some of the faults and inaccuracies of the Latin translation did not lead to other errors being avoided. Significantly, the Cracow version was originally devoid of additional regulations derived from the Magdeburg judgments. This is evidenced by texts in the Florian (Flor.), Częstochowa (AJG) and Kielce (Kiel.) manuscripts.

Texts belonging to the two versions were not made uniform. With the *versio Sandomiriensis*, two "lines" of development can be distinguished. The first starts with the oldest surviving text of the Latin *Weichbild*—manuscript No. 104 from the Gniezno Archdiocesan Archive. It contains several characteristic omissions and modifications that appear in several other manuscripts from the 15th and early 16th centuries (Dział. I, Przem., Plesz., BOZ). The other "line" (F 143, BN 12600, Q II 157 (2), Q II 157 (1), BJ 4405) lacks these omissions. It is worth mentioning that *Weichbild* users compared the copies available to them and the additions to the deficiencies in the first development "line" were marked in the form of notes.

It is also necessary to mention the two texts preserved in the Działyński IV codex (Kórnik Library of the Polish Academy of Sciences, 800) and the manuscript stored in the University of Warsaw Library (no. 5). They share many features with the Cracow version, but at the same time they are heavily truncated, as selected articles also present in the Saxon Mirror were removed from them. This feature makes it possible to distinguish the Wawel variant of the Cracow version. The name for this variant comes from the fact that the Latin wording of Dział. IV and Warsz. contains modifications that correspond to the features of the German *Weichbild* preserved in the manuscript of the High Court of German Law at the Royal Castle of Wawel (BJ 168). It should be noted that in the Dział. IV manuscript the copyist included a dozen passages from Chełmno Law (*ius Culmense*).

The present edition takes into account composite manuscripts as well. By this term I mean manuscripts containing texts that are a compilation of the Sandomierz and Cracow versions. We can distinguish three such manuscripts devoid of additional Magdeburg judgments (AJG, Kiel., Flor), and two that are generally based on the Sandomierz version and are supplemented with the additional Magdeburg judgments (951b, BN 3068).

The research carried out so far ultimately makes it possible to identify the following groups of texts:

- Sandomierz version, first variant: a developmental line running from the oldest manuscript of Gn.,
- Sandomierz version, second variant: a different developmental line, devoid of the characteristic features of the Gn. line and thus originally closer to the German base of the *Weichbild* known from the 1308 manuscript used by the Cracow city council (BJ 169),
- Cracow version devoid of additional Magdeburg judgments that appear in composite manuscripts,
- Wawel variant preserved in manuscripts Dział. IV and Warsz.,
- Cracow version with additional Magdeburg judgments,
- composite manuscripts devoid of the additional judgments,
- composite manuscripts with the additional judgments.

The medieval evolution of the *Weichbild*, culminating in the official text issued by Jan Łaski in *Commune incliti Poloniae Regni privilegium*.

3 Selection of Texts for Editing

When embarking on the editorial work, it was necessary to decide in what form the *Weichbild* texts should be textually arranged and prepared for publication today. The fundamental question, valid for all legal texts, is: which form of editing is more useful to the researcher? Should an edition of all the texts be made available, since each was used on an equal footing in legal practice, or should a uniform critical edition be prepared, an edition that, yes, would include all the variations in the complex footnote apparatus (in the case of the twenty surviving texts of the *Weichbild*), but would force the user to reconstruct the wording of a particular text? It should be noted that so far two *Weichbild* texts have been published in "classic" paper form in the Silesian-Małopolska compilation. Witold Maisel published a text present in the Pleszew town register, containing about half of the articles.[8] The full text from the oldest surviving Gniezno manuscript was published in a monograph on the *Weichbild* in the medieval Kingdom of Poland.[9]

In the case of legal texts, it is desirable to edit all surviving copies, as each of them had the value of an equal authentic text in practice. This was the approach of the editors of 15th-century Polish land statutes, Bolesław Ula-

8 Witold Maisel, "Prawo magdeburskie miasta Pleszewa" [Magdeburg Law of the City of Pleszew], *Studia i Materiały do Dziejów Wielkopolski i Pomorza* 9/1 (1963), pp. 67–82.

9 Maciej Mikuła, *Municipal Magdeburg Law*, pp. 388–430.

nowski, Franciszek Piekosiński and Stanisław Kutrzeba.[10] On the other hand, leaving the researcher without tools to compare the surviving texts is an insufficient solution. An electronic edition meets both demands. The preserved Latin texts of the Magdeburg *Weichbild* of the Silesian-Małopolska compilation have been published in full in the knowledge base "IURA. Sources of Law from the Past".[11] In addition, a concordance table has been prepared and provided with hyperlinks referring to individual articles. The use of the Collatex tool, in turn, makes it possible to carry out an automatic comparison of the texts.

A critical edition not only provides source material, but also constitutes a kind of culmination of analytical work. In the case of legal texts, it can be the closure of research on the meaning and fate of legal regulations, showing the evolution of texts the task of which was to shape social reality. Note that in the case of the Statutes of Casimir the Great (1333–1370) we have an edition of the individual surviving texts in the *Archiwum Komisji Prawniczej* (Law Commission Archive), but there is also a successful reconstruction of the Statutes of Wielkopolska,[12] a critical reconstruction of the Statutes of Małopolska[13] and a critical edition according to the text printed in the 1488 *Syntagmata*.[14] The edition included in the present volume is the result of a critical analysis of the legal text and a compilation of texts showing the most important developmental lines of the *Ius municipale Magdeburgense* in Poland.

The present edition consists of three texts. The first is the Sandomierz version, for which the basic text is that from the Dział. I manuscript of 1455. This choice requires justification. None of the surviving texts of the Sandomierz version can be considered compatible with the "autograph text" of Konrad of Sandomierz. In particular, none includes the oldest surviving text of Gn.—as has already been mentioned, it contains minor deficiencies that are not present in other manuscripts comprising the Sandomierz version: Dział. I, Przem., Plesz.,

10 The editions were included in the *Archiwum Komisji Prawniczej* [Law Commission Archives] series.

11 https://iura.uj.edu.pl/dlibra/collectiondescription/5 (accessed 21.01.2023).

12 *Statuty Kazimierza Wielkiego. Cz. 2, Statuty wielkopolskie* [Statutes of Casimir the Great. Part 2, Statutes of Wielkopolska], ed. Ludwik Łysiak (Poznańskie Towarzystwo Przyjaciół Nauk, Warszawa: PWN, 1982).

13 *Statuty Kazimierza Wielkiego* [Cz. 1] [Statutes of Casimir the Great. [Part 1]], ed. Oswald Balzer, from a posthumous manuscript published by Zdzisław Kaczmarczyk, Michał Sczaniecki, Stefan Weyman (Poznań: Poznańskie Towarzystwo Przyjaciół Nauk, 1947).

14 *Polskie statuty ziemskie w redakcji najstarszych druków (Syntagmata)* [Polish land statutes in the redaction of the oldest printed copies (Syntagmata)], eds. Ludwik Łysiak, Stanisław Roman (Wrocław, 1958) [Starodawne Prawa Polskiego Pomniki, seria II, Pomniki Prawa Polskiego, dział I: Prawo ziemskie, t. 2]

BOZ and 951b. On the other hand, among the manuscripts without these deficiencies, none has the provisions featured in the texts derived from Gn. The choice of Dział. I was dictated by the fact that it is the most complete text. First, it contains a complete list of rubrics in the form of a separate register (some of the rubrics also appear next to the provisions themselves). It contains a prologue as well as an elaborate *incipit* and *conclusio libri*. It also contains a group of articles characteristic of the Sandomierz version. Moreover, mistaken omissions from the text by the original copyist were completed by a later commentator, as noted. The commentator also inserted the passages missing from Gn., Dział. I, Przem., Plesz., BOZ and 951b. Dział. I is also the most heavily commented manuscript of the Sandomierz version. Numerous notes contain translations of terms into Polish as well as *regulae iuris*.

The Cracow version is published together with the Sandomierz version. The basis here could only be two manuscripts: BN 12607 and II Q 4. They are the only ones that have preserved a basically complete text, including characteristic additions taken from the Magdeburg judgments. Oss., as a result of the loss of several pages, lacks more than thirty of the original articles. BN 12607 has been chosen as a text probably older and more complete than II Q 4. The textual footnotes indicate variations that appear in Oss. and II Q 4 (the Cracow version with judgments), Dział. IV and Warsz. (the Wawel variant), AJG, Kiel, Flor. (composite manuscripts—including passages corresponding to the Cracow version), and additions of Magdeburg judgments, that also appear in the composite manuscripts 951b and BN 3068.

The official text in the Statute of Jan Łaski was published separately. The text was based on aforementioned texts of the Sandomierz and Cracow versions. The editors of the Statute would often construct a given provision by drawing on both versions, seeking to provide the broadest possible content. One example is Article 1. Its form in the Statute includes additions characteristic of both versions. The method used in the drafting of the Statute text makes the inclusion of comments on the Statute expressed in Dział. I or BN 12607 inadvisable. The inclusion of the Statute variations would make the present edition unreadable. That is the main reason why the Statute was published separately (an exception is the Prologue). It is worth mentioning that previous research has shown significant similarities between the text of the Statute, and the *Weichbild* contained in manuscripts BJ 4405 and II Q 4.

In the present edition, Jan Łaski's official statutory text is accompanied by an English translation.

This edition does not include the German texts of the Silesian-Małopolska compilation. Again, the rationale for and against including these texts had to be carefully considered. Elsewhere I have called for a critical study of the oldest law book of the Cracow city council from 1308 (manuscript BJ 169) and the legal collection of the High Court of German Law at the Castle of Wawel (manuscript BJ 168), which contain two of the five surviving German texts. In the end, without prejudging whether all five German texts would be published separately or together with other texts of Saxon-Magdeburg law, in the present editions of the manuscripts in question, I decided to focus on the selected Latin texts.

4 Rules for Providing Variations in Footnotes

The first letter-note to the article informs us which manuscripts have been included for comparison with the basis of either the Sandomierz or Cracow versions. This is important especially in the case of texts classified as composite, since both versions were used in their creation. The footnote also indicates cases where the article was omitted by the copyist or the text has not been preserved due to lost manuscript pages. The order of comparison is listed below, article numbers are given after the Dział. I:

Texts of the Sandomierz version—variations in Dział. I [S^6]

Gn. [S^1]	complete articles of the Sandomierz version
F 143 [S^2]	missing articles: prologus, 31, 48, 55, 71, 94, 95, 98, 110–117
II Q 157 (1) [S^3]	missing articles: prologus, 68, 113–117
BN 12600 [S^4]	missing articles: 110, 114, 116, 117
II Q 157 (2) [S^5]	missing articles: 110, 114, 116, 117
Plesz. [S7]	missing articles: 55–117
BJ 4405 [S^8]	missing articles: prologus, 38, 111–117; gloss on Article 95 and gloss on Article 97 at the Cracow version
Przem. [S^9]	missing articles: prologus, 110–117
BOZ 90 [S^{10}]	missing articles: 95, 105, 113, 114

Composite texts

AJG [K^1]	arrangement of articles according to the Cracow version, variations are presented in the edition of the Cracow version except for articles 37, 55, 76, 77—variations of these articles are presented in the edition of the Sandomierz version; articles 76 and 77 are from the Sandomierz version; missing articles: prologus, 54, 57
Kiel. [K^2]	arrangement of articles according to the Cracow version, divergences are presented in the edition of the Cracow version

	except for articles 37, 55, 76, 77—variations of these articles are presented in the edition of the Sandomierz version; articles 76 and 77 are from the Sandomierz version; missing articles: prologus, 54, 57
Flor. [K3]	articles 1–60 according to the Cracow version, articles duplicated 60–end according to the Sandomierz version; there is a prologus; variations in articles 57, 60–109 are presented in the edition of the Sandomierz version, variations in articles 1–56, 58–60 are presented in the edition of Cracow version
951b [K4]	arrangement of articles according to the Sandomierz version, variations are presented in the edition of the Sandomierz version except for article 66; three articles not appearing in the Sandomierz version (according to BN 12607 numbering Art. 123 pars 2, 124, 125) are presented in the edition of the Cracow version; additions characteristic of Cracow version are presented by articles 12, 13, 14, 18, 68, 73, 74, 90, 95, 97, 105; missing articles: prologus
BN 3068 [K5]	arrangement of articles according to the Sandomierz version, variations are presented in the edition of the Sandomierz version except for article 3, divergences for duplicated articles 38, 66, 77, 85 are presented in editions of both versions (*versio Sandomiriensis* and *versio Cracoviensis*); article not appearing in Sandomierz version (according to numbering BN 12607 art. 83) is presented in the Cracow version; additions characteristic of the Cracow version are presented by articles 7, 9, 12, 58, 68, 73, 74 (the addition occurs twice in the manuscript, both versions included), 97; missing articles: prologus

Texts of the Wawel variant—variations in BN 12607 [C1]

Dział. IV [W1]	arrangement of articles according to the Cracow version; article 37 in the Sandomierz version, but an appendix from the Chełmno Law in this article in the Cracow version; missing articles: 55–57, 81
Warsz. [W2]	arrangement of articles according to the Cracow version; missing manuscript pages resulted in missing articles: 1–74

Texts of the Cracow version—divergences posted at BN 12607 [C1]

Oss. [C2]	lack of manuscript pages resulted in missing articles: 1–29, 31, 62–64
II Q 4 [C3]	articles in German only: 8, 113

The composite nature of AJG, Kiel, Flor. and BN 3068 is evident in the duplication of articles from both versions: *versio Sandomiriensis* and *versio Cracoviensis*. That is why in the case of the Florian manuscript, Article 60, and in the Częstochowa, Kielce and BN 3068 manuscripts, different versions of Article 77 are compared with the basic text of both the Sandomierz and Cracow versions. In the case of the Leipzig manuscript (951b), the variations are marked in the Dział. I manuscript, but passages from the Cracow version have been compared with the BN 12607 manuscript. In addition, although the articles of AJG, Kiel. and Dział. IV are generally compared within the framework of the Cracow version, a comparison with Art. 37 has been made with regard to Dział. I, since they are closer in this case to the Sandomierz version than to the Cracow version, and Articles 55 and 76 are missing from the Cracow version altogether. On the other hand, Article 83 is missing in the Sandomierz version according to the numbering of BN 12607, and since it appears in BN 3068—it has been compared with the basis of the Cracow version.

5 Article Rubrics

Rubrics belonged to those fragments of medieval legal texts that copyists could modify freely. Hence the considerable number of textual variations, especially since some texts were also provided with registers of titles. An index of rubrics—a register—occurs in several texts, Dział. I and BN 12607, which form the basis of the present edition—and in AJG, Kiel., Flor., Przem. and 951b. In Dział. I and BN 12607 the index precedes the regulations, in the others it is placed at the end of the *Weichbild*. Sometimes the lack of a separate register was compensated by placing headings next to the articles. In several cases the texts contain both a register and rubrics next to articles. These approaches are specified in the following summary:

Texts of the Sandomierz version

Gn.	no register; set of rubrics next to articles; variations placed adjacent to Dział. I
F 143	no register; rubrics next to Articles 4, 7, 8, 10, 13–19, 42, 45, 46, 54, 93, 97; variations placed adjacent to Dział. I
Q II 157 (1)	no register; rubrics next to Articles 2–26, 57–61, 69; variations next to Dział. I; rubrics placed adjacent to articles that resulted from the division of the original provisions into smaller ones are included in footnotes in the text of the articles
BN 12600	no register; set of rubrics next to articles; variations placed adjacent to Dział. I

Q II 157 (2)	no register; set of rubrics next to articles; variations next to Dział. I
Dział. I	rubric register: basis of the edition; no rubrics next to Articles 32–52, 64–117, variations from rubrics next to articles marked *ad articulum*
Przem.	in rubric register, Article 59 is omitted; no rubric next to Article 1; variations next to Dział. I, variations from rubrics next to register marked *in indice rubricarum*
Plesz.	no register; no rubrics next to Articles 1–6; variations placed adjacent to Dział. I
BJ 4405	no register; no rubric next to Art. 1; variations next to Dział. I
BOZ	no register; complete rubrics next to articles; variations placed adjacent to Dział. I

Composite texts

AJG	Article 1 omitted from rubric register; no rubric next to articles; variations placed adjacent to Dział. I
Kiel.	Article 1 omitted from rubric register; no rubrics next to articles; variations placed adjacent to Dział. I
Flor.	Articles 110–117 omitted from rubric register; rubrics present next to Articles 3, 4, 5, 6, 11; variations placed adjacent to Dział. I, variations in rubrics next to articles marked *ad articulum*
951b	register present and set of rubrics next to articles; rubrics and subrubrics repeat the initial passage of the provision—not included as variations
BN 3068	no register; no rubrics next to articles 1, 2, 22, 47, 66, 109; complete rubrics next to Dział. I, in BN 12607 only Article 83 (according to the numbering of BN 12607); rubrics next to articles that resulted from the division of the original provisions into smaller ones are included in the footnotes in the text of the articles

Wawel variant

Dział. IV	no register; rubrics are missing next to articles 103, from 114 to the end (according to BN 12607 numbering); full text of rubrics is given next to BN 12607
Warsz.	no register; text incomplete, rubrics next to articles 80–88, 90–97, 100–102, 104–113 (according to BN 12607 numbering); full wording of rubrics next to BN 12607

Text of the Cracow version

BN 12607	register the basis of the edition; rubrics next to the articles are missing
Oss.	no register; text incomplete, rubrics next to surviving articles; full wording of rubrics next to BN 12607 is given; rubrics next to articles that resulted from the division of the original rules into smaller ones are provided in footnotes in the text of the articles
11 Q 4	no register; rubrics next to articles written in lighter ink by author of basis, missing next to articles: 12, 19, 35, 48, 50–55, 58–61, 59–73, 75–94, 96–112, 115–127 (according to numbering of BN 12607); full wording of rubrics next to BN 12607

Text in the Statute no register; complete rubrics given in the edition of the *Weichbild* in the Statute

Dział. 1 Register consists of short summaries. The main text lacks rubrics next to Articles 32–52 and from Article 64 onward. Those that are next to the provisions are almost identical to the wording of the Register, except for minor differences next to Articles 7, 12, 15, 17, 23 and 61, as noted in the Register edition. Numerous provisions have a distinctive *Item* at the beginning of the rubric (a detail retained only in the Register in Przem.). Rubrics 76 and 77 were placed in reverse order present in the articles.

In BN 12607 the rubrics are generally the initial wording of the articles, with the original *folio* number indicated. Titles are not repeated with individual articles.

The register in Flor. is structured similarly to that in Dział. 1—the rubric is a very short summary along with the article number. The two texts are similar, with the list in Flor. ending with the Jewish oath, and therefore not including the provisions attached to the *Weichbild* from the "Constitution of Courts" (otherwise known as the "Treaty on the Constitution of Magdeburg"). The Florian manuscript lacks rubrics next to the rules except for a few succinct ones next to Articles 3, 4, 5, 6 and 11, as noted in the edition. The rubrics in the register correspond to the articles of the Sandomierz version and variations have been included next to the rubrics of the Dział. 1.

In the register in the AJG, a short summary (similar to that of Dział. 1) is followed by a few initial words of the provision. The summary usually begins with *De*. Rubrics do not occur with provisions. The list of rubrics comes from the Sandomierz version and does not correspond to the contents of the *Weichbild* in the AJG, which is a compilation of the Sandomierz and Cracow versions. As a result, two rubrics appear in the register with no corresponding articles (Articles 54 and 57 according to the numbering of Section I). The register in Kiel. is nearly identical to that of the AJG, there are only minor linguistic differences noted in the footnotes.

In Przem. the register essentially consists of an abbreviated version of the headings, placed adjacent to the articles. In addition, several words of the provision (1–9, 11–20) are given next to the first dozen or so titles. A few articles (61, 106, 108/109) were divided into smaller units in the rubric list, one (59) was omitted from the register. Four articles (24, 51, 76, 100)—which applies to both the provisions, rubrics and their register—are divided into smaller ones relative to the articles in Dział. I. The wording of the rubrics of these smaller units (subrubrics) is given in a footnote within the provision. In the edition the text of the rubrics next to the provisions is included as a default, and the register of the rubrics is included only when the text differs from that next to the provisions in other ways than just by their summaries.

The register in the Leipzig manuscript 951b generally consists of the initial words of the articles. For this reason their contents are not cited in the edition. The titles in the register mostly follow the rubrics next to the articles, the differences being a shorter or longer wording of the phrase taken from the beginning of the provision. Only in Articles 1–5 are the headings almost identical to Dział. I; the differences (in Articles 1 and 3) are cited in this edition. Numerous articles in the Leipzig manuscript are divided into smaller units (Articles 2, 4, 5, 6, 7, 9, 11, 14, 16, 18, 20, 23, 24, 25, 26, 32, 35, 36, 37, 39, 42, 46, 47, 49, 51, 57, 60, 61, 65, 77, 80, 86, 87, 102, 105, 116 and 121). They, too, have their headings in the register and next to the articles, and the wording is the same as the beginning of the provisions they announce. For this reason they are not included in the edition. In two cases (Articles 13 and 14) the passage transcribed from the Cracow version has its heading only in the register and its wording, too, is the initial passage of the provision in question. Articles 105 part 3 and 116 part 2 have their headings exclusively in the register. In addition, the register mentions the last two articles, which have not survived in the manuscript.[15]

The division of articles into smaller units also occurs in Q II 157 (1), Oss. and in BN 3068. Unlike in the Leipzig manuscript, their titles usually have the original wording. They are marked in the lettered footnotes introduced in the edition of the main text—as either rubric or subrubric, depending on whether an article is divided into two smaller ones or parts are highlighted within one article.

15 [*126*] De eo. Hic intelligere et audire potestis. [*127*] De eo. Eodemmodo sicut scultetus citat burgravium.

Variations of the wording of rubrics are included for F 143, II Q 157 (1), BN 12600, II Q 157 (2), AJG, Kiel., Flor., Przem., Plesz., BN 4405, BOZ, BN 3068 in the edition of Dział. I. In contrast, the rubrics in Oss., II Q 4, Dział. IV and Warsz. are so diverse that the variations have been abandoned and their full wording is introduced in the footnotes to BN 12607 (refecences between asterixes). Rubrics for the Statute of Jan Łaski are included in his edition next to the provisions. For those texts in which rubrics appear both in the index and next to the articles, when wording variants are provided, they were marked *in indice rubricarum* and *ad articulum*, respectively.

The variants of rubrics in Dział. I do not take into account the original (usually misleading) numbering of articles. Additions of summaries of regulations by later commentators, even if put in the place of the rubric, are noted in the critical apparatus as notes next to the text of the regulations. When reading the edition, it is useful to take into account the contents of the list in the section "4. Rules for providing variations in footnotes", which helps to determine which articles were missing rubrics.

6 Features of Individual Texts

The characteristics of the manuscripts (especially their content) are described in the already mentioned monograph *Municipal Magdeburg Law*. The main features of the individual *Weichbild* texts are summarized below, largely on the basis of the findings published in that monograph.

Text from the Gniezno manuscript (Archdiocesan Archives of Gniezno, 104). The oldest surviving text of the 1359 Magdeburg *Weichbild* came from the hand of the scribe Mikołaj of Cieszyn (died before 1359). It contains an incipit and excipit, as well as a prologue. The copyist omitted passages relative to the archetype of the Sandomierz version: Articles 24, 46 and 83; their absence makes the text incomplete. The text was introduced carefully, the titles of the articles were written in red ink, as were the initials of the first words of the provisions. A particularly ornate initial begins the first article. Users' notes are only corrections to the text, and are included in the present edition. The text has been published before.[16]

Text from the manuscript of the Library of the Russian Academy of Sciences in St. Petersburg, Ban F 143. Work on the second oldest text was completed by

16 See footnote 9.

the copyist on 26 February 1368. A significantly modified Sandomierz version was introduced in neat handwriting, with the initials of the articles inscribed in red ink and the titles of the articles underlined in red as well. These modifications sometimes also come close to the features of the Cracow version (but without additional Magdeburg judgments); hence the likelihood that the time of preparation of the Cracow version should be dated before 1368. The text does not contain a set of articles or a set of rubrics. The writer made numerous modifications to the basic text, and also made authorial additions, such as Article 1, regarding the powers of the city council to elect a mayor.

Text from the manuscript of the National Library in Warsaw, BN 12600 III / second text in the manuscript of the National Library of Russia in St. Petersburg, Lat. Q II 157. Dated 1421, the text in BN 12600 was compiled by Mikołaj of Smogorzewo. It is nearly identical to that of the second of the *Weichbild* texts, contained in manuscript Q II 157. Both are characterized by peculiar changes in wording that do not fundamentally affect the content of the rules. Yet there are also numerous omissions and, unfortunately, erroneous *lectiones*. That makes both texts translations of a broken legal text that was nevertheless used in practice with all its consequences. BN 12600 is two-column neat work, the titles of the articles are alternately introduced in either red or blue ink, as are the initials of the first words. The text of Q II 157 (2) was written carelessly, the rubrics are framed and the whole is in uniform brown ink.

First text in the manuscript of the National Library of Russia in St. Petersburg, Lat. Q II 157 (1429). The text of the *Weichbild* in the manuscript in question was written in neat hand. The copyist left space for rubrics and decorative initials, which were only partially entered in red ink. This is a text that features a number of individual deviations from the Sandomierz version. These include omissions and modifications, like the substitution of "Magdeburg" for "Środa Śląska" in Article 4. Another significant addition is a passage in Article 17, according to Gn. numbering, which requires a sick person to be able to sit on a horse in order for a legal act of that sick person to be valid. More than a dozen summaries of the articles were introduced by two commentators (hand A and hand B).

Text from the manuscript of the Library and Archives of the Pauline Monastery in Częstochowa (AJG II-3, Częstochowa manuscript, before 1423) / text from the manuscript of the Library of the Diocesan Seminary in Kielce (RK 45/25, Kielce manuscript, 1429). The twin texts of the *Weichbild* are of composite nature, having been created from the texts of the Sandomierz version and the Cracow version. In terms of the selection and sequence of provisions, features of the Sandomierz version in both texts include the presence of three of the four articles characteristic of the text (according to the Gn. numbering, these are Articles 55, 76 part 1 and 3, 77, with only 57 missing). On the other hand, the text shares with the Cracow version the order of the provisions (52–54, 60–61, 96–97, 102–103, 108–109 according to Gn. numbering) as well as set of *Weichbild* articles from the Constitution of Courts. The *Weichbild* in the AJG was probably written before 1423—an inference suggested by the absence from this text of the 1421/1423 Cracow-Warta Statute, which was usually added immediately after the Statutes of Casimir the Great (these are present in the AJG). The text has a register consisting of a red abstract and the beginning of the article in black ink. Ornate initials in red and blue, sometimes multi-coloured, decorate the individual articles. Kiel. also contains a register constructed similarly to that of the AJG, but the writing of the *Weichbild* text is decidedly careless, the initials being two lines high, written in red ink. The copyist of Kiel. was Peter *pauperus*, parish priest (rector) of Potok. He completed the work on 4 August 1429. Although no direct filiation between the texts can be proven, they are nevertheless characterized by a number of shared modifications, which are marked in the present edition.

Text from the manuscript from the National Library in Warsaw, 12607 III (first half of the 15th century). This is one of the three surviving manuscripts containing the *Weichbild* in the Cracow version with Magdeburg judgments, provided alongside the German text. Typical of the Cracow version is the order of the articles and their selection (including a set of articles from the Constitution of Courts, without articles Gn. 55, 57, 76 part 1 and 3, and 77). The polymorphic structure of the manuscript makes only approximate dating possible. A carefully written text, accompanied by two-page high red initials for the first words of the provisions, precedes the register of articles. The two-paragraph neat text was produced by a scribe different from the one who produced the later register of articles. A characteristic feature of the *Weichbild* in BN 12607 is the significant number of hands—authors of marginal notes. As can be seen, the set consisting of the bilingual *Weichbild*, the Saxon Mirror and a separate set of Magdeburg judgments provided valuable support for legal practice. The register was accompanied by numerous notes. Although they were introduced by several users, one of them (marked B) significantly expanded its content—often starting the phrase *et ibidem* just below the commented provision, the user referred to regulations that were not announced by the original author of the register. The use of different writing materials, the need to enter notes in a limited space as well as, especially, their succinctness make it difficult to identify confidently the commentators' hands. Notes on the article register were entered by several users. The proposed identification is approximate—the limited material makes it impossible to group writing hands with certainly. For the rubric register, the writing hands are distinguished based on the following criteria:

A author of the basis
B fine and neat, dense writing
C tall, slightly slanted letters, characteristic slant to the left in the letter "d", defective writing tool needs correction, ink paler than the black of the main text
D shapely writing, neat, ink paler than the base text
E dark ink, writing not very neat
F dark ink, angular writing, thin pen,
G light ink, thin writing tool, entry full of light, with large letters and wide spacing
H pale ink, thick writing tool
X entry unrelated to the *Weichbild*

Nearly 50 entries were recorded next to the *Weichbild* text, which can be classified as marginal notes. Unfortunately, their succinctness makes it difficult and sometimes impossible to identify unambiguously the writing hands. Hence the following proposal for identifying the phrases that are undoubtedly in the same writing hand:

α clear writing, not very neat, ink without peculiarities, capital Q and capital S consist of several combined elements; similar to hand B in the article register
β careful ductus, clear ink, simple letters
γ less careful ductus, light ink
δ clear writing, thick writing tool, ink insufficiently covered the paper giving the impression of the text being erased,
ε dark ink, shapely letters with a tendency to roundness
ζ dark ink, thick writing tool, no rounding
η clear writing, dark ink, fine ductus

An additional explanation of the term "Franconian field" is placed and the end of the text.

Text from the manuscript from the Sankt-Florian Monastery Library in Austria (Florian, 1453). The *Weichbild* from the Florian manuscript also belongs to the texts that are a composite compilation of the Sandomierz and Cracow versions (without Magdeburg judgments, similar to the *Weichbild* in II Q 4). The main difference is that it is an almost mechanical compilation. There are articles up to Article 59 that contain features of the Cracow version. In addition, a provision is devoted to the *gerada* (women's household items; according to Gn./Dział. I Article 60) occurring twice and containing features from both versions. The text was written carelessly, the space left for initials being only partially filled in. The whole is supplemented with an article register.

Text from the manuscript from the Kórnik Library of the Polish Academy of Sciences, 801 (Działyńscy Codex I, 1455). The so-called Działyńscy Codex I is one of the most interesting medieval legal collections in Poland. The *Weichbild* was probably written down by two people, as is evidenced by the change of writing hand after the first three pages of the *Weichbild*. As a result, Article 7 appears twice. The entire collection was completed in 1455 by S[tanisław] of Opatów in the small town of Solec. Still another hand drew up the register of articles, while the same scribe annotated the rules with red initials. At least two hands of commentators can be distinguished. Their entries next to the text include corrections to the text, as well as legal rules (*regulae iuris*) and translations of legal terms into Polish.

Text from the manuscript from the Kórnik Library of the Polish Academy of Sciences, 800 (Działyńscy Codex IV, 1472) / text from the manuscript of the University of Warsaw Library (Shelfmark 5). Zygfryd Rymaszewski classified the Latin text of the Saxon Mirror in this manuscript as *versio Sandomiriensis II*. In doing so, he wanted to emphasize the dissimilarities between this text and Konrad of Sandomierz's translation. In the case of the *Weichbild*, comparative studies justify the introduction of the name "Wawel variant", as the text shares some passages with the manuscript kept at the High Court of German Law at the Castle of Wawel (Jagiellonian Library manuscript, 168 III). There are also numerous similarities with the Warsaw manuscript, which unfortunately is preserved only in part (from article 75 onward, according to Gn. numbering). Both texts contain a set of articles present in the Constitution of Courts, characteristic of the Cracow version; in addition, Dział. IV includes a prologue. The author of the Wawel variant carefully compared the *Weichbild* with the Saxon Mirror and excluded some of the repeated provisions, which he clearly indicated. Dział. IV contains interesting additions from Chełmno Law (*ius Culmense*), used here as comparative material. The handwriting of the Dział. IV manuscript is excessively careful; the rubrics are in red ink. The handwriting in Warsz. 5 is more careful, the rubrics of the articles are in red as well.

Text from the manuscript from the State Archive in Przemyśl, Archives of the City of Przemyśl 428 (*Liber legum*, 1473–1474). According to currrent research, the *Weichbild* kept in Przemyśl is probably a copy of the text that was used by the Przemyśl city council. Szymon of Jaworów (15th century), the scribe of the Book of Laws, used this text and finished copying the *Weichbild* on 5 March 1473 for use by the chapter of the Przemyśl. The handwriting in the *Weichbild* is neat, the rubrics are introduced with a larger ductus, the initials are decorative, especially the first one. Individual features of the text were introduced deliberately and significantly changed the rules. Thus, the *Weichbild* in the Book of Laws is an example of a legal text being adapted to local needs. In terms of content layout, the copyist dispensed not only with the prologue, which is common in *Weichbild* texts, but also with the rules derived from the Constitution of Courts, inserted after the Jewish oath. The indexes of the rubrics in the Book of Laws, drawn up carelessly in a different hand, begin with the *Weichbild*.

Text from the manuscript from the Ossoliński National Institute, 832/I (Opatów manuscript, 1488). Another text of the Cracow version was written down by Mikołaj, a cleric of the Gniezno diocese (completion date 15 February 1488). Unfortunately, the manuscript is damaged, missing the opening pages and one page inside, as a result of which more than 30 articles of the *Weichbild* (1–30, 68–71) have not survived. The copyist's handwriting is careless, the main text and the headings are in red ink. The numbering of the articles is inadequate. The text contains additions from the Magdeburg judgments and the layout of the articles is typical of the Cracow version. After the articles from the Constitution of Courts, the copyist added an explanation of the term "Franconian field", as in BN 12607.

Text from the manuscript from the Jagiellonian Library, 4405 (manuscript of Żegota Pauli, second half of the 15th century). Next to Dział. I, this is the second text closest in its content to the oldest manuscript of the Gn. However, it lacks the prologue and the provisions taken from the Constitution of Courts; Article 38 is missing as well. The careful double-page text contains red rubrics and initials of the same kind. There are also marginal notes, probably introduced by one hand. They go beyond the *Weichbild* regulations in their content. A text close to BJ 4405 was the basis for Jan Łaski's team working on the *Weichbild* in the Statute. It could not have been BJ 4405 directly, or at least not as the sole text of the Sandomierz version, due to its deficiencies.

Text from the manuscript from the Wrocław University Library, II Q 4 (Żagań manuscript, 15th century). The *Weichbild* in the Żagan manuscript was not written with great care. It is a bilingual text, with the copyist initially attempting to enter small portions of the German text alternately with the Latin text, but later abandoning this idea and entering the German text of full provisions second. On the first two pages the copyist used red ink to distinguish rubrics and certain phrases in the text. The rubrics are written inconsistently, mostly in lighter ink and in equally careless handwriting, and presumably their authorship is the same as that of the base. Articles 9 (according to Dział. 1/Gn. 8) and 114 (according to Dział. 1/Gn. 113), are in German only. The *Weichbild* in II Q 4 represents the Cracow version, because of the selection and arrangement of the articles, and of their content. In addition, some of its features suggest that a text similar to II Q 4 must have been the basis for the work of Jan Łaski's team, as is exemplified by the addition to Article 1 of the statement that: *Et hoc non dimittendo ratione amoris, molestie, ire vel munerum, sicut eos iuvet Deus et sancti eius.*

Text from the Pleszew council register from before 1483 (State Archive in Poznań, Pleszew Town Records, 1/2). The *Weichbild* in the Pleszew council register encompasses about half of the content of the Sandomierz version, that is, 54 articles. According to the editor of the text Witold Maisel,[17] two provisions, not originally part of this text, were subsequently added in other hands. The second is probably a judgment issued by one of the higher courts of German law in Wielkopolska. The initials of the first words and the rubrics were written in red in ink, but only from Article 7 onward. Also, the decorative "P" at the end of the articles serving as a period was written in red. The *Weichbild* from the Pleszew register is close to the Gniezno manuscript in its content and undoubtedly belongs to manuscripts comprising the Sandomierz version.

Text from the manuscript from the Leipzig University Library "Albertina", 951b (Leipzig manuscript, 15th/16th century). The *Weichbild* present in the Leipzig manuscript can be classified as a composite text. Although the basis is the Sandomierz version, similarly to another late text from the BOZ 90 manuscript, the scribe made additions to it, drawn from the Magdeburg judgments, as well as other additions that are characteristic of the Cracow version. At first he did this in the margins of the already copied text, but in the second part he incorporated these additions directly into the main body of the text. One can conclude that the copyist originally had only the text of the Sandomierz version available, and then, having also the second (similar in content to

17 Witold Maisel, "Prawo magdeburskie miasta Pleszewa", p. 66.

the Statute of Jan Łaski), he made the relevant additions. At the end of the manuscript there is a register of articles. The copyist used red ink for the rubrics and decorative initials. The two-column text is written very neatly, with incidental notes that probably did not come from the hand of the author of the base text.

***Weichbild* from the manuscript from the National Library in Warsaw, 3068 III (early 16th century).** The *Weichbild* from the BN 3068 manuscript is one of the most elaborate. The copyist, Tomasz of Bydgoszcz, worked at the beginning of the 16th century and he may have had access to the Statute of Jan Łaski. This composite text uses the Sandomierz version as a basis, which is supplemented with additions characteristic of the Cracow version, with rules of law (*regulae iuris*), and with translations of terms in Polish and other explanations—all of it introduced directly into the main text. Some of these additions, which go beyond the text of the *Weichbild* itself, are similar to the marginal notes present in the Dział. I manuscript. The neatly written text is interspersed with passages in red ink. Compared with the Gn. manuscript, numerous articles are divided into smaller units, which are provided with their own titles. The BN 3068 manuscript can be seen as a private collection of Magdeburg law, containing the author's adaptation of its contents. Undoubtedly, this manuscript requires further, comprehensive and in-depth research.

***Weichbild* from the manuscript from the National Library in Warsaw, Shelfmark BOZ 90 (1513).** The copyist of the *Weichbild* in manuscript BOZ 90 was Marcin Zabowski of Lwówek. This late copy is part of the group of texts comprising the Sandomierz version, close to the Leipzig manuscript. Significant deviations from the Gn. are primarily the omission of three articles (13, 95 and 105 according to the Gn./Dział. I numbering) and more than a dozen substantive differences in the content of the rules. Other dissimilarities are not substantive, but linguistic. The text contains blank spaces for the introduction of initials, and lacks ornamentation, but the titles of the articles are in larger ductus.

***Commune incliti Poloniae Regni privilegium...* by Jan Łaski (1506).** Although the manuscripts referenced above (BN 3068, BOZ) are more recent than the official text in the Statute of Jan Łaski, nevertheless the *Weichbild* contained in *Commune incliti Poloniae Regni privilegium* is presented in this edition at the very end, as the culmination of the evolution of one medieval legal text, crowned by the official approval of the text by King Alexander I (1501–1506). A minimum of fourteen parchment copies were accompanied by an edition of more than 80 paper copies.[18] The present edition of the main text is based on a copy held in the Jagiellonian Library, St. Dr. Cim. 8002, a copy classified as the B2 version.[19] A comparison of the text of the *Weichbild* in the A and B versions allows us to conclude that there were no differences between them.[20] My analyses confirm that the *Weichbild* in the Statute was a compilation that included both Latin versions. Although the BN 3068 manuscript discussed above contains numerous additions derived from the *regulae iuris*, the *Weichbild* in the Statute is the most complete expression in terms of the basic text, including both the full text of the Sandomierz version, and additions specific to the Cracow version. The importance of the *Weichbild* version contained in the Statute is evidenced by the marginal notes of its users. For purposes of the present edition, dozens of copies of the Statute of Jan Łaski have been verified. We also know that some copies were lost after 1939.[21] I was unable to reach several of the printed versions, despite my attempts, which were also hindered by the dramatic circumstances of the Russian invasion of Ukraine.[22] There are

18 Wojciech Graś, "Rozważania nad problemem nakładu Statutu Jana Łaskiego" [Some considerations on the question of the volume of copies of the Statute by Jan Łaski], *BIBLIOTEKA* 26/35 (2022), p. 131. Cf. Piotr Tafiłowski, *Jan Łaski (1456–1531) kanclerz koronny i prymas polski* [Jan Łaski (1456–1531): Grand Chancellor of Poland and Primate of Poland] (Warszawa, 2007), p. 296. Also Edward Potkowski, *Książka rękopiśmienna w kulturze Polski średniowiecznej* [The Handwritten Book in the Culture of Medieval Poland] (Warszawa, 1984), p. 176.

19 This edition uses the original early print folio.

20 Two versions A and B, corresponding in principle to the print on parchment and on paper, are distinguished by Maria Cytowska (*Bibliografia druków urzędowych XVI wieku* [Bibliography of 16th Century Legal and Government Documents] (Wrocław, 1961), pp. 53–54). More variants (A, B1, B3), see *Polonia Typographica Saeculi Sedecimi*, z. IV: *Jan Haller Kraków 1505 1525*, introduction, list of printed copies, eds. Helena Kapełuś, Alodia Kawecka-Gryczowa (Wrocław–Warszawa–Kraków, 1962), p. 40, there is also information about the B variant being stamped on parchment. Another list of variant B (B1, B2, B4) in: Marian Malicki, Ewa Zwinogrodzka, eds., Marian Malicki, Małgorzata Gołuszka, Wanda Ptak-Korbiel, Zofia Wawrykiewicz, Ewa Zwinogrodzka, coop., *Katalog poloników XVI wieku Biblioteki Jagiellońskiej* [Catalogue of Polonica from 16th Century in Jagiellonian Library], 1: A–Ł (Kraków, 1992), pp. 425–427.

21 An example is the collection of the Milanów library, also containing a copy of *Commune incliti Poloniae Regni Privilegium*, which was destroyed and dispersed. See: Albin Koprukowniak, *Biblioteka Włodzimierza księcia Światopełka Czetwertyńskiego w Milanowie* [Library of Vladimir Prince Światopełk Czetwertyński in Milanów], in: *Drogą historii. Studia ofiarowane prof. Józefowi Szymańskiemu w 70. rocznicę urodzin*, eds. Piotr Dymmel, Krzysztof Skupieński, Beata Trelińska (Lublin, 2001), p. 401. A copy from the Płock Theological Seminary Cim. 2. o 482 was stolen in 1940 by the Nazis.

22 Vasyl Stefanyk National Scientific Library of Ukraine in Lviv CT.IV.21212 and CT.IV.21273; V.I. Vernadski National Library of Ukraine, Pal. 1077 I, Pal. 1588, Pal. 1588a, Pal. 1588b. Des-

also incomplete copies, without the *Weichbild*.[23] More than thirty copies of the *Weichbild* lack notes situated next to the text.[24] They do occur, in various forms (sometimes only as *maniculae*), in more than fourty other copies, as summarized in the following list, which includes the sigla used in the present edition:

Bydgoszcz

JL[1] Kazimierz Wielki University Library in Bydgoszcz, S 104; 41 notes

Cracow

JL[2] Czartoryski Library in Cracow (branch of the National Museum in Cracow), Cim. 13 III; the "X" next to selected provisions seems to signify an important passage

JL[3] Czartoryski Library in Cracow (branch of the National Museum in Cracow), Cim. 30 III; with Magdeburg judgments, two notes

JL[4] Czartoryski Library in Cracow (branch of the National Museum in Cra-

---

pite various attempts, it proved impossible to obtain data on the copy stored in the Hebrew Union College Jewish Institute of Religion Cincinati K 2099.

23 Jagiellonian Library St. Dr. Cim. 51, St. Dr. Cim. 8008 and St. Dr. Cim. 8009; The British Museum C.107.g.14. (I used the microfilm Monumenta Germaniae Historica—mf. V 318); Poznań Society for the Advancement of Arts and Sciences 11495 III; Adam Mickiewicz University Library in Poznań SD 9017 III.

24 Staatsbibliothek zu Berlin 4″ Ho 15050; Universitäts und Landesbibliothek Bonn Sav 4′ 152; Książnica Cieszyńska in Cieszyn, CL 1212 III; Emeryk Hutten-Czapski Museum (branch of the National Museum in Cracow): VIII XVI.134, MNK VIII-XVI.190, MNK VIII-XVI.1308; Scientific Library of the Polish Academy of Art and Science and the Polish Academy of Science in Cracow St.Dr. 4022; Gdańsk Library Polish Academy of Science In 20146 4°; Archdiocesan Archives of Gniezno: PL 346, PL 398; Central Library of the Kaunas University of Technology, KTUB Es 72; Kórnik Library of the Polish Academy of Sciences: Cim.F.4117, Cim.F.4139 and Cim.F.4240; Hieronim Łopaciński Provincial Public Library in Lublin P 16 f 26; The John Paul II Catholic University of Lublin, University Library: XVI.1738, XVI.1741, XVI.1760, XVI.1820, XVI.1874; Harvard Library Hollis Houghton Library f typ 556.06.706; Nieborów and Arcadia Musem (branch of the National Museum in Warsaw) I/62; Olomouc Research Library II 7.937; University Library, University of Warmia and Mazury in Olsztyn: ZZ102516, SD BGST.30; Polish Library in Paris, FA 38439 III; Płock Scientific Society XVI.185; Poznań Society of Friends of Learning 14989 III; Raczyńscy Library in Poznań III.J.a.6.; Książnica Pomorska in Szczecin ST7511 (XVI.491.II); Uppsala University Library Sv. Rar. fol. 10:31; The Central Archives of Historical Records in Warsaw dok. perg. no. 5632, SD.III.50; Library of the Higher Metropolitan Seminary of the Archdiocese of Warsaw D.17.D15.(50935); National Library in Warsaw: SD XVI.F.9, SD.XVI.F.88, SD.XVI.F.211, SD.XVI.F.335, SD.XVI.F.350, SD.XVI.F.735; National Museum in Warsaw SD 348; University of Warsaw Library Sd.612.523 and Sd.612.540; Warsaw Public Library XVI. F. 74; Ossoliński National Institute in Wrocław: XVI.F.4088, XVI.F.4089, XVI.F.4092, XVI.F.4320, XVI.F.4654; Wrocław University Library St. Dr. 401097.

cow), Shelfmark Cim. III 1239; sixteen notes

JL^{5} Emeryk Hutten-Czapski Museum (branch of the National Museum in Cracow), 4022; one note

JL^{6} Jagiellonian Library in Cracow, St. Dr. Cim. 8002; seven notes

JL^{7} Jagiellonian Library in Cracow, St. Dr. Cim. 8004; 33 notes

JL^{8} Jagiellonian Library in Cracow, St. Dr. Cim. 8006; thirteen notes, two writing hands (default A, additionally marked B: manus B)

JL^{9} Jagiellonian Library in Cracow, St. Dr. Cim. 8470; *maniculae* only

JL^{10} Scientific Library of the Polish Academy of Art and Science and the Polish Academy of Science in Cracow, 4017 (= 4483W VIIII.-1); two notes

Gdańsk

JL^{11} Gdańsk Library Polish Academy of Science, Uph. F. 1393; sixteen notes

Gniezno

JL^{12} Archdiocesan Archives of Gniezno, PL 388; ten notes

Katowice

JL^{13} Silesian Library in Katowice, ZS III 224111; five notes

Kalisz

JL^{14} Adam Asnyk City Public Library in Kalisz, ST 000020 zb. spec.; seven notes

Kielce

JL^{15} Witold Gombrowicz Provincial Public Library in Kielce, Pol. 1522; two notes

Kórnik

JL^{16} Kórnik Library of the Polish Academy of Sciences, Cim.F.4118; three notes

JL^{17} Kórnik Library of the Polish Academy of Sciences, Cim.F.4119; almost three hundred notes, two writing hands can be discerned (default A, additionally marked B: manus B); author of most notes (A) reveals familiarity with the practice of law in Lviv

Lublin

JL^{18} Hieronim Łopaciński Provincial Public Library in Lublin, P-16-f-61; three notes

Łódź

JL^{19} Library of University of Łódź, 1022575; one note

New Haven

JL^{20} Yale University Beinecke Rare Book and Manuscript Library, P4-5 R9 +506; one note

Płock

JL^{21} Płock Scientific Society, XVI.184; one note

Poznań

JL^{22} Adam Mickiewicz University Library in Poznań, SD 372 III; one note

JL^{23} Adam Mickiewicz University Library in Poznań, SD 1994 III; 31 notes

JL^{24} Adam Mickiewicz University Library in Poznań, SD 188 III; three notes, marginalia only on f. 177^{r}, 179^{v}–180^{r} (underlining of text fragment, 181^{v})

JL^{25} Raczyńscy Library in Poznań, 194.III; six notes, two hands (manus A, B)

JL^{26} Raczyńscy Library in Poznań, 246.III; six notes, two hands (manus A, B)

JL^{27} Raczyńscy Library in Poznań, IV.G.a.8; five notes, three writing hands (manus A, manus B, manus C)

Praha

JL^{28} National Library of the Czech Republic, P 009015; almost a hunderd notes, mostly in Polish, two writing hands A and B; then hand C on p. 188^{r} (most likely A, additionally marked manus B, manus C)

Riga

JL^{29} National Library of Latvia in Riga, Rare books RW3S/179; five notes

Tarnów

JL^{30} Juliusz Słowacki Public Library in Tarnów, SD 173; one note

Toronto

JL^{31} Toronto Thomas Fisher Rare Book Library Rare Book Collection, hutt f 00004; 35 notes, two writing hands (default A, additionally marked B: manus B)

Toruń

JL^{32} Nicolaus Copernicus University Library in Toruń, Pol. 6.III.106; one note

JL^{33} Książnica Kopernikańska in Toruń, Gzw 101788; 28 notes

Vatican

JL[34] Vatican Apostolic Library, Shelfmark Barberini FF.IV.8; six notes

Vilnius

JL[35] Martyno Mažvydo National Library of Lithuania, Vilnius, Shelfmark Clot. 1/506/155672; three notes

JL[36] Vilnius University Library, BAV.I.12b; nineteen notes, four writing hands (default A, additionally marked manus B, manus C, manus D)

JL[37] Vilnius University Library, II-2223-224; five notes

Warsaw

JL[38] Library of the Royal Castle in Warsaw, Shelfmark 43; more than a hundred notes, two writing hands (default A, additionally marked B: manus B)

JL[39] National Library in Warsaw, SD XVI.F.57; six notes, glossary of legal terms

JL[40] National Library in Warsaw, SD XVI.F.337; two notes

JL[41] National Library in Warsaw, SD.XVI.F.432; six notes

JL[42] University of Warsaw Library, Sd.612.545; one note

JL[43] University of Warsaw Library, Sd.612.553; five notes

Zielona Góra

JL[44] Provincial and Municipal Public Library in Zielona Góra, S III 260; one note

Only notes on legal issues are included in the edition.

Principles of the Edition

General principle. The edition was prepared on the basis of Adam Wolff's *Draft publishing instructions*,[1] with the exceptions noted below. The overriding rule was the least possible interference with the text. The normative text had a strong perlocutionary function. Even small changes could lead to modification of the meaning of the provision and could have an effect in the outside world. In the case of any normative texts, it is worth exercising restraint in any amendments.

Presentation of the basic text. The present edition of the Sandomierz version and of the Cracow version is based on the basic texts of Dział. I and BN 12607. For the sake of clarity, graphic features such as the use of coloured ink, embellishments and the like have been dispensed with. Deletions and mistakenly repeated words in the basic texts are indicated in footnotes. As previously mentioned, the basis for the edition of the *Weichbild* in *Commune incliti Poloniae Regni privilegium…* is the copy held at the Jagiellonian Library (BJ St. Dr. Cim. 8002).

Textual variations; *apparatus*. The preserved texts of the Sandomierz and the Cracow versions show numerous linguistic variations. The purpose of the edition, that is, to provide sources to observe the evolution of the legal text, ruled out the inclusion of all linguistic variants, the notation of which would have immeasurably expanded the critical apparatus. For this reason, the following differences were not included:

- changes in genus/number/mood/tense that do not change the meaning;
- *ac / et, aut / seu / vel, aut / vero, et /* comma, *et / eciam, absque / sine, et tunc/ extunc* and similar;
- other conjunctions and particles that do not change the meaning, such as *autem, enim* and similar;
- equivalent expressions such as *iuraverunt / fecerunt iuramentum*;
- the order of words in a sentence.

In the editions of *versio Sandomiriensis* and *versio Cracoviensis* the lettered footnotes (small letters) contain textual variations in the copies used, notes on the texts that form the basis of the edition, as well as notes by the authors of the

1 Adam Wolff, "Projekt instrukcji wydawniczej dla pisanych źródeł historycznych do połowy XVI wieku" [Draft Publishing Instructions for Written Historical Sources up to the Middle of the 16th Century], *Studia Źródłoznawcze* 1 (1957), pp. 155–181.

basis and later users whose purpose was to interfere with the text. This apparatus thus serves to mark phenomena relevant to the wording of the *Weichbild*. The lettered footnotes (small letters in {} brackets), on the other hand, contain user notes that were not intended to interfere with the wording of the regulations. These include Polish and German translations of Latin terms, legal rules (*regulae iuris*) appearing in Dział. I and BN 3068, additions from Chełmno Law contained in Dział. IV. In the case of *Commune incliti Poloniae Regni privilegium*, there was no need for a division of the apparatus into two parts, as there are relatively few comments on the text. Explanations have been included in the numbered footnotes accompanying the English translation. References to articles in the *Weichbild* and to other texts are the main subject of the explanations accompanying the Latin texts.

Additions by authors of the main text and commentators. Any additions placed outside the main text (in the margins, interlineated) are indicated in parentheses ⟨ ⟩. If they came from a commentator, the text in similar parentheses (⟨ ⟩) was written on the top line. A footnote accompanies the commentator's addendum only if it is possible to attribute authorship to one of the writing hands.

Copyists' errors. The surviving copies of the Latin *Weichbild* are characterized by a significant number of errors. Several types can be identified in the surviving *Weichbild* texts:

- grammatical errors, such as in conjugation and declension;
- spelling errors, among which are probably those that arose as a result of the scribe's inattention while copying the text;
- copyists' errors involving the writing of completely different words than in the underlying text, which makes the text lose its meaning even despite the correct spelling or grammatical consistency.

Errors in Dział. I, BN 12607 and Statute that make the text difficult to understand are marked [*s*]. The editor's corrections are clearly described in the text footnotes, taking into account the exceptions below.

The peculiarities of the spelling of the authors of the basic texts of the edition have been left intact. Thus, in Dział. I and BN 12607 we have the infinitive *prostestare* instead of *protestari*; moreover, in BN 12607 the indicative mood has been left consistently used, although the verb should be introduced in the conditional mood. Grammatical errors were corrected only if leaving them would make the text difficult to read.

Errors that can be regarded with a high degree of probability as obvious were corrected without any comments in the footnotes. These are words whose spelling could not have been intended, as is evidenced primarily by the form of the words elsewhere in the text (for example, *iuducium* instead of *iudicium*). In such a situation, the correct wording was given in the edition, along with a textual footnote giving the wording in the manuscript. On the other hand, in the early printed copy of *Commune incliti Poloniae Regni privilegium* there are typical typographical errors replacing the letter "n" with "u" and vice versa, for example in words such as *seu* (*sen* in the printed copy) or "Schartavia" ("Schartania" in the printed copy). In the case of obvious mistakes, a correction was made without indication by a footnote. However, the lack of attention to the use of "n" and "u" fonts could lead to significant differences in the meaning of the text in the words *uoluerit* / *noluerit* or *iudicare* / *indicare*. If, after comparison with other surviving *Weichbild* texts, the *lectio* in the *Commune* turned out to be different, the possible improvement was annotated in a footnote.

As a rule, the critical apparatus does not mark errors occurring in texts other than Dział. I, BN 12607 and Statute, unless they lead to a completely different meaning of the text.

Standardization of orthography. Manuscript texts from the 14th–16th centuries, an early printed text from 1506, and user notes from the 15th and 16th centuries are characterized by widely varying orthography. In accordance with the general principle from the Wolff's *Draft Publishing Instructions*, in making the standardization separately within each published text, I took into account the prevailing wording.

In terms of the Latin text, the spelling of "v", "u" and "w" has been standardized, for example, *uel* for *vel*. A certain deviation from the *Draft Publishing Instructions* is the replacement of "w" with "v" or "vu". "J" is written as "I"—for example, *jure* as *iure* (the spelling "j" has been retained in the users' notes on copies of *Commune incliti Poloniae regni privilegium...*, dating from the 16th and 17th centuries). When relevant, *quit* is rendered as *quid* (Dział. I, BN 12607), *capud* as *caput* (Dział. I, BN 12607), *optineo* as *obtineo* (Dział. I), *forizare* as *forisare* (Dział. I), *iccirco* as *idcirco* (Statute). The spelling of *verumptamen* and *dampnum* in Dział. I. and also *condempnatus* in BN 12607 has been retained.

There is inconsistency in the use of the letter "c" / "t" (*eciam* / *etiam*). The spelling has been made uniform according to the prevailing wording—in manuscripts "c", e.g. *tercium, quociens, peticio*; in the printed book "t".

Many discrepancies concern the spelling of n/m: "con", "cun", "inp" / "com", "cum", "imp", for example: *comparuit, ubicumque, impedimentum*. In Dział. I entries with "n" predominate. In addition, words such as *co[m]mitto, co[m]paret* and **cu[m]que* are abbreviated. The predominant spelling "n" was adopted as a rule, with the exceptions mentioned above. There is a lack of consistency in BN 12607, where we find varying spellings of the same words. The spelling has been standardized in accordance with the prevailing "n" notation. Consistently, the spelling with "m" is found in **cumque* and prevails in *impedio* and *imperium*—the spelling with "m" has been retained in these. The editors of the Statute used the classical notation with "m" except in **cunque* and this exception has been retained.

There is no consistency in the spelling of double letters in the published texts. Thus, we have *amittit, ammittit* and *ammitit, oportet* and *opportet, equm* and *equum, suppellectilia, supelectilia* and *supellectilia*, and many other examples. Again, the spelling prevalent within the copy in question has been adopted, with any additions made in square brackets.

In the case of proper names, fidelity to the grapheme of the message has been maintained (including "ẏ" and "ÿ", for example: *Meẏdborg, Maẏdenburg*). The spelling of Polish phrases is presented as faithfully as possible, without modernization, except for the long "s".

According to the present rules, the spelling of uppercase and lowercase letters has been rendered. The notation of Roman numerals is given in capital letters.

Abbreviations. The abbreviations were clearly marked in the copies of the *Weichbild*. Therefore, the shortened text is shown in full without any markings. The brackets were used when the writer did not use an abbreviation mark or when the cut edge of the folio made it impossible to read the abbreviation with certainty. The exceptions to these rules concern the notes made by users of prints of the *Commune incliti Poloniae Regni privilegium*. Their notes were very short and often careless, and the abbreviation marks were not used consistently. For this reason, brackets were only used in cases where the reading was doubtful, or the words were cut off at the edges. The number of dots in brackets does not represent the number of missing letters—it was impossible to determine this.

Punctuation. The placement of punctuation marks in legal texts can have far-reaching consequences in the wording of regulations. Only in the Statute of Jan Łaski is there any extensive punctuation and the associated spelling of capital letters. The choices made in the text of the Statute very rarely correspond to the spelling of capital letters in manuscript texts. Significantly, the preservation of the Statute's punctuation does not make the reading of the *Weichbild* relaxed. Some sentences are far too long; it is not uncommon for a period and a capital letter to divide logically related two parts of speech that should be one sentence divided by a comma. For this reason, it became necessary to modernize the punctuation, standardizing it across all surviving copies. Sentences were divided in a way that ensured the most accurate rendering of the content. Footnotes mark those situations where it became necessary to divide a sentence into two, while the Statute lacks any punctuation mark or a capital letter for the first word of the separated sentence. This intention was abandoned when two sentences were combined or a sentence was split where any punctuation mark appeared in the original.

The point of reference for punctuation in the basis of the Sandomierz version and the Cracow version is the punctuation in the Statute.

Numbering of articles. The model for the numbering of the articles is the *Weichbild* text from the Gniezno manuscript, which had already been published.[2] Almost fully consistent with it is the numbering in the Działyńscy Codex 1—the two texts differ in the different location of articles 76 and 77. All the *Weichbild* texts have been juxtaposed with the layout of the text in Gn./Dział. 1. It is worth mentioning that the original numbering, if present in the surviving texts, is usually burdened with numerous errors. For the sake of order, the concordance of articles is included in the first footnote to each article. In addition, the editing is preceded by the summary of the article numbers of the text from *Commune incliti Poloniae Regni privilegium* with the Dział. 1 and BN 12607.

Editorial marks. The following characters are included in the edition:

⟦⟧	repeated word
[]	additions of the publisher
⟨Item⟩	annotation of the author of the basis
⟨^{Item}⟩	annotation of the commentator
⊢⊣	deletions, erasures
a.c.	before amendment
cf.	compare
corr.	correction
deest, desunt	missing word(s), without deciding whether this was intended by the copyist
del.	deleted when it is necessary to indicate by whose hand it occurred
in marg.	in margin

2 Maciej Mikuła, *Municipal Magdeburg Law*, pp. 388–430; there is also a concordance table of articles (pp. 245–265).

in ms.	in manuscript
org.	original wording before correction in an edition
p.c.	after amendment

Notes on translations. The basis of the translation is the official text of the *Ius municipale Magdeburgense* in *Commune incliti Poloniae Regni privilegium*. It represents the culmination of the evolution of the Latin text of the *Weichbild* in the Silesian-Małopolska compilation. The translation has been compiled to faithfully convey the meaning of the Latin text. For this reason, at times the wording of the translation deviates from the literary one and indicates clumsiness in the wording of the original. This has been guided by both the terminology introduced in the monograph on the *Ius municipale*, as well as the glossary compiled by Maria Dobozy, the translator of the Saxon Mirror.[3] Although some of the provisions of the Magdeburg *Weichbild* have their roots in the Saxon Mirror, the Latin text used in the Kingdom of Poland diverged from the original. Above all, the *Weichbild* was written for cities and its content was modelled accordingly, including at the stage of medieval Latin translations from German. Hence the not uncommon differences also in the translation of the corresponding provisions of the Saxon Mirror and the Weichbild, to mention, as one example, the replacement of the term *Morgengabe* by the Latin *dotalicium*. Necessary explanations are included in the footnotes to the translation.

Biblical quotations are given after The New Revised Standard Version, Catholic Edition (NRSV-CE), and in the case of Ps 2:12 according to the Myles Coverdale translation (the departure from current modern editions of the Bible is due to the fact that 16th-century translations reflect the wording in the Latin source much more accurately than these more current translations do). Where a wording from a German source was needed, reference was made to the Jagiellonian Library manuscript 169 of 1308.

A note on the use of AI. The reading of manuscripts and early printed books was done without the use of handwritten text recognition (HTR) tools.

3 The Saxon Mirror: *A "Sachsenspiegel" of the Fourteenth Century*, translated by Maria Dobozy (University of Pennsylvania Press, 1999) [The Middle Ages Series].

Concordatio articulorum

Statute	Dział. I	BN 12607
Art. 1–6	Art. 1–6	Art. 1–6
Art. 7	Art. 7	Art. 7–8
Art. 8	Art. 8	Art. 9
Art. 9	Art. 9	Art. 10–1
Art. 10	Art. 10	Art. 12
Art. 11	Art. 11	Art. 13
Art. 12	Art. 12	Art. 14
Art. 13	Art. 13	Art. 15–6
Art. 14–5	Art. 14	Art. 17–8
Art. 16	Art. 15	Art. 19
Art. 17–8	Art. 16	Art. 20
Art. 19	Art. 17	Art. 21
Art. 20–1	Art. 18	Art. 22–3
Art. 22	Art. 19	Art. 24
Art. 23	Art. 20	Art. 25
Art. 24	Art. 21	Art. 26–27
Art. 25	Art. 22	Art. 28
Art. 26–7	Art. 23	Art. 29–30
Art. 28–30	Art. 24	Art. 31
Art. 31	Art. 25	Art. 32
Art. 32	Art. 26	Art. 33
Art. 33	Art. 27	Art. 34
Art. 34	Art. 28	Art. 35
Art. 35	Art. 29	Art. 36
Art. 36	Art. 30	Art. 38
Art. 37	Art. 31	Art. 37
Art. 38	Art. 32	Art. 39
Art. 39	Art. 33	Art. 40
Art. 40	Art. 34	Art. 41
Art. 41	Art. 35	Art. 42
Art. 42	Art. 36	Art. 43
Art. 43	Art. 37	Art. 44
Art. 44	Art. 38	Art. 45
Art. 45	Art. 69	Art. 74

 | DOI:10.1163/9789004735033_004

(*cont.*)

Statute	Dział. I	BN 12607
Art. 46	Art. 39	Art. 46
Art. 47	Art. 40	Art. 47
Art. 48	Art. 41	Art. 48
Art. 49	Art. 42–3	Art. 49–50
Art. 50	Art. 44	Art. 51
Art. 51	Art. 45	Art. 52
Art. 52	Art. 46	Art. 53
Art. 53	Art. 47	Art. 54
Art. 54	Art. 48	Art. 55
Art. 55	Art. 49	Art. 56
Art. 56	Art. 50	Art. 57
Art. 57	Art. 51	Art. 58
Art. 58	Art. 52	Art. 61
Art. 59	Art. 53	Art. 59
Art. 60	Art. 54	Art. 60
Art. 61	Art. 55	–
Art. 62	Art. 56	Art. 63
Art. 63	Art. 57	–
Art. 64	Art. 58	Art. 64
Art. 65	Art. 59	Art. 65
Art. 66	Art. 60	Art. 62
Art. 67–8	Art. 61	Art. 66
Art. 69	Art. 62	Art. 67
Art. 70	Art. 63	Art. 68
Art. 71	Art. 64	Art. 69
Art. 72	Art. 65	Art. 70
Art. 73	Art. 66	Art. 71
Art. 74	Art. 67	Art. 72
Art. 75	Art. 68	Art. 73
Art. 76	Art. 70	Art. 75
Art. 77	Art. 71	Art. 76
Art. 78	Art. 72	Art. 77
Art. 79	Art. 73	Art. 78
Art. 80	Art. 74	Art. 79
Art. 81	Art. 75	Art. 80
Art. 82	Art. 77 p.1,3	–

(*cont.*)

Statute	Dział. I	BN 12607
Art. 83	Art. 76	–
Art. 84	Art. 77 p. 2	Art. 81
Art. 85	Art. 78	Art. 82
Art. 86	–	Art. 83
Art. 87	Art. 79	Art. 84
Art. 88	Art. 80	Art. 85
Art. 89	Art. 81	Art. 86
Art. 90	Art. 82	Art. 87
Art. 91	Art. 83	Art. 88
Art. 92	Art. 84	Art. 89
Art. 93	Art. 85	Art. 90
Art. 94	Art. 86	Art. 91
Art. 95–6	Art. 87	Art. 92
Art. 97	Art. 88	Art. 93
Art. 98	Art. 89	Art. 94
Art. 99	Art. 90	Art. 95
Art. 100	Art. 91	Art. 96
Art. 101	Art. 92	Art. 97
Art. 102	Art. 93	Art. 98
Art. 103	Art. 94	Art. 99 p. 1
Art. 104–5	Art. 95	Art. 99 p. 2
Art. 106	Art. 97	Art. 100
Art. 107–8	Art. 96	Art. 101–2
Art. 109	Art. 98	Art. 103
Art. 110	Art. 99	Art. 104
Art. 111	Art. 100	Art. 105
Art. 112	Art. 101	Art. 106
Art. 113	Art. 103	Art. 107
Art. 114	Art. 102	Art. 108
Art. 115	Art. 104	Art. 109
Art. 116	Art. 105	Art. 110
Art. 117	Art. 106	Art. 111
Art. 118	Art. 107	Art. 112
Art. 119 p. 1	Art. 108	Art. 113 p. 1
Art. 119 p. 2	Art. 109	Art. 113 p. 2
Art. 120 p. 1	Art. 110	Art. 114 p. 1

(*cont.*)

Statute	Dział. I	BN 12607
Art. 120 p. 2	Art. 111 p. 1	Art. 114 p. 2
Art. 121–2	Art. 111 p. 2	Art. 115–6
Art. 123	Art. 112	Art. 117
Art. 124	Art. 113	Art. 118
Art. 125	Art. 114	Art. 119
Art. 126	Art. 115	Art. 120
Art. 127–8	Art. 116	Art. 117
Art. 129 p. 1	Art. 117	Art. 123 p. 1
Art. 129 p. 2	–	Art. 123 p. 2
Art. 130	–	Art. 124
Art. 131	–	Art. 125
Art. 132	–	Art. 126
Art. 133	–	Art. 127

Ius Municipale Magdeburgense
Versio Sandomirsiensis (Dział. 1)
Versio Cracoviensis (BN 12607)

Rubricae

S^{6} (Dział. I)

130r

(aHic sequitur numerus Iuris Municipalis. Primo ipsius prologus, deinde nota numerum.a)

[*1*] (bPrimo(c) de cezare Ottone, qui fundavit templum in Meÿdeburgb) (d). Capitulum primum

[*2*] (eItem de iure penesticorum (fet (g) comestibilia vendenciumf). Capitulum IIe)

[*3*] (hItem de iniustis mensuris et iniustis(i) pensis(j) (k). Capitulum IIIh)

[*4*] (lItem de tribus iudiciis provincialibus (madvocati provinciem)(n). Capitulum IIIIl)

[*5*] (oItem de iudicio burgravii. Vo)

[*6*] (pItem de iure(q) sculteti (rin(s) tribus iudiciisr). (t) VIp)

(a) Sequitur registrum libri municipalis. K^{3} Hic incipitur aliud registrum. Sequitur de cesare Ottone, qui fundavit templum in Meydeburg et sequitur. In nomine Patris, et Filii, et Spiritus Sancti. Amen. K^{4} *titulus indicis rubricae deest* K^{1} K^{2} (b) Hic incipitur fundamentum S^{4} Incipit fundamentum S^{5} Hic incipitur de cesare Ottone, qui fundavit templum in Meÿdeburg, qui ius municipale transmutavit de Theutonico in Latinum. Capitulum primum. *ad articulum* K^{4} (c) Incipitur S^{1} S^{10} (d) et primo incipit S^{10} (e) De hominibus, qui penestici vocantur S^{8} K^{1} K^{2} ⟨De penesticis et eorum pena.⟩ K^{5} (f) *desunt* S^{5} S^{9} (g) aliorum S^{5} (h) De metretis mensuris. Capitulum 2. *ad articulum* K^{3} De iniustis mensuris et metretis et pensis. K^{5} *rubrica deest* S^{8} K^{1} K^{2} (i) metretis et K^{5} *deest* S^{4} S^{5} (j) ponderis S^{4} S^{5} S^{9} (k) ac ponderibus S^{1} aut metretis K^{4} (l) De iudiciis provincialibus. S^{2} De tribus iudicis. Capitulum 3. *ad articulum* K^{3} De tribus magnis iudicis. K^{5} (m) sic dicens S^{4} sequitur S^{5} *deest* S^{9} K^{1} K^{2} (n) *deest* S^{8} K^{3} (o) De stupro et obsidio. Capitulum 4. *ad articulum* K^{3} Adire iudicium castella[ni]. K^{5} (p) De sculteto. Capitulum quintum. *ad articulum* K^{3} De tribus iudiciis sculteti. K^{5} (q) iudicio S^{10} (r) dicit sic K^{1} sequitur K^{2} (s) de S^{9} S^{4} et S^{10} (t) ⊢IIII⊣ S^{6}

Rubricae

C[1] (*BN 12607*)

⟨Iudex Iudicium Clerus Sponsalia Crimen I⟩[1](a) Incipitur registrum super corpus iuris et scias, quod per hunc modum debes invenire quodlibet capitulum primi, secundi, terti et quarti libri, primo perlege inicium capituli, secundum quod hic habetur et post hoc vide numerum folii et in quo folio invenias numerum in eodem folio erit capitulum etc. 15ra

[*1*]*(b)* Cesar Octo. Hoc capitulum est primum libri huius et tractat de consulibus, super quid habent potestatem iudicandi et alia faciendi. Require in primo folio primi libri.

[*2*]*(c)* Qui penestici vocantur. Hoc capitulum tractat de penesticis. Require in primo folio primi libri. ⟨Ibidem qui statu[tu]m civitatis infregerit⟩(d)

[*3*]*(e)* Si metrete aut alie mensure. Require in primo folio primi libri.

[*4*]*(f)* Ille supremus iudex. Hoc capitulum tractat de tribus legalibus iudiciis et sic de aliis. Require in primo folio primi libri.

[*5*]*(g)* Stuprum, obsidia et irruencias domiciliorum. Require in secundo folio primi libri.

[*6*]*(h)* Scultetus etiam habet tria iudicia legialia. Require in secundo folio primi libri. ⟨Ibidem de penis⟩(i)

(a) *manus X* C[1] (b) De cesare Othone, qui fundavit templum in Meydburg et dedit cuilibet municipale ius ac de iudicio consulum etc. W[1] Capitulum primum. De ortu iuris municipalis. C[3] (c) De pena penasticarum erga consules. II W[1] Capitulum secundum. Qui penastici vocantur. C[3] (d) *manus B* C[1] (e) De modis et mensuris. III W[1] Capitulum tercium. De iudicio consulum. C[3] (f) Qui dies dimittur legali seu tria sunt magna iudicia. IIII W[1] Capitulum IIII. De tribus iudiciis burgrabii vel scultetii. C[3] (g) De stupro, obsidio et irreverenciis dommicillarum [*s*]. Quinto W[1] Capitulum quintum. De iudice violenciarum. C[3] (h) De tribus iudiciis legalibus scolteti facto. VI W[1] Capitulum VI. De iudicio sculteti. C[3] (i) *manus B* C[1]

---

1 *libri Decretalium Gregorii IX*

[*7*] (aItem de clamore (bin(c) vulneribusb) (det (ein(f) monomachalibus vulneribus(g)e)d) (h).a) VII

[*8*] (iItem de conflictu, qui sit in die aut (jtempestate(k) noctisj).i) VIII

[*9*] (lItem de diffinicionibus sentenciarum (met(n) quid sit iuris (o) debitism).l) IX

[*10*] (p(qItem de(r) querimonia, que(s)q) pernoctaverit pro vulneribus.p) X (t)

[*11*] (uItem de stupro et (v) insidiis(w) (xet irruenciis domicilii (yet iure(z) burgraviiy)x). Capitulum XIu)

[*12*] (aa) (bbItem (ccde homine(dd), qui multiscc) vulneribus fuerit vulneratus.bb) XII

(a) De vulneribus et corporis profunditate. S^{2} De homine vulnerato clamante. K^{5} (b) et vulneribus monomachalis K^{2} (c) *deest* K^{1} (d) monomachalibus *ad articulum* S^{6} (e) modo K^{1} (f) *deest* S^{7} (g) *deest* S^{8} (h) legitur S^{5} (i) De conflictu tempore noctis. S^{2} De conflictu nocturno ac diurno. K^{5} (j) *desunt* K^{1} (k) tempore S^{4} (l) Quod scabinus non tenetur invenire sentencia extra iudiciales dies nisi in casibus. K^{5} (m) *desunt* S^{4} S^{5} S^{7} S^{8} K^{1} K^{3} (n) *deest* S^{10} (o) de S^{1} S^{9} (p) De vulneribus pernoctatis. S^{2} Quid si querimonia pernoctatur. K^{1} De vulneribus pernoctatis. K^{5} (q) Quodsi querimonia S^{8} (r) Si S^{7} (s) *deest* S^{7} (t) ├Item de conflictu, qui sit in die aut tempestate noctis. XI┤ ├Item de diffinicionibus sentenciarum et quit sit iuris debitis. XII┤ ├Item de querimonia, que pernoctaverit pro vulneribus. XIII┤ S^{6} (u) C[apitulum] X. De stupro. *ad articulum* K^{3} Iudicium burgrabii de stupris, obsidiis et irruenciis domiciliorem [*s*]. K^{5} (v) de K^{1} (w) obsidiis S^{7} S^{8} K^{1} K^{2} obsidium S^{10} (x) *desunt* S^{4} S^{5} (y) *desunt* S^{7} S^{8} S^{9} (z) Meyburgensii S^{10} (aa) Sequitur S^{5} (bb) Quod si homo multis vulneribus K^{1} K^{2} Quod si homo multis vulneribus vulneratur. S^{8} De vulnerato cum clamore. K^{5} (cc) Si homo S^{7} (dd) vulnere *ad articulum* S^{6}

[*7*] *(a)* Quodsi homo vulneratus fuerit, si clamorem proclamaverit et si ceperit. Require in secundo folio primi libri. ⟨de vulneribus cum clamore⟩(b)

[*8*] Si quis fideiusserit aliquod iudicio pro aliquo (c) adiutorio presentare ex parte homicidii. Require in secundo folio primo libri. ⟨de fideiussoribus⟩(d) ⟨Rarum⟩(e)

[*9*]*(f)* Si contingerit criminale nephas aut conflictus. Require in secundo folio primi libri. ⟨de criminalibus⟩(g)

[*10*] *(h)* | Nec castellano, nec sculteto tenetur scabinus sentenciam aliquam 15rb
extra veros dies iudiciales diffinire, nisi sit factum manifestum. Require in secundo folio primi libri.

[*11*] ⟨Ille dicitur hospes⟩(i) Ille dicitur esse hospes, qui ultra undecim miliaria extra iudicium habuerit mansionem. Require in tertio folio primi libri.

[*12*]*(j)* Quodsi vir vulneratus fuerit et eodem die iudicium non quesierit, et sua querimonia pernoctaverit. Require in tercio folio primi libri. ⟨Sed si vir vulneribus⟩(k)

[*13*]*(l)* Stuprum et obsidium, et irruencia domicilia burgravius iudicat nec alter ullus. Require in tercio folio primi libri. ⟨domorum irruencia⟩(m) ⟨stuprum et obsidium⟩(n)

[*14*]*(o)* Quicumque vulneratus fuerit, si clamorem proclamaverit et ad iudicium devenerit, de quocumque querulatur. Require in tercio folio primi libri. ⟨Quicumque vulneribus⟩(p)

(a) De capto vulneratore et convicto, es[s]et fideiuss[i]onis coadiutor. VII W[1] Capitulum VII. De capto et vulnerato. C[3] (b) *manus B* C[1] (c) ⊢j⊣ C[1] (d) *manus C* C[1] (e) *manus E* C[1] (f) De inculpacione nocturnali. VIII W[1] Capitulum VIII. De inculpacione nocturnali violencia. C[3] (g) *manus B* C[1] (h) Qui potest iudicare pro peccunia absque testimonio. IX W[1] De presentacione hospitis ad manus et distancia ipsius. C[3] (i) *manus B* C[1] (j) De querimonia, que pernoctaverit pro vulneribus. X W[1] Capitulum X C[3] (k) *manus H* C[1] (l) De stupro et obsidiis et irruenciis domiciliorum et iure burgrabii. XI W[1] De vulnerato multis vulneribus. XII W[1] Capitulum XI. De capto viro propter violacionem. C[3] (m) *manus C* C[1] (n) *manus H* C[1] (o) Capitulum XII. De irruenciis et clamore. C[3] (p) *manus B* C[1]

[*13*] (aItem de obligacione pignerum.a) XIII

[*14*] (bItem de iure feminarum, (csi partes (dpuerorum eradicati fuerintd)c).b) XIIII

[*15*](e) (fItem de publicacione(g) seu(h) fiscacione(i) (j) possessionis(k) (l).f) XV

[*16*] (mItem (nde pacis firmitate(o) etn) de dono infra annum possesso(p) (q).m) XVI

[*17*] (r) Item de dono in (sinfirmitate donatos)(t) (u). XVII

(a) De bonis mobilibus in debito obligatis. K^3 K^5 (b) De viro, qui moritur et habet pueros. S^2 Uxor nichil habet in bonis mariti, nisi dotalicium et vite promissionem. K^5 (c) *desunt* S^4 et dotalicio et suppellectili S^9 sequitur S^5 et K^1 K^2 (d) desunt K^1 K^2 (e) *error: rubrica postea inserta ad Art.* [*17*] Capitulum XVII K^3 (f) De bonorum. K^5 (g) fiscacione K^1 K^2 (h) *deest* S^2 *deest ad articulum* S^6 (i) *deest* S^2 K^1 K^2 (j) et *ad articulum* S^6 (k) bonorum S^2 *in ms.* possessione [*s*] S^6 (l) sic dicit S^4 (m) De possessione bonorum S^2 De possessione per annum et diem. K^5 (n) *desunt* S^4 S^5 S^7 S^8 K^1 K^2 (o) firmacione S^9 (p) *deest* S^{10} (q) sequitur S^5 (r) *error: rubrica antea inserta ad Art.* [15] Capitulum XV K^3 (s) lecto egritudinis S^2 K^5 quod datur in infirmitate S^3 egritudinis lecto W^1 (t) dato *ad articulum* S^6 (u) sequitur S^5

[*15*]^(a) Obligat aliquis mercimonia aut alia bona mobilia pro debito ex parte iudicii. Require in tercio folio primi libri. ⟨de obligacionibus⟩^(b)

[*16*] Nullus eciam hospes ab alio advena, et contra, indiget pignus recipere. Require in tercio folio primi libri.

[*17*]^(c) ⟨De successione bonorum hereditarium⟩^(d) Si aliquis ducit uxorem et si vir de hac luce decedit, uxor nichil habet in suis bonis. Nulla mulier potest vite provisionem. Quodsi sibi maritus mulieri nichil in suis bonis dederit. Si vir oves habuerit. Et si pueri | ⟨Si aliqui pueri fuerint exhereditati⟩^(e) vellent dotalicium 15va mulieri infringere, servare. Si vir pueros habuerit, aut mulier, quecumque ex eis exhereditati. Require quarto folio primi libri. ⟨Et ibidem de dotalicio⟩^(f)

[*18*] Deservitum precium, racionale debitum debent solvi de bonis mortui viri pro dotalicio. Require quarto folio primi libri.

[*19*]*^(g)* Quando alicui sua possessio publicata fuerit iuste ac iudicialiter. Require quarto folio primi libri.

[*20*]*^(h)* ⟨Quidquid oppositum habes, ibi conqueritur x capitulo⟩^(i) Quidquid masculus dat sub banno, si possidebit pacifice ⟨anno dieque⟩^(j) ac quiete absque contradiccione. Require quarto folio primi libri. ⟨Ibidem quod si scabini mortui fuerunt⟩^(k)

[*21*]*^(l)* ⟨Nemo⟩^(m) Nemo masculus, nec ulla mulier potest in lecto egritudinis de suis bonis. Require quarto folio primi libri.

---

^(a) De obligatione pignorum. XIII W¹ Capitulum XIII. De debitis et pignore. C³ ^(b) *manus C* C¹ ^(c) Si mulieri nihil resignatum fuerit et maritus moriatur. XIIII W¹ Capitulum XIIII. De iure mulieris vel uxoris et dotalicio eius, si uxori nihil assignatum fuerit et vir moritur. C³ ⟨De viduis quomodo sunt foveri⟩ K² ^(d) *manus C* C¹ ^(e) *manus E* C¹ ^(f) *manus B* C¹ ^(g) De publicacione seu fiscacione possessione [*s*]. XV W¹ Capitulum XV C³ ^(h) Quidquid masculus dat sub anno. XVI W¹ Capitulum XVI. De prescripcione possessionis vel de re possessa. C³ ^(i) *manus B* C¹ ^(j) *manus B* C¹ ^(k) *manus B* C¹ ^(l) De dono in egritudinis lecto. XVII W¹ Capitulum XVII. De dono egritudinis. C³ ^(m) *manus B* C¹

[*18*] (aItem de hereditate, ubi nec fratres nec sorores reperiuntur(b).a) XVIII

[*19*] (cItem de firmacione pacis (ddonacioni pro hereditated).c) XIX

[*20*] (eItem(f) pro debito per iuris extorsionem aquisito(g) (h).e) XX

[*21*] (iItem de impedimento ad limina sanctorum (jextra provinciamj) (k).i) XXI

[*22*] (lItem de pena illius(m), qui scabinum illicitis(n) verbis obruit(o).l) XXII

[*23*] (p)Item de(q) concordia et (rrancore, (sque(t) coram iudicio (ufacta(v) fuerit r)(w)u)s) (x). Capitulum XXIII

(a) De hereditate recipienda. S^2 De defectu fratrum et sororum. K^5 (b) recipiunt S^{10} *deest* S^5 K^1 K^2 (c) De dono cognicionis. S^2 De solido scabinali. K^5 (d) *desunt* S^4 S^5 S^7 S^8 K^1 K^2 (e) De debiti per vim extorsione. S^7 De debito iure aquisito. S^9 De debitis. K^5 (f) Sequitur S^5 (g) *deest* S^4 S^5 S^8 K^1 K^2 (h) et de iudicio, ubi conqueritur et fatetur S^1 S^{10} K^3 (i) De limina sanctorum vulgariter poszwÿaczÿ. Qui ad limina sancta vadit. K^5 (j) *desunt* S^4 S^5 S^9 S^7 S^8 K^1 K^2 (k) aut ad nundinas S^1 sequitur S^5 aut nundinas S^{10} aut ad nundinas aut extra terminos K^3 (l) De increpante scabinum. K^5 (*in ms. Art. 8*) (m) *deest* S^7 K^1 K^2 (n) turpibus S^7 S^8 K^1 K^2 *deest* S^9 (o) in sede iudiciali obruit S^1 S^4 S^5 S^9 S^{10} in sede iudiciali obruit vel improperaverit K^3 *deest* K^1 K^2 (p) de iudicio S^4 S^5 De concordia. K^5 (q) et S^5 (r) recompensacione S^7 (s) *desunt* S^8 K^1 K^2 (t) *deest* S^9 (u) *deest ad articulum* S^6 (v) concordata S^1 S^4 S^5 K^3 concordia S^{10} (w) *deest* S^9 (x) aut absque iudicio S^1 S^9 S^{10} K^3

[22] *[(a)]* ⟨Quando sit defectus in legittimis successoribus⟩[(b)] Quodsi hereditas in fratribus seu sororibus defectum habuerit. Require quinto folio primi libri.

[23] *[(c)]* Qui autem in possessione, si bene sacerdos sit, aut manserit, tamen suppellectilia. Require quinto folio primi libri.

[24]*[(d)]* ⟨Quidquid masculus⟩[(e)] Quidquid masculus dat in iudicio bannito coram iudice et scabinis. Require in quinto folio primi libri.

[25]*[(f)]* ⟨Quicumque⟩[(g)] Quicumque aliquem coram iudicio pro debito inpulsaverit. Si autem querimonia. Require in quinto folio primi libri. ⟨Ibidem de penis cum debitum non solverit⟩[(h)]

[26] *[(i)]* | ⟨Limina sanctorum⟩[(j)] Si aliquis ad limina sanctorum aut ad. Require 15vb
in quinto folio primi libri.

[27] *[(k)]* ⟨Si uni⟩[(l)] Et si uni viro testimonium adiudicatum fuerit, inducias. Require in quinto folio primi libri. ⟨de testimonio⟩[(m)]

[28]*[(n)]* Quicumque scabino in scampno iudiciali inproperaverit aut turpibus verbis. Require in quinto folio primi libri. ⟨de scabini et eciam XXVI⟩[(o)]

[29] *[(p)]* ⟨de concordia⟩[(q)] Quando concordia inter discordantes ordinata fuerit coram iudicio. Require in quinto folio primi libri.

[30] *[(r)]* Ubi concordia et fremitus diuturnus coram iudicio confirmata fuerit. Require in [(s)] VI folio primi libri.

[(a)] De hereditate fratre et sorore carente. XIX W^1 C[apitulum] XVIII. De hereditatis divisione. C^3 [(b)] *manus C* C^1 [(c)] Capitulum XIX. De sacerdotis hereditate. C^3 [(d)] Memoriale ad iudicium avandi [s] sunt. XX W^1 Capitulum XX. De arra scabinorum de dono in iudicio. C^3 [(e)] *manus B* C^1 [(f)] De debito necessario, quem acquisito et de debito requi[si]to. XXI W^1 XXI. De debito querela. C^3 [(g)] *manus B* C^1 [(h)] *manus B* C^1 [(i)] De volente visitare limina sanctorum. XXII W^1 Capitulum XXII. De debito ipsorum, qui vult ire liminam sanctorum. C^3 [(j)] *manus C* C^1 [(k)] Capitulum XXIII. De induciis testimoni. C^3 [(l)] *manus E* C^1 [(m)] *manus C* C^1 [(n)] Scabino in iudicio redarguto. XXIIII W^1 XXIIII. De scabino in iudicio redarguto. C^3 [(o)] *manus B* C^1 [(p)] De testimonio concordie iudicialis. XXV W^1 XXV. De testimonio concordie iudicialis, de compensacione etc. C^3 [(q)] *manus C* C^1 [(r)] De concordia et satisdacione. XXVI W^1 XXVI. De concordia et satisdacione non conservata. C^3 [(s)] ⊢quinto⊣ *del. manus A* C^1

[*24*] (a Item de filio (b excipere(c) coram iudicio et mercede deservita(d) b) (e). a) xxiiii (f)

[*25*] (g Item (h) de (i hereditate aut i) dono, (j quod datur viro vel femine j) (k). g) xxv

[*26*] (l Item de hiis(m), que pertinent(n) ad hereditatem (o). l) xxvi

130v [*27*] | (p(q Item de viro, qui q) alterum vulnerat (r vitam suam defendendo r) (s). p) Capitulum xxvii

[*28*] (t(u Item de duobus, qui u) de stirpe Sclavica (v se(w) mutuo vulnerant v) (x). t) Capitulum xxviii

[*29*] (y Item de causa, (z de qua z) promittitur coram iudicio (aa) terminari(bb) (cc). y) Capitulum xxix

[*30*] (dd) (ee Item de duobus, qui se mutuo(ff) vulneraverint equaliter(gg). ee) Capitulum xxx

---

(a) De filio, quem pater potest ter eximere coram iudicio. K^3 Pater ter eximit filium. K^5 (b) *desunt* K^1 K^2 (c) excepto S^8 (d) deservito S^6 (e) iudicialiter optinere S^1 S^7 S^{10} (f) *titulus articuli separati* [*24*] De precio famuli. S^{10} (g) De dono coram iudicio facto. K^5 (h) Sequitur K^1 K^2 (i) *desunt* S^4 S^5 (j) *desunt* S^7 S^8 K^1 K^2 (k) coram iudicio S^1 S^9 S^{10} K^3 in iudicio bannito S^4 coram iudicio bannito sequitur S^5 (l) De suppellectilibus. S^7 De supellectili ⟨hereditate⟩ S^8 De suppellectilibus sequitur. K^1 K^2 Que spectant ad hereditatem. K^5 (m) rebus S^4 S^5 (n) spectant S^4 S^5 (o) sic dicit S^4 sequitur S^5 (p) De vulnerato per alterum in defensione vite. K^5 (q) Quod si vir S^8 K^1 K^2 Si vir S^7 (r) *desunt* K^1 K^2 (s) et eciam solus fuerit vulneratus S^1 S^7 S^8 S^{10} K^3 et solus fuerit vulneratus S^9 sequitur S^5 (t) De eo quod respondet nemo tenetur nisi ydiomate. K^5 (u) Si duo se S^7 S^8 K^1 K^2 Sequitur S^5 (v) fuerint et se S^5 *deest* S^9 in K^1 K^2 (w) et de S^4 *deest* S^7 (x) intra ius municipale S^1 S^7 K^3 (y) Sequitur de causa. K^1 K^2 De causa que absque iudicio terminari debuit. K^5 (z) que S^9 (aa) bannito S^4 S^5 (bb) determinari S^{10} *deest* S^5 S^7 S^8 S^9 (cc) sic dicit S^4 (dd) Sequitur S^5 (ee) Si vir alterum vulnerat S^7 S^8 Si vir alterum vulnerat equaliter K^1 K^2 De duobus invicem vulneratis et unus conqueritur coram iudice et alter coram quat[t]uor bancis. K^5 (ff) *deest* S^4 S^5 (gg) *deest* S^4 S^9 S^{10}

[*31*]*(a)* ⟨famulus⟩(b) ⟨merces famulorum⟩(c) Et quivis vir potest filium suum ter excipere. Et famulus potest mercedem suam, promeruit, quinque soli[dos] etc. Require in sexto folio primi libri.

[*32*]*(d)* ⟨donum⟩(e) Donum, quod mulieri vel viro datum fuerit in iudicio bannito. Si moritur, femina absque herede. Require in sexto folio primi libri. ⟨Ibidem de argento informato et de pulmentaris⟩(f)

[*33*]*(g)* Ista sunt, que ad hereditatem pertinent. Require in sexto folio primi libri. ⟨Ista sunt que pertinet ad hereditatem⟩(h)

[*34*]*(i)* ⟨De vulneribus per totum⟩(j) Vulnerat quis alium vitam suam defendendo. Require in septimo folio primi libri. ⟨et ibidem de pernoctacione⟩(k)

[*35*]*(l)* Quodsi se duo mutuo vulneraverint. Require in septimo folio primi libri. ⟨Sequitur de vulneribus per totum⟩(m)

[*36*]*(n)* | Quodsi querimonie duorum virorum dilate fuerint in iudicio ban- 16ra
nito coram iudice. Require in septimo folio primi libri.

[*38*]*(o)* Quodsi se duo mutuo vulneraverint equaliter, ex hiis unus vadet ad iudicem. Require VIII folio primi libri.

(a) De empcione inculpati filii iurando per patrem et quando testes et actor iurare debet. XXVII W^1 XXVII. De exempcione filii inculpati scilicet pater, capitulo LXXXVIIo. C^3 (b) *manus E* C^1 (c) *manus C* C^1 (d) De dono viro ac mulieri asignato, et si mulier absque herede moriatur. XXVIII W^1 XXVIII. De dono viri ac mulieri coram iudicio et si mulier moritur absque herede. C^3 ⟨De donacione inter virum et mulierem⟩ K^2 (e) *manus B* C^1 (f) *probabiliter manus B* C^1 (g) De hiis, que ad hereditatem pertinent. XXIX W^1 Capitulum XXIX. Que [ad] hereditatem pertinent. C^3 (h) *manus E* C^1 (i) De viro, qui alterum vulnerat vitam suam defendendo et de antequerelis. XXX W^1 Capitulum XXXIII [*s*]. Quando primum vi repellere lic[et]. XXX C^3 (j) *manus E* C^1 (k) *manus B* C^1 (l) De diverse ydiomatis querela. XXXI W^1 Capitulum XXXI C^3 (m) *manus E* C^1 (n) De iudiciis concordium. XXXII W^1 XXXII. De causa que est concordata cum voluntate iudicis. C^3 (o) De visitantibus scamnam scabinalia propter latronem. XXXIIII W^1 XXXIII. Qui primam querelam debet servare. C^3

[*31*] (a) (bItem de duobus, qui se mutuo(c) vulneraverint equaliter(d)(e).b) XXXI

[*32*] (f(gItem de virof), qui alterum vulnerat (het si (i) in manifesto facto deh) (j).g) XXXII

[*33*] (k[(lDe duobus, quil) se mutuo vulneraverint: unus cultello et alter gladio.]k)

[*34*] (mItem de vulneribus, que pernoctaverint (net de(o) quibusn) (p).m) XXXIII

[*35*] (qItem de duobus, qui se vulneraverunt et ambo coram iudicio conparent(r).q) XXXV

[*36*] (s(tItem de viro, quit) alterum vulneraverit (uet ipsis pax indicta fueritu).s) XXXVI

[*37*] (v(wItem de duobus, quiw) se mutuo vulneraverint (xet ambo coram(y)x).v) XXXVII (z)

(a) Sequitur S[5] (b) Si duo equaliter vulnerantur. K[1] K[2] Si duo equaliter se vulnerant et conquerantur equaliter. S[7] Si duo equaliter se vulnerant. S[8] De duobus equaliter vulneratis. K[5] (c) *deest* S[5] (d) et querulantur equaliter S[1] S[9] K[3] sic dicens S[4] (e) *deest* S[4] (f) Si vir detinet alterum S[7] S[8] K[1] K[2] (g) De vulneratore de facto cum clamore ad iudicium deducto. K[5] (h) in facto recenti sic dicens S[4] et cum clamore protestaverit S[7] S[8] in facto recenti sequitur S[5] (i) ad iudicium S[1] S[9] S[10] (j) deductus fuerit S[1] S[9] S[10] K[3] (k) *adsunt* S[1] S[7] S[10] K[3] *desunt* S[6] De duobus, qui se vulneraverint: unus gladio, alter cutello. S[4] Sequitur de duobus, qui se vulneraverint: unus gladio, alter cutello vide. S[5] Quod si se duo vulneraverint mutuo: unus cultello et alter gladio S[9] Quod si se duo vulneraverint K[1] De eo si se duo vulneraverint K[2] De vulneribus cum cutello aut gladio. K[5] (l) Si duo S[10] (m) De duobus, qui se vulneraverit, et causa eorum pernoctavit. S[4] S[5] Pernoctaverint eodem die non fit querimonia. *ad articulum* S[8] De eo, qui pernoctaverit eodem die non fuit querimonia. *in indice rubricarum* S[9] De vulneribus dilatis ad proximum iudicium. K[5] (n) *desunt* K[1] K[2] (o) *deest* S[7] (p) eodem die sit querimonia S[1] S[10] eodem die K[3] querulatur eodem die S[7] S[8] (q) Si vir alterum vulnerat. S[7] S[8] Si vir alterum vulnerat et ambo. K[1] K[2] De vulneribus et de pugilli duello mercenario. K[5] (r) conquirent S[1] *deest* K[3] (s) De caucione fideiussoria pro vulneribus usque ad iudicium. S[4] S[3] Si vir alterum vulnerat et ipsis pax indicta fuerit. S[8] Si vir alterum vulnerat et ipsis pax. K[1] K[2] De vulneratore fideiusso et post ea vulnerato occiso. K[5] (t) Si vir S[7] (u) pace indicta *in indice rubricarum* S[9] (v) De duobus invicem vulneratis et cum unus incepcionem littis in vulneribus moritur. K[5] (w) Si duo S[7] S[8] K[1] K[2] (x) et querimonia usque ad iudicium dilatata fuerit. S[4] et querimonia usque ad iudicium dilatata. S[5] (y) querulaverint, et querimonia usque ad iudicium disposita fuerit S[1] querulantur, et querimonia usque ad iudicium fuerit S[9] querulaverint, et querimonia usque ad iudicium disposita fuerit vel dilata K[3] querulaverint S[7] S[8] (z) ⊢Item de viro, qui alterum.⊣ S[6]

[*37*]*(a)* ⟨de vulneribus⟩(b) Et si se duo mutuo vulneraverint equaliter et querulantur equaliter. Require in septimo folio primi.

[*39*]*(c)* Si aliquis detinet hunc, qui ipsum vulneravit in facto recenti. Require viii folio primi libri.

[*40*]*(d)* Quodsi se duo mutuo vulneraverint: cultello unus, alter gladio. Require octavo folio primi libri. ⟨Si duo se vulneraverint⟩(e)

[*41*]*(f)* Eciam si alter alterum vulneraverit et causam suam pernoctaverint. Require octavo folio primi libri.

[*42*]*(g)* Si duo vulneraverint se et ambo coram iudicio conpareant. Require nono folio primi libri.

[*43*]*(h)* Si vulnerat vir alterum, et si caucionem fideiussorie fecerit usque ad iudicium. Require nono folio primi libri.

[*44*]*(i)* Si se duo mutuo vulneraverint et ambo coram iudicio conpar[e]ant. Require nono folio primi libri.

(a) De duobus se mutuo vulnerantibus equaliter. xxxiii W^1 xxxiiii. De duello abtestari propter vulnera. C^3 (b) *manus C* C^1 (c) De duello obtente propter vulneracionem. xxxv W^1 lii. De vite racione alicuius vulnerantis. liii. De teste. C^2 xxxv. De testimonio homicidii vel vulneris. C^3 (d) De pugnacione gladiferi et cultiferi. xxxvi W^1 liiii. De vulneracione per cultellum. C^2 xxxvi. De mutilacione gladio et cultello. C^3 (e) *manus F* C^1 (f) De vulnere duellari pernoctato. xxxvii W^1 lv. De vulneribus pernoctatis. xxxvii. C^2 De vulnere duellari et pernoctata. (g) De protestacione ante querele. xxxviii W^1 lvi. De duobus vulnerantis coram iudicio comparentis. C^2 xxxviii. De vulneribus duellaria. C^3 (h) De fideiussoria vulnerum non retenta. xxxix W^1 lvii. De vulneracione unus alterum. C^2 xxxix. De pace coram iudicio facta. C^3 (i) De iudiciis vulnerum et de evasione homicidii. xl W^1 lviii. De vulneracione mutua duorum. C^2 xl. De iudiciis vulneris. C^3

[*38*] [(a]Item de eo[(b)], quid[(c)] [(d]in equo[d)] cum venditur, promitti teneri[(e)] debeat [(f)].[a)] XXXVIII

[*39*] [(g]Item de fure, qui in die tres solidos [(h] aut[(i)] in[(j)] nocte sex[(k)] denarios[h)] [(l)].[g)] XXXIX

[*40*] [(m]Item [(n]de eo[(o)], qui[n)] super alium [(p]querimoniam [(q]fecerit[p)] [(r]pro bonis[q)r)] [(s)].[m)] XL

[*41*] [(t]Item de hereditariis censualibus [(u]bonis[(v)] a claustro aut [(w)] alio domino[u)] [(x)].[t)] XLI

[*42*] [(y]Item de testimonio pro[(z)] persolutis debitis [(aa]aut proprio metseptimus[aa)].[y)] XLII

[*43*] [(bb]Item de testimonio [(cc]pro debito[cc)] persoluto[(dd)].[bb)] XLIII

[*44*] [(ee]Item de viro habente filium et viduam [(ff]ducit [(gg]habentem pueros[gg)ff)].[ee)] XLIIII

[*45*] [(hh)] [(ii]Item [(jj]de viro, qui [jj)]bona sua in iudicio [(kk]bannito uxori sue[(ll)] aut[(mm)kk)] [(nn)].[ii)] XLV

[(a)] De equo, quia in eo convenitur, quod promitti. S^7 *rubrica deest* S^8 De equo, quid in eo convenitur. K^1 K^3 De equo vendito, quid promitti debet. K^5 [(b)] equo S^5 S^9 [(c)] d *superscriptum* S^6 [(d)] *desunt* S^5 [(e)] *deest* S^4 S^{10} K^3 [(f)] sic dicens in omniam S^4 [(g)] De fure in die deprehenso tribus solidis. K^5 [(h)] subtraxerit S^{10} *deest* K^1 K^2 [(i)] et S^8 [(j)] *deest* S^7 S^9 [(k)] vii S^5 [(l)] aut plus, subtraxerit S^1 K^3 aut plus, subtraxerit sic S^4 aut plus, subtraxerit sequitur S^5 furatur S^7 [(m)] De hereditate et possessione. K^5 [(n)] Sequitur S^5 Si vir S^7 S^8 Si K^1 K^2 [(o)] viro S^1 S^4 S^5 S^9 S^{10} [(p)] conqueritur S^9 [(q)] *desunt* K^1 K^2 [(r)] *desunt* S^5 [(s)] que sibi dicit esse innata S^1 S^9 S^{10} hominibus, qui sibi innata hereditate S^7 que sibi innata sunt S^8 que sibi dicit innata K^3 [(t)] De bonis habitis a monasterio. K^5 [(u)] etc. S^4 sequitur S^5 *desunt* S^7 S^8 K^1 K^2 [(v)] *deest* S^9 [(w)] ab S^{10} [(x)] datis S^{10} [(y)] De testimonio. S^2 De testimonio super proprium alterius. K^5 [(z)] *deest* S^8 K^1 K^2 [(aa)] sic dicitur etc. S^4 *deest* S^5 S^7 S^8 K^1 K^2 super proprium metseptimus aut mettercius S^{10} [(bb)] De victione debitorum. K^5 [(cc)] *desunt* S^2 S^8 K^3 [(dd)] *deest* S^2 S^8 K^1 K^2 [(ee)] Quando vir habens primum ducit uxorem cum prius bona non habentes et post ea bona acquirunt, qui pueri succedunt. K^5 [(ff)] *desunt* K^1 K^2 [(gg)] *desunt* K^3 [(hh)] Iura raro fallunt. S^{10} [(ii)] De bonis, que pueris dantur. S^2 De donacione absque contradictione successoris per annum et diem. K^5 [(jj)] Si vir S^7 S^8 Quod si vir K^1 K^2 [(kk)] *desunt* K^1 K^2 [(ll)] et S^5 [(mm)] ante S^7 ac pueris suis S^{10} [(nn)] pueris suis dederit S^1 S^4 S^9 K^3 pueris S^5 pueros suos dededit S^7 pueris dederit S^8

[45]*(a)* Si vir equum vendiderit, promittere debet. Require nono folio primi libri.

[46]*(b)* | Si vir clara luce diei deprehensus fuerit, qui bone fame. Require 16rb
decimo folio primi libri.

[47]*(c)* Conqueritur vir super alterum pro bonis, quod sua sit vera hereditas. Require X folio primi libri. ⟨pro bonis hereditariis optimum⟩(d)

[48]*(e)* Si homo habuerit hereditaria censualia et bona a quodam monasterio. Require X folio primi libri.

[49]*(f)* Si vir debet producere testimonium super proprium. Require X folio primi libri. ⟨de testibus et producendo⟩(g)

[50]*(h)* Si aliquis debet persoluta debita probare. Require X folio primi libri. ⟨Si vir debet persoluta debita probare⟩(i)

[51]*(j)* Si vir ducerit uxorem viduam, que unum aut plures pueros habuerit. Require X folio primi libri. ⟨Si vir ducerit uxorem viduam⟩(k)

[52]*(l)* Si aliquis vir dederit suis pueris aliqua sua bona, et sue uxori, in iudicio bannito circa vitam suam, et bone racionis. Require XI folio primi libri. ⟨Si quis aliquid in iudicio dederit⟩(m)

(a) Vir si equ[u]m vendiderit, hoc tum certificet. XLI W^1 LVIIII. De li[bero] vendicione equi. C^2 XLI. De satisdacione equi venditi. C^3 (b) De querela ex parte furti nocturnalis vel diei. XLII W^1 LX. De furis deprehensione. C^2 XLII. De querela ex parte furti. C^3 (c) De bonis, que dum alienantur. XLIII LXI. De bonis conquestione. C^2 XLIII. De querela super hereditatem. C^3 (d) *manus C* C^1 (e) Si vir habuerit bona censualia a monasterio seu alio domino. XLIIII W^1 LXII. De hereditariis censualibus bonis. C^2 (f) De testimonio septem virorum vel tercium pro hereditate aut debito soluto. XLV W^1 LXIII. De produccione testimonium super proprium. C^2 XLV. De testimonio septem virorum vel cum pro hereditate vel debitis solutis. C^3 (g) *manus C* C^1 (h) De debito persoluto. XLVII W^1 Capitulum LXIIII. De protestac[i]one solutorum debitorum. C^2 (i) *manus E* C^1 (j) De viro habente filium ducentem uxorem viduam habentem pueros ambo peccuniam carentes. XLVI W^1 LXV. De viro ducente viduam. C^2 (k) *manus E* C^1 (l) De bonis, que alienis a viro aliquam assignantur et prius mulieri seu pueris iudicialiter fuerit attributa. XLVII W^1 LXVI. De viro dante pueris sua bona. C^2 (m) *manus C* C^1

[*46*] (aItem de hereditariis censualibus bonis(b) (cet edificiisc) (d).a) XLVI

[*47*]*(e)* Item de iure (fliberi(g) in emendis f)sine(h) obnoxii (i). XLVII

[*48*] (jItem (kde viro, quik) absque herede moritur (let(m) (nnepotem ex filian)l) (o).j) X[LVIII]

[*49*] (p(qItem si aliquisq) manum alterum(r) abtestare voluerit pro falso.p) XLIX

[*50*] (s(tItem de (ueot), si(v) viru) moritur, qui pueros habuerit (w).s) L

[*51*] (xItem de (y) querimonia(z) (aaet testimonioaa), (bbqui cum criminosis violenciisbb) (cc).x) LI

[*52*]*(dd)* (eeItem de querimonia, (ffquomodo unus conqueritur super aliumff).ee) LII

(a) De dono uxoris. S^2 De donacione edificiorum mulieri facta. K^5 (b) *deest* S^7 S^8 (c) *desunt* S^5 K^1 K^2 (d) super censualia bona donacione uxore coram iudicio S^1 K^3 super censualia bona donata uxore coram iudicio S^9 S^{10} super censualibus bonis vel censualia bona S^7 super censualia bona S^8 sic dicit S^4 (e) *rubrica deest* K^5 (f) *desunt* S^8 (g) liberti S^{10} K^1 K^2 abbatis S^9 (h) sui S^7 (i) et in successionibus in bonis naturalibus et in iniuriis S^1 et in successionibus in bonis naturalibus S^9 K^3 in successionibus in bonis S^7 S^8 (j) De nepote in bonis avi succedente. K^5 (k) Si vir S^7 S^8 K^1 K^2 (l) *desunt* S^4 S^5 (m) habente S^9 (n) non K^1 K^2 (o) habuerit S^1 S^7 S^8 S^{10} K^3 (p) De abtestacione manus pro falso aut vulneribus. S^1 S^5 S^8 De abtestacione manus pro falso aut vulneribus sic dicit. S^4 De abtestacione manus pro falso aut vulneribus. S^7 De abtestac[i]one manus. S^9 De abtestacione manus pro falso. K^1 K^2 Quomodo manus abtestatur pro falsitate. K^5 (q) De eo, qui vir S^{10} (r) suam S^{10} (s) De tutore puerorum. K^5 (t) *desunt* S^7 S^8 (u) viro, qui S^1 S^4 S^5 (v) qui S^9 (w) qui ad annos discrecionis nondum pervenerunt S^1 K^3 sic dicit S^4 qui ad annos pubertatis S^7 ad annos discrecionis perventos S^8 (x) De qualibet querimonia et testimonio, quod ad iudicium pervenerit. S^1 De cuiuslibet querele attestatione, que ad iudicium pervenerit. S^7 De querinoniis [s] testimoniis circa violencias. K^5 (y) equalibus S^4 S^5 qualibet S^8 K^1 K^2 omni S^9 S^{10} (z) querela *in indice rubricarum* S^9 (aa) *desunt* S^5 (bb) *desunt* S^{10} K^1 K^2 quod ad iudicium pervenerit S^4 S^5 S^8 (cc) cum clamore ad iudicium in facto manifesto deprehense K^3 (dd) *deest in indice rubricarum* K^3 (ee) De obsidiis et spolio. S^1 S^4 S^5 Pro insidiis et spoliis. S^7 S^8 K^1 K^2 De querela super insidiatorem. K^5 (ff) desunt S^9 S^{10}

*[53]**(a)* ⟨Si vir⟩(b) ⟨Ibidem habitur quod vir censualia bona non potest dare⟩(c) Si vir sue uxori sua edificia dederit, que super bona censualia edificia sunt, coram domino proprietatis, et coram suis vicinis, tempore sue vite. Si vir mercimonia aut mobilia. Require XI folio primi libri. ⟨Bona censualia non potest dare sine le[git]im[i]s successoribus⟩(d)

*[54]**(e)* Ubi alicuius monasterii obnoxius suam penam demeretur. Require XI folio primi libri.

*[55]**(f)* | ⟨Si moritur vir⟩(g) ⟨De successione⟩(h) Si moritur vir absque herede et 16va
nepotem ex filia habuerit, que exhereditata fuerit. Require XII folio primi libri. ⟨Ibidem stat. Si pater filium a se dimiserit, extunc filii filiorum et filiarum recipient equalem divisionem⟩(i)

*[56]**(j)* Si unus abtestari voluerit alteri manum suam. Require XII folio primi libri.

*[57]**(k)* Cum moritur vir, qui pueros habuerit, qui ad annum discrecionis nondum pervenerint. Require XII folio primi libri. ⟨Cum moritur vir⟩(l)

*[58]**(m)* Omnis querimonia ac testimonia, que cum criminosis violenciis cum clamore ad iudicium, in facto manifesto deprehense. Require XII folio primi libri. ⟨Omnis querimonia quomodo vinci debet in facto manifesto et in secundo li[bro] c. lxiiii⟩(n)[1]

*[61]**(o)* Sic stat Cunradus et conqueritur super Heynricum. Require XIIII folio primi libri.

(a) Si mulier bona censualia, edificia a viro habuerit. XLVIII W^1 LXVIII. De viro dante uxori sua edif[icia]. LXVI. De viro habente mercimonia. C^2 (b) *manus C* C^1 (c) *manus B* C^1 (d) *manus B* C^1 (e) De resignacione obnoxii bonorum monesterii erga dominum suum. LIX W^1 LXVII. De obnoxio alicuius monasterii. C^2 (f) Vir habens filiam maritatam carens hiis liberis. L W^1 LXVIII. De morte viri habente [*s*] nepotem ex filia. C^2 (g) *manus E* C^1 (h) *manus C* C^1 (i) *manus B* C^1 (j) De abtestificacione manus pro falsitate vel vulnere. LI W^1 LXIX. De abtestacione unius alteri. C^2 LII. De abtestatione manus. C^3 (k) De mundiburdio puerorum. W^1 C^3 LII LXX. De morte viri, qui pueros habuerit. C^2 LIII. (l) *manus E* C^1 (m) De querela violente. LIII W^1 LXXI. De querimoniis de in facto manifesto. LXXII. De facto manifesto gladii aut cultelli. LXXIII. De stupro et obsidio in facto manifesto. LXXIIII. De pacis violencia mulieris. C^2 (n) *manus E* C^1 (o) De querela super insidiatorem. LVI W^1 LXXVIII. De querela racione Cunradus super Henricum. C^2

---

1 *Speculum Saxonum, eodem manuscripto, fol. 90ra, articulus:* Qui captivatur in facto manifesto eo modo, ut fuerit detentus [*SSp. 1.66§1*]

[*53*] (a(bItem si(c)b) vulneratus vir (dad iudicium cum clamore deductus fueritd) (e).a) LIII

[*54*] (f(gItem quando vir g)furem(h) aut spoliatorem protestare voluerit.f) LIIII

[*55*] (iItem(j) ubi vir alterius verbum loqui debet.i) LV

[*56*] (kItem de (l) monomachali incitacione et(m) iure duelli (net testimonion) (o).k) LVI

[*57*] (pItem de eo, qui alium(q) ad iudicium aut(r) mortuum(s) aut(t) vulneratum perduxerit (u).p) LVII

131r [*58*] | (vDe viro(w), qui vitam aut manum (xpecunia redimeritx).v) LVIII

[*59*] (y(zDe fideiussoria caucione pro (aaviroz) ad statuendum coram iudicioaa) (bb).y) LIX

[*60*] (ccDe suppellectili (ddfeminarum (eeet quid ad hoc pertinet(ff)dd)ee).cc) LX

(a) De viro, qui vulneratus fuerit in facto manifesto. S^{4} S^{5} Quod si unus vir vulneratus fuerit in facto manifesto S^{8} Quod si unus vir K^{1} K^{2} De querela per vulneratum in facto manifesto deprehensum. K^{5} (b) De eo, si S^{10} (c) qui S^{9} (d) fuit in facto manifesto S^{7} (e) in facto manisfesto S^{1} K^{3} (f) De fure vel raptore obtestare in facto manifesto. S^{1} De furto aut spolio. S^{2} De fure vel raptore abtestare in facto manifesto sic loquitur. S^{4} De fure vel raptore in facto manifesto etc. S^{5} De fure et raptore obtestare. S^{7} De fure vel raptore. S^{8} De fure et latrone. K^{1} K^{2} De protestacione super furem aut spoliatorem et querela. K^{5} (g) De eo, qui S^{9} (h) *deest* S^{10} (i) De eo, qui alterius prolocutor fuerit in iudicio. S^{1} S^{5} De alterius fuerit prolocutor in iudicio, sic dicitur etc. S^{4} De eo, qui alterius prolocutor fuerit. S^{8} De eo, qui alterum ad iudicium aut. K^{1} K^{2} Quando quis compellitur ad loquendum alicuius verbum in facto manifesto. K^{5} (j) De eo S^{9} (k) De eo, qui alterius proloqutor sue. K^{1} K^{2} Qui aliquem equaliter salutat seu alloquitur ad duellum. K^{5} (l) iure S^{10} (m) vel S^{4} S^{5} (n) sic dicit S^{4} deest S^{5} S^{9} (o) monomachali S^{1} S^{8} K^{3} (p) De incitacione monomachali. K^{1} K^{2} Qui actor in probacione deficit eodem iudicio iudicatur. K^{5} (q) *deest* S^{5} (r) *deest* S^{4} S^{5} S^{8} (s) occisum S^{4} S^{5} (t) *deest* S^{5} (u) et ipsum pacis violatorem devincere voluerit S^{1} (v) De iure privatis et infamibus. K^{5} (w) eo S^{9} K^{1} K^{2} (x) *desunt* K^{1} K^{2} (y) Qui aliquem fideiusserit ad statuendum pro crimine ad statuendum. K^{5} (z) Qui fideiusserit virum pro scelere ad statuendum S^{8} Qui eciam fideiusserit unum virum pro scelere S^{10} Qui fideiusserit virum pro scelere K^{1} K^{2} (aa) scelere S^{4} scelere conqueratur S^{5} (bb) pro aliquo scelere S^{1} S^{9} S^{10} K^{3} (cc) Quando mulier recipit supellectilia, quid viro manere debet. K^{5} (dd) sic dicit S^{4} (ee) *desunt* K^{1} K^{2} (ff) spectat S^{9}

[*59*]*(a)* ⟨de vulneribus⟩(b) Si vulneratus vir ad iudicium deductus fuerit cum clamore in facto manifesto, et si ita inbecillis aut debilis fuerit, quod per tutorem querulari oportet. Require XIII folio primi libri. ⟨Ibidem de prescripcionibus et eciam quomodo proposicio debet transferre⟩(c)

[*60*]*(d)* ⟨De furtis. Quando vir furem⟩(e) Quando vir furem aut spoliatorem protestare voluerit, qui cum manifesto facto ad iudicium cum clamore productus fuerit. Require XIIII folio primi libri. ⟨Ibidem quod circa factum manifestum opportet homo iurare methseptimus⟩(f)

[*articulus deest*]

[*63*]*(g)* | ⟨Qui monomachaliter suum salutare⟩(h) Qui monomachaliter suum equa- 16[vb]
lem salutare seu alloqui voluerit, hunc iudicem petere oportebit. Require XV folio primi libri. ⟨Ibidem de satisdacionibus alias gwarem⟩(i)

[*articulus deest*]

[*64*]*(j)* Qui vitam aut manum pecunia eximerit, quod iure meruerit. Require XVII folio primi libri. ⟨Ibidem de periurio, qui est perluens⟩(k)

[*65*]*(l)* ⟨de fideiussoribus⟩(m) ⟨Qui eciam fideiusserit⟩(n) Qui eciam fideiusserit virum unum pro scelere ad statuendum. Require XVII folio primi libri. ⟨Ibidem quod nemo debet proscribi, nisi sibi vadetur ad vitam⟩(o)

[*62*]*(p)* | Si mulier recipit suppellectilia, ad que spectant oves et modele, 16[va]
et omnia cibaria. Require XV folio primi libri. ⟨Et ibidem quomodo mulier debet decorare suum stratum⟩(q)

(a) De querela manifeste actionis. LIIII W[1] LXXV. De viro vulnerato et deducto ad iudicium. LXXVI. De induciis, que pernoctaverit. C[2] (b) *manus C* C[1] (c) *manus B* C[1] (d) De querela super furem. LV W[1] LXXVII. De protestacione viri super furem et spoliatorem. C[2] (e) *manus C* C[1] (f) *manus B* C[1] (g) LXXX. De uno pacis violatorio monomachali. LXXXI. De paupere, qui suam querimoniam meliorare potest ante satisdacionem. C[2] (h) *manus E* C[1] (i) *manus B* C[1] (j) De furis perditis. LVIII. LIX W[1] LXXXII. De exem[p]cione vite cum pecunia et. LXXXIII. De bonis unius v[i]ri pluribus adinventis. C[2] LX. Ista sunt iure privati. C[3] (k) *manus B* C[1] (l) De promissione presentacionis. LX W[1] LXXXIIII. De fideiussoria pro scelere. LXXXV. De prescripcione. C[2] LXI. Qui fideiussit statuere aliquem ad iudicium. C[3] (m) *manus C* C[1] (n) *manus E* C[1] (o) *manus E* C[1] (p) Viro mortuo, tum suppellectilia succedetur mulieri. LVII W[1] LXXIX. De recep[to] suppellectile a muliere ad quam pertinet. C[2] LVIII. suppellectilia quod pertinet. C[3] (q) *manus B* C[1]

[*61*]*(a)* (bDe armis bellicis (cet suppellectili feminarum (det(e) sacerdotumd)c) (f).b) LXI

[*62*] (gDe diffinicionibus sentenciarum (h). g)LXII

[*63*] (iDe iudicio (j(kin iudiciumj) et loqucione virik) (l).i) LXIII

[*64*]*(m)* (nDe fideiussoria (opro boniso).n) LXIIII

[*65*] (p(qDe viro, quiq) fustibus aut baculis percussus fuerit (r).p) LXV

[*66*]*(s)* (t) De hereditate, (uque(v) (wmortuo domino permanet(x) sine successorew)u) (y). LXVI

[*67*] (zDe viro, qui (aaoccisus fuerit et pueros (bb) habueritaa) (cc).z) LXVII

[*68*] (dd(eeDe viroee), qui alteri coram iudicio (ffiurare debuitff) (gg).dd) LXVIII

[*69*] (hh) (iiDe arestacione equorum(jj).ii) LXIX

(a) *in indice rubricarum rubrica et tres subrubricae:* De armis bellicis et supellectili feminarum; De eo, ubi pupilli annos non habent; De eo, post arma bellica; De eo, si puer intraverit religionem. S^{9} (b) De suppellectilibus mulierum S^{4} S^{5} (c) *desunt* S^{8} K^{5} (d) *desunt ad articulum* S^{6} *desunt* K^{1} K^{2} (e) aut S^{9} (f) iure ac monachorum S^{1} seu monachorum S^{9} iure et monomachorum [*s*] S^{10} iure ac eciam monachorum K^{3} (g) De sentenciis et collo quis. K^{5} (h) sic dicens dicit etc S^{4} (i) De procuratore quod unus cum constituit procuratorem apte non loquitur. K^{5} (j) iudicum S^{1} S^{4} S^{5} S^{8} *desunt* S^{9} S^{10} (k) *desunt* S^{5} K^{1} K^{2} (l) sic dicit S^{4} (m) *deest rubrica* K^{3} (n) De iudicio sequitur K^{1} De iudicio iuris K^{2} De fideiussore pro debito. K^{5} (o) bonorum S^{8} K^{1} K^{2} (p) Quod si vir baculis. K^{1} K^{2} De vulneribus fustis et flaveis. K^{5} (q) Quod si vir S^{8} (r) ita quod verbera inflata fuerint S^{1} S^{10} ita quod vulnera inflata fuerint K^{3} (s) *deest rubrica* K^{5} (t) Sequitur S^{5} (u) post mortem domino pertinet S^{10} (v) *deest* S^{4} S^{5} (w) caret herede S^{8} K^{1} K^{2} (x) *deest* S^{5} (y) sic dicit etc. S^{4} (z) Cum unus aliquem evaserit pro homicidio aliis pro eodem non tenetur respondere. K^{5} (aa) pueros tres aut plures K^{1} K^{2} (bb) tres aut plures S^{1} S^{8} S^{10} K^{3} (cc) duos aut plures S^{9} (dd) De iuramentis. K^{5} (ee) Sequitur de viro S^{5} (ff) *desunt* K^{1} K^{2} (gg) sic dicens S^{4} (hh) Sequitur S^{5} (ii) De equo subtracto et arestato. K^{5} (jj) bonorum K^{1}

[*66*]*(a)* | ⟨Quid pertinet ad arma bellica et quid ad suppellectile[m]⟩(b) Mulier pro armis bellicis dare debet gladium mariti vel suum etc. Require xvii folio primi libri. ⟨Et ibidem senior dividit et iunior eligit⟩(c) 16[vb]

[*67*]*(d)* De qua sentencia prius requiritur, de hec prius diffiniri debet. Require xix folio primi libri.

[*68*]*(e)* In omni loco iuris est, ut iudex iudicet cum sentenciis. Require xix folio primi libri.

[*69*]*(f)* ⟨fideiussoria⟩(g) ⟨Si vir pro pecunia aut pro debito⟩(h) Si vir pro pecunia aut pro debito fideiussor fuerit et idem vir moritur. Require xix folio primi libri.

[*70*]*(i)* ⟨si vir (j) aut cum fustibus⟩(k) Si vir cum fustibus aut baculis percussus fuerit. Require xix folio primi libri. ⟨Si vir cum (l) fustibus percussus⟩(m)

[*71*]*(n)* Si hereditas mortaliola sine herede inventa fuerit. Require xx folio primi libri.

[*72*]*(o)* Si vir occisus fuerit, qui pueros tres aut plures habuerit. Require xx folio primi libri.

[*73*]*(p)* Si eciam iuramenta promissa venerint super diem ligatum. ⟨de iuramentis⟩(q)

[*74*]*(r)* | ⟨de expensis in lite factis⟩(s) Si aliquis arestat equum et dicit, quod sibi sit subtractus aut eo sit spoliatus. Require xx folio primi libri. ⟨de furtis aut spolio equorum et ibidem de [e]xpensis in (t) lite factis⟩(u) 17[ra]

(a) Sacerdos dividit cum fratribus et monachis. lxi W[1] De armis bellicis. Capitulum lxx[x]vi C[2] (b) *manus B* C[1] (c) *manus B* C[1] (d) De interlocutorio. lxii W[1] (e) Vir habens prolocutorem marito non loquatur. lxiii W[1] (f) De mortuo fideiussore. lxiiii W[1] (g) *manus C* C[1] (h) *manus B* C[1] (i) De percusso cum baculo. lxv W[1] (j) ⊢pro partem⊣ *del. manus E* C[1] (k) *manus E* C[1] (l) ⟦cum⟧ C[1] (m) *manus C* C[1] (n) De obmortua hereditate. lxvi W[1] xciii. Si hereditas sine herede invenitur. C[2] (o) De viro mortificato habente plures pueros. lxvii W[1] xciiii. Si vir occiditur, tres aut plures pueros habet et. C[2] xciiii. Si vir occiditur, tres aut plures pueros habet et. C[2] (p) De iuramentis absque pena. lxviii W[1] xcv. Iuramenta super diem ligatum venientia, iudex iuramenta prorogare potest pro alia die. C[2] (q) *manus B* C[1] (r) De impedicione equorum. lxix W[1] xcvi. Si arestat aliquis equ[u]m et dixit, esse eum sibi subtractum aut eo spoliatum. C[2] lxx. De arestacione equorum. C[3] (s) *manus C* C[1] (t) ⟦in⟧ *manus C* C[1] (u) *manus C* C[1]

[70] De pena iudicis [(a]et hereditate[a)] [(b)]. LXX

[71] [(c(d(e]De viro, qui vulneratus [(f)] aut [d)]percussus fuerit et querulari[(g)] noluerit[(h)].[e)c)] LXXI

[72] [(i)] [(j]De bonis illius, qui ad mortem condempnatur[(k)].[j)] LXXII

[73] [(l]De viro, qui [(m]pueros habeat [(n]et moritur et[(o)] bona[n)m)] [(p)].[l)] LXXIII

[74] [(q]De etate[(r)] puerorum, [(s]quando[(t)] tutores [(u]eligere[(v)] possunt[u)s)].[q)] LXXIIII

[75] [(w]De viro, qui[(x)] suam libertatem[(y)] possit[(z)] probare.[w)] LXXV

[77] [(aa]De pecunia [(bb(cc]ludo aut[(dd)bb)] taxillis acquisita[cc)].[aa)] LXXVI

[76] [(ee]De bonis[(ff)], que alicui [(gg]danda[(hh)] fuerint[(ii)] ad servandum[gg)] [(jj)].[ee)] LXXVII

[78] [(kk(ll]De eo[ll)], qui se a[(mm)] descripcione iuramento expurgat[(nn)].[kk)] LXXVIII

[(a)] *desunt* S^8 K^5 [(b)] sic dicit etc. S^4 sequitur S^5 [(c)] Nullus compellitur ad querelam. K^5 [(d)] Si vir S^8 K^1 K^2 [(e)] De eo, qui trucidatus fuerit et querulari voluerit S^4 S^5 [(f)] fuerit S^9 [(g)] *in ms.* querulare S^6 [(h)] voluerit S^{10} *deest* K^1 K^2 [(i)] Sequitur S^5 [(j)] De proscriptis. K^5 [(k)] deest K^1 K^2 [(l)] Si vir moritur, qui habet bona. K^1 K^2 De puerii post mortem patris. K^5 [(m)] moritur et pueros legittimos S^4 moritur et qui pueros legittimos etc. S^5 [(n)] *desunt* S^8 [(o)] eciam K^3 [(p)] habuerit nulli donata S^1 S^9 S^{10} K^3 [(q)] Puer in duodecim annis eligit quem vult in tutorem. K^5 [(r)] hereditate S^5 [(s)] qui tutor K^1 K^2 [(t)] quam S^5 [(u)] habuerit S^4 S^5 [(v)] esse S^8 [(w)] Quomodo homo suam libertatem habet probare. S^8 Quomodo homo suam libertatem. K^1 Quomodo homo suam hereditatem liber. K^2 De illiberis. K^5 [(x)] quomodo S^1 quando S^4 S^5 S^{10} [(y)] hereditatem S^9 [(z)] debet S^5 [(aa)] De servo bona domini perdente vel sua propria. K^5 [(bb)] *desunt* S^8 K^1 K^2 [(cc)] taxillorum aut in ludo acquisita S^4 S^5 [(dd)] et S^9 [(ee)] De bona ad servandum traditis aut obligatis. K^5 [(ff)] illis S^4 S^5 [(gg)] dantur K^1 K^2 [(hh)] data S^9 S^{10} [(ii)] *deest* S^{10} [(jj)] in deposito S^1 est ipse etc. S^4 [(kk)] Qui se extraxerit a descripcione et si solutus. S^8 De servicio deservito. K^5 [(ll)] *desunt* K^1 K^2 [(mm)] ex S^4 S^5 [(nn)] *deest* K^1 K^2

[*75*]*(a)* Quando iudex suam extorquet penam, ulterius nec aliquam aliam super hanc potest extorquere. Require XX folio primi libri.

[*76*]*(b)* Si vir vulneratus aut trucidatus fuerit. Require XXI folio libri primi.

[*77*]*(c)* Et si vir proscriptus fuerit (d) aut ad sentenciam mortis iudicatus. Require XXI folio libri primi.

[*78*]*(e)* Si vir moritur, qui habeat pueros. Require XXI folio primi libri. ⟨Si vir mo[ritur]⟩(f)

[*79*]*(g)* ⟨Quando puer duodecim annorum fuerit⟩(h) Quando puer duodecim est annorum, tunc potest eligere pro sua voluntate quem voluerit pro tutore. Require XXI folio primi libri.

[*80*]*(i)* Si vir alloquitur aliquem, qui suus sit illiber. Require XXI folio primi libri.

[*articulus deest*]

[*81*]*(j)* ⟨Expenses [*s*] si quis comederit⟩(k) ⟨post sequitur capitulum si quis expensas apud aliquam comederit sive habuerit⟩(l) Si aliquis super aliquem conqueritur pro debito aut pecunia ludo taxillis acquisita. Require XXI folio primi libri.

[*82*]*(m)* Qui se extraxerit a descripcione et solutus, iudicatus fuerit. Require XXI folio primi libri.

(a) De pena iudicis. LXX W[1] XCVII. De extorsione pene pro iudice, ulterius ius nec aliam potest extorquere. C[2] (b) De uno vulnerato querulari nolente. LXXI W[1] XCVIII. Si vir vulneratus aut truncatus [*s*] fuerit. C[2] (c) De homine diffamato vel suspenso. LXXII W[1] XCIX. Nullus bona prescripti aut ad mortem damnati recipit in hereditate. C[2] (d) ├ad┤ *del. manus A* C[1] (e) Vir si moritur bona sua heredibus succedunt. LXXIII W[1] (f) *manus D* C[1] (g) Quando puer potest eligere mundibordium. LXXIIII W[1] CI. Puer XII annorum pro sua voluntate tutorem eliget et tutor matri et puero racionem faciat, et in eadem etate iudicio sisti debet. C[2] (h) *manus B* C[1] (i) De probacione illibertatis. LXXV W[1] W[2] CII. Alloquitur aliquis aliquem, quod suus sit illiber et suam libertatem protestari debet. C[2] (j) De debitis expensarum et ludorum. K[5] Pro debito tesserato. LXXVI W[1] De debito tasserato. LXXVI W[2] CIII. Si quis conqueritur pro debito aut pecunia pro ludo taxillorum aquisita, pro eo non respondebit. C[2] (k) *manus C* C[1] (l) *manus G* C[1] (m) De extracto a proscripcione. LXXVII W[1] W[2] CIIII. Subtraccio a proscripcione et solutus fuerit, penam iudex obtinet. C[2]

[*articulus deest*]

[*79*] (a) (b(cDe viro, super quem (d) c)querulatum fuerit pro debito (e).b) LXXIX

[*80*] (fDe querela, que facta fuerit super aliquem et ipse pecierit (g).f) LXXX

[*81*] (hDe facto manifesto, quod(i) (jad iudicium fuerit(k)j) .h) LXXXI

[*82*] (lDe iudicio burgravii Meÿdeburgensis(m).l) LXXXII

[*83*] (nDe iudicio iudicis etc.n)(o) LXXXIII

[*84*] (pDe fiscacione(q) seu(r) publicacione bonorum(s).p) LXXXIIII

(a) Sequitur S^5 (b) Si super virum querulatum fuerit. K^1 K^2 De debitis negatis et confessis. K^5 (c) Si super virum S^8 (d) in S^2 S^3 S^7 S^8 S^9 K^4 K^5 (e) sic dicet S^4 (f) De satisdacione petenda. S^8 K^1 K^2 De satisdacione sic dicit etc. S^4 De satisdacione sic dicitur. S^5 De satisdacione. K^5 (g) satisdacionem S^1 S^9 S^{10} (h) Quod querela in facto manifesto sit cum clamore. K^5 (i) *deest* K^1 (j) *desunt* K^1 K^2 (k) aductum fuerit S^5 deductum fuerit, sic dicit S^4 fuerit deductum S^9 S^8 S^{10} (l) De iudicio burgrabii pro debitis. K^5 (m) pro debitis K^5 *deest* S^1 S^4 S^5 S^9 S^8 S^{10} K^1 K^2 (n) Quod iudex omni die iudicat. K^5 (o) sic dicit S^4 (p) De bonis publicatis et fiscatis. K^5 (q) satisdacione K^1 K^2 (r) et S^8 (s) S^{10} K^1 K^2

[*83*]*(a)* ⟨Si servus deservitum⟩(b) Si servus deservitum precium super suus(c) dominum obtinuerit. Require XXII folio primi libri.

[*84*]*(d)* ⟨Cum testibus debitum⟩(e) Si vir conqueritur super alterum pro suo debito cum testibus. Require XXII folio primi libri.

[*85*]*(f)* | ⟨De satisdacione⟩(g) Si vir super virum conquestus fuerit et satisda- 17rb
cionem petit. Require XXII folio primi libri.

[*86*]*(h)* ⟨de furtis et aliis criminibus ad vitam transferentibus⟩(i) Omnis querela, que ad iudicium pro capitali crimine in facto manifesto deducta fuerit, debet conqueri cum clamore. Require XXII folio primi libri.

[*87*]*(j)* In iudicio burgravii ⟨de magnis iudiciis⟩(k) Maydeburgensis ⟨In iudicio burgravii⟩(l) potest vir pro debito bene querulari. Require XXII folio primi libri.

[*88*]*(m)* Iudex debet iudicium exercere et de eo temptare cottidie in vero iudicii loco. Require XXIII folio primi libri.

[*89*]*(n)* Si viro sua bona publicata seu fiscata fuerint. Require XXIII folio primi libri. ⟨Ibidem habes quod debes ibi manere tribus diebus et tribus noctibus comedere et bibere⟩(o)

(a) De sercivio deservito. K^5 Quando precium iure obtentum solvatur. LXXVIII W^1 W^2 CV. Servus deservitum precium super domino obtinet et nullam penam demeretur, si dominus eodem die deservitum solverit. C^2 (b) *manus C* C^1 (c) *a.c.* super C^1 (d) De querela testimonio debitorum. LXXIX W^1 CVI. Conqueritur quis pro debito cum testibus fidedignis, qui in iure non possunt reprobari et ille dicit se innocentem. C^2 (e) *manus B* C^1 (f) Quid satisdacio signat. LXXX W^1 W^2 CVII. Peticio satisdacionis per actorem reus negare non potest et ab quivis ipse caucionari debet. C^2 (g) *manus F* C^1 (h) CVIII. Querela pro capitali crimine in facto manifesto cum clamore, quod ostenditur manifestum. C^2 (i) *manus D* C^1 (j) De querela peccuniarum cum testimonio coram burgrabio. LXXXII W^1 *ibidem, numerus articuli* LXXXI W^2 CIX. In iudicio burgrabii Meydeburigensi vir potest querulari pro debito. C^2 LXXXIII. De absolucione reconpense et pene et emende. C^3 (k) *manus C* C^1 (l) *manus F* C^1 (m) De tempore et loco iudiciorum. LXXXIII W^1 *ibidem, numerus articuli* LXXXII W^2 CX. Iudex debet iudicium exercere quottidie in vero iudicii loco. C^2 (n) De impedicione pannorum et aliarum rerum. [*error scribae, titulus articuli sequentis*] LXXXIV W^1 CXI. Vir bona sua publica fiscata iure in eo illi possideat, quis iustificacionem induxerit. C^2 (o) *manus B* C^1

131^{v} [*85*] | [(a]De bonorum[(b)] arestacione, [(c(d]similiter et[d)] equorum[c)] [(e)].[a)] LXXXV

[*86*] [(f]Si vir conqueritur [(g]post debitum[g)] a manu mortua.[f)] LXXXVI

[*87*] [(h(i]De viro, qui [(j(k]probabiliter aut[(l)] scienter[j)i)] contra alium ad iusticiam[k)] [(m)].[h)] LXXXVII

[*88*] [(n(o)]De mulieribus[(p)], que [(q]in manifesto [(r]facto[q)] detente fuerint[r)].[n)] LXXXVIII

[*89*] [(s]De viro, [(t]qui habeat[t)] duplices pueros [(u)].[s)] LXXXIX

[*90*] [(v]De inproperacione scabinorum [(w)].[v)] LXXXX

[(a)] De arrestacione rerum mobilium. K^5 [(b)] rerum S^5 [(c)] *desunt* S^5 S^8 K^1 K^2 [(d)] seu S^9 S^{10} vel S^4 [(e)] sic dicit S^4 [(f)] De debito post manum mortuam, sic dicit in iuramenta. S^4 De debito post manum mortuam. S^5 De informacione debitorum post manum mortuam. S^8 De informacione bonorum debitorum. K^1 De informacione debitorum. K^2 De debitis post mortuam manum. K^5 [(g)] pro debito S^{10} [(h)] De viris se mutuo vulnerantibus. K^5 [(i)] Si vir S^8 De eo, si vir K^1 K^2 [(j)] *desunt* S^4 [(k)] oportet ad iusticiam se exhibuerit S^5 [(l)] *deest* S^9 ac S^{10} [(m)] se exhibuerit S^9 S^8 S^{10} K^3 exhibuerit, sic dicit S^4 [(n)] De femina in facto manifesto deprehensa, ubi iurat metseptima et semper sola K^5 [(o)] Sequitur S^5 [(p)] vulneribus K^1 K^2 S^5 S^8 facto mulierum S^9 [(q)] manifeste S^9 [(r)] *desunt* K^1 K^2 [(s)] De duplicibus pueris S^4 S^5 S^8 K^1 K^2 [(t)] *desunt* K^5 [(u)] habente K^5 [(v)] Quando aliquis scabinum in sede increpaverit. K^5 [(w)] sequitur S^5

[*90*]*(a)* ⟨Si vir alloquitur⟩(b) ⟨de furtis⟩(c) Si vir alloquitur bona vel pannos aut quidquam suarum rerum fuerit. Require XXIII folio libri primi. ⟨et ibidem de arestacione equorum⟩(d)

[*91*]*(e)* Si vir super virum conqueritur pro (f) debito manu mortis, et ipsum informari voluerit. Require XXIIII folio primi libri. ⟨post mortuam manum⟩(g)

[*92*]*(h)* Si vir cum scitu ad iusticiam contra alium se exhibuerit, et alter noluerit aut spreverit. Require XXIIII folio primi libri. ⟨de vulneribus⟩(i) ⟨se defendit⟩(j)

[*93*]*(k)* ⟨ubi femina vinci potest et ubi eam nemo vincere potest⟩(l) ⟨de vulneribus ubi femina vi[ncere] potest⟩(m) Si femina deprehensa fuerit in facto manifesto in homicidio aut vulneribus duello dignis. Require XXIII folio primi libri. ⟨et ibidem quomodo eam, nemo eam vincere potest⟩(n)

[*94*]*(o)* ⟨Si vir duplic[es] pueros habue[rit]⟩(p) ⟨Ubi duplices pueri sunt; de succes[s]ione⟩(q)
Si vir duplices pueros | habuerit et pueros antea exradicavit. Require XXIIII 17va
folio primi libri.

[*95*]*(r)* Si vir scabinum in scampno incidenter in iudicio bannito increpaverit. Require XXV folio primi libri. ⟨de eodem in quinto folio⟩(s)[1]

(a) De debito mortue manus. LXXXVI [*error scribae, titulus articuli sequentis*] W^1 De impedicione pannorum et aliarum rerum. LXXXIIII W^2 CXII. De subtraccione panni aut similium iuramentum decernitur, ut iudicat sentencia et de equi subtraccione. CXIII. Pars si ad venditorem trahit, et si dixerit, quod eum in foro libero emerit et venditorem habere non possit. C^2 (b) *manus D* C^1 (c) *manus C* C^1 (d) *manus B* C^1 (e) De debito mortue manus. LXXXVI W^1 W^2 CXIII. Vir super virum conqueritur pro debito manu mortis et ipsum infamare voluerit in iure. C^2 (f) ├duo┤ *del. manus A* C^1 (g) *manus E* C^1 (h) Pater potest filium proprie manus iuramento eximere. LXXXVII W^1 W^2 CXIIII. De infiscacione vulnerum et vulneratus venit ad defensionem. C^2 (i) *manus C* C^1 (j) *manus G* C^1 (k) De accione manifesta mulierum. LXXXVII W^1 *ibidem, numerus articuli* LXXXVIII W^2 CXIIII. Si femina deprehensa fuerit in facto manifesto in homicidio aut in vulneribus, vir propior est eam vincere metseptimus. C^2 (l) *manus D* C^1 (m) *manus G* C^1 (n) *manus B* C^1 (o) De viro duplices habente pueros. LXXXIX W^1 W^2 CXV. Vir duplices pueros habens, a primis bona affert et secundis dat et moritur. C^2 (p) *manus D* C^1 (q) *manus C* C^1 (r) De scabino coram iudicio male tractato. XC W^1 W^2 CXVI. Si vir scabinis in scamno incidentaliter in iudicio bannito increpaverit et probaverit per suos sodales. C^2 XCI. De scabinis maletractatis. C^3 (s) *manus B* C^1

1 *cf. art. 28, fol. 31va–b, fol. or. Vv*

[*91*] [(a]De homicidio [(b]aut[(c)] vulneribus[b)] [(d)].[a)] LXXXXI

[*92*] [(e]De contencione, [(f]que [(g]facta fuerit[g)] in die aut [(h]tempore noctis[h)f)].[e)] LXXXXII

[*93*] [(i]De peticione[(j)] prolocutoris.[i)] LXXXXIII

[*94*][(k)] [(l]De suppellectili feminarum[(m)].[l)] LXXXXIIII

[*95*][(n)] [(o]De iuramento incolatus [(p)].[o)] LXXXXV

[*96*] [(q]De tutoribus pupillorum.[q)] LXXXXVI

[*97*] [(r]De iuramento [(s]pro enormibus[(t)] verbis[s)] [(u]coram iudicio[u)].[r)] LXXXXVII

[*98*] [(v]De civibus Meÿdeburgensibus.[v)] LXXXXVIII

[(a)] De obligato ad temporalem dum super bona. K[5] [(b)] *desunt* K[1] S[8] sequitur K[2] [(c)] et S[10] [(d)] dicit S[4] [(e)] De probo homine et contencione ac[c]usato. K[5] [(f)] aut homicidio, quod sit clara die S[8] facta nocte aut die S[9] homicidio K[1] K[2] [(g)] sit S[4] *desunt* S[5] [(h)] in nocte S[4] S[5] [(i)] De procuratoribus. K[5] [(j)] iure S[2] [(k)] *error: rubrica ex sequenti articulo* S[8] Sequitur S[5] De eo K[1] K[2] [(l)] Oves ad supellectilia pertinent et alia in littera. K[5] [(m)] sic dicit S[4] dicitur S[5] [(n)] De eo. S[8] [(o)] Quod nemo potest probare suum incolatus. K[5] [(p)] Sic dicit etc. S[4] [(q)] De pupillis tutore carentibus. K[5] [(r)] De promisione iuramenti. S[2] De iudicio enormium. S[8] Qui promittit iuramentum ab eo non solvitur nisi ex voluntate iudicis. K[5] [(s)] *desunt* S[10] [(t)] malis S[4] S[5] [(u)] *desunt* S[4] S[5] S[9] [(v)] Quod nemo trahat alium ad iudicium alienum. K[5]

[*96*]*(a)* Si super virum querimonia facta fuerit(b) pro homicidio aut vulneribus, et ipse se ac[c]omodaverit circa suam hereditatem. Require XXV folio primi libri.

[*97*]*(c)* Si casu contencio oritur clara die, si probus vir pro eo accusetur. Require XXV folio primi libri.

[*98*]*(d)* Quem vir provocato rogaverit. Require XXV folio primi libri.

[*99*]*(e)* Et quando vir moritur, tunc uxori debent dare et suppellectilia. Require XXV folio primi libri. ⟨et ibidem de exaccione civitatis⟩(f)

[*101*]*(g)* Quando pupilli suum verum tutorem non poterint habere. Require XXVI folio primi libri. ⟨extunc modo tenentur respondere pro dictis bonis ad annos discrecionis⟩(h)

[*102*]*(i)* Si vir super alterum conqueritur, quod sibi aliquid abedificavit. Require XXVI folio primi libri. ⟨Si quid uni abedificatur⟩(j)

[*100*]*(k)* Ubi eciam vir iuramentum promiserit coram iudicio pro enormibus verbis. Require XXVI folio primi libri. ⟨Ibidem quod iudex debet dare secundum voluntatem ad dimittendum iuramenta⟩(l)

[*103*]*(m)* Eousque cives Maydeburgenses veram accionem aut responsionem. Require XXVI folio primi libri.

(a) De promissa fideiussionis ex parte homicidii super hereditatem et excessionem fideiussionis. XCI W[1] *ibidem,* fideiussoria *loco* fideiussionis W[2] CXVII. Si super virum querimonia facta fuerit pro homicidio aut vulneribus et se fideiusserit in sua hereditate comparendum. CXVIII. Nullus vir potest cogi caucionem fideiussorie facere suam recompensam. C[2] (b) *in ms.* fuerint [*s*] C[1] (c) De inculpacione nocturnali. XCII W[1] De inculpacione diuturnali. XCII W[2] (d) CXXI. Rogat vir quem, ut advocatus fiat et causam suam foveat. C[2] (e) Mortuo viro mulieri ad suppelle[cti]lia oves assignantur. XCIIII W[1] W[2] CXXII. Quando vir moritur, tunc uxor debet dare omnia suppellectilia exceptis causis in sentencia insertis scriptis. C[2] (f) *manus B* C[1] (g) Pueri carentes mundibordio non coartantur. XCVI W[1] W[2] LXXIIII. Quando pupilli verum tutorem habere non possunt. C[2] (h) *manus B* C[1] (i) Si quis alteri sue hereditatis quidquam edificaverit. XCVII W[1] *ibidem,* abedificaverit *loco* edificaverit W[2] CXXV. Vir alterum super [*s*] loquitur, quod sibi aliquid abedificat de suis bonis hereditariis. C[2] (j) *manus D* C[1] (k) De iuramento male tractatoris. XCV W[1] W[2] CXXII. Promitit iuramentum coram iudicio pro malis verbis depillacione eciam ex consensu iudicis. CXXIII. Actor si reum pro iuramentis causa Dei vel peticionis hominum dimittere vellet absolutum etc. C[2] (l) *manus B* C[1] (m) LXXVI. Nullus in iudicio in alieno iure cives Meydeburigenses conveniat, nisi coram domino. C[2]

[*99*] (aDe inpedimento (b) coram iudicio (c).a) LXXXXIX

[*100*] (dDe sculteto, si aliquem inpedierit in (esua(f) querelae).d) C

[*101*] (gIudicium super advocatum.g) CI

[*102*] (h) De irruencia (i) domiciliorum (j). CII

[*103*] (kDe obsidiis (let quod femine stuprantur l) (m).k) CIII

[*104*] (nDe promissione querele tenenda(o).n) CIIII

[*105*] (pDe debitis ex parte patris.p) CV

(a) Nullus alium impediat coram iudicio. K[5] (b) quod sit K[1] K[2] S[8] (c) sequitur S[5] (d) Quod si scultetus aliquem impedierit. S[8] De eo, quod si scultetus aliquem. K[1] K[2] De iudicio alique in querela impedire. K[5] (e) iudicio etc. S[4] iudicio S[5] (f) *deest* S[9] (g) De advocato. S[4] De advocato sequitur. S[5] De advocato, si aliquis impedierit. S[8] K[1] K[2] De advocato iniuste iudicante et quis ipsum iudicat. K[5] (h) Hic vide S[4] (i) ├super┤ S[6] (j) sequitur S[5] (k) De iudiciis burgrabii. K[5] (l) *desunt* K[1] S[8] (m) sequitur S[5] (n) De tenenda querela coram iudicio. S[4] De tenenda querela coram iudicio sequitur. S[5] De concordia in causa inchoata. K[5] (o) tenere et concordia facta fuerit S[10] *deest* S[9] (p) De debito post patrem obligato. K[5]

[*104*]*(a)* | Nullus alterum impedire debet coram iudicio. Require XXVI folio primi libri. ⟨De impedimentis iudicialibus⟩(b) ⟨de impedimenstis in iudicio⟩(c) 17vb

[*105*]*(d)* Nunc attendatis super eo, si scultetus aliquem impedierit. Require XXVI folio primi libri. ⟨Ibidem de reconpensa hominum in fine⟩(e)

[*106*]*(f)* Nunc de advocato attendatur, si non iuste iudicaverit cum sibi querulatur. Require XXVI folio primi libri. ⟨de advocato⟩(g)

[*108*]*(h)* Si aliquis alteri fecerit domorum irruenciam die ac nocte. Require XXVIII folio primi libri. ⟨domorum i[r]ruencia⟩(i) ⟨Si quis fecerit domorum⟩(j) ⟨Si quis fecerit domorum⟩(k)

[*107*]*(l)* Insidias et stupra, et domorum irruenciam burgravius iudicat. Require XXVIII folio primi libri. ⟨domorum ir[r]uencia⟩(m)

[*109*]*(n)* Et si vir suam promiserit (o) tenere querelam. Requiri XXVIII folio primi libri.

[*110*]*(p)* Si vir querulatur super alterum pro debito, quod sibi pro suo patre teneatur. Requiri XXVIII folio primi libri. ⟨post mortuam manum debitum patris⟩(q)

(a) De impedimento coram iudicio. XCIX W^1 W^2 CXXVII. Nullus alterum impedire debet in iudicio postquam banirato [*s*] fuerit pro iniuria et ipsum querela impediat. CXXVIII. Si hoc peractum fuerit in iudicio castellani aut in iudicio sculteti, extunc tria. C^2 (b) *manus G* C^1 (c) *manus B* C^1 (d) De sculteto nolente iudicare. C W^1 W^2 CXXIX. Si sculteto [*s*] aliquem in sua querela impedierit et sibi iusticiam non fecerit, sinistre recusando. CXXX. Si pro facto criminali pro quo iudicium facere recusavit, sive pro homicidio. CXXXI. Vir pro debito in captivitatem publicam presentatus fuerit pro crimine, quod transit ad collum. C^2 (e) *manus B* C^1 (f) Advocatus si iniuste iudicaverit. CI W^1 W^2 CXXXII. De viro advocato, qui iniuste iudicaverit, cum sibi querulatur et hoc propter amorem aut munera, aut ob. C^2 (g) *manus C* C^1 (h) De probacione violenciarum. CII W^1 De capto propter inquisiciones nocturnales. CIII W^1 W^2 CXXXIIII. Si quis fecerit alteri domorum irruenciam nocte ac die, et si ille detentus fuerit in facto manifesto cum clamore et ad iudicium adducitur. C^2 (i) *manus C* C^1 (j) *manus F* C^1 (k) *manus E* C^1 (l) De violenciarum probacione. CIII W^1 *ibidem, numerus articuli* CII W^2 CXXXIII. Nullus alius iudicat irruenciam domorum nisi burgrabius aut scultetus, ut patet in sentencia. C^2 (m) *manus E* C^1 (n) De concordia querularum. CIIII W^1 W^2 CXXXV. Promittit quis tenere querelam et post concordia sequetur, tunc iudici penam succumbet. C^2 (o) ⊢te⊣ *del. manus A* C^1 (p) De debito mortue manus. CV W^1 W^2 CXXXVI. Querulatur quis pro debito super alterum, qui sibi pro suo parte tenetur. C^2 (q) *manus G* C^1

[*106*]*(a)* (bDe pecudibus(c), que noxam inferunt(d).b) CVI

[*107*] (eDe eo, quis spoliat (fcivitates aut suos concivesf).e) CVII

[*108*] De iuramento (g) Iudeorum (h). CVIII

[*109*]*(i)* (j) (kSic iurabit Iudeus(l) (m).k) CIX

[*110*] (nExplicit numerus Iuris Municipalis. Incipit de statutis Imperii terris Saxonie. Capitulum primumn)

132r [*111*] | (oDe imperio (pquamdiu stetitur(q)p) .o) Capitulum primum; Capitulum II [*s*]

[*112*] (rDe mercatoribus (sin quo permanere possents).r) Capitulum II

[*113*]*(t)* De civitate Meÿdeburg(u) (vac eius fundacionev). Capitulum III

(a) *in indice rubricarum divisio articuli in tres minores:* De pecudibus, que noxam faciunt. Qui caucionem servat. Si homo occidit canem. S^{9} (b) De hiis, qui dampnum faciunt in peccudis. S^{4} De hiis, qui dampnum faciunt peccudis. S^{5} De animali noxam faciente. K^{5} (c) animalibus S^{8} K^{1} K^{2} (d) faciunt S^{8} S^{9} (e) De qui cives suos spoliat, sic dicit in ista litera. S^{4} Qui suos cives spoliat. S^{8} K^{1} K^{2} Cum aliquis suos cives spoliat. K^{5} (f) cives suos. Sequitur S^{5} cives suos S^{9} (g) pessimo S^{10} (h) sic dicens S^{4} et rota ipsorum K^{5} (i) *deest rubrica* S^{5} K^{5} (j) Sequitur S^{10} (k) Quod tu in hac causa sis. *in indice rubricarum* S^{9} (l) deest S^{1} K^{1} K^{2} S^{8} (m) ut in litera ista S^{4} (n) Explicit liber iuris municipalis domini Nicolai viri famosi, civis Sandomiriensis, dicti Paczonow. S^{1} *desunt* S^{10} K^{1} K^{2} De iure municipali unde originem sumpsit. K^{5} (o) De iudicio super imperatorem. S^{4} S^{5} De imperio Grecorum. K^{5} (p) *desunt* S^{1} (q) in potencia steterit K^{1} K^{2} (r) Hic sequitur videre. S^{4} De iure mercatorum, quod eis dedit imperator, quod dicitur municipale. K^{5} (s) *desunt* S^{4} S^{5} S^{10} K^{1} K^{2} (t) *deest articulus* S^{10} (u) Meẏdborg K^{5} (v) *desunt* S^{1} S^{4} S^{5} K^{1} K^{2} K^{5}

[*111*]*(a)* Si quis equum aut canem habuerit vel aliquod pecus. Requiri XXVIII folio primi libri. ⟨Si quis equum⟩(b)

[*112*]*(c)* Si quis spoliaverit suos civitatum [*s*], qui proprium aut feodum vel hereditatem habuerit. Require XXIX folio primi libri.

[*113*](d) Hoc est illud iudicium et iuramentum, per quod vel cum quo Iudeus iurare debet sue evadere. Require XXIX folio primi libri. ⟨Iuramentum Iudeorum⟩(e)

[*114 pars 1*]*(f)* | Nunc placeat audire et intelligere, quomodo presens scrip- 18ra
tum informat ex relacione. Primo de Imperio. Require XXX folio primi libri.

[*114 pars 2*]

[*115*](g) Nunc audire [et] intelligere potestis, quod [de] principibus et baronibus, et his omnibus, qui digne nomen sorciuntur. Require XXXI primi libri.

[*116*](h) Nunc attendatis, quis cesarem iudicare debet. Require XXXI folio primi libri.

[*117*]*(i)* Extunc mercatores dicebant ad cesarem, quod libenter scire vellent, in quo permanere possent. Require XXXI folio primi libri.

[*118*]*(j)* Nunc attendatis de civitate Maydeburg. Cum primo Maydeburg locata fuerit. Require XXXII folio primi libri. ⟨et ibidem quam advocatus non debet iudicare sine scabinis⟩(k)

(a) De cane aut equo damnum faciente. CVI W^1 W^2 CXXXVII. De bruto vinco quocumque, quod si fecerit damnum. C^2 (b) *manus E* C^1 (c) Si quis spoliat suos civitatenses. CVII W^1 W^2 CXXXVIII. Spoliat quis suos cives seu civitatis homines, qui proprium aut feodum vel hereditatem habuerit. Et de stupro virginis. C^2 (d) De Iudeorum iuramento. CVIII W^1 W^2 CXXXIX. Iuramentum Iudei contra Christianum ex iure imperatorum. C^2 CIX. Iudei iuramentum C^3 (e) *manus C* C^1 (f) CXXXX. De imperio, quomodo terre Saxonie ius suum fuerit constitutum et confirmatum. C^2 CX. De imperio unde ortum habuit C^3 (g) CXXXXI. De regimine imperii quo iure imperiali debet permanere. C^2 (h) De iudicio cesaris, quis illum debeat iudicare, nunc restat dicere. C^2 (i) CXLIII. De mercatoribus videndum est in presenti. CXLIIII. Pax fuit confirmata per beatum Petrum Apostolum. C^2 (j) CXLV. De fundacione civitatis Meydeburk restat in presenti dicere. CXLVI. Numerus scabinorum et de prelacione prime sentencie sculteti restat dicere. C^2 (k) *manus F* C^1

[*114*]*(a)* (bDe civitate Hallis, (cubi (dsentenciam recipere debeantc)d).b) Capitulum IIII

[*115*] (eDe (freprobacione sentencie, (gubi eam quereregf).e) Capitulum V

[*116*]*(h)* (iDe (jpalacia, (kper quem medium ipse feceritk)j).i) Capitulum VI

[*117*]*(l)* (m(nDe reprobacione sentenciem), quantum (o) dare opportet.n) Capitulum VII

[*articulus deest*]

[*articulus deest*]

[*articulus deest*]

[*articulus deest*]

[*articulus deest*]

(a) *deest articulus* S^4 S^5 S^{10} (b) De civitate Hallis, ubi reprobata. K^1 Nunc attendatis de Hallis civitate, de civitate Hallis, ubi reprobata. K^2 Ubi de Hallis sentencia recipitur cum reprobatur. K^5 (c) *desunt* S^1 K^1 (d) *desunt* K^1 K^2 (e) Cum in Meÿdburg sentencia reprobatur trahitur in Scarthow et de Scarthow in pallaciam. K^5 (f) Meÿdenburg K^1 K^2 (g) *desunt* S^1 S^4 S^5 (h) *deest articulus* S^4 S^5 (i) Quando pallacia super Othonem imperatorem facta. K^5 (j) civitate Hallis K^1 K^2 (k) *desunt* S^1 (l) *desunt rubricae* S^1 K^1 K^2 *deest articulus* S^4 S^5 (m) *desunt* S^{10} (n) Quid succumbet aut sive reprobatur. K^5 (o) plus S^{10}

[*119*]*(a)* Nunc attendatis de Hallis, ubi ius suum querere debent. Require XXXIII folio primi libri.

[*120*]*(b)* Nunc atten[den]dum est, si Maydeburg sentencia reprobaretur. Require XXXIII folio primi libri.

[*121*](c) Nunc attendatis de pallacia, per quem modum ipse pallaciam fecerit. Require XXXIII folio primi libri.

[*122*](d) Et cum sentencia ante pallaciam fuerit data. Require XXXIIII folio primi libri.

[*123 pars I*]*(e)* Nunc attendatis, quantum plus dare oportet. Require XXXIIII folio primi libri. ⟨Ibidem habes de scabinis et eorum emendis⟩(f)

[*123 pars II*]

[*124*]*(g)* | Nunc dicere volo nobis de pallacia, quomodo illa debeat conve- 18rb
niri. Require XXXIIII folio primi libri.

[*125*]*(h)* Scultetus de Maydeburg debet recipere lit[t]eram civitatis cum sigillo ipsius pendente. Requiri XXXV folio primi libri.

[*126*]*(i)* Hic audire et intelligere potestis, quomodo hii omnes domini debent citari. Require XXXV folio primi libri.

[*127*]*(j)* Eodem modo sicut scultetus citat burgravium. Sic burgravius debet citare hos tres principes. Require XXXV folio primi libri. ⟨Iste eciam est primum et in glosis usque ad capitulum, ubi domini se confederarent iuramento periuro⟩(k)

(a) CXLVII. De [H]aliis videndum est, ubi suum ius querere debent. C^2 (b) CXLVIII. Si sentencia in Meydeburg reproba[re]tur, ubi querere debet, hoc in presenti videre debet. C^2 (c) CLIX. De pallacia videndum est. Idem dicendum est de sentencia procedenti. C^2 (d) CL. Predictis viris viginta octo debent dare cuilibet unum solidum per se ut patet. C^2 (e) CLI. De penis, qui reprobant sentenciam. Et de emenda iniuste reprobata. C^2 (f) *manus B* C^1 (g) CLII. Pallacia, quomodo debet conveniri et diffiniri. C^2 (h) CLIII. Scultetus debet recipere litteram civitatis sigillo ipsius pendente et hanc mittere debet supremo advocato. C^2 (i) CLIIII. Sentencia ad premissa cum pena regali trium marcarum aurearum. C^2 (j) CLV. Burgravius predictas tres principes citat sub banno regio. C^2 (k) *manus C* C^1

[*articulus deest*]

Conclusio libri huius sequitur. Capitulum VIII

[*128*]*[a]* Nota. De latitudine ac longitudine mansi Franconici.

Conclusio libri.

---

[a] *rubrica ad articulum* C[1] CLVI. Mansus quot virgas et quot iugera habeat, nunc dicendum est. C[2]

Prologus[(a)]

137v [(b)] [(c]Incipit prologus [(d]super librum Iuris Municipalis[c)][d)].

In nomine [(e)] Patris et Filii et Spiritus Sancti. Amen. [(f]Primo dicit de Sancta Trinitate et fide, et[f)] hoc opus locatum est supra [(g)] fundamentum, de quo dicit Apostolus: et fundamentum aliud nemo ponere potest [(h)] id[(i)], quod positum est, quod est [(j)] Christus [*1 Cor. 3, 11*]. Ubi enim Christus fundamentum non est, ibi nullius boni operis[(k)] potest esse[(l)] edificium ad invocacionem summe et individue [(m)] Trinitatis. Exemplum laudabile me conpellit et racio violenta, quia hoc[(n)] a maioribus factum[(o)] esse dinoscitur, quod[(p)] a minoribus[(q)] [(r]sit[(s)] conpletum[r)]. Et mos [(t)] retinendus est[(u)] fidelissime vetustatis; licet enim non exemplis, sed[(v)] legibus est iudicandum, verumptamen exemplum potest aliquis sequi maxime, ubi recte factum [(w)] aliquod intuetur ad probandum. Siquidem[(x)] quod[(y)] in quolibet principio a gloria Trinitatis debeat auxilium peti, sola racio sufficere potest; cuiuslibet enim rei potissima[(z)] pars est principium, et ex hiis, que inordinate inchoata sunt, non potest ordinaliter[(aa)] agi. Quod[(bb)] per se patet, qualiter[(cc)] bene et laudabiliter omnia geruntur, si principium fuerit decens et amabile Deo, et vix[(dd)] [(ee)] [(ff]est, ut[ff)] [(gg)] bono[(hh)] peragantur exitu, que[(ii)] malo [(jj)] inchoata sunt inicio. Quibus omnibus luce clarius[(kk)] apparet, quia filius[(ll)] laudabilis a bono
138r dependent principio | et tamquam suo maiori subiacet [(mm]et [(nn)] maioribus maius[(oo)] vertitur et ibi caucius est agendum[mm)]. Ipsa est enim[(pp)] benedicta Trinitas, in cuius nomine et consilio omnis actus progreditur. Sic enim ad[(qq)] omnipotentis Dei auxilium[(rr)] debemus oculos erigere, ut non[(ss)] in armis[(tt)] sciencie vel elloquencie iaculis [(uu]confidere valeamus[(vv)][uu)], sed[(ww)] omnem

---

(a) S^1 S^4 S^5 S^6 S^{10} K^3 K^4 W^1 JL (b) Et sic S^{10} (c) Hic prologus fuerit. Incipitur de cesare Ottone, qui fundavit templum in Meydeburg. Et sequitur. K^4 Prologus in ius Maÿdeburgense JL (d) *desunt* S^1 libri iuris municipalis sive civilis deTheutunico translatus in Latinum etc. W^1 (e) ├Domini amen┤ S^6 Dei W^1 (f) *desunt* JL (g) firmum S^1 S^4 S^5 S^{10} K^3 K^4 W^1 JL (h) preter S^1 S^4 S^5 S^6 S^{10} K^3 K^4 W^1 JL (i) illud W^1 (j) scilicet K^3 (k) *deest* W^1 S^{10} (l) superesse S^1 S^4 S^5 S^{10} K^3 K^4 JL (m) Sancte K^3 (n) quod JL (o) *deest* K^3 (p) id JL (q) maioribus S^4 S^5 (r) quoque observari debeat JL (s) est, ut sit S^{10} (t) quippe JL (u) *deest* S^{10} (v) sit S^4 S^5 W^1 (w) est W^1 (x) si S^{10} K^4 sed JL (y) quidquid K^4 S^{10} (z) potentissima K^4 S^{10} potissime [*s*] S^4 S^5 (aa) aliquid ordinate JL (bb) ⟨Quod⟩ K^4 *deest* S^{10} JL (cc) qui aliter S^5 (dd) *deest* S^4 S^5 (ee) primus S^1 uno S^4 S^5 in uno S^{10} K^4 (ff) *desunt* S^{10} K^4 JL (gg) in S^{10} W^1 (hh) *deest* S^{10} ⟨ut bono⟩ K^4 (ii) quam S^4 (jj) iam S^4 S^5 (kk) *deest* S^{10} (ll) finis S^1 S^4 S^5 S^{10} K^3 K^4 W^1 (mm) In quo quidem principio cautius est agendum. Cum enim inceptio omnum est gravissima, ne is, qui se putat stare, in foribus delinquat, ad causam causarum, ut pro auxilio recurrat, necesse est. JL (nn) in S^4 W^1 (oo) magnis S^4 (pp) nanque JL (qq) *deest* S^4 (rr) presidium JL (ss) *deest* W^1 (tt) artis S^{10} (uu) confidamus JL (vv) debeamus S^{10} (ww) si K^3

spem, omnem propositum erigamus ad providenciam Trinitatis, ipsa enim laborantibus[(a)] aurem apperit et inclinat [(b)]: Apprehendite etenim[(c)] disciplinam [(d]et sapienciam[d)], nequando irascatur Dominus et [(e)] pereatis de via iusta [*Ps 2,12*]. Nos[(f)] sermo propheticus exhortat, felix exhortacio, dulce consilium; qui [(g]enim apprehendit sapienciam[(h)], Christum, ut verum, fateor, apprehendit [(i)]. Ipse[g)] enim est sapiencia, iusticia, veritas, fortitudo, sancitas. Et qui ignorat sapienciam et Scripturas, Christum ignorare Scripture[(j)] testimonio perhibetur. Christus etenim Dei virtus est [(k]sapiencia, ignorancia autem Scripturarum ignominia est Christi[k)] iuxta apostolicum. Apprehendit siquidem sapienciam, qui insipienciam[(l)] procul pellit, egressus enim unius alterius operatur ingressum. Cum[(m)] renunciatur inprobitati, nascitur[(n)] virtus [(o)]. Qui enim[(p)] sapienciam non apprehendit, inproperabitur ei a Domino, et ideo sacerdocio non fungetur[(q)] et [(r]in tenebris[r)] ignorancie latitans[(s)], mentis oculis excecatus iusticiam invenire non poterit. Sine qua, etsi ceterarum [(t)] virtutum in ipso fulgeant radii, pro nichilo [(u)] repu-
138^v tantur, ipsa [(v)] est[(w)] enim, que[(x)] inter ceteras virtutes | perfectissima dicitur, que iura omnibus[(y)] distribuit et ex[(z)] causa iusticia[(aa)] appellatur, [(bb]ut legitur[(cc)] in auctoritatibus[(dd)],[bb)] ut[(ee)] omnes [(ff)] obediant iudicio[(gg)]. Hec est[(hh)]enim illa virtus laudabilis, que diffinicione nobili[(ii)] diffinitur. Iusticia ergo[(ij)] est[(kk)] constans et perpetua voluntas, ius suum cuique tribuens [*D. 1.1.10 pr.*], que concupiscencie conatus sua virtute conprimit ac [(ll)] [(mm]desiderat refrenare[(nn)], ut in prohemio *Decretalium*[1] [mm)]. Cum igitur subiectum libri presentis nullum sit aliud ponere preter ius[(oo)] et iusticiam et felix liber [(pp)] cui tam nobile famulatur subiectum, et felix, inter cuius ubera[(qq)] liber iste tamquam mirre [(rr)] fasciculus poterit commorari. Merito igitur, qui[(ss)] opus tantum aggreditur, ut librum signatum septem sigillis[(tt)] apperiat, summe[(uu)] Trinitatis [(vv)] auxilium expetet et imploret. Ego siqui-

[(a)] errantibus S^5 [(b)] propter quod nos sermo propheticus exhortatur JL [(c)] enim S^5 *deest* JL [(d)] *desunt* S^4 S^5 [(e)] ne S^4 S^5 S^{10} K^4 [(f)] Ne [*s*] S^4 *deest* S^5 [(g)] *desunt* S^{10} [(h)] ⟨sapienciam⟩ K^4 [(i)] summum bonum JL [(j)] ex scriptore S^{10} [(k)] *desunt* S^5 [(l)] in sapiencia S^4 [(m)] *deest* S^4 [(n)] nacisscitur S^1 W^1 [(o)] et cum eiicitur superbia, adest humilitas. Et iterum JL [(p)] *deest* JL [(q)] finietur S^5 [(r)] inteletur S^4 S^5 [(s)] latinitas [*s*] K^4 [(t)] in K^4 [(u)] tamen JL [(v)] iusticia JL [(w)] *deest* S^{10} [(x)] *deest* K^3 [(y)] *deest* S^4 [(z)] ea S^{10} ea de JL [(aa)] iusta K^4 [(bb)] *desunt* JL [(cc)] elegit S^{10} [(dd)] auctoribus K^3 K^4 S^{10} [(ee)] Illius JL [(ff)] ├┤ S^6 [(gg)] *deest* S^4 S^5 [(hh)] *deest* S^4 S^5 [(ii)] obiliter [*s*] S^{10} [(ij)] *deest* S^5 JL [(kk)] *deest* S^{10} [(ll)] de [*s*] S^1 S^6 [(mm)] desideria refrenat JL [(nn)] confrenare S^4 S^5 reservare S^{10} K^4 [(oo)] iudicium W^1 [(pp)] est S^4 S^5 [(qq)] verba S^1 K^4 JL [(rr)] ├e┤ S^6 [(ss)] cum S^4 S^5 [(tt)] ⟨sigillis⟩ S^1 [(uu)] supreme S^4 S^5 [(vv)] est S^4

1 *Bulla Rex pacificus Gregorii papae IX*: iustitia conatus eius sua virtute reprimeret.

dem(a) (b) inter ceteros lectores(c) minimum me reputans (det ignorancie mee tenebrasd) non ignorans, excusare me deberem, cum propheta dicente: •A,•a,•a• Domine Deus, ecce(e) nescio loqui, quia(f) puer ego sum [*Jr 1,6*], quoniam(g) altus est puteus (h) sapiencie, et non est cum quo hauriam, quemadmodum mulier Chananea (i), cum de Dei omnipotentis (j), qui aquam vivam distribuit et largitur, (k) confisus (l) misericordia(m) (n) opus presens aggredior spem gerens firmissimam, quod de fonte graciarum suarum ad siccitatem meam rivulum derivando(o), de pane sue consolacionis, ne in via deficiam, buccelam michi porrigat. (p) Ne igitur (q) prolixitas, que frequenter parit fastidium, sermonem protrahat(r) in(s) inmensum, (tsed attendens, quam omne artificium per exercicium recipit incrementumt), (unon
139^{r} in armisu) sciencie vel elloquencie iaculis confisus, | sed omnem spem, omnem propositum referens ad omnipotentis Dei legis consilium, que (v) est omnium vera(w) salus. (xSed quoniam scriptum est(y), ut nemo alciorem locum in scolis teneat, nisi cui laborum assiduitas et studiorum prolixitas suffragatur. Egox) fundo principium super(z) lapidem angularem, qui est Christus Ihesus(aa), (bb) Alpha et O[mega], principium et finis etc. (cc)

(a) si quid W^{1} (b) illud scriptum attendens, quod nemo altiorem locum in scholis quibusvis teneat, nisi cui laboris assiduitas et studiorum prolixitas suffagatur, quamvis JL (c) ⟨lectores⟩ S^{1} (d) *desunt* W^{1} (e) nichil S^{5} *deest* S^{10} (f) qui S^{1} (g) qui S^{4} (h) sciencie S^{10} JL (i) locuta est JL (j) Filio JL (k) tamen JL (l) de S^{10} JL (m) minime W^{1} (n) eius JL (o) demonstrando S^{10} (p) Sed JL (q) inter W^{1} (r) *deest* K^{3} (s) *deest* S^{5} S^{10} (t) brevibus iam orationem meam absolvam JL (u) *desunt* S^{10} (v) lex JL (w) naturaliter JL *deest* K^{3} (x) *desunt* JL (y) *deest* K^{4} (z) sub S^{4} (aa) *deest* K^{3} S^{10} (bb) hoc est K^{3} (cc) Hic finitur prologus. S^{1} W^{1} Amen S^{4} S^{5} K^{3} Explicit prologus S^{10} ⟨modum⟩ K^{3} Sequitur K^{4}

Incipit

82ra S^{1}: | ⟨Insuper ius municipale cum huius racione⟩ Hic incipitur ius municipale de Theutonico translatum in Latinum per Conradum notarium quondam Sandomiriensem ac civem civitatis supradicte.

S^{4}: Hic incipitur ius municipale per Cunradum civem Sandomiriensem de Theutonico translatum in Latinum.

S^{5}: Incipit ius municipale per Cunradum civem Sandomirinesem de Theutunico translatum in Latinum.

S^{10}: Incipit ius municipale de Theutonico in Latinum.

K^{4}: Hic incipitur de cesar Ottone, qui fundavit templum in Meÿdeburg, qui ius municipale transmutavit de Theutonico in Latinum.

K^{5}: Liber primus incipit felicit[er].

Incipit

W[1]: Incipiunt iura municipalia.
C[3]: In nomine Patris, et Filii, et Spiritus Sancti. Amen. Incipiunt tres libri Meydburgenses[1].

1 *Liber primus: Ius municipale Magdeburgense (Weichbildrecht); liber secundus: Speculum Saxonum; liber tertius: Sententiae scabinorum Magdeburgensium.*

Versio Sandomiriensis

S[6] (*Dział. I*)

Articulus 1 (a)

139r [*1*] | (b) ⟨Regula iuris. Mutare quis consilium non potest in alterius detrimentum. Item quod omnes tangit debet ab omnibus (c) approbari⟩{a} (dCesar Otto Ruffus(e) fundavit templum in Meÿdeburg etd) dedit civibus(f) municipale ius ⟨powÿszschone prawo⟩{b} secundum(g) eorum arbitrium (het secundum consilium seniorumh). (i) Extunc (jarbitrati sunt, quod eligerentj) scabinos ac consules, ⟨arbitrium voluntas consensus vulgariter uchwalona wola⟩{c} scabinos ad (kdiuturnum temporis(l)k) et consules ad unum annum. (m) Qui tunc iuraverunt et(n) nunc(o) iurant (p) annis singulis, {d} dum(q) eliguntur, ius (rac profectumr) et honorem custodire(s) ⟨civitatis⟩(t) et agere(u), quanto (vcaucius acv) (w) melius (xsciant autx) possunt, cum consilio (yac iuvaminey) seniorum (z). (aaConsules exponunt suum conventum secundum(bb) suum placitum ac voluntatem cum(cc) seniorum consensu.aa) ⟨conventum id est consilium alias gromada mÿesczska⟩{e} (dd) (eeConsules eciam(ff) habent potestatem iudicandi {f} super quamlibet vacuam mensuram ac pondera iniusta, ac coretos iniustos et cuiuslibet(gg) cibi seu potus mercimonia.ee) ⟨Regula iuris. Contractus ex convencione legem

---

(a) S[1] S[2] S[3] S[4] S[5] S[6] S[7] S[8] S[9] S[10] K[4] K[5] *Art. 1* (b) ⟨Incipit fundamentum. Cesar Otho Ruffus fundit templum Maydiburk et dedit civibus municipale ius secundum eorum arbitrium et secundum consilium seniorum⟩ *manus A* S[3] (c) ⊢approbari⊣ *del. manus A* S[6] (d) Cum Maydeburgensis civitas primo plantabatur, S[2] (e) Crassus S[7] (f) incolis S[2] (g) *deest* S[10] (h) *desunt* S[10] (i) Cum Maydeburgensis civitas primo plantabatur, datum fuit incolis ipsius ius municipale iuxta ipsorum arbitrium. S[2] Vobis dedit civibus municipale ius secundum eorum arbitrium et secundum consilium seniorum. S[3] Regula iuris K[5] (j) decrevunt eligere S[2] (k) longa tempora S[2] (l) *deest* S[1] S[2] S[3] S[4] S[5] S[7] S[8] S[9] S[10] K[4] K[5] (m) ⟨Iuramentum consulum⟩ K[5] (n) sicut S[2] (o) tunc S[10] (p) tria seu alia S[2] (q) cum novi S[2] quando S[4] S[5] (r) *desunt* S[2] (s) et fructum civitatis conservare S[2] (t) *manus B* S[6] ⟨civitatis⟩ K[4] *deest* S[6] S[7] S[10] (u) dilatare S[2] (v) *desunt* S[2] (w) aut S[3] S[9] (x) *desunt* S[2] (y) *desunt* S[2] (z) civitatis S[2] ⟨et hoc non dimittendo non racione amoris molestie ire vel munerum sicut eos iuvet Deus et sancti eius; Consules ex ac [*?*]⟩ K[4] (aa) *desunt* S[2] (bb) sive S[7] (cc) et K[5] (dd) *subrubrica:* Consulum iudicium. K[5] (ee) Consules hanc habent potestatem, qui iudicant super omnem forum defr[a]u[d]osum [*?*] in comestibilibus et bibilibus, super iniustas pensas, mensuras et libras. S[2] (ff) hanc S[2] (gg) tunas S[7]

{a} *manus A* S[6] ⟨Arbitrium id est voluntas census vchwala wolna, alias dicitur wyelkyerz wsziithkÿch liber primus incipit felicit[er]⟩ K[5] {b} *manus A* S[6] {c} *manus A* S[6] {d} ⟨Conventum id est consilium vulgariter Gromada mieszczka⟩ K[5] {e} *manus A* S[6] {f} ⟨Municipale ius vulgariter powÿêszone prawo⟩ K[5]

Versio Cracoviensis

C^1 (*BN 12607*)

Articulus 1 (a)

[*1*] | ⟨Liber primus et folium primum⟩ (b) Cesar Octo(c) Ruffus fundavit templum in Maÿdeburg et dedit civibus municipale ius secundum eorum | arbitrium et secundum consilium seniorum. Extunc(d) arbitrati sunt, quod(e) eligerent(f) (g scabinos ac consules g), scabinos ad diuturnum tempus(h) et consules ad unum annum. Qui tunc(i) iuraverunt et nunc(j) iurant(k) annis singulis, dum(l) eligentur, ius ac profectum et (m) honorem custodire civitatis et agere(n), quanto caucius(o) ac melius sciant (p aut possunt p), cum consilio aut iuvamine seniorum. (q) Consules exponunt suum conventum secundum suum(r) placitum ac voluntatem cum seniorum consensu (s). Consules eciam habent potestatem iudicandi super quamlibet vacuam mensuram ac pondera iniusta, ac coretos iniustos (t) et quelibet cibi aut potus mercimonia(u). Et quicumque hoc(v) violaverit, demeretur tres Sclavonicas marcas, 27ra I

(a) K^1 K^2 K^3 W^1 C^1 C^3 *Art. 1* W^2 C^2 *deest folium* (b) ⟨iurant sic consules et scabini⟩ C^3 ⟨Otto⟩ C^3 (c) Otto K^1 C^3 Ottho K^2 Otho K^3 (d) Et tunc qui K^1 K^2 (e) ut K^1 K^2 (f) *in ms.* elegerent [*s*] C^1 (g) *desunt* W^1 (h) temporis W^1 (i) autem K^1 K^2 (j) *deest* K^2 (k) iuratis K^1 K^2 (l) quod C^3 (m) ad K^3 (n) augmentare et conservare C^3 (o) aut K^3 (p) *desunt* C^3 (q) Et hoc non dimittendo ratione amoris, molestie, ire vel munerum, sicut eos iuvet Deus et sancti eius. C^3 *in glossa* K^4 ⟨legum ius⟩ C^3 (r) *deest* K^3 (s) ⟨artificum⟩ C^3 ⟨Consules⟩ C^3 (t) ⟨xxxv⟩ C^3 (u) institoria K^3 (v) *deest* K^3

accipere dimescuntur. Item. Quod semel placuit amplius disciplire non potest.⟩{a} (aEt quicumque hoc violaverit, demeretur tres Slavicas marcas, ⟨slowÿenÿskÿe grzywnÿ⟩{b} qui faciunt triginta sex(b) solidos.a) {c} (c) (dQuando consules suum conventum (e) exponunt, extunc quidquid ibi statutum fuerit aut compromissum in isto conventu, (fquod(g) iure Divino non contradicitf), ⟨Regula
139v iuris. Nullus ex consilio dummodo frandulentum non fuerit obligatur⟩{d} | firmum(h) et (inon(j) violabiliteri) debet observari. Et quicumque (k) violaverit, hoc consules habent(l) agere (m).d) (n) (oEt quicumque ad conventum (p) venire neglexerit, cum(q) signum datur per campanam, demeretur sex denarios.o) Sin autem conventus(r) sibi pronunciatus(s) fuerit, (t) demeretur quinque(u) solidos. (v) ⟨Solidus habet videlicet XII alenses quem precium szelag.⟩{e}

Articulus 2 (w)

[2] {f} (x) Qui penestici vocantur, si in aliquo delinquerint vel si in aliquo demerentur (y) statutis civitatis, ⟨Communitas Gmÿn mÿesczski emenda pokup emendare pokupÿcz⟩{g} (zita ut (aacivitatisz) (bbautaa) consulumbb) decreta⟨ustawÿ⟩{h} violaverint, si in hoc convicti(cc) fuerint, demerentur

---

(a) Et qui in istis delinquit, hic suum ius tres marcas Sclavonicas demeretur, que in numero faciunt triginta sex solidos. S^{2} (b) tres S^{10} K^{4} (c) Consules inter se eligunt proconsulem et exponunt legale suum iudicium, quando volunt, cum consilio sapienciorum. S^{2} *subrubrica:* De constitucione consulum. K^{5} (d) De civitate et quidcumque tunc in iudicio fieri decreverint, hoc debet inviolabiliter observari. Si quis istud statutum infringit, hoc consules repetant. S^{2} (e) faciunt aut S^{10} eligunt virum magistrum inter se K^{5} (f) *desunt* S^{3} S^{4} (g) pro S^{9} (h) est K^{5} *deest* S^{4} S^{5} (i) invio[la]bile S^{8} (j) *deest* S^{4} (k) hoc K^{5} (l) debent S^{10} (m) contra ipsum S^{9} ⟨iudicare⟩ K^{4} (n) *subrubrica*: Qui ad conventum venire neglexerit. K^{5} (o) Qui ad iudicium non venerit, cum campana pulsator, solvet sex denarios. S^{2} (p) ⟨de con[ventu] eme[?]⟩ K^{4} (q) dum S^{3} S^{4} S^{5} S^{7} S^{8} (r) iudicium S^{2} (s) publicatum S^{2} (t) et tunc non venerit S^{2} (u) VI K^{5} (v) Si mensure alique aut pense minis [*s*] parve sint aut iniuste, hoc consules bene repetant secundum decretum civitatis, aut recipiant melioracionem in emenda triginta sex solidorum. S^{2} ⟨consul a consulendo vel a iudicando nam et hoc consules veteres vocantur; vim aduc remanet illud rogat bonum consulitis et bonum iudicialis⟩ S^{8} Solidus hic valet XII allenseles K^{5} (w) S^{1} S^{2} S^{3} S^{4} S^{5} S^{6} S^{7} S^{8} S^{9} S^{10} K^{4} K^{5} *Art. 2* (x) ⟨de iure penesticorum conmestibilia vende[n]cium⟩ ⟨de penesticis⟩ *manus A* S^{3} (y) in S^{1} S^{2} S^{3} S^{4} S^{5} S^{7} S^{8} S^{9} S^{10} K^{4} K^{5} (z) *desunt* K^{4} (aa) *desunt* S^{9} (bb) consilium S^{10} (cc) detenti seu devicti S^{8} *deest* S^{7}

{a} *manus A* S^{6} {b} *manus A* S^{6} ⟨Sclavonica marca vulgariter Szlowaczka Grzÿwna⟩ K^{5} {c} ⟨Regula iuris. Mutare quis consilium non potest in alterius detrimentum. Item quod omnes tangit debet ab omnibus approbari. Eciam. Regula iuris. Quod semel placuit amplius disciplinere non potest.⟩ K^{5} {d} *manus A* S^{6} {e} *manus A* S^{6} ⟨prossiela pro decreto ├faciendo┤ in hac controver[sia] ferendo, dolozila tesz tego actorea pars, ze czo a nie ze tego nie pravu nie wzywa ·N· ÿ nie od⟩ K^{5} {f} Com[m]unis pecunie vero Szlacz. K^{5} {g} *manus A* S^{6} ⟨Decreta id est statuta vulgariter ustawÿ⟩ K^{5} {h} *manus A* S^{6}

que faciunt xxxvi solidos. Quando consules suum conventum exponunt, extunc ibi quidquid statutum fuerit aut(a) commissum in isto conventu, firmum et inviolabiliter debet observari (b). (cEt quicumque (d) violaverit, hoc consules habent iudicare.c) (e) Et quicumque ad conventum venire neglexerit, dum signum datur per campanam, demeretur vi d[enarios] (f). Si autem sibi conventus pronunciatus fuerit, demeretur vi(g) solidos. Capitulum primum. {a}

Articulus 2 (h)

[*1*] | (i) Qui penestici vocantur, si in aliquo demerentur vel si in aliquo delin- 27rb
querint in statutis (j) civitatis, aut consulum decreta violaverint, si in hoc convicti fuerint, demerentur cutem cum crinibus aut tres solidos. Hoc (k) arbitrio

(a) ac K^3 (b) ⟨tene[re]⟩ C^3 (c) *desunt* W^1 (d) hoc K^3 K^2 (e) Et quicumque hoc violaverit consules habent iudicare. K^1 (f) ⟨d[e] pen[a]⟩ C^3 (g) V K^1 K^2 K^3 W^1 C^3 (h) K^1 K^2 K^3 W^1 C^1 C^3 Art. 2 W^2 C^2 *deest folium* (i) ⟨penastici II⟩ C^3 (j) aut W^1 (k) consilio et K^3

{a} ⟨Digestum continet statuta Romanorum | Codex continet statuta imperatorum | Autentica sunt, que ex comperta, eciam filia istorum et dedita per Tylos et Tyli, per [*s*] Agachos per Agachi, per collatores⟩ C^3 ⟨Item liber [*?*] | Item in legibus item liber accionum post alphabetum abc coll. pre in [*?*]⟩ C^3

cuttem (a) cum crinibus ⟨id est statuam et aurum abscissionem cum pilis⟩(b) aut tres solidos. Et hoc arbitrio consulum(c) committitur, quod horum recipere velint. Quando penesticus consulum aut ⟨agere c o n a c z⟩{a} civitatis statutum infringerit foro infronito(d), ⟨id est edicto publico item quat[t]uor angulos civitatis si eo arbitro, quod civitas ipsa cum senioribus statuit de consensu sue communitatis⟩(e) ita quod cuttem cum crine demeretur et cum pena(f) ⟨pecunia⟩(g) (h) redimet, (ihic maneti) sine iure et non potest amodo aliquod forum comestibilem absque civitatis aut consulum consensu(j) exercere. (k) {b} Et si alii homines, qui communitatem seu(l) fraternitatem habent (min comestibilibusm), consulum seu civitatis compromissum (n), hos opportet emendam dare secundum ius et edictum civitatis, et non possunt ulterius(o) aliqua {c} comestibilia vendere(p), (qnec communitatemq) habere seu acquirere absque consensu consulum et(r) civitatis.

Articulus 3 (s)

[*3*] (t) Si metrete aut alie mensure parve seu (uiniuste fuerint (vetu) iniustev) pense, quod consules bene(w) agere possunt secundum honorem civitatis aut cum ⟨Sentencia o r t e l Talentum R u b l et facit viginti ex argenti purii in sua summa in
140r hoc loco⟩{d} (x) | triginta (y) solidis emendare. (z)

(a) ⟨et crine⟩ K^4 (b) *manus A* S^6 ⟨Cutem cum crinibus et statuam et aurum abscis[s]ionem cum pilis demerint⟩ K^5 (c) suo S^4 S^5 *deest* S^3 (d) infrunito S^1 S^2 S^3 S^4 S^5 S^8 S^{10} K^5 infinito S^7 infranico S^9 in fanito S^{10} infirmito K^4 vel in frumento K^5 (e) *manus A* S^6 ⟨Quando statutum civitatis penesticus infringit hic foro in frumento id est foro edicto publico in quat[t]uor angulos civitatis scilicet illo arbitrio, quod civitas ipsa cum senioribus statuit de consensu sue concivitatis.⟩ K^5 (f) pecunia S^2 S^3 S^4 S^5 S^7 S^8 S^9 S^{10} K^5 (g) *manus B* S^6 (h) ⟨hoc⟩ K^4 (i) *desunt* S^5 (j) *deest* S^9 (k) *subrubrica:* De fraternitatibus. K^5 (l) *deest* S^9 S^{10} (m) *desunt* S^{10} (n) fregerint S^2 seu edictum infregerint ⟨id est statutum⟩ K^5 (o) *deest* S^3 (p) *deest* S^3 (q) aut fraternitatem S^3 (r) aut S^3 S^5 (s) S^1 S^2 S^3 S^4 S^5 S^6 S^7 S^8 S^9 S^{10} K^4 *Art. 3* (t) ⟨de mensura ponderis⟩ *manus A* S^3 (u) *desunt* S^5 (v) aut S^2 (w) tunc S^7 (x) ⟦tri⟧ S^6 (y) ⟨sex⟩ K^4 (z) De iudicio pensarum et parvarum mensurarum require plenius libro secundo Registro item. [*SSp. II.13§3*] S^2

{a} *manus A* S^6 {b} Regula iuris. Nullus ex consulibus, dummodo fraudulentus non fuerit, obligatur. K^5 {c} ⟨Emenda vulgariter p o k u p⟩ K^5 {d} *manus A* S^6

consulum committitur(a), quod horum recipere velint. (b) Quando penesticus consulum aut civitatis statutum infringerit foro (c) (din fremitod), ita quod cutem cum crine(e) de|meretur et cum pecunia redimet, hic manet sine 27va
iure{a} et non potest ammodo adire(f) forum conmestibilium absque civitatis et(g) consulum consensu(h) exercere. Aut si alii homines, qui communitatem seu fraternitatem habent in conmestibilibus, consulum seu civitatis conpromissum (i), (j) hos oportet emendam dare secundum ius et edictum civitatis, (k) et non possunt ulterius aliqua conmestibilia vendere, nec communitatem acquire absque consensu consulum et civitatis

Articulus 3 (l)

[*3*] (m) Si metrete aut alie mensure parve seu iniuste fuerint aut(n) pense(o) (p), quod(q) consules bene agere possunt secundum honorem civitatis aut cum triginta sex solidis emendare. (r) {b}

(a) *deest* K^1 (b) ⟨consules⟩ C^3 (c) vel K^3 (d) infirmito K^3 W^1 K^1 K^2 infrumito C^3 (e) pelle K^1 K^2 (f) *deest* K^1 K^2 K^3 W^1 C^3 (g) aut W^1 (h) licencia K^1 K^2 (i) infringerit K^3 C^3 (j) seu W^1 (k) ⟨emenda⟩ C^3 (l) K^1 K^2 K^3 K^5 W^1 C^1 C^3 *Art. 3* W^2 C^2 *deest folium* (m) ⟨III mensure⟩ C^3 (n) et K^5 (o) *a.c.* parve C^3 (p) iniuste K^5 W^1 (q) hoc W^1 C^3 (r) *subrubrica:* De mercibus falsificatis. Si que res mercionales falsificantur, sive ulnas duas vel libras habuerint, ille honore privatur et satis consulibus facere compellitur. Si quis parvulus convictus fuerit, ille honore privatur et satisfacere consulibus compellitur, et iudici solvere penam ius. *subrubrica:* Primo pertinet ad consulem. Consulum est civitati sic procedere et singulis erupcionibus et in iure mechanici et pauper populus sic valeat suficere ac sustinere, quod ipsi non efficiantur periuri. K^5

{a} gwarra K^1 K^2 {b} ⟨A tak poczÿtha ssobie strona powodna liepÿ sluzącze ⊢sobie⊣ prawo mieczku theÿ rolÿ, nÿ zebÿ stroneÿ obzalowaneÿ zapÿ[...]⟩ K^5

Articulus 4 [(a)]

[*4*] Ille supremus iudex, qui in(b) Meÿdeburg(c) iudicio presidet, hoc est(d) castellanus, qui sedet(e) tria(f) iudicia provincialia(g) (hin annoh) (i): unum iudicium(j) (k) in die sancte Agate, secundum in die(l) sanctorum (mJohannis (net Paulim),n) tercium in octava sancti Martini. Si (oceciderit (p) auto) evenerit (q) aliquod horum iudiciorum(r) ad diem celebrem aut feriatum, ⟨feriatus dies debet dies dominicus, Ec[c]lesie dies naroczÿti dzen⟩{a} (s) extunc (t) ammisit suum iudicium. Et si scultetus aut solus castellanus ad iudicium non venerit, (uquia scultetus {b} (v) castellano primam sententiam debet invenire, {c} et si scultetus non veneritu) ad castellanum, (w) extunc decem talenta demeretur, nisi legale impedimentum (x), ⟨sprawyedlÿwa przekaza vel nagabanÿe⟩{d} quod probare(y) potuerit, ut ius dictaverit. (z)

Quidquid criminalis(aa) (bb) cause factum (ccseu commissumcc) fuerit quattuordecim diebus ante suum iudicium (dd), hoc castellanus debet iudicare (eeet nemo aliusee). (ff)

Articulus 5 (gg)

[*5*] Stuprum ⟨odlyeganie dzewstina⟩{e} et obsidia ⟨zasadzenÿa⟩{f} et irruenciam (hhdomiciliorum ⟨uderzenÿe na dom⟩{g} iudicathh) castellanus (ii) et nullus alter. Sed si castellanus presens esse non poterit, extunc cives (jj) eligunt

(a) S^1 S^2 S^3 S^4 S^5 S^6 S^7 S^8 S^9 S^{10} K^4 K^5 *Art. 4* (b) *deest* S^4 S^5 (c) Novo Foro S^3 (d) ⟨est⟩ S^8 *deest* K^4 (e) *deest* S^4 S^5 (f) tam [*s*] K^5 (g) ter S^2 (h) *desunt* S^7 (i) ⟨iudicare⟩ K^4 (j) *deest* S^2 K^5 (k) in anno S^8 (l) festo S^2 (m) *locus nominum inscribendorum* S^2 (n) Apostoli S^{10} ⟨et Pauli⟩ S^8 (o) *desunt* S^2 (p) ⟨de rebus iudiciis castellani⟩ *manus A* S^3 (q) ad S^{10} (r) *deest* S^9 (s) ⟨Cum scultetus aut castellanus ad iudicium non venerit⟩ K^5 (t) totum S^2 (u) *desunt* S^2 (v) cum S^{10} (w) qui si sit tempus iudicii K^5 (x) assignaverit, si S^2 impediverit S^8 ipsum impediret S^{10} ipsum impediverit K^5 (y) *deest* S^2 (z) *subrubrica:* Quid castellanus iudicat. K^5 (aa) terminalis S^{10} (bb) nephas seu K^5 (cc) *desunt* S^2 (dd) comissi fuerint S^4 S^5 (ee) *desunt* S^7 (ff) Que et quot sint legalia impedimenta quere libro 2 Registro VII. [*SSp II.7*] S^2 (gg) S^1 S^2 S^3 S^4 S^5 S^6 S^7 S^8 S^9 S^{10} K^4 K^5 *Art. 5* (hh) *desunt* S^{10} (ii) seu burgrabius K^5 (jj) unum S^8

{a} *manus A* S^6 ⟨feriatus dies est vulgariter Deicus dies vel celebris et solemnis dies vulgariter naroczÿszthÿ dzÿen⟩ K^5 {b} ⟨Sentencia vulgariter orthel⟩ K^5 {c} Talentum vulgariter rubl et facit xx grossos argenti puri in sua summa. K^5 {d} *manus A* S^6 ⟨Legale impedimentum vulgariter sprawyedlÿwa przekaza vel nagabanÿe⟩ K^5 {e} *manus A* S^6 {f} *manus A* S^6 ⟨Obsidium vulgariter zaszadzenye na drodze⟩ K^5 {g} *probabiliter manus B* S^6 ⟨Irruencia domiciliorum vulgariter uderzenÿe na dom⟩ K^5

Articulus 4 [(a)]

[4] | Ille supremus[(b)] iudex, qui in Meÿdeburg [(c]iudicio[(d)] presidet[c)], hoc [(e)] 27vb est castellanus, qui sedet tria iudicia provincialia in anno: unum [(f)] in die sancte Agathe, secundum in festo sanctorum Johannis et Pauli, tercium in octava sancti Martini. Si evenerit aliquod horum iudiciorum ad diem celebrem aut feriatum, extunc suum iudicium amisit. [(g]Dies ligati sunt omnes dies dominicales et festivi[(h)] dies [(i)]: dies rogationum ante[(j)] Pentecostes et adventus Christi, et septuaginta dies ante Pascha, in quibus diebus non debent iudicari.[g)] Et si [(k]scultetus aut solus castellanus[(l)] ad iudicium non venerit[k)], quia scultetus castellano[(m)] primam sentenciam debet invenire, et si scultetus non venerit ad castellanum[(n)], extunc X talenta demeretur, nisi legittimum[(o)] impedimentum sit[(p)], [(q)] quod probare poterit, ut[(r)] ius dictaverit. Quidquid [(s)] [(t]criminalis cause omne[t)] factum seu[(u)] commissum fuerit quat[t]uordecim diebus ante suum[(v)] iudicium, hoc castellanus[(w)] iudicare debet[(x)] et nemo alius.

Articulus 5 [(y)]

[5] | [(z)] Stuprum, obsidia et irruencias domiciliorum iudicat castellanus[(aa)] 28ra
et nemo alius. Sed si castellanus presens[(bb)] esse non[(cc)] poterit, extunc II

(a) K^1 K^2 K^3 W^1 C^1 C^3 *Art. 4* W^2 C^2 *deest folium* (b) summus W^1 (c) iudicat C^3 (d) *deest* K^2 (e) ⟨die⟩ C^3 (f) iudicium K^3 (g) *desunt* K^1 K^2 K^3 W^1 ⟨ligati dies⟩ C^3 (h) alii C^3 (i) celebres et festi C^3 (j) aut C^3 (k) eciam pre[si]det suum iudicium, si illac non venerit vel scultetus ibi non fuerit C^3 (l) burgrabius K^3 (m) burgrabio K^3 C^3 (n) burgrabium K^3 (o) legale W^1 (p) *deest* K^1 K^2 scilicet impeditus C^3 (q) sic K^1 K^2 si K^3 in C^3 (r) et W^1 (s) eciam C^3 (t) criminalis esse K^1 K^2 criminalis cause K^3 W^1 criminaliter C^3 (u) se K^1 K^2 (v) *deest* W^1 (w) burgrabius K^3 (x) habet K^3 (y) K^1 K^2 K^3 W^1 C^1 C^3 *Art. 5* W^2 C^2 *deest folium* (z) ⟨de iudic[io] princeps [*s*] V⟩ C^3 ⟨Gewette. De pena burgravii vel emenda castellani⟩ C^3 (aa) burgrabius K^3 (bb) paratus W^1 *deest* C^3 (cc) *deest* C^3 ⟨de iudic[io] princeps [*s*] V⟩ C^3 ⟨De pena burgravii vel emenda castellani⟩ C^3

unum iudicem loco (a) castellani, pro excessu(b) manifesto. (c) (dCastellani pena(e) et recompensad) ⟨glowna zaplata⟩{a}, quod acquisitum fuerit in iudicio bannito, debet solvi(f) per sex ebdomadas. Pena castellani (g) (htria(i) talentah), (j) pena sculteti octo solidi. (k) Quando castellanus surgit (let iudi-
140v catl), (m) tunc iudicium suum expirat (n) (oet statim | iudicium sculteti disponitur a proximo(p) ad duas septimanaso)(q).

Articulus 6 (r)

[6] Scultetus habet eciam(s) tria iudicia legalia in(t) anno: unum in Epiphania Domini(u) aut (v) die sequenti, secundum(w) tercia feria post (x) conductum Pasche, tercium feria tercia post festum (y) Trinitatis. Post hec disponit (zsua(aa) iudiciaz) continue(bb) ad duas ebdomadas(cc). Si dies iudicialis evenerit ad diem celebrem, bene(dd) potest ultra(ee) unam(ff) diem aut duos (gg) (hhpost diem celebremhh) iudicium suum(ii) disponere. (jj) Iudicium sculteti nemo potest(kk) (ll) indicare, nisi scultetus solus vel preco, (mmnec suus famulusmm). Quodsi scultetus in domo non fuerit (nnet si(oo) criminale nephas exortum (pp) fueritnn) (qq), cives(rr) statuant unum iudicem pro crimine manifesto. (ss) Scultetus eciam debet habere legalitatem ⟨id est ius vel iusticiam⟩(tt) a domino (uu) terre et cum(vv) eo(ww) debet esse feodatus(xx) ⟨id est hereditatus⟩(yy)

(a) iudicis S4 S5 (b) accessu S4 (c) ⟨Pene et recompense castellani⟩ K5 (d) recompensam S10 (e) ⟨pena⟩ K4 (f) *deest* S5 (g) sunt K5 (h) 30 solidi S2 (i) tam [*s*] S10 (j) Talentum autem signat ⊢decem⊣ XX solidos. K5 (k) *subrubrica:* ⟨Quando iudicium castellani expirat.⟩ K5 (l) a iudicio S2 (m) ⟨de stupro idem⟩ ⟨de rebus iudiciis sculteti⟩ *manus A* S3 (n) pena ad sex ebdomadas solvi debet, emenda post penam ad XIIII dies. Si autem vir emendam ante penam acquisierit, exsolvi debet ad sex ebdomadas et pena post hoc ad XIIII dies. Recompensa debet solvi ad XII ebdomadas ad domum illius, cui debitum tenetur, ante solis occasum, aut in propria domo, si ibi domum non habuerit. K5 *subrubrica:* De debito persoluto. Quin debitum persolutum vir persolvisse hic mettercius protestari debet post iudicium castellani. K5 (o) *desunt* S2 (p) primo S7 (q) ebdomadas S3 (r) S1 S2 S3 S4 S5 S6 S7 S8 S9 S10 K4 K5 *Art. 6* (s) *deest* S2 (t) *deest* S10 (u) *deest* S4 S5 S8 S9 K5 (v) in S9 (w) *deest* S9 (x) ad S5 (y) Sancte S2 S4 S5 K4 (z) sentenciam K4 (aa) *deest* K5 (bb) *deest* S9 (cc) septimanas S2 (dd) tunc S7 (ee) *deest* S4 S10 ⟨ultra⟩ S9 (ff) *deest* S5 (gg) dies S9 (hh) *desunt* K5 (ii) *deest* S2 S3 K4 (jj) ⟨Quod nemo nisi scultetus indicat suum iudicium⟩ K5 (kk) habet S2 (ll) hominum S1 S2 S3 S4 S5 S7 S8 S9 S10 K5 (mm) *desunt* S2 (nn) *desunt* S3 (oo) *deest* K4 S10 (pp) commissum S8 (qq) sive commissum fuerit ⟨Legalitatem id est ius seu iusticiam⟩ K5 (rr) consules K5 (ss) ⟨Quis debet elegi in scultetum⟩ K5 (tt) *manus A* S6 (uu) rege seu K5 (vv) sibi S2 (ww) ⟨eo⟩ S8 (xx) infeudatus K5 (yy) *manus A* S6

{a} *manus A* S6 Recompensa vulgariter glow[na] zaplata⟩ K5

cives eligunt unum iudicem loco castellani, [(a]pro excessu[a)] manifesto[(b)]. Castellani[(c)] pena et reconpensa, quid acquisitum fuerit bannito iudicio, debet solvi ad sex ebdomadas. Pena castellani sit[(d)] tria talenta, 〈Talentum xx solidorum〉[(e)] pena sculteti octo solidi. Quando castellanus[(f)] surgit et iudicat, tunc iudicium [(g)] sculteti disponitur a proximo die ad duas septimanas. [{a}]

Articulus 6 [(h)]

[*6*] | [(i)] Scultetus eciam habet tria iudicia legalia in anno: unum in Epi- 28rb
phania Domini aut die sequenti, secundum feria tercia post festum vel [(j)] conductum Pasche, tertium feria tercia post festum [(k)] Trinitatis. Post hec disponit sua iudicia continue ad duas ebdomadas. Si dies iudicialis evenerit ad diem celebrem, bene potest ultra diem unam aut duos post diem celebrem iudicium suum disponere. Iudicium sculteti nemo potest[(l)] hominum iudicare[(m)], nisi scultetus solus aut preco, nec[(n)] suus famulus. Quid[(o)] si scultetus in domo non fuerit et si criminale nephas exortum fuerit, cives substituent[(p)] unum iudicem pro crimine manifesto. Scultetus eciam debet habere legalitatem[(q)] a domino terre [(r]et cum [(s)] debet esse feodatus et verum suum

---

(a) processu K^1 K^2 (b) manu facto K^2 (c) Burgrabii K^3 (d) *deest* K^1 K^2 W^1 (e) *manus α* C^1 (f) burgrabius K^3 (g) suum expiravit et statim iudicium W^1 (h) K^1 K^2 K^3 W^1 C^1 C^3 *Art. 6* W^2 C^2 *deest folium* (i) 〈Sculteto〉 C^3 (j) post K^3 (k) Sancte K^3 (l) habet K^1 K^2 K^3 W^1 C^3 (m) *deest* C^3 (n) vel K^3 (o) Quod K^3 W^1 C^3 (p) statuant K^1 K^2 K^3 W^1 C^3 (q) bannum C^3 (r) *desunt* C^3 (s) eo K^1 K^2 K^3 W^1

{a} In Colmensi. Pena sculteti secundum Colmense quatuor solidi alias XVI quadrantes. W^1 〈w e r g e l t recompensa dicta et pena iudici g e w e t t e solvit; 2 ebdomadas〉 C^3

et verum(a) suum feodum esse debet. (bInsuper liber(c) esse debetb) et legittime natus de terra.

Articulus 7 (d)

[7] (e) Quodsi homo vulneratus fuerit, si clamorem proclamaverit et si(f) ceperit hunc, qui ipsum vulneravit, et eum ad iudicium usque(g) deduxerit, et si(h) tunc ipsum cum hiis, qui clamorem suum audierunt, protestare poterit(i) metseptimus, propius est ipsum(j) vincere, quam ille possit eum evadere. Pro vulnere manum, pro homicidium collum (k). Si vulnus profunditatem (l) unguis et longitudinem membri habuerit, acquirit homo duellum pro uno(m) vulnere, (net si victor fuerit, victus a victo[re] pro vulneren)
140r manum, pro homicidio homicidio caput(o). |(p)

Articulus 8 (q)

[8] (r) ⟨VIII⟩ Si continget criminale nephas aut conflictus (s) nocte vel (t) die et si probus homo pro eo accusetur(u), propius est evadere metseptimus, quam ille possit super(v) eum(w) (x) protestare, quia in isto loco conflictus per neminem visus est(y).

(a) *deest* S3 (b) *desunt* S2 (c) *deest* S8 (d) S1 S2 S3 S4 S5 S6 S7 S8 S9 S10 K4 K5 *Art. 7* (e) ⟨de vulneratis⟩ *manus A* S3 (f) *deest* S2 S3 S8 S9 K4 (g) *deest* S4 S5 (h) *deest* K5 (i) *deest* S5 (j) *deest* S2 S3 (k) amputando S2 ⟨Pro vulnere manum, pro homicidio collum⟩ K5 *subrubrica:* Quoquo vulnere homo duellum adquirit. K5 (l) habuerit S4 S5 habet unius S9 (m) *deest* S3 (n) *desunt* S7 (o) collum S1 S2 S3 S4 S5 S7 S8 S9 S10 K4 K5 (p) ⟨pro vulneracione⟩ S10 *mutatio scriptoris, articulus 7 iteratus* S6 (q) S1 S2 S3 S4 S5 S6 S7 S8 S9 K4 S10 *Art. 8* K5 *Art. 9* (r) ⟨de conflictu duorum⟩ *manus A* S3 (s) fuerit K3 (t) in S2 S4 S5 K5 (u) densetur [*s*] S3 (v) *deest* S3 S10 (w) *deest* K4 (x) vincere seu S10 (y) *deest* S1 S9

feodum esse debet, et ligittime natus de terra. (aSumma iuris actus legittimi cum condicionem non recipiunt neque diem r).a)

Articuli 7–8 (b)

[*7*] | (c) Quodsi homo vulneratus fuerit et (d) clamorem proclamaverit, et si 28va ceperit hunc, qui ipsum vulneravit, et eum ad iudicium usque deduxerit, et si(e) tunc ipsum cum hiis, qui suum clamorem audierint, protestare poterit metseptimus, propius est eum vincere, quam ille possit evadere. Pro vulnere manum, pro homicidio collum. {a} Si vulnus profunditatem unguis et longitudinem membri habuerit, (f) acquirit homo duellum, (g) pro vulnere (h) manum, pro homicidio collum.

[*8*] (iSi quis eciam fideiusserit aliquod iudicio(j) pro aliquo adiutorio presentare ex parte homicidii ⟨de eodem XVII fo[lio] li[bri] primi⟩(k) et eundem non representat, extunc fideiussorem dare oportet querulatori unam reconpensam {b}, videlicet XVIII talenta, et iudici suam penam octo solidos (l). Si autem sentenciam fuerit pro uno vulnere duellari, protunc (mfideiussor det unam mediam reconpensam querulanti m), scilicet novem talenta, et iudici suam penam octo solidos, istorum nummorum, qui in eodem iudicio sunt transeuntes(n) communiter et dativi. i)

Articulus 9 (o)

[*9*] [*28vb*] Si contingerit criminale nephas aut conflictus (p) nocte vel die et si probus vir (q) accusetur, propius est evadere metseptimus, quam ille(r) possit super eum protestare, quia in isto loco conflictus per neminem visus est.

(a) *desunt* K^1 K^2 K^3 W^1 (b) K^1 K^2 K^3 W^1 W^2 C^1 *Art. 7–8* K^5 *Art. 7 pars 2, pars* Si—dativi C^2 *deest folium* C^3 *Art. 7* (c) ⟨De vulnerato hoc est occiso⟩ C^3 (d) si K^3 W^1 K^1 K^2 (e) *deest* W^1 (f) si W^1 C^3 (g) et triumphaverit, pro tunc convictus C^3 ⟨dum⟩ C^3 (h) demeretur C^3 (i) ⟨De fideiussione vulneracionis⟩ Sed si per fideiussoriam obligat alterum pro iuvamine homicidii et non potest eum statuere, tunc fideiussor tenetur actori dare plenam recompensam, hoc sunt XIIII talenta. ⟨Recompensa plena talentum quid signat⟩ Talentum quis facit XX solidos denariorum et iudici emendam viii solidos, tali peccunia sic in districtu solet forisari. K^5 (j) *deest* C^3 (k) *manus δ* C^1 (l) ⟨emenda⟩ C^3 (m) *desunt* C^3 (n) presentes C^3 (o) K^1 K^2 C^1 *Art. 9* K^3 W^1 *Art. 8* W^2 C^2 *deest folium* C^3 Art. 9 *deest textus Latinus* (p) fuerit K^3 (q) pro eo K^1 K^2 K^3 W^1 (r) *deest* K^1 K^2

{a} ⟨emenda wer[gelt]⟩ C^3 {b} ⟨recompensa werg[elt]⟩ C^3

Articulus 9 (a)

[*9*] (b) Nec sculteto, nec castellano (ctenetur scabinusc) nec civis (daliquam sentenciamd) (e) extra veros dies iudiciales diffinire, nisi sit factum manifestum, ut(f) vulnera mortalia aut homicidia(g), vel furta seu alia criminalia ⟨contingerint⟩(h). (i) Castellanus et scultetus bene(j) possunt (komni diek) iudicare pro debito, (lpro quol) absque testimonio agitur, nisi si(m) (n) civis agat contra hospitem et(o) hospes super(p) (q) civem pro debito cum(r) testimonio, 141v de quo alter alteri fassus est, quod bene(s) potest sine | mora iudicari. Et si uni(t) adiudicatur(u) debitum(v), (w) habet(x) solvere sequenti die, quod tenetur. Sed hospitem(y) opportet iuramento protestare(z), quod sit alienigena(aa) et (bb) ita remote domicilium habeat, quod una die ad iudicium venire non possit.

Articulus 10 (cc)

[*10*] (dd) (eeQuodsiee) vir vulneratus fuerit et eodem die iudicium non quesierit (ffet sua querimonia pernoctaverit et, qui inculpatur, (ggtunc comparetgg), evadit eum metseptimus (hh) {a}, quam ille super eum possit(ii) protestare(jj).ff) Sed si tribus iudiciis non comparet, quarto iudicio describetur, ita tamen, si iusto modo (kk) citatus (ll) et super eum conquestus fuerit. (mm)

(a) S^1 S^2 S^3 S^4 S^5 S^6 S^7 S^8 S^9 S^{10} K^4 *Art. 9* K^5 *Art. 10* (b) ⟨de iure castellani et sculteti cum criminibus⟩ *manus A* S^3 (c) nec scabinis S^{10} (d) *desunt* S^4 S^5 (e) de diffinicione suarum S^2 (f) aut S^{10} (g) *deest* S^2 (h) *manus B* S^6 (i) *subrubrica:* Pro debito omni die iudicatur. K^5 (j) tamen S^7 (k) omnium S^4 omnia S^5 (l) *desunt* S^9 (m) *deest* S^{10} K^5 (n) ⊢cicius⊣ S^6 (o) vel S^2 K^5 (p) contra S^2 S^9 K^5 (q) ⟨de hospite contra civem agente vel e converso pro debito⟩ K^5 (r) absque S^2 (s) tamen (t) *deest* S^2 S^{10} (u) abiudicatur S^4 (v) debitor S^{10} (w) quod S^9 (x) debet S^2 (y) hospes S^7 (z) probare S^1 S^2 S^3 S^4 S^5 S^7 S^8 S^{10} K^4 K^5 (aa) *a.c.* aligenigena S^6 aliena K^5 (bb) quod S^2 (cc) S^1 S^2 S^3 S^4 S^5 S^6 S^7 S^8 S^9 S^{10} K^4 *Art. 10* K^5 *Art. 11* (dd) ⟨de vulneratis⟩ *manus A* S^3 (ee) Si alias S^2 (ff) et si inculpatus post ea iudicio paret, evadit eum sola manu possibilius propius pernoctacio, quam vulneratus eum querere possit. S^2 (gg) *desunt* S^9 (hh) ⟨suis vicinis⟩ K^4 (ii) ⟨possit⟩ K^4 (jj) *deest* S^3 (kk) iure S^7 (ll) fuerit S^8 K^5 (mm) Qui in prescripcione rapitur, quid pro eo sustineat et quomodo convinci possit, quare libro 1 Registro S[peculi] S[axonici]. [*SSp. 1 68§1*] S^2

{a} ⟨Evadet vulgariter o z b a d z ÿ c⟩ K^5

Articuli 10–11 [(a)]

[*10*] Nec castellano[(b)] nec sculteto tenetur scabinus [(c)] sentenciam aliquam extra veros dies iudiciales diffinire, nisi sit[(d)] factum manifestum crimen[(e)]. Castellanus[(f)] [(g)] et scultetus bene possunt omni die iudicare pro debito, pro quo absque testimonio agitur, nisi [(h)] civis agat contra[(i)] hospitem vel hospes contra civem pro debito cum testimonio, de quo alter alteri fassus [(j)], quod bene iudicari potest sine mora. Et si uni[(k)] adiudicatur hospiti debitum, [(l)] debet sibi solvi sequenti die, quod tenetur. Sed hospes[(m)] iurare[(n)] tenetur vel oportet, quod sit alienigena [(o]et ita remote domicilia habuerit, quod die una ad iudicium | venire non possit[o)]. 29ra

III

[*11*] [(p][(q]Ille dicitur esse hospes, qui ultra XI miliaria extra iudicium habuerit mansionem.[p)] Hospes, si hospiti vel alteri, qui in [(r)] iudicio non habuerit possessionem, racione debiti per manum fuerit presentatus, hunc iudex illi servare debet tamdiu, quousque se de debito expurget iuridice vel persolvet.[q)]

Articulus 12 [(s)]

[*12*] Quodsi vir vulneratus fuerit et eo die | iudicium non quesierit, et sua querimonia pernoctaverit et, qui inculpatur, tunc conparuerit, evadet eum metseptimus [(t]suis vicinis [(u)], quam ille possit protestare[t)]. Sed[(v)] tribus iudiciis non conparet, [(w)] quarto [(x)] iudicio describetur, ita tamen, si [(y]iusto modo[y)] citatus et super ipsum conquestus[(z)] fuerit. 29rb

---

[(a)] K^{1} K^{2} C^{3} *Art. 8* K^{3} W^{1} *Art. 9* K^{5} *Art. 10 pars 2, pars* Ille—persolvet W^{2} C^{2} *deest folium* C^{1} *Art. 10–11* [(b)] burgrabio K^{3} [(c)] nec civis K^{1} K^{2} K^{3} W^{1} C^{3} [(d)] *deest* K^{1} K^{2} [(e)] ut vulnera mortalia vel forsan alia criminalia K^{1} K^{2} ut vulnera mortalia vel furtum seu alia criminalia W^{1} *deest* C^{3} [(f)] Burgrabius K^{3} [(g)] ut W^{1} [(h)] sit W^{1} [(i)] *a.c.* extra C^{3} [(j)] sibi K^{1} K^{2} est C^{3} [(k)] *deest* K^{3} [(l)] debitor K^{1} K^{2} [(m)] hospitem K^{1} K^{2} K^{3} W^{1} C^{3} [(n)] iudicare K^{1} K^{2} [(o)] *in glossa* C^{3} [(p)] *in glossa* C^{3} [(q)] *desunt* K^{1} K^{2} K^{3} W^{1} Hospes dicitur ille esse, qui videlicet xi miliaria suum domicilium habet et si pro aliquo datur vir alieni[g]ena per ⟨Tradatur reus actorem in debito actus ad servandum⟩ manum in modum pignoris, iudex tenetur eum dare ad observandum, quousque debitum persolvat. Etiam non debet aliquis hospes nec aliena unus ab alio aliquod pignus accipere ⟨Quomodo pignus accipitur⟩ pro debito quem fatetur, sed si hoc pignus reciperit, hec debet iure obtinere ⟨De pignore hospitis⟩ et acquirere in iudicio, sicut alii homines, exceptis si hoc pignus recipit cum prolocucione et excepcione. K^{5} [(r)] isto C^{3} [(s)] K^{1} K^{2} K^{3} W^{1} C^{3} *Art. 10* W^{2} C^{2} *deest folium* C^{1} *Art. 12* [(t)] *desunt* C^{3} [(u)] pocius K^{1} K^{2} [(v)] Sed si K^{1} K^{2} K^{3} Et si C^{3} [(w)] tunc C^{3} [(x)] in K^{1} K^{2} [(y)] iuste eum C^{3} [(z)] conquester C^{1}

Articulus 11 (a)

[*11*] (b) Stuprum et obsidium et irruenciam domiciliorum burgravius(c) iudicat(d) (e) nec alter ullus. Si aliquis irruit super alterius(f) domicilium tempore nocturno aut diurno, {a} temeraria violencia, nulla procedente querimonia, et si(g) in manuali ⟨manifesto⟩(h) facto deprehensus fuerit cum clamore, et si clamorem cum(i) auditoribus metseptimus (jsuorum vicinorumj) hoc ostendendo (k) probare poterit secundum iuris exigenciam, malefactor collum demeretur. Sin autem (l) manifestum factum(m) non fuerit, extunc propius est evadere metseptimus, quam aliquo testimonio vinci possit.

Articulus 12 (n)

[*12*] Quicumque vulneratus fuerit, si clamorem proclamaverit et ad iudicium
142r pervenerit, de quocumque | querulatur, qui presens(o) fuerit, et si habuerit hos, qui clamorem suum audierunt, et quot(p) vulnera habuerit, tot homines potest inculpare. (q) (rSin autem hii homines(s) comparuerint, duellum(t) in ipsis acquirere potest.r) Sin autem plures iudicialiter(u) infestaverit, quam vulnera habuerit, alii omnes(v) evadent suo iure(w) ⟨iuramento⟩(x), quivis metseptimus. (y)

(a) S^1 S^2 S^3 S^4 S^5 S^6 S^7 S^8 S^9 S^{10} K^4 *Art. 11* K^5 *Art. 12* (b) ⟨de stupro obsidio et irruenciam domicilii⟩ *manus A* S^3 (c) ⟨burgrabius⟩ S^1 (d) ⟨iudicat⟩ S^1 (e) ⊢et⊣ S^6 (f) alicius S^4 S^5 (g) ⟨si⟩ K^3 (h) *manus B* S^6 (i) *deest* K^5 (j) *desunt* S^2 (k) protestari et K^5 (l) manu S^4 S^5 S^7 S^8 K^4 (m) *deest* S^3 (n) S^1 S^2 S^3 S^4 S^5 S^6 S^7 S^8 S^9 S^{10} K^4 *Art. 12* K^5 *Art. 13* (o) prius S^{10} prius K^5 (p) ⟨quot⟩ *manus B* S^6 (q) ⟨de vulnerato recenti cum clamore ad iudicium veniente⟩ *manus A* S^3 (r) *desunt* S^2 (s) omnes S^9 (t) *deest* S^8 (u) *deest* S^2 (v) homines S^8 S^9 K^5 (w) iuramento S^4 S^5 (x) *manus B* S^6 (y) ⟨Quando evadunt plures inculpati, quam vulnera de causa pernoctata⟩ Etiam si alter alterius vulnerat et causa sua pernoctata fuerit, et vulnus monachale non fuerit, et si comparuerit iudici, debet sibi ad iudicium proximum. ⟨de vulnere monachali⟩ Si autem vulnus monachale fuerit, tunc statim continuo iudicium sibi iudex formare debet pro facto manifesto. K^5

{a} ⟨Temeraria violencia vulgariter Szmÿalem gwaltem⟩

Articulus 13 [a]

[*13*] [b] Stuprum et obsidium et irruencia[m][c] domicilii burgravius iudicat nec[d] alter ullus[e]. Si aliquis irruit super alterius[f] domicilium tempore nocturno aut diurno, temeraria violencia procedente [g], et si in manuali facto deprehensus fuerit cum clamore, et si clamorem cum auditoribus metseptimus suorum vicinorum hoc ostendendo actor[h] probare poterit secundum iuris exigenciam, malefactor collum demeretur. Si autem [i] factum[j] manifestum non fuerit, extunc propius est reus[k] evadere metseptimus, quam aliquo testimonio vinci possit.

Articulus 14 [l]

[*14*] | Quicumque vulneratus fuerit, si clamorem proclamaverit, ad iudi- 29va
cium devenerit, de quocumque querulatur, qui presens fuerit, et [m] habuerit hos, qui suum clamorem audiverunt, et quot vulnera habuerit, tot homines potest inculpare. Si autem hii homines conparuerint, duella in ipsis acquirere potest. Si autem plures iudicialiter[n] infestaverit[o], quam [(p]vulnera habuerit[p)], alii omnes[q] evadent suo iuramento[r], [(s]quivis[t] sua sola manu pro eo[u] quo adiutorio racione homicidii vel vulneris duellaris, vel mettercius ad hoc [v], si pro eo cum testibus fuerit inpulsatus[s)].

(a) K^1 K^2 K^3 W^1 C^3 *Art. 11* W^2 C^2 *deest folium* C^1 *Art. 13* (b) ⟨Quis iudicat⟩ C^3 (c) violenciam K^1 K^2 (d) et nullus K^1 K^2 (e) *deest* K^1 K^2 (f) *deest* K^3 (g) ita querimonia K^1 K^2 ulla querimonia K^3 W^1 C^3 (h) *deest* K^1 K^2 K^3 W^1 C^3 (i) ├manu┤ *del.* C^1 (j) malefactum C^3 *deest* K^3 W^1 (k) *deest* K^1 K^2 K^3 W^1 C^3 (l) K^1 K^2 K^3 W^1 C^3 *Art. 12* K^4 *Art. 12 in glossa, pars* quivis—impulsatus C^1 *Art. 14* W^2 C^2 *deest folium* (m) si K^1 K^2 W^1 C^3 (n) *deest* K^3 K^1 K^2 (o) manifestaverit W^1 (p) vulnera fuerit, et tot viri destituentur, quod vulnera fuerint K^3 (q) homines K^3 (r) iure K^3 (s) *desunt* K^1 K^2 K^3 W^1 *in glossa* K^4 (t) ⟨quilibet⟩ C^3 quilibet K^4 (u) *deest* C^3 (v) ⟨metseptimus⟩ C^3

Articulus 13 (a)

[*13*] {a} (b) Obligat aliquis(c) mercimonia aut alia bona mobilia(d) pro debito ex parte iudicii, et(e) ille pronunciet tribus iudiciis, ut est iuris, et quarto iudicio (fsuper eo ⟨iudicialiter⟩(g) dominiumf) (h) receperit (iac appropriatum sibi(j) fueriti), et cognoscencie donum(k) dederit coram iudice et scabinis. Et (lsi istel) in posterum ad repetendum(m) sua bona pervenerit, possidens (n) propius est (o) suum pignus servare cum scabinis ac iudice, quam ille, qui caret possessione.

Articulus 14 (p)

[*14*] Si aliquis ducit uxorem et (qsi virq) (rde hacr) luce decessit (s), uxor nichil habet in suis bonis, (t) nisi sibi(u) dederit pro dotalicio aut vite ⟨provisionem⟩(v) pro sua vita in iudicio bannito. Nulla (wuxor seuw) mulier potest vite (x) provisionem(y) nec dotalicium hereditarie(z) (aa) observare. Et cum (bbde hac luce deceditbb), ad heredes revertitur sui mariti. Quodsi(cc) (dd) maritus mulieri nichil dederit in suis bonis, in possessione bonorum(ee) sui mariti debet per-
142^{v} manere, et pueri(ff) | sibi(gg) necessaria ministrabunt, quousque in viduitate et (hh) sine marito permanere voluerit. (ii) (jjSi vir oves habuerit, quas mulier recipiet ad supellectile[m].jj) Et si pueri(kk) (ll) vellent dotalicium infringere, servare potest testimonio virorum ac mulierum metseptima(mm), qui tunc(nn) presentes fuerunt. (oo) Si vir pueros habuerit aut mulier, quicumque ex hiis (pp) exhereditati(qq) sunt, ⟨si moritur vir, hii pueri, qui in hereditate patris[(rr)] sunt, [(ss]recipiunt bona et non hii, qui exhereditati fuerint[ss)]⟩(tt) sed(uu) hereditatem

---

(a) S^{1} S^{2} S^{3} S^{4} S^{5} S^{6} S^{7} S^{8} S^{9} K^{4} *Art. 13* S^{10} *articulus deest* K^{5} *Art. 14* (b) ⟨de pignoribus et debitis⟩ *manus A* S^{3} (c) autem quis K^{3} (d) *deest* K^{4} (e) in S^{9} (f) ad propria S^{2} (g) *manus B* S^{6} (h) habuerit ac S^{8} (i) *desunt* S^{2} (j) *deest* K^{5} (k) dominii S^{7} K^{5} (l) iuste S^{4} S^{5} iste K^{5} (m) recipiendum S^{8} (n) ut K^{4} (o) quam [*s*] K^{5} (p) S^{1} S^{2} S^{3} S^{4} S^{5} S^{6} S^{7} S^{8} S^{9} K^{4} *Art. 14* S^{10} *Art. 13* K^{5} *Art. 15* (q) *desunt* S^{2} (r) *desunt* S^{10} (s) uxore vita permanente S^{2} (t) quod S^{9} (u) *deest* S^{10} ⟨sibi⟩ K^{4} (v) *manus B, a.c.* promissionem S^{6} promissione S^{3} S^{10} provisionem S^{1} S^{2} S^{4} S^{5} S^{7} S^{8} S^{9} K^{4} K^{5} (w) *desunt* S^{1} S^{2} S^{3} S^{4} S^{5} S^{6} S^{7} S^{8} S^{9} S^{10} K^{4} K^{5} (x) ⟨de eo, qui moritur et uxor relinquitur in bonis viri vel [*?*]⟩ *manus A* S^{3} (y) *manus B, a.c.* promissione S^{6} promissione S^{3} S^{10} provisionem S^{1} S^{2} S^{4} S^{5} S^{7} S^{8} S^{9} K^{4} K^{5} (z) possidere nec hereditatem K^{4} (aa) possidere S^{10} ⊢possidere⊣ S^{6} (bb) mulier moritur S^{2} moritur S^{3} (cc) Et si S^{2} S^{9} K^{5} Sed si S^{7} quod K^{4} (dd) sibi S^{1} S^{3} S^{4} S^{5} suus S^{7} (ee) tamen S^{2} *deest* S^{9} K^{5} (ff) primum K^{5} (gg) ipsi S^{2} (hh) si S^{1} S^{4} S^{3} S^{5} K^{4} (ii) Item S^{8} (jj) *desunt* S^{3} (kk) *deest* S^{8} (ll) mulieri S^{2} S^{3} S^{4} S^{5} S^{7} S^{8} K^{5} (mm) *deest* K^{5} (nn) iure K^{5} (oo) Item S^{8} (pp) ⟨qui⟩ K^{4} (qq) hereditati S^{8} (rr) *deest* K^{5} (ss) *desunt* S^{6} K^{5} (tt) *manus B* S^{6} *deest* S^{10} *in glossa* K^{4} (uu) *deest* S^{10}

{a} ⟨obligare vulgariter szastawÿ⟩ K^{5}

Articuli 15–16 (a)

[*15*] | ⟨Obligatio⟩(b) Obligat aliquis mercimonia aut alia bona mobilia(c) pro 29vb debito ex parte iudicii, et ille pronunciat tribus iudiciis, ut iuris est, (d) et quarto iudicio super eo dominium(e) receperit aut appropriatum(f) sibi fuerit, et cognoscencie donum dederit coram iudicio(g) et scabinis. Et si(h) ille in posterum ad repetendum sua bona pervenerit, possidens est propius suum pignus servare cum scabinis et iudice, quam ille, qui caret possessione.

[*16*] (iNullus eciam(j) hospes ab alio | advena et contra, indiget(k) pignus reci- 30ra pere pro debito (l) recognito. Si(m) autem (nreceperit, extuncn) ipsum acqui- IIII rere et prosequi prout alter vir iuridice oportebit, nisi aliter fuisset inter eos ordinatum verbotenus in contractu.i)

Articuli 17–18 (o)

[*17*] (p) Si aliquis ducit uxorem et si vir (qde hac luce decedit,q) uxor nichil habet in suis bonis, nisi sibi dederit pro dotalicio aut(r) vite provisione pro eius vita in iudicio bannito. Nulla mulier po[te]st vite provisionem nec dotalicium hereditarie observare(s). (t) Et cum moritur, ad heredes revertitur sui mariti. Quodsi sibi(u) maritus mulieri nichil in suis bonis dederit, in possessione(v) bonorum sui mariti debet permanere, et pueri sibi necessaria ministrabunt, eousque in viduitate(w) et sine marito voluerit permanere. (x) Si vir oves habuerit, mulier ad suppellectilia recipiet. Et si(y) pueri vellent dotalicium mulieri infringere, servare potest testimonio virorum ac mulierum metseptima, qui tunc presentes fuerunt. ⟨Si aliqui pueri fuerint exhereditati⟩(z) Si vir pueros habuerit, aut mulier, quicumque ex hiis exhereditati fuerint, (aa) si moritur vir, hii pueri, qui in hereditate(bb) patris | sunt, recipiunt (ccbona 30rb et non hii, qui exhereditati suntcc), sed hereditatem vendere non possunt absque coheredum consensu. Hii pueri, (dd) qui in potestate patris tempore

---

(a) K^1 K^2 K^3 W^1 C^3 *Art. 13* K^4 *Art. 13 in glossa, pars* Nullus—contractu W^2 C^2 *deest folium* C^1 *Art. 15–16* (b) *manus β* C^1 ⟨de debitis⟩ C^3 (c) *deest* W^1 (d) ⟨insuper⟩ C^3 (e) bonum K^2 (f) aprobatum K^1 K^2 (g) iudice K^3 W^1 (h) *deest* K^3 W^1 C^3 (i) *desunt* K^1 K^2 K^3 W^1 *in glossa* K^4 (j) *deest* K^4 (k) indigenam C^3 (l) ⟨dic⟩ C^3 (m) Sed K^4 C^3 (n) *desunt* C^3 (o) K^1 K^2 K^3 K^4 W^1 C^3 *Art. 14* K^4 *Art. 14 in glossa, pars* Deservitum—voluerit W^2 C^2 *deest folium* C^1 *Art. 17–18* (p) ⟨De dotalicio⟩ C^3 ⟨et uxor⟩ C^3 (q) moriatur K^3 (r) et W^1 (s) conservare W^1 (t) ⟨in ea aliquis mater⟩ *lectio incerta* C^3 (u) *deest* K^1 K^2 (v) *in ms.* possessionem [*s*] C^1 (w) *abbreviatio* viduitate[m] [*s*] C^1 (x) ⟨dotalicium⟩ C^3 (y) *deest* K^1 K^2 (z) *manus β* C^1 (aa) ⟨causam [*?*]⟩ C^3 (bb) deest K^1 K^2 K^3 W^1 (cc) *desunt* W^1 (dd) ⟨qui cum his [*?*]⟩ C^3

vendere non possunt absque heredum(a) consensu. (b) Hii pueri, qui in potestate(c) patris (dmortis(e) tempore fuerunt, si ex hiis unus(f)d) moritur, istius partem dividunt inter se equaliter, tam exhereditati(g), quam(h) domestici ⟨id est dimis[s]i[t] exhereditavit⟩(i). (j)

Articulus 15 (k)

[*15*] Quando alicui sua possessio publicata(l) fuerit iuste (m) ac iudicialiter(n), quociens exit vel intrat, tociens penam iudici demeretur(o), ita si publicacio super ipsum rite ac iuste sit aquisita. (p)

Articulus 16 (q)

[*16*] (r) (sQuidquid masculus dat sub banno, sis) possidet pacifice et quiete absque arestacione(t) aliqua(u) anno et die, hoc propius et melius obtinere potest cum iudice et scabinis, quam (vab(w) ipsov) aliquis possit exbrigare. Quodsi iudex et scabini sunt mortui(x), quod(y) tamen bene(z) cum(aa) aliis fidedignis ad minus duobus scabinis et quat[t]uor viris probitate probatis ⟨deponeri possunt⟩(bb) testimonio (cc), (ddet sicdd) bona sibi donata obtinebit.

(a) *deest* S^{10} (b) Item S^{8} (c) hereditate K^{5} (d) *desunt* S^{5} (e) mortui K^{5} (f) bonis S^{7} (g) ex *adscriptum* K^{4} hereditati K^{5} (h) ⟨quam⟩ K^{4} quam eciam sive K^{5} (i) *manus B* S^{6} ⟨vite provisionem aut dotalicium nulla mulier hereditarie observarepotest, sed cum moritur ad heredes revertitur sui mariti⟩ S^{8} (j) ⟨de viduis quomodo sunt foveri⟩ K^{2} (k) S^{1} S^{2} S^{3} S^{4} S^{5} S^{6} S^{7} S^{8} S^{9} K^{4} *Art. 15* S^{10} *Art. 14* K^{5} *Art. 16* (l) publice S^{2} (m) ⟨de publicacione possessionum⟩ *manus A* S^{3} (n) abiudicata S^{2} (o) solvit S^{10} (p) Si autem filius uxorem duxerit vivente patre, si moritur filius absque divisione patris in hereditate, tunc pueri eiusdem filii hereditatem patris partem patris recipient, sed non pueri filie seu ancille. Sin autem filium a se diviserit cum hereditate, tunc cum sui pueri recipient partem equalem in hereditate ave, sed in hereditate ave equalem divisionem tam filiorum pueri, quam filiarum. K^{5} (q) S^{1} S^{2} S^{3} S^{4} S^{5} S^{6} S^{7} S^{8} S^{9} K^{4} *Art. 16* S^{10} *Art. 15* K^{5} *Art. 17* (r) ⟨de resignacione possessionum in bannito iudicio⟩ *manus A* S^{3} (s) Quidquid alicui datur aut porrigitur in bannito iudicio, quod S^{2} (t) contradiccione S^{2} (u) *deest* S^{2} K^{5} (v) *desunt* K^{5} (w) sub S^{7} (x) non S^{10} (y) *deest* K^{5} (z) *deest* S^{4} S^{5} S^{9} (aa) *deest* K^{5} (bb) *manus B* S^{6} (cc) probet S^{8} K^{5} (dd) ut K^{5}

mortis fuerunt, si ex hiis unus moritur, istius partem dividunt inter se equaliter, tam exhereditati, quam domestici. {a}

[*18*] (aDeservitum(b) precium, rationabile debitum debent solvi de bonis mortui | viri pro dotalicio, ad(c) hoc si mulier fuerit dotata pecuniis in promp- 30va
tis(d). Si autem dotata fuerit in hereditate (evel proprioe), tunc suum dotalicium pre aliis debitis iure valeat obtinere. Eciam quivis vir(f) habens mansionem infra municipale, ille sue conthorale dare potest pro dotalicio suam propriam(g) hereditatem, quam in posse habet alienandi, et eciam in aliis bonis suis mobilibus, in quantum voluerit.a)

Articulus 19 (h)

[*19*] Quando(i) alicui(j) sua possessio publicata(k) fuerit iuste ac iudicialiter, quociens (l) exiit(m) vel intrat, tociens penam iudici demeretur(n), (oita si publicacioo) super ipsum (prite ac iuste fuerit acquisitap).

Articulus 20 (q)

[*20*] | ⟨Quidquid masculus et dat⟩(r) Quidquid (smasculus dats) sub banno, si pos- 30vb
sidebit(t) pacifice ac quiete absque contradiccione anno et die, hoc propius (u) ac melius (v) obtinere (w) potest cum iudice et scabinis, quam aliquis possit (xab ipsox) exbrigare(y). Quodsi iudex et scabini mortui fuerint, quod(z) tamen bene(aa) cum aliis fidedignis(bb) ad(cc) minus (dd) duobus scabinis et quat[t]uor viris (ee) (ffprobitate probatisff) (ggtestimonio(hh) deponi potestgg), (iiet sic (jj) bona donata obtinebitii).

(a) *desunt* K^1 K^2 K^3 W^1 *in glossa, manicula* K^4 (b) Sed deservitum C^3 K^4 (c) et C^3 (d) paratis K^4 (e) propria K^4 C^3 (f) *deest* C^3 (g) ipsam K^4 C^3 (h) K^1 K^2 K^3 W^1 C^3 *Art. 15* W^2 C^2 *deest folium* C^1 *Art. 19* (i) Ubi C^3 (j) alia K^3 (k) fundata C^3 (l) hic C^3 (m) erit K^2 (n) solvet C^3 (o) nisi fiscacio C^3 (p) possessionem sibi fuerit iuridice allucrata C^3 (q) K^1 K^2 K^3 W^1 C^3 *Art. 16* W^2 C^2 *deest folium* C^1 *Art. 20* (r) *manus α* C^1 ⟨de re possessa per annum et diem⟩ C^3 ⟨de donis prescripcio⟩ C^3 ⟨dic⟩ C^3 (s) vir dederit C^3 (t) possessor hoc C^3 (u) est W^1 (v) possessor K^1 K^2 K^3 W^1 C^3 (w) propius W^1 (x) *desunt* C^3 (y) possidere W^1 K^1 K^2 possidere seu alienare C^3 (z) hoc K^1 K^2 *deest* C^3 (aa) donacio valeat possideri C^3 (bb) iudicialibus C^3 (cc) ac K^3 (dd) cum K^1 K^2 C^3 (ee) veris W^1 (ff) iudicialibus C^3 *desunt* K^1 K^2 (gg) probat K^1 probet K^2 (hh) *deest* K^3 W^1 (ii) obtinebit ille suum dominium C^3 (jj) sibi K^1 K^2

{a} In Colmensi. Dividit uxor cum viro bona per medium, si bona directe ad virum spectant et e converso. W^1

Articulus 17 (a)

143r [*17*] | Nemo masculus nec ulla mulier possunt in lecto(b) egritudinis (c) de suis bonis alicui ultra tres solidos dare(d) absque heredum consensu (eseu voluntatee) (f).

Articulus 18 (g)

[*18*] (h) Quodsi hereditas in(i) fratribus et(j) sororibus defectum {a} habuerit, extunc omnes hii, qui se (k) linea equali consanguinitatis ostendere poterint, in hereditate succedunt equaliter (l). (m) (nQui autem in possessione est, si bene sacerdos est(o) aut manserit, tamen supellectilia (precipit, quod(q) si(r) nulla puella fuerit(s). (tSin) autem puella et sacerdos fuerintt), tunc supellectilia (u) interp) se dividunt ⟨equaliter⟩(v).

Articulus 19 (w)

[*19*] Quidquid (xmasculus datx) in iudicio bannito coram iudice et scabinis, ibi(y) recipiens dat unum solidum (z) pro doni cognicione, quem (aa) recipiunt scabini.

(a) S^1 S^2 S^3 S^4 S^5 S^6 S^7 S^8 S^9 K^4 *Art. 17* S^{10} *Art. 16* K^5 *Art. 18* (b) facto S^4 S^5 loco S^7 S^{10} K^4 K^5 (c) quam S^2 (d) ⟨dare⟩ S^4 *deest* S^5 (e) *desunt* S^8 et consensu [*s*] K^5 (f) nisi tali racione videlicet quando aliquis esset in aliqua manifesta, tunc sellabitur [*s*] sibi equus et induat se arma bellica vel vestes suas meliores, et si posset equ[u]m asscendere de lapide, qui esset altus ad unam ulnam, vel de aliquo, et tunc equitaret ad iudicium, et sedens in equo potest, quidquid vult resignare, ita [*?*] quod simul posset ad similem lapidem descendere de equo. S^3 ⟨vide aliquis potest sua bona dare in infirmitate positus⟩ *manus A* S^3 ⟨et alibi additur, nec mulier sine consensu viri⟩ S^8 ⟨nec mulier sine consensu viri⟩ K^4 (g) S^1 S^3 S^4 S^5 S^6 S^7 S^8 S^9 K^4 *Art. 18* S^2 *Art. 18–19* S^{10} *Art. 17* K^5 *Art. 19–20* (h) ⟨de hereditate privata fratribus et sorobibus⟩ *manus A* S^3 (i) *deest* S^3 (j) aut S^2 (k) in S^2 S^{10} (l) ⟨[sive] sint masculi [sive femi]ne, ex paterna [et materna] consanguineitate⟩ K^4 (m) *rubrica:* De divisione suppellectilium. S^2 *rubrica:* De filia et fratre sacerdote. K^5 (n) Si in possessione hereditatis aliqua virgo sit, illa principaliter recipit S^2 *deest* S^3 (o) *deest* K^5 (p) *deest* S^{10} (q) *deest* S^8 (r) *deest* K^5 (s) *deest* K^5 (t) et si sacerdotem in fratrem habet S^2 Et sacerdos fuerit K^5 (u) equaliter S^2 S^8 (v) *manus B* S^6 ⟨equali forma⟩ K^4 (w) S^1 S^3 S^4 S^5 S^6 S^7 S^8 S^9 K^4 *Art. 19* S^2 *Art. 20* S^{10} *Art. 18* K^5 *Art. 21* (x) masculo datur S^5 (y) *deest* S^{10} K^4 (z) de dono recognosciencie, quorum sunt solidorum S^{10} K^4 (aa) pro se K^5

{a} ⟨linea vulgariter k r e s z a consanguineitatis vulgariter p o k o l e n y a k r e w n e g o⟩ K^5

Articulus 21 (a)

[*21*] ⟨Nemo⟩(b) Nemo masculus, nec ulla mulier potest in (clecto egritudinisc) de suis bonis alicui ultra tres solidos dare (d) absque heredum consensu (eseu voluntatee), (fnec mulier sine consensu viri(g)f).

Articuli 22–23 (h)

[*22*] | (i) Quodsi hereditas in(j) fratribus seu(k) sororibus defectum habuerit, 31ra
extunc (l) hii, qui se (m) linea equali consanguinitatis ostendere poterint(n), v
in hereditate succedunt equaliter (o).

[*23*] Qui autem in possessione(p), si bene(q) sacerdos sit, manserit(r), tamen(s) suppellectilia recipit, quodsi puella (t) nulla fuerit. Si autem sacerdos et puella (u) fuerint, (v) suppellectilia inter se (w) dividunt (x).

Articulus 24 [(y)]

[*24*] Quidquid masculus dat in iudicio bannito coram iudice et scabinis, ibi recipiens dat unum solidum pro doni cognicione, quem(z) recipiunt scabini.

(a) K^1 K^2 K^3 W^1 C^3 *Art. 17* C^2 W^2 *deest folium* C^1 *Art. 21* (b) *manus η* C^1 ⟨de testamentis⟩ C^3 (c) egritudine K^1 K^2 (d) ⟨eo racione⟩ *lectio incerta* C^3 (e) *desunt* C^3 (f) *desunt* K^1 K^2 *in glossa* K^4 (g) mariti W^1 C^3 (h) K^1 K^2 K^3 K^4 C^3 *Art. 18–19* W^1 *Art. 18* W^2 C^2 *deest folium* C^1 *Art. 22–23* (i) ⟨hereditas⟩ C^3 ⟨dic⟩ C^3 (j) *deest* K^3 (k) seu in K^1 aut in K^2 in C^3 (l) omnes W^1 K^1 K^2 C^3 (m) in C^3 (n) *deest* K^1 K^2 K^3 W^1 C^3 (o) sive sint masculi sive femine, ex paterna et materna consanguneitate. C^3 *in glossa* K^4 (p) *in ms.* possessionem [*s*] C^1 (q) *deest* K^1 K^2 K^3 W^1 C^3 (r) *deest* K^1 K^2 K^3 W^1 C^3 (s) tunc K^1 K^2 W^1 C^3 (t) ibi K^3 C^3 (u) ibi K^3 C^3 (v) extunc K^1 K^2 W^1 C^3 (w) eciam K^3 (x) equaliter C^3 (y) K^1 K^2 K^3 C^3 *Art. 20* C^1 *Art. 24* W^1 *Art. 19* C^2 W^2 *deest folium* (z) quod K^1 K^2

Articulus 20 (a)

[20] Quicumque aliquem coram iudicio(b) (c) (dpro debitod) inpulsaverit, {a} si(e) debitum coacto(f) iure(g) consecutus fuerit, opportet eodem die solvere et iudex in eo suam penam acquisivit. (h) Sin autem querimonia facta fuerit (i) super aliquem pro debito, de quo fatetur(j), (k) solvere tenetur infra duas ebdomadas, et si (ltempore statutol) debitor(m) non solverit, extunc iudex in eo suam(n) penam acquisivit. ⟨Regula iuris. Debitor in regere si non plene satisfecerit, proscribetur. [(o)Item. Minus[o)] est exactio, quam excusat inopia debitoris.⟩{b} Extunc solvere(p) mandat ad octo dies, deinde ad tres dies, extunc sequenti die. (q)
143v Quociens tunc (rmandatum | debitorr) adimplere neglexerit, tociens (spenam suam in ⟨fiscacione⟩(t) eo iudex acquisivits) (u). Si penam(v) iudici(w) et debitum creditori solvere contempserit, {c} extunc fiscatur sua possessio. Per hac compellitur, quod(x) debitum creditori et pena iudici persolvatur. Si autem possessione caruerit, extunc banno compellitur, extunc (y) bene potest(z) {d} comprehendi, ubi visus fuerit, pro debito et (aa) pena. Et quicumque ipsum ultra hoc tenuerit, (bb) penam iudici demeretur.

Articulus 21 (cc)

[21] ⟨Regula iuris. Non prestat impedimentum, quod de iure sortitum fuit ad effectum.⟩{e} Si aliquis ad limina sanctorum aut(dd) ad(ee) nundinas extra provinciam (ffaut extra terminosff) ire voluerit, et si ipsum aliquis pro(gg) debito (hh) inpedire voluerit, (ii) hoc fieri non debet(jj), (kk) opportet(ll) ius suum (mmcoram suo(nn)

(a) S^1 S^3 S^4 S^5 S^6 S^7 S^8 S^9 K^4 *Art. 20* S^2 *Art. 21* S^{10} *Art. 19* K^5 *Art. 22* (b) iudice S^7 (c) aliquem S^9 (d) *desunt* S^8 (e) oportet K^5 (f) acto S^7 tacto S^9 S^8 (g) modo S^2 (h) ⟨De debito coactum ius aquisito⟩ K^5 (i) ⟨de solucione debitorum et pena, qui negligens solvere [debet]⟩ *manus A* S^3 (j) profatetur K^5 (k) quod S^8 qui K^5 (l) debito vel statuto modo S^9 (m) *deest* S^8 S^9 K^5 (n) *deest* S^9 (o) istis. In cuius K^5 (p) solvi rite K^5 (q) ⟨Causa solvendorum⟩ S^4 (r) mandare debitori et S^2 (s) iudici demeretur S^3 (t) *manus B* S^6 (u) nisi se iure excusaverit S^9 (v) autem S^9 (w) *deest* S^3 (x) *deest* S^2 (y) eum K^5 (z) *deest* S^{10} (aa) pro S^1 S^2 S^3 S^7 S^8 K^5 (bb) aut S^1 ⊢aut⊣ S^6 (cc) S^1 S^3 S^6 S^7 S^8 S^9 *Art. 21* S^2 S^4 S^5 *Art. 22* S^{10} *Art. 20* K^4 *Art. 19* K^5 *Art. 23–24* (dd) *deest* S^4 S^5 (ee) *deest* S^8 S^{10} K^5 (ff) *desunt* S^2 (gg) *deest* K^5 (hh) ipsum S^9 (ii) ⟨vide extra locum proprium, potest quis pro debito duellari⟩ *manus A* S^3 (jj) potest S^2 oportet S^8 (kk) *rubrica:* De testibus infra tria iudicium statuendis. K^5 (ll) sed S^{10} (mm) aut iudicem S^2 (nn) *deest* K^5

{a} ⟨Impulsaverit per querulaverit vulgariter pozalowalbÿ⟩ K^5 {b} *manus A* S^6 *adest* K^5 {c} ⟨Creditor Gÿszczyrcz albo dzwyerdza; fiscat vel pignorat vulgariter ma bÿcz czÿa dzana⟩ K^5 {d} ⟨Sua possessio vulgariter gyego wladza albo gyego gÿmÿenye⟩ K^5 {e} *manus A* S^6 De limina sanctorum vulgariter poszwÿaczÿ. *ad rubricam* K^5

Articulus 25 (a)

[25] | ⟨Quicumque aliquem⟩(b) Quicumque aliquem coram iudicio(c) (d) (e pro 31rb
debito e) impulsaverit, si debitum(f) coacto iure consecutum fuerit, oportet eodem die solvere et iudex in eo suam penam acquisivit. Si autem querimonia facta fuerit super aliquem pro debito, si (g) fatetur, solvere tenetur per duas ebdomadas, et si (h) tempore(i) (j) statuto debitor non solverit, extunc iudex in eo penam suam acquisivit. (k) Extunc solvere mandat ad octo dies, deinde ad tres dies, extunc die sequenti. Quociens tunc debitor mandatum adimplere neglexerit, tociens in eo penam iudex acquisivit. Si penam iudici et debitum(l) creditori(m) (n solvere contempsit, n) tunc fiscatur(o) sua possessio. Per hoc conpellitur, quod debitum creditori et iudici penam persolvet. Si autem possessione caruerit, extunc banno conpellitur, extunc bene potest conprehendi, ubi visus fuerit pro debito et pena. Et quicumque ipsum(p) ultra hoc tenuerit, penam iudici demeretur.

Articuli 26–27 (q)

[26] | ⟨Si quis ad limina sanctorum⟩(r) Si aliquis ad limina sanctorum aut ad(s) 31va
nundinas extra provinciam ire voluerit, et (t si aliquis t) ipsum (u pro debito u) voluerit, hoc fieri non debet, oportet suum ius recipere coram iudice suo.

(a) K^1 K^2 K^3 C^3 *Art. 21* W^1 *Art. 20* W^2 C^2 *deest folium* C^1 *Art. 25* (b) *manus α* C^1 (c) iudice K^1 K^2 (d) bannito C^3 (e) *desunt* W^1 (f) *deest* K^1 K^2 (g) de quo C^3 (h) in C^3 (i) ad tempus vel W^1 (j) debito et K^3 (k) ⟨de debito recognito⟩ K^3 (l) penam K^1 K^2 (m) debitori W^1 (n) contempserit W^1 non persolverit C^3 (o) fundatur C^3 (p) *deest* W^1 (q) K^1 K^2 *Art. 22* K^3 C^3 *Art. 22–23* W^1 *Art. 21* W^2 C^2 *deest folium* C^1 *Art. 26–27* (r) *manus ε* C^1 ⟨de debito⟩ C^3 (s) *deest* K^3 (t) *desunt* W^1 (u) *desunt* K^3

iudice[mm)] recipere. Et si uni testimonium[(a)] adiudicatum fuerit, inducias [{a}] trinas [(b)] duas ebdomadas [(c)] obtinebit, quodcumque elegerit aut[(d)] iudicio proximo.

Articulus 22 [(e)]

[22] ⟨Regula iuris. [(f]Contra eum[f)] qui legem dicere potuit apertius est interpretacio facienda. Item. Nemo potest plus iuris conferre, quam sibi competere dinoscatur. Item. Ad facinus duplex non sufficit ulcio simplex.⟩[{b}] [(g)] Quicumque scabinum in scampno iudiciali[(h)] improperaverit aut turpibus verbis [(i)] obruerit, scabinis lucratur suam emendam triginta solidos, et iudex suam penam acquirit. [(j)] Obruitur autem scabinus[(k)], postquam sua[(l)] sentencia diffinita sit et consensus[(m)] aliorum scabinorum preterierit, extunc[(n)] omnes emendas acquirunt et iudex penas, et quot emende[(o)] fuerint, totidem et pene iudici acquiruntur.

Articulus 23 [(p)]

[23] Quando concordia inter discordantes coram iudicio ordinata fuerit, [(q)] diuturnus fremitus, ⟨hoc⟩[(r)] homo[(s)] protestare potest, cum iudice et scabinis. Quodsi scabini[(t)] mortui fuerint, tunc protestatur cum[(u)] hominibus [(v)] fidedignis, qui [(w)] iudicio affuerunt. [(x)] Quidquid scabini protestantur [(y)], hoc [(z)] iudex cum ipsis debet protestare, simul[(aa)] et confirmare. [(bb)] Sed ubicumque concordia ordinata[(cc)] fuerit [(dd]extra iudicium[dd)], hoc facilius potest [(ee)] probare vir cum[(ff)] sex[(gg)] testibus solus[(hh)] septimus, qui interfuerunt et[(ii)] [(jj)] viderunt[(kk)] concordiam esse factam. Ubi concordia [(ll]et vera[(mm)]

(a) debitum S^2 (b) per S^8 S^{10} in S^9 (c) ad solvendum S^2 (d) a S^{10} (e) S^1 S^3 S^6 S^7 S^8 S^9 K^4 *Art. 22* S^2 *Art. 23* S^4 S^5 S^{10} *Art. 21* K^5 *Art. 8, 25* (f) *desunt* K^5 (g) ⟨Quis scabinum turpiter obiurgavit⟩ *manus A* S^3 (h) sede S^9 K^5 (*Art. 8*) (i) eum S^4 S^5 (*art. 25*) (j) ⟨non⟩ S^1 (k) *manicula* S^1 (l) *deest* S^4 (m) sensus K^5 (*Art. 8*) (n) extra K^5 (*art. 25*) (o) pene S^4 S^5 (*art. 25*) (p) S^1 S^3 S^4 S^5 S^6 S^7 S^8 S^9 K^4 *Art. 23* S^2 *Art. 24* S^{10} *Art. 22* K^5 *Art. 26–27* (q) aut S^3 (r) *manus B* S^6 (s) non K^5 (t) *deest* S^4 S^5 (u) *deest* S^7 S^8 (v) ⟨de firmacione concordie inter litigantes⟩ *manus A* S^3 (w) in K^4 S^{10} (x) ⟨nota⟩, *manicula* S^8 *rubrica:* De testimonio scabinorum. K^5 (y) aut confirmant S^4 S^5 S^7 S^8 (z) eciam S^2 (aa) *deest* S^4 S^5 (bb) *subrubrica:* De concordia extra iudicium. K^5 (cc) facta S^{10} K^4 (dd) *desunt* S^{10} (ee) protestare seu K^4 (ff) assumptis sibi S^2 (gg) tribus S^3 (hh) *deest* S^2 (ii) aut S^5 (jj) audierunt et S^7 S^8 (kk) audierunt S^2 (ll) *desunt* K^5 (mm) *deest* S^2

{a} vulgariter r o k ÿ K^4 {b} *manus A* S^6 *adest* K^5

[27] ⟨Si uni viro⟩(a) Et si uni(b) viro(c) testimonium(d) adiudicatum fuerit, inducias (e) trinas (fduas ebdomadasf) obtinebit(g), quodcumque elegerit(h) aut (i) iudicio proximo.

Articulus 28 (j)

[28] ⟨Quicumque⟩ (k) Quicumque scabinum in scampno iudiciali vituperaverit(l) aut turpibus verbis eum(m) ob|ruerit, scabinus lucratur suam emendam 31vb
xxx solidos, et iudex (nocto solidosn) suam penam acquirit. Obruitur autem scabinus, postquam sua(o) sentencia diffinita (p) sit et ubi(q) consensus aliorum scabinorum preterierit, extunc omnes emendas(r) acquirunt, et iudex tot penas (s), quot fuerint emende (t). ⟨Item de eodem XXVI⟩(u) {a}

Articuli 29–30 (v)

[29] ⟨Quando concordia⟩(w) Quando concordia inter discordantes ordinata fuerit coram iudicio aut(x) diuturnus fremitus(y), hoc homo(z) protestare potest cum iudice et scabinis. Quodsi scabini mortui fuerint, tunc(aa) protestatur cum hominibus(bb) fidedignis, qui iudicio profuerunt(cc). Quidquid scabini protestantur (ddet confirmantdd), hoc et(ee) iudex debet cum eis protestare, simul et confirmare. Sed ubi concordia extra iudicium ordinata fuerit, hoc probare facilius potest vir cum sex(ff) testibus (gg) metseptimus, qui interfuerunt | et viderunt concordiam esse factam. {b} 32ra

VI

(a) *manus η* C1 ⟨Testimonium⟩ C3 (b) vir K3 (c) *deest* K1 K2 W1 (d) testis K1 K2 (e) extunc C3 (f) quindenarium C3 (g) eiusdem habuerit C3 (h) voluerit C3 (i) in C3 (j) K1 K2 *Art. 23* K3 C3 *Art. 24* W1 *Art. 22* W2 C2 *deest folium* C1 *Art. 28* (k) ⟨Qui scabinos maletra[cta]t⟩ C3 (l) improperaverit K1 K2 W1 C3 (m) *deest* K1 K2 W1 C3 (n) *desunt* K1 K2 K3 W1 C3 (o) *deest* C3 (p) fuerit K2 (q) *deest* K1 K2 K3 (r) *deest* K3 (s) acquirit C3 (t) totidem pene iudici aquiruntur K1 K2 K3 W1 (u) *manus β* C1 (v) K1 K2 *Art. 24–25* K3 C3 *Art. 25–26* W1 *Art. 23–24* W2 C2 *deest folium* C1 *Art. 29–30* (w) *manus ε* C1 ⟨De concordia coram iudicio⟩ C3 (x) *deest* K1 K2 (y) *in ms.* diuturno [s] *C1* (z) *deest* W1 (aa) nil W1 (bb) omnibus K1 (cc) affuerunt C3 (dd) *desunt* K1 K2 (ee) eciam K1 (ff) septem W1 (gg) solus K1 K2

{a} In Colmensi. Consuli et scabino ferto cuilibet et quot fertones, tot sculteto quatuor solidi. W1 {b} In Colmensi. Arbitri quecumque recognoverunt , licet extra iudicium sit concordia facta vadit in rem iudicatam. W1

fremitus(a) (bdiurna etb)(ll) diuturna(c) coram iudicio confirmata(d) fuerit, si ipsam violat adversa pars, et si vincetur, ut ius dictaverit(e), (f) cum iudice et scabinis, pro vulnere manum, pro homicidio collum. (g) Sin autem contingeret, quod alter eam(h) infringeret, hunc (itamen(j) emendare cum recompensai) opportet, pro vulnere novem talenta, pro homicidio decem et octo taleta, nisi se possit excusare (ksecundum iuris(l) edictumk).

Articulus 24 (m)

[*24*] Et vir quivis(n) filium suum ter(o) potest eximere(p), quem habet in potestate, coram iudicio(q) pro quolibet crimine capitali tacto sacramento metseptimus secundum ius municipale(r). Similiter(s) et vir potest filium suum, quem in potestate ⟨Regula iuris. Imputari ei non debet per quem non stat, si non faciet quod
144v per eum fuerat faciendum.⟩{a} | habet, tribus vicibus(t) eximere(u), ubi aut(v) ad(w) collum aut(x) ad(y) manum pertransit(z). (aa) Quarta vero vice ipsum (bbsolum propria in personabb) respondere(cc) opportebit, et patrem(dd) in suo iure(ee) non inpediet, si filius prius(ff) bene respondisset. (gg) Sin autem pater (hh) cum (ii) filio (jj) simul(kk) in eodem crimine coram iudicio inpulsati fuerint, extunc pater filium eximere non potest, nisi prius ⟨pater⟩(ll) se ab(mm) eodem crimine expurgabit. (nn) Famulus potest mercedem suam, quam promeruit, quinque solidos(oo) probare(pp) (qq) tacto sacramento mettercius(rr) (ss⟨ita tamen [(tt]si sibi[tt)] dominus consentire voluerit[(uu)]. Si autem dominus(vv) iuraverit(ww) tacto

(a) *p.c.* ⟨firmitas⟩ *manus B* S^6 (b) *desunt* S^1 S^2 S^3 S^4 S^5 S^7 S^8 S^9 S^{10} K^4 K^5 (c) *deest* S^{10} (d) seu ordinata S^4 S^5 (e) declaravit S^8 (f) coram iudicio S^2 (g) ⟨Quando concordia infringitur⟩ K^5 (h) concordiam S^2 (i) cum emenda satisfacere S^2 (j) tunc S^7 (k) *desunt* S^4 S^5 (l) deest S^{10} (m) S^1 S^4 S^5 S^6 S^7 S^8 K^4 *Art. 24* S^2 *Art. 25–26* S^3 S^9 *Art. 24–26* S^{10} *Art. 23–24* K^5 *Art. 28* (n) qui⟨vis⟩ S^8 (o) *deest* S^3 S^5 K^2 (p) *deest* S^3 (q) *deest* S^3 (r) provinciale K^5 (s) Si ex amore S^3 ⟨de redempcione filii per patrem pro crimine notorio⟩ *manus A* S^3 (t) iudiciis S^9 (u) eximere potest K^5 *deest* S^3 S^4 S^5 S^7 S^8 (v) autem S^7 S^8 S^{10} K^4 K^5 *deest* S^3 S^5 (w) ⟨ad⟩ S^4 *deest* S^9 K^5 (x) *deest* K^5 (y) ⟨ad⟩ S^4 *deest* S^7 S^8 K^5 (z) percusit S^{10} (aa) ⟨Quarta vice ipsum iudicabit⟩ K^5 (bb) *desunt* S^8 (cc) iudicare K^5 (dd) primum S^7 (ee) nomine S^7 (ff) propius S^4 S^5 (gg) ⟨De precium famuli deservicio, quod famulus habet obtinere in iudicio.⟩ S^3 ⟨De patre et [fi]lio in eodem crimine deprehensis⟩ K^5 (hh) filii S^7 prius S^{10} K^4 (ii) suo S^8 (jj) suo K^5 (kk) *deest* S^7 (ll) *manus B* S^6 (mm) alii S^4 (nn) *rubrica:* De precio famuli deservicio, quod famulus habet optinere in iudicio. S^3 ⟨de precio famulorum deservito⟩ *manus A* S^3 *subrubrica:* Capitulum de eodem S^9 *rubrica:* De precio famuli. S^{10} ⟨De mercede famuli⟩ K^5 (oo) *in ms.* solidis [*s*] S^6 (pp) obtinere S^7 K^5 (qq) et obtinere S^9 (rr) metseptimus S^4 S^5 (ss) *manus B* S^6 *textus adest in* S^2 S^3 S^4 S^5 S^7 S^8 S^9 S^{10} K^5 (tt) *desunt* S^7 (uu) noluerit S^3 S^9 (vv) *deest* S^3 (ww) voluerit S^4 S^5 voluerit probare S^9 S^{10} K^5

{a} *manus A* S^6

[*30*] (a) Ubi concordia et fremitus diuturnus coram iudicio confirmata fuerit, si ipsam violat adversa pars(b), et si vincetur, ut ius dictaverit, cum iudice et scabinis, pro vulnere manum, pro homicidio collum. Si autem contingeret, ut(c) alter eam infringeret, hunc cum(d) (e emenda satisfacere e) oportet, pro vulnere novem talenta, (f pro homicidio XVIII talenta f), nisi se(g) poterit(h) excusare secundum edictum iuris.

Articulus 31 (i)

[*31*] | ⟨Pater suum filium ter potest eximere(j)⟩(k) Et(l) quivis (m) vir (n) potest filium 32rb
suum(o) ter excipere(p), quem habet in potestate, coram iudicio pro quolibet crimine capitali tacto sacramento metseptimus secundum ius municipale. (q (r Eciam(s) (t) potest filium suum, quem in potestate habet, tribus vicibus (u), ubi ad collum aut ad manum pertransit. Quarta vero vice ipsum propria in persona respondere oportebit, et primum(v) in suo iure non impediet, si bene filius prius respondisset. r) Si autem pater cum filio simul in eodem crimine (w coram iudicio w) inculpati fuerint, extunc pater filium (x) eximere non potest, nisi prius se(y) de eodem crimine expurgabit. q) ⟨famulus potest⟩(z) Et(aa) famulus potest mercedem(bb) suam, quam promeruit, (cc) quinque solidos tacto sacramento probare, ita (dd) si ut(ee) sibi dominus consentire voluerit. (ff) (gg Si autem dominus iuravit tacto sacramento mettercius, quod sibi persolvit, tunc propius est evadere, quam (hh famulus

---

(a) ⟨de compensacione⟩ C3 (b) *deest* K1 K2 K3 W1 C3 (c) quod K1 K2 vel W1 (d) tamen K1 K2 K3 W1 (e) emendare et satisfacere K3 (f) *desunt* K2 W1 (g) *deest* K1 K2 C3 (h) fecerit K1 K2 (i) K1 K2 *Art. 26* K3 C3 *Art. 27* W1 *Art. 25* W2 C2 *deest folium* C1 *Art. 31* (j) *in ms.* exhymere [*s*] C1 (k) *manus γ* C1 ⟨De domino et servi precio⟩ C3 (l) Quod K1 W1 (m) ⟨quis⟩ C3 (n) iure suo reprobatus C3 (o) *deest* C3 (p) extrahere K3 (q) *desunt* K1 K2 (r) *desunt* C3 (s) Simili vir W1 (t) vir K3 (u) extrahere K3 exemere W1 (v) patrem K3 W1 (w) *desunt* C3 (x) de iure K3 (y) *deest* W1 (z) *manus β* C1 (aa) *desunt* K2 K3 W1 C3 (bb) maritum W1 (cc) continuo K3 (dd) ⊢ut⊣ C1 (ee) *deest* K1 K2 K3 W1 C3 (ff) ⟨merces servorum⟩ C3 (gg) *desunt* K1 K2 (hh) famulum obtinere W1

sacramento mettercius etc. sibi⟩ss), quod sibi(a) persolvit, tunc propius est (b) evadere, quam famulus obtinere. Sin autem famulus (csuam mercedemc) super suum dominum obtinuerit coram iudicio, pro eo dominus iudici(d) nullam penam demeretur, sed(e) (fdominus famulof) eadem mercedem eodem die solvere tenetur indilate(g). (h) Si alter alterum pro vino aut (i) alio potu(j) inculpare voluerit, evadet ut(k) aliud debitum, in(l) quo nullum dominium(m) ostendere poterit aut probare(n) ⟨protestari⟩(o).

Articulus 25 (p)

[25] (q) Donum(r), quod viro vel mulieri datum fuerit in iudicio bannito, in eo mulier cum sua parte sive dono pro suo arbitrio facere potest absque omni(s) contradiccione quidquid (t) placet. Idem (u) potest (v) vir cum parte(w) sui doni, quidquid(x) deliberaverit(y) modo simili, quam ipse suscepit. (z) Si moritur femina absque herede, ita quod nullum heredem(aa) (bb) a suo marito(cc) pepererit, ipsa heredat(dd) (ee) sua (ff) successoria seu sua(gg) pro-
145r spera fortuna acquisita, super suum proximum | (hhnaturalem(ii) successoremhh), sive(jj) sit(kk) masculus sive (ll) femina, qui sibi sit paris condicionis ⟨in natura⟩(mm). {a} (nnIdem facit vir (ooilli, qui sibi fuerit paris condicionisoo).nn) Insuper omne aurum et argentum informatum(pp), et omnis siligo et carnes cum cervisia et vino, et panis, que vel quod aut quantum post(qq) trecesimum (rr) (sspermansit, (tt) velss) permanserunt, totum cedit heredibus viri

(a) *deest* S[4] S[5] (b) protestare aut S[9] (c) *desunt* S[10] K[4] (d) inde K[4] (e) *deest* S[10] (f) famulus K[5] (g) *deest* S[10] (h) *subrubrica:* De iure debitorum pro vino aut. S[3] *subrubrica:* Capitulum de eodem. S[9] *subrubrica:* De debito vini vel potus. K[5] (i) pro K[4] (j) *deest* S[3] (k) et S[5] (l) ut K[4] (m) dominum S[7] damnum S[9] S[10] K[5] (n) protestari S[1] S[2] S[3] S[7] S[8] S[9] S[10] K[4] K[5] probare, protestare S[4] S[5] (o) *manus B* S[6] (p) S[1] S[4] S[5] S[6] S[7] S[8] S[10] K[4] *Art. 25* S[2] S[3] S[9] *Art. 27* K[5] *Art. 29* (q) ⟨de donis viri aut mulieris⟩ *manus A* S[3] ⟨de donacione inter virum et mulierem⟩ K[2] (r) Bonum K[4] (s) viri S[3] (t) ei K[5] (u) ⟨Idem⟩ S[8] (v) facere S[7] S[8] S[9] (w) *deest* S[8] (x) *deest* S[10] (y) ⟨de⟩liberaverit S[8] *deest* K[4] S[10] (z) *subrubrica:* De bonis femine sine prole decedentis. K[5] (aa) *deest* S[4] S[5] (bb) absque S[3] (cc) viro S[9] (dd) hereditat et S[7] (ee) data S[4] S[5] (ff) bona S[10] (gg) *deest* S[8] (hh) ⟨naturalem successorem⟩ K[4] (ii) natalem S[7] (jj) *deest* K[4] (kk) *deest* K[5] (ll) sit S[3] (mm) *manus B* S[6] (nn) *desunt* S[9] (oo) desunt S[5] (pp) ⊢non⊣ S[6] non informatum S[1] S[9] S[10] K[4] (qq) *deest* K[5] (rr) annui S[10] (ss) *desunt* S[3] (tt) ⟨De suppellectile post tricesinum⟩ K[5]

{a} ⟨Paris condicionis id est heres legittime naturis secundum formam Sancte Ecclesie vulgariter czýsthego loza polozonÿ⟩ K[5] protestare[hh)].[gg)] Si autem famulus suam merdecem super dominum suum obtinuerit ([a]coram iudicio[a)]), pro eo dominus nullam penam iudici demeretur, sed dominus famulo eandem mercedem die eodem solvere tenetur indilate[(b)]. Si alter alterum pro vino aut alio potu inculpare voluerit, evadet sicut[(c)] debitum, in quo nullum | dominium[(d)] ostendere poterit aut protestare. 32[va]

Articulus 32 [(e)]

⌊32⌋ ⟨Donum quod vir potest dare mulieri et e converso⟩[(f)] ⟨Donum bonorum capitulum⟩[(g)] Donum, quod mulieri vel viro datum fuerit in iudicio bannito, [(h)] ([i]in eo[i)]) mulier cum sua parte sive dono pro suo[(j)] arbitrio facere potest absque omni contradiccione quidquid placet[(k)]. Idem potest vir cum parte sui doni, quidquid deliberaverit modo simili, quam ipse suscepit. ⟨De eodem IIII folio primi libri et XI eiusdem libri⟩[(l)] Si moritur vir[(m)], femina[(n)] absque herede, [(o)] ita quod nullum heredem a viro[(p)] suo [(q)] perceperit, ipsa [(r)] heredat[(s)] sua successoria, [(t)] seu prospera fortuna acquisita super suum proximum naturalem successorem, sive[(u)] sit masculus sive femina, qui sibi sit paris condicionis. ([v]Idem facit vir illi, qui sibi sunt paris condicionis.[v)]) Idem[(w)] insuper [(x)] omne aurum et argentum informatum[(y)], et omnis siligo et carnes cum cervisia, vino, et pane, et[(z)] quantum post tricesimum permanserit,

---

(a) *desunt* K^1 K^2 (b) *deest* K^3 (c) ut aliud K^1 K^2 K^3 W^1 si aliud C^3 (d) dampnum K^2 (e) K^1 K^2 *Art. 27* K^3 C^3 *Art. 28* W^1 *Art. 26* W^2 C^2 *deest folium* C^1 *Art. 32* (f) *manus* γ C^1 (g) *manus* δ C^1 (h) ⟨De dotalicio et donum coram iudicio⟩ C^3 (i) *desunt* K^3 (j) *deest* K^3 (k) voluerit W^1 (l) *manus* δ C^1 (m) *deest* K^1 K^2 K^3 W^1 C^3 (n) mulier K^3 (o) ⟨dic uxor[...] aliquam mar[...]⟩ C^3 (p) marito K^1 K^2 K^3 C^3 (q) ⊢successoria seu prospera fortuna⊣ C^1 (r) mulier C^3 (s) hereditat K^3 W^1 (t) ⊢super suum proximum naturalem⊣ C^1 (u) *deest* K^1 K^2 (v) *desunt* W^1 C^3 (w) *deest* K^1 K^2 K^3 W^1 C^3 (x) super K^1 K^2 (y) non formatum K^3 (z) que vel quot aut W^1

et non mulieris(a), exceptis pulmentariis, de(b) quibus mulier recipit (c) partem(d) ⟨seu medietatem⟩(e) {a} et heredes viri reliquam mediam tollunt(f) partem(g,g)

Articulus 26 (h)

[*26*] (i) Ista (jsunt, quej) ad hereditatem spectant(k): omne aurum et argentum informatum(l), omnia vasa argentea, et tela ⟨et pannus⟩(m), que non (n) incisa ⟨vel incisus⟩(o) (paut formatap) ⟨vel formatus⟩(q) (r) ad muliebria vestimenta, (s) et sartagines, que a loco non moventur, et dolea, et vasa distillatoria, {b} et omnia (t) caldaria(u) excepto caldari (v), in quo liquescit cera, quod spectat ad supellectile[m]. {c} Omne proprium, quod locando possessum est, et omnia arma et omnes gladii, et eciam omnes olle (weree(x) ac morsere(y)w), et cinguli, bracciles, et annuli viri, hec predicta spectant ad (z) hereditatem. Mense et lavatoria, omnes ciste (aa) planis cooperimentis(bb) et sedilia (ccspectant ad hereditatemcc), (dd) pelves cupree(ee){d}, (ffet ciste pharine(gg),ff) et ciste (hh) annonarum, et porci, qui in curiis sive in domibus nutriuntur(ii), eciam
145v spectant ad hereditatem. Et omnes porci inpinguati (jj) | (kk) spectant ad pulmentaria ubi pulmentaria dantur, et omnis expensa domestica, que in(ll) potestate viri est (mm), et omnes vaccue(nn) cuppe(oo). Pulmentaria(pp) (qq) recipit uxor mariti, et non sua cognata(rr) proxima.

(a) mulieribus S^{10} femine K^5 (b) *deest* S^{10} (c) mediam S^1 S^2 S^3 S^4 S^5 S^7 S^8 S^9 S^{10} K^4 K^5 (d) *deest* S^{10} (e) *manus B* S^6 (f) tenebunt S^4 S^5 (g) *deest* S^5 (h) S^1 S^4 S^5 S^6 S^7 S^8 S^{10} K^4 *Art. 26* S^2 S^3 S^9 *Art. 28* K^5 *Art. 30* K^5 (i) ⟨Que res spectant ad hereditatem⟩ *manus A* S^3 (j) *desunt* S^{10} (k) pertinent S^{10} (l) non fortunatum S^{10} (m) *manus B* S^6 (n) fuerint S^8 est S^9 (o) *manus B* S^6 (p) desunt S^3 S^4 S^5 (q) *manus B* S^6 (r) fuerint S^7 (s) non S^1 ⊢non⊣ S^6 (t) ⊢caldaria⊣ S^6 (u) *a.c.* cadaria, *correctio probabiliter manu commentatoris B* S^6 (v) magno S^7 S^8 (w) *desunt* S^{10} (x) omnes herree K^5 (y) morsere S^2 S^3 K^4 morsaria S^7 morsoria S^8 (z) ⊢suplli⊣ S^6 (aa) cum S^9 (bb) quod perinentis S^4 (cc) *desunt* S^4 S^5 S^8 (dd) Mense et lavatoria et S^7 (ee) cuspa (ff) *desunt* K^5 (gg) *deest* S^{10} (hh) annorum S^9 (ii) *deest* S^{10} (jj) ⟦spectant⟧ S^6 (kk) eciam K^4 (ll) ex S^4 S^5 (mm) tempore mortis S^7 S^8 S^9 K^5 (nn) *deest* S^{10} (oo) *deest* S^4 S^5 S^7 S^8 (pp) pulmentario [*s*] S^1 S^4 S^5 S^6 (qq) ⟦recipit⟧ S^6 (rr) agnata S^{10} K^4 ⟨Magdeburg⟩ S^2

{a} ⟨pulmentaria vulgariter jarzýnÿ⟩ {b} ⟨vasa distillatoria szadý spusczadlne sicut in braxatorio et in cellario in quibus reconditur [*2 verba difficilia*]⟩ K^5 {c} Proprium dicitur hereditas sicut domus, arca, fundus, predium et omnes agri, ortus, vinea, humulentus vulgariter chmÿenÿk. K^5 {d} ⟨Cuspa dicitur cussa vel eciam tok potest dici in hoc loco⟩ K^5

hoc[a] cedit heredibus | viri[b] et non mulieris, exceptis pulmentariis, de qui- 32vb
bus mulier recepit medietatem et heredes viri aliam recipiunt partem. {a}

Articulus 33 [(c)]

[33] ⟨Ista⟩[d] Ista[e] sunt, que ad hereditatem pertinent[f]: omne aurum et
argentum informatum, omnia vasa argentea, et tela, que non est incisa aut
formata ad[g] muliebria vestimenta, et sartagines, que a loco non moventur,
dolea, et vasa distillatoria, et omnia[h] caldaria, excepto caldari, in quo lique-
fecit[i] ceram, quod spectat ad suppellectile[m]. Omne proprium, | ⟨Ista sunt, 33ra
que pertinent ad hereditatem⟩[j] quod locando possessum[k] [l] est, et[m] omnia VII
arma et gladii [n], et olle eree ac morsee, et cinguli, bractiales[o], et annuli
viri[p], hec spectant ad hereditatem. Mense, lavatoria et omnes ciste [q]planis
cooperimentis[q], cupree[r], et cist[e] annonarum, et ciste pro pharine[s], et
porci, qui in curiis aut in domibus nutriuntur, [t]spectant ad hereditatem[t].
Et omnes porci inpinguati spectant ad pulmentaria. Ubi pulmentaria dan-
tur et omnes expense domestice, que in potestate viri sunt, et omnes vacue
cuppe[u], [v] pulmentaria recipit uxor [w], et non cognata sua[x]. {b}

(a) totum K¹ K² (b) *deest* W¹ (c) K¹ K² *Art. 28* K³ C³ *Art. 29* W¹ *Art. 27* W² C² *deest folium* C¹ *Art. 33* (d) *manus γ* C¹ (e) Statuta W¹ (f) spectant K¹ (g) aut K¹ (h) *deest* K¹ K² (i) liquesit K¹ K² K³ W¹ C³ (j) *manus γ* C¹ (k) *deest* W¹ (l) non C³ (m) ut K³ (n) omnes K³ (o) *probabiliter* bractile *aut* briachiale (p) viriles K³ (q) pelves, cooperimenta W¹ (r) sedilia, pulvinaria K¹ K² pelves cupree K³ (s) farine K¹ K² K³ W¹ C³ (t) *desunt* W¹ (u) crÿpe K³ (v) vasa et C³ (w) mariti K¹ K² K³ W¹ C³ (x) proxima K¹ K² W¹ sua proxima K³ proxima ipsius mariti C³

{a} Discrepat hic Colmense. Quia si moritur mulier sine prole, extunc proximi mulieris medietatem omnium bonorum, qui directe ad eos pertinebatur, recipiant et dicitur directe, quia forsitan viri aut mulieris prevignus vel previgna ibi fuerit cuius bona paterna aut materna, quorum bona dicti prevignus vel previgna racione paternorum vel e converso tollunt. Vir vero vel mulier, qui supervixit, quarta parte gaudebit. Prevignus vero vel previgna racione patris vel matris non mortui aliam quartam partem sublevabunt. W¹ {b} In Colmensi. Quicumque mobilia bona ab alto et basso pro bonis hereditariis computantur. W¹

Articulus 27 (a)

[27] ⟨Regula iuris. Actus legitimi condicionem non receperit neque diem.⟩{a} (b) Vulnerat quis(c) alterum vitam suam defendendo super viam publicam, quod ille ipsum percuttit aut vulnerat, et si clamore proclamaverit, et (d) invasor(e) comparet violenter seu proterve, et conqueritur (f iudici, et hic(g) non potest (h nec audet,h) {b} pre(i) inbecillitate sui corporis tunc comparere et in posterum (j) eo die compareat et conqueraturf), iudici (k et scabinis, et ostendatk) sua vulnera, et protestatur per hos, qui suum clamorem audierunt, quod inicium(l) contencionis(m) sui adversarii fuerit et non(n) suum, et quod ipse se(o) (p) defenderit in defensione vite sue, (q) (r et ipser) acquirit querimoniam primam. Sed si pernoctabit, extunc hoc(s) fieri non potest.

Articulus 28 (t)

[28] (u) Quodsi(v) duo se vulnerant (w de stirpe Sclavicaw) mutuo in(x) iure municipali, qui ambo processerunt(y) de stirpe Sclavica et tamen Sclavi(z) non sunt, compareat unus(aa) et conqueratur in Sclavico (bb ydiomate, alterum(cc) non opportet(dd) sibi(ee) respondere, si (ff) placet, nisi conqueraturbb) (gg) ydiomate, quod sibi ⟨Regula iuris. Item. Cum sunt partium (hh) iura, reo pocius est
146r fovendum quam actori. Item. Scienti et non facienti non est iniuria necque dolus.⟩{c} | innatum est per ius municipale.

(a) S[1] S[4] S[5] S[6] S[7] S[8] S[10] K[4] *Art. 27* S[2] S[3] S[9] *Art. 29* K[5] *Art. 31* (b) Si S[2] ⟨de eo, qui alterum vulnerat se defendendo⟩ *manus A* S[3] (c) unus vir K[4] S[10] (d) si K[5] (e) *deest* S[4] S[5] (f) *desunt* S[2] S[9] (g) *deest* K[4] (h) *desunt* S[1] (i) pure S[7] (j) tunc S[5] S[7] S[8] K[5] (k) *desunt* S[10] (l) nuncium K[5] (m) *deest* K[4] S[10] (n) *deest* S[4] S[5] inter K[5] (o) *deest* S[2] (p) de se S[10] (q) hoc fecit S[10] (r) si protestatur S[2] S[8] (s) *deest* S[2] (t) S[1] S[4] S[5] S[6] S[7] S[8] S[10] K[4] *Art. 28* S[2] S[3] S[9] *Art. 30* K[5] *Art. 32 pars 2* (u) ⟨Quid duo municipale vulnerantur⟩ *manus A* S[3] *cf. Art. 61 pars:* que ad supellectilia—ad heredes K[5] (v) Et S[2] (w) *desunt* S[1] S[2] S[3] S[4] S[5] S[7] S[8] S[9] S[10] K[4] K[5] (x) *deest* S[4] S[5] (y) sint nati S[2] (z) scabini [s] K[5] (aa) *deest* S[4] S[5] S[10] (bb) *desunt* S[3] (cc) alter S[2] (dd) debet S[2] (ee) *deest* S[8] K[5] (ff) sibi S[7] S[8] K[5] (gg) in eo S[1] S[2] S[3] S[4] S[5] S[7] S[8] S[9] S[10] K[4] K[5] (hh) ⟦sunt⟧ S[6]

{a} *manus A* S[6] ⟨Regula iuris. A[ctus] legittimi [co]ndicionem non recipiunt neque diem.⟩ K[5] {b} ⟨pre imbecillitate corporis vulgariter dla mgloszczÿ czyeleszneÿ⟩ K[5] {c} *manus A* S[6] ⟨Regula iuris. Cum fuit parto iura, reo pocius est faciendum quam actori.⟩ K[5] ⟨Regula iuris. Sciente et non faciente non est iniuria neque dolus.⟩ K[5]

Articulus 34 (a)

[*34*] | ⟨Sequitur capitula de vulneribus per totum⟩(b) Vulnerat quis alium vitam suam 33rb defendendo super viam publicam, quod ille ipsum percutit aut vulnerat, et si(c) clamorem proclamaverit, et si(d) invasor conparet violenter, seu proterve, et conqueritur iudici, et hic(e) non potest(f), nec(g) audet(h), pre inbecillitate sui corporis tunc conparere, et in posterum eodem die conpareat et conqueratur iudici et scabinis, et ostendat sua vulnera, et protestetur per hos, qui suum clamorem audierunt, et quod inicium contencionis sui adversarii fuerit et non(i) suum, et quod ipse se defenderit in defensione sue vite, ipse acquirit querimoniam(j) primam. Sed si pernoctaverit, tunc hoc fieri non potest. {a}

Articulus 35 (k)

[*35*] | Quodsi se duo mutuo vulneraverint in iure municipali, qui ambo sint 33va nati de stirpe Sclavica(l) et (mtamen(n) Sclavim) non sunt, conpareat unus et conqueratur in Sclavico ydiomate, alter sibi non debet(o) respondere, si placeat sibi(p), nisi conqueratur in eodem(q) ydiomate, quod sibi innatum est per ius municipale. {b}

(a) K^1 K^2 *Art. 29* K^3 C^3 *Art. 30* W^1 *Art. 28* W^2 C^2 *deest folium* C^1 *Art. 34* (b) *manus β* C^1 (c) *deest* W^1 (d) *deest* K^1 K^2 (e) *deest* K^3 (f) *deest* K^1 K^2 (g) non W^1 *deest* K^1 K^2 (h) *deest* K^3 (i) si K^1 K^2 (j) querelam C^3 (k) K^1 K^2 *Art. 30* K^3 C^3 *Art. 31* W^1 *Art. 29* W^2 C^2 *deest folium* C^1 *Art. 35* (l) *in ms.* Sclavicica C^1 (m) ad W^1 (n) cum K^1 K^2 (o) oportet K^3 (p) *deest* K^1 K^2 K^3 (q) Sclavico K^2

{a} In Colmensi. Dummodo scabini aut consules hec viderint et protestati fuerint, nisi sit concordiam factum, alias nisi sit violator concordie, cui dictum est uno in campo. W^1 {b} In Colmensi. Potest per procuratorem sive mundiburdium. W^1

Articulus 29 (a)

[29] (b) Quodsi(c) duorum virorum querimonie dilate fuerint in iudicio bannito ⟨coram iudice et scabinis⟩(d) de voluntate iudicis et consensu ⟨ac libero arbitrio parcium utriusque⟩(e) et parcium(f) (garbitrium ut(h) earumque(i)g), (j) quod(k) inter ipsos concordia extra iudicium debeat terminari(l), nec ultra (m) causam peragendam, et(n) (o) se arbitri(p) (qad(r) hocq) electi de causa(s) intromittant concordandi(t), absque iudicio et querimoniam(u) (v) non(w) repetendo(x) cum(y) consensu iudicis. Et si alter(z) ex eis suam querimoniam in posterum vellet renovare pro hac causa (aacoram iudicio, (bbiste sibi suus adversarius (cc) respondere non tenebituraa) (ddcoram iudiciobb), sidd) protestare potuerit cum iudice et scabinis, quod (ee) causa absque(ff) iudicio debeat terminari(gg).

Articulus 30 (hh)

[30] (ii) Quodsi(jj) se(kk) duo (ll) mutuo vulneraverint (mmequaliter, ex hiismm) unus vadat ad iudicem in domum suam et querimoniam faciat, alter veniat ad quat[t]uor ⟨consules⟩(nn) bancos (oo) (ppet conqueraturpp) cum clamore scabinis et iudicio astantibus, et vulnera ostendat, et mittat pro iudice et conqueratur, ipse primam querimoniam obtinebit, si testes (qqsuper hocqq) habuerit a scabinis aut astantibus iudicio, quod inter quat[t]uor bancos querimoniam fecerit.

(a) S^1 S^4 S^5 S^6 S^7 S^8 K^4 Art. 29 S^2 S^3 S^9 Art. 31 K^5 Art. 33 (b) ⟨de dilacione querimonie utriusque partis⟩ *manus A* S^3 (c) Et S^2 (d) *manus B* S^6 coram iudice S^7 K^5 (e) *manus B* S^6 (f) precium S^{10} (g) *desunt* S^2 (h) in S^4 et S^5 *deest* S^1 S^2 S^3 S^7 S^8 S^9 S^{10} K^4 K^5 (i) utrum S^{10} utracumque K^5 (j) quam S^7 (k) *deest* K^5 (l) ordinari S^7 S^8 (m) uniquam S^9 (n) quod S^2 (o) si S^9 (p) arbitrari S^{10} K^4 (q) ab S^{10} (r) super S^2 (s) hac S^2 (t) concordia S^2 (u) causam S^3 (v) amovendo S^7 in omni modo K^5 (w) *deest* S^4 S^5 (x) impetendo S^7 (y) ex S^2 (z) *deest* S^9 (aa) *desunt* S^4 S^5 (bb) *desunt* S^7 K^5 (cc) sibi S^{10} (dd) *desunt* S^5 (ee) ista S^2 (ff) ⟨absque⟩ S^8 (gg) diffiniri S^2 (hh) S^1 S^4 S^5 S^6 S^7 S^8 S^{10} K^4 Art. 30 S^2 S^3 S^9 Art. 32 K^5 Art. 34 (ii) ⟨Quod duo conqueruntur, unus iudici, alter scabinis pro vulneracione⟩ *manus B* S^3 (jj) Et S^9 (kk) *deest* S^3 (ll) viri S^4 (mm) *desunt* S^2 (nn) *manus B* S^6 (oo) aut scabinos S^9 ⟨scampna scabinalia⟩ K^4 (pp) *desunt* S^5 (qq) *desunt* S^{10} K^4

Articulus 36 (a)

[*36*] (b) Quodsi querimonie duorum virorum dilate fuerint in iudicio bannito coram iudice et de voluntate iudicis et consensu (cet parciumc) arbitrio utrarumque(d), quod(e) inter ipsos concordia extra iudicium debeat terminari, nec ultra causam peragendam, et (f) se arbitri ad hoc electi de causa intromittant concordiam(g) absque iudicio et querimonia non repetendo cum
consensu iudicis. Et si(h) alter | ex eis in posterum suam causam(i) vellet reno- 33vb
vare pro hac causa coram iudicio, ille sibi(j) suus(k) adversarius respondere non tenetur (lcoram iudiciol), si(m) protestare poterit cum iudice et scabinis, quod causa(n) absque iudicio debeat finiri(o).

Articulus 38 (p)

[*38*] | (q) (rQuodsi se(s) duo mutuo vulneraverint equaliter, ex hiis unus(t) 34ra
vadet ad iudicem in domum suam et querimoniam facit, alter veniet ad VIII
quat[t]uor bancos et conqueratur cum clamore scabinis et iudicio astantibus(u), vulnera ostendat, etr) mittat pro iudice et conqueratur, ipse primam querimoniam obtinebit, et si testes super hoc(v) habuerit a scabinis aut(w) astantibus iudicio, quod inter quat[t]uor bancos querimoniam fecit. {a}

(a) K^1 K^2 *Art. 31* K^3 C^3 *Art. 32* W^1 *Art. 30* W^2 C^2 *deest folium* C^1 *Art. 36* (b) ⟨de vulneribus⟩ C^3 (c) *desunt* W^1 (d) *in ms.* utrorumque [*s*] C^1 (e) actorumque C^3 (f) si K^1 K^2 (g) *deest* W^1 (h) *deest* W^1 (i) querimoniam K^1 K^2 K^3 W^1 C^3 (j) *deest* K^1 (k) *deest* K^3 (l) cum iudice K^1 K^2 (m) *deest* W^1 (n) ita K^1 K^2 (o) diffiniri K^1 K^2 K^3 W^1 (p) K^1 K^2 W^1 *Art. 32* K^3 *Art. 34* W^2 C^2 *deest folium* C^1 *Art. 38* C^3 *Art. 33* (q) ⟨de vulneribus⟩ C^3 (r) *deest folium* C^2 (s) *deest* K^1 K^3 C^3 (t) *deest* K^1 (u) attestantibus K^1 (v) *deest* W^1 (w) *deest* K^3

{a} In Colmensi. Cum prius ad iudicium venerit vel ad scabinos, ille apud Colmensem principium actionis obtinebit. W^1

Articulus 31 (a)

146v [*31*] | (b) Et si se(c) duo mutuo vulneraverint equaliter (d), quicumque ex eis in alterum duellum (e) acquisierit, (f) tunc eius(g) adversarius manum(h) demeretur. Ita cum(i) si vulnus monomachale fuerit. (j) Et si alter ex eis, antequam duellum acquisitum fuerit, moritur, adversarius collum demeretur.

Articulus 32 (k)

[*32*] (l) Si aliquis detinet hunc, qui ipsum vulneravit, in facto recenti et ipsum cum clamore ad iudicium deducit, qui sic queruletur cum prolocutore(m): “Domine iudex, ego cum querela propono super istum virum, quod ipse venit intra municipalia vel infiscata(n) ⟨in strata⟩(o) regia, et in me pacem violavit, et me spoliavit (p in meo p) corpore et in(q) (r) meis bonis, et me vulneravit, dum pacem in me confregit. Tunc ego (s) vidi ipsum in persona propria et proclamavi (t) ipsum(u) cum clamore, et ipsum captivum (v) huc ad iudicium deduxi, et volo eum (w mittere sed eum volo w) vincere per eos, qui clamorem meum audierunt, et cum(x) meo testimonio vero, ut ius michi diffinierit. Et in sentencia requiro, quomodo hoc probare debeam(y), ita ut (z) michi proficiat in meo iure” Extunc satisdacionem adversarius rectam(aa) petat pro hac querimonia, et dicat se (bb de facto bb) (cc) innocentem. Ille, qui ipsum (dd captivum(ee) in dd) manifesto facto(ff) detinuit, facilius eum(gg) vincere potest cum testimonio, quam ipse (hh captivus(ii) cum testimonio hh)
147r evadere (jj) possit. | Si, ut iuris est, probaverit testimonio, ille(kk) solvet collum, si est homicidium, vel ad(ll) manum, si vulnus est(mm) monomachale(nn)

(a) S^{1} S^{4} S^{5} S^{6} S^{7} S^{8} S^{10} K^{4} *Art. 31* S^{2} *articulus deest* S^{3} S^{9} *Art. 33* K^{5} *Art. 35* (b) ⟨Quod duo mutuo se vulneraverint et querulantur equaliter⟩ S^{3} (c) ⟨se⟩ S^{9} (d) et querulantur S^{1} S^{2} S^{3} S^{4} S^{5} S^{8} S^{9} S^{10} K^{4} K^{5} et querulantur equaliter S^{7} K^{5} (e) ├con┤ S^{6} (f) quod S^{4} sed S^{5} (g) ⟨eius⟩, *a.c.* ius S^{5} (h) collum S^{4} S^{5} (i) tamen S^{1} S^{2} S^{3} S^{4} S^{5} S^{7} S^{8} S^{9} S^{10} K^{4} tamen, quod ei K^{5} (j) ⟨monomachalia est singulare testamen⟩ S^{8} (k) S^{1} S^{4} S^{5} S^{6} S^{7} S^{8} S^{10} K^{4} *Art. 32* S^{2} *Art. 33* S^{3} S^{9} *Art. 34* K^{5} *Art. 36* (l) ⟨de eo, qui aliquis alterum vulnerat, et eiusdem in facto recenti detinet⟩ *manus A* S^{3} (m) *in ms.* proloqutore S^{6} (n) in strata S^{1} S^{2} S^{3} S^{4} S^{5} S^{7} S^{8} S^{9} S^{10} K^{4} K^{5} (o) *manus B* S^{6} (p) *desunt* S^{3} (q) *deest* S^{3} (r) rebus S^{10} (s) ipse S^{3} S^{4} S^{5} (t) super S^{9} (u) in eum K^{5} (v) et communitum K^{5} (w) *desunt* S^{1} S^{2} S^{3} S^{4} S^{5} S^{7} S^{8} S^{9} S^{10} K^{4} K^{5} (x) *deest* S^{3} (y) valeam K^{4} (z) debeam S^{3} (aa) relictam S^{3} S^{5} *deest* K^{5} (bb) *desunt* S^{7} K^{5} (cc) esse S^{4} (dd) *desunt* S^{10} (ee) *deest* K^{5} (ff) *deest* S^{10} (gg) *deest* S^{3} (hh) *desunt* S^{4} S^{5} (ii) captus K^{5} (jj) ├cum testimonio┤ S^{6} (kk) illi S^{1} S^{2} S^{3} S^{4} S^{5} (ll) *deest* S^{7} (mm) *deest* K^{4} (nn) monachale K^{5}

Articulus 37 (a)

[*37*] | Et(b) si se duo mutuo vulneraverint equaliter et querulantur(c) equaliter, 33vb quicumque ex eis duellum (din alterumd) acquisierit, tunc eius adversarius manum(e) demeretur. Ita tamen, si vulnera ambo(f) monomachalia(g) fuerint. Et si(h) alter ex eis, antequam duellum acquisitum fuerit(i), moritur, adversarius collum demeretur. {a}

Articulus 39 (j)

[*39*] | Si aliquis detinet hunc (k), qui ipsum vulneravit in facto recenti et ipsum 34ra cum clamore ad iudicium deducit, ille sic queruletur (l): "Domine iudex, ego(m) cum querela propono super istum virum, | quod(n) ipse(o) venit (pin(q) 34rb municipiap) et(r) in strata regia, et in me pacem violavit, (set me spoliavits) in meo corpore et (t) bonis meis, et me vulneravit, dum pacem in me fregit. Tunc vidi(u) (vego ipse ipsum in persona propria et proclamavi eumv) (w) cum clamore, et ipsum captivum huc ad iudicium deduxi(x), et volo eum vincere per hos, qui meum clamorem audierunt, et (y) meo testimonio vero, ut ius michi diffinierit. Et in sentencia requiro, quomodo (z) hoc probare debeam, ut michi proficiat in iure meo." Extunc adversarius relictam(aa) petit satisfaccionem(bb) {b} (ccpro haccc) querimonia, et dicat se de(dd) facto esse(ee) innocentem. Ille, qui ipsum captivum(ff) in(gg) manifesto facto detinuit, facilius ipsum vincere potest cum testimonio, quam ipse captivus (hhcum testimoniohh) evadere (iipotest, seuii) possit. Si autem(jj), ut iuris est, probaverit testimonio, illi solvet collum, si est homicidium, vel (kk) si vulnus est monomo-

---

(a) K^1 K^2 K^3 *Art. 33* W^1 *Art. 31* W^2 C^2 *deest folium* C^1 *Art. 37* C^3 *Art. 34* (b) Ut K^2 (c) conquerantur C^3 (d) *desunt* K^1 K^2 W^1 (e) marcam W^1 (f) *deest* K^1 K^2 W^1 (g) duellaria K^3 mortale, *a.c.* monomachale C^3 (h) *deest* K^3 (i) *deest* W^1 (j) K^1 K^2 *Art. 34* K^3 C^3 *Art. 35* W^1 *Art. 33* C^1 *Art. 39* W^2 C^2 *deest folium* (k) ipsum C^3 (l) cum prolocutore K^1 K^2 K^3 C^2 C^3 (m) *deest* K^1 K^2 (n) *deest* K^1 K^2 (o) *deest* C^3 (p) intra municipalia W^1 (q) intra K^4 K^1 C^2 *deest* K^3 (r) vel K^1 K^2 K^3 W^1 C^3 (s) *desunt* W^1 (t) in K^3 (u) *in ms.* vide [*s*] C^1 (v) ego ipse te proclamavi ipsum persona in propria et K^1 K^2 (w) per C^2 (x) adduxi K^3 (y) cum K^3 (z) quo W^1 (aa) rectam C^2 (bb) satisdacionem K^3 C^2 ⊢satisdationem⊣ ⟨g e w e r e satisfaction[em]⟩ C^3 (cc) probat C^2 (dd) *deest* K^1 (ee) *deest* K^3 (ff) *deest* C^2 (gg) aut C^3 (hh) *desunt* C^2 (ii) *desunt* K^1 K^2 K^3 W^1 C^2 C^3 (jj) *deest* C^3 (kk) ad manum K^1 K^2 W^1 manum K^3 C^3

{a} Duellum quamvis dicitur duorum bellum, hic tamen accipitur pro illo, qui obtinet principium agendi. [*probabiliter de iure Culmensi*] W^1 {b} g w a r r a z a d a C^2

{a}, cum(a) ad iudicium ipsum cum(b) (c) manifesto facto deduxerit(d). Pro teste potest quivis vir alteri ⟨testes⟩ astare, qui in suo iure non possit argui, excepto patre et(e) fratre(f), et filio et mercenario (g).

Articulus 33 (h)

[*33*] (i) Quodsi se duo mutuo(j) vulneraverint: unus cultello et alter gladio, et si(k) vulnera utriusque monomachalia(l) fuerint, illi(m) cum gladio solvit manum, illi(n) cum cultello solvit collum, quia cultellus infert furtivam mortem. (o)

Articulus 34 (p)

[*34*] ⟨Regula iuris. Actus legitimi condicionem non recipiunt neque diem. Item. Factum retractarii non debet legitime, licet casus postea eveniat a quo non potuit inchoari.⟩{b} (q) Eciam(r) si alter alterum vulneraverit et(s) causa sua pernoctaverit, sibi(t) debet indici(u) in(v) iudicium proximum. Et si (w) vulneratus fuerit et vulnus monomachale non fuerit, et si (x) comparuerit, (ysibi indici(z)y), et conquestus fuerit, debet ad iudicium proximum. (aaSi autem(bb) vulnus monomachale fuerit, tunc continuo(cc) sibi (dd) iudex (ee) formare(ff) debet ⟨iudicium si exigerit pro facto manifesto⟩(gg) pro facto manifesto.aa)

(a) *deest* S^4 S^5 (b) in S^3 S^7 S^8 *deest* S^{10} (c) ⟨Ille debet esse testis, qui non est in iure reprobatus⟩ K^5 (d) *deest* K^5 (e) aut S^7 (f) matre S^3 S^{10} (g) ⟨Eciam [ullo] precio c[onventi] in aliquib[us causis non] valent cont[estari], qui eici iu[re possunt.]⟩ K^4 (h) S^1 S^4 S^5 S^6 S^7 S^8 S^{10} K^4 *Art. 33* S^2 *Art. 34* S^3 S^9 *Art. 35* K^5 *Art. 37* (i) ⟨de vulneracione duorum cum cultello et alter cum gladio⟩ *manus A* S^3 ⟨qui mutuo se vulnerant in via⟩ K^2 (j) *deest* S^4 S^5 (k) *deest* S^7 S^8 (l) monachalia K^5 (m) ille S^7 K^5 (n) ille S^7 K^5 (o) ⟨Ad huc si ambo in recenti accione cum clamore ad iudicium fuerint deducti.⟩ K^4 (p) S^1 S^4 S^5 S^6 S^7 S^8 S^{10} K^4 *Art. 34* S^2 *Art. 35* S^3 S^9 *Art. 36* K^5 *Art. 38* (q) ⟨Quando alter alterum ex causa vulneraverit⟩ *manus B* S^3 (r) *deest* S^{10} (s) *a.c.* ex, *corr. manus B* S^3 (t) similiter S^9 (u) indicari S^9 (v) ad S^2 S^9 (w) vir S^1 S^3 S^4 S^5 alias vir S^2 ⟨vir⟩ K^4 (x) non S^8 (y) si indicari S^9 (z) iudici S^8 (aa) *desunt* K^5 (bb) vero S^3 *deest* S^4 S^5 (cc) incontinenti S^8 (dd) iudicium S^9 ⟨iudicium⟩ S^8 (ee) ⟨statim⟩ K^4 (ff) *a.c.* formavi S^6 (gg) *manus B* S^6 iusticiam S^2 si exigerit S^9

{a} ⟨szmÿerthelnye⟩ K^5 {b} *manus A* S^6

chale(a), cum ad iudicium ipsum in facto manifesto adduxerit. (b) Pro teste potest quivis vir(c) alteri astare(d), qui in suo iure non possit argui, excepto patre aut(e) fratre, (fet filio,f) et(g) mercenario(h). (i)

Articulus 40 (j)

[*40*] | (k) Quodsi se duo mutuo vulneraverint: cultello unus, alter gladio, 34va
et si vulnera utriusque monomachalia(l) fuerint, illi(m) cum gladio | solvet 34vb
manum, illi(n) cum cultello solvit collum, quia cultellus furtivam infert mortem. (o) {a}

Articulus 41 (p)

[*41*] (q) Eciam si alter alterum vulneraverit et causa sua pernoctaverit, sibi debet indici(r) ad iudicium proximum. Et si vir (s) vulneratus fuerit (t) {b}, et si conparuerit et conquestus fuerit, sibi indicari debet(u) ad iudicium proximum. Si autem vulnus monomachale(v) fuerit, tunc continuo sibi iudex statui(w) debet(x) pro facto manifesto(y), (zet statim debet iudicariz).

(a) duellare K^{3} (b) *rubrica:* Pro teste. C^{2} (c) *deest* W^{1} (d) atestare K^{1} K^{2} (e) *deest* C^{3} (f) *deest* W^{1} (g) aut K^{1} K^{2} (h) famulo C^{3} (i) Eciam nulli precio convenienti in aliquibus causis valeat contestari, qui eici iure possunt. C^{3} *in glossa* K^{4} (j) K^{1} *Art. 35* K^{2} *Art. 35 pars 1* K^{3} C^{3} *Art. 36* W^{1} C^{2} *Art. 34* W^{2} *deest folium* C^{1} *Art. 40* (k) ⟨In mutuo se vulnerant in via⟩ K^{2} (l) duellaria K^{3} (m) ille K^{3} W^{1} (n) ille K^{3} W^{1} (o) et hoc si ambo in recenti accione cum clamore ad iudicium fuerint deducti C^{3} *in glossa* K^{4} (p) K^{1} *Art. 36* K^{2} *Art. 35 pars 2* K^{3} C^{3} *Art. 37* W^{1} C^{2} *Art. 35* W^{2} *deest folium* C^{1} *Art. 41* (q) ⟨Causa pernoctata⟩ C^{3} (r) indicari W^{1} (s) ⟨de vulneribus⟩ C^{3} (t) et vulnus monomachale non fuerit K^{1} K^{2} et vulnus duellare non fuerit K^{3} W^{1} C^{3} (u) *deest* C^{3} (v) duellare K^{3} C^{3} (w) formari W^{1} (x) *deest* W^{1} (y) *deest* K^{1} K^{2} K^{3} (z) indicari C^{2} *desunt* K^{1} K^{2} K^{3} W^{1} C^{3}

{a} In Colmensi. Qualecumque quocumque vulnus infligitur, eodem pondere trutinatur a vulnere in facie vel in capite, vel in alia parte corporis, dum mortale est, leso tres marce. Si autem fuerit in alia parte corporis et mortale, extunc due sexagene, sculteto pro pena quatuor solidi. W^{1} {b} Arana smyertellna C^{2}

Articulus 35 (a)

[*35*] (b) Si duo (c) vulneraverint et ambo coram(d) iudicio(e) comparent et querimonias proponent, qui primam precellentem(f) querimoniam et protestare 147v poterit, (g) apud suum adversarium duellum acquirit, si(h) ipsum(i) | isto(j) ⟨iusto⟩(k) modo salutavit, et(l) si(m) vulnus monomachale fuerit. Sin autem (nad diemn) duellum dilatum fuerit et si alter pugilem convenerit(o) super alterum, et si(p) ille(q) protestare poterit, quod pugil sit mercenarius, extunc sibi(r) iure a(s) duello cedere potest. (t)

Articulus 36 (u)

[*36*] (v) Si vulnerat vir alterum, et si caucionem fideiussorie (w) fecerit usque ad iudicium, et si(x) iudex ipsis pacem indixerit. Et si(y) ipsum postea occiderit, et si(z) fideiussores posuerit pro causa eadem, ipse tamen(aa) propius est(bb) evadere metseptimus de homicidio, quam (cc) ipsum(dd) aliquis(ee) protestare possit. Sin autem coram iudicio comparuerint, et si (ff) in iudicio bannito(gg) manu pax promissa fuerit coram iudice et scabinis pro primo vulnere, et si(hh) ipsum postea occiderit, hoc melius potest super eum protestare, quam ipse evadere possit.

Articulus 37 (ii)

[*37*] (jj) Si se(kk) duo vulneraverint (ll) mutuo et ambo (mmcoram iudiciomm) comparent et querulose proponant, et(nn) querimonia usque ad iudicium(oo)

(a) S1 S4 S5 S6 S7 S8 S10 K4 *Art. 35* S2 *Art. 36* S3 S9 *Art. 37* K5 *Art. 39* (b) Quod S2 ⟨Si duo vulnerantur et ambo coram iudicio compareant⟩ *manus B* S3 (c) viri S8 se S2 S4 S5 S10 viri se K5 (d) *deest* S5 (e) iudice S7 (f) *possibilis* precellerit S6 (g) ⟨Duellum causam mortalem prima⟩ K5 (h) super S7 S8 (i) *deest* S10 (j) in S6 S9 si S7 (k) *manus B* S6 iusto S1 S2 S3 S4 S5 S7 S8 S9 S10 K4 K5 (l) eciam S2 (m) *deest* S4 S5 S8 (n) *desunt* K5 (o) convenerit S7 querulaverit ⟨convenerit⟩ S8 querint K5 (p) *deest* S10 (q) ille K4 S10 (r) sibi S2 (s) *deest* S4 S5 (t) ⟨duellum et vel mortalitas alias burdmet duellum dicitur poyed[ynek]⟩ K5 (u) S1 S4 S5 S6 S7 S8 S10 K4 *Art. 36* S2 *Art. 37* S3 S9 *Art. 38* K5 *Art. 40* (v) ⟨de caucione vulneris⟩ *manus B* S3 (w) non S2 (x) hic S4 S5 *deest* S3 (y) *deest* S2 S3 S10 K5 (z) *deest* K5 (aa) tunc S7 (bb) *deest* S10 (cc) super S4 S5 (dd) ipsis S3 ipse S7 (ee) *deest* K5 (ff) tunc S7 (gg) *deest* S8 S10 (hh) *deest* K5 (ii) S1 S4 S5 S6 S7 S8 S10 K4 *Art. 37* S2 W1 *Art. 38* S3 S9 *Art. 39* K1 *Art. 40, 38 pars 2* K2 *Art. 39, 37 pars 2* K5 *Art. 41* (jj) ⟨de dilacione querimonie ad iudicium et cum in dilacione ex vulneribus aliquis moritur⟩ *manus A* S3 (kk) *deest* W1 (ll) pariter K4 S10 (mm) ⟨coram iudicio⟩ S4 (nn) autem K4 si autem S10 (oo) iudicem K5

Articulus 42 (a)

[42] | Si duo vulneraverint se et ambo coram iudicio conpareant et queri- 35ra
monia[m] proponunt, qui primam querimoniam precellente[m] protestare IX
poterit, ad(b) suum adversarium duellum acquirit, et si(c) ipsum (d) iusto modo salutaverit (e), et si(f) vulnus monomachale(g) fuerit. Si autem duellum ad diem dilatum fuerit et si(h) alter pugillem convenerit super alterum, et si ille protestare poterit, quod pugil mercennarius(i) sit, extunc iure a(j) duello sibi(k) cedere possit.

Articulus 43 (l)

[43] (m) Si (n) vulnerat vir alterum et si (o) caucionem fideiussorie fecerit usque (p) ad iudicium (q), et(r) si(s) iudex ipsis pacem(t) indixerit, et si(u) ipsum
postea occiderit, et si fideiussores | (v) posuerit super(w) (x) pro causa eadem, 35rb
(y) ipse tamen(z) propius evadet metseptimus de homicidio, quam (aa) ipsum aliquis protestare possit. Si autem coram(bb) iudicio conparuerint, et si in iudicio bannito (cc) manu pax promissa fuerit coram iudice et scabinis pro(dd) primo vulnere, et ipsum postea(ee) occiderit, hoc melius potest super ipsum protestare, quam ipse evadere possit(ff).

Articulus 44 (gg)

[44] Si se duo mutuo vulneraverint et ambo coram iudicio conpareant et querulose proponant, et querimonia usque ad iudicium dilata fuerit, qui(hh)

(a) K^1 *Art. 37* K^2 W^1 C^2 *Art. 36* K^3 C^3 *Art. 38* W^2 *deest folium* C^1 *Art. 42* (b) apud K^1 K^2 K^3 W^1 C^3 (c) *deest* C^2 (d) in C^2 (e) incitaverit C^2 (f) *deest* K^3 (g) duellare K^3 (h) *deest* K^3 W^1 (i) *deest* W^1 (j) de K^3 (k) *deest* K^3 W^1 (l) K^1 *Art. 38 pars 1 Art. 39* K^2 *Art. 37 pars 1 Art. 38* K^3 C^3 *Art. 39* W^1 C^2 *Art. 37* C^1 *Art. 43* W^2 *deest folium* (m) ⟨de pace⟩ C^3 (n) unus K^3 (o) unus K^3 (p) ad iudicem vel C^2 (q) dilata fuerit K^1 K^2 (r) ut K^2 (s) *deest* W^1 (t) partem C^2 (u) *deest* W^1 (v) ⟨de homicidio et vulneribus⟩ C^3 (w) qui K^1 K^2 deest K^3 (x) ipsum C^2 (y) que gerebatur K^1 K^2 (z) *deest* C^2 (aa) super C^2 (bb) in K^1 K^2 (cc) ⟨de homicidio et vulneribus⟩ C^3 (dd) quod K^1 K^2 (ee) *deest* C^3 (ff) *deest* C^3 (gg) K^3 C^3 *Art. 40* W^2 *deest folium* C^1 *Art. 44* C^2 *Art. 38* (hh) *deest* C^2

dilata(a) fuerit(b), qui primo (c) querulatus fuerit, moriatur ab hiis vulneribus, mortuus ad iudicium portetur(d), et alter(e) vulneratus eciam(f) (g) comparuerit, et unus de(h) mortui(i) agnatus(j) loquatur super(k) vulneratum cum(l)
148r testimonio, quod ipse suum affinem occiderit, et pro | eo (mpetat iudiciumm). Extunc ille petat satisdacionem(n) de iure et(o) ostendat suam(p) innocenciam cum suo(q) testimonio evadendo(r) homicidium. Si hoc, ⟨ut⟩(s) iuris est, (t) protestaverit, propius est evadere, quam ille (usuper eumu) poterit protestare(v), quia ambo coram iudicio querimoniam(w) inceperunt. Sed (xsuum(y) testimoniumx) sic debet procedere, quod inicium contencionis illius (z) fuerit, et non(aa) suum. Et (bbsi suos(cc)bb) testes incontinenti habere non potuerit, terminum sex ebdomadas acquirit, tunc facilius potest evadere homicidium(dd) metseptimus(ee), quam ille(ff) cum testimonio ipsum (gg) vincere possit. {a} Sin autem ille ipsum monomachaliter alloquitur alloquitur, extunc(hh) ipsum(ii) pro(jj) suo collo pugnare opportebit.

Articulus 38 (kk)

[*38*] (ll) Si(mm) mas(nn) equ[u]m vendiderit, promittere debet in eo(oo) equo, quod stabilis non(pp) fuerit, ita quod a loco discedere tempore se offerente noluerit(qq), et videre(rr) quod(ss) apparens (tt) sit cecus(uu), et eciam a iusta(vv) arestacione (ww).

(a) delata K^5 (b) *deest* K^1 K^2 (c) ad iudicium venerit et S^3 (d) deportetur W^1 (e) ⟨alter⟩ S^8 (f) ⟨eciam⟩ S^8 (g) ad iudicium S^7 S^9 K^1 K^2 W^1 in iudicio S^8 K^5 (h) *deest* S^3 S^9 K^1 K^2 W^1 (i) *deest* W^1 (j) cognatus S^3 K^5 *a.c.* cognatus S^6 (k) contra S^4 S^5 (l) *deest* S^{10} K^4 (m) *desunt* S^3 (n) satisfaccionem K^1 K^2 (o) ut K^5 (p) *deest* S^4 S^5 (q) *deest* K^2 (r) evadere duo S^4 S^5 (s) *manu commentatoris* S^6 ut S^1 S^3 S^4 S^5 S^6 S^7 S^8 S^{10} K^1 K^2 K^4 K^5 W^1 vult S^9 *deest* S^2 (t) si S^9 (u) *desunt* W^1 (v) vincere K^1 K^2 (w) *deest* S^3 (x) sub testimonio S^{10} (y) sine S^7 (z) mortui S^7 (aa) non S^4 S^5 (bb) quos S^{10} (cc) *deest* K^1 K^2 (dd) *deest* S^9 (ee) mettercius W^1 (ff) *deest* K^1 K^2 (gg) *deest* S^4 W^1 (hh) *deest* K^5 (ii) *deest* K^1 K^2 W^1 (jj) *deest* S^2 (kk) S^1 S^4 S^5 S^6 S^7 S^{10} K^4 *Art. 38* S^2 *Art. 39* S^3 S^9 *Art. 40* S^8 *articulus deest* K^5 *Art. 42* (ll) ⟨Si quis equum vendiderit⟩ *manus B* S^3 (mm) *deest* S^{10} (nn) quis S^9 vias [*s*] vir K^5 (oo) *deest* S^4 S^5 (pp) *deest* K^5 (qq) voluerit S^3 S^4 S^7 (rr) *deest* S^1 S^2 S^3 S^4 S^5 S^7 S^9 S^{10} K^4 K^5 (ss) utrum S^2 K^5 (tt) si S^5 (uu) *p.c.* equus, *manus B* S^6 (vv) iniusta K^5 (ww) fuerit S^9

{a} ⟨Monomachaliter et duellatorie vulgariter Szmyertelnye⟩ K^5

primo querulatus fuerit(a), moriatur ab his vulneribus, et mortuus ad iudicium portetur, et alter vulneratus eciam | ad iudicium conpareat, unus, 35va
mortui cognatus(b), loquatur super vulneratum cum testimonio sine duello, quod ipse suum proximum affinem occiderit, et pro eo petit iudicium. Extunc ille petit satisdacionem de iure, (c hoc tamen c) propius est evadere metseptimus(d), quam (e ille super eum poterit (f) protestare(g) e). (h) (i Et si (j) evadet i) (k), tunc(l) suum(m) testimonium ita(n) debet sic procedere, quod (o inicium contecionis o) illius (p) fuerit et non suum (q). Et si quis(r) (s suos testes s) incontinenti(t) habere non poterit, (u terminum (v) (w sex ebdomadas w) u) acquirit, ex hiis sibi eligat unam quindenam, quamcumque voluerit. (x Si autem ille ipsum monomachaliter allocutus fuerit, extunc pro suo collo respondere oportet. x) {a}

Articulus 45 (y)

[*45*] | ⟨De equorum vendicione⟩(z) Si vir equum vendiderit, (aa) promittere debet 35vb
(bb in eodem loco bb)(cc), quod stabilis (dd non fuerit dd), (ee ita quod a loco discedere tempore(ff) se offerente noluerit(gg), et videre apparens sit cecus, et eciam ab iniusta(hh) arestacione ee). {b}

(a) *deest* C^2 (b) agnatus K^3 (c) hic K^3 (d) *deest* K^3 (e) vincere possit C^3 (f) ⊢post⊣ C^1 (g) metseptimus K^3 (h) Si autem ille ipsum duellarie fuit alloqutus, extunc ipsum pro suo collo respondere oportet. K^3 Si autem alias cognatus ipsius mortui duellarie salutaverit ipsum, tunc pro collo suo respondere opportet. C^3 (i) Si autem evaserit cum testimonio K^3 (j) autem C^3 (k) cum testibus C^3 (l) extunc C^3 (m) *deest* C^3 (n) *deest* K^3 C^2 C^3 (o) exordium C^3 (p) mortui C^3 (q) ipsius C^3 (r) *deest* C^3 (s) *deest* K^3 (t) statim C^3 (u) extunc inducias trium quindenarum C^3 (v) ad C^2 (w) trium quindenarum K^3 (x) *desunt* C^3 (y) K^1 K^3 C^3 *Art. 41* K^2 *Art. 40* W^1 C^2 *Art. 39* W^2 *deest folium* C^1 *Art. 45* (z) *manus* η C^1 ⟨de quis⟩ C^3 (aa) hoc tam in eodem K^3 (bb) *desunt* K^1 K^3 (cc) equo K^2 W^1 (dd) sit K^3 (ee) nec cecus, et quod non in iuste impeticionis, et eciam a iusta arestacione K^3 (ff) ipse C^3 (gg) voluerit C^2 (hh) iusta K^1 K^2 W^1

{a} In Colmensi. Mortuus vulneratus condemnat collum, vivi vulnerati tum mortui sit man[u]m. W^1 {b} In Colmensi. Iudicibus mercipotariis pro rebus, quibus mercipotarii solent et apparent [*org.* apantur [*s*]], [reus] purgatur et honorem conservat, sed rem emptam si aliena fuerit sibi vendita perdit cum penis, que circa talia consueverunt fieri. W^1

Articulus 39 (a)

[*39*] ⟨Regula iuris. Semel malus semper presumitur esse malus. Item. Non parcas pravis, studeas bonus esse suavis. Fautor amicorum nec sis protector eorum.⟩{a} (b) Si fur(c) clara luce diei deprehensus fuerit, qui bone fame sit (d), et furtum minus quam tres solidos valeat, (ecuttem cum(f) crine demerentur. Sed si furtum ultra tres(g) solidos valeat(h),e) (i) reus est(j) patibulo. De hiis denariis(k) tres solidi medium ferto-
148v nem debent ponderare. (l) Sin autem fur(m) | tempestate noctis deprehensus fuerit cum sex(n) denariis, reus est(o) suspendio(p). (q)

Articulus 40 (r)

[*40*] ⟨Regula iuris. Possessor male fidei ullo tempore non prescribit. Item. Pro possessore habetur, qui dolo desivit possidere. Item. Non confirmatur tractu temporis, quod de iure ab inicio non subsistit. Regula iuris. Successoriam naturam sequi congruit principalis. Item. Ius naturale ante omnia obtinet privatum.⟩{b} (s) Conqueritur vir super alium (tpro bonist), quod vera(u) sua(v) hereditas sit, et quod(w) ille teneat cum(x) iniuria, et (y) sua vera(z) sit (aa) successio a patre suo(bb), (cc(ddvel ab(ee) alio suodd) cognato(ff) ⟨amico⟩(gg), aut a(hh) suocc) predecessore, et si ille comparet, super quem querela(ii) proposita fuerit, et dicit se habere(jj) bonorum defensionem(kk), et (ll) bona possiderit pacifice et quiete, anno et die, contradiccione qualibet non obstante et est(mm) iuste(nn) ac rite(oo) meum(pp) predium censuale, ipsum opportet suum defensorem nominare, et ad dies statuere, si potest, et cum(qq) (rrdefendentem seurr) defensorem conservat sua bona

---

(a) S^1 S^4 S^5 S^6 S^7 S^8 S^{10} K^4 *Art. 39* S^2 *Art. 40* S^3 S^9 *Art. 41* K^5 *Art. 44* (b) ⟨de eo, qui de luce furatur⟩ *manus B* S^3 (c) quis S^2 (d) sic S^3 (e) *desunt* K^5 (f) vel S^{10} (g) *deest* S^8 (h) habuerit S^2 (i) ⟨Solidus hic valet tres grossos⟩ K^5 (j) *deest* S^4 S^5 S^{10} (k) solidis S^9 (l) ⟨Ultra solidos tres furtum⟩ K^5 (m) vir S^7 S^8 *deest* S^2 (n) VII S^2 *deest* S^4 S^5 (o) *deest* S^4 S^5 (p) patibulo S^2 S^3 S^9 patibulo seu suspendio S^{10} K^4 (q) Si vir aliqua bona scilicet vel quicquid suarum rerum, qui sibi subtractum vel raptum fuerit, ad hoc se trahere debet tacto sacramento, ut iuris est. (*cf. Art. 85 in initio*) K^5 ⟨solidus facit 2 grossos⟩ *manus A* S^3 ⟨solidi VI duos grossos⟩ K^2 (r) S^1 S^4 S^5 S^6 S^7 S^{10} K^4 *Art. 40* S^2 *Art. 41* S^3 S^9 *Art. 42* S^8 *Art. 39* K^5 *Art. 45* (s) ⟨De viro, qui tenet bona alterum minus iustum⟩ *manus B* S^3 *manicula* S^6 At si S^7 (t) *desunt* K^4 (u) *deest* S^2 (v) *deest* S^5 (w) *deest* S^2 (x) ad S^9 (y) quod S^8 K^5 (z) *deest* S^5 (aa) hereditaria S^2 (bb) *deest* S^8 K^5 (cc) *desunt* S^5 (dd) *desunt* S^{10} (ee) *desunt* S^3 S^8 (ff) agnato S^1 S^2 S^7 S^8 S^9 S^{10} K^4 (gg) *manus B* S^6 (hh) *deest* S^8 K^5 (ii) querimonia S^3 (jj) huic S^5 (kk) defensorem S^1 S^2 S^3 S^4 S^5 S^7 S^8 S^9 K^5 (ll) quod S^2 (mm) *locus ad verbum* S^3 (nn) ⟨iuste⟩ S^1 (oo) recte S^8 *deest* S^3 (pp) medium S^8 (qq) tunc S^7 (rr) *desunt* S^2

{a} *manus A* S^6 *adest* K^5 {b} *manus A* S^6 *adest* K^5

Articulus 46 [(a)]

[*46*] [(b)] Si vir[(c)] clara luce diei deprehensus fuerit, qui bone fame sit, [(d][(e]in furto et[e)] non plus quam[d)] tres solidos valeat [(f)], [(g)] cutem cum crinibus demeretur. [(h]Sed[(i)] si[h)] furtum[(j)] ultra tres solidos valeat, reus est[(k)] suspendio. [(l]De hiis denariis[l)] tres solidi [(m]medium [(n)] fertonem[(o)] debent[(p)] ponderare[m)]. Si autem fur[(q)] [(r]tempore noctis[r)] deprehensus fuerit cum sex denariis, reus est patibulo[(s)].

Articulus 47 [(t)]

[*47*] | [(u)] Conqueritur vir super alterum pro bonis, quod sua sit vera[(v)] here- 36ra
ditas, et quod ille teneat[(w)] cum iniuria, et sua vera sit successio a suo X
patre, [(x]vel ab alio suo amico, [(y)] [(z]a suo[z)] predecessore[x)], et si[(aa)] ille compareat super quem querimonia proposita fuerit, et dicet se habere bonorum defensorem {a}, et bona possid[er]it pacifice et quiete [(bb)] anno[(cc)] et die, contradiccione qualibet non obstante et est[(dd)] iuste [(ee)] ac rite meum predium censuale, ipsum oportet defensorem[(ff)] suum nominare et ad dies statuere, [(gg)] et cum [(hh)] defensore [(ii)] conservet sua[(jj)] bona, si defensus

---

(a) K^1 K^3 C^3 *Art. 42* K^2 *Art. 41* W^1 C^2 *Art. 40* W^2 *deest folium* C^1 *Art. 46* (b) ⟨fur⟩ C^3 (c) fur K^2 K^3 C^2 (d) et furtum W^1 (e) et furtum C^3 (f) commiserit W^1 (g) in eo K^3 (h) Quodsi C^3 (i) *deest* K^3 (j) vero in furto K^3 (k) *deest* K^1 K^2 (l) Horum denariorum K^3 (m) dimidium debent solvere faccionem K^3 (n) ⊢marcam⊣ C^1 (o) *deest* W^1 (p) *deest* K^1 (q) *deest* W^1 (r) de nocte K^3 (s) pati K^1 K^2 (t) K^1 K^3 C^3 *Art. 43* K^2 *Art. 42* W^1 C^2 *Art. 41* W^2 *deest folium* C^1 *Art. 47* (u) ⟨hereditas⟩ C^3 (v) *deest* W^1 (w) veniet C^2 (x) decessore K^3 (y) aut W^1 (z) vel K^1 K^2 C^3 (aa) *deest* K^3 (bb) ⊢vini⊣ C^1 ⟨dic⟩ C^3 (cc) *deest* C^2 (dd) *deest* K^3 (ee) ac recte C^2 (ff) censuale C^2 (gg) si possit, W^1 (hh) eo W^1 (ii) suo W^1 (jj) *deest* C^3

{a} z a c h o c z c z a vel w a r m a n a C^2

[(a]in eo[a)], [(b)] si defensus fuerit, ut iuris est, [(c]a defensore[c)]. Sin autem sibi[(d)] defectus fuerit in defensore[(e)], actor [(f)] conservat[(g)] suam legalem proprietatem[(h)], in bonis eisdem, quia quivis homo conservat suam innatam hereditatem[(i)], [(j]sive naturalem[(k)] porcionem[j)], facilius, [(l]quam alter emptam hereditatem[l)][(m)] [(n]aut obligatam hereditatem[(o)], aut datam proprietatem[n)], [(p]aut predium censuale[p)], [(q]cum inpossibile sit[(r)] aliquem de[(s)] naturali porcione defraudari[q)].

Articulus 41 [(t)]

[*41*] [(u)] Si[(v)] homo habuerit hereditaria[(w)] censualia et bona a [(x)] quodam monasterio[(y)] [(z]aut alio domino[z)], et si[(aa)] dominus aut abbas sibi[(bb)] non
149^{r} fatetur[(cc)], aut conventus, hic vir | potest hoc[(dd)] metseptimus protestare[(ee)] suorum heredum, qui[(ff)] [*s*] quilibet iurabit singulariter, quod iustum ac successorum[(gg)] suum[(hh)] sit predium censuale. Et si dominus seu abbas [(ii)] hiis septem de ipsorum bonis denegaverit aut fateri noluerit[(jj)], extunc quivis[(kk)] ipsorum metseptimus suorum coheredum bona[(ll)] sua obtinebit.

Articulus 42 [(mm)]

[*42*] [(nn)] Si debet vir producere testimonium super proprium alterius metseptimus, aut mettercius, hoc facere[(oo)] [(pp)] opportet cum possessis[(qq)] hominibus, [(rr]qui in suo iure argui non possunt, et[rr)] qui iudicio astare solent, et domicilia habentibus in[(ss)] iudicio supradicto. Sin autem debet vir persoluta debita protestare super proprietatem alterius, hoc iterum[(tt)] esse[(uu)]

(a) *desunt* S^{2} (b) quod S^{3} (c) ad defensorem S^{4} S^{5} S^{10} (d) *deest* S^{8} K^{5} (e) defensione S^{4} S^{3} S^{8} (f) non S^{3} (g) *deest* S^{9} observat K^{5} (h) possessionem K^{5} (i) proprietatem S^{3} (j) ⟨seu porcionem⟩ K^{4} *deest* S^{10} (k) natalem S^{7} (l) *desunt* S^{10} K^{4} (m) proprietatem S^{2} S^{3} S^{4} S^{5} S^{7} S^{8} (n) *desunt* S^{4} S^{5} (o) proprietatem S^{7} (p) *desunt* S^{3} (q) *desunt* S^{2} (r) si S^{3} S^{10} K^{4} (s) *deest* K^{5} (t) S^{1} S^{4} S^{5} S^{6} S^{7} S^{10} K^{4} *Art. 41* S^{2} *Art. 42* S^{3} S^{9} *Art. 43* S^{8} *Art. 40* K^{5} *Art. 46* (u) Conqueritur vir super alterum S^{10} (v) qui S^{10} (w) hereditatem S^{4} S^{5} *a.c.* hereditatem, *correctio manus B* S^{6} (x) quo S^{3} (y) abbate S^{10} (z) *desunt* S^{2} S^{3} S^{4} S^{5} S^{7} (aa) *deest* S^{9} (bb) *deest* S^{8} S^{10} K^{5} (cc) confitetur S^{4} S^{5} (dd) S^{6} S^{9} K^{4} (ee) probare S^{8} K^{5} (ff) quorum S^{2} S^{7} S^{8} K^{5} quia K^{4} *deest* S^{4} S^{5} S^{9} S^{10} (gg) successorem S^{2} S^{5} (hh) *deest* S^{7} S^{8} (ii) de S^{2} (jj) voluerit S^{4} S^{5} (kk) dominus S^{2} (ll) *deest* S^{10} (mm) S^{1} S^{4} S^{5} S^{6} S^{7} S^{10} K^{4} *Art. 42* S^{2} *Art. 43–44* S^{3} S^{9} *Art. 44* S^{8} *Art. 41* K^{5} *Art. 47* (nn) ⟨nota⟩ S^{8} (oo) probare S^{4} S^{5} (pp) debet vel S^{10} K^{4} (qq) possessionatis S^{7} (rr) *desunt* S^{2} S^{3} S^{4} S^{5} S^{7} S^{8} (ss) *deest* S^{4} S^{5} (tt) eciam S^{7} (uu) *deest* K^{5}

fuerit, ut iuris est[a], a[b] defensore. [c] Si autem sibi[d] defectus fuerit [e] defensore[f], actor[g] conservat suam [h]legittimam seu[h] legalem proprietatem[i] in bonis eisdem, quia quivis homo conservat[j] suam innatam | heredi- 36rb
tatem [k] facilius, quam alter emptam proprietatem aut obligatam [l]proprietatem, aut datam proprietatem[l], aut predium censuale.

Articulus 48 [m]

[*48*] [n] Si homo habuerit hereditaria[o] censualia et bona a quodam monasterio [p], et si[q] dominus vel abbas[r] sibi[s] non fatetur, aut conventus[t], hic vir potest met|septimus protestare suorum coheredum[u], quorum quilibet 36va
iurabit singulariter, quod iustum est[v] ac successorum[w] suum sit predium censuale. Et si[x] dominus seu abbas[y] hiis septem de ipsorum bonis denegaverit[z] aut fateri noluerit[aa], extunc quivis metseptimus suorum coheredum[bb] bona sua obtinebit.

Articulus 49 [cc]

[*49*] [dd] Si vir debet producere testimonium super proprium alterius metseptimus aut mettercius[ee], hoc facere debet cum possessis hominibus, [ff] qui[gg] [hh] iudicio astare solent et domicilia habentibus et in iudicio supradicto. Si autem vir debet persoluta debita debet[ii] protestare super proprietatem alterius[jj], hoc[kk] iterum esse debent possessi homines domicilia

(a) *deest* C^2 (b) *deest* W^1 (c) ⟨[*2 verba difficilia*] dic⟩ C^3 (d) *deest* C^3 (e) in K^1 K^2 K^3 W^1 C^2 C^3 (f) defensione defensore K^1 defensione K^2 (g) alter C^2 (h) *desunt* K^1 K^2 K^3 W^1 C^2 C^3 (i) hereditatem W^1 (j) *deest* K^1 K^2 (k) seu porcionem ⟨pignus oportet⟩ K^1 seu porcionem oportet K^2 seu porcionem K^3 seu porcionem naturalem W^1 sive porcionem C^3 (l) *desunt* C^2 (m) K^1 K^3 C^3 *Art. 44* K^2 *Art. 43* W^1 C^2 *Art. 42* W^2 *deest folium* C^1 *Art. 48* (n) ⟨XLIIII. De testimonio⟩ C^3 (o) hereditatem, W^1 (p) aut alio domino K^1 K^2 (q) *deest* K^3 (r) conventus C^3 (s) *deest* K^3 (t) abbas C^3 (u) heredum K^1 K^2 (v) *deest* K^1 K^2 K^3 W^1 (w) *in ms.* successorem [s] C^1 C^3 (x) *deest* K^3 (y) *deest* K^1 K^2 (z) negaverit K^3 (aa) voluerit C^2 (bb) heredum K^1 K^2 (cc) K^1 C^3 *Art. 45* K^2 *Art. 44* K^3 *Art. 45 pars 1* W^2 *deest folium* W^1 C^2 *Art. 43* C^1 *Art. 49* (dd) ⟨de testimonio⟩ C^3 (ee) octavus C^2 (ff) ⟨dic⟩ C^3 (gg) quia K^1 (hh) in W^1 (ii) *deest* K^3 W^1 (jj) *deest* K^3 (kk) hoc W^1

debent(a) possessi(b) homines domicilia habentes (c), si hoc in iudicio non viderunt, nec in iudicio (dfuerit confirmatumd). (e)

Articulus 43 (f)

[*43*] (g) Si aliquis debet(h) persoluta debita probare(i), (jprotestando pro debitoj), hoc facere debet cum talibus hominibus (k), qui in suo iure argui non possunt.

Articulus 44 (l)

[*44*] Si vir ducit viduam, que unum filium (m) aut plures pueros(n) habuerit et ipse (o) nulla bona habuerit nec (pipsa, et vir unum filium habuerit cum sua(q) prima uxorep), et si fortuna arridente (r) per suos labores bona habuerint et(s) proprietatem sive hereditatem emerint(t), aut super bona mobilia sive
149v mercimonia posuerint, | et in posterum vir moritur et uxor, extunc filius viri propius est recipere hereditatem, quam (u) pueri femine, aut(v) pueri(w) sororis (xsue(y), vel eciam nepotes (zseu neptez)x) ex filia sua. Ita tamen, si filius

(a) ⟨debent⟩ S^{8} (b) possessionati S^{7} (c) ⟨in eodem iudicio⟩ S^{8} (d) audierunt K^{5} (e) ⟨In nullis causis precio conventi seu empti possunt esse testes, quia iure possunt eici.⟩ S^{8} (f) S^{1} S^{4} S^{5} S^{6} S^{7} S^{8} S^{10} K^{4} *Art. 43* S^{2} S^{3} S^{9} *Art. 45* K^{5} *Art. 48* (g) ⟨Magdeburg⟩ S^{2} (h) voluerit S^{2} (i) protestari S^{2} S^{9} (j) *desunt* S^{2} S^{10} (k) mettercium K^{5} (l) S^{1} S^{4} S^{5} S^{6} S^{7} S^{10} K^{4} *Art. 44* S^{2} S^{3} S^{9} *Art. 46* S^{8} *Art. 43* K^{5} *Art. 49* (m) habeat S^{10} (n) *deest* S^{4} S^{5} (o) eciam similiter, que S^{10} (p) ipse S^{10} (q) *deest* K^{4} (r) quod S^{2} (s) aut S^{2} S^{4} S^{5} (t) promeruit S^{2} habuerit seu emerit K^{5} (u) filii seu S^{10} (v) et S^{7} (w) *deest* S^{5} (x) *desunt* S^{3} (y) sive S^{10} (z) *desunt* S^{5}

habentes, si hoc in iudicio non (a) fuerit confirmatum. (bIn nullis causis precio conventi seu empti valeant protestare, quia iure possunt eici(c).b) {a}

Articulus 50 (d)

[*50*] | (e) Si aliquis debet persoluta debita (f) probare, protestante(g) pro 36vb
debito(h), hoc facere debet talibus cum hominibus, qui in suo iure argui non possunt mettercius(i). {b}

Articulus 51 (j)

[*51*] (k) Si vir duxerit uxorem viduam(l), que unum aut plures pueros habuerit et ipse nulla bona habuerit nec ipsa, et(m) vir unum filium habuerit cum sua prima uxore, et si(n) fortuna aridente(o) per suos labores bona habuerint, aut(p) proprietatem sive hereditatem emerint, aut super bona mobilia sive(q) mercimonia posuerint, et(r) si(s) vir moritur et uxor, extunc filius viri
proprior | ⟨De successione heredum⟩(t) est recipere(u) hereditatem, quam pueri 37ra
femine, aut pueri(v) sororis sue, vel eciam nepotes seu neptes ex filia sua. XI

(a) viderunt, nec in iudicio K^1 K^2 W^1 (b) *desunt* W^1 (c) vinci C^2 (d) K^1 C^3 *Art. 46* K^2 *Art. 45 Art.* K^3 *45 pars 2* W^1 C^2 *Art. 44* W^2 *deest folium* C^1 *Art. 50* (e) ⟨probare⟩ C^3 (f) protestari vel C^2 (g) *deest* C^2 (h) quo K^3 (i) *deest* K^1 K^2 K^3 W^1 C^3 (j) K^1 C^3 *Art. 47* K^2 K^3 *Art. 46* C^2 W^1 *Art. 45* C^1 *Art. 51* W^2 *deest folium* (k) *manicula* C^1 ⟨[…] […] mater iure […] aliqua [*?*]⟩ [*3 verba difficilia*] C^3 (l) *deest* W^1 (m) nec K^3 (n) *deest* K^3 (o) accedente K^3 (p) et K^1 K^2 (q) *deest* C^3 (r) aut K^3 (s) in posterum K^1 K^2 K^3 W^1 C^3 (t) *manus γ* C^1 (u) accipere K^1 (v) *deest* W^1

{a} In Colmensi. Cum scabinis vel consulibus, si autem mortui fuerint, et unus illorum manserit, tunc loco illorum cuiuslibet mortui duobus posses[s]ionatis, quibus fides adhiberi debent, super proprio probari potest. W^1 {b} In Colmensi. Cum consulibus, scabinis, arbitris, et iudicibus mercipotariis solummodo debitorum probari potest, non aliis hominibus. W^1

patri paris condicionis fuerit. Proxima cognata uxoris[(a)] recipit supellectilia [(b]de iure[b)].

Articulus 45 [(c)]

[*45*] [(d)] Si vir aliquis dederit pueris suis [(e)] aliqua bona sua, et sue uxori in iudicio bannito circa vitam suam et bone racionis, et si sibi pueri[(f)] paris condicionis [(g)] fuerint, et si desuper [(h]vera[(i)] pax [(j)] ac[(k)] firmata fuerit[h)], et [(l)] in posterum alteri in eisdem bonis aliquid dederit [(m]aut heres fuerit[m)] aut[(n)] ⟨non⟩[(o)], ille, cui prima donacio sit[(p)] data[(q)], bene[(r)] contradicere potest de iure. Ita tamen, si testimonium desuper iudicis habuerit et scabinorum, quod[(s)] sibi[(t)] primum donum donatum [(u)] sit absque contradiccione[(v)] illius, qui ad hoc successor fuerit infra annum et diem. Extunc contradicere non potest ⟨possunt⟩[(w)], si illi[(x)] desuper testes habuerint.

Articulus 46 [(y)]

[*46*] Si vir sue uxori sua[(z)] edificia dederit, que super bona censualia edificata fuerint, coram ⟨domino⟩[(aa)] proprietatis et coram suis vicinis, tempore vite sue, et inducit eam in possessionem, et si discedit ab hac luce sine prole, si heres suus super bona [(bb)] eadem loqui voluerit post mortem viri [(cc)], nichil in eis poterit obtinere, si mulier protestaverit, quod sibi datum fuerit. [(dd)]
150r Sin autem [(ee]apparatus et[ee)] edificia viri proprium[(ff)] fuerit, extunc heres |

(a) *deest* S^{9} (b) *desunt* S^{10} K^{4} (c) S^{1} S^{4} S^{5} S^{6} S^{7} S^{10} K^{4} *Art. 45* S^{2} S^{3} S^{9} *Art. 47* S^{8} *Art. 44* K^{5} *Art. 50* (d) *manicula* S^{4} ⟨de donacionibus per actorem habetur⟩ K^{2} (e) ad huc S^{2} (f) filius S^{4} S^{5} (g) pueri S^{2} (h) pueris bona firmata sunt K^{5} (i) firma K^{4} *deest* S^{10} (j) ├desierit┤ S^{6} (k) *deest* S^{1} S^{2} S^{3} S^{4} S^{5} S^{7} S^{8} S^{9} S^{10} K^{4} K^{5} (l) si S^{4} S^{3} S^{5} S^{8} K^{5} (m) *desunt* S^{2} S^{5} (n) tunc S^{2} S^{7} S^{8} K^{5} et S^{5} (o) *manus B* S^{6} (p) sic S^{3} (q) *deest* S^{4} S^{3} S^{5} S^{7} S^{8} (r) *deest* S^{2} (s) quando S^{10} K^{4} (t) *a.c.* si, *correctio manus B* S^{6} si S^{9} (u) ├est┤ S^{6} (v) *a.c.* condicione, *correctio manus B* S^{6} (w) *manus B* S^{6} (x) ibi K^{5} (y) S^{1} S^{4} S^{5} S^{6} S^{7} S^{10} K^{4} *Art. 46* S^{2} S^{3} S^{9} *Art. 48* S^{8} *Art. 45* K^{5} *Art. 51, 52 pars 1* (z) *deest* S^{9} S^{10} (aa) ├iudicio┤ *correctio manus B* S^{6} domino S^{1} S^{2} S^{3} S^{4} S^{5} S^{7} S^{8} S^{9} S^{10} K^{4} K^{5} (bb) sua S^{10} K^{4} (cc) sui K^{5} (dd) ⟨Qui donatio infringitur⟩ K^{5} (ee) *desunt* S^{4} S^{5} (ff) *deest* S^{2}

Ita tamen, si filius patri sit paris condicionis. Proxima cognata uxoris recipit suppellectilia de(a) iure(b). {a}

Articulus 52 (c)

[52] ⟨Bonum⟩(d) Si aliquis vir dederit suis pueris aliqua sua bona, et sue uxori, in (e) iudicio bannito circa vitam suam, et bone racionis, et si(f) sibi(g) paris condicionis pueri fuerint, et si (hdesuper vera pax firmata fuerit, eth) (i) in posterum alteri in eisdem bonis aliquid dederit aut heres fuerit, aut non, ille, cui prima donacio sit data, bene contradicere potest de iure. Ita tamen, si testimonium iudicis desuper habuerit(j) et scabinorum, quod(k) | [37rb] sibi primum(l) donum donatum(m) fuerit absque contradiccione illius, qui ad hoc successor fuerit infra annum (net diemn). Extunc contradicere non potest(o), si(p) ille super hoc testes habuerit.

Articulus 53 (q)

[53] (r) Si vir sue uxori sua edificia dederit, que super(s) bona censualia edificata sunt, coram domino proprietatis et coram(t) suis vicinis, tempore sue vite, et(u) inducit eam in possessionem, et si (vdiscedit de hac lucev) sine prole, et si heres suus super bona eadem loqui voluerit post mortem (w), nichil in eis poterit obtinere, si mulier protestare poterit, quod ei datum

(a) *deest* K^3 W^1 C^2 (b) *deest* K^3 W^1 (c) K^1 C^3 *Art. 48* K^2 K^3 *Art. 47* W^1 C^2 *Art. 46* W^2 *deest folium* C^1 *Art. 52* (d) *manus η* C^1 ⟨donacio uxori⟩ C^3 (e) suo C^2 (f) *deest* C^3 (g) ergo K^1 K^2 (h) desunt K^3 (i) si K^1 K^2 (j) fuerit C^2 (k) si K^1 K^2 (l) *deest* W^1 (m) datum K^3 (n) *desunt* W^1 (o) *deest* K^1 (p) sed K^1 (q) K^1 C^3 *Art. 49* K^2 K^3 *Art. 48* W^1 *Art. 47* W^2 *deest folium* C^1 *Art. 53* C^2 *Art. 47–48* (r) ⟨municipale ius⟩ C^3 ⟨donacio uxori⟩ C^3 (s) desuper K^1 K^2 (t) *deest* W^1 (u) ut K^3 (v) vir moriatur K^3 (w) viri K^1 K^2 K^3 W^1 C^3

{a} In Colmensi. Si vir viduam duxerit, ut dicitur in capitulo, que puerum unum vel plures habuerit, et similliter vir, mortuo vero viro pueri viri racione paternorum bonorum hereditariorum et maternorum medietatem bonorum tollunt, pueri vero uxori cum iure medietatem, ita quod quarta pars cedit illis pueris racione paternorum. Si autem alii pueri fuerint ex eadem uxore, n[i]chilominus pueri patris modo mortui medietatem recipiunt racione partis materne et eidem pueri cum pueris primis uxoris eius, et posteris quartam partem illorum bonorum equaliter condividere debent, ita quod nulli pueri primi patris modo mortui habeant in illa quarta parte paternam porcionem, similiter pueri primi, et pote posteri in eadem parte quarta eciam primam porcionem obtinebunt, materno vero porcio utriusque pueris in alia quarta parte bonorum circa morem reservatur. W^1

mulieri infringere potest, nisi donacio(a) in iudicio bannito (b) fuerit confirmata. (c) Quia nullus (dsuum propriumd) dare potest, nisi(e) in iudicio bannito, vel(f) coram iudice et scabinis, (gnisi suus heres contradicatg). (h) Sin autem (i) hereditaria censualia bona fuerint, extunc sue(j) uxori dare (knon potestk) absque(l) heredum consensu(m), vel absque(n) domini proprietatis consensu, in cuius bonis sunt. (o) Si vir(p) mercimonia aut (q) bona mobilia habuerit, quod cum bonis emerit eisdem (rsuccessoriis(s) paterna successione, hoc sue uxori dare non potest, nisir) in iudicio bannito coram iudice et scabinis. Sin autem (t) habuerit bona mobilia aut mercimonia, que sibi propriis laboribus aut(u) prospera fortuna accreverint (v), que(w) potest dare(x) in(y) valitudine vite sue cuicumque placet, cuiuslibet(z) sine contradiccione(aa). (bb)

Articulus 47 (cc)

[*47*] (dd) (eeUbi(ff) alicuius monasterii obnoxius suam penam demeretur, hoc sunt triginta solidi, obnoxius (gg) bene potest bona sua resignare et iterum suscipere et dare cui placet, contradiccione qualibet non obstante, quod(hh) propriis laboribus acquisivit.ee) Ubi obnoxius ⟨census⟩(ii) suo domino suum(jj) censum subtraxerit, pro eo tria talenta ⟨talenta⟩ demeretur. (kk) Quidquid obnoxius criminalis cause commiserit, pro eo (ll) nullus(mm) queret iudicium, nisi (nn) domini advocati. Quando obnoxius moritur, extunc (oosuo domino autoo) suo(pp) advocato opportet dare denarios obnoxietarum(qq) [*s*]
150v et meliorem equ[u]m, quem habet. (rr) Idem opportet facere sacerdotem | suo archipresbitero (ss), dum moritur, tunc sibi opportet dare suum(tt) meliorem equ[u]m.

(a) *deest* S^{8} K^{5} (b) vel coram iudice et scabinis S^{3} (c) ⟨De donacione coram iudicio⟩ K^{5} (d) *desunt* K^{4} S^{10} (e) *deest* S^{2} (f) *deest* S^{2} S^{7} (g) *desunt* S^{7} (h) ⟨De bonis hereditariis aut censualibus, que donari non debent⟩ K^{5} (i) bona mobilia aut S^{7} (j) *deest* S^{10} (k) *desunt* S^{10} (l) *deest* S^{7} (m) *deest* S^{8} (n) *deest* S^{8} K^{5} (o) *rubrica:* De mercimoniis et bonis mobilibus. K^{5} (p) *deest* K^{5} (q) alia S^{10} K^{4} (r) ⟨successoriis paterna successione, hoc sue uxori dare non potest, nisi⟩ S^{8} (s) successionis S^{7} sunt cens[u]ariis S^{10} sunt cesaris K^{4} (t) vir S^{1} S^{2} S^{3} S^{4} S^{5} S^{7} S^{8} S^{9} S^{10} K^{4} K^{5} (u) ac S^{2} S^{3} S^{8} K^{5} hac S^{4} (v) cum sua uxore S^{2} S^{3} S^{4} S^{5} S^{7} S^{8} (w) *deest* S^{2} (x) *deest* K^{4} (y) *deest* S^{7} (z) cui⟨us⟩ S^{8} (aa) condicione K^{5} (bb) De iure liberti/liberi in emendis sive obnoxii et in successionibus in bonis naturalibus. *Titulus sequentis articuli erronee adnexus* S^{10}/K^{4} (cc) S^{1} S^{4} S^{5} S^{6} S^{7} S^{10} K^{4} *Art. 47* S^{2} S^{3} S^{9} *Art. 49* S^{8} *Art. 46* K^{5} *Art. 52 pars 2* (dd) ⟨De obnoxio domino censum subtrahente⟩ K^{5} (ee) *desunt* K^{5} (ff) Si S^{7} (gg) tamen S^{9} (hh) que S^{2} S^{10} (ii) *manus A?* S^{6} (jj) *deest* S^{2} S^{9} (kk) ⟨De obnoxio criminale nephas comitente⟩ K^{5} (ll) quod S^{3} qui S^{5} (mm) *deest* S^{1} (nn) sui S^{3} S^{9} (oo) *desunt* S^{8} (pp) *deest* S^{2} (qq) obnoxietatis S^{7} (rr) Hoc S^{2} (ss) aut suo seniori K^{5} (tt) *deest* S^{2} S^{4} S^{5} S^{10} K^{4}

fuerit. Si (aautem fundusa) et edificia proprialiter(b) viri fuerint, extunc heres mulieri infringere potest, nisi donacio in | iudicio bannito(c) fuerit confir- 37va
mata. (d) Quia nullus suum proprium dare potest, nisi in iudicio bannito coram iudice et scabinis, quin(e) suus(f) heres contradicat. Si autem hereditaria censualia(g) bona fuerint, extunc (h) uxori dare non potest absque heredum consensu, vel absque(i) domini proprietatis consensu, (jin cuius bonisj) sunt. Si vir(k) mercimonia aut mobilia bona habuerit, quod cum bonis emerit (leisdem(m) successoribusl) paterna successione (n), hoc sue uxori dare non potest, nisi in(o) iudicio bannito coram iudice et scabinis. (p) Si autem vir habuerit bona mobilia aut mercimonia, que sibi propriis laboribus aut prospera fortuna accreverint cum sua uxore, (q) potest dare in valitudine vite sue cuicumque placet, cuiuslibet(r) sine contradiccione.

Articulus 54 (s)

[*54*] Ubi alicuius monasterii obnoxius suam penam demeretur, hoc sunt triginta solidi. Obnoxius bene potest sua bona resignare et iterum(t) suscipere et dare cui placet, contradiccione qualibet non obstante, que propriis laboribus(u) acquisivit. Ubi obnoxius suo domino (v) suum censum subtraxerit(w), pro eo demeretur tria talenta. Quidquid obnoxius (xcriminalis causex) commiserit, pro eo nullus querat iudicium nisi domini(y) sui(z) (aa) advocati. Quando obnoxius moritur, extunc suo domino (bb) advocato (cc) oportet dare denarios obnoxiorum(dd) et meliorem equum, quem habet. Idem oportet (ee) sacerdotem suo(ff) archipresbitero, dum moritur, tunc (gg) suum(hh) dare oportet equum meliorem.

(a) autem apparatus K1 K2 apparatus W1 (b) *deest* K1 K2 W1 (c) *deest* C3 (d) ⟨regula⟩ C3 (e) nisi K1 K2 W1 (f) proximus K1 (g) *deest* W1 (h) sue K1 K2 K3 W1 C3 (i) *deest* C2 (j) cuius bona W1 C3 (k) *deest* K1 K2 (l) sibi C3 (m) *deest* W1 (n) innatis W1 (o) coram W1 (p) *rubrica:* De viro habente mercimonia. C2 (q) hoc W1 que C3 (r) *deest* C3 (s) K1 C3 *Art. 50* K2 K3 C2 *Art. 49* W1 *Art. 48* W2 *deest folium* C1 *Art. 54* (t) item W1 (u) *deest* W1 (v) ⊢advocato⊣ C1 (w) protraxerit C3 (x) noxe W1 (y) domicili C2 (z) *deest* K1 K2 C2 (aa) aut sui W1 (bb) aut W1 (cc) debet et C2 (dd) obnoxietarum K1 K2 K3 W1 (ee) fateri K1 facere K2 K3 W1 C3 (ff) *deest* K1 K2 (gg) sibi C3 (hh) sibi K1 K2 K3

Articulus 48 (a)

[*48*] Si moritur vir absque herede et nepotem ex filia habuerit, que exheredata fuerit circa suam(b) vitam, idem nepos maiori iure recipit {a} bona avi materni(c), quam iudicium, qui (d) sibi(e) est(f) paris condicionis. (g⟨Sed iudicium recipit (h) arma bellica⟩g).

Articulus 49 (i)

[*49*] Si unus alteri manum suam abtestare voluerit(j) pro(k) falso, hoc opportet, quod faciat mettercius (l) cum(m) talibus hominibus, qui in suo iure argui non possunt. Sin autem facere debet(n) (o) pro vulnere in facto(p) manifesto, opportet, quod hoc(q) faciat metseptimus, per iusticiam pacis(r), ita tamen, si manifestum factum cum malefactore(s) ad iudicium deductum fuerit.

Articulus 50 (t)

[*50*] ⟨de etate pueri liber iste LXXX capitulum. Item in provinciali[1] LXXII et LXXIII⟩(u) Cum moritur vir, qui pueros habuerit, qui ad annos discrecionis nondum pervenerunt, proximus agnatus(v) (w) debet ipsorum esse tutor, (x) eousque ad annos pubertatis pervenerint(y). (zEt si(aa) idem non⟨dum⟩(bb) adhuc(cc) annos(dd) pubertatis attingeritz), adiutor(ee) suus (ff) esse(gg) debet (hhproximus agnatus(ii) suus(jj)hh), eousque ipse(kk) ad annos (ll) pervenerit discrecionis, et

(a) S^1 S^4 S^5 S^6 S^7 S^{10} K^4 *Art. 48* S^2 *articulus deest* S^3 S^9 *Art. 50* S^8 *Art. 47* K^5 *Art. 53* (b) *deest* K^5 (c) mortui S^{10} K^4 (d) si S^3 (e) *deest* S^7 (f) *deest* S^{10} K^4 (g) *manus A* S^6 *textus adest in* S^3 S^4 S^5 S^7 S^8 K^5, *manu commentatoris in* S^1 (h) cum S^5 (i) S^1 S^4 S^5 S^6 S^7 S^{10} K^4 *Art. 49* S^2 *Art. 50* S^3 *Art. 51* S^9 *Art. 55* S^8 *Art. 48* K^5 *Art. 54* (j) debuerit S^7 *deest* S^4 S^5 voluerit ac debuerit K^5 (k) *deest* S^{10} (l) ⟨pro vulnere autem sic⟩ K^5 (m) *deest* S^7 S^8 (n) *deest* S^{10} K^4 (o) ⟨manifestum factum⟩ K^5 (p) *deest* S^9 (q) *deest* S^2 S^{10} K^4 (r) peragat S^{10} (s) malediccione S^3 (t) S^1 S^4 S^5 S^6 S^7 S^{10} K^4 *Art. 50* S^2 S^9 *Art. 51* S^3 *Art. 52* S^8 *Art. 49* K^5 *Art. 55* (u) *manus A* S^6 *adsunt* K^5 (v) cognatus S^4 S^5 *a.c.* cognatus, *correctio manus B* S^6 (w) ita S^3 (x) eorum S^2 (y) attingerit S^9 (z) *desunt* S^9 (aa) *deest* S^5 (bb) *manus B* S^6 dum S^1 S^2 S^3 S^4 S^5 S^7 S^8 S^9 S^{10} K^4 K^5 (cc) ad K^5 (dd) *deest* S^4 S^5 (ee) *deest* S^{10} (ff) eousque S^4 S^5 (gg) *deest* S^3 (hh) *desunt* S^{10} K^4 (ii) cognatus S^4 S^5 *a.c.* cognatus, *correctio manus B* S^6 (jj) *deest* S^8 (kk) *deest* S^2 (ll) pubertatis S^{10}

{a} ⟨nepos dicitur w n u k avus d z ÿ a d⟩ K^5

1 *Speculum Saxonum in eodem manuscripto, error: articuli* LXXII *et* LXXIII (*fol. 192ʳ*) *de banno regio et de banno comitis, cf. SSp. I.23§2.*

Articulus 55 (a)

[*55*] | ⟨Si moritur⟩(b) Si moritur vir absque herede et nepotem(c) ex filia habue- 38ra
rit, que exheredata(d) fuerit circa vitam suam, idem nepos(e) maiore recipit XII
iure bona (f) (g avi materni(h), quam g) iudicium, qui(i) si(j) sibi est(k) paris con-
dicionis, sed iudicium(l) recipit sua arma bellica. (m Si eciam filius ducerit
uxorem tempore vite sui patris, et premoriatur patri indivisus sua hereditate,
extunc ipsius filii hereditatem (n) avi recipiunt, (o) et non filii filiarum(p). Si
autem pater(q) filium a se diviserit, protunc filii filiorum et filiarum | in bonis 38rb
sui(r) avi equalem recipiunt porcionem. Sed in hereditatibus s[ue](s) (t avie
filii t) filiorum et aliarum(u) iuridice sunt equales. m) ⟨vide XXI et ibi videbis signum
crucis ex toto in Tewtunico⟩1

Articulus 56 (v)

[*56*] (w) Si unus abtestari voluerit alteri manum suam(x) pro falso, hic oportet, quod faciet mettercius cum talibus hominibus, (y qui in(z) suo iure argui non possunt y). Si autem facere(aa) debet pro (bb) vulnere in facto manifesto, oportet, quod hoc(cc) faciat metseptimus, pro iusticia pacis, ita tamen, si manifestum factum cum malefactore(dd) ad iudicium fuerit deductum.

Articulus 57 (ee)

[*57*] | ⟨Cum moritur⟩(ff) Cum moritur vir, qui pueros habuerit, qui ad annos 38va
discrecionis nondum pervenerint, proximus cognatus(gg) eorum(hh) debet
esse eorum tutor(ii), usque ad annos pubertatis pervenerint. Et si idem nondum adhuc pubertatis annos attingerit, adiutor suus debet propior (jj)

(a) K^1 C^3 *Art. 51* K^2 K^3 C^2 *Art. 50* W^1 *Art. 49* W^2 *deest folium* C^1 *Art. 55* (b) *manus η* C^1 ⟨de hereditate⟩ C^3 (c) puerum K^3 (d) exhereditata K^3 C^3 (e) in ipso K^3 (f) sua C^3 (g) porcionem sui patrui secundum C^2 (h) *deest* C^3 (i) de hoc C^2 (j) *deest* K^1 K^2 W^1 (k) *deest* W^1 (l) iudex K^1 K^2 (m) *desunt* K^1 K^2 K^3 W^1 (n) sui C^3 (o) equaliter cum suis patruis C^3 (p) filiorum C^2 (q) avus C^3 (r) suis C^2 (s) *deest* C^2 C^3 (t) avi filie C^2 (u) filiarum C^2 filiarum recipienda C^3 (v) K^1 C^3 *Art. 52* K^2 K^3 C^2 *Art. 51* W^1 *Art. 50* W^2 *deest folium* C^1 *Art. 56* (w) ⟨scilicet testes⟩ C^3 (x) *deest* C^3 (y) astantibus ac fidedignis C^3 (z) *deest* K^2 (aa) protestari K^3 (bb) uno K^3 (cc) *deest* K^1 K^2 (dd) viro W^1 (ee) K^1 C^3 *Art. 53* K^2 K^3 C^2 *Art. 52* W^1 *Art. 51* W^2 *deest folium* C^1 *Art. 57* (ff) *manus β* C^1 ⟨de tutore⟩ C^3 (gg) agnatus W^1 (hh) *deest* K^2 (ii) mundibordius W^1 (jj) suus K^1 K^2 K^3 W^1 C^3

1 *error, textus Germanicus (fol.* XXI *= fol. 47*^{va}*) non congruit textui Latino in eodem manuscripto; manus ζ* C^1

racionem de(a) anno ad annum (bde bonisb) pupillorum (ccoram vero ipsorum tutorec) facere (d) tenetur.

Articulus 51 (e)

[*51*] (f) Omnis querimonia(g) et (h) testimonia, (ique cumi) criminosis(j) violenciis cum clamore ad iudicium in facto manifesto |
151r deprehense et deducte fuerint, virum metseptimum protestare opportet(k) circa ius pacis, exceptis vulneribus, que monomachales non fuerint. (l) Manifestum factum ibi(m) esse(n) dicitur, (oubi vir captivatur(p) cum furto aut (q) spolio(r), deprehensus ducitur ad iudicium cum clamore. Insuper(s) eciam manifestum factum (tibi essest) dicitur,o) ubi viro cultellus aut gladius, (uaut alia ⟨arma⟩(v) siccau)(w) in sua manu deprehensa fuerint, cum qua pacem(x) infregit, aut si in fuga facti deprehensus fuerit et captivus ad iudicium cum clamore ductus fuerit. Hunc actor metseptimus vincere (y) debet(z) circa ius pacis. Et ⟨hoc est unum⟩(aa) si(bb) factum manifestum (cccum viro ad iudicium deductum(dd) fueritcc), (ee) stuprum et obsidium, et irruenciam domicilii, homicidium(ff), furtum, spolium(gg), (hhprobat(ii) homo(jj)hh) protestando(kk) metseptimus(ll). (mm) Si vir(nn) de istis(oo) conqueritur, extunc sua querimonia sic debet procedere: "Domine iudex ⟨et domini scabini⟩(pp), ego(qq) conqueror Deo et vobis, quod hic(rr) homo iste(ss) venit intra municipalia, et in me pacem violavit, et(tt) me stupravit (uu) corpore, rebus et honore muliebri, de quo (vv) sufficiens habeo testimonium per eos, qui meum clamorem audierunt, et ostendere(ww) volo (xx) factum(yy), (zzut(aaa) de(bbb) iure (ccc(dddteneozz) autddd)

(a) *deest* S1 S3 S4 S5 (b) *desunt* K5 (c) *desunt* S10 K4 (d) debet vel K4 S10 (e) S1 S4 S5 S6 S7 S10 K4 *Art. 51* S2 S9 *Art. 52–53* S3 *Art. 53* S8 *Art. 50* K5 *Art. 56* (f) De eo. K4 (g) querela S3 S4 S7 S8 (h) omnia K4 (i) quecumque S10 K4 (j) cum clamore et S10 (k) debet S9 (l) De eo. K4 *subrubrica:* Quid sit factum manifestum. K5 (m) et K5 (n) *deest* S2 (o) *desunt* S4 S5 (p) rapitur S2 (q) cum S9 (r) *deest* S2 (s) *deest* S2 (t) *desunt* S9 (u) *desunt* S10 (v) *manus B* S6 (w) furtiva S2 facta S8 arma S9 litiosa K5 (x) potestate S3 (y) potest vel S4 S5 (z) opportebit S2 (aa) *manus B* S6 (bb) *deest* S2 S3 (cc) dicitur, quam quis scienter claves ad furta gesserit, aut ea in sua defensione tenuerit, nec sint tam parva [*s*], quod ad fenestram [*?*] cellarii reponi sive ipsius scitu valeant. S2 (dd) ⟨deductum⟩ S8 (ee) sicut est S7 S8 K5 ⟨de protestacione criminum et ipsa querela⟩ K5 (ff) *deest* S2 (gg) *deest* S2 (hh) probantur S2 (ii) tunc probare debet S7 S8 (jj) hoc S4 S5 (kk) *deest* S10 (ll) cum VII testibus S2 (mm) *subrubrica:* De rebus concessis seu obligatis. S9 *subrubrica:* De eo. K4 (nn) vero S2 (oo) damnosis violenciis S9 (pp) *manus B* S6 (qq) ecce K5 (rr) *deest* S3 S9 (ss) *deest* S7 S8 K5 (tt) aut S2 (uu) et spoliavit S2 S3 S4 S5 et spoliavit in S7 S8 (vv) ├f┤ S6 (ww) protestare S2 (xx) hoc S2 (yy) *deest* S4 S5 (zz) et demere teneor S10 (aaa) sed S4 S5 (bbb) *deest* S2 S7 S8 K4 (ccc) habeo S4 S5 teneor aut habeo S9 (ddd) *desunt* S2 S3 S8

agnatus(a) esse, quousque ad annos pervenerit (b) discrecionis(c), et racionem (d) anno ad annum (e(fde bonisf) pupillorume) coram vero ipsorum tutore(g) facere(h) tenetur, (ivel coram consulibus aut scabinisi).

Articulus 58 (j)

[*58*] Omnis querimonia ac(k) testimonia, que cum(l) criminosis violenciis cum clamore ad iudicium in facto manifesto deprehense et deducte fuerint, virum metseptimum protestare oportet circa ius pacis, exceptis vulneribus, que monomach⌊al⌋es(m) non sunt (n). Manifestum factum ibi esse dicitur, ubi vir captivatur cum furtu aut spolio et deprehensus ducitur (oad(p) iudiciumo) cum clamore. (q) Eciam manifestum factum(r) esse ibi(s) dicitur, | [38vb] ubi viro gladius aut cultellus, aut alia arma sua(t) (uin suau) manu deprehensa fuerint, cum qua pacem infregit, aut si (vin fuga factiv) deprehensus fuerit et captivus ad iudicium cum clamore deductus fuerit(w). Hunc actor metseptimus vincere oportet(x) circa ius pacis. (y) Et si(z) factum manifestum cum viro ad iudicium deductum fuerit (aa), stuprum et obsidium, et irruenciam(bb) domiciliorum, homicidium, furtum et spolium probat(cc) homo metseptimus(dd) protestando. Si vir de istis conqueritur (ee), extunc sua querimonia(ff) sic debet procedere: (gg) "Domine iudex, ego conqueror Deo et vobis, quod hic(hh) homo iste(ii) venit intra municipalia, et (jjin mejj) pacem (kk) violavit, et (ll) me stupravit et spoliavit (mm) corpore, rebus et honore muliebri, de quo sufficiens habeo testimonium per hos, qui meum clamorem audierunt, et ostendere volo factum, (nn) de iure (oo) debeo (ppet requiro(qq) in sentencia

---

(a) cognatus K^1 K^2 C^3 (b) pubertatis seu C^2 (c) pubertatis W^1 (d) de K^1 K^2 (e) *desunt* W^1 (f) *desunt* K^3 (g) mundibordio W^1 (h) *deest* K^3 (i) quidquid factum fuerit cum hiis bonis C^3 *desunt* K^1 K^2 K^3 W^1 (j) K^1 *Art. 54* K^2 *Art. 53* K^3 *Art. 53–54* W^1 *Art. 52* W^2 *deest folium* C^1 *Art. 58* C^2 *Art. 53–56* C^3 Art. 54 (k) aut K^1 K^2 (l) in C^2 (m) monomochalia K^1 K^2 duellaria W^1 monomachalia et duellaria C^2 (n) vel mortalia C^2 (o) W^1 (p) in C^2 (q) *rubrica:* De facto manifesto gladii aut cultelli. C^2 Si C^2 (r) *deest* K^3 (s) *deest* K^1 K^2 (t) *deest* K^3 W^1 (u) *desunt* C^3 (v) fugator K^1 K^2 (w) *deest* W^1 (x) debet K^3 C^2 (y) *rubrica:* De stupro et obsidio in facto manifesto. C^2 (z) *deest* K^3 (aa) cum clamore C^3 (bb) violenciam K^2 (cc) probus K^3 (dd) mettercius W^1 (ee) pro stupro C^3 (ff) querela W^1 (gg) *rubrica:* De pacis violencia mulieris. C^2 (hh) *deest* K^1 W^1 (ii) *deest* K^3 W^1 C^2 (jj) *desunt* C^2 (kk) fregit seu K^1 K^2 (ll) in C^3 (mm) me W^1 (nn) et K^1 ut K^2 K^3 W^1 C^3 (oo) habeo et C^2 (pp) *desunt* W^1 (qq) quero C^2

debeo(ccc), et requiro in sentencia diffinitiva, quomodo (a) ipsum vincere debeam, ut michi proficiat in iure meo." Extunc ille petit satisdacionem, si vult, quam(b) sibi facere (c) opportet, et dicat se(d) de facto esse(e) innocentem. Tunc tutor(f) mulieris interroget in sentencia diffinitiva, si mulier(g) 151v violenciam melius | (h) protestare poterit cum hiis, qui clamorem suum audierunt, quam ille(i) possit evadere, cum ad iudicium ⟨in facto manifesto⟩(j) sit deductus. Tunc diffinitur ⟨de⟩(k) iure, quod possit ipsum possibilius vincere cum hiis, qui suum clamorem audierunt, quam (l) evadere possit. Et si hoc protestabitur(m), ut iuris est, adversarius collum demeretur. Idem vero(n) iudicium super irruenciam domicilii(o) iudicatur.

Articulus 52 (p)

[52] (q) Hic(r) stat Conradus(s) et conqueritur super Henricum(t) Deo et vobis, nostro domino(u), regi aut(v) duci, aut(w) vobis, domine iudex ac toti universitati civitatis(x), (y) divitibus ac(z) pauperibus, quod ipse inter(aa) municipale(bb) ven[er]it ad locum talem, ubi(cc) Conradus(dd) pace(ee) et quiete perfrui(ff) debuerat et sibi(gg) obsidium fecit in strata regia(hh), (ii) (jjet in(kk) regia pacejj), et in eo municipale(ll) infregit ac ipsum vulneravit ac destruxit ac (mm) spoliavit in(nn) corpore et (oo) rebus (pp), et in eo talem(qq) strepitum perfecit, quem bene probare potest; cum ipse (rrin eorr)(ss) pacem violavit(tt) et strepitum (uuin eouu) commisit(vv), tunc (wwpropria in personaww) vidit(xx) ipsum(yy) et (zz) ipsum clamore proclamavit(aaa). (bbbSi hocbbb)(ccc) fatetur, diligit(ddd), sin autem negabit, ipse eum vincere intendit (eeeper eoseee), qui

---

(a) eo S^{2} (b) quomodo K^{5} (c) debet seu S^{10} K^{4} (d) *deest* S^{9} (e) *deest* S^{2} K^{4} (f) *deest* S^{10} (g) femina S^{7} K^{5} (h) et citius S^{2} (i) *deest* S^{2} (j) *manus B* S^{6} in manifesto facto S^{4} S^{5} (k) *manus B* S^{6} (l) ipse S^{7} S^{8} ille K^{5} (m) probaverit S^{10} (n) *deest* S^{2} (o) dominus S^{10} domus K^{4} (p) S^{1} S^{4} S^{5} S^{6} S^{7} S^{10} K^{4} *Art. 52* S^{2} S^{3} S^{9} *Art. 54* S^{8} *Art. 51* K^{5} *Art. 57* (q) Si vir insidiatorem et K^{5} (r) Si S^{10} (s) D K^{5} *deest* S^{7} (t) A S^{7} N S^{8} H K^{5} (u) *deest* S^{4} S^{5} S^{8} (v) ac S^{8} K^{5} (w) ac K^{5} *deest* S^{2} (x) *deest* S^{10} K^{4} (y) tam S^{2} (z) quam S^{2} (aa) *deest* S^{10} (bb) nuptialem [*s*] K^{5} (cc) vir S^{7} (dd) A S^{7} N S^{8} C K^{5} (ee) pacifice S^{7} (ff) persuadi S^{10} (gg) si S^{5} (hh) *deest* S^{3} (ii) ⟦et in regia⟧ S^{6} (jj) *desunt* S^{2} (kk) *deest* S^{10} K^{4} (ll) municipali pacem S^{1} S^{3} S^{5} S^{7} mutuam pacem S^{2} meam pacem S^{4} nuptialem [*s*] pacem K^{5} (mm) ipsum S^{2} (nn) *deest* S^{4} S^{5} (oo) in S^{3} S^{4} S^{5} S^{10} K^{4} eciam in K^{5} (pp) suis S^{2} S^{7} (qq) *deest* S^{2} (rr) *desunt* S^{3} (ss) me S^{2} (tt) *deest* S^{10} (uu) *desunt* S^{2} K^{5} (vv) *deest* S^{3} (ww) in propria K^{5} (xx) vidi S^{2} (yy) *deest* S^{7} S^{8} (zz) in propria persona S^{2} S^{10} (aaa) proclamavi S^{2} (bbb) Sic S^{5} (ccc) tunc S^{2} *deest* S^{4} (ddd) *deest* S^{9} K^{4} S^{10} (eee) *desunt* S^{4} S^{5}

diffinitiva, quomodo ego ipsum(a) vincere debeam,pp) ut(b) michi (c) proficiat in(d) iure meo." Extunc(e) ille petat satisdacionem(f) {a}, si vult, quam sibi facere oportet, et dicat (g) de facto esse innocentem. Tunc tutor mulieris interrogat in sentencia diffinitiva(h), si(i) mulier violenciam melius protestare poterit cum hiis, qui clamorem suum audierunt, (j) quam ille possit evadere, cum in facto manifesto ad iudicium sit deductus. (k) Tunc diffinitur de iure, quod possit ipsum possibilius | vincere cum hiis, qui suum clamo- 39ra rem audierunt, quam (l) evadere possit. Et si(m) hoc protestabitur, ut iuris est, XIII adversarius collum demeretur. Idem vero(n) iudicium super irruenciam(o) domicilii iudicatur.

Articulus 61 (p)

[*61*] | (q) Hic stat Kunradus(r) et conqueritur super Heynricum(s) Deo et (t) 40va domino nostro(u), regi (vaut(w) duci, autv) vobis domine iudex aut(x) toti universitati civitatis, (ytam divitibus quam pauperibusy), (z) quod ipse inter(aa) municipale venerit ad locum talem, ubi (bb) Kunradus(cc) pace ac quiete perfrui(dd) debuerat et sibi obsidium(ee) fecit in strata regia pacem(ff), et in eo munici[palem](gg) pacem(hh) infregit ac ipsum vulneravit (ii) (jjac ipsum(kk) spoliavitjj) in corpore et in(ll) rebus suis(mm), et in eo talem strepitum perfecit(nn), quem bene ipse(oo) perficere(pp) potest; (qqcum (rripse(ss)qq) inrr) eo pacem violavit et in eo strepitum commisit(tt), tunc(uu) (vv) in persona propria (ww) ipsum cum(xx) clamore proclamavit. Si hoc fa|tetur, diligit, (yy) si autem 40vb

(a) *desunt* C3 (b) et C2 (c) nichil C2 (d) a C3 (e) Et tunc C2 (f) satisfaccionem K1 K2 (g) se K1 K2 K3 (h) diffinita K1 K2 (i) utrum W1 (j) tunc mulier ipsum melius vincere iure potest K3 (k) Hiis K1 K2 (l) ipse W1 ille C2 (m) *deest* K3 W1 (n) *deest* C3 (o) inquisitos W1 (p) K1 C3 *Art. 57* K2 K3 *Art. 56* W1 *Art. 55* W2 *deest folium* C1 *Art. 61* C2 *Art. 60* (q) Quomodo conqueratur super insidiatorem, ut dicit. W1 Si conqueritur super insidiatorem et dicit. C3 ⟨Insidiator⟩ C3 (r) N K3 W1 C3 (s) P K3 hoc W1 N C3 (t) vobis K1 K2 K3 (u) meo K1 K2 C3 (v) et C3 (w) ac W1 (x) ac K3 W1 C3 (y) pauperibus ac divitibus K3 (z) ac terre C3 (aa) intra K1 K2 (bb) ipse K2 (cc) N K3 W1 C3 (dd) frui C2 (ee) insidium [*s*] W1 (ff) in regia pace K3 et in pace regia W1 C3 *deest* K1 K2 (gg) *deest* C2 (hh) *deest* K2 K3 W1 (ii) ac destruxit K1 K2 K3 (jj) *desunt* W1 (kk) *deest* K3 (ll) *deest* W1 (mm) *deest* K3 W1 (nn) fecit K2 (oo) *deest* K1 K2 K3 C3 (pp) probare K3 protestare W1 ostendere C3 (qq) et C3 (rr) *desunt* K1 (ss) *desunt* K2 (tt) permisit C3 (uu) cum K1 K2 (vv) vidit W1 C3 (ww) vidit et K3 (xx) et ipsum W1 et C3 *deest* K1 K2 K3 (yy) ⟨et qui in legibus⟩ C3

{a} idem gwar C2

suum clamorem audierunt [(a]ac suo testimonio[a)]. Et sicut eum[(b)] [(c)]in manifesto facto deduxit [(d]ad iudicium[d)], sic[(e)] in sentencia requirit, quomodo ipsum vincere debeat, ut[(f)] sibi proficuum sit in suo iure.

Articulus 53 [(g)]

[*53*] [(h]Si vir[h)] vulneratus ad iudicium [(i]cum clamore[i)] decuctus fuerit [(j]in[(k)]
152ʳ facto manifesto, et | si[(l)] ita [(m]inbecillis aut[m)][(n)] debilis fuerit[j)], quod[(o)] per tutorem[(p)] ipsum querulari opportet et prolocutorem[(q)] per sentenciam[(r)] petat, extunc tali modo sua[(s)] procedat querimonia: "Domine iudex ⟨et domini scabini⟩[(t)], si me huic vulnerato dedistis pro advocato, extunc in sentencia requiro, si per[(u)] iusticiam[(v)] insidias per[(w)] aliquem pati debeam, [(x]quam iure tereri[(y)] [*s*] debeam[x)] aut sustinere, cum [(z)] suam [(aa)] causam propter iuris[(bb)] exigenciam teneo." [(cc]Extunc sibi[(dd)] diffinitur[(ee)], quod non [(ff)]. Extunc sibi petat correccionem. Cum obtinuerit [(gg]correccionem[(hh)],[cc)] tunc[gg)] petat colloqium [(ii]pro consilio[ii)]. Et cum colloquium[(jj)] habuerit, [(kk)] tunc requirat, qualiter suam[(ll)] [(mm)] inchoare[(nn)] debeat ⟨querimoniam⟩[(oo)], et hoc[(pp)] per sentenciam diffinitivam, ut sibi proficiat in suo iure. Extunc[(qq)] diffinitur ⟨sibi⟩[(rr)] cum clamore. Tunc interrogetur sentencialiter[(ss)], si requiri debeat de[(tt)] ore [(uu)] ad[(vv)] os, a quo suam habeat lesionem. Tunc sibi diffinitur, quod debeat. Extunc emittuntur duo scabini et cum[(ww)] ipsis preco, aut[(xx)] duo viri, qui iudicio astare consueverunt, qui ab[(yy)] ipso solo audiant, a quo sua receperit vel habuerit dampna[(zz)], aut quis in eo pacis federa confregerit. {a} Extunc requiritur sentencialiter[(aaa)], si[(bbb)] requiri[(ccc)]

(a) *desunt* S^2 (b) ipsum captum K^5 *deest* S^4 S^5 (c) captivum S^7 S^8 (d) *desunt* S^3 (e) *deest* S^{10} K^4 (f) et K^5 (g) S^1 S^4 S^5 S^6 S^7 S^{10} K^4 *Art. 53* S^2 S^3 *Art. 55* S^9 *Art. 56* S^8 *Art. 52* K^5 *Art. 58* (h) Ubi S^3 Si K^5 (i) *desunt* S^2 (j) *desunt* S^3 (k) *deest* S^{10} (l) *deest* S^2 S^{10} (m) *desunt* S^4 S^5 (n) et S^2 (o) ut S^2 *deest* S^{10} (p) prolocutorem S^3 (q) *deest* S^3 (r) suam S^7 (s) sic S^2 (t) *manus B* S^6 (u) propter S^7 (v) iustas K^4 (w) *deest* S^2 (x) *desunt* S^2 S^3 S^9 S^{10} (y) teneri S^2 S^3 S^5 S^7 S^9 S^{10} K^4 terrestri S^4 ⊢terreri⊣ ⟨tenere⟩ S^8 terreni K^5 (z) verbum S^4 S^5 (aa) aut S^4 S^5 (bb) talis facti S^2 (cc) *desunt* K^5 (dd) *deest* S^3 (ee) *a.c* finitur, *correctio manus B* S^6 (ff) ⟨ut si ipsum in aliquo neglexerit, quod se contingere poterit per se ispum aut alium⟩ S^8 (gg) *desunt* S^3 (hh) *deest* S^2 S^4 S^5 S^8 hoc S^7 (ii) *desunt* S^{10} K^4 (jj) *deest* S^{10} (kk) pro consilio S^4 S^5 (ll) *deest* K^4 (mm) querelam S^2 S^3 S^7 S^8 S^9 causam S^{10} K^5 (nn) incipere S^4 (oo) *manus B* S^6 (pp) *deest* S^{10} K^4 (qq) Ex⟨tunc⟩ S^1 (rr) *manus B* S^6 sibi S^2 S^4 S^5 S^7 S^8 K^5 non S^9 (ss) finaliter S^9 (tt) ab S^2 S^3 S^4 S^5 S^8 ex S^9 (uu) suo S^{10} (vv) et K^4 (ww) *deest* K^4 K^5 (xx) ut S^4 et S^5 (yy) *deest* S^{10} (zz) suam lesionem S^2 (aaa) finaliter S^9 (bbb) *deest* K^4 S^{10} (ccc) interrogari S^2 S^3 S^4 S^5 S^7 S^8 K^5

{a} ⟨Federa pacis vel firmatam pacem vulgariter u c z y w y e r d z o n ý m ý r⟩ K^5

negabit, ipse eum vincere intendit(a) per hos, qui(b) suum clamorem(c) audierunt ac suo testimonio. Et(d) sicut ipsum (e) in(f) manifesto facto (g) deduxit ad iudicium, sic in(h) sentencia requirit, quomodo ipsum vincere debeat, ut sibi(i) proficuum sit in suo iure. (jEt sic diffinitur cum clamore metseptimus eum vincere debet.j)

Articulus 59 (k)

[*59*] | (l) Si vulneratus vir ad iudicium deductus fuerit cum clamore in facto manifesto, et(m) si ita (ninbecillis autn) debilis fuerit, quod(o) per tutorem (p) querulari oportet et prolocutorem per(q) sentenciam petat, extunc tali modo procedat sua querimonia: “Domine iudex, si me huic vulnerato dedistis pro advocato, extunc in sentencia requiro [et] si(r) per(s) iusticiam(t) insidias per aliquam pati debeam, | quas iure tenere debeam aut sustinere, cum suam causam propter(u) iuris exigenciam teneo.” Extunc sibi diffinitur, quod non, extunc sibi(v) petat correccionem. Cum (w) obtinuerit, tunc petat colloquium pro consilio. Extunc cum(x) colloquium habuerit, tunc requirat, qualiter suam (y) querelam inchoare debeat, et hoc per sentenciam diffinitivam, ut sibi proficiat in suo iure. Extunc diffinitur sibi cum clamore. Tunc interrogetur (zper sentenciam (aaseuz) sentencialiteraa), si requiri debeat ab ore ad os, a quo suam habeat lesionem. Tunc sibi diffinitur, quod debeat. Extunc emittuntur duo scabini et (bbcum ipsis bb)preco, aut duo viri, qui in(cc) iudicio astare consueverunt, qui ab ipso solo audiant, a(dd) quo suam (eereceperit autee) habuerit lesionem, vel quis(ff) in eo pacis federa infregerit. Extunc requiritur(gg) sentencialiter, ut(hh) interrogari debeant circa(ii) iuramentum

39rb 39va

(a) vult C3 (b) *deest* C3 (c) *deest* C3 (d) ut W1 (e) captivum K3 (f) *deest* K1 K2 (g) hoc C3 (h) *deest* K3 (i) fieri K3 (j) tunc diffinitur metseptimus W1 *desunt* K1 K2 K3 C2 C3 (k) K1 K3 C3 *Art. 55* K2 *Art. 54* W1 *Art. 53* W2 *deest folium* C1 *Art. 59* C2 *Art. 57–58* (l) ⟨vulneratus⟩ C3 (m) ut W1 (n) *desunt* W1 C3 (o) *deest* C2 (p) ipsum K1 K2 K3 W1 C2 C3 (q) *deest* C3 (r) qui K3 (s) *deest* K1 (t) sententiam K3 (u) per C2 (v) *deest* W1 (w) hanc W1 (x) non W1 *deest* C3 (y) causam vel C3 (z) *desunt* W1 (aa) *desunt* C3 (bb) *desunt* C2 (cc) *deest* K3 (dd) *deest* C2 (ee) *deest* K1 K2 W1 C3 (ff) qui K1 K2 quia C2 *deest* K3 (gg) queratur K3 (hh) si K1 K2 K3 W1 C3 (ii) tunc W1

debeant (a) circa iuramentum prestitum aut(b) ius civitatis, quid ab eo audie-
rint. (cAudita responsiva (d), tunc (e⟨unus interrogetur ad dicendum, quid ab eo audie-
rint, tunc⟩e)c) in sentencia requiratur, (fsi iam(g) profeceritf)(h) ⟨seu perfectus
est⟩(i), (jcum(k) sibi diffinitur, quod sic(l). Et eciam secundus et tercius interro-
getur, extunc sibi diffinitur, quod (m) profecerit(n). Extunc querelam(o) inci-
152^{v} piat: "Domine | iudex ⟨et domini scabini⟩(p), (q) placeat j)attente audire. Tunc
hic conqueritur (r) super virum(s) •N•(t) et super (u) •N•(v), quod ipsi vene-
runt intra municipale et in eo pacem infregerunt, et ipsum vulneraverunt
aut suum affinem proximum(w) (x) trucidaverunt, si homicidium fuerit, et
ipsum spoliaverunt corpore et rebus, et pro eo iudicium petit." Extunc illi(y)
ter(z) vocantur. Quando(aa) ⟨vero⟩(bb) vocati(cc) per clamorem ter(dd) fuerint,
tunc conqueratur ulterius et nominent malefactores, ut prius querulatum
fuerit. Idem faciat tercia vice. Extunc inducie {a} indicentur(ee) per noctem.
Si tunc non comparent, describentur(ff). Sin autem comparent, duellum in
eis acquiri potest.

Articulus 54 (gg)

[*54*] Quando vir furem aut spoliatorem protestare voluerit, qui cum (hh) manifesto facto ad iudicium (iicum clamoreii) [d]eductus fuerit, qui conqueritur sic(jj): "Domine iudex, (kk) conqueror(ll) Deo et vobis super meum furem, quem cum (mmapparenti furtumm) captivavi et ligatum ad iudicium usque(nn) perduxi(oo), quod venit intra meos quat[t]uor(pp) angulos et subtraxit michi(qq) mea bona, super quo bonum habeo testimonium cum(rr)

(a) interrogari debeat S^{9} (b) ac S^{1} S^{3} S^{4} S^{5} S^{7} S^{8} K^{5} (c) Tunc unus interrogetur ad dicendum, quid ab eo audierint. Audita responsiva, tunc S^{1} S^{3} S^{4} S^{5} S^{7} S^{9} K^{4} K^{5} Tunc unus interrogetur ad dicendum, quid ab eo audierint. Audita sentencia responsiva, tunc S^{2} Tunc unus interrogetur ad dicendum, quid ab eo audierint. Audita responsiva ⟨sua⟩, tunc S^{8} (d) ⟨sua⟩ S^{8} (e) *manus B* S^{6} (f) quod fecerit S^{4} S^{5} (g) *deest* K^{4} (h) proferat S^{3} perfecerit K^{5} (i) *manus B* S^{6} (j) deinde S^{2} (k) tunc S^{7} S^{9} S^{8} (l) sit S^{3} (m) sic S^{4} S^{5} sibi K^{5} (n) perfecerit S^{8} S^{10} (o) querimoniam K^{5} (p) *manus B* S^{6} (q) si S^{5} (r) rebus S^{2} vobis S^{3} N K^{5} (s) unum S^{2} S^{3} S^{5} S^{8} K^{4} *deest* S^{9} (t) T K^{5} (u) unum S^{8} (v) Henricum S^{2} P K^{5} (w) *deest* S^{8} (x) pervicum K^{5} (y) *deest* S^{2} (z) tibi S^{3} (aa) quoniam S^{7} (bb) *manus B* S^{6} tibi S^{3} (cc) citati S^{2} (dd) *deest* S^{3} S^{8} (ee) *a.c.* indicantur S^{6} inducantur S^{2} iudicantur S^{7} (ff) proscribentur S^{2} *p.c.* proscribentur, *correctio manus B* S^{6} (gg) S^{1} S^{4} S^{5} S^{6} S^{7} S^{10} *Art. 54* S^{2} S^{3} K^{4} *Art. 56* S^{9} *Art. 57* S^{8} *Art. 53* K^{5} *Art. 59* (hh) in S^{9} (ii) *desunt* S^{3} S^{4} S^{5} (jj) *deest* S^{2} (kk) ego K^{4} (ll) *deest* S^{7} (mm) apprehendi in furto S^{10} (nn) *deest* S^{9} (oo) deduxi S^{2} S^{3} (pp) *deest* K^{5} (qq) *deest* S^{4} S^{9} (rr) in S^{7}

{a} vulgariter r o k ÿ K^{4}

prestitum aut ius civitatis, quid ab eo audiverunt(a). Tunc unus interrogetur a[d] dicendum, quid ab eo audierunt. Audita responsiva(b) sua, tunc in(c) sentencia requiritur, (dsi(e iam profecerit, cum sibi diffiniturd), quod sic. (f) Eciam(g) interrogetur, (h(iextunce) sibi diffinitur,i) quod sic(j) profeceriteh) secundus et tertius. Deinde querela[m] incipit sic(k): "(lDomine iudex, placeat(m) attente audire.l) Tunc hic N conqueritur(n) (o) vobis(p) super (qunum N (ret Nq), quodr) ipsi venerunt intra unum(s) municipale, et pacem | 39vb in eo fregerunt(t), et ipsum vulneraverunt aut suum affinem proximum(u) trucidaverunt(v), si homicidium fuerit, et spoliaverunt ipsum(w) (x) corpore et rebus, et pro eo iudicium petit." Extunc (yilli tery) vocantur. Quando ter(z) vocati(aa) per(bb) clamorem fuerint, tunc conqueratur ulterius et nominet malefactores, ut prius querulatum fuit. Idem facit tercia vice. (cc) Extunc inducie (dd) indicantur(ee) per noctem. Si tunc non conparent, (ffproscribentur(gg). Si autem conpareantff), duellum in eis acquiri potest.

Articulus 60 (hh)

[*60*] | 40rb Quando vir furem aut spoliatorem protestare voluerit, qui cum manifesto facto ad iudicium cum clamore productus(ii) fuerit, qui(jj) (kk) con- XIIII queratur(ll): "Domine iudex, conqueror Deo et vobis super meum furem, quem cum apparenti furto captivatum et ligatum ad iudicium usque(mm) deduxi(nn), quod (oo) venit intra meos quat[t]uor angulos(pp) et subtraxit in(qq) mea bona, super quo bonum habeo testimonium cum aliis, qui meum

(a) audivit vel audiverit W[1] (b) responsione K[1] K[2] (c) *deest* K[1] K[2] (d) *desunt* W[1] (e) sentencia profecit, cum K[1] K[2] (f) extunc K[3] (g) et sic W[1] (h) *desunt* W[1] (i) *desunt* K[3] (j) *deest* C[3] (k) sic dominus C[2] *deest* K[1] K[2] K[3] W[1] C[3] (l) multis audire verba huiusdem attente K[3] (m) *deest* C[3] (n) requiritur K[1] K[2] (o) Deo et K[3] (p) *deest* W[1] (q) S et V K[1] K[2] N et P K[3] unum N et T C[2] P D R W[1] (r) et si C[3] (s) *deest* K[1] K[2] K[3] W[1] (t) infregerunt K[1] K[2] K[3] W[1] C[3] (u) *deest* W[1] (v) occiderunt W[1] (w) cum K[1] K[2] (x) in W[1] (y) tribus K[1] (z) vero W[1] ubi C[3] (aa) citati ipsi W[1] (bb) *deest* K[1] K[2] (cc) *rubrica:* De induciis, que pernoctaverit. C[2] (dd) illis W[1] (ee) inducentur W[1] durant C[2] (ff) *deest* K[3] (gg) perscribentur W[1] (hh) K[3] *Art. 57* W[1] *Art. 54* W[2] *deest folium* C[1] *Art. 60* C[2] *Art. 59* C[3] *Art. 56* (ii) deductus K[3] W[1] (jj) sic hic W[1] (kk) ita K[3] sic C[3] (ll) querulatur K[3] (mm) huc C[3] (nn) adduxi K[3] (oo) ipse C[3] (pp) parietes K[3] (qq) michi K[3] W[1] C[2] hiis, qui meum clamorem audierunt, et ipsum vincere(a) volo(b) (c) iure meo ac meo(d) testimonio, ut (e) hic(f) michi(g) ius dictaverit. Et requiro ⟨in sentencia⟩(h), quomodo ipsum vincere debeam, ut michi proficiat in iure meo." ([i]Tunc sibi[i]) diffinitur metseptimus, si(j) furtum presens(k) fuerit. Idem iudicium fiat(l) pro spolio et super raptorem.

Articulus 55 (m)

153r [*55*] | Ubi(n) vir alterius verbum loqui debet, ad(o) quod sentenciis scabinorum vel iure compellitur in facto manifesto, dicat sic: "Domine iudex, me dedistis illi homini prolocutorem, extunc requiro in sentencia, si ab aliquo pro eo ([p]inimicicias ([q]aut timorem[p]) habere[q]) debeam, quod verbum suum pro iuris loquar exigencia quantum melius possum ([r]aut valeo[r])." Quando sibi(s) hoc diffinitum fuerit, tunc sibi diffiniat correccionem, quod si ipsum in aliquo neglexerit, quod (t) se corrigere(u) poterit mecum, aut per me, aut(v) (w) alterum advocatum. ([x]Cum sibi hoc diffinitum[x]) fuerit, petit colloquium, si vult, et requirat in sentencia, quando querelam inchoare debeat, ut sibi proficiat in suo iure. Cum (y) hoc diffinitum fuerit, tunc in sentencia interroget, si(z) lesus interrogari debeat(aa), quis in eo pacem infregerit, etsi ita fuerit debilis, (bb) quod suum malefactorem nominare non possit. Cum(cc) igitur hoc diffinitum fuerit et ipsum(dd) iudex aut duo scabini aut duo viri, qui iudicio astare viderint consueti(ee), requirat in sentencia, si ipsi causa iusticie dicere(ff) debeant(gg) circa iuramentum ipsorum et ius civitatis, quod notum(hh) ipsis de hoc(ii) facto sit. Cum hoc(jj) sibi(kk) diffinitur ([ll]ab uno[ll]) ad secundum et tercium, extunc requirat in sentencia (mm), si iam profecerit. Cum sibi hoc(nn) diffinitum fuerit et pacis violator citatus per clamorem fuerit, ut iuris est, extunc dicat sibi(oo): "Domine iudex, placeat
153v audire verbum suum. Tunc(pp) conqueritur vobis(qq) super hunc | N(rr), quod

(a) *deest* S^{10} (b) *deest* K^{5} (c) in S^{5} (d) vero S^{9} (e) his S^{1} (f) *deest* S^{8} S^{10} (g) *deest* K^{5} (h) *manus B* S^{6} (i) Et sic S^{10} K^{4} (j) *deest* S^{5} (k) prius K^{5} (l) *deest* S^{4} S^{5} (m) S^{1} S^{4} S^{5} S^{6} S^{10} K^{2} K^{4} *Art. 55* S^{2} *articulus deest* S^{3} *Art. 57* S^{8} *Art. 54* S^{9} *Art. 58* K^{1} *Art. 56* K^{5} *Art. 60* (n) Qui K^{1} (o) et S^{8} S^{9} K^{1} K^{2} K^{5} (p) nunciam K^{5} (q) ac amorem hic S^{3} (r) a valore [*s*] K^{5} (s) *a.c.* si, *correctio manus B* S^{6} *deest* S^{3} S^{4} S^{5} S^{8} (t) in S^{4} a S^{5} (u) negligere S^{4} S^{5} (v) *deest* S^{4} S^{5} (w) per S^{10} K^{4} K^{5} (x) *desunt* S^{10} (y) sibi S^{1} S^{3} S^{4} S^{5} S^{8} S^{9} S^{10} K^{1} K^{2} K^{4} K^{5} (z) sit K^{5} (aa) *deest* S^{3} (bb) ⊦fuerit⊣ S^{6} (cc) Quando S^{5} (dd) sibi S^{3} (ee) solent S^{1} S^{3} S^{4} S^{5} S^{8} S^{9} S^{10} K^{1} K^{2} K^{4} K^{5} (ff) *deest* S^{10} K^{1} K^{2} (gg) *deest* K^{1} K^{2} (hh) notorium S^{1} S^{3} S^{4} S^{5} S^{8} S^{10} K^{1} K^{2} K^{4} K^{5} sibi notorium S^{9} (ii) *deest* S^{9} K^{1} K^{2} (jj) *deest* S^{3} (kk) ipsi S^{3} S^{4} S^{5} S^{8} (ll) *desunt* S^{4} S^{5} (mm) sua K^{5} (nn) *deest* K^{1} K^{2} (oo) *deest* S^{1} S^{3} S^{4} S^{5} S^{8} S^{10} K^{1} K^{2} K^{4} (pp) Quod S^{5} Hic N S^{9} (qq) *deest* S^{9} (rr) Mathiam S^{9} P K^{1}

clamorem audierunt, et ipsum volo vincere iure meo ac meo testimonio, ut ([a]hic michi[a]) ius dictaverit. Et requiro(b) (c), quomodo ipsum vincere debeam, ut michi proficiat in iure meo." Tunc sibi diffinitur metseptimus, (d) si furtum presens fuerit. ([e]Idem iudicium fiat ([f]pro spolio et[e]) super raptorem[f]).

[*articulus deest*]

(a) *desunt* W[1] (b) quero C[2] (c) in sentencia W[1] sentencialiter sciscitando C[3] (d) et hoc C[3]
(e) Et ad querela transsit C[3] (f) cum spoliatore W[1]

ipsum in (astrata liberaa) infestavit ac(b) intra municipalia(c) in eo pacem infregit, ac ipsum vulneravit et violenciam in eo peregit, quam(d) probando ostendere potest, et ipsum depredavit corpore et rebus, et tantum(e) recepit sibi, quod non(f) minus valeat, nisi bene(g) duellum mereatur. Et super eo a vobis iustum(h) petit(i) iudicium." Extunc pacis violator(j) proclamatur primo et secundo et tertio, per nomen suum, •N• (k), et iterum suam querimoniam renovet in hunc modum: "(l) Vobis conqueritur super ⟨virum⟩(m) •N• (n), quod ipse venit intra municipale in strata regia, in eo Dei(o) pacem infringendo, et ipsum rebus et corpore sanitatis depredavit ac ipsum vulneravit et in eo(p) strepitum fecit, quam(q) apparenter(r) potest demonstrare." Et pro eo petit iudicium, et sic tercia vice faciat. Tunc ostendet vulnus et interroget in sentencia diffinitiva(s), si(t) suum pacis violatorem in aliquo loco invenerit, si ipsum licite arestare possit ex parte(u) iudicii(v). Cum igitur (w) fuerit(x) diffinitum, tunc petat pacem, qui(y) [*s*] sibi indici debet.

Articulus 56 (z)

[*56*] Qui(aa) monomochaliter suum equalem salutare seu alloqui voluerit, hunc iudicem petere opportebit, ut se intromittere possit de uno suo(bb) pacis violatore, quem videat in presenti. Cum hoc sibi per sentenciam diffinitum fuerit(cc), tunc eciam in | 154r sentencia requirat, per quem modum se(dd) (eede ipsoee) intromittere debeat, ut sibi in suo iure proficere possit. Tunc sibi de iure diffinitur, curialiter(ff) ⟨criminaliter per finum et⟩(gg) per oram vestimenti(hh). Et cum se de ipso (iiintromittat, pronunciet sibi causam, pro qua se de ipsoii) intromiserit, quod statim(jj) facere (kkpotestkk), si vult, aut pro eo habere colloquium. Tunc ipsum inculpare opportebit, quod pacem in eo infregerit (llaut in strata regia, aut in villa(mm), qualiter(nn) infregeritll), eodem modo(oo) queruletur super eum. Tunc ipsum iterum inculpet, quod ipsum

(a) *desunt* S^3 (b) aut S^9 hanc K^5 (c) nupcialia [*s*] K^5 (d) nam K^5 (e) tamen S^{10} enim K^5 (f) sibi K^5 (g) *deest* S^3 K^5 (h) *deest* S^3 (i) *deest* K^1 (j) spoliator K^5 (k) vel •P• K^1 (l) Domine iudex S^3 K^5 (m) virum S^1 S^3 S^4 S^5 S^9 S^{10} K^1 K^2 K^4 K^5 unum S^8 (n) vel •P• K^1 P K^5 (o) *deest* S^4 S^5 S^9 die C^3 (p) *deest* K^4 (q) quem S^8 S^9 K^5 quasi K^1 K^2 (r) a proprio talis K^1 a proprio taliter K^2 (s) *deest* K^1 K^2 (t) *deest* S^8 (u) *deest* S^4 S^5 (v) gladii K^1 K^2 (w) hoc S^3 S^4 S^5 S^8 (x) *deest* S^3 (y) que S^4 S^5 S^8 S^9 S^{10} K^1 K^2 K^4 K^5 (z) S^1 S^4 S^5 S^6 S^{10} K^4 *Art. 56* S^2 *Art. 57* S^3 *Art. 58* S^9 *Art. 59* S^8 *Art. 55* K^5 *Art. 61* (aa) Si S^{10} (bb) ⟨suo⟩ S^1 *deest* S^{10} (cc) *deest* S^4 (dd) *deest* K^4 S^{10} (ee) *desunt* S^2 (ff) criminaliter K^5 (gg) *manus B* S^6 (hh) *p.c.* vestimenta sua, *correctio manus B* S^6 (ii) *desunt* S^2 K^5 (jj) factum K^5 (kk) ⟨potest⟩ K^2 (ll) *desunt* S^2 (mm) via K^5 (nn) quantum S^3 (oo) *deest* S^{10}

Articulus 63 (a)

[63] | ⟨Qui monomachaliter suum et etc.⟩(b) Qui monomochaliter(c) suum equalem (d(esalutare seud) alloqui voluerite), hunc iudicem petere oportebit, ut se intromittere possit de uno suo(f) pacis violatore, quem (gvideat in presentig). Cum hoc per sentenciam diffinitum fuerit, tunc(h) eciam in sentencia (i) requirat, per quem modum se de ipso intromittere debeat, ut sibi in suo(j) iure (kproficere possitk). Tunc sibi (lde iurel) diffinitur, curialiter (mper horam vestimentim)(n). Et cum de ipso se intromittat, pronunciat sibi causam, pro qua se de ipso intromiserit, quod statim facere(o) potest, si vult, aut pro eo habere colloquium. Tunc ipsum inculpare oportebit, quod in eo pacem infregerit aut in strata regia, aut in villa, qualiter(p) infregerit, eodem modo super eum queruletur(q). Tunc ipsum iterum inculpet, quod ipsum 41rb

(a) K^1 K^3 C^3 *Art. 59* K^2 *Art. 58* W^1 *articulus deest* W^2 *folium deest* C^1 *Art. 63* C^2 *Art. 62–63* (b) *manus α* C^1 (c) duellarie K^3 (d) *desunt* C^2 C^3 (e) salutaverit K^3 (f) *deest* C^2 (g) ibi videt C^2 (h) cum K^1 K^2 (i) requiratur aut C^2 (j) *deest* K^3 (k) proficiat K^3 (l) *deest* K^2 (m) *deest* C^2 (n) *in ms.* resti[men]ci C^1 (o) *deest* K^3 (p) equaliter C^2 (q) conqueritur C^2

depredavit(a) et eam vim(b) in eo fecerit(c), quam bene (d) probare(e) poterit. Tunc (f) vulnus(g) aut(h) cicatricem demonstret, si vulnus sanatum fuerit. Tunc ulterius conqueratur, (iquod ipsum spoliaverit bonis suis et de ipsis (jsibi tantaj) receperit(k) ⟨quod nichil peius⟩(l), quod bene duellum meretur(m). Hec tria criminalia(n) facta omnia simul conquerantur i), de quoqumque horum trium(o) (pde unop) obliviscitur aut tacuerit, extunc suum duellum ammisit. Tunc loquatur ulterius: "Tunc ipsum solum, hoc(q) est(r) in persona propria, ⟨ipsum solum vidi, hoc est in persona propria⟩ ⟨vidi⟩(s) et ipsum clamore(t) proclamavi. Si fateri voluerit, quod(u) diligo(v), et si non fatebitur, (w) ipsum omni(x) iure vincere volo, ut michi vulgus iudicaverit, aut scabini, (ysi sub banno regio fuerity)." Extunc ille petat satisdacionem, (zquam sibi facere debet. Tamen vir potest suam querimoniam(aa) meliorare ante(bb) satisdacionemz), si voluerit. Facta ⟨aut⟩(cc) satisdacione, ille exhebebat [s] ⟨ostendat⟩(dd) suam innocenciam, hoc est iuramentum, quod ipsum iurare 154v opportet, et iuramentum(ee) | monomochale, si(ff) ipsum iure(gg) incitaverit (hhet si ibi fuerit, hoc esthh), perficere si(ii) potuerit pre inbecillitate sui corporis.(jj) (kkQuivis(ll) vir potest se(mm) a duello excusare illi viro, qui sibi paris condicionis non fueritkk) ⟨in natura⟩(nn). Ille autem, qui(oo) nobilioris(pp) nature fuerit, (qqille preesse(rr) non potest (ss), qui deterioris nature fueritqq), si ipsum alloquetur (tt). (uu) A duello eciam(vv) cedere(ww) (xx) potest, qui post meridiem allocutus fuerit, nisi ante meridiem esset (yy) inchoatum(zz). (aaa) Iudex eciam habere(bbb) debet clipeum(ccc) et gladium illi, super quem allocutum fuerit. (ddd) A duello eciam potest accipere(eee) (fff) suos ⟨capitulum de

(a) damnavit S^{10} (b) dum S^{4} (c) infregit K^{5} (d) in eo K^{4} S^{10} (e) protestari S^{2} (f) aut S^{2} (g) ⟨vulnus⟩ S^{4} (h) ac S^{10} (i) *desunt* S^{10} (j) tantum S^{2} (k) facerit S^{4} (l) *manus B* S^{6} (m) detur S^{4} *p.c.* demeretur, *correctio manus B* S^{6} (n) anumeralia [*s*] K^{5} (o) *deest* K^{5} (p) *desunt* S^{2} (q) *deest* S^{2} K^{4} (r) *deest* S^{2} K^{5} (s) *manus B* S^{6} vidi S^{2} ipsum solum vidi, hoc est in persona propria S^{3} S^{10} K^{4} (t) *deest* S^{4} (u) *deest* S^{2} S^{10} (v) duellum S^{4} *deest* S^{10} (w) michi S^{3} (x) cum S^{3} (y) *desunt* S^{2} (z) *desunt* S^{2} (aa) querelam S^{8} (bb) aut K^{5} (cc) *manus B* S^{6} (dd) *a.c.* exhebebat, *correctio manus B* S^{6} exhibeat S^{1} S^{2} S^{3} S^{4} S^{5} S^{8} S^{9} S^{10} K^{4} K^{5} (ee) manifestum S^{4} (ff) *deest* S^{10} K^{4} (gg) iurare K^{4} *deest* S^{10} (hh) *desunt* S^{2} (ii) *desunt* S^{2} (jj) ⟨Quilibet cum im pari non habet duellum⟩ K^{5} (kk) Si S^{9} (ll) Quis S^{10} (mm) *deest* K^{5} (nn) *manus B* S^{6} (oo) *deest* S^{10} (pp) melioris S^{2} (qq) *desunt* S^{10} (rr) posse K^{5} (ss) illi S^{2} (tt) nobiliorum nature S^{9} (uu) ⟨Qui cedit a duello⟩ K^{5} (vv) *deest* S^{2} S^{9} *a.c.* eum, *correctio manus commentatoris* S^{8} (ww) *deest* S^{10} (xx) non S^{9} (yy) ⟨inchoatum aut⟩ S^{8} (zz) inculpatum S^{8} (aaa) ⟨Quando debet iudex habere ad duellum⟩ K^{5} (bbb) dare S^{2} (ccc) duellum S^{4} (ddd) A duello excusare illi viro, qui sibi paris condicionis non fuerit. Ille autem nobilioris nature fuerit, ille preesse non potest [illi], qui deterioris nature fuerit, si ipsum alloquetur. A duello eciam potest, qui post meridiem allocutus fuerit, nisi ante meridiam [*s*] fuerit inchoatum, iudex eciam debet habere clipeum et gladium illi, super quem allocutum fuerit. S^{10} (eee) excipere S^{2} S^{3} S^{9} S^{10} K^{4} (fff) vir S^{2} homo K^{5}

depredaverit et eam(a) vim in eo fecerit, quam bene probare poterit. Tunc vulneratus(b) cicatricem demonstrat, si vulnus sit sanatum. Tunc ulterius conqueratur, quod ipsum spoliaverit (cbonis suis etc) de(d) ipsis (e) tanta receperit, quod bene duellum | (f) meretur. Hec tria criminalia facta omnia 41va
demeretur(g) simul, de quocumque horum(h) trium (ide uno obliviscitur aut tacuiti), extunc suum duellum(j) amisit. Tunc(k) loquatur ulterius: "Tunc(l) ipsum solum, (mhoc (n) in persona propria (o) etm) ipsum proclamavi clamore. Si fateri(p) voluerit, quod(q) diligit, et si (rnon fatebiturr), ipsum(s) omni iure vincere volo, ut michi vulgus(t) iudicaverit(u), aut scabini, si sub banno(v) regio fuerit." Extunc ille petat satisfaccionem(w), quam sibi facere debet. (x) Tamen(y) vir potest suam querimoniam meliorare ante satisfaccionem(z), si voluerit. Facta satisdacione(aa) ille suam exhibeat innocenciam, hoc est(bb) iuramentum monomachale(cc), si(dd) ipsum (eeiure incitaverit et si hoc(ff) fuerit, (ggibi(hh) estgg)(ii), si perficere (jj) potuerit pro inbecillitate sui corporisee). (kk) Quivis vir potest(ll) se a duello excusare (mm) illi viro, qui sibi paris condicionis non fuerit. Ille autem, qui nobilioris nature(nn) fuerit, (ooille preesse non potest [illi], qui deterioris nature(pp) fuerit,oo) si(qq) ipsum alloquitur. A duello eciam cedere(rr) potest, qui post meridiem allocutus fuerit, nisi ante meridiem esset inchoatum, iudex autem eciam habere debet clipeum (ss) illi, super quem allocutum fuerit. (ttA duello eciam excipere(uu)

(a) talem K^3 (b) *in ms.* vulnus C^1 (c) nomine, sive K^1 K^2 (d) *deest* K^3 (e) sibi K^3 (f) dici K^3 (g) conqueratur K^1 K^2 K^3 C^3 (h) *deest* C^3 (i) obtinuerit K^3 (j) *deest* K^3 (k) Cum K^1 K^2 (l) ego ipse K^3 (m) vidi K^3 (n) est K^1 K^2 C^3 (o) viderit K^1 K^2 (p) facere K^1 (q) hoc K^3 (r) noluerit K^3 (s) cum K^1 K^2 tunc ipsum K^3 (t) vulnere K^1 K^2 (u) hic diffinierit K^3 (v) banito C^2 (w) satisdacionem K^3 C^2 C^3 (x) *rubrica:* De paupere, qui suam querimoniam meliorare potest ante satisdacionem. C^2 (y) Pauper C^2 (z) satisdacionem K^3 C^2 C^3 (aa) satisfaccione K^1 K^2 (bb) *deest* K^3 C^2 (cc) quod ipsum iurare oportet et iuramentum monomachale K^3 C^2 *deest* C^3 (dd) quod C^3 (ee) iurare oportet C^3 (ff) ibi K^3 (gg) *desunt* C^2 (hh) hoc K^3 (ii) *desunt* K^2 (jj) non K^2 (kk) ⟨Regula⟩ C^3 (ll) deest K^1 (mm) ⟨de duello quomodo sit⟩ C^3 (nn) *deest* C^3 (oo) *desunt* K^1 K^2 (pp) *deest* C^3 (qq) *deest* C^3 (rr) se excusare C^3 (ss) ac gladium C^3 (tt) Item duobus congre[g]atis potest quivis prohibere duellum, dummodo iuret metseptimus, eos ita vicinos [esse], quod de iure non debent monomachale inire. C^3 (uu) accipere K^3

duello⟩(a) affines ⟨seu nepotes⟩(b), si uterque suus affinis ⟨fuerit⟩(c) et ita(d) consanguineitatis linea coniuncti (e) fuerint, quod(f) simul pugnare(g) non poterint. Iudex eciam duos nuncios dare(h) debet cuilibet hiis, qui pugnare debent, qui videant, ut(i) habeant attinencia secundum veram consuetudinem. (j) {a} Coreum(k) et linea ⟨vestimenta vel⟩(l) indumentum induere possunt(m), quantum placet, caput et pedes antea nudi sint, in manibus cirotecas habeant. Unum gladium (nnudum(o) in manun) (pet alio cinctus, aut duobus, hocp) arbitrio eorum committitur(q), et unum clippeum rotundum (rin manur), ubi non aliud, quam(s) lignum aut coreum sit, preter(t) manutectorium ⟨manutectorium debet eciam umbo prope p u k e l in medio clipei⟩{b}, quod potest(u) esse ferreum. Unam tunicam absque manicis (vsuper preparamentav). (w) Eciam iudex debet indicere pacem circa collum, quod nemo eos (x) inpediat circa duellum. Cuilibet ipsorum iudex (y) unum virum habeat(z), qui
155r flangam(aa) ferat(bb) (cc), qui ipsos (ddin nichilodd) inpedire | debent, (ee) si(ff) autem(gg) unus ceciderit, quod flangam(hh) interponat, aut(ii) si(jj) vulneratus fuerit. Aut si(kk) flangam(ll) desiderat, hoc idem facere(mm) ⟨debet⟩(nn), nisi voluntas iudicis fuerit, (oo) (ppnon potestpp). Postquam circulo pax indicta fuerit, ambo debent circulum affectare, quem ipsis(qq) iudex licenciare(rr) (ss) debet. (ttFinalia(uu) ferrimenta(vv) de vaginis(ww) gladiorumtt) deponere(xx) debent, nisi a iudice licenciam habuerint(yy). Ambo ornati(zz) ire debent ante iudicem (aaaet ambo iurare debentaaa): unus, scilicet actor, quod causa sit vera, pro qua super ipsum querelam fecerit, et respondens(bbb), quod sit innocens. Sic ipsis Deus adiuvet ad(ccc) suum duellum. (dddSol eciamddd) dividi ipsis(eee) debet ⟨equaliter⟩(fff) recte(ggg), quando primo conveniunt. Si vincetur ille, super quem conqueritur, tunc iudicetur sentencia capitali. Sin

---

(a) *manus B* S6 (b) *manus B* S6 (c) *manus B* S6 fuerit S4 S8 S9 (d) iter [*s*] K5 (e) si K5 (f) *deest* K5 (g) *in ms.* pungnare S6 (h) habere S9 (i) qui S2 (j) *subrubrica:* Quibus uti debent in duello. K5 (k) ├ycoreum┤ ⟨Coreum⟩ S8 (l) *manus B* S6 (m) possint aut debent K5 (n) in manum nudum S3 (o) *deest* S2 S10 (p) *desunt* S4 (q) admittitur K4 S10 (r) *desunt* S3 (s) nisi S3 (t) nisi S3 potest [*s*] K5 *deest* S10 (u) debet S2 (v) supra preparata K5 (w) ⟨Quando iudex debet facere ad duellum⟩ K5 (x) duos S2 (y) presens S9 dare K5 (z) dare debet S2 *p.c.* ⟨debet⟩ S8 (aa) *p.c.* falangam, *correctio manus B* S6 (bb) facerit [*s*] S9 (cc) suam S8 (dd) non S2 (ee) nisi S1 S2 S3 S4 S5 S8 S9 S10 K4 K5 (ff) *deest* S4 S8 (gg) *deest* S1 S2 S3 S4 S5 S8 S9 S10 K4 K5 (hh) *p.c.* falangam, *correctio manus B* S6 (ii) *deest* S10 (jj) *deest* S4 (kk) *deest* S2 S8 (ll) *p.c.* falangam, *correctio manus B* S6 (mm) *deest* S3 (nn) *manus B* S6 debet S10 (oo) facere S3 (pp) *desunt* S2 (qq) *deest* S10 (rr) licere S2 (ss) iure S8 de iure K5 (tt) Lucros [*?*] ferreos S9 (uu) et in alia S4 (vv) fragmenta S2 (ww) virgis S2 (xx) affringere S9 (yy) possunt obtinui S9 (zz) armati S9 K5 (aaa) desunt S9 (bbb) reus respondeat S2 (ccc) et S8 S9 S10 K4 (ddd) Soli et S2 (eee) *deest* S10 K4 (fff) *manus B* S6 equaliter S9 (ggg) directe S8 K5 *deest* S9 per medium S10 K4

{a} Item linea [*s*] vestimentum vulgariter p a r c z ÿ a n e d z y e n y e K5 {b} *probabiliter manus A* S6

potest vir(a) suos affines, si uterque suus affinis (bfuerit, (choc probare debet metseptimus tacto sacramentoc)b), et(d) ita sangui|nitatis(e) linea coniuncti 41vb fuerint, quod simul pungnare non poterint.tt) Iudex eciam duos nunccios dare debet cuilibet hiis(f), qui pungnare debet, qui videant, ut(g) habeant attinencia secundum suam(h) veram consuetudinem. Coreum et linea (i) indumenta induere possunt, (jquantum placetj). (kCaput et pedes ante(l) nudi sunt, in manibusk) cirotecas habeant, unum(m) gladium nudum(n) in manu et alio cincti, aut duobus, hoc (o) arbitrio eorum committitur(p), (qunum(r) clipeumq) rotundum in (s) manu, (t) non aliud quam (u) lignum aut coreum sit, preter (vmanutectoriumv), quod debet(w) esse ferreum, unam tunicam absque manicis super preparamenta. Eciam iudex debet indicere pacem (x) (ycirca collumy), quod nemo eos impediat circa duellum. Cuilibet ipsorum iudex(z) unum virum (aadare debetaa), qui flangam (bbferat, qui ipsos in nichilo impedire debet, nisi si unus cecidit, quod flangambb) (cc) desiderat. Quod(dd) idem facere (ee), nisi voluntas iudicis fuerit, non potest. Postquam circulo(ff) (gg) pax indicta fuerit, (hh) ambo debent circulum affectare, quem ipsis iudex licenciare debet. Finalia ferrimenta de vaginis gladiorum(ii) deponere debent, nisi a iudice licenciam habuerint. Ambo ornati ire debent (jjante iudicem, | et ambo iurare debentjj): unus, scilicet actor, quod causa 42ra sit vera, pro qua super ipsum querelam fecerit, et respondens, quod sit inno- XVI cens. (kk) Ipsos Deus adiuvat et suum duellum. Sol eciam ipsis (ll) debet dividi recte(mm), quando primo conveniunt. Si vincetur ille, super quem conqueritur, (nn) iudicetur sentencia capitali. Si autem vincerit, dimittetur cum pena

---

(a) *deest* K3 (b) *desunt* K3 (c) *desunt* K1 K2 (d) quod C2 (e) consanguineitatis K1 K2 K3 (f) *deest* C3 (g) et K1 (h) *deest* K1 K2 K3 C3 (i) vestimenta seu C2 (j) *desunt* C3 (k) Nude capite et parte pedum anteriori denudati, pugnabunt, et nihil in manibus preter, quam C3 (l) una K1 antea K2 K3 (m) *deest* C3 (n) nondum C2 (o) sed in C3 (p) *deest* C3 (q) non clipeo [*s*] C1 unum scutum C3 (r) *deest* C2 (s) rotundum C3 (t) ubi K3 (u) aliud K1 (v) umbonem puckleum [*s*] C3 (w) potest K3 (x) vel preco communis C3 (y) sub pena capitali C3 (z) *deest* K1 (aa) habeat K3 (bb) *desunt* K2 (cc) interponat, aut si vulneratus fuerit. Aut si plangam K3 (dd) Hoc C3 (ee) debet K2 (ff) *deest* C2 (gg) iam C3 (hh) iam C2 (ii) *deest* K2 C2 (jj) *desunt* C3 (kk) Sic K1 K2 K3 C3 (ll) vel inter ipsos K1 K2 (mm) *deest* C3 (nn) tunc K1 K2 K3

autem vincerit, dimittetur cum pena et emenda. Actor primo circulum intrabit. [(a]Si alter diu tardaverit[a)], iudex debet ipsum[(b)] per[(c)] preconem mittere[(d)] vocare in illa domo, ubi se[(e)] preparaverit, et duos scabinos[(f)] cum ipso mittere debet. Sic citari[(g)] debent[(h)] [(i]primo et[i)] secundo et tercio, et si ad terciam citacionem non venerit, tunc querulator surgat et se ad duellum [(j)] exhibeat. Et statim percuciet duos ictus et semel[(k)] surgat[(l)] contra ventum, cum eo[(m)] ipse suum adversarium devicit tali causa sive [(n)] querela, pro qua ipsum fuerat allocutus. Et iudex sibi[(o)] iudicare debet, sicut[(p)] [(q)] fuisset duello convictus, sic mortuus [(r)] debet[(s)] convi[n]ci[(t)], si[(u)] in furtu aut [(v)] rapina, aut
155v in[(w)] tali[(x)] crimine | occisus fuerit. Sin autem mortuus [(y)] cum[(z)] septem testibus protestari poterit, extunc ad duellum se[(aa)] non indiget exhibere contra ipsum. Sin autem [(bb)] alter cognatus[(cc)] mortui, quiscumque fuerit, loco ipsius [(dd)] per duellum se [(ee]exhibuerit, [(ff)] hic[ee)] extinguet[(gg)] omne testimonium, quia tunc ipsum absque duello vincere non potest, ut[(hh)] superius est expressum. Sin[(ii)] vincetur eciam ille[(jj)], qui ad duellum captivatus aut salutatus[(kk)] fuerit, aut promittit aut fideiussorie caucionem fecerit [(ll)] et non comparuerit ad iustam[(mm)] responsivam[(nn)].

Articulus 57 [(oo)]

[57] Quicumque occisum seu vulneratum virum captivum ad iudicium deduxerit et ipsum pacis violatorem accusaverit, per duellum vel absque duello, si non[(pp)] probaverit [(qq)] secundum iuris exigenciam ipse aut[(rr)] super ipsum[(ss)], idem iudicium iudicari debeat[(tt)], quod super illum[(uu)] procedere debuerat, ac si iudicio [(vv)] convictus fuisset, et hoc per iusticiam pacis. [(ww)] Si vulneratus vir[(xx)] hunc alloquetur[(yy)], qui ipsum vulneravit, per duellum et si[(zz)] pre[(aaa)] debilitate corporis duellum perficere non possit, et si tutorem

---

(a) *desunt* S^{10} (b) *deest* K^5 (c) *deest* S^{10} K^5 (d) *deest* S^3 S^6 S^{10} (e) *deest* S^{10} (f) iuratos S^2 (g) civitati [*s*] esse K^5 (h) *deest* S^2 S^3 (i) *desunt* S^4 ⟨primo⟩ S^8 (j) induci S^2 (k) eciam S^2 (l) figat S^1 S^2 S^3 S^4 S^5 S^8 S^9 S^{10} K^4 (m) *deest* S^4 (n) cum K^5 (o) *deest* S^{10} K^4 (p) *deest* S^3 (q) si S^2 S^3 (r) si S^2 (s) fuerit S^2 (t) *deest* S^2 (u) quia sicut S^2 (v) in S^{10} K^4 (w) *deest* S^8 (x) simili S^{10} K^4 (y) est S^4 (z) tunc S^2 (aa) si K^5 *deest* S^2 (bb) ipsum S^{10} K^4 (cc) agnatus S^1 S^3 S^8 S^9 S^{10} K^4 K^5 (dd) pro eo S^8 (ee) *desunt* S^{10} (ff) tunc K^5 (gg) confrengerit S^2 (hh) *deest* K^5 (ii) Sic S^1 et S^8 (jj) *deest* S^4 S^5 (kk) solutus S^2 (ll) comparere S^1 S^2 S^3 S^4 S^5 S^8 S^9 S^{10} K^4 K^5 (mm) iusticiam S^4 S^5 K^4 instantiam S^{10} (nn) responsionem S^9 *a.c* recompensam, *correctio manus commentatoris* S^8 (oo) S^1 S^4 S^5 S^6 S^{10} K^4 *Art. 57* S^2 *Art. 58–59* S^3 *Art. 59–60* S^9 K^3 *Art. 60* S^8 *Art. 56* K^5 *Art. 62* (pp) *deest* S^{10} (qq) ut iuris est vel S^9 (rr) *deest* S^4 S^5 (ss) *deest* S^5 (tt) oportet S^8 K^5 (uu) ⟨illum⟩ S^9 (vv) ⟨nota⟩ S^9 (ww) *rubrica:* De viro, qui ad duellum allocutus fuerit. S^3 ⟨De vulnerato [pri]mo valente duellare⟩ K^5 (xx) *deest* S^{10} K^4 (yy) alloquetur S^6 (zz) autem S^8 *deest* S^2 S^{10} K^4 (aaa) *deest* S^{10}

et emenda. Actor primo circulum intrabit. Si alter diu tardaverit (a), iudex debet ipsum per preconem mittere(b) vocare in illa domo, ubi se preperaverit, et duos (c) iuratos(d) cum ipso mittere debet. Sic debet citare primo, secundo, tercio, et si ad terciam citacionem non venerit, tunc querulator surgat et se ad duellum exhibeat. Et percuciat statim duos ictus et tercium(e) figat(f) contra(g) ventum, cum eo (h) suum adversarium devicit(i) tali (jcasu(k) (lsivej) querelal), pro qua ipsum fuerat allocutus. Eciam(m) iudex sibi iudicare debet(n), sicut(o) esset duello convictus. Sic mortuus convictus(p), si(q) in furtu aut in rapina, aut in tali casu(r) occisus fuerit. (sSi autem mortuuss) (t) cum septem testibus protestare poterit, extunc ad duellum se non indiget exhibere contra(u) ipsum. Si autem alter agnatus(v) mortui, quiscumque fuerit, loco | 42rb ipsius ad duellum se exhibuerit, hic(w) extinguet omne testimonium, quia tunc ipsum absque duello(x) vincere non potest, (y(znisi fuerit proscriptusz), ut superius est expressumy). Sic(aa) vincetur et ille, qui ad duellum captivatus (bbaut salutatusbb) fuerit, (ccaut promittitcc) aut caucionem(dd) fideiussorie fecerit, conparaverit(ee), conparere (ffet non conparueritff) (ggad iustam responsivam(hh)gg).

[*articulus deest*]

(a) aliquid C^3 (b) multe K^3 *deest* C^3 (c) scabinos vel C^3 (d) scabinos K^3 (e) semel K^3 C^2 (f) agat K^2 (g) extra K^1 K^2 (h) ipse K^3 (i) vicit in C^2 (j) *desunt* C^3 (k) causa K^1 K^2 K^3 C^2 (l) *desunt* C^2 (m) Et K^1 K^2 K^3 C^3 (n) *deest* C^3 (o) sic C^2 (p) debet convici K^3 (q) *deest* K^1 K^2 (r) crimine K^1 K^2 K^3 C^2 C^3 (s) *desunt* K^1 K^2 (t) fuerit C^2 (u) extra K^1 K^2 (v) cognatus K^1 K^2 C^3 (w) *deest* C^3 (x) testimonio C^3 (y) *desunt* C^3 (z) *desunt* K^1 K^2 K^3 (aa) Si K^3 (bb) *desunt* C^2 (cc) *desunt* C^3 (dd) *deest* K^2 (ee) *deest* K^1 K^2 K^3 C^2 C^3 (ff) quod compareat K^1 K^2 (gg) *desunt* C^3 (hh) responsionem K^1 K^2

non habuerit, qui pro eo pugnare velit, inducie sibi (a) ordinari(b) debent, quousque suum duellum perficere possit.

Articulus 58 (c)

[*58*] ⟨Regula iuris. Infamibus porte non pateant dignitatum.⟩{a} Qui vitam aut manum pecunia redimerit(d), quod iure demeruerit, hic iure suo privetur.

Articulus 59 (e)

156r [*59*] | Qui eciam fideiusserit(f) unum virum pro scelere ad statuendum ipsum coram iudicio, et ipsum statuere non (g) potuerit, recompensam(h) ipsum solvere opportet, et sibi in(i) suo iure non (joberit illij), qui fuerat fideiussor. (k) Et(l) nemo describi debet(m), nisi(n) culpa (o) ad collum sive ad manum (psibi proceditp).

(a) indicari et S^{10} K^{4} (b) dari S^{2} (c) S^{1} S^{4} S^{5} S^{6} S^{10} K^{4} *Art. 58* S^{2} *Art. 60 pars 1* S^{3} S^{9} *Art. 61* S^{8} *Art. 57* K^{5} *Art. 63 pars 1* (d) exemerit S^{2} S^{3} S^{8} eximerit seu redimerit K^{5} (e) S^{1} S^{4} S^{5} S^{6} S^{10} K^{4} *Art. 59* S^{2} *Art. 60 pars 2* S^{3} *Art. 62–63* S^{8} *Art. 58* S^{9} *Art. 62* K^{5} *Art. 64* (f) iusserit K^{5} (g) possit seu S^{10} (h) recompensacionem S^{2} (i) *deest* S^{3} (j) obedierit ille S^{4} S^{5} (k) *rubrica:* Prescripcione hominibus. S^{3} (l) extunc S^{2} (m) potest S^{8} (n) ⟨nisi⟩ S^{2} (o) que S^{2} (p) pertransit S^{2}

{a} *manus A* S^{6} *ad textum rubricae* K^{5}

Articulus 64 (a)

[*64*] | (b) Qui vitam aut manum pecunia eximerit(c), (dquod iure meruerit d), 43va hic (e) iure privetur. (f) (g(hQui (i) manum (j) eximerit (k) iure perditam(l), (m) iure privetur.h) Si tempore (n) unius viri plura bona fuerint adinventa, quam quod(o) suo iuramento exaccionaliter conprobasset, et si fatetur eadem bona esse sua, tunc periurus extitit(p) et perdit ius suum civile et caret iure, propter quod dicitur infamis. Et quicumque periurus debeat (q) protestari, hoc coram(r) iudicio fieri(s) oportet, (t) quod causa sibi nominatur propter quam sit periurus. Et si fateatur (uvel siu) bona sub ipso valeant premonstrari(v), pro quibus patenter iuravit, extunc periurus est convictus, omni(w) iure carens et suum perdit ius civile.g)

Articulus 65 (x)

[*65*] | ⟨Qui eciam fideiusserit⟩(y) Qui eciam fideiusserit virum unum pro scelere(z) 43vb ad statuendum ipsum coram iudicio, et (aa) ipsum statuere non potuerit, reconpensam ipsum solvere oportet, et sibi(bb) in suo iure non oberit(cc) illi, qui fuerat fideiussor. (dd) Et nemo proscribi(ee) debet, nisi culpa ad collum vel(ff) ad(gg) manum pertransit(hh).

(a) K^1 C^3 *Art. 60* K^2 *Art. 59* K^3 *Art. 61* K^5 *Art. 63 pars 2, pars* Qui manum—civile W^1 *Art. 57* W^2 *deest folium* C^1 *Art. 64* C^2 *Art. 64–65* (b) ⟨Quis peccunia vitam redemerit privatur iure infamis⟩ C^3 (c) redimerit K^3 (d) *desunt* C^2 (e) suo K^1 K^2 K^3 C^3 (f) *rubrica:* De bonis unius v[i]ri pluribus adinventis. C^2 (g) *desunt* K^1 K^2 K^3 W^1 Et si eciam circa vitam unus vir plura bona invenerit, quam sub iuramento adidiam [*s*] dederit secundum arbitrium civitatis, ille homo est periurus, sic homo debet fieri et perdit omne ius suum, si bona illa fatetur, quod sua sint. Et si homo vincetur, quod periurus sit, hoc quod debet fieri coram iudicio bannito et si factum et actum, queritur, quare periurus factus sit et si fatetur, possunt bona dicta sub potestate inveniri, pro quibus iuramentum prestitit ac inquit, quod possunt protestari, tunc ius suum perdit et honorem et hominem. K^5 (h) De bonis unius viri pluribus adinventis. C^2 (i) vitam aut C^3 (j) pecunia C^3 (k) quod C^3 (l) meruerit C^3 (m) hic suo C^3 (n) vite C^2 C^3 (o) *deest* C^2 (p) *in ms.* exstitit C^1 (q) probari vel C^2 (r) eciam C^2 (s) *deest* C^2 (t) ita C^3 (u) quod C^2 (v) periurari C^3 (w) et est C^3 (x) K^1 C^3 *Art. 61* K^2 *Art. 60* K^3 *Art. 62* W^1 *Art. 58* W^2 *deest folium* C^1 *Art. 65* C^2 *Art. 66–67* (y) *manus ε* C^1 (z) noxa C^3 (aa) si C^2 (bb) *deest* C^3 (cc) obedit C^3 (dd) *rubrica:* De proscripcione. C^2 (ee) prescribi C^3 (ff) et K^2 *deest* K^1 (gg) *deest* K^2 (hh) sibi procedit K^3

Articulus 60 (a)

[*60*] Si mulier recipit supellectilia, ad(b) quod spectant: (c) oves, (d(ead quode) et modele(f)d) [*s*]; et omnia cibaria domestica, de quibus vir indiget ad unius anni(g) revolucionem, que in sua possessione(h) inveniuntur(i), ad mulierem(j) pertinet medietas. Cum(k) viro(l) uxor moritur, proxima sua (m) cognata(n) recipit supellectilia, que debet donare(o) viro sua(p) strata(q), ut stetit, cum uxor sua vixit (r), cum(s) (t) cussino, (usuum(v) sedileu) cum(w) pulvinari, suum stratum (xcum lecto, cussinis et (ycolcidra(z)x), suam sedem cum sedisy) tectorio, quod singulis diebus desuper(aa) iacuit, suam mensam cum(bb) mensali et manutergio. (ccHec nulla recipit pulmentaria.cc)

Articulus 61 (dd)

[*61*] Mulier pro armis bellicis (ee) (ff) mariti gladium (gget suumgg) (hh) dextrarium(ii) meliorem sellatum et meliora arma, que(jj) habuit (kkpro corporekk) unius viri, cum decessit, in sua potencia, deinde(ll) debet dare pulvinar bellicale, (mmhoc estmm) lectum et duos(nn) kussinos(oo), (ppet duo lintea-
156v mina(qq)pp), et unum mensale, et duas pelves, unum(rr) manutergium. | Hec sunt universalia(ss) arma bellica. Sed tamen(tt) aliqui(uu) homines diversa apponunt(vv), que tamen ad ea non pertinent. Sed quidquid (wwex hiisww) nominatis mulier(xx) non habuerit et (yy) hoc, (zzquod det(aaa)zz), compelli

(a) S^{1} S^{4} S^{5} S^{6} S^{10} K^{4} *Art. 60* S^{2} *Art. 61–62* S^{3} *Art. 64* S^{8} *Art. 59* S^{9} K^{3} *Art. 63* K^{5} *Art. 65* (b) *deest* S^{5} S^{4} (c) omnes S^{9} (d) *deest* S^{2} S^{9} (e) *deest* S^{3} S^{8} (f) medelle [*s*] K^{4} medule [*s*] K^{5} (g) *deest* S^{3} (h) proprietate S^{2} (i) pertinet S^{3} reperiuntur S^{4} S^{9} ceperunt S^{5} (j) minorem S^{3} (k) Si S^{2} (l) vero S^{10} (m) agnata vel S^{9} (n) agnata K^{3} agnata seu neptis K^{5} (o) ornare S^{2} ordinare S^{10} K^{5} (p) suo S^{9} S^{10} K^{4} K^{5} (q) hec debet viro sic stratum decorare scilicet S^{9} (r) videlicet cum lectu, cussinis, lintiaminibus cum teqalia [*?*], cum culcitra sedem suam, S^{9} (s) *deest* S^{2} (t) karissimo [*s*] S^{4} (u) *desunt* S^{9} (v) sive S^{2} (w) vel S^{2} (x) staminum S^{9} (y) *desunt* S^{10} (z) culcitram suam K^{3} (aa) *deest* K^{3} K^{5} (bb) *deest* S^{2} (cc) *desunt* S^{2} (dd) S^{1} S^{4} S^{5} S^{6} S^{10} K^{4} *Art. 61* S^{2} *Art. 63–65* S^{3} *Art. 65–66* S^{9} K^{3} *Art. 64* S^{8} *Art. 60* K^{5} *Art. 66 et 32 pars 1: que ad suppelectilia—ad heredes* (ee) debet dare S^{2} K^{4} (ff) mortui S^{9} (gg) *desunt* S^{3} S^{10} (hh) runcinum vel S^{1} S^{4} S^{5} S^{9} S^{10} K^{3} K^{4} K^{5} runcinum S^{2} vel S^{3} rutincum [*s*] ⟨runcinum⟩ vel S^{8} (ii) *deest* S^{2} (jj) *deest* K^{5} (kk) *desunt* S^{3} (ll) de iure S^{4} S^{5} ipsi K^{5} (mm) desunt S^{2} (nn) *a.c.* duo, *correctio probabiliter manus B* S^{6} (oo) *a.c.* kussino, *correctio probabiliter manus B* S^{6} (pp) *desunt* S^{2} (qq) *in ms.* lintiamina S^{6} (rr) *desunt* S^{4} S^{5} (ss) omnia S^{2} (tt) cum S^{3} (uu) *a.c.* alloqui, *correctio manus B* S^{6} diversi K^{5} (vv) componunt K^{5} (ww) *desunt* S^{3} (xx) *deest* K^{3} K^{5} (yy) ad S^{2} S^{3} S^{8} S^{9} K^{3} K^{4} K^{5} ⟨ad⟩ S^{1} (zz) *desunt* S^{2} S^{9} (aaa) *a.c.* debet S^{8} deberet K^{5}

Articulus 62 (a)

[*62*] | ⟨De eodem XVIII folio eiusdem libri⟩(b) ⟨Was czu der gerade gehőret⟩(c) Si(d) mulier 41ra
recipit suppellectilia, ad que spectant: (e) (foves et modele [*s*], etf) omnia XV
cibaria et domestica, de quibus (gvir indigetg) ad unius anni revolucionem, que in sua possessione inveniuntur, ad mulierem pertinet medietas. Cum (h) uxor moritur, (i) proxima uxoris cognata recipit suppellectilia, que debet viro(j) (k) decorare suum(l) (m) stratum, (n) ut stetit, cum uxor(o) sua (p) vixit, (q(rcum (s) cussino, (tsuum(u) sedile cum pulvinarir), suum stratum cum (vlecto, cussinis etv) colcitra{a} suam(w), sedem cum sedis(x) tectoriot),q) quod singulis diebus desuper iacuit, suam mensam cum mensali et manutergio. Hec(y) (z) nulla(aa) (bb) recipit pulmentaria.

Articulus 66 (cc)

[*66*] (dd) Mulier(ee) pro armis bellicis dare debet gladium (ff) mariti vel(gg) suum ru[n]cinu[m] vel dextrarium (hh) meliorem sellatum et meliora arma, que habuit pro corpore | ⟨Das Capitulum Beweysset das was gehoyret czu der hergewette 44ra
und czu der Leypgeding⟩(ii) unius viri, cum decessit, in sua potencia(jj), deinde(kk) XVIII
dare debet pulvinar (llbellicale, (mmhoc estmm)ll) (nn) lectum (ooet duo cussina, et duo linthiamina, et unum(pp) mensale, et duas pelves, et unum manutergium. Hec sunt universalia arma bellica. Sed tamen diversa conponunt(qq) aliqui homines, que (rrtamen ad earr) non pertinent. Sed quidquid ex eis nominatis (ss) mulier non habuerit, ad hoc (tt) non debet(uu) conpelli, si(vv)

(a) K^1 K^3 C^3 *Art. 58* K^2 *Art. 57* W^1 *Art. 56* W^2 *deest folium* C^1 C^2 *Art. 62* (b) *manus δ* C^1 (c) *manus commentatoris Germanici* C^1 (d) *deest* W^1 (e) omnes C^2 (f) omnia vascula et capisteria K^3 vasa et capisteria, et C^3 (g) iura indigent K^1 K^2 (h) viro K^1 K^2 K^3 W^1 C^3 (i) tunc W^1 C^3 (j) *deest* K^1 K^2 (k) suo C^3 (l) *deest* C^3 (m) sic W^1 (n) scilicet W^1 (o) uxore K^3 C^2 (p) dum K^3 (q) scilicet cum lectulo, cum cussinis, cum lintiamibus, cum tegali [*?*], cum culcitra, sedem suam cum cussino, scamnum suum ad cum pulvinari, et cum scamni tectoris, W^1 (r) *desunt* K^3 (s) lecto et C^3 (t) linteamina, culcitra et tectura, sedem suam cum cussino, scampnum suum cum pulvinari et scampnali [*s*] C^3 (u) *deest* K^1 K^2 (v) *desunt* K^1 K^2 (w) suum K^3 (x) *deest* K^2 (y) Sed W^1 (z) eadem cognata C^3 (aa) mulier C^2 (bb) hec W^1 (cc) K^1 *Art. 62* K^2 *Art. 61* W^2 *deest folium* W^1 *Art. 59* C^1 *Art. 66* C^2 *Art. 68* C^3 *Art. 62* (dd) ⟨Suppellectilia⟩ C^3 (ee) Qualiter C^2 (ff) sui W^1 (gg) et K^1 K^2 W^1 C^3 (hh) suum W^1 (ii) *manus commentatoris Germanici* C^1 (jj) possessione W^1 (kk) de iure C^2 (ll) et C^3 (mm) in C^2 (nn) unum W^1 (oo) *deest folium* C^2 (pp) *deest* W^1 (qq) apponunt C^3 (rr) *deest* C^3 (ss) ista W^1 (tt) ut det K^1 K^2 dandum W^1 (uu) potest K^1 K^2 W^1 C^3 (vv) sed C^3

{a} coldra C^2

(a) non potest, (b si (c) iuramento b) probaverit(d) pro qualibet re per se. (e Si vero e) ostendere patenter(f) poterit, ibi vir nec mulier per iuramentum evadere potest. (g) Ubi duo (h) aut tres (i) ad(j) una(k) bellica arma nati fuerint, senior recipit gladium pro se et cetera divident inter se equaliter. ⟨Ita tamen, quod senior dividit et iunior elegit.⟩(l) (m) Et ubi pupilli(n) annos pubertatis nondum(o) attigerint, et eorum senior(p) agnatus(q) recipit arma bellica solus(r), et in eis tutor est puerorum quousque ad annos discrecionis pervenerint; extunc ipsis (s) reddere tenetur et insuper ipsorum omnia bona, nisi racionem fecerit(t) eis, quo ea ad eorum (u) profectum(v) converterit, aut per spolium (w) aut per(x) apparens(y) infortunium et absque sua voluntate ammiserit. (z) Ipse eciam est(aa) vidue tutor(bb), quousque maritum ducet, si(cc) paris condicionis sibi(dd) fuerit(ee). (ff) Post(gg) arma bellica, mulier vite provisionem(hh) recipit et alia omnia, (ii que(jj) ad suppellectilia pertinent(kk), hoc(ll) sunt: omnes oves et auce (mm) et (nn) ciste cum(oo) elevatis tecturis(pp), (qq) omnia strata(rr), (ss) pulvinaria(tt), kussini, linteamina mensalia(uu), pelves, manutergia, lucibula, (vv kandelabra, semen lini, linum(ww)vv) et omnia muliebria vestimenta, (xx) (yy annuli et brachialia, et crinalia, psalteria yy) et omnes libri, in quibus mulieres legere(zz) consueverunt, qui(aaa) ad Dei cultum(bbb) pertinent, sedilia ⟨ladule⟩(ccc) ac scrinia(ddd), tapecia, {a} dorsalia,
157^{r} vela(eee) (fff) tectoria, (ggg) balneamina | et omnia pepla, et alia(hhh) ornamenta capitis muliebria, (iii hoc est(jjj), quod ad femine spectat(kkk) supellectile iii). Et

(a) non debet seu K^5 (b) manifesto S^5 (c) manifesto K^5 (d) obtinuerit S^2 approbaverit S^9 (e) Si vir S^1 K^3 Si ubi S^2 Sed si vir S^3 Sed quod vir S^4 Sed qui vir S^5 Sed ubi S^8 S^9 K^5 Vero K^4 (f) *deest* S^{10} (g) ⟨Qui recipiunt arma bellica et qualiter⟩ K^5 (h) ⟨nota⟩ S^9 (i) viri S^9 (j) et S^{10} (k) unica S^4 S^5 (l) *manus B* S^6 Ita tamen, quod senior dividit et iunior eligit. S^9 Ita quod senior dividet et minor eliget. Ubi eciam duo vel plures unam simul habuerit hereditatem, ibi unus alium ad divisionem iure valeat coartare. K^4 (m) ⟨Quis pupil[l]orum sit tutor⟩ K^5 (n) *mutatio instrumenti scriptorii* S^6 (o) non S^3 S^4 S^5 S^8 (p) *deest* S^4 S^5 (q) *a.c.* cognatus, *correctio manus B* S^6 cognatus S^4 S^5 (r) *deest* S^3 (s) racionem S^{10} (t) facet S^6 ⟨fecerit⟩ *manus B* S^6 (u) usus S^2 S^9 usus seu K^4 (v) *deest* S^2 S^9 (w) aut furticinium S^9 (x) *deest* S^3 S^4 S^5 S^8 (y) patens S^2 (z) ⟨Quod post arma bellica mulier recipit dotalicium et alia⟩ K^5 (aa) *deest* S^3 (bb) tractor S^5 mundibordius S^9 (cc) qui K^4 *deest* S^9 (dd) *deest* S^{10} (ee) *deest* S^9 (ff) *rubrica:* De vite promissione mulieris. S^3 (gg) Postea K^4 (hh) promissionem S^4 S^{10} K^4 recipit suum dotalicium aut suam vite promissionem K^5 (ii) *etiam in Art. 32* K^5 (jj) *deest* S^8 (kk) pertinencia S^8 (ll) sicuti K^3 (mm) et anete S^2 K^4 K^5 (nn) si S^4 (oo) et S^3 (pp) *deest ad Art. 32* K^5 (qq) et cooperimentis S^9 (rr) *deest* S^4 S^5 (ss) seu S^2 seu lectisternia S^9 (tt) pulmentaria S^4 S^5 (*ad Art. 32*) K^5 (uu) viorisalea [*s*] (*ad Art. 32*) K^5 (vv) *desunt* S^4 S^5 (ww) *deest* (*ad Art. 32*) K^5 (xx) crateramina K^5 (yy) *desunt* (*ad Art. 32*) K^5 (zz) *deest* S^4 S^5 (aaa) *in ms.* que [*s*] S^6 (bbb) servicium S^2 S^9 (ccc) *manus B* S^6 ladule S^9 (ddd) strinia ⟨scrinia⟩ S^8 semina K^5 (eee) *deest* S^{10} (*ad Art. 32*) K^5 (fff) vel S^{10} K^4 lecti (*ad Art. 32*) K^5 (ggg) vel S^4 (hhh) omnia S^9 K^5 (iii) *desunt* K^5 (jjj) *deest* S^{10} (kkk) sociat S^3 pertinet S^4 S^5 S^8 S^9 K^4

{a} c z e p c z e (*ad Art. 32*) K^5

iuramento probaverit (a) pro qualibet re (b per se b). Sed ubi patenter(c) ostendi poterit, ibi (d) vir nec(e) mulier per iuramentum evadere possunt. Ubi duo vel tres (f) ad una(g) arma bellica nati fuerint, (h) senior recipit gladium pro se et cetera dividunt inter se equaliter, (i ita (j) quod senior dividit et iunior eligit. (k Ubi duo vel plures unam simul habuerint hereditatem, ibi unus alium ad divisionem (l) valeat coartare. i) k) Et ubi pupilli (m) annos pubertatis non(n) attingerint, (o) eorum senior agnatus(p) recipit arma bellica solus, et in eis est tutor(q) puerorum(r) quousque ad annos discrecionis(s) pervenerint; extunc ipsis reddere tenetur et insuper omnia ipsorum(t) bona, nisi eis racionem fecerit, quo ea(u) ad eorum usum converterit, aut per spolium aut per apparens infortunium absque (v) voluntate ami|serit. Ipse eciam est(w) 44rb vidue tutor(x), quousque maritum duxerit, qui paris (y) condicionis fuerit. Post(z) arma bellica mulier (aa) vite provisionem recipere potest et alia omnia, que ad supellectilia pertinent, hoc sunt: omnes oves (bb et (cc) auce bb), ciste cum elevatis tecturis, (dd (ee) omnia strata, pulmenta(ff) dd), cussina, linthiamina mensalia, (gg pelves, manuteria, gg) lucibula, candelabra, semen lini (hh) et omnia muliebria vestimenta, (ii annuli et brachialia, et ii) crinicalia(jj) [*s*], psalteria et omnes libri, in quibus mulieres legere consueverunt, qui ad Dei servicium pertinent, sedilia et scrinia(kk), capecia, vela, dorsilia, tectoria, balniamina et omnia pepla, (ll et alia(mm) ll) ornamenta capitis muliebria, hoc est, quod ad suppellectilia femine pertinent. (nn Et ad[h]uc diversa clenodia, que

---

(a) quod non habeat W^1 (b) specialiter W^1 (c) quid W^1 (d) neque W^1 nec C^3 (e) neque W^1 (f) viri W^1 (g) vii K^1 K^2 unica C^3 (h) ibi W^1 (i) *desunt* K^1 K^2 (j) tamen W^1 (k) *desunt* W^1 (l) iure C^3 (m) ad K^1 (n) nondum K^1 K^2 W^1 C^3 (o) ibi W^1 (p) cognatus C^3 (q) mundibordius eorum W^1 (r) *deest* K^1 K^2 (s) pubertatis W^1 (t) istorum W^1 (u) evadere W^1 (v) sua W^1 (w) *deest* C^3 (x) mundibordius W^1 (y) sibi W^1 (z) Postea K^1 K^2 (aa) suam W^1 (bb) *desunt* C^3 (cc) omnes W^1 (dd) et omnes lectus pulvinaria W^1 (ee) aucas C^3 (ff) *deest* C^3 (gg) *desunt* C^3 (hh) linum C^3 (ii) *desunt* K^1 K^2 (jj) *a.c.* crinialia C^1 crinalia K^1 K^2 W^1 C^3 (kk) ladule W^1 (ll) *desunt* W^1 (mm) omnia K^1 (nn) *desunt* W^1

ad hoc diversa sunt clenodia(a), que (bad supellectiliab) pertinent, (c) singulariter ea(d) (enon nominoe)(f), sicut sunt(g) seticule, (h(ipectines, forpices, specula. Sedi) tela non incisa, nec aurum, nec(j) argentum (k) non textum non pertinent ad(l) feminas(m)h). Et(n) quidquid extra(o) prenominata in(p) rebus fuerit inventum, (qpertinet ad heredes.ii) Si aliquid ex hiis obligatum fueritq) circa vitam viri, qui mortuus est, exemet(r) (s), si(t) vult, ad quem de(u) iure(v) pertinet. (w) Sacerdos dividet cum fratre, sed(x) non qui(y) monachus est(z). ⟨de religiosis⟩(aa) Si(bb) puer in annis pubertatis religionem intraverit(cc), bene potest exire(dd), si vult, (eeintra (ff) annos(gg)ee) et ius observat feodale et terrestre. Sin autem vir, qui (hh) dum(ii) (jj) annos pubertatis inplevit et religionem (kkintraverit, hic se a iure terrestri ac(ll) feodali alienavitkk), et sua feoda vacant, quia(mm) (nnscutum(oo) bellicum resignavit. Quod(pp)nn) hoc possit protestari (qqper hos,qq) cum(rr) quibus (sssimilem vitam visus est suscepissess).

Articulus 62 (tt)

[*62*] De(uu) qua sentencia (vv) prius requiritur, hec prior diffiniri debet. (wwAmbo(xx) (yy) actor et (zz(aaaille, hoc estzz)(bbb) super quem conqueritur, (ccc) respondens(ddd) est siveaaa) reusww), possunt habere colloquia pro qualibet causa tribus(eee) vicibus, eousque eos preco revocet.

(a) *deest* S^4 S^5 (b) *desunt* S^4 S^5 (c) sed S^8 K^5 (d) *deest* S^2 S^3 S^4 S^5 S^9 K^4 K^5 (e) *desunt* S^9 tamen nomina K^5 (f) domino S^5 nominati K^4 ⟨nomine⟩ S^3 (g) *deest* S^4 K^3 (h) desunt (*ad Art. 32*) K^5 (i) specula specialia. Sed S^4 specialia S^5 (j) ⟨Sed⟩ S^2 vel S^3 (k) informatum seu S^9 (l) ⟨ad⟩ S^4 (m) mulieres S^2 S^9 K^4 (n) Sed S^2 S^3 S^9 K^4 (o) ex tria S^{10} (p) *deest* S^{10} (q) *desunt* K^3 (r) redimet S^2 K^4 (s) hic S^8 sibi K^5 (t) qui S^9 (u) *deest* K^3 S^8 S^9 K^5 (v) *deest* K^3 (w) ⟨Sacerdos habet partem de iure⟩ K^2 (x) *deest* S^8 sed K^5 (y) *deest* S^9 K^5 ⟨qui⟩ K^2 (z) *deest* S^3 S^9 (aa) *manus commentatoris* S^6 (bb) Sed S^4 S^5 (cc) hic S^9 (dd) exime [*s*] K^5 (ee) *desunt* S^2 (ff) ter S^{10} (gg) anni spacium S^4 S^5 (hh) est S^{10} (ii) *deest* S^2 (jj) ⊢ad⊣ S^6 (kk) *deest* S^5 (ll) aut S^6 (mm) si S^2 per S^3 et S^9 (nn) *desunt* S^2 (oo) *deest* S^4 S^5 (pp) Si S^9 Qui S^{10} (qq) metseptimus S^2 (rr) *deest* S^3 (ss) qui eum monachali vita viderunt S^2 (tt) S^1 S^4 S^5 S^6 S^{10} K^4 *Art. 62* S^2 *Art. 66* S^3 *Art. 67–68* S^9 S^8 *Art. 61* K^3 *Art. 65* K^5 *Art. 67* (uu) Si S^4 S^5 (vv) vir K^4 (ww) Et reus seu respondens S^2 (xx) ille K^5 *deest* S^2 K^4 (yy) scilicet S^{10} (zz) *desunt* S^{10} (aaa) *desunt* K^4 (bbb) *deest* S^8 (ccc) scilicet S^{10} hoc K^5 (ddd) respondet [*s*] K^5 (eee) tamdiu et tot S^2

ad suppellectilia pertinent,[nn)] singulariter [(a]non nominata[a)], [(b]sicut sunt[b)] seticule, pectines, forpices, specula. Sed tela non[(c)] incisa, nec argentum, nec aurum non textum non pertinet ad mulieres. Sed[(d)] quidquid extra [(e)] in rebus inventum fuerit, [(f)] [(g]pertinet ad heredes. [(h)] Si aliquid ex hiis obligatum fuerit[g)] circa vitam viri, qui mortuus est[(i)], [(j)] redimerit, si vult, ad quem de[(k)] iure pertinet. [(l)] Sacerdos dividet cum fratre, [(m]sed non, qui[(n)] monachus sit[m)][(o)]. [(p)] Si puer infra[(q)] | annos pubertatis religionem intra- 44va verit, [(r)] bene potest exire inter[(s)] annos, si vult, et[(t)] ius observet[(u)] feodale [(v]et terrestre[v)]. [(w]Si autem vir, qui dum pubertatis annos adimplevit[(x)], intraverit religionem, hic se a iure terrestri ac feodali[w)] alienavit, et sua feoda[(y)] vacant[(z)], quia scutum bellicum resignavit. Quod[(aa)] hoc possit protestari per hos, [(bb]cum quibus[bb)] similem vitam visus est suscepisse.[oo)]

Articulus 67 [(cc)]

[67] | De qua sentencia prius[(dd)] requiritur, de[(ee)] hec prius diffiniri debet. 45ra
Ambo[(ff)] actor et reus [(gg]seu respondens[gg)] possunt habere colloquia pro XIX
qualibet causa [(hh]ter seu[hh)] tribus vicibus, eosque ipsos preco revocet.

[(a)] nominando ea K^1 K^2 sunt, que non nomine W^1 [(b)] videlicet K^1 K^2 [(c)] *deest* W^1 [(d)] Si K^1 [(e)] prenominata K^1 K^2 W^1 C^3 [(f)] hoc W^1 [(g)] *desunt* K^1 K^2 [(h)] ⟨et sive in [*?*] monachus cum recipit dic [*6 verba difficilia*] C^3 [(i)] *deest* K^1 [(j)] hoc W^1 [(k)] *deest* W^1 [(l)] ⟨Sacerdos habet partem de iure⟩ K^2 [(m)] et non monachus W^1 [(n)] *deest* C^3 [(o)] *deest* C^3 [(p)] Sed W^1 [(q)] non perveniens K^1 K^2 [(r)] hic W^1 [(s)] infra C^3 intra K^1 K^2 W^1 [(t)] ut K^2 [(u)] servat K^1 K^2 obtinet W^1 [(v)] *desunt* C^3 [(w)] Qui C^3 [(x)] implevit K^1 K^2 [(y)] feodalia W^1 [(z)] nominata K^1 K^2 [(aa)] Si K^1 K^2 [(bb)] qui K^1 [(cc)] K^1 *Art. 63* K^2 *Art. 62* W^1 *Art. 60* W^2 *deest folium* C^1 *Art. 67* C^2 *deest folium* C^3 *Art. 63* [(dd)] vir primus W^1 [(ee)] *deest* K^1 K^2 W^1 C^3 [(ff)] *deest* W^1 [(gg)] *desunt* W^1 C^2 [(hh)] *desunt* K^1 K^2 W^1 C^3

Articulus 63 (a)

[*63*] In omni loco iuris est, ut(b) (ciudex iudicet(d) cum sentenciisc) ⟨scabinorum⟩(e). Aperte (f) vir(g) ⟨non⟩(h) loquatur (i) iudicio, postquam pro-
157v locutorem(j) (k) habuerit, nisi ⟨si⟩(l) iudex eum requisierit. | Si in(m) verbo consenciat sui (n) advocati, (o) bene dicere potest ⟨ita vel non⟩(p), (qsic aut(r)q) non sic, aut desuper petere(s) colloquium.

Articulus 64 (t)

[*64*] Si (uhomo (vet(w) ubiu) virv) pro pecunia (xaut (y) debitox) fuerit(z) fideiussor(aa) et moritur (bb) vir(cc), (dd) sui(ee) pueri (ffaut heredes suiff)(gg) non tenentur (hhpro eohh) solvere. (iiSi vir pro pecunia fideiussor fuerit, fideiussorem pecuniam solvereii) opportet solum(jj), aut probare, quod pecunia sit integraliter persoluta (kk).

Articulus 65 (ll)

[*65*] Si vir cum fustibus aut baculis percus[s]us fuerit supra dorsum (mm) aut supra ventrem, et(nn) verbera (oofusca ⟨livida⟩(pp) aut(qq) flavea fuerint et inflata, si desuperoo) pro teste iudicem habere potuerit et homines (rr), qui hoc(ss) viderunt (ttet(uu) audieruntt), ipse (vv) (wwest(xx) duellumww) propius super eos acquirere(yy) (zz), quam ipsi eum(aaa) evadere possent suo iure. Sin saltem(bbb) super caput et(ccc) (ddd) brachia percussus fuerit, quod alter

(a) S^{1} S^{4} S^{5} S^{6} S^{10} K^{4} *Art. 63* S^{2} S^{3} S^{9} K^{3} *Art. 66* S^{8} *Art. 62* K^{5} *Art. 68* (b) *deest* K^{5} (c) homo S^{2} (d) *deest* S^{3} K^{4} (e) *probabiliter manus B* S^{6} scabinorum K^{4} (f) voce S^{3} S^{4} S^{5} S^{8} S^{9} (g) *deest* S^{2} (h) *probabiliter manus B* S^{6} non S^{1} S^{2} S^{3} S^{4} S^{5} S^{8} S^{9} S^{10} K^{4} K^{5} (i) coram S^{2} S^{4} S^{5} S^{8} S^{9} K^{4} K^{5} in S^{10} (j) *in ms.* proloqutorem S^{6} (k) sive advocatum S^{2} (l) *probabiliter manus B* S^{6} si S^{1} S^{2} S^{3} S^{4} S^{5} S^{8} S^{9} S^{10} K^{3} K^{4} (m) *deest* S^{2} (n) prolocutoris seu K^{4} (o) tunc K^{4} (p) *probabiliter manus B* S^{6} (q) ita vel S^{2} *deest* S^{4} (r) *deest* S^{5} (s) habere S^{3} (t) S^{1} S^{4} S^{5} S^{6} S^{10} K^{4} *Art. 64* S^{2} *Art. 68* S^{3} *Art. 70* S^{8} *Art. 63* S^{9} K^{3} *Art. 67* K^{5} *Art. 69* (u) *desunt* S^{2} K^{4} (v) *desunt* S^{5} S^{9} K^{5} (w) aut S^{3} S^{8} (x) *desunt* S^{2} (y) pro K^{4} K^{5} (z) ⟨fuerit⟩ S^{8} (aa) ⟨fideiussor⟩ S^{1} *deest* K^{3} (bb) idem S^{2} K^{4} (cc) *deest* S^{8} S^{9} K^{3} (dd) si S^{9} veri K^{3} (ee) *deest* S^{9} (ff) heredes K^{5} *desunt* S^{2} K^{4} (gg) *deest* S^{10} (hh) *desunt* S^{10} (ii) *desunt* K^{3} (jj) *deest* S^{2} K^{4} (kk) ⟨mettercius⟩ S^{8} (ll) S^{1} S^{4} S^{5} S^{6} S^{10} K^{4} *Art. 65* S^{2} *Art. 69* S^{3} *Art. 71* S^{8} *Art. 64* S^{9} K^{3} *Art. 68* K^{5} *Art. 70* (mm) suum K^{4} (nn) aut S^{9} (oo) plana habuerint, et S^{2} (pp) *manus B* S^{6} (qq) aut S^{6} S^{9} (rr) iudicio dignos K^{4} (ss) *deest* K^{4} (tt) *desunt* S^{10} (uu) aut K^{3} (vv) eum S^{9} (ww) cum duello K^{3} (xx) *deest* S^{10} (yy) ⟨acquirere⟩ S^{3} (zz) potest S^{10} (aaa) *deest* S^{10} K^{5} (bbb) autem K^{5} (ccc) aut S^{2} S^{3} S^{4} S^{5} S^{8} S^{9} S^{10} K^{4} K^{5} (ddd) super S^{10}

Articulus 68 (a)

[*68*] In omni loco iuris est, ut iudex iudicet(b) cum sentenciis (c). (dAperte vird) non loquatur coram iudicio, postquam advocatum(e) habuerit (fsive prolocutoremf), nisi (g) iudex eum requisierit. Si in verbo consenciet(h) sui advocati(i), (j) bene potest dicere, ita vel (k) non, aut desuper petere(l) colloquium.

Articulus 69 (m)

[*69*] <Si vir pro pecunia aut pro debito fideiussor fuerit>(n) Si(o) vir (ppro pecunia aut pro debitop) fideiussor fuerit et (qidem virq) moritur, sui pueri | non tenentur 45va pro eo solvere(r). Si autem vir fideiussor pro pecunia fuerit, fideiussorem(s) solum pecuniam solvere oportet, aut probare mettercius(t), quod pecunia(u) sit integraliter(v) persoluta.

Articulus 70 (w)

[*70*] (x) Si vir cum fustibus aut baculis percussus fuerit supra dorsum aut supra ventrem, et verbera(y) flavea aut fusca fuerint et inflata, si desuper iudicem pro teste habere poterit et (z) homines, qui hoc viderunt et audierunt, ipse est duellum propius super eos aquirere, quam(aa) ipse eum(bb) evadere possit suo iure, (ccid est vincere eum cum testibus, quam ipse cum testibus evadere possitcc). Si autem super caput aut brachia percussus fuerit,

(a) K1 *Art. 64* K2 *Art. 63* W1 *Art. 61* W2 *deest folium* C1 *Art. 68* C2 *deest folium* C3 *Art. 64* (b) ⟨iudicat⟩ C3 (c) scabinorum W1 C3 (d) manifeste vero W1 (e) prolocutorem W1 C3 (f) *desunt* W1 C3 (g) si W1 (h) consenciet C1 (i) prolocutoris W1 locutoribus C3 (j) extunc W1 (k) aut W1 (l) rogare W1 (m) K1 *Art. 65* K2 *Art. 64* W1 *Art. 62* W2 *deest folium* C1 *Art. 69* C2 *deest folium* C3 *Art. 65* (n) *manus α* C1 (o) Ubi W1 (p) *desunt* W1 (q) *desunt* W1 (r) *deest* W1 (s) hanc fideiussionem W1 (t) *deest* W1 C3 (u) *deest* W1 (v) *deest* W1 (w) K1 *Art. 66* K2 *Art. 65* W1 *Art. 63* W2 *deest folium* C1 *Art. 70* C2 *Art. 72* C3 *Art. 66* (x) *manicula* C1 (y) vulnera W1 (z) iudicio dignos W1 *eciam* C3 (aa) *deest* W1 (bb) *deest* W1 (cc) *desunt* W1 C3

⟨aliter⟩(a) ostendere(b) non(c) possit, illi homines melius(d) ostendere(e) possunt, quam ipse super eos probare(f) possit (g) suo iure. Sin autem fatentur, quivis ammittit emendam(h) et iudex acquirit suam penam. Sin autem verbera(i) mortalia(j) fuerint, respondere tenentur cum duello, qui pro eo iudicialiter inpulsati(k) fuerint. Sin autem mortales [*s*] non fuerint, respondebit unus(l) cum duello et alii respondebunt(m) absque duello, (n(oquia ipsi evadunt(p)n) (q) suo iuramento o).

Articulus 66 (r)

158r [*66*] | Quod(s) si hereditas mortaliola(t) [*s*] absque (u) heredibus inventa seu reperta (v) fuerit, ⟨ita quod nullus se trahat ad hanc infra annum et diem (w) cedat in quam regie maiestati, nisi legale impedimentum [(x)]ipse prepedierit[(x)]]⟩(y) (zregie cedet maiestati z). {a}

Articulus 67 (aa)

[*67*] Quod(bb) si vir qui pueros habuerit, occisus fuerit, tres aut plures, et si vir unus iudicialiter pro (cc) inpulsatus fuerit et evaserit, ut ius (dd) dictaverit, ⟨et si super eandem querelam fuerit aliqua refricacio [{b]et si sibi[b}]⟩(ee) et si sibi(ff) super eam querimoniam vera satisdacio(gg) facta fuerit, ⟨hoc⟩(hh) non (iitenetur, nec ii) debet (jjab aliis pueris jj) in posterum pro eodem homicidio infestari(kk) (ll) {c}.

(a) *manus B* S^{6} (b) *deest* S^{10} (c) *deest* S^{4} S^{5} (d) *deest* S^{2} (e) *p.c.* evadere, *correctio manus B* S^{6} evadere S^{2} S^{3} S^{4} S^{5} S^{8} K^{4} (f) protestare K^{4} (g) super S^{4} S^{5} (h) *deest* S^{2} (i) vulnera S^{2} S^{3} (j) mortalitas S^{10} (k) conflati K^{5} (l) *deest* S^{3} S^{4} S^{5} (m) evadet S^{2} (n) quilibet S^{2} (o) pro eo iudicialiter impulsati fuerint S^{3} (p) *deest* K^{5} (q) cum S^{1} S^{4} S^{5} S^{8} K^{3} K^{5} (r) S^{1} S^{4} S^{5} S^{6} S^{10} *Art. 66* S^{2} *Art. 70* S^{3} *Art. 72* S^{8} *Art. 65* S^{9} K^{3} *Art. 69* K^{5} *Art. 71* (s) *deest* S^{2} (t) aliqua S^{2} mortali S^{3} mortalia S^{4} (u) mortuis K^{5} (v) ⟨anno et die⟩ S^{8} (w) ⊢habentem⊣ S^{6} hoc inquit S^{9} (x) impedierit S^{9} (y) *manus B* S^{6} *adest* S^{9} (z) *desunt* S^{9} (aa) S^{1} S^{4} S^{5} S^{6} S^{10} K^{4} *Art. 67* S^{2} *Art. 71* S^{3} *Art. 73* S^{8} *Art. 66* S^{9} K^{3} *Art. 70* K^{5} *Art. 72* (bb) *deest* S^{2} K^{4} (cc) eo S^{2} S^{3} S^{4} S^{5} S^{8} S^{9} S^{10} K^{3} K^{4} K^{5} ⟨eo⟩ S^{1} (dd) declaraverit seu S^{8} (ee) *manus B* S^{6} *adest* K^{5} (ff) *deest* K^{5} (gg) *a.c.* satisdacione S^{6} (hh) *probabiliter manus B* S^{6} (ii) *desunt* S^{2} K^{4} (jj) *desunt* S^{3} (kk) manifestum S^{10} (ll) et quid infestans perdat pro eo quere S^{2}

{a} Hereditas obmortua vulgariter dzẏedzẏna odumarla albo puszcza przes dzyedzẏcza. K^{5} {b} vel invocacio vulgariter wsznowyenye K^{5} {c} Infestari id est inculpari vgaban vel obvẏnyon. K^{5}

([a]etsi qualiter[a]) ostendi non possit, illi homines(b) melius(c) evadere possunt, quam ille super eos probare possit suo iure ([d]id est sua sola manu[d]). Si autem fatentur, (e) quivis (f) amittit emendam ([g]XXX solidos[g]) et iudex acquirit (h) suam penam •([i]VIII• solidos[i]). Si autem verbera(j) mortalia fuerint, (k) respondere | tenentur cum duello ([l]et cum testibus[l]), qui pro eodem iudicia- 45vb
liter fuerint inpulsati. Si autem mortales [*s*] non fuerint (m), (n) respondebit unus cum duello et alii respondebunt absque duello, quia ipsi evadunt cum suo iuramento.

Articulus 71 (o)

[*71*] | Si(p) hereditas mortaliola(q) [*s*] ([r]([s]sine herede inventa fuerit aut reman- 46ra
serit anno et die,[s]) regie cedet maiestati[r]). XX

Articulus 72 (t)

[*72*] (u) Si vir occisus fuerit, qui pueros tres aut plures habuerit, et vir unus ([v]pro eo[v]) iudicialiter inpulsatus fuerit et evaserit, ut ([w]ius dictaverit[w]), et si(x) sibi super eadem querimoniam(y) veram(z) satisdacio facta fuerit, (aa) non debet in posterum ab(bb) aliis pueris pro eodem homicidio (cc) infestari.

(a) quod alter W^1 C^3 (b) *deest* W^1 (c) *deest* C^3 (d) *desunt* W^1 C^3 (e) extunc W^1 (f) eorum W^1 (g) *desunt* W^1 C^3 (h) in eo W^1 (i) *desunt* W^1 C^3 (j) vulnera C^3 (k) extunc W^1 (l) *desunt* W^1 C^3 (m) ex re W^1 (n) extunc W^1 (o) K^1 *Art. 67* K^2 K^4 *Art. 66* W^1 *Art. 64* W^2 *deest folium* C^1 K^5 *Art. 71* C^2 *Art. 73* C^3 *Art. 67* (p) Quod C^3 (q) obmoriatur K^4 K^5 W^1 obmortaliola [*s*] C^3 (r) ita quod nullus se trahat ad eandem infra annum et diem, hoc pertinet ad regiam maiestatem K^4 K^5 C^3 (s) ita quod nullus se trahat ad hanc infra annum et diem, hoc nu[n]quam W^1 (t) K^1 C^3 *Art. 68* K^2 *Art. 67* W^1 *Art. 65* W^2 *deest folium* C^1 *Art. 72* C^2 *Art. 74* (u) Quod C^3 (v) *desunt* C^3 (w) iuris est W^1 (x) *deest* C^3 (y) querelam W^1 (z) vera W^1 C^3 (aa) hoc W^1 (bb) in W^1 (cc) seu querela W^1

Articulus 68 [(a)]

[*68*] Si vir alteri iuraverit coram iudicio [(b]digne et sine pena[b)], potest [(c)] superponere[(d)] et deponere ab licencia ⟨[iudicis]⟩[(e)], quod[(f)] per[(g)] hoc ⟨[nichil]⟩[(h)] non ammittit.

Articulus 69 [(i)]

[*69*] Si aliquis[(j)] arestat equ[u]m et dicit, [(k]quod [(l)] sibi[k)] aliquis [(m]subtraxerit aut[m)] subtractus fuerit[(n)] aut eo[(o)] sit[(p)] spoliatus, ad hoc se[(q)] trahere[(r)] debet, ut iuris est[(s)], extunc ille bene ad suum venditorem se[(t)] trahere potest et venditorem[{a}] nominare debet[(u)], [(v)] super quem se[(w)] traxerit, et iurare tenetur[(x)] tacto sacramento, quod ad verum se trahat venditorem. [(y]Quocumque [(z]sibi nominaverit[z)], ibi ipsum sequi opportet[y)], non autem [(aa)] sequi ipsum[(bb)] debet [(cc]ultra Mare[cc)] Aquilonis ⟨[z a m o r z e n a p o l n o c z ÿ]⟩[{b}]. [(dd]Et si sibi[(ee)] [(ff]defectus fuerit et neminem pro se habuerit respondentem, utpote[ff)] [(gg)] venditorem[(hh)] habere [(ii)] poterit, ut se coram iudicio[(jj)] iacticavit,[dd)] et [(kk]tunc sibi[kk)] fideiussorie faciat caucionem [(ll)]iudici pro pena
158v et pro[(mm)] expensis, quas adversarius | suus expendit, et diem [(nn)] nominare, quando [(oo]ibidem debeat pervenire[(pp)]. [(qq)] Sin autem dixerit, quod [(rr)] equ[u]m in[oo)] foro communi et[(ss)] libero emerit, extunc suam pecuniam, quam pro eodem[(tt)] equo[(uu)] dedit, integraliter ammittit, et illi suum equ[u]m reddere opportet[(vv)], et nullam penam pro eo ammittit [(ww)]. [(xx)]

[(a)] S[1] S[4] S[5] S[6] S[10] *Art. 68* S[2] *Art. 72* S[8] *Art. 67* S[9] K[3] *Art. 71* K[4] *Art. 68* K[5] *Art. 73* [(b)] bene S[2] hic bene S[9] [(c)] bene K[4] [(d)] ponere digittos S[10] [(e)] *manus B* S[6] iudicis S[9] S[10] K[4] [(f)] *deest* S[9] [(g)] *deest* S[8] [(h)] *manus B* S[6] [(i)] S[1] S[4] S[5] S[6] S[10] *Art. 69* S[2] *Art. 73* S[3] *Art. 74* S[8] *Art. 68* S[9] K[3] *Art. 72* K[4] *Art. 71* K[5] *Art. 74 et Art. 43 pars 1* [(j)] homo S[8] [(k)] *desunt* S[10] [(l)] equus *in Art. 43* K[5] [(m)] *desunt* S[2] S[8] [(n)] *deest* S[2] S[10] [(o)] *deest* S[4] S[5] [(p)] *deest* S[3] [(q)] *deest* S[4] S[5] [(r)] retrahere K[5] [(s)] *deest* S[10] [(t)] *deest* K[3] [(u)] *deest* K[3] [(v)] si S[4] S[5] [(w)] *deest* S[8] [(x)] debet S[2] S[9] S[10] K[4] [(y)] *desunt* S[4] S[5] [(z)] se traxerit S[2] [(aa)] cum K[5] [(bb)] *deest* S[2] S[3] S[4] S[5] S[8] S[9] K[3] K[4] K[5] [(cc)] iurare [s] S[10] [(dd)] *desunt in Art. 43* K[5] [(ee)] *deest* S[4] S[5] [(ff)] *desunt* S[2] [(gg)] iudicio K[4] [(hh)] *deest* S[3] [(ii)] non S[9] S[10] K[4] [(jj)] iudice S[2] [(kk)] ibi *in Art. 43* K[5] [(ll)] non satisfaciat *in Art. 43* K[5] [(mm)] *deest* S[4] S[5] [(nn)] non S[2] S[4] S[5] [(oo)] *desunt* K[5] [(pp)] querere S[2] [(qq)] ⟨Cum in foro communi emitur⟩ *in Art. 43* K[5] [(rr)] eundem S[2] K[4] [(ss)] aut S[1] S[3] S[4] S[5] S[8] S[9] *in Art. 43* K[5] [(tt)] *deest* S[3] [(uu)] *deest in Art. 43* K[5] [(vv)] debet S[10] [(ww)] sibi hoc probaverit, ut iuris est S[2] [(xx)] Quod si habuerit hospitem, qui marcipotum benedixit. *in Art. 43* K[5]

[{a}] ⟨vel sub tutorem vulgariter n a z a c h o c z c z a a l b o s p l a c z c z a⟩ K[5] [{b}] *manus commentatoris* S[6] ⟨Ultra mare [z] a m o [rz] e n a [p] u l n o [cz] ẏ⟩ K[5]

Articulus 73 (a)

[*73*] ⟨Si eciam iuramenta⟩(b) (cSi eciam iuramenta promissa venerint super diem ligatum, hec(d) iudex protrahere (e) potest super alium diem iudicialem, qui venerit extra dies ligatos. Et si eciam vir(f) bal|buciens vel alter, seu testis 46rb
ipsius fuerit impeditus, ita quod inperfecte suum dixerit iuramentum, ille seipsum emendare valeat, quociens impeditur et manebit de huiusmodi sive dampno.c) Si vir alteri iurare debet coram iudicio (gdigne et sine penag), (h) bene potest superponere (i) absque licencia, quod per hoc non amittit.

Articulus 74 (j)

[*74*] ⟨Cum quis equum arestat⟩(k) Si aliquis arestat equum et dicit, quod (l) sibi (m) sit subtractus aut eo(n) sit spoliatus, ad hoc (o) trahere debet, ut iuris est, tunc ille se bene ad suum venditorem(p) (q) trahere potest et venditorem(r) bene(s) nominare, super quem se(t) traxerit, et iurare debet tacto sacramento, quod se(u) ad verum trahat venditorem(v). Quocumque(w) | nominaverit(x), 46va
ibi eum sequi oportet, non autem ipsum sequi debet ultra Mare Aquilonis. (ySed si sibi(z) defectus fuerit (aaet neminem pro se respondentem habuerit, utpoteaa) iudicio venditorem(bb) habere non poterit, ut se coram iudicio iactavit, extunc fideiussorem(cc) fideiussorie sibiy) faciat caucionem (dd) iudici pro pena et pro expensis, quas (eeadversarius suusee) expendit, et diem (ffnominare, quando ibidem debeat pervenireff). (gg) Si autem dixerit, quod in foro communi vel(hh) libero (ii) emerit eundem equum, extunc suam pecuniam, quam pro eodem equo(jj) dedit, integraliter amittit, (kket illi suum equum reddere oportet, et nullam penam pro eo amittitkk).

(a) K^1 *Art. 69* K^2 *Art. 68* K^4 *Art. 69–70 pars* Si eciam—dampno K^5 *Art. 73 pars* Si eciam - dampno W^1 *Art. 66* W^2 *deest folium* C^1 *Art. 73* C^2 *Art. 75* C^3 *Art. 69* (b) *manus α* C^1 (c) *desunt* K^1 K^2 W^1 Si homini iuramenta pervenerint ad dies feriatos, iudex bene potest postponere ad secundum et tertium diem iuramenta. Si eciam homo, qui non est facundus ad loquendum, aut si testes imperiti fuerint, quod iuramentum bene loqui non potest, tunc potest bene se reiterare quantum voluerit et si nichil nocebit. K^5 (d) et C^3 (e) debet aut C^2 (f) *deest* C^3 (g) *desunt* W^1 (h) hic W^1 (i) et deponere K^1 K^2 W^1 C^3 (j) K^1 C^3 *Art. 70* K^2 *Art. 69* K^5 *Art. 43 pars 1* W^1 *Art. 67* W^2 *deest folium* C^1 *Art. 74* C^2 *Art. 76* (k) *manus ζ* C^1 (l) equ[u]s K^5 (m) subtraxerit K^5 (n) *deest* K^5 (o) se K^5 (p) tutorem W^1 (q) se K^5 (r) tutorem W^1 (s) debet W^1 C^3 K^5 (t) *deest* W^1 (u) *deest* W^1 C^3 (v) tutorem W^1 (w) Quemcumque sibi K^5 (x) eum nominaverit sibi W^1 sibi eum nominaverit C^3 (y) Et ibi fideiussoriam K^5 (z) *deest* W^1 (aa) ita quod sibi W^1 (bb) tutorem W^1 (cc) *deest* W^1 C^3 (dd) non satisfaciat K^5 (ee) *desunt* W^1 (ff) debet ibidem nominare perveniendi C^3 (gg) ⟨Cum in foro communi emitur⟩ K^5 (hh) et in K^5 (ii) foro C^3 (jj) *deest* K^5 (kk) Quod si habuerit hospitem, qui marcipotum benedixit. K^5

Articulus 70 [a]

[70] Quando iudex suam extorquet penam, ulterius[b] nec aliquam [c] super hanc penam potest extorquere. ⟨pena concordie⟩[d] Et si[e] vir iudicialiter alloquitur ⟨bona sua⟩[f], ut iuris est, vel hereditatem, pro eo non indiget iudici dare[g] [h] quidquam, cum[i] ipse[j] sibi ad[k] iusticiam iuvare teneatur. Et si homo[l] [m] suam querelam tenere promiserit, etsi [n] per bonum pacis medio tempore concordatum fuerit, pro eo non plus ammittit, quam iudex acquirit suam penam. [o]

Articulus 71 [p]

[71] {a} Vir, si vulneratus [q]aut trucidatus[q] fuerit et [r] conqueri noluerit[s], iudex ipsum [t] compellere[u] nec[v] ad aliquam querimoniam potest [w] ultra suam voluntatem.

Articulus 72 [x]

[72] {b} Et si vir descriptus[y] fuerit et[z] [aa] penam[bb] mortis iudicatus [cc] fuerit, sua bona nullus recipere habet[dd], quam[ee] sui veri[ff] [gg] heredes [hh].

---

[a] S^{1} S^{4} S^{5} S^{6} S^{10} *Art. 70* S^{2} *Art. 74–75* S^{3} *Art. 75–76* S^{8} *Art. 69* S^{9} K^{3} *Art. 73* K^{4} *Art. 72* K^{5} *Art. 75* [b] alterus S^{5} [c] aliam K^{4} [d] *manus B* S^{6} [e] ⟨si⟩ S^{8} *deest* S^{4} S^{5} [f] *manus B* S^{6} bona S^{1} S^{2} S^{3} S^{4} S^{5} S^{8} S^{9} S^{10} K^{3} K^{4} K^{5} [g] tenere K^{3} [h] ⟨Quid sit pena a [= *ius municipale Magdeburgense in eodem codice*] [*Art.*] v, b [= *Speculum Saxonum in eodem codice*] CCCLVII [*error*], C [= *collectio iuris in eodem codice:* Tertius tractus, *fol. 125^r*] CXXVII. De mutilacione sepius contingenti nivuo membro⟩ K^{5} [i] sed K^{4} [j] *deest* S^{2} [k] per S^{2} *deest* S^{9} [l] vir S^{2} S^{3} [m] ⟨nondum⟩ S^{9} [n] hoc K^{4} [o] *manicula* S^{6} [p] S^{1} S^{4} S^{5} S^{6} S^{10} *Art. 71* S^{3} *Art. 77* S^{8} *Art. 70* S^{9} K^{3} *Art. 74* K^{4} *Art. 73* K^{5} *Art. 76* [q] *desunt* S^{4} S^{5} [r] si S^{8} [s] voluerit S^{3} S^{4} S^{5} S^{10} [t] conquerere seu conqueri voluerit, iudex ipsum S^{10} [u] *deest* K^{4} [v] *deest* K^{5} [w] popter et S^{9} [x] S^{1} S^{4} S^{5} S^{6} S^{10} *Art. 72* S^{2} *Art. 76* S^{3} *Art. 78* S^{8} *Art. 71* S^{9} K^{3} *Art. 75* K^{4} *Art. 74* K^{5} *Art. 77* [y] proscriptus S^{2} K^{4} K^{5} [z] aut S^{2} S^{4} S^{5} S^{8} K^{4} *deest* K^{3} [aa] ad S^{1} S^{2} S^{3} S^{4} S^{5} S^{8} S^{9} S^{10} K^{3} K^{4} K^{5} [bb] sentenciam S^{2} K^{4} [cc] vel condempnatus S^{2} [dd] debet K^{3} [ee] nisi S^{3} [ff] viri S^{10} [gg] et legitimi K^{3} [hh] et legitimi cognati. K^{5}

{a} ⟨trucidatus vulgariter szmordowanÿ⟩ *ad rubricam* K^{5} {b} ⟨Proscriptus vulgariter wẏszwÿeczon.⟩ *ad rubricam* K^{5}

Articulus 75 (a)

[*75*] | (b) Quando iudex (c) extorquet penam, (d) ulterius(e) (f nec aliquam aliam 46vb
super hanc f) (g) potest extorquere. Et si vir bona iudicialiter(h) alloquitur, ut iuris est, aut hereditatem, pro eo non (i indiget iudicare i) quidquam (j), cum(k) ipse sibi ad(l) iusticiam iuvare teneatur. Et si sibi(m) suam querelam tenere promiserit, etsi medio tempore concordatum per bonum pacis fuerit, pro eo non plus amittit, (n) quam iudex suam acquirit penam.

Articulus 76 (o)

[*76*] | Si vir vulneratus aut trucidatus fuerit et conqueri noluerit(p), iudex 47[ra]
ipsum nec ad aliquam querimoniam conpellere potest ultra(q) suam volun- XXI
tatem.

Articulus 77 (r)

[*77*] Et si vir proscriptus(s) fuerit(t) aut ad(u) sentenciam mortis (v iudicatus vel v) condempnatus fuerit, sua bona nullus recipere potest(w), quam sui veri heredes.

(a) K[1] C[3] *Art. 71* K[2] *Art. 70* W[1] *Art. 68* W[2] *deest folium* C[1] *Art. 75* C[2] *Art. 77* (b) ⟨De penis⟩ C[3] (c) suam C[3] (d) extunc W[1] (e) super hoc C[3] (f) super aliquem hanc non W[1] (g) penam C[3] (h) sua W[1] (i) debet iudici C[3] (j) dare W[1] (k) sed W[1] (l) *deest* C[3] (m) vir W[1] (n) nisi C[3] (o) K[1] C[3] *Art. 72* K[2] *Art. 71* W[1] *Art. 69* W[2] *deest folium* C[1] *Art. 76* C[2] *Art. 78* (p) voluerit C[2] (q) sed circa K[1] K[2] (r) K[1] C[3] *Art. 73* K[2] *Art. 72* W[1] *Art. 70* W[2] *deest folium* C[1] *Art. 77* C[2] *Art. 79* (s) prescriptus C[2] (t) *deest* C[2] (u) *deest* W[1] C[2] (v) *desunt* W[1] (w) habet C[3]

Articulus 73 (a)

[*73*] Quando(b) vir moritur(c), qui (dhabeat pueros et sid) bona donata nulli habuerit, sibi succedunt pueri(e) (f), si equalis sibi nature fuerunt. (g) Et si ex hiis pueris unus (h) decesserit, mater sibi in sua parte succedit(i). (jEt mater cum hiis bonis(k) nichil facere potest absque (l) heredum consensu ac(m) voluntate.j)

Articulus 74 (n)

159r [*74*] | (o) Quando puer(p) est(q) duodecim annorum, tunc potest eligere pro sua voluntate quem voluerit(r) pro tutore. Et qui suus fuerit tutor, (s) matri racionem facere habetur(t) (uet adolescentiu), quid cum (v) bonis factum fuerit.

(a) S^{1} S^{4} S^{5} S^{6} S^{10} *Art. 73* S^{2} *Art. 77* S^{3} *Art. 79* S^{8} *Art. 72* S^{9} K^{3} *Art. 76* K^{4} *Art. 75* K^{5} *Art. 78* (b) Si S^{2} S^{4} S^{5} K^{4} K^{5} Si autem S^{3} S^{8} (c) *deest* S^{10} (d) *desunt* S^{2} K^{4} (e) *deest* K^{3} (f) sui S^{2} K^{4} (g) Et scire debet, quilibet legens, ubi scribitur agnatus, designat ex parte patris et ex parte gladii. Et ubi cognatus, ex parte matris designatur. S^{2} (h) puer S^{10} (i) succepit K^{5} (j) *desunt* S^{4} S^{5} (k) *deest* S^{10} (l) suorum K^{4} (m) aut S^{2} S^{9} K^{4} (n) S^{1} S^{4} S^{5} S^{6} S^{10} *Art. 74* S^{2} S^{3} *Art. 80* S^{8} *Art. 73* S^{9} K^{3} *Art. 77* K^{4} *Art. 76* K^{5} *Art. 79* (o) ⟨anni pueri⟩ K^{5} (p) *deest* S^{3} (q) *deest* S^{8} (r) *deest* S^{10} (s) hic K^{4} (t) habet S^{1} S^{2} S^{3} S^{4} S^{5} S^{8} K^{3} K^{4} K^{5} debet S^{9} tenetur S^{10} (u) *desunt* S^{10} (v) ipsis S^{10}

Articulus 78 (a)

[*78*] (b) Si vir moritur, (cqui habeat pueros etc) bona habuerit nulli donata, pueri sui(d) sibi succedunt, si equales (e) sibi fuerint (fin naturaf). Et si ex hiis pueris(g) unus decesserit, (hmater sibi in sua(i) parte succedit (j). Et mater cum hiish) bonis nichil(k) facere potest absque suorum heredum consensu (laut(m) voluntatel). (nSi autem omnes pueri(o), patre mortuo(p), moriuntur, extunc bona sua heredant(q) super suam matrem, et si (rpost hocr) mater(s) decesserit ab hac luce, pro(t) tunc eadem omnia bona heredant super | suos 47rb proximiores heredes, sive sint masculi, sive femine, ex paterna vel(u) materna consanguineitate. Eciam mater cum(v) talibus innatis mobilibus bonis facere et dimittere potest sine suorum heredum consensu, sed cum heredibus(w) [*s*] stantibus et propriis nichil facere potest sine (xconsensu etx) voluntate propinquorum (y) heredum suorum(z).n)

Articulus 79 (aa)

[*79*] ⟨Quando puer XII annorum fuerit⟩(bb) Quando puer XII est annorum, tunc potest eligere pro sua voluntate quem voluerit pro tutore. Et qui suus tutor fuerit, (cc) matri racionem facere habet et adolescenti, quid cum bonis

---

(a) K1 C3 *Art. 74* K2 *Art. 73* K4 *Art. 74 pars* Si autem - heredum suorum W1 *Art. 71* W2 *deest folium* C1 *Art. 78* C2 *Art. 80* K5 *Art. 79 cf. pars* Si autem—heredum suorum K5 *Art. 53 cf. pars* Si autem—heredum suorum (b) *manicula* C1 (c) *desunt* K1 K2 (d) *deest* W1 (e) ⟨de⟩ C3 (f) innatam W1 (g) *deest* W1 (h) *desunt* C3 (i) *deest* K1 K2 (j) ⊢seu successerit⊣ C1 (k) *deest* W1 (l) *desunt* W1 (m) ac C2 (n) *desunt* K1 K2 W1 Si autem moriuntur pueri omnes post mortem patris, tunc heredant sua bona super matrem. Si moritur mater, tunc bona statim spectant ad agnatos sive cognatos mulieris, quicumque fuerint paris condicionis. Etsi mulier non potest talem hereditatem dare nec vendere, ⟨absque consensus heredum non potest vendi hereditas⟩ sed cum rebus mobilibus potest facere, quid vult. Sed cum hereditate quicquam non potest facere absque consensu heredum. (*ad eundem Art.*) K5 Si moriuntur omnes pueri ⟨Post mortem filiorum hereditas spectat ad matrem et post ea ad ipsius heredes. Idem⟩ post mortem, tunc hereditas spectat ad matrem. Si moritur mulier post hoc, tunc hereditas spectat ad heredes mulieris, qui sunt sibi paris condicionis, sive sunt de patre sive de matre. Vir sive mulier eciam non potest iure eciam cum tali hereditate quicquam facere absque heredum con[sen]su, que spectat post mortem ipsius. Sed tamen cum rebus mobilibus et immobilibus potest facere quid voluerit absque consensu heredum. (*ad Art. 53*) K5 (o) *deest* C3 (p) mortui ⟨vivente⟩ C2 (q) heredita[n]t C2 (r) postea C3 (s) puer C2 (t) *deest* C3 (u) et C3 (v) deest C2 (w) hereditatibus C2 (x) *desunt* C3 (y) sive innatorum C3 (z) deest C3 (aa) K1 C3 *Art. 75* K2 *Art. 74* K4 *Art. 76 pars* Cum—coartari K5 *Art. 79 cf. pars* Cum—coartari W1 *Art. 72* W2 *deest folium* C1 *Art. 79* C2 *Art. 81* (bb) *manus α* C1 (cc) hoc C3

Articulus 75 (a)

[75] Si alloquitur vir aliquem, quod (b) fuisset(c) illiber(d), si potest suam libertatem protestare(e) {a}, propius est(f) (g) evadere, quam (hille ipsumh) vincere possit. Libertatem suam vir probare potest cum (itribus cognatis(j) (ket tribusi) agnatisk), sic metseptimus esse debet, sive sint viri sive femine. (lEt hoc scire debet (m) quilibet (nlegens, ubi(o) scriturn) agnatus, (p) designat(q) ex parte patris et ex parte (r) gladii. Et ubi scribitur(s) cognatus, (t) ex parte matris (u) designatur(v).l)

Articulus 76 (w)

[76] Quicumque alteri(x) bona sua(y) dederit ad servandum aut in deposito(z) posuerit(aa), si sibi(bb) subtracta(cc) fuerint, (ddaut spoliatus (ee) eis(ff) fueritdd), aut combusta, (ggvel sigg) mortuum fuerit, si equ[u]s vel pecora(hh) fuerint, non debet aliquod dampnum (iipro eoii) sustinere, si presumpserit iurare(jj), quod absque sua culpa ammissum fuerit. (kk) (llSed(mm) quidll) viro concessum(nn) fuerit(oo) aut obligatum fuerit, hoc indestructum reddere tenetur aut solvere(pp) secundum suum valorem. Sin autem equ[u]s moritur(qq) aut pecus (rrinfra obligacionemrr) (ss) absque (tt) illius culpa, cui obligatum fuerat, (uusi hoc probaverituu) (vv), (wwet siww) iuramentum (xxpro eoxx) prestare presumserit, quod sine sua(yy) culpa decesserit, non solvit

(a) S1 S4 S5 S6 S10 *Art. 75* S2 S3 *Art. 81* S8 *Art. 74* S9 K3 *Art. 78* K4 *Art. 77* K5 *Art. 80* (b) suus S1 S2 S3 S4 S5 S8 S9 S10 K4 K5 (c) sit S1 S2 S3 S4 S5 S7 S8 S9 S10 K3 K4 K5 (d) liber S10 (e) probare S3 protestare et ostendere S9 ap[p]robare seu protestari K5 (f) *deest* S10 (g) eum S2 (h) cum ipse K5 (i) *desunt* S10 (j) *p.c.* agnatis, *correctio probabiliter manus B* S6 (k) *desunt* S4 S5 (l) *desunt, cf. Art. 73* S2 *desunt* S3 (m) ⟨Nota⟩ S1 (n) *desunt* S10 (o) quod qunado K4 (p) ⟨Quid sit agnatus et quid cognatus⟩ K5 (q) significat S10 (r) patris S5 (s) *deest* K4 (t) ibi ⟨vide⟩ S9 (u) et ex parte fuse K4 (v) significat S10 K4 (w) S1 S4 S5 S10 *Art. 77* S2 S3 *Art. 83* S6 S8 *Art. 76* S9 *Art. 81–82* K1 *Art. 77 pars 4* K2 *Art. 76 pars 4* K3 *Art. 80* K4 *Art. 79* K5 *Art. 82* (x) *deest* S1 S2 S3 S4 S5 S6 S8 S9 S10 K1 K2 K3 K4 (y) *deest* S3 (z) ⟨in deposito fuerit⟩ *manus A* S3 (aa) ⟨posuerit⟩ *manus A* S3 habuerit S9 habuerit seu posuerit S10 (bb) *deest* S2 (cc) sublata S8 (dd) desunt S2 (ee) in S10 (ff) *a.c.* eius S6 (gg) *desunt* S2 (hh) alia S2 pecunia K3 (ii) *desunt* S2 (jj) intrare [s] K5 (kk) *subrubrica:* De rebus concessis seu obligatis. S9 (ll) Quod autem S2 Quicquid S9 (mm) Si S8 K3 (nn) confessum K5 (oo) *deest* S9 K1 K2 K5 (pp) ⟨solvi⟩ S3 (qq) *deest* S9 (rr) in secunda obligacione K1 K2 (ss) absque obligacione S2 (tt) quod S8 (uu) *desunt* S4 S5 (vv) sacramento S10 (ww) aut S2 (xx) super S8 (yy) ipsius S2 ⟨sua⟩ S9 *deest* S3 S4 S5 S8

{a} ⟨Illiber alias [o]bnoxius vulgariter nyewolnýk alias vulgariter servus⟩ K5

factum fuerit. [(a]Cum eciam puer fuerit XII annorum, extunc mundiburdius est [(b)] factus[(c)]; et potest in eo iudicio perpetrare et eciam sua bona a se sine tutore alienare. Sed innatam hereditatem et proprium debet dare cum consensu heredum. Eciam iste puer ad responsionem [(d]de iure valeat coartari[d)].[a)]

Articulus 80 [(e)]

[*80*] | Si vir alloquitur aliquem, qui[(f)] suus [(g)] sit illiber, [(h)] si potest | suam 47[va]
libertatem protestare[(i)], propius [(j]est [(k)] evadere[j)], quam ille[(l)] ipsum vincere 47[vb]
possit. Libertatem [(m]suam si[m)] probare[(n)] potest cum tribus cognatis [(o]et cum[(p)] tribus agnatis[o)], sic[(q)] metseptimus esse debet [(r)], sive sint viri sive femine[(s)].

[*articulus deest*]

[(a)] *deest* K[1] K[2] W[1] Eciam quando duodecim annorum et antiqu[u]s, nunc potest sua bona absque tutore vendere cui vult, excepta hereditate sive domorum [*s*], hoc debet dare cum consensu heredum, qui [*s*] ad hoc spectant, qui eciam pueris opportet ostendere coram iudicio iure. K[5] [(b)] ⟦est⟧ C[1] [(c)] *deest* C[2] [(d)] potest compelli C[3] [(e)] K[1] C[3] *Art. 76* K[2] W[2] *Art. 75* W[1] *Art. 73* C[1] *Art. 80* C[2] *Art. 82* [(f)] quod W[1] W[2] C[2] C[3] [(g)] sibi W[1] [(h)] iste W[2] [(i)] probare W[2] [(j)] *desunt* C[2] [(k)] sibi W[1] W[2] [(l)] *deest* K[2] [(m)] vir W[1] W[2] [(n)] protestare W[1] W[2] [(o)] *desunt* C[2] [(p)] sicut C[2] *deest* K[1] K[2] C[3] W[2] [(q)] eciam W[1] *deest* W[2] [(r)] suorum amicorum W[1] W[2] [(s)] mulieres W[1] W[2]

159v ⟨quidquam⟩[(a)], | sed[(b)] suam recompensam ammittit, [(c]in qua[c)] sibi[(d)] fuerat obligatum. [(e)]

Articulus 77 [(f)]

[77] Si[(g)] servus bona domini sui[(h)] deluserit[(i)] taxillis, aut obligat aut vendit, dominus bene[(j)] potest [(k)] arestare denuo[(l)] iure, ut[(m)] se ad ea bona[(n)] trahat, ut iuris sit. Sin autem ⟨servus⟩[(o)] propria bona sua[(p)] deluserit aut quocumque modo a se alienaverit sua voluntate, dominus super ea[(q)] nichil[(r)] alloqui potest, quia servus[(s)] solvere ⟨non⟩[(t)] tenetur, [(u]et sic[(v)u)] domino pro servi bonis non est licitum respondere. [(w]Si eciam aliquis conqueritur super aliquem pro [(x]debito[(y)] aut [(z)] pecunia[x)] ludo seu taxillis acquisita, [(aa]pro eo[aa)] sibi[(bb)] [(cc]non potest[cc)(dd)] respondere.[w)] [(ee)] [(ff]Sin autem servo suus[(gg)] equ[u]s vel alia bona sua[(hh)] furtive aut spoliando [(ii)] recepta fuerint absque culpa servi[(jj)] in domini servicio, hoc opportet[(kk)] dominum solvere servo[(ll)], et pro eo opportet dominum[(mm)] respondere, si super eo queruletur [(nn)].[ff)] [(oo)] ⟨Si quis eciam conqueritur super eum pro cibariis preparatis et coctis hoc propius est hoc obtinere iuramento, quam ille ipsum evadere possit suo iuramento.⟩[(pp)]

[(a)] *manus commentatoris* S^6 [(b)] sibi K^5 [(c)] quia S^5 [(d)] *deest* K^5 [(e)] ⟨primam⟩ S^8 [(f)] S^1 S^4 S^5 S^{10} *Art. 76* S^2 *Art. 82, 78* S^3 *Art. 82, 102* S^6 *Art. 77* S^8 *Art. 75* S^9 *Art. 79–80* K^1 K^2 *Art. 77 pars 1–3* K^3 *Art. 79* K^4 *Art. 78, 80* K^5 *Art. 81* [(g)] Quando S^{10} [(h)] *deest* S^{10} K^1 K^2 K^3 K^4 [(i)] perluserit S^1 S^2 S^4 S^5 S^8 K^5 [(j)] *deest* S^4 S^5 S^9 [(k)] ea S^2 [(l)] suo S^2 de S^9 [(m)] quod S^8 K^5 [(n)] *deest* S^2 [(o)] *probabiliter manus B* S^6 [(p)] *deest* S^3 S^{10} K^4 [(q)] sua bona S^4 S^5 [(r)] bene K^3 iure K^5 [(s)] servo S^8 S^{10} K^5 [(t)] *probabiliter manus B* S^6 non S^8 K^5 [(u)] de S^{10} [(v)] *deest* K^4 [(w)] *desunt* S^{10} [(x)] *desunt* S^3 [(y)] *deest* S^9 [(z)] pro S^2 [(aa)] reus S^3 [(bb)] *deest* K^5 [(cc)] nemo habet S^2 [(dd)] habet S^9 K^2 debet K^1 K^5 [(ee)] Eadem si conqueritur quis de alio pro cibariis preparatis preparatis aut coctis, hic propius est obtinere iuramento, quam ille ipsum evadere poterit iuramento. S^2 ⟨[...]um [...]nius [...]dit [...]ser [...]icio⟩ K^5 [(ff)] *desunt* S^4 S^5 [(gg)] suo S^8 *deest* K^5 [(hh)] *deest* K^3 K^4 S^{10} [(ii)] amiserit vel sibi K^1 K^2 [(jj)] *deest* K^4 S^{10} [(kk)] debet S^2 [(ll)] *deest* S^3 [(mm)] *deest* S^2 [(nn)] ter de bonis, que alicui data sunt ad servandum K^1 K^2 [(oo)] [...]debi [...]per [...]utum qui [...]ro⟩ Si conqueritur homo super alium pro peccuniis taxillis acquisita coram iudicio, ille non debet respondere sibi. Si conqueritur hospes super hospitem pro expensis suis comestibilibus, tunc hospes suas melius potest obtinere sub iuramento tacto sacramento, quam ille possit evadere. K^5 [(pp)] *manus B* S^6 *adest* K^5

Articulus 81 [(a)]

[*81*] [(b)] Si aliquis super aliquem conqueritur pro [(c(d]debito aut[d)] pecunia [(e)] [(f]ludo [(g)] taxillis acquisita[f)c)], pro eo respondere [(h)] non habet[(i)]. [(j]Eciam si conqueritur quis [(k]de alio[k)] pro cibariis preparatis [(l]et coctis[l)], hic propius est[(m)] obtinere [(n)] iuramentis, quam ille ipsum evadere possit iuramentis[(o)].[j)]

[(a)] K^1 *Art. 78* K^2 C^3 *Art. 77* K^5 *Art. 83* W^2 *Art. 76* W^1 *Art. 74* C^1 *Art. 81* C^2 *Art. 83* [(b)] *manicula* C^1 ⟨ludus⟩ C^3 [(c)] pecunia detasserata W^1 W^2 [(d)] *desunt* K^5 [(e)] de K^1 K^2 [(f)] detasserata K^5 [(g)] aut C^3 [(h)] sibi K^1 K^2 K^5 W^1 W^2 C^3 [(i)] debet K^5 [(j)] *desunt* C^3 [(k)] super aliquem W^1 W^2 super alium K^5 [(l)] *desunt* W^1 W^2 [(m)] *deest* C^2 [(n)] hoc W^2 [(o)] suo iuramento K^5 W^1 W^2

Articulus 78 (a)

[*78*] Qui se extraxerit(b) a descripcione, et(c) solutus diiudicatus fuerit, iudex tamen in eo suam(d) obtinet penam. Et si sibi(e) iudex fateri noluerit(f), ipse (g) eum(h) ⟨bene potest⟩(i) deponere per unum (j), qui (k) eodem interfuit iudicio, quia nec captivus iudicio comparuit, nec proclamatus. Sin autem iudex ipsum(l) in posterum obiurare(m) (n) voluerit(o), ipsum in(p) nullo ulterius(q) obiurare(r) potest, quam(s) ad suam penam, si super(t) eo testes habuerit, quod se(u) extra descripcionem obiuravit.

[*articulus deest*]

⟨Si servus deservitum suum precium super suum dominum obtinebit coram iudicio, hoc bene post obtinere cum viris fidedignis, qui in suo iure argui non possunt, et dominus servo solvere hoc tenetur eodem die.⟩(v)

Articulus 79 (w)

[*79*] ⟨Regula iuris. Pluralis locucio duorum numero est contenta. Regula iuris. Actus ligitimi condicionem non recipiunt neque diem. Item factum legitimum retractari non debet, licet casus postea eveniat a quo non potuit inchoari.⟩{a} Si vir conqueritur super alterum
160r pro suo(x) debito cum testibus (y), hoc bene potest obtinere (z) cum viris | (aafidedignis, qui in suo iure non possunt reprobari. Ita tamen, si ille(bb) dicit se esse(cc) innocentem. Sin autem respondens(dd) dixerit se esse(ee) debitum persolvisse, extunc inpedit sibi(ff) suum testimonium. Hoc bene potest probare cum probis(gg) viris metseptimus(hh) ⟨tercius⟩(ii) tacto sacramentoaa).

(a) S1 S4 S5 S6 S10 *Art. 78* S2 *Art. 79* S3 K5 *Art. 84* S8 *Art. 77* S9 *Art. 83* K3 K4 *Art. 81* (b) eximit K5 (c) ut si S4 S5 si S8 et si K5 (d) *deest* S10 (e) *deest* S2 (f) voluerit [*s*] S4 S5 S10 K5 (g) super S9 (h) *deest* S2 S10 (i) *manus B* S6 bene potest S1 S2 S3 S4 S5 S8 S9 S10 K3 K4 bene K5 (j) virum S9 (k) in S9 (l) *deest* K4 (m) obiudicare K5 (n) ⟨conservare⟩ [*?*] S8 (o) noluerit S4 (p) *deest* K3 (q) *deest* S8 K5 (r) obiudicare K5 (s) *deest* S4 S5 (t) in K3 (u) *deest* S4 S5 (v) *manus B* S6 (w) S1 S4 S5 S6 S10 *Art. 79* S2 *Art. 84* S3 *Art. 85* S8 *Art. 78* S9 *Art. 84* K3 *Art. 82* K4 *Art. 83* K5 *Art. 86* (x) *deest* S3 S9 (y) coram iudicio K4 (z) mettercius S2 (aa) tacto sacramento, aut ille evadere cum testibus S2 (bb) *deest* K4 (cc) *deest* S10 K3 K4 (dd) reus hoc K4 (ee) *deest* K5 (ff) *deest* S9 (gg) fidedignis K4 (hh) metseptimus S1 S6 mettercius S3 S5 S8 S9 S10 K3 K4 metseptimus et mettercius S4 (ii) *manus B* S6

{a} *manus A* S6 ⟨Regula iuris. Pluralis locucio duorum numero est contenta.⟩ K5

Articulus 82 [(a)]

[*82*] Qui se extraxerit a descripcione[(b)], et solutus iudicatus fuerit, iudex [(c)] suam in[(d)] eo obtinebit penam. Et si sibi iudex [(e)] fateri noluerit[(f)], ipsum [(g)] bene potest | [(h]deponere id est protestare[h)] per unum, qui eodem inter- 48ra fuit iudicio, quia nec captivus [(i)] iudicio apparuit[(j)], nec proclamatus [(k)]. Si XXII aut[em] ipsum iudex in posterum obiurare[(l)] voluerit, ipsum [(m]in nullo ulterius[m)] [(n)] obiurare[(o)] [(p]id est agravare[p)] potest, quam ad suam penam, si[(q)] super[(r)] eo testes habuerit, quod se [(s]extra descripcionem[s)][(t)] obiuravit [(u)].

Articulus 83 [(v)]

[*83*] [(w)] Si servus deservitum [(x)] precium [(y]super suum dominum[y)] obtinuerit[(z)] coram [(aa]iudicio, pro eo dominus[(bb)] nullam iudici[aa)] demeretur penam et dominus servo solvere hoc[(cc)] tenetur die eodem.

Articulus 84 [(dd)]

[*84*] | Si vir conqueritur super alterum pro suo debito cum testibus [(ee)], hoc 48rb bene potest obtinere cum viris[(ff)] fidedignis, qui in suo iure non[(gg)] possunt reprobari [(hh)]. Ita tamen, si ille se dicit [(ii)] innocentem. Si autem respondens[(jj)] se[(kk)] dixerit debitum persolvisse, extunc impedit[(ll)] sibi suum testimonium. Tamen[(mm)] bene probare potest cum viris[(nn)] fidedignis mettercius tacto sacramento.

(a) K^1 *Art. 79* K^2 C^3 *Art. 78* W^1 *Art. 75* W^2 *Art. 77* C^1 *Art. 82* C^2 *Art. 84* (b) prescripcione W^1 proscripcione W^2 C^2 (c) tamen K^1 K^2 W^1 C^3 (d) pro K^1 K^2 (e) factum W^1 (f) voluerit [*s*] C^2 (g) eum K^1 K^2 W^1 C^3 (h) eum deponere K^1 K^2 W^1 C^3 protestari C^2 (i) in K^2 (j) comparuit W^1 W^2 C^3 (k) fuit C^2 (l) obviare W^2 (m) nullomodo K^1 K^2 (n) potest W^1 W^2 (o) obviare C^2 (p) *desunt* K^1 K^2 W^1 C^3 (q) nisi C^2 (r) pro W^1 in K^3 (s) ex prescripcione W^1 ex proscripcione W^2 (t) proscripcionem C^2 (u) id est per iuramentum liberatur C^2 (v) K^1 *Art. 80* K^2 C^3 *Art. 79* K^4 *Art. 82* K^5 C^2 *Art. 85* W^1 *Art. 76* W^2 *Art. 78* C^1 *Art. 83* (w) ⟨mortes⟩ C^3 (x) suum K^1 K^2 K^4 K^5 W^1 W^2 C^3 (y) dominium W^1 W^2 *deest* C^3 (z) obiurgaverit K^4 (aa) iudice C^2 (bb) *deest* W^1 C^2 (cc) *deest* W^1 (dd) K^1 *Art. 81* K^2 C^3 *Art. 80* W^1 *Art. 77* W^2 *Art. 79* C^1 *Art. 84* C^2 *Art. 86* (ee) coram iudicio W^1 W^2 (ff) iure K^1 (gg) *deest* C^3 (hh) mettercius C^3 (ii) esse K^1 (jj) reus W^1 W^2 (kk) hoc W^1 W^2 (ll) infringit W^1 W^2 C^3 (mm) Hoc K^1 K^2 W^1 W^2 C^3 (nn) *deest* K^1

Articulus 80 [(a)]

[*80*] Si super virum conquestum fuerit et [(b)] satisdacionem pecierit, alter eam sibi negare [(c]non potest, quin[c)] eam sibi[(d)] faciat, si ipsum per sentenciam ad hoc compulerit. Sin autem satisdacionem fecerit sibi, ad suum ius non nocet, nec [(e)] plus lucratur [(f)] satisdacione, [(g)] qui eam[(h)] petit, nisi quod ipsum[(i)] nullus[(j)] amicorum suorum [(k)] inpedire[(l)] amodo [(m)] potest[(n)] pro hac causa. [(o]Satisdacione facta[o)] suam querimoniam meliorare non[(p)] potest.

Articulus 81 [(q)]

[*81*] Omnis querela, que[(r)] ad iudicium pro[(s)] capitali crimine in facto[(t)] manifesto deducta fuerit, debet conqueri cum[(u)] clamore propter factum manifestum, quod ostendi potest[(v)]. [(w)] Manifestum factum [(x]ibi[(y)] est[x)] et ubi vir cum furtu [(z)] [(aa]aut [(bb)] preda[aa)] captivus ad iudicium [(cc]deductus fuerit[cc)] cum clamore. [{a}] Item[(dd)] factum manifestum eciam est ibi[(ee)], ubi [(ff)] virum[(gg)] cum gladio aut cultello aut alia sicca[(hh)] in via[(ii)] deprehenditur, cum quo pacem infregit[(jj)], aut si[(kk)] in [(ll]fuga facti captivatus[ll)] [(mm]fuerit et captivus[mm)] ad iudicium deductus[(nn)] fuerit cum clamore. Hunc actor metseptimus vincere debet circa ius pacis, si factum manifestum cum reo[(oo)] ad iudicium deductum fuerit.

(a) S^1 S^4 S^5 S^6 S^{10} *Art. 80* S^2 S^9 *Art. 85* S^3 *Art. 86* S^8 *Art. 79* K^3 *Art. 83* K^4 *Art. 84* K^5 *Art. 87* (b) ipse S^3 K^3 K^5 (c) *desunt* S^4 S^5 (d) *deest* S^3 (e) ille S^1 S^2 S^3 S^4 S^5 S^8 S^9 S^{10} K^3 K^4 ipse K^5 (f) cum S^1 S^2 S^4 S^5 S^8 K^4 (g) nisi S^3 (h) eciam K^3 (i) alter K^4 (j) in illis S^{10} (k) ipsum K^4 (l) *deest* S^2 (m) non S^8 (n) valeat K^4 (o) Per quam satisdacionem fecit infestare S^2 (p) *deest* K^5 (q) S^1 S^4 S^5 S^6 S^{10} *Art. 81* S^2 S^9 *Art. 86* S^3 *Art. 87* S^8 *Art. 80* K^3 *Art. 84* K^4 *Art. 85* K^5 *Art. 88* (r) ⟨que⟩ S^4 (s) ⟨pro⟩ S^8 (t) *deest* S^4 S^5 (u) *deest* S^2 (v) potest et debet S^{10} debet S^1 S^3 S^4 S^5 S^8 S^9 K^3 K^4 *deest* K^5 (w) ⟨Quid sit manifestum factum⟩ K^5 (x) *desunt* S^4 S^5 (y) *deest* S^2 K^5 (z) aut spolio S^9 (aa) *desunt* S^2 (bb) cum S^3 (cc) *desunt* S^{10} (dd) *deest* S^1 (ee) *deest* S^9 S^{10} (ff) apud S^1 S^2 S^3 S^4 S^5 S^8 K^5 (gg) unum S^1 S^2 S^3 S^4 S^5 S^9 K^4 S^{10} (hh) defendicula S^1 offendicula S^2 re K^3 ⟨arma⟩ S^8 (ii) via S^6 K^3 manu S^1 S^2 S^3 S^4 S^5 S^8 S^9 S^{10} K^4 K^5 (jj) violavit S^1 S^2 (kk) *deest* S^{10} (ll) recenti facto vel in fuga factus fuerit K^5 (mm) *desunt* S^2 (nn) *deest* S^{10} (oo) eo S^9 S^{10}

{a} ⟨Regula iuris. Actus legitimi condicionem non recipiunt neque diem. Factum legitimum retractari non debet, licet causus [*s*] postea eveniat a quo non poterit [inchoari].⟩ K^5

Articulus 85 [a]

[*85*] Si vir[b] super virum conquestus fuerit et satisdacionem[c] pecierit, alter eam [d] negare non [e], quin[f] eam[g] sibi faciat, si per sentenciam ipsum ad hoc conpulerit[h]. Si autem satisdacionem[i] fecerit sibi, ad suum ius non nocet, nec ille plus lucratur cum [j] satisdacione[k], qui eam petit, nisi quod ipsum[l] nullus amicorum suorum [m] ammodo | impedire potest[n] 48va
pro[o] hac causa. [p]Satisfaccione facta suam querimoniam meliorare non[q] potest[p].

Articulus 86 [r]

[*86*] [s] Omnis querela, que ad iudicium pro capitali crimine in facto manifesto deducta fuerit, debet conqueri cum clamore propter[t] factum manifestum, quod ostendi debet. Manifestum factum ibi est, ubi vir cum furtu aut preda captivus ad iudicium deductus cum clamore fuerit. Item[u] manifestum factum est ibi[v] eciam, ubi apud unum cultellus aut gladius aut alia arma[w] in manu sua deprehensa fuerint, cum qua pacem violaverit, aut si in fuga captivus fuerit [x]et [y] captivus ad iudicium deductus fuerit[x] cum clamore. Hunc actor metseptimus vincere debet circa ius pacis, si manifestum factum cum reo ad iudicium deductum fuerit. [z]Manifestum factum p r o b a cum clamore metseptimus. Sequitur in Thewtunico capitulum.[z]

(a) K^1 *Art. 82* K^2 C^3 *Art. 81* C^1 *Art. 85* W^1 *Art. 78* C^2 *Art. 87* W^2 *Art. 80* (b) *deest* K^1 K^2 W^1 W^2 C^3 (c) satisfaccionem K^1 (d) sibi K^1 K^2 W^1 W^2 C^2 C^3 (e) potest K^1 K^2 W^1 W^2 C^2 C^3 (f) quia C^3 (g) *deest* C^3 (h) *in ms.* conpulserit C^1 (i) satisfaccionem K^1 (j) ⊢sed⊣ C^1 (k) satisfaccione K^1 (l) ipsorum K^1 K^2 alter C^3 (m) consensu C^3 (n) valeat C^3 (o) *deest* W^1 (p) nec querelam meliorare W^1 W^2 (q) nullus C^3 (r) K^1 *Art. 83* K^2 *Art. 82* C^1 *Art. 86* C^2 *Art. 88* C^3 *Art. 82* (s) *manicula* C^1 (t) per C^2 (u) *deest* C^3 (v) *deest* C^3 (w) sicca K^1 K^2 defendicula C^3 (x) bene C^3 (y) cum K^1 K^2 (z) *desunt* K^1 K^2 W^1 W^2 C^3

Articulus 82 (a)

[*82*] In iudicio burgravii Meydeburgensis(b) potest vir (c) (dpro debitod) bene(e) querulari(f), super (g) actorem, aut(h) opportet ab uno iudicio burgravii ad aliud(i) iudicium suam sequi querelam, ita quod semper(j) suo(k) adversario denunciet. Si autem super virum(l) querimonia cum testimonio (m) facta fuerit (nin eodem iudicio (o) pro debiton), et si dicit, quod persolverit, hoc probabit per homines fidedignos ⟨mettercius melius⟩(p), quam ille ipsum vincere possit, quod facere potest incontinenti, si vult, aut per sex ebdomadas in(q) iudicio sculteti. Sin autem vir(r) iuramentum (s) unica manu prestare(t) (u) debet, quod(v) in eodem iudicio(w) facere opportet.

Articulus 83 (x)

[*83*] Iudex debet (y) iudicium ⟨suum omni die⟩(z) (aaexercere et (bb) (cceo(dd) temptare(ee)cc) cottidieaa) in vero iudicii loco, nisi (ffsit, quodff) vir absque testibus conqueri(gg) voluerit ⟨pro debito⟩(hh), quod(ii) statim(jj) iudicare (kk) potest sine mora. Recompensam et emendam et penam iudicis(ll) solvere debent ad diem, ut(mm) fuerit diffinitum ⟨cum denariis⟩(nn), (oo(pput(qq) tunc pagamentum (rr) consuetum fueritpp), (ssrecompensam et (ttemendam actori et penamtt) iudici solvetur(uu)ss)oo) (vv).

(a) S^{1} S^{4} S^{5} S^{6} S^{10} *Art. 82* S^{2} S^{9} *Art. 87* S^{3} *Art. 88* S^{8} *Art. 81* K^{3} *Art. 85* K^{4} *Art. 86* K^{5} *Art. 89* (b) Meydburgensi K^{5} (c) virum S^{2} (d) probare S^{3} (e) *deest* S^{10} (f) *in ms.* querulare S^{6} (g) ⟨alibi habetur sed actorem opportet⟩ S^{8} (h) *deest* S^{2} S^{3} (i) *deest* S^{3} S^{4} S^{5} S^{8} (j) super S^{3} S^{10} (k) *deest* S^{4} (l) *deest* S^{3} (m) ⟨nota⟩ S^{9} (n) coram iudicio S^{2} (o) Meydburiensi S^{2} (p) *manus B* S^{6} propius S^{2} mettercius K^{5} (q) *deest* S^{10} (r) *deest* S^{2} (s) vi [*?*] K^{3} (t) protestare K^{5} (u) potest seu S^{4} S^{5} (v) hoc S^{2} K^{5} (w) officio S^{10} (x) S^{1} S^{4} S^{5} S^{6} S^{10} *Art. 83* S^{2} S^{9} *Art. 88* S^{3} *Art. 89* S^{8} *Art. 82* K^{3} *Art. 86* K^{4} *Art. 87* K^{5} *Art. 90* (y) suum K^{5} (z) *probabiliter manus B* S^{6} (aa) suum omni die attemptare S^{9} (bb) de S^{2} K^{4} ├in┤ ⟨de⟩ S^{8} (cc) *p.c.* attemptare, *correctio probabiliter manus B* S^{6} (dd) id S^{1} *deest* S^{10} (ee) ├temptare┤ ⟨atemptare⟩ S^{8} contemptare S^{10} tempore K^{5} (ff) *desunt* S^{9} (gg) querulari K^{4} S^{10} (hh) *probabiliter manus B* S^{6} pro debito S^{4} S^{2} S^{3} S^{5} S^{8} S^{9} S^{10} (ii) hoc K^{4} (jj) ubilibet K^{4} (kk) debet et S^{10} (ll) *deest* S^{10} (mm) et S^{4} S^{5} K^{3} (nn) *manus B* S^{6} cum talibus denariis K^{4} (oo) iure S^{9} (pp) *desunt* S^{8} in eodem iudicio sunt transeuntes et dativi sive daturi K^{4} (qq) prout K^{4} (rr) ibidem S^{3} S^{4} S^{8} illud S^{5} (ss) *desunt* S^{4} S^{5} (tt) penam et emendam S^{9} (uu) *deest* S^{1} S^{2} S^{3} S^{4} S^{5} S^{8} S^{10} K^{3} K^{4} (vv) in pagamento S^{9}

Articulus 87 (a)

[*87*] | (b) In iudicium burgravii Maÿdeburgensis(c) potest vir pro debito (d) 48vb
bene(e) querulari, sed(f) actorem oportet de uno iudicio burgravii(g) ad aliud
iudicium suam sequi querelam, ita (hsemper(i) quodh) suo adversario(j) de-
nunciet. Si autem querimonia(k) super virum cum testimonio facta fuerit
in eodem iudicio pro debito, et si dicit, quod persolverit, hoc probabit per
homines fidedignos (l), quam ille ipsum vincere possit, quod(m) facere potest
incontinenti, si vult, | aut per (nsex ebdomadasn) in iudicio sculteti. Si autem 49ra
vir iuramentum unica manu prestare debet, hoc in eodem iudicio facere XXIII
oportet.

Articulus 88 (o)

[*88*] Iudex debet (p) iudicium (q) exercere (ret de eo temptare cottidier) in
vero iudicii loco, nisi sit(s), (tquod virt) conqueri(u) pro debito absque testi-
bus voluerit, quod(v) ubilibet(w) iudicare potest (xsine morax). (yIudex eciam
iudicium tenetur(z) conportare(aa), (bb) et non actor neque reus.y) Reconpen-
sam et emendam et penam iudicis | solvere debet ad diem, ut fuerit (cctunc 49rb
pagamentum (dd) consuetum (ee) diffinitumcc). Reconpensam et emendam
actor[i](ff) et(gg) penam iudici. {a}

(a) K^1 *Art. 84 pars 1* K^2 *Art. 83 pars 1* C^1 *Art. 87* W^1 *Art. 79* C^2 *Art. 89* C^3 *Art. 83* W^2 *Art. 81* (b) *manicula* C^1 (c) *deest* W^1 W^2 (d) pecuniali W^1 W^2 (e) ipsi K^1 K^2 (f) super K^1 K^2 C^3 (g) *deest* C^3 (h) tamen quod semper W^1 W^2 (i) *deest* C^3 (j) reo W^1 W^2 (k) querela W^1 W^2 (l) propius K^1 K^2 C^3 melius W^1 W^2 pocius C^2 (m) et hoc W^1 W^2 (n) tres quindenas W^1 W^2 (o) K^1 *Art. 84 pars 2* K^2 *Art. 83 pars 2* C^1 *Art. 88* W^1 *Art. 80* C^2 *Art. 90* C^3 *Art. 84* W^2 *Art. 82* (p) suum W^1 W^2 (q) omni die W^1 W^2 (r) attemptare W^1 W^2 (s) sic K^1 K^2 (t) ubi W^1 W^2 (u) querulari C^2 C^3 (v) hoc W^1 C^3 W^2 (w) videlicet W^1 W^2 (x) *desunt* W^1 W^2 C^2 (y) *desunt* K^1 K^2 W^1 W^2 (z) oportet C^3 *deest* C^2 (aa) coordinare C^3 (bb) quando iudicare debet C^3 (cc) diffinitum cum denariis, prout extunc valent in pagamento W^1 W^2 diffinita cum talibus denariis, prout tunc in eodem iudicio sunt transeuntes C^3 (dd) ibidem C^2 (ee) fuerit K^1 K^2 (ff) *deest* W^1 W^2 (gg) sed C^3

{a} ⟨pena gewette, vergelt recompensa⟩ C^3

Articulus 84 (a)

[*84*] {a} Si viro sua(b) bona (cpublicata seu fiscatac) fuerint iure(d), in eo (eille possideate), qui hoc in fiscacionem deduxit(f) (gcum fiscacioneg) tribus diebus et tribus noctibus(h). Insuper in(i) eo debet comedere et bibere (jcum(k) fiscacionej), similiter(l) et dormire. Deinde debet(m) coram iudicio pronun-
161r ciare (n) tribus vicibus semper ad duas ebdomadas(o), ad quartum iudicium | iudex(p) sibi pacem desuper formare(q) ⟨firmare⟩(r) debet(s), ⟨et sibi⟩(t) appropriare(u) (v), (wet(x) sentenciisw) scabinorum vendere(y). Extunc (z) vendere potest(aa) cum scitu ⟨bonorum hominum⟩(bb). Si(cc) tunc aliquid(dd) ultra suum debitum (ee) superfuerit(ff), (gg) (hhcum scituhh) illi reddere debet, cuius fuit hereditas. Sed si deficit, ⟨tunc⟩(ii) agat ulterius. ⟨donec ex integro suum debitum consequetur⟩(jj)

Articulus 85 (kk)

[*85*] {b} (llSi vir (mm) aliqua(nn) bona ⟨pannos⟩(oo) vel quidquid suarum rerum fuerit(pp), (qqquod sibi (rr) subtractum aut raptum fueritqq), (ss) ad hoc se unica manu trahere debet(tt) (uuet iurare debetuu)(vv) tacto sacramento, quod tunc suum fuit et nunc suum sit, cum sibi subtractum (ww) fuerit. ll)(xxSin

(a) S^1 S^4 S^5 S^6 S^{10} *Art. 84* S^2 S^9 *Art. 89* S^3 *Art. 90* S^8 *Art. 83* K^3 *Art. 87* K^4 *Art. 88* K^5 *Art. 91* (b) aliqua K^4 (c) *desunt* K^4 (d) concessa K^4 *deest* S^2 (e) *desunt* S^2 (f) *deest* K^3 (g) *desunt* K^3 (h) *deest* S^9 (i) *deest* S^3 (j) *desunt* S^2 (k) *deest* K^5 (l) *deest* K^5 (m) coram S^{10} (n) diebus S^2 (o) septimanas S^9 (p) *deest* K^5 (q) firmare S^9 K^5 (r) *manus B* S^6 (s) *deest* S^8 (t) *manus B* S^6 et sibi S^1 S^2 S^3 S^4 S^5 S^8 S^9 S^{10} K^3 K^4 K^5 (u) *a.c.* probare, *correctio manus commentatoris* S^8 properare S^{10} (v) debet S^1 S^3 S^4 S^5 S^8 S^{10} K^3 (w) per sentenciam S^9 K^4 (x) in S^{10} (y) *deest* S^2 S^9 K^4 (z) bene S^9 K^4 (aa) *deest* S^{10} (bb) *manus B* S^6 bonorum hominum S^9 hominum proborum K^4 (cc) *deest* S^9 (dd) *deest* S^9 (ee) aliquid de hoc S^9 et de hoc K^4 (ff) fuerit S^4 S^5 (gg) eo S^1 (hh) hoc S^9 K^4 (ii) *manus B* S^6 extunc K^4 (jj) *manus B* S^6 (kk) S^1 S^4 S^5 S^6 S^{10} *Art. 85* S^2 S^9 *Art. 90* S^3 *Art. 91* S^8 *Art. 84* K^3 *Art. 88* K^4 *Art. 89* K^5 *Art. 92 et Art. 43 pars 2: Si viro—Mare Aquilonis* (ll) Si eciam aliquis arestat equum, quem sibi aliquis subtraxerit vel subtractus fuerit aut spoliatus, ad hoc se trahere potest, ut iuris est, supradictum. ⟨Qualiter equus arestatur⟩ K^5 (mm) alloquitur S^3 S^4 S^5 S^9 S^8 K^4 (nn) *deest* S^3 S^4 S^5 S^8 (oo) *a.c.* per annos, *correctio manus B* S^6 pannos S^1 S^3 S^4 S^5 S^8 S^9 S^{10} K^3 K^4 aut annos K^5 (pp) *deest* S^{10} (qq) *desunt* S^3 (rr) *manicula* S^8 (ss) arestavit S^{10} (tt) *deest* S^4 S^5 (uu) *desunt* S^9 (vv) *desunt* S^2 K^4 K^5 (ww) aut raptum S^1 S^2 S^3 S^4 S^5 S^8 S^9 S^{10} K^3 K^4 (xx) Quod si quis arestat equ[u]m vel *ad Art. 43* K^5

{a} ⟨fiscata, ob[li]gata id est in […]diata vulgariter z a s t h a w a⟩ K^5 {b} Alloquitur vel arestaverit vulgariter n a r z e t e l n ý z a s t h a w K^5

Articulus 89 (a)

[*89*] ⟨Si viro sua bona⟩(b) Si viro (c) sua(d) bona(e) (f publicata seu f) fiscata(g) fuerint(h) iure(i), (j in eo (k) ille possideat, qui hoc infiscacionem(l) induxerit cum fiscacione tribus diebus ac noctibus. Insuper(m j)m) in eo debet(n) comedere et bibere, similiter(o) et dormire (p). (q Deinde debet coram iudicio pronunciare tribus vicibus(r) semper ad duas ebdomadas q), ad quartum iudicium iudex sibi(s) pacem desuper formare(t) debet, et sibi appropriare, et(u) sentenciis scabinorum. (v) Vendere potest (w) cum scitu (x). Si(y) aliquid (z ultra suum debitum z) (aa) superfuerit, (bb(cc cum scitu cc) illi reddere | debet, cuius 49va
fuit hereditas bb). (dd(ee Sed si deficit ee), (ff) agat ulterius. dd)

Articulus 90 (gg)

[*90*] (hh Si vir alloquitur bona (ii) vel pannos aut quidquam suarum rerum(jj) fuerit, quod sibi subtractum (kk) fuerit, ad hoc se unica manu trahere debet et (ll) iurare tacto sacramento, quod tunc(mm) suum fuit et nunc (nn suum sit nn), cum sibi subtractum seu raptum fuerat. Si autem equus fuerit, (oo quem vir

---

(a) K^1 C^3 *Art. 85* K^2 *Art. 84* W^1 *Art. 81* W^2 *Art. 83* C^1 *Art. 89* C^2 *Art. 91* (b) *manus* ɳ C^1 (c) vir C^2 (d) aliqua W^1 W^2 (e) possessio C^3 (f) *desunt* W^1 W^2 C^3 (g) protestata W^1 infiscata C^3 (h) *deest* C^2 (i) *deest* K^1 K^2 C^3 (j) extunc ille qui possessionem infiscacionem precepit cum fiscacione per tres dies et noctes debet possidere. Eciam ipse C^3 (k) iura K^1 K^2 (l) iustificacionem W^1 (m) tribus K^1 K^2 W^1 W^2 (n) *deest* K^1 K^2 W^1 W^2 (o) *deest* W^1 W^2 C^2 C^3 (p) cum fiscacione W^1 W^2 (q) Postea vero eadem bona exhibere debet in tribus iudiciis continue per quindenam C^3 (r) *deest* W^1 (s) si W^1 *deest* K^1 K^2 (t) indicare C^3 formare W^2 (u) cum C^3 (v) Et tunc bene W^1 W^2 Extunc C^3 (w) eadem bona C^3 (x) hominum proborum W^1 W^2 hominum honestorum C^3 (y) Sed tunc K^1 Sed si tunc K^2 Si autem W^1 W^2 (z) de hiis C^3 (aa) de hoc W^1 W^2 (bb) hoc illi instituere debet C^3 (cc) hoc W^1 W^2 (dd) Si autem defectum in hoc habuerit, extunc ulterius ipsum impetere oportebit. C^3 (ee) Si sibi sufficit K^1 Si sibi non sufficit K^2 (ff) tunc W^1 W^2 (gg) K^1 *Art. 86* K^2 *Art. 85* K^5 *Art. 43 pars. 2* C^1 *Art. 90* W^1 *Art. 82* C^2 *Art. 92–93* C^3 *Art. 86* W^2 *Art. 84* (hh) Si eciam aliquis arestat equum, quem sibi aliquis subtraxerit vel subtractus fuerit aut spoliatus, ad hoc se trahere potest, ut iuris est, supradictum. ⟨Qualiter equus arestatur⟩ Quod si quis arestat equ[u]m vel quod si subtractus fuerit aut spoliatus fuerit, ad hoc se unica manu trahere debet tacto sacramento, qui tunc suus fuit et nunc suum quando sibi subtractum fuit et se trahere debet K^5 (ii) aliqua W^2 sua C^2 C^3 (jj) *deest* C^2 (kk) aut raptum K^1 K^2 W^1 W^2 C^2 C^3 (ll) debet C^3 (mm) *deest* K^1 K^2 (nn) sumpsit K^1 *desunt* K^2 (oo) *desunt* C^3

autem equ[u]s (a), (bquem vir alloquiturb),xx) quod sibi(c) subtractus sit(d) aut(e) eo(f) spoliatus sit(g), ad hoc se(h) trahere debet: (i) (jcum suo dextro pede calcare debetj) equo super (k) pedem anteriorem(l) {a}, et (m) sinistra manu equ[u]m capere per dextram aurem, et petere debet reliquias et(n) prolocutorem. Et iurabit equo(o) (ptacto sacramentop) super caput, (q) quod tunc suus fuerit et nunc suus(r) sit, cum(s) sibi subtractus ⟨aut⟩(t) (uab(v) eo depredatusu) fuerit. Et tunc ille ad suum se(w) trahat venditorem(x) (yet(z) ipsum(aa) iurare (bbopportet super sanctosbb), quod trahat se (cc) cum equo ad (dd) verum venditorem(ee),y) (ffibi eumff) sequi opportet, nisi(gg) trans(hh) Mare Aquilonis. (iiSin autem (jj) dicit, quod equ[u]m emerit in foro libero (kk) et venditorem habere non possit, tunc(ll) equ[u]m ammittit et (mm) argentum (nn) pro eo(oo) datum, et(pp) non (qqammittit(rr) (ss) aliquam penamqq).ii)

Articulus 86 (tt)

[*86*] (uuSi viruu) conqueritur super virum (vvpro debito(ww)vv) (xxa manu mortuaxx), et ipsum infestare(yy) ⟨informare⟩(zz) voluerit (aaasecundum edictum iurisaaa), hoc facere potest unica manu sacramento tacto, (bbb) si ille (ccc) consenserit. Sin autem dixerit hic, super quem querimonia prolata fuerit, quod(ddd) de debito (eeenesciat vel in eo (fffnon(ggg) sitfff) obligatuseee),

---

(a) fuerit S^3 S^4 S^5 S^2 S^8 S^9 K^4 (b) *desunt* S^4 S^5 (c) si *ad Art. 43* K^5 (d) *deest* S^2 S^3 S^4 S^5 S^8 S^9 K^4 (e) *deest* S^9 (f) *deest* S^{10} *ad Art. 43* K^5 (g) *deest* S^{10} (h) *deest* S^4 S^5 se unica manu *in Art. 43* K^5 (i) tacto sacramento, qui tunc suus fuit et nunc suum quando sibi subtractum fuit et se trahere debet, *ad Art. 43* K^5 (j) *desunt* S^4 S^5 (k) suum S^1 S^2 S^3 S^4 S^5 S^8 K^4 K^5 (l) anteriorem sinistrum K^5 (m) si S^{10} (n) ⟨et⟩ S^8 (o) *deest ad Art. 43* K^5 (p) *desunt* S^9 (q) quem equum trahat se ad verum tutorem K^4 (r) *deest ad Art. 43* K^5 (s) et K^5 (t) *manus B* S^6 aut S^1 S^2 S^3 S^4 S^5 S^8 S^9 S^{10} K^3 K^4 K^5 *ad Art. 43* K^5 (u) eodem die predatus K^5 aut depredatus *ad Art. 43* K^5 (v) de S^2 *deest* S^1 S^3 S^4 S^5 S^8 S^9 S^{10} K^3 K^4 (w) *deest* S^{10} (x) tutorem K^4 (y) *desunt ad Art. 43* K^5 (z) ut K^5 (aa) *deest* K^4 (bb) debet tacto sacramento K^4 (cc) ├cum┤ S^6 (dd) suum S^4 S^5 (ee) tutorem S^9 K^4 (ff) ad quem ille ipsum iure K^4 (gg) a S^5 non autem K^4 (hh) ultra S^2 K^4 (ii) et de ceteris ut supra S^4 *deest* S^5 (jj) vir S^9 (kk) aut communi S^2 (ll) *deest* S^2 (mm) suum S^2 K^4 (nn) quod K^4 (oo) equo S^2 (pp) sed S^2 S^9 (qq) iudici demeretur S^2 (rr) perdet K^4 (ss) pro eo S^9 K^4 (tt) S^1 S^4 S^5 S^6 S^{10} *Art. 86* S^2 *Art. 91* S^3 S^9 *Art. 92* S^8 *Art. 85* K^3 *Art. 89* K^4 *Art. 90* K^5 *Art. 93* (uu) Quis S^5 (vv) *desunt* S^9 (ww) pecunia K^4 (xx) postmortuam manum K^4 (yy) informare S^8 K^4 (zz) *probabiliter manus B* S^6 (aaa) de hoc, ut iuris est K^4 (bbb) et hoc K^4 (ccc) sibi K^4 (ddd) *deest* K^4 (eee) esse ignorantem K^4 (fff) *desunt* S^3 (ggg) ut S^4 S^5

{a} p r z e d n o S^4 S^5

alloquitur, quod sibi subtractus aut eo[(a)] spoliatus sit, et[oo)] ad hoc se trahere debet[hh)]: [(b)] cum[(c)] suo dextro pede calcare debet equo[(d)] supra suum[(e)] pedem anteriorem [(f)], et sinistra manu equum [(g)] capere [(h]per dextram aurem, et petere debet reliquias et prolocutorem[(i)h)]. | Et iurabit equo[(j)] 49vb
super caput [(k]tacto sacramento[k)], quod tunc suus fuit et nunc[(l)] suus sit[(m)], cum sibi [(n)] subtractus aut eo[(o)] depredatus fuerit[(p)]. [(q)] [(r]Extunc ille se[(s)] ad suum venditorem[(t)] trahit[r)(u)], [(v]ibi eum sequi oportet[(w)], nisi [(x)]trans Mare Aquilonis[v)]. [(y(z]Arestatur oportet iurare, quod se trahit ad verum suum venditorem.[z)] Si autem [(aa)] dixerit, quod equum emerit in foro libero [(bb]et[(cc)] communi[bb)] et venditorem[(dd)] habere non possit, extunc equum amittit et argentum[(ee)] [(ff)] pro eo datum, et non[(gg)] amittit[(hh)] aliquam [(ii)] penam.[y)]

Articulus 91 [(jj)]

[*91*] | ⟨post mortuam manum⟩[(kk)] Si vir super virum ⟨de eodem quem XXVIII folio⟩[(ll)] 50ra
conqueritur pro debito [(mm]manu mortis[mm)], et ipsum [(nn)] informari[(oo)] vol- XXIII
uerit [(pp]secundum edictum iuris[pp)], [(qq)] hoc facere potest [(rr)] tacto sacramento, [(ss)] si [(tt)] consenserit [(uu]sola manu[uu)]. Si autem dixerit[(vv)] hic, super quem[(ww)] querimonia prolata[(xx)] fuerit, [(yy]quod de[(zz)] debito nesciat [(aaa]vel[(bbb)] in eo sit obligatus[aaa)], aut quod[(ccc)] ille persolvit[(ddd)yy)], hoc [(eee)]

(a) *deest* W1 W2 (b) quod K1 K2 (c) *deest* K5 (d) *deest* W1 W2 (e) *deest* K5 (f) sinistrum K5 (g) debet W1 W2 (h) reliquias, id est calcare et prolocutorem C2 (i) procuratorem K5 (j) *deest* C3 K5 (k) *desunt* W1 W2 (l) tunc K1 K2 (m) *deest* C2 (n) sit C3 (o) *deest* K5 (p) *deest* W1 W2 (q) *rubrica:* Pars si ad venditorem ⊢ter⊣ trahit, et si dixerit, quod eum in foro libero emerit et venditorem habere non possit. C2 (r) Extunc ipse se trahat ad suum tutorem et ipsum iurare oportet super sanctos, quod trahat se cum equo ad verum tutorem W1 Extunc ipse se trahat cum equo ad verum tutorem et ipsum iurare oportet super sanctos, quod trahat se cum equo ad verum tutorem W2 (s) *deest* K1 K2 (t) tutorem C3 (u) *deest* K1 K2 (v) et iurare debet tacto sacramento, quod equum trahat ad verum tutorem, ad quem ille ipsum iure sequi debet, non autem ultra Mare Aquilonis C3 (w) et C2 (x) ad W1 W2 (y) *desunt* K5 (z) *desunt* K1 K2 W1 W2 C2 C3 (aa) vir W1 W2 (bb) *desunt* C3 (cc) aut K1 K2 W1 W2 (dd) tutorem W1 W2 (ee) pecuniam W1 W2 (ff) suum C3 (gg) *deest* K2 (hh) perdet C3 (ii) pro eo W1 W2 (jj) K1 C3 *Art. 87* K2 *Art. 86* W1 *Art. 83* W2 *Art. 85* C1 *Art. 91* C2 *Art. 94* (kk) *manus γ* C1 (ll) *manus δ; manicula* C1 (mm) post mortuam manum C3 (nn) de hoc C3 (oo) infestare K1 K2 infamare C2 (pp) ut iuris est C3 (qq) ⟨pecunia debita⟩ C3 (rr) unica manu K1 K2 W1 W2 C3 sola manu C2 (ss) dixerit W1 hoc C3 (tt) ille K1 K2 ipse W1 iste sibi W2 (uu) ille sibi C3 *desunt* K1 K2 W1 W2 C2 (vv) *deest* K1 K2 (ww) *deest* K1 K2 (xx) probata K1 (yy) se debitum ignorare, aut quod alter persolverit, ex parte cuius fuerit, ex parte cuius fuerit impulsatus C3 (zz) ipse de W2 *deest* W1 (aaa) *desunt* W1 W2 (bbb) nec K1 K2 (ccc) *deest* W1 W2 (ddd) sit obligatus K1 K2 (eee) eum W1 W2

aut quod[(a)] [(b)] persolverit, [(c)] hoc opportet iuramento probare metseptimus[(d)] tacto sacramento. [(e)]

Articulus 87 [(f)]

[*87*] Si[(g)] vir cum scitu [(h]contra alium[h)] ad iusticiam se exhibuerit, et alter noluerit[(i)] aut spreverit, et vulneret[(j)] illum non querulando absque iure, et ille[(k)], qui[(l)] vulneratus [(m]sit, inveniet[m)] [(n)] defensionem et mutuo[(o)] vulneret illum, et[(p)] hic[(q)], qui primo vulneravit suum adversarium, primo ad iudicium veniat et conqueratur, et alter, [(r]in quo pax violata[r)] sit, eciam postea[(s)] veniat ⟨eodem die⟩[(t)] circa lucem [(u)] diei et dicat, quod inicium[(v)] illius fuerit et non suum. Si hoc, ut[(w)] iuris fuerit[(x)], metseptimus protestabitur cum probis[(y)] hominibus, qui [(z)] viderunt et audierunt, [(aa)] qui presentes fuerunt, acquirit primam querelam. [(bb)] [(cc]Unus[(dd)] vir potest filium suum[(ee)] eximere[(ff)] [(gg)] unica manu, qui est in pane suo non uxoratus, tacto sacramento, [(hh)] quod [(ii)] filius suus reus non sit.[cc)] ⟨Huius facti. Si autem noxa una tam super patrem, quam super filium simul fuerit querulata, extunc patrem se ipsum oportebit primo eximere de tali facto.⟩[(jj)]

(a) *deest* S^{10} (b) ille K^4 (c) ex parte cuius fuerit inculpatus K^4 (d) *deest* S^3 (e) Si autem dixerit, quod solus illi debitum hoc persolvisset, hoc iurare debet mettercius tacto sacramento cum hominibus fidedignis. K^4 (f) S^1 S^4 S^5 S^6 S^{10} *Art. 87* S^2 S^9 *Art. 92* S^3 *Art. 93* S^8 *Art. 86* K^3 *Art. 90* K^4 *Art. 91* K^5 *Art. 94* (g) *deest* S^{10} (h) *desunt* S^2 (i) voluerit S^{10} (j) vulnera inter S^{10} (k) *deest* S^2 (l) *deest* S^2 K^4 (m) veniet ad S^2 K^4 (n) et ad K^5 (o) inicium S^3 (p) ut S^9 (q) *deest* S^2 (r) cui facta facta violencia S^2 (s) violenta K^5 *deest* S^3 S^{10} (t) *manus commentatoris* S^6 (u) eiusdem S^2 (v) iudicium S^9 (w) quod ⟨ut⟩ S^8 (x) *deest* S^3 (y) fidedignis S^3 (z) hoc S^2 (aa) vel S^2 K^4 (bb) Item S^8 ⟨Pater eximit filium⟩ K^5 (cc) Sed si sua querela pernoctabitur, hoc facere non potest. S^2 *desunt* S^3 (dd) *deest* S^9 K^4 (ee) *deest* K^3 K^4 (ff) extunc K^5 (gg) ⟨Nota⟩ S^9 (hh) sic S^4 S^5 S^8 K^4 (ii) iuret S^8 iuret sic, quia S^9 (jj) *manus B* S^6 post mortem tuam manum. Hoc potest facere in eodem iudicio aut per sex ebdomadas querimonia facta aliter norunt [*?*]. Si autem noxa una tam super patrem, quam super filium fuerit querulata simul, extunc patrem se ipsum oportebit primo eximere de tali facto. K^5 Si autem pater et filius ambo pro uno facto fuerint impulsati, extunc patrem oportet se primo de facto iuridice expurgare. K^4

oportet iurare(a) metseptimus (btacto sacramento (cpost mortuam manum, hoc statim facere potest(d)b)c). (e)

Articulus 92 (f)

[92] | ⟨Si vir cum⟩(g) Si vir cum scitu ad iusticiam (hcontra aliumh) se exhibuerit, et alter noluerit(i) aut spreverit, et vulneret illum(j) non(k) querulando absque iure, et ille vulneratus venerit ad defensionem et vulneret(l) illum mutuo, et (m) hic, qui(n) primo vulneravit suum adversarium, prius(o) ad iudicium veniat et conqueratur, alter, in quo pax violata sit, eciam (ppostea veniatp) circa lucem diei et dicat, quod inicium illius fuerat et non suum. Si hoc, (qut(r) iuris fuerit,q) metseptimus protestabit[ur] cum probis hominibus, qui (s) viderunt et audierunt, vel qui (t) presentes fuerunt(u), (v) aquisivit primam querelam. Vir potest filium suum(w) (xunica manux) eximere, qui est in pane suo non uxoratus, tacto sacramento sic(y), quod filius suus (z) reus non sit. (aa) 50rb

(a) protestari W^1 W^2 (b) ipsum W^1 W^2 (c) *desunt* K^1 K^2 C^3 (d) *deest* C^2 (e) Si autem dixerit, quod solus illi soli hoc debitum persolvisset, hoc iurare debet mettercius tacto sacramento cum hominibus fidedignis. C^3 (f) K^1 C^3 *Art. 88* K^2 *Art. 87* K^4 *Art. 91* W^1 *Art. 84* W^2 *Art. 86* C^1 *Art. 92* C^2 *Art. 95* (g) *manus η* C^1 (h) *desunt* W^1 W^2 (i) voluerit C^2 (j) alium C^3 (k) *deest* K^1 K^2 (l) voluerit C^2 (m) primo C^2 (n) *deest* K^1 (o) *deest* C^2 (p) post adveniat eodem die et W^1 postea deveniat eodem die et W^2 (q) *desunt* C^3 (r) *deest* C^2 (s) hoc K^2 (t) tunc W^1 W^2 (u) *deest* K^1 (v) extunc W^1 W^2 (w) *deest* C^3 (x) vincat iuramento W^1 vincat manu W^2 (y) *deest* C^3 (z) huius facti W^1 W^2 (aa) Si autem noxa una tam super patrem, quam filium fuerit querulata simul, extunc patrem semper primo oportet eximere de tali noxa. W^1 W^2 Si autem pater et filius ambo pro uno facto fuerint impulsati, extunc patrem oportet se primo de facto veridice expurgare. C^3

Articulus 88 (a)

[*88*] Si mulier(b) deprehensa fuerit in facto manifesto (c) in homicidio aut (d) vulneribus (e) duello dignis, (f hanc(g) ipsam f) ⟨vir⟩(h) propius(i) est vincere metseptimus(j) cum hominibus fidedignis, quam innocens fieri pos-
162r sit. Extunc ipsam | iudicium pati(k) opportet. Si autem vir querulatur super feminam pro homicidio aut vulneribus, quod eodem die factum fuerit aut(l) visum, et si femina(m) fideiussorie caucionem fecerit supra ius, de quo femina propius est(n) evadere cum hominibus fidedignis metseptima, quam ultra(o) aliquam vim(p) in ea agere(q) possit. Si autem femina(r) inculpatur pro querimoniis pernoctatis, eo(s) propius evadere femina (t) unica manu tacto sacramento potest(u), quam eam(v) aliquis vincere possit aut aliquid (w in posterum w) contrarium(x) pati (y pro eo y).

Articulus 89 (z)

[*89*] Si vir duplices pueros habuerit et primos(aa) (bb antea eradicavit bb) {a} exponendo, et si postea secundis(cc) pueris aliquid dederit in suis bonis, et moriatur idem vir, hoc secundi pueri ante tollunt. Et quidquid superfluum fuerit(dd) aut(ee) supermanserit(ff), hoc equaliter (gg inter se gg) dividunt, cum omnes equales sibi(hh) fuerint in natura.

(a) S1 S4 S5 S6 S10 *Art. 88* S2 S9 *Art. 93* S3 *Art. 94* S8 *Art. 87* K3 *Art. 91* K4 *Art. 92* K5 *Art. 95* (b) femina S1 S2 S3 S4 S5 S8 S9 S10 K4 K5 (c) sic est S4 sicut est S5 (d) in S9 (e) duellaribus seu K4 (f) ac ipsorum K5 (g) ac S1 S4 S5 S9 S10 K3 actor S3 (h) *manus commentatoris* S6 S8 vir K3 K4 (i) proxima K5 (j) *deest* S3 (k) *deest* K5 (l) ac S3 S8 K4 ad S4 ad ⟨et⟩ S5 (m) *in ms.* femine [*s*] S6 (n) *deest* S2 (o) *deest* S3 K4 ├ultra┤ ⟨in⟩ S8 (p) *deest* S2 K3 K4 ├vim┤ S8 (q) vincere S2 K4 ├agere┤ ⟨vincere⟩ S8 (r) mulier aut vir S2 mulier K4 (s) et S1 S10 *deest* S9 (t) aut vir S2 (u) est S2 S3 S4 S5 S8 S9 S10 K4 K5 *deest* K3 (v) *deest* S3 S8 (w) ipsorum K5 (x) *deest* S4 S5 (y) *desunt* S1 S2 S3 S4 S5 S8 S9 S10 K3 K4 (z) S1 S4 S5 S6 S10 *Art. 89* S2 S9 *Art. 94* S3 *Art. 95* S8 *Art. 88* K3 *Art. 92* K4 *Art. 93* K5 *Art. 96* (aa) ⟨primos⟩ S8 (bb) ante ea hereditavit K5 (cc) aliis S2 (dd) *deest* S4 S5 (ee) *deest* S2 S4 S5 K4 (ff) *deest* S2 K4 (gg) *desunt* K5 (hh) manserit K5 *deest* S9

{a} ⟨hereditavit id est dimis[s]it vulgariter o d d z ÿ e l ẏ l o d s z y e b y e⟩ K5

Articulus 93 (a)

[*93*] | ⟨Quando femina vinci potest et quomodo evadere potest bonum⟩(b) Si femina depre- 50va
hensa fuerit in facto manifesto (c) in(d) homicidio aut vulneribus (e duello
dignis e), hanc(f) vir propius est(g) vincere metseptimus (h cum hominibus
fidedignis h), quam (i) innocens fieri possit. Extunc ipsam iudicium pati(j)
oportet. Si autem vir querelam(k) super feminam pro homicidio aut(l) vul-
neribus, (m quod eodem die m) factum sit ac visum, et si femina caucionem
fideiussorie | fecerit supra ius, (n de quo n) femina propius est evadere met- 50vb
septima cum hominibus(o) fidedignis, quam aliquis eam vincere possit. Si
autem mulier inculpatur pro querimoniis(p) pernoctatis, (q de quo q) propius
est evadere femina(r) propria(s) manu tacto sacramento, quam eam(t) aliquis
vincere possit, aut aliquid (u in posterum contrarium u) pati(v).

Articulus 94 (w)

[*94*] ⟨Si vir duplices pueros habuerit⟩(x) Si vir duplices pueros habuerit et primos
antea(y) | exradicavit exponendo(z), et si secundis(aa) aliquid postea dederit 51ra
in suis bonis, et moriatur idem vir, hoc secundi(bb) pueri (cc ante tollunt cc). XXV
Extunc quidquid superfluum fuerit, hoc(dd) equaliter inter se dividunt(ee),
cum(ff) omnes equales sibi(gg) fuerint in natura.

(a) K^1 C^3 *Art. 89* K^2 *Art. 88* W^1 *Art. 85* W^2 *Art. 87* C^1 *Art. 93* C^2 *Art. 96* (b) *manus γ* C^1 (c) sicud W^1 W^2 (d) *deest* C^3 (e) duellaribus W^1 W^2 C^3 (f) *deest* W^1 (g) *deest* C^3 (h) hominibus K^1 K^2 (i) ipsa W^1 W^2 (j) attingere K^1 K^2 (k) querulatur K^1 K^2 W^1 W^2 C^3 (l) tunc K^1 (m) *desunt* K^1 K^2 (n) extunc W^1 W^2 (o) *deest* C^3 (p) querelis W^1 W^2 (q) et K^1 quod K^2 eo W^1 W^2 de eo C^2 unc C^3 (r) *deest* W^1 (s) unica K^1 K^2 C^3 unica sua W^1 W^2 (t) *deest* W^1 (u) pro eo W^1 W^2 (v) *deest* C^3 (w) K^1 C^3 *Art. 90* K^2 *Art. 89* W^1 *Art. 86* W^2 *Art. 88* C^1 *Art. 94* C^2 *Art. 97* (x) *manus β* C^1 (y) ante ea K^1 K^2 (z) excipiendo C^3 (aa) secundis pueris K^1 K^2 W^1 W^2 C^2 aliis pueris C^3 (bb) *deest* W^1 W^2 C^3 (cc) attolunt W^1 W^2 (dd) *deest* C^3 (ee) condividunt W^1 W^2 (ff) quia W^1 W^2 (gg) *deest* C^2

Articulus 90 [(a)]

[*90*] Si vir scabinum [(b]in [(c)] scampno[b)] indecenter[(d)] in iudicio bannito [(e)] increpaverit[(f)] [(g)], si hoc probaverit per suos consodales, qui [(h)] audiverunt, illum opportet dare emendam [(i]scabino et iudici suam[(j)] penam[i)]. [(k)]

Articulus 91 [(l)]

[*91*] Si super virum querimonia[(m)] facta pro homicidio fuerit aut pro[(n)] vulneribus, et ipse ⟨se ad ius⟩[(o)] accomodaverit circa suam hereditatem ad comparendum, et si[(p)] profugus factus fuerit, quod[(q)] non comparet, tunc debet vocari cum[(r)] clamore, ut iuris est. Et si non comparet [(s)] iudicio eodem [(t)],
162ᵛ tunc debet describi [(u]et | recompensa super[(v)] suam hereditatem iudicatur[(w)], et iudici sua pena. [(x]Et eciam[x)] nullus[(y)] alcius cogi potest caucionem facere fideiussoriam, quam [(z)] se sua extendit recompensa, nisi sit [(aa)] pro debito, quod maius[(bb)] sit[u)]. [(cc)]

Articulus 92 [(dd)]

[*92*] Si casu contencio [(ee)] oritur[(ff)] [(gg)] clara die[(hh)], si probus vir[(ii)] in eo accusetur [(jj)], qui [(kk)] ibi visus non fuerit, de quo propius est evadere metsepti-

---

(a) S^1 S^4 S^5 S^6 S^{10} *Art. 90* S^2 S^9 *Art. 95* S^3 *Art. 96* S^8 *Art. 89* K^3 *Art. 93* K^4 *Art. 94* K^5 *Art. 97* (b) *desunt* S^8 (c) sede aut S^9 (d) iudiciali sive S^8 (e) indecenter S^9 (f) improperaverit S^8 (g) aut turpibus verbis obruerit S^3 (h) hoc S^3 (i) scabinis xxx solidos. Ignorant quousque ad iudicium tercium, tunc sentenciam debent invenire, longius non tardare K^5 (j) *deest* S^4 S^5 S^8 S^{10} (k) Quod sit emenda aut pena conpare libro 20 Registro [*SSp. III.32§10*] S^2 (l) S^1 S^4 S^5 S^6 S^{10} *Art. 91* S^2 S^9 *Art. 96* S^3 *Art. 97* S^8 *Art. 90* K^3 *Art. 94* K^4 *Art. 95* K^5 *Art. 98* (m) querela S^8 (n) *deest* S^2 S^4 S^5 S^8 S^{10} K^5 (o) *manus commentatoris* S^6 se ad ius S^9 se S^3 S^4 S^5 S^8 K^5 (p) *deest* S^2 S^9 (q) *deest* S^2 S^9 (r) *deest* S^2 S^3 S^4 S^5 S^8 (s) in K^3 S^9 (t) secundo S^2 die S^{10} K^4 (u) *desunt* S^4 S^5 (v) ⟨su⟩per S^8 (w) computatur S^2 computatur seu iudicatur S^3 S^9 (x) *desunt* S^9 (y) ⟨nemo⟩ S^8 *deest* K^3 (z) ut S^2 (aa) ⟦sit⟧ S^6 (bb) *deest* K^3 (cc) Nullus alcius fideiubetur, quam sua se extendit recompensa. K^5 (dd) S^1 S^4 S^5 S^6 S^{10} *Art. 92* S^2 S^9 *Art. 97* S^3 *Art. 98* S^8 *Art. 91* K^3 *Art. 95* K^4 *Art. 96* K^5 *Art. 99* (ee) fuerit vel S^9 K^3 K^5 (ff) moritur S^{10} (gg) in S^2 (hh) luce diei vel tempestate noctis S^9 die luce K^5 (ii) *deest* S^2 (jj) ⟦in eo⟧ S^6 (kk) est S^{10}

Articulus 95 (a)

[95] ⟨de eodem f[olio] V⟩ (b) Si vir (c scabinum in scampno c) incidenter(d) in iudicio bannito increpaverit, si hoc probaverit (e per suos consodales, qui hoc(f) audierunt e), illum oportet (g) emendam dare scabino(h) et iudici penam. (i Scabini si in una sentencia non fuerint unanimes vel eam ignorantes, extunc eandem ad secundum(j) vel ad tercium(k) proximum(l) iudicium (m valeant dilatare m), extunc eam(n) inferre(o) debent(p) vel mittere eam(q), ferre illuc quo conpetit, si nequeant invenire et non diucius prolongare. i)

Articulus 96 (r)

[96] | (s) Si super virum querimonia(t) facta fuerit pro homicidio aut (u) vulne- 51rb
ribus, et ipse (v) accomodaverit (w) circa suam hereditatem ad conparendum, et si(x) non conparet, et profugus factus fuerit, tunc debet vocari(y) clamore, (z ut iuris est. Et si non conparet z) iudicio (aa), tunc debet proscribi(bb) et reconpensa super suam hereditatem conputatur, et iudici sua pena(cc). (dd) Et eciam nullus alcius cogi potest vir(ee) caucionem(ff) iure(gg) (hh fideiussorie facere hh), nisi prout extendit (ii fideiussorie nullus alcius ponat, quam sua reconpensa, nisi debitum se ad maius se extendit, tunc oportet ii) sua reconpensa, nisi (jj) pro debito (kk), quod maius sit.

Articulus 97 (ll)

[97] | Si casu(mm) contencio oritur (nn) clara die, si probus vir pro eo accuse- 51va
tur, qui ibi(oo) visus non fuerit, de quo propius est evadere metseptimus cum

(a) K^1 C^3 *Art. 91* K^2 *Art. 90* K^4 *Art. 94 pars* Scabini–prolongare C^1 *Art. 95* W^1 *Art. 87* C^2 *Art. 98* W^2 *Art. 89* (b) *manus β* C^1 ⟨Scabinum increpaverit⟩ C^3 (c) *desunt* W^1 W^2 (d) incidentaliter C^2 (e) *desunt* K^1 K^2 (f) *deest* W^1 C^3 W^2 (g) eum C^3 (h) *deest* K^1 K^2 (i) *desunt* K^1 K^2 W^1 W^2 (j) *in ms.* secundam [*s*] C^1 (k) *in ms.* terciam [*s*] C^1 (l) *deest* C^2 (m) possunt C^3 (n) *deest* C^2 (o) proferre C^3 (p) *deest* C^3 (q) *deest* C^3 (r) K^1 C^3 *Art. 92* K^2 *Art. 91* C^1 *Art. 96* W^1 *Art. 88* C^2 *Art. 99–100* W^2 *Art. 90* (s) *manicula* C^1 (t) querela W^1 W^2 (u) pro W^1 W^2 (v) se K^1 K^2 C^2 C^3 se ad ius W^1 W^2 (w) et fideiusserit C^2 (x) *deest* W^1 C^2 (y) invocari W^1 W^2 (z) in W^1 C^2 W^2 (aa) eodem K^1 K^2 W^1 W^2 C^3 (bb) describi C^3 (cc) ⟨pena⟩ C^2 (dd) *rubrica:* Nullus vir potest cogi caucionem fideiussorie facere suam recompensam. C^2 (ee) nisi K^1 K^2 C^3 *deest* W^1 W^2 (ff) *deest* W^1 W^2 (gg) *deest* K^2 (hh) fideiussores ponere W^1 W^2 (ii) racio K^1 se W^1 W^2 C^2 *deest* C^3 K^2 (jj) sit K^1 K^2 W^1 C^2 C^3 W^2 (kk) peccuniali W^1 W^2 (ll) K^1 C^3 *Art. 93* K^2 *Art. 92* C^1 *Art. 97* W^1 *Art. 89* C^2 *Art. 101* W^2 *Art. 91* (mm) *in ms.* causu [*s*] C^1 (nn) in W^1 W^2 (oo) *deest* C^3

mus cum hominibus fidedignis, qui presentes fuerunt, quam in(a) eo duellum acquirere possit. Si autem super virum ydoneum circa noctis tempestatem (b) pro(c) homicidio aut vulneribus duello dignis (d(ealloqutum(f) fuerit d), quod noctis tempore factum sit e) (g), de quo propius evadet metseptimus cum hominibus probitate(h) probatis, circa quos tunc fuit, (icum hoc(j) factum(k) perpetratum est, cum(l) (m) sit de facto innocens i).

Articulus 93 (n)

[*93*] Quem vir pro advocato(o) rogaverit, hunc (psuam causam tenere p) opportet iure(q), nisi(r) se excusaverit cum pena. ⟨apud iudicem⟩(s)

Articulus 94 (t)

[*94*] Et (u) quando vir moritur, tunc (v) uxori (woves presentari debent ad(x) supellectilia w), (yubicumque ierint(z). Anete y), colcidre, (aa) (bbvela(cc), tecture currum(dd) bb), olle picte eciam(ee) ad supellectilia pertinent.

Articulus 95 (ff)

[*95*] Nemo potest nec pro homicidio nec pro vulneribus nec pro aliquo debito suum(gg) (hh) probare incolatum ⟨iuramento aut eciam pro effusione sanguinis. Et si promiserit virum iuramentum coram iudicio pro enormibus verbis, aut verberibus seu depilacione, vel sanguinis effusione, de quo solutus dimitti non potest, nisi voluntas aut consensus ad hoc fuerit iudicis.⟩(ii)

(a) *deest* S[5] (b) querimonia facta fuerit S[2] S[9] K[4] querulatum fuerit S[3] (c) quod K[5] (d) *desunt* S[3] ⟨allocutum fuerit⟩ S[8] (e) *desunt* S[2] (f) accusatum S[4] S[5] (g) ⟨allocutum fuerit⟩ S[8] (h) bonitate S[2] S[3] S[4] S[5] S[8] K[4] (i) *desunt* S[4] S[5] (j) *deest* S[2] (k) *deest* S[9] (l) *deest* S[2] K[4] (m) aut ita quod S[2] ita quod K[4] ⟨ita quod⟩ S[8] (n) S[1] S[4] S[5] S[6] S[10] *Art. 93* S[2] S[9] *Art. 98* S[3] *Art. 99* S[8] *Art. 92* K[3] *Art. 96* K[4] *Art. 97* K[5] *Art. 100* (o) prolocutore K[4] (p) verbum suum loqui K[4] (q) *deest* S[2] S[3] S[9] (r) ubi S[3] (s) *manus commentatoris* S[6] (t) S[1] S[4] S[5] S[6] S[10] *Art. 94* S[2] *articulus deest* S[3] *Art. 100* S[8] *Art. 93* S[9] *Art. 99* K[1] *Art. 94 pars 2* K[2] *Art. 93 pars 2* K[3] *Art. 97* K[4] *Art. 98* K[5] *Art. 101 pars 1* (u) si K[1] K[2] (v) sue S[3] S[9] (w) pulmentarii suppellectilia et oves K[1] K[2] (x) et S[9] (y) et ubi erunt S[9] (z) eciam erunt K[2] (aa) et qui habet S[9] (bb) *desunt* S[10] (cc) *deest* K[2] (dd) *deest* K[5] (ee) que S[9] (ff) S[1] S[4] S[5] S[6] *Art. 95* S[2] S[10] *articulus deest* S[3] *Art. 103* S[8] *Art. 94* S[9] *Art. 100* K[3] *Art. 98* K[4] *Art. 99–100* K[5] *Art. 101 pars 2* (gg) suo S[3] S[9] (hh) iuramento S[3] S[4] S[5] S[8] S[9] K[4] (ii) *manus A* S[6]

hominibus fidedignis, qui presentes fuerint, quam in eo duellum acquirere possit. Si autem super virum ydoneum circa noctis [(a]tempestatem querimonia[a)] facta fuerit pro homicidio aut [(b]vulneribus duello dignis[b)], que tempore noctis facta sunt, de quo propius [(c)] evadet metseptimus [(d]cum hominibus bonitate probatis[d)], circa quos tunc [(e]fuit, cum[e)] hoc factum[(f)] perpetratum erat, ita[(g)] quod[(h)] sit[(i)] de facto innocens.

Articulus 98 [(j)]

[*98*] | Quem vir pro advocato[(k)] rogaverit, hunc [(l]causam suam tenere oportet 51vb
[(m)] iure[(n)][l)], nisi se excusaverit cum pena.

Articulus 99 pars 1 [(o)]

[*99 pars 1*] Et [(p)] quando vir moritur, tunc uxori debent dari ad[(q)] suppellectilia oves [(r]et de[(s)] iure inserere[r)], ubi ierint[(t)].

Articulus 99 pars 2 [(u)]

[*99 pars 2*] Nemo potest nec pro homicidio, aut [(v)] vulneribus, seu pro aliquo debito[(w)] suum iuramentum probare incolatum[(x)]. [(y]Consules si iuramentum unius viri receperint, quod [(z)] secundum [(aa]iustam senteciam[(bb)] civitatis et statutam[aa)] consuetudinem exaccionem dedisset, et si[(cc)] tunc post mortem illius[(dd)] iurantis plura bona sub ipsius possessione fuerint inventa, quam perexaccionata[(ee)] fuissent, illa bona consules non habent recipere, sed ipsius defuncti heredes, nisi aliquis heredum denegata eadem

---

(a) horam querela W^1 W^2 (b) vulnere duellari W^1 W^2 (c) eum K^1 K^2 (d) fidedignis W^1 W^2 C^3 (e) *desunt* W^1 (f) *deest* W^1 W^2 (g) *deest* W^1 W^2 (h) *deest* W^1 W^2 C^2 (i) *deest* C^3 (j) K^1 *Art. 94 pars 1* K^2 *Art. 93 pars 1* W^1 *Art. 90* W^2 *Art. 92* C^1 *Art. 98* C^2 *Art. 102* C^3 *Art. 94* (k) prolocutore W^1 W^2 (l) verbum suum loqui oportet W^1 W^2 (m) cum C^3 (n) *deest* K^1 K^2 tamem C^2 (o) W^1 C^1 *Art. 91 pars 1* W^2 *Art. 93 pars 1* C^2 *Art. 103 pars 1* C^3 *Art. 94 pars 1* (p) si W^1 C^3 (q) et C^1 ⟨ad⟩ C^3 omnia C^2 (r) iure W^1 W^2 (s) *deest* C^2 (t) transeant C^3 (u) S^8 *Art. 94* (*in glossa*) *pars* Consules–arbitratur K^1 *Art. 94 pars 3* K^2 *Art. 93 pars 3* K^4 *Art. 100 pars* Consules–arbitratur W^1 *Art. 91 pars 2* W^2 *Art. 93 pars 2* C^1 *Art. 99 pars 2* C^2 *Art. 103 pars 2* C^3 *Art. 94 pars 2* (v) pro W^2 (w) *deest* C^2 (x) auxilium W^1 W^2 (y) *in glossa* S^8 *desunt* K^1 K^2 W^1 W^2 (z) iuste K^4 (aa) civitatis statuta et K^4 (bb) summam S^8 (cc) *deest* K^4 (dd) *deest* C^2 (ee) exaccionata S^8 C^2

Articulus 96 (a)

[*96*] ⟨Regula iuris. In pari delicto vel causa pocior est condicio possidentis. In penis benignior est interpretacio facienda. Item. Non debet aliquis alterius odio pregravari.⟩{a} Quando pupilli suum verum tutorem habere(b) non poterint, eousque nullus ipsos ad aliquam iudicialem responsivam deducere potest (c), nisi prius ad annos (d) pubertatis pervenerint. (e) Et si vir super alterum conqueritur, quod sibi abedificaverit [*s*] aliquid de suis bonis aut hereditate, hoc ille possibilius obtinet, qui habet(f) in possessione unica manu, nisi ipsum cum testimonio alloqutus fuerit. (gExtunc possessor cum testibus servat, si voluerit.g) (h)

Articulus 97 (i)

[*97*] Ubi(j) eciam vir iuramentum (k) promiserit coram iudicio pro enormibus verbis aut depilacione, aut verberibus, aut effusione sanguinis, de quo solutus(l) dimitti non potest, nisi voluntas fuerit iudicis et(m) consensus.

(a) S^1 S^6 S^8 S^{10} *Art. 96* S^2 *Art. 100–101* S^3 *Art. 104–105* S^4 S^5 *Art. 97* S^9 *Art. 101* K^3 *Art. 99* K^4 *Art. 102* K^5 *Art. 103–104* (b) *manicula* S^1 (c) ⟦deducere potest⟧ S^6 (d) discrecionis seu K^5 (e) *subrubrica:* De abedificacione. K^5 (f) *deest* S^4 (g) *desunt* S^4 (h) Quando ad annos pubertatis pervenerit quere libro. S^2 (i) S^1 S^4 S^6 *Art. 97* S^2 *Art. 99* S^3 K^4 *Art. 101* S^5 *Art. 96* S^8 S^{10} *Art. 95* S^9 K^5 *Art. 102* K^3 *Art. 100* (j) Qui S^{10} K^5 (k) prestare S^3 (l) solus S^9 *deest* S^3 (m) aut S^2

{a} *manus A* S^6

bona coram iudicio vel sedenti consilio recipere abrenunciasset, extunc | 52ra
ipsa bona consulibus pro utilitate civitatis permanerent, quemadmodum XXV
arbitratur (a).y)

Articuli 101–102 (b)

[*101*] | (c) Quando pupilli suum verum tutorem(d) non poteri[n]t habere, (e) 52rb
eousque nullus ipsos ad aliquam (fresponsionem (gseu responsivamg) iudicialemf) deducere potest, nisi prius ad annos pervenerint pubertatis(h).

[*102*] ⟨Si aliquid fuerit abedificatum⟩(i) Si vir super alterum conqueritur, quod sibi aliquid abedificaverit [*s*] de (jsuis bonis aut dej)(k) hereditate, hoc ille (lpossibilius obtinetl), qui (m) habet(n) in (o) possessione (p) unica manu, nisi (q) ipsum cum(r) testimonio fuerit allocutus. (sExtunc possessor cum testibus servat (t), si vult mettercius(u).s)

Articulus 100 (v)

[*100*] (w) Ubi(x) eciam vir(y) iuramentum promiserit coram iudicio pro enormibus (z) verbis(aa) aut depilacione, (bb) verberibus(cc) vel(dd) sanguinis ef[f]usione, de quo solutus dimitti non potest, nisi (eevoluntas iudicis fuerit aut consensusee). (ff) (gg(hhActor eciam si(ii) reum pro iuramentis promissis (jj) causa Dei vel peticionis hominum (kk) dimittere(ll) voluerit(mm) absolutum(nn), extunc(oo) iudici(pp) eciam conpetit ad hoc dare suam voluntatem.

(a) seu per arbitrum dimissumm est S^{8} (b) K^{1} *Art. 96–97* K^{2} W^{2} *Art. 95–96* W^{1} *Art. 93–94* C^{1} *Art. 101–102* C^{2} *Art. 106–107* C^{3} *Art. 97–98* (c) Interim W^{1} W^{2} (d) mundibordium W^{1} W^{2} (e) tamdiu C^{3} (f) iudicialia W^{1} W^{2} (g) *desunt* C^{3} (h) discrecionis C^{2} (i) *manus* γ C^{1} (j) sua W^{1} W^{2} (k) sua C^{3} (l) *desunt* W^{1} W^{2} (m) eam W^{1} W^{2} (n) est K^{2} *desunt* K^{1} (o) sua W^{1} W^{2} (p) melius oportet W^{1} W^{2} (q) ille W^{1} W^{2} (r) *deest* W^{1} W^{2} (s) *desunt* C^{3} (t) illa W^{1} W^{2} (u) *deest* K^{1} K^{2} W^{1} W^{2} (v) S^{8} *Art. 95* (*in glossa*) *pars* Actor–eciam K^{1} *Art. 95* K^{2} K^{4} *Art. 101 pars* Actor–eciam K^{5} *Art. 102 cf. pars* Actor–eciam W^{1} *Art. 92* W^{2} *Art. 94* C^{1} *Art. 100* C^{2} *Art. 104–105* C^{3} *Art. 96* (w) ⟨iuramento⟩ C^{3} (x) Si W^{1} W^{2} (y) per K^{1} K^{2} vir unum W^{1} W^{2} (z) vulneribus C^{2} (aa) insidiis K^{1} K^{2} (bb) vel C^{3} (cc) vulneribus W^{1} W^{2} (dd) *deest* W^{1} (ee) fuerit cum iudicis consensu W^{1} W^{2} (ff) *rubrica:* Actor si reum pro iuramentis causa Dei vel peticionis hominum dimittere vellet absolutum etc. C^{2} (gg) *in glossa* S^{8} (hh) *desunt* K^{1} K^{2} W^{1} W^{2} Et si voluerit actor propter Deum et peticionem bonorum hominum dimittat, iudex vero eciam suum consensum adhibere debet, ut sibi decet, et si postea iudex voluerit consentire, tunc actor oportet iuramentum recipere aut illum ad penam iudici remittere. K^{5} (ii) *deest* S^{8} (jj) ⊢culta Dei⊣ C^{1} (kk) proborum C^{2} C^{3} (ll) mittere S^{8} K^{4} (mm) *deest* C^{3} (nn) solutum K^{4} (oo) ex ante C^{3} (pp) iudicia C^{2} *deest* K^{4}

Articulus 98 (a)

[*98*] Eousque civis Meÿdeburgenses(b) veram accionem seu responsivam(c) tenuerint et se(d) coram suo(e) domino pontifice et burgravio ac sculteto ad iusticiam se(f) [*s*] exibuerint circa civitatis ius, tunc nemo eos extra civitatem in (g) alio iure(h) (i) occupare seu contra eos agere in iudicio alieno (j).

Articulus 99 (k)

[*99*] Nullus alterum (l) (minpedire debetm) coram iudicio, postquam (n) iudicium(o) bannitum fuerit, cum iniuriis (ptalibus inpedimentis,p) (q) que ipsum inpedire possint in sua querela, sicut (r) clamore aut turpiloquiis(s), aut ceteris insolenciis. Si hoc contra iusticiam ⟨Regula iuris. Non est sine culpa, qui rei que ad
163v eum non pertinent, se inmiscet.⟩{a} | fecerit(t), et si paciens ipsum protestaverit cum iudice et (u) scabinis, extunc suam acquirit emendam(v) et iudex acquirit(w) suam penam. (xSi contingerit in iudicio castellani, tunc(y) tria talenta demerentur, et in(z) iudicio sculteti(aa) octo solidi. Et ubi homo suam emendam acquirit, ibi obtinet(bb) iudex suam penam.x) (cc)

(a) S^1 S^4 S^5 S^6 *Art. 98* S^3 *Art. 106* S^8 S^{10} *Art. 97* S^9 K^4 *Art. 103* K^3 *Art. 101* K^5 *Art. 105* (b) in Novo Foro aut in Meÿdeburc S^3 Meydburgenses K^5 (c) responsionem S^9 (d) si K^5 (e) *deest* S^{10} K^3 (f) *deest* S^3 S^4 S^5 S^8 (g) aliquo S^{10} (h) iudicio S^4 S^5 (i) debet S^3 (j) ⟨potest⟩ S^8 potest K^4 K^5 (k) S^1 S^4 S^5 S^6 *Art. 99* S^2 K^3 *Art. 102* S^3 *Art. 107* S^8 S^{10} *Art. 98* S^9 K^4 *Art. 104* K^5 *Art. 106* (l) impediat aut K^5 (m) *desunt* S^{10} (n) in S^3 S^4 S^5 K^4 (o) *deest* S^2 (p) *desunt* K^5 (q) ⊢qui⊣ S^6 (r) cum S^3 S^{10} (s) queriloquiis S^3 (t) fuerit S^3 (u) duobus K^4 (v) *deest* K^3 (w) *deest* S^8 (x) *desunt* S^4 S^5 (y) *deest* S^2 (z) *deest* S^9 (aa) *deest* S^9 (bb) *acquisivit* S^2 K^4 (cc) Quid sit emenda et quid pena et quid reconpensacio quere libro 20 Registro. [*SSp. II 20§2*] S^2 ⟨Magdeburg⟩ S^2

{a} *manus A* S^6

Et si suum consensum noluerit(a) adhibere, tunc actorem iuramenta accipere(b) oportebit vel iudici demeretur (cin penac) octo solidorum et non plus pro causis singulis specialitergg), et(d) (equibus ius eciame).hh)

Articulus 103 (f)

[*103*] (g) Eousque(h) Meÿdebur|genses veram (iaccionem (j) aut(k)i) responsionem(l) tenuerint et se coram suo domino pontifice(m) aut burgravio aut(n) sculteto(o) ad(p) iusticiam exhibuerint circa civitatis ius, tunc nemo eos extra civitatem in alio iure occupare, (qseu contra eos agereq) in iudicio potest alieno(r). 52va

Articulus 104 (s)

[*104*] ⟨Nullus alterum debet impedire in iudicio⟩(t) Nullus alterum impedire debet coram iudicio, postquam(u) in(v) iudicium(w) bannitum fecerit(x) cum iniuria (y) talibus impedimentis, que ipsum impedire possint in sua(z) querela, sicut clamore aut turpiloquiis, aut ceteris(aa) insolenciis (bb). Si hoc contra iusticiam fecerit, et si paciens(cc) ipsum(dd) protestare poterit cum iudice et (ee) scabinis, extunc suam (ff) acquirit penam(gg). (hh) Si (ii) contingerit in iudicio castellani, tunc tria talenta demeretur, et in(jj) iudicio sculteti octo solidos. Et ubi homo(kk) suam (llemendam acquirit, ibi et iudex suamll) penam(mm) acquirit.

(a) voluerit C^2 (b) recipere C^3 K^4 (c) *desunt* C^3 (d) *a.c.* ex C^1 (e) quibus suis K^4 quod quibusvis C^2 quibusvis C^3 (f) K^1 *Art. 98* K^2 W^2 *Art. 97* W^1 *Art. 95* C^1 *Art. 103* C^2 *Art. 108* C^3 *Art. 99* (g) ⟨dic⟩ C^3 (h) Quousque K^1 K^2 C^2 Ex quo W^1 W^2 (i) in C^3 (j) in C^2 (k) *deest* W^1 W^2 (l) responsivam K^1 K^2 W^1 W^2 C^2 (m) episcopo W^1 W^2 C^3 (n) *deest* W^2 (o) *deest* W^1 W^2 (p) *deest* W^1 (q) *desunt* W^1 W^2 (r) aliquo W^1 (s) K^1 *Art. 99* K^2 W^2 *Art. 98* W^1 *Art. 96* C^1 *Art. 104* C^2 *Art. 109–110* C^3 *Art. 100* (t) *manus γ* C^1 (u) e quo W^1 ex quo W^2 (v) *deest* K^1 K^2 W^1 W^2 C^2 C^3 (w) *deest* W^1 W^2 (x) fuerit K^1 K^2 W^1 W^2 C^2 C^3 (y) cum W^1 W^2 (z) alia K^1 K^2 (aa) certis K^1 K^2 (bb) fecerit W^1 (cc) percuciens C^2 (dd) in publico K^1 K^2 *deest* W^1 W^2 (ee) duobus W^1 C^3 W^2 (ff) acquirit emendam et iudex suam W^1 W^2 (gg) pecuniam C^3 (hh) *rubrica:* Si hoc peractum fuerit in iudicio castellani aut in iudicio sculteti, extunc tria. C^2 (ii) hoc W^1 W^2 (jj) *deest* C^3 (kk) *deest* C^2 (ll) *desunt* K^1 K^2 (mm) pecuniam C^3

Articulus 100 [(a)]

[*100*] Nunc attendatis [(b]super eo[b)], si scultetus[(c)] aliquem [(d)] inpedierit [(e)] in sua querela et sibi[(f)] iusticiam [(g]non fecit seu[g)] non fecerit, et [(h)] hoc sibi iniuste recusat, si pro eo coram castellano aut advocato inpulsatus fuerit [(i)] cum testibus [(j)] evadere opportet[(k)],[(l)] [(m]⟨cum qualicumque testimonio super iudicem querularus fuerit [(n]cum testimonio[n)] ipsum iudicem[(o)] evadere oportebit⟩[m)] sive sint scabini aut alii astantes [(p)] iudicio. Sin autem hoc[(q)] coram iudicio bannito actum fuerit, tunc[(r)] melius vinci potest [(s)] testibus iure, quam ipse[(t)] [(u)] testibus[(v)] evadere possit. [(w]Sin autem vir[(x)] cedere voluerit[(y)] a testimonio et ipsum inculpare [(z)] pro[(aa)] suo scitu, de quo unica manu evadere potest.[w)] Quando querimonia super ipsum coram advocato [(bb)] fuerit pro hac causa, pro eo respondere tenetur sine mora, ita quod ibi[(cc)] sit iudicium bannitum, quia ipsum opportet ibi[(dd)] esse presentem [(ee)], nisi legale inpedimentum [(ff]ipsum occupaverit, quod inpedimentum[ff)] statim probare opportet. [(gg]Si hoc non[(hh)] ostenderit[(ii)] et non nominare velit, et hoc per iusticiam[(jj)] facere denegaverit, se excusare de sua iniuria, quam exercuit[(kk)], et se ad iusticiam exhibere ⟨voluerit⟩[(ll)], extunc condempnatur [(mm)] advocato
164r ⟨scultetus⟩[(nn)] in decem talentis | idem advocatus[(oo)] et illi[(pp)] suum debitum, de quo [(qq]denegavit facere iusticiam[qq)]; et medio [(rr)] quo illo[(ss)] non solvit solus[(tt)], aut se iure [(uu)] excusaverit iudicio proximo, tunc nullus iudex[(vv)] esse [(ww)] potest, nisi se[(xx)] ex hac culpa eximerit, secundum ut est premissum. Sin autem pro facto criminali, [(yy]pro quo[yy)] iudicium facere recusavit, sicut pro vulneribus aut homicidio, [(zz]aut furtu,[zz)] aut spolio, aut ecclesie[(aaa)]

(a) S^1 S^4 S^5 S^6 *Art. 100* S^2 K^3 *Art. 103* S^3 *Art. 108* S^8 S^{10} *Art. 99* S^9 *Art. 105–106* K^4 *Art. 105* K^5 *Art. 107* (b) *desunt* S^2 (c) advocatus K^4 (d) impediat seu K^5 (e) in iudicio et S^4 S^5 (f) si S^4 S^5 (g) non fecerit. Nunc K^4 *deest* S^1 S^2 S^3 S^4 S^5 S^8 S^9 S^{10} K^3 K^5 (h) si S^2 (i) cum testibus, extunc S^1 S^2 S^3 S^4 S^5 S^8 S^9 K^3 K^4 (j) ipsum S^1 S^3 S^4 S^5 S^8 S^9 K^3 K^4 nisi S^2 (k) potest S^2 (l) *subrubrica:* De querela super iudicem. S^9 (m) *manus B* S^6 *textus adest* S^1 S^2 S^3 S^4 S^5 S^8 S^9 S^{10} K^4 cum quolibet testimonio super iudicem quam tali iudicio ipsum evadere K^5 (n) *desunt* S^{10} (o) *deest* S^2 K^3 (p) in S^5 (q) *deest* S^8 (r) cum K^3 (s) cum K^5 (t) *deest* S^2 (u) cum S^2 K^4 (v) *deest* S^4 S^5 (w) *desunt* S^{10} (x) *deest* S^4 S^5 (y) noluerit S^3 (z) ⟨quod sic scit esse⟩ S^8 (aa) cum S^2 (bb) facta S^2 S^3 S^4 S^5 S^8 S^9 K^4 K^5 (cc) sibi S^{10} K^5 (dd) sibi S^3 (ee) ⟨circa talem iudicium⟩ S^8 (ff) *desunt* K^5 (gg) *desunt* S^4 S^5 (hh) *deest* K^5 (ii) probaverit S^3 (jj) iniusticiam K^5 (kk) excusaverit K^5 (ll) *probabiliter manus B* S^6 (mm) ab S^8 S^9 S^{10} K^4 (nn) *manus B* S^6 se castellano K^5 (oo) scultetus S^2 S^3 K^5 advocatus ⟨scultetus⟩ S^1 advocatus ⟨seu scultetus⟩ S^8 (pp) ille K^5 (qq) de quo facere iusticiam denegavit. Quod impedimentum statim iusticiam vacat, K^5 (rr) tempore S^2 S^9 ⟨tempore⟩ S^8 (ss) *in ms.* illa [*s*] S^6 (tt) *deest* S^3 (uu) ⟨scilicet nam⟩ S^8 (vv) iudicio K^4 (ww) non K^4 (xx) *deest* S^{10} (yy) *desunt* S^2 (zz) *desunt* S^9 (aaa) *deest* S^2

Articulus 105 (a)

[*105*] ⟨Si iudex aliquem impedierit in sua querela vide infra⟩(b) Nunc attentatis super eo, si scultetus(c) aliquem impedierit in sua querela et sibi(d) iusticiam non fecerit, et hoc sibi iniuste recusat, si pro(e) eo coram (fcastellano autf) advocato impulsatus fuerit cum testibus, extunc ipsum cum testibus evadere oportet. (g) Testimonio super iudicem querulatum fuerit, tali ipsum testimonio iudicem evadere oportebit, sive sint scabini aut alii astantes iudicio. Si autem coram(h) iudicio bannito actum(i) fuerit, tunc(j) melius potest vinci testibus iure(k), quam (lipse cuml) testibus evadere possit(m). Si autem(n) vir cedere voluerit a(o) testimonio et ipsum inculpare pro suo (pscitu, dep) quo unica manu evadere potest. Quando querimonia(q) coram advocato super ipsum(r) scultetum(s) facta fuerit, pro | hac causa, pro eo respondere opor- 53ra
tet(t) sine mora, ita quod ibi(u) (v) iudicium bannitum, quia(w) ipsum oportet, XXVII
ibi(x) esse presentem, nisi legale impedimentum fuerit(y), quod(z) (aa) statim probare oportet. Si hoc non ostenderit et non nominaverit, et (bb) hoc pro iusticia facere denegaverit(cc), se excusare (ddde sua(ee) iniuriadd), quam exercuit, et se ad iusticiam(ff) exhibere [debet], extunc condempnatur advocato in decem talentis idem scultetus et illi suum debitum, (gg) de quo negavit facere iusticiam; et (hhmedio temporehh) quo illo(ii) non solvit solus, aut(jj) se(kk) iure excusaverit iudicio proximo, (ll) nullius(mm) iudex esse (nnpotest, nisinn) se ex hac culpa eximerit, secundum ut(oo) est(pp) premissum. (qq) Si autem pro facto (rrcriminali (ssfuerit rr), pro quo iudiciumss) facere recusavit, sicut(tt) pro homicidio aut vulneribus, (uuaut(vv) furtu(ww),uu) aut(xx) spolio,

(a) K^1 *Art. 100–101* K^2 *Art. 99–100* W^1 *Art. 97* W^2 *Art. 99* C^1 *Art. 105* C^2 *Art. 111–113* C^3 *Art. 101* (b) *manus γ* C^1 (c) advocatus K^1 K^2 C^3 (d) si per K^1 K^2 (e) super W^1 W^2 (f) *desunt* W^1 W^2 (g) Cum qualicumque K^1 K^2 W^2 C^2 C^3 Cum qualicumque quia W^1 (h) *deest* C^3 (i) factum W^1 W^2 C^3 (j) extunc W^2 (k) iurare W^1 (l) *desunt* K^1 K^2 (m) *deest* W^1 (n) *deest* C^3 (o) *deest* C^2 (p) *desunt* C^2 (q) querela W^1 W^2 (r) *deest* C^2 (s) *deest* K^1 K^2 W^1 W^2 (t) tenetur K^1 K^2 W^1 W^2 C^2 C^3 (u) sibi K^1 C^2 (v) sit C^3 (w) esse baniratum [s] tunc C^2 (x) *deest* K^1 K^2 W^1 W^2 C^3 (y) occupaverit ipsum W^1 W^2 ipsum preoccupaverit C^3 *deest* K^1 K^2 W^1 W^2 (z) *deest* K^1 K^2 (aa) impedimentum eum W^1 W^2 impedimentum C^3 (bb) ├p┤ C^1 (cc) negaverit K^1 (dd) demeretur W^1 (ee) *deest* W^2 (ff) iudicium iure W^1 W^2 (gg) cum C^2 (hh) iterim W^1 W^2 (ii) illi W^1 W^2 C^2 *deest* C^3 (jj) *deest* C^3 (kk) *deest* W^1 (ll) tunc K^1 K^2 W^1 W^2 C^3 (mm) nullus W^1 W^2 (nn) in sese C^2 (oo) ut K^1 K^2 quod C^3 (pp) ius C^2 (qq) *rubrica:* Si pro facto criminali pro quo iudicium facere recusavit, sive pro homicidio. C^2 (rr) civili K^1 K^2 (ss) *desunt* C^3 (tt) sed W^1 W^2 (uu) *desunt* C^3 (vv) aut K^1 K^2 (ww) facto W^1 (xx) *deest* K^1 K^2

violent[i]a, aut incendio[(a)], aut hiis similibus[(b)], que [(c]crimina capitalia[c)] tanguntur.[gg)] Idem iudicium super eum ⟨ire debet⟩[(d)], quod super illum ire debuit, pro eo nec recompensam, [(e]nec aliquid[e)] facere potest, si[(f)] in hiis vincitur, ut iuris est. Sin autem unus[(g)] vir [(h]pro delicto[(i)h)] in captivitatem publicam[(j)] ⟨pro debito⟩[(k)] presentatus fuerit ad tenendum [(l)] iure, si[(m)] ipsum ammiserit [(n)] aut si[(o)] evaserit absque sua culpa aut[(p)] negligencia pro crimine, quod transit ad collum, pro eo solvet integram recompensam. Sin autem pro manu, tunc mediam solvit recompensam et[(q)] [(r)] hoc ipsum[(s)] iuramento probare[(t)] [(u)] opportet [(v]tacto sacramento[v)], [(w)] si[(x)] sibi parcere noluerit[(y)], quod ipsum[(z)] absque omni sua[(aa)] culpa ammiserit[(bb)] [(cc)]. ⟨Integra recompensa⟩[(dd)] [(ee)] Integra recompensa facit decem et octo talenta, [(ff]media recompensa[(gg)] facit novem talenta[ff)]. [(hh)]

Articulus 101 [(ii)]

[*101*] Nunc attendatis de advocato, si non iuste iudicaverit, cum sibi querulatur, et hoc propter amorem aut [(jj)] munera[(kk)], aut[(ll)] [(mm)] [(nn]ob aliquam[nn)] causam dimittit, vel si solus[(oo)] noxam fecerit iniustam[(pp)], quod de iure
164v facere [(qq)] non debuit: postquam ad iudicem electus | sit ius confortare et iniurias[(rr)] [(ss)] suffocare[(tt)] [(uu)]. Si querela super ipsum in suo iudicio facta fuerit, tunc scultetus iudex esse debet [(vv)] super advocatum[(ww)] et per hoc cogitur cum sentenciis, [(xx]quod ante ipsum opportet respondere [(yy)], ut in

---

(a) *in ms.* incendium [*s*] S^{6} (b) *in ms.* similia [*s*] S^{6} (c) criminalia capitalia S^{2} (d) *probabiliter manus B* S^{6} ⟨ire debet⟩ S^{8} ire debet S^{4} S^{5} K^{4} (e) aliquam S^{2} (f) nisi K^{3} (g) *deest* S^{2} S^{3} (h) *desunt* S^{9} productus S^{2} (i) debito S^{1} S^{2} S^{10} K^{3} (j) *deest* S^{2} (k) *manus B* S^{6} (l) dum S^{2} (m) *deest* S^{2} K^{5} (n) advocatus S^{9} (o) *deest* S^{2} (p) pro S^{3} ac S^{4} S^{5} (q) ut S^{3} (r) homicidium K^{5} (s) *deest* S^{2} (t) *deest* S^{2} (u) iurare S^{2} S^{3} S^{4} S^{5} (v) *desunt* S^{3} K^{5} (w) ita S^{4} S^{5} quod S^{2} S^{8} S^{9} K^{3} (x) ⟨si⟩ S^{8} *deest* S^{9} K^{3} (y) voluerit S^{4} S^{5} S^{10} K^{5} (z) *deest* S^{4} S^{5} (aa) *deest* K^{3} (bb) evaserit S^{2} S^{3} S^{4} S^{5} S^{8} (cc) vel amiserit S^{8} K^{5} (dd) *probabiliter manus B* S^{6} (ee) Omne aurum et argentum non informatum, et omnis siligo et carnes, cervisia et vinum, et panis, que vel quod aut quantum post tricessinum permansit, vel permanserit, totum cedit heredibus viri et non mulieri, exceptis pulmentariis, de quibus mulier mediam recipit partem. Et heredes viri mediam reliquam tollunt etc. S^{9} (ff) *desunt* S^{4} S^{5} (gg) *deest* S^{8} (hh) Ubi eciam vir promiserit iuramentum coram iudicio pro enormibus verbis aut depilacione, aut verberibus, aut effusione sanguinis, de quo solitus dimitti non potest, nisi voluntas fuerit iudicis et consensus etc. K^{5} (ii) S^{1} S^{4} S^{5} S^{6} *Art. 101* S^{2} K^{3} *Art. 104* S^{3} *Art. 109* S^{8} S^{10} *Art. 100* S^{9} *Art. 107* K^{4} *Art. 106* K^{5} *Art. 108* (jj) propter S^{4} S^{5} K^{5} (kk) iniuria K^{5} (ll) *deest* S^{10} (mm) quod K^{4} S^{10} (nn) obliquam K^{3} (oo) sibi K^{5} *deest* S^{3} (pp) iniusticiam S^{10} (qq) non debet vel K^{3} (rr) iniusticiam K^{5} (ss) fugare seu K^{3} ⊢con⊣ S^{6} (tt) humiliare S^{2} (uu) seu debilitare K^{4} (vv) advocati seu K^{4} S^{10} (ww) burgravium K^{4} (xx) *desunt* S^{2} (yy) per sentenciam K^{5}

aut ecclesie violencia, aut incendio, aut hiis similibus(a), que criminalia(b) facta tangunt, idem iudicium super (ceum irec)(d) debet, (equod super illum(f) ire debuerat,e) pro eo nec reconpensam, nec aliquid (g) facere potest, si(h) in hiis vincitur, (iut iurisi) est(j). (k) Si autem unus(l) vir (m) pro debito(n) in captivitatem publicam presentatus fuerit ad tenendum iure, si ipsum evaserit aut (o) amiserit absque sua culpa ac(p) negliencia (q) pro crimine, quod transit ad collum, (rpro eor) solvet integram(s) reconpensam (t) (uet hoc ipsum (v) (wtacto sacramentow) iurare oportet, si(x) | sibi parcere noluerit(y), (zquod 53rb
ipsumz) absque omni sua(aa) culpa evaserit.u) Integra reconpensa facit(bb) XVIII talenta, media (ccreconpensa facitcc) novem talenta.

Articulus 106 (dd)

[*106*] | ⟨Hic attendatur, si advocatus (ee) iniuste iudicaverit⟩(ff) Nunc de advocato(gg) 53vb
attendatur, si non iuste iudicaverit, cum sibi querulatur, et hoc(hh) propter amorem aut munera(ii), aut ob aliquam causam dimittit, vel si solus noxam fecerit iniustam, (jjquod de iure facere non debuit;jj) postquam ad(kk) iudicem sit electus ius confortare et (lliniurias debilitarell). Si querela super eum in iudicio suo(mm) fuerit facta, tunc scultetus iudex esse debet super advocatum(nn) et (ooper hocoo) cogitur cum sentenciis, quod ante ipsum oportet respondere, ut in posteris patebit. Petat advocatum(pp) surgere per

---

(a) *in ms.* similia [*s*] C¹ (b) noxalia W¹ W² (c) exire K¹ exigere K² (d) habere C² (e) in quo C³ (f) *deest* W¹ (g) aliud in hiis W¹ W² (h) nisi W¹ W² (i) et ritus C² (j) *deest* W¹ (k) *rubrica:* Vir pro debito in captivitatem publicam presentatus fuerit pro crimine, quod transit ad collum. C² (l) sibi W¹ *deest* C³ (m) videlicet W¹ (n) delicto K¹ K² W¹ W² (o) alter eum C³ (p) aut K¹ K² W¹ W² C² (q) ad hoc W¹ W² tunc C³ (r) *desunt* C³ (s) mediam K¹ plenam W¹ W² *deest* K² (t) Si autem pro manu, tunc mediam solvit reconpensam K¹ K² C² Si autem pro manu, mediam solvet reconpensam W¹ W² (u) *desunt* C³ (v) iuramento K¹ K² W¹ W² (w) *desunt* W¹ W² (x) quod C² (y) voluerit W¹ (z) *desunt* C² (aa) sua W¹ W² (bb) *deest* W² (cc) *desunt* C³ (dd) K¹ C³ *Art. 102* K² *Art. 101* W¹ *Art. 98* W² *Art. 100* C¹ *Art. 106* C² *Art. 114* (ee) ⊢iust⊣ *del. manus γ* C¹ (ff) *manus γ* C¹ (gg) burgravio C³ (hh) *deest* W¹ W² (ii) amiciciam K¹ K² dona W¹ W² (jj) *desunt* C³ (kk) *deest* W¹ (ll) ut iuris debilitate K¹ non debilitare K² (mm) *deest* W¹ (nn) burgravium C³ (oo) *desunt* C³ (pp) burgravium C³

posteris patebit. Petat advocatum (a) surgere(b) per sentenciam(xx), quod super ipsum habeat querulari(c) et per sentenciam petat, ut alium iudicem ponat (d) loco suo, quod ipsum facere opportet. Et tunc locet scultetum, (e) qui sibi iudicare debet. (f)Simili modo(f), (g)ut advocatus super scultetum iudicare debuit(g). Eodem modo(h) scultetus iudicet advocatum. Idcirco advocatus iudicium bannitum habere non potest absque sculteto, quia coram eo se iure debet(i) exhibere, si super ipsum aliquis(j) voluerit querulari(k). Si hoc contra(l) iusticiam anno (m)et die(m) (n) recusaverit, tunc domino terre iudicium vacat, quod habuit (o), et regi bannum, si prosecutus(p) fuerit cum veris sentenciis. (q)

Articulus 102 (r)

[*102*] Si aliquis (s) irruenciam domicilii fecerit nocte aut(t) (u) die, et si ille eum detinuerit in facto manifesto, (v)et ipsum(v) captivum(w) cum clamore ad iudicium perduxerit ⟨et ipsum non pernoctando per querulaverit⟩(x), si super eo (y)homines, qui suum clamorem audierunt(y), habuerit(z) metseptimus (aa) suorum vicinorum, (bb) factum ostendere possit, ut(cc) iuris sit, (dd) illi ad collum transit. Sin autem manifestum factum ostendi non potest, extunc(ee) ille(ff) propius est evadere metseptimus, quam per(gg) eum vinci possit.

Articulus 103 (hh)

165r [*103*] | Obsidia et (ii)quod femine stuprantur(ii), et irruenciam domiciliorum burgravius iudicat(jj) et(kk) nullus alter nec scultetus. Si irruencia(ll) domicilii

---

(a) seu burgravium K^{4} cum sentenciis K^{5} (b) *deest* S^{3} (c) *in ms.* querulare S^{6} (d) in S^{4} S^{5} (e) ⊢qui sibi⊣ S^{6} (f) *desunt* S^{3} (g) *desunt* K^{4} (h) *deest* K^{3} (i) opportet seu respondere S^{9} (j) *deest* S^{3} (k) *in ms.* querulare S^{6} (l) *deest* S^{4} S^{5} (m) *desunt* S^{4} S^{5} (n) quod S^{2} (o) ab eo S^{8} S^{9} K^{4} K^{5} (p) perfectus K^{5} (q) ⟨Quilibet iudex post resignacionem sui officii debet pausare L diebus in eodem loco, ubi talem officium exercuit, offerens se responsurum omnibus de se querulantibus publiceque sua quevis negocia et non latenter disponere.⟩ S^{8} (r) S^{1} S^{6} S^{8} S^{10} *Art. 102* S^{2} *Art. 106* S^{3} *Art. 111* S^{4} S^{5} *Art. 103* S^{9} K^{4} *Art. 108* K^{3} *Art. 105* K^{5} *Art. 110* (s) alteri S^{2} S^{8} S^{9} K^{4} K^{5} (t) ac K^{4} (u) in S^{2} (v) *desunt* K^{3} (w) *deest* S^{4} S^{5} (x) *manus B* S^{6} (y) clamatores K^{4} (z) debet K^{5} (aa) eorum S^{4} S^{5} (bb) et si K^{4} (cc) cum S^{5} (dd) manifestum est K^{5} (ee) *deest* K^{5} (ff) *deest* S^{8} (gg) *deest* S^{5} S^{10} K^{4} (hh) S^{1} S^{6} *Art. 103* S^{2} *Art. 105* S^{3} *Art. 110* S^{4} S^{5} *Art. 102* S^{8} S^{10} *Art. 101* S^{9} K^{5} *Art. 109* K^{3} *Art. 106* K^{4} *Art. 107* (ii) stupra K^{4} (jj) *deest* S^{10} (kk) ut K^{5} (ll) *a.c.* irruenciam S^{6}

sentenciam, quod super ipsum habeat[(a)] [(b]querelam seu[b)] querulare et sen-
tencialiter petat, ut alium ponat iudicem loco suo, hoc ipsum facere oportet.
Et tunc locet scultetum, qui[(c)] sibi debet iudicare simili modo, [(d]ut advocatus
super scultetum iudicare[(e)] debuit. Eodem modo[d)] scultetus[(f)] iudicet advo-
catum[(g)]. Idcirco advocatus [(h)] bannitum iudicium absque sculteto habere[(i)]
non potest, quia coram eo[(j)] se ad ius debet | exhibere, si[(k)] super ipsum lite[(l)] 54ra
aliquis[(m)] querulatur. Si autem hoc contra iusticiam anno et die recusaverit, XXVIII
extunc [domino][(n)] terre iudicium vacat, quod ab eo habuit, et regi bannum,
si cum sentenciis [(o)] observatur[(p)].

Articulus 108 [(q)]

[*108*] ⟨De domorum irruencia⟩[(r)] [(s]Si quis alteri fecerit[s)] [(t]domorum irruenciam[t)]
die ac nocte, et si[(u)] ipse illum detinuerit [(v]in facto manifesto, et ipsum cap-
tivum[(w)] cum[(x)] clamore[(y)] | adduxerit[(z)] ad iudicium, si super [(aa)] clamato- 54va
res habere poterit [(bb]metseptimus suorum vicinorum, et si factum ostendi
potest, ut iuris est, illi ad collum transit. Si autem factum manifestum ostendi
non potest[v)], extunc ille propius est evadere metseptimus, quam per eum
vinci possit[bb)].

Articulus 107 [(cc)]

[*107*] | ⟨De irruencia domiciliorum⟩[(dd)] Insidias[(ee)] [(ff]et stupra,[ff)] et domorum 54rb
irruenciam burgravius iudicat et nullus alter nec eciam scultetus. Si

---

[(a)] debeat W^1 W^2 [(b)] *desunt* K^1 K^2 C^2 W^1 [(c)] *deest* W^1 [(d)] *desunt* C^3 [(e)] *deest* W^1 querulari W^2 [(f)] advocatus W^1 W^2 [(g)] scultetum W^1 W^2 burgravium C^3 [(h)] esse W^1 in C^3 [(i)] facere W^1 W^2 [(j)] *deest* C^2 [(k)] qui C^3 [(l)] *deest* K^1 K^2 W^1 W^2 C^2 C^3 [(m)] *deest* K^1 K^2 C^3 [(n)] domino K^1 K^2 W^1 W^2 C^2 C^3 [(o)] veris K^1 K^2 W^1 W^2 C^2 C^3 [(p)] prosequatur W^1 W^2 K^1 consequitur K^1 C^2 sequitur C^3 [(q)] K^1 *Art. 103* K^2 W^2 *Art. 102* W^1 *Art. 99–99a* C^1 *Art. 108* C^2 *Art. 116* C^3 *Art. 104* [(r)] *manus ζ* C^1 [(s)] Insidias et stupra K^1 K^2 [(t)] violenciam C^3 [(u)] *deest* W^2 [(v)] burgravius iudicat et nullus alter nec eciam scultetus. Si domorum irruencia proba[bi]liter potest ostendi cum vulneribus vel edificio vulnerato, si super iudicem et clamatores in testimonium poterit habere K^1 burgravius iudicat et nullus alter nec eciam scultetus. Si domorum irruencia probabiliter potest ostendi cum vulneribus vel edificio vulnerato, si super iudicem et clamatores in testimonium non poterit habere K^3 [(w)] *deest* W^1 W^2 [(x)] *deest* W^1 C^3 [(y)] *deest* C^3 [(z)] deduxerit W^1 W^2 perduxerit C^3 [(aa)] hoc W^1 W^2 C^2 C^3 [(bb)] testimonium habere, extunc ille propius cum duello debet respondere, quam suo possit evadere iuramento. W^1 [(cc)] K^1 *Art. 104* K^2 C^3 *Art. 103* W^1 *Art. 100* W^2 *Art. 101* C^1 *Art. 107* C^2 *Art. 115* [(dd)] *manus ζ* C^1 [(ee)] Obsidia K^1 K^2 [(ff)] stuprantur K^1

probabitur, potest ostendi cum vulneribus (a et cum a) vulneratis edificiis; si super hoc (b iudicem et homines b), qui clamorem audierunt, habere potuerit in(c) testimonium (d), (e) opportet desuper respondere cum duello, quam cum(f) iuramento evadere possit.

Articulus 104 (g)

[*104*] Etsi vir querelam suam tenere promissit, et si tempore medio concordia facta fuerit (h), extunc pro eo non plus(i) ammittit, nisi iudici dat suam penam.

Articulus 105 (j)

[*105*] Si vir conquerulatur [*s*] super alterum (k pro debito k), quod (l) sibi(m) a(n) patre suo teneatur et ipse debet super eo certificare(o), ut iuris est. Sin autem iurare voluerit, quod (p) pater suus (q) debitum persolverit, hoc ipsum facere opportet metseptimus, post manum mortuam. Sin autem dixerit, quod ipsum(r) (s) persolverit, hoc iurabit mettercius(t) ⟨cum talibus hominibus, qui in suo iure argui non possunt⟩(u).

(a) *desunt* S2 (b) homines ad iudicem S9 (c) *deest* S4 S5 (d) metseptimus K5 (e) extunc ille sibi propius K4 (f) suo K4 *deest* S10 (g) S1 S4 S5 S6 *Art. 104* S2 K3 *Art. 107* S3 *Art. 112* S8 S10 *Art. 103* S9 *Art. 110* K4 *Art. 109* K5 *Art. 111* (h) inter eos S9 (i) prius K5 (j) S1 S4 S5 S6 *Art. 105* S2 K3 *Art. 108* S3 *Art. 113* S8 *Art. 104* S9 *Art. 111* S10 *articulus deest* K4 *Art. 110* K5 *Art. 112* (k) *desunt* K4 (l) si K5 (m) *deest* K4 (n) pro S8 S9 K4 K5 (o) informari K4 testari K5 (p) sibi S2 (q) hoc K4 (r) hoc debitum K4 ipse S4 (s) solus K5 (t) metseptimus S4 S3 K3 *a.c.* metseptimus, *corr. commentatoris* S1 (u) *manus A* S6 domorum(a) irruencia probabiliter(b) ostendi potest cum vulneribus vel(c) (dedificio vulneratod); si(e) super (f) iudicem et clamatores(g) in testimonium poterit habere, extunc ille propius sibi(h) cum duello debet(i) respondere(j), quam ille(k) (lsuo possitl) evadere (m) iuramento(n).

Articulus 109 (o)

[*109*] Et si vir suam tenere promisserit querelam, et si(p) medio tempore concordia fuerit facta, extunc(q) pro eo non plus amittit, nisi(r) iudici penam (s).

Articulus 110 (t)

[*110*] Si vir querulatur super alterum (upro debitou), | ⟨Pro debito patris⟩(v) quod sibi(w) pro suo patre teneatur, ipse debet super eo, ut iuris est, (xinformari. Si autem voluerit(y)x) iurare, quod pater suus (zhoc debitumz) persolvisset, hoc (aa) ipsum(bb) facere oportet metseptimus, (cc) post mortuam manum. Si autem dixerit, quod hoc debitum solus persolverit, hoc mettercius iurabit heres(dd). (eeSi de(ff) debito sui patris recognoscit, hoc solvere(gg) debet, in quantum recepta hereditas se extendit. Et (hh) si solvere noluerit (iivel heredes hoc consentire recusant(jj)ii), tunc sibi(kk) hereditas (llsua vel propriumll) potest (mm) iudicio possideri (nnpro isto debito et acquirinn), aliter ille(oo) constringi(pp) non potest suam hereditatem (qqet qq) proprium(rr).ee) 54vb

(a) *deest* C^3 (b) *deest* K^2 (c) et K^1 K^2 (d) cum edificiis vulneratis K^1 K^2 (e) et K^1 K^2 (f) hoc K^1 K^2 W^1 W^2 C^2 C^3 (g) homines, qui clamorem audierunt K^1 K^2 (h) *deest* W^1 W^2 (i) oportet K^1 K^2 (j) videre W^2 (k) eum scilicet reus C^2 *deest* K^1 K^2 C^3 (l) *deest* K^1 K^2 (m) cum K^1 K^2 (n) *deest* C^3 (o) K^1 C^3 *Art. 105* K^2 *Art. 104* W^1 *Art. 101* W^2 *Art. 103* C^1 *Art. 109* C^2 *Art. 117* (p) *deest* C^3 (q) *deest* W^1 W^2 (r) quam K^2 (s) meretur K^1 demeretur W^1 W^2 C^2 (t) K^1 C^3 *Art. 106* K^2 *Art. 105* K^4 *Art. 110 pars* Si–proprium C^1 *Art. 110* W^1 *Art. 102* W^2 *Art. 104* C^2 *Art. 118* (u) *desunt* C^3 (v) *manus γ* C^1 (w) si W^1 W^2 C^3 (x) *desunt* C^3 (y) debuerit W^2 (z) *desunt* C^3 (aa) idem K^2 W^2 (bb) *deest* K^1 C^3 (cc) in W^2 (dd) K^1 K^2 W^1 W^2 (ee) *desunt* K^1 K^2 W^1 W^2 (ff) *deest* C^3 K^4 (gg) exsolvere C^3 (hh) sibi C^3 (ii) *desunt* C^3 (jj) excusant C^2 (kk) *desunt* C^3 (ll) *desunt* C^3 (mm) cum C^3 (nn) *desunt* C^3 (oo) illi K^4 (pp) confringi K^4 (qq) *desunt* C^3 (rr) ad vendendum C^3 K^4

Articulus 106 [a]

[*106*] Si aliquis habuerit equ[u]m vel canem aut aliquod [b] pecus quodcumque [c], [d] loquela careat, et noxam sive dampnum fecerit [e], sin autem dicit suum non esse dampno perpetrato, sibi in suo iure non nocebit. [f]

Articulus 107 [g]

[*107*] Si aliquis spoliaverit cives suos, qui[h] proprium aut[i] feodum aut here-
165ᵛ ditatem [j] intra municipale ha|beat[k] et si[l] hoc non[m] prehabita querela faciat ante[n] dominum terre vel[o] [p] suum iudicem, illi sua edificia abiudicare ⟨debent⟩[q] [r] supra curiam suam[s] et secari, et illa[t] edificia erunt communia et omnibus publicantur hominibus. Sin autem edificium[u] [v] iudicialiter fiscatum[w] fuerit [x], [y] ita quod ibi puella aut femina stuprata fuerit intra[z] illud edificium, [aa] debet resecari et abinde[bb] milles[cc] [*s*] duci. [dd]

(a) S^1 S^4 S^5 S^6 *Art. 106* S^2 K^3 *Art. 109* S^3 *Art. 114* S^8 *Art. 105* S^9 *Art. 112* S^{10} *Art. 104* K^4 *Art. 111* K^5 *Art. 113* (b) animal seu S^9 (c) sit S^2 S^3 K^4 (d) quod S^1 S^2 S^3 S^4 S^5 S^8 S^9 S^{10} K^3 K^4 K^5 (e) solvere tenetur S^9 (f) De hoc quere plenius Libro 2 Registro. [*SSp. II.40*] S^2 Qui canem servat oculte mordentem vel feram indomitam aut avem vel ursum aut simeam, qualecumque damnum faciunt, solvere tenetur. Et si eas dampno perpetrato alienaverit, per hoc non est innocens, si mettercius poterint protestare et probare, quod eas detinuerit, quousque dampnum facientem. Si homo eradit [*s*] canem vel feram vel ursum, cum sibi nocere voluerit, manere debet sine satisfaccione, si hoc tacto sacramento probare presumpserit, quod se defendendo hoc fecerit. Qui feras bestias extra gaya banita servare voluerit, debet ea servare sub custodia. S^9 (g) S^1 S^4 S^5 S^6 *Art. 107* S^2 K^3 *Art. 110* S^3 *Art. 115* S^8 *Art. 106* S^9 *Art. 113* S^{10} *Art. 105* K^4 *Art. 112* K^5 *Art. 114* (h) aut S^{10} (i) *deest* S^4 S^5 (j) ⟨aut dampnum fecerint⟩ K^2 (k) *deest* S^{10} (l) *deest* S^2 (m) *deest* S^9 K^5 (n) aut S^5 (o) et S^4 S^5 S^8 ut S^3 (p) ad S^1 S^9 S^{10} K^3 K^5 ante S^2 S^3 K^4 (q) *probabiliter manus B* S^6 debent S^2 S^4 S^3 S^5 S^9 K^4 K^5 (r) domino K^4 (s) *deest* S^4 S^5 (t) alia K^5 (u) *deest* S^3 (v) iudici S^{10} (w) astatum S^3 (x) abiudicata K^4 (y) aut femina stuprata fuerit S^3 (z) ⟨intra⟩ *probabiliter manu commentatoris* K^5 (aa) eciam S^2 S^9 ⟨eciam⟩ S^8 (bb) de iure K^5 (cc) nullus S^1 S^2 S^3 S^4 S^5 S^8 S^9 S^{10} K^3 K^4 (dd) *subrubrica:* De debito per patrem obligato in hereditate. Si autem milles [*s*] querulatur pro debito patris sui super heredem, ille debet persolvere, ita ut hereditas valeat. Si autem non vult persolvere debitum et quod sibi heredes consentire nolunt, tunc potest sibi hereditas appropriari et cum iudicio protestari querelam, eciam extorquere pro debito, aliter non potest agravare hereditatem. K^5

Articulus 111 (a)

[*111*] ⟨Si pecus fecerit dampnum⟩(b) Si quis equum aut canem habuerit(c) vel aliud pecus quodcumque sit suum, quod careat loquela, si hoc fecerit dampnum,
et si dicit suum non esse dampno perpetrato, sibi(d) hoc in suo iure | non 55ra
nocebit. XXIX

Articulus 112 (e)

[*112*] Si quis spoliaverit suos (f civitatum homines f), qui proprium aut feodum vel hereditatem(g) habuerit (h) intra municipale (i) et si hoc non prehabita faciat querela ante dominum (j) vel ante(k) suum iudicem, illi sua edificia adiudicari debent supra (l) curiam et execari, et edificia illa erunt omnia(m), et hoc(n) omnibus hominibus publicatur. Si autem iudicialiter(o) edificia fuerint abiudicata(p), ita quod femina aut puella ibi fuerit(q) (r stuprata intra illud edificium r), eciam debet resecari et abinde(s) nullas(t) [*s*] deduci.

(a) K^1 *Art. 107* K^2 *Art. 106* W^1 *Art. 103* W^2 *Art. 105* C^1 *Art. 111* C^2 *Art. 119* C^3 *Art. 107* (b) *manus* γ C^1 (c) *deest* W^1 W^2 (d) sic K^1 K^2 (e) K^1 C^3 *Art. 108* K^2 *Art. 107* C^1 *Art. 112* C^2 *Art. 120* W^1 *Art. 104* W^2 *Art. 106* (f) civitatenses K^1 K^2 W^1 W^2 C^3 cives seu civitatis homines C^2 (g) proprietatem K^1 K^2 (h) ⟨aut dampnum fecerint⟩ K^2 (i) ius C^2 (j) terre K^1 K^2 W^1 W^2 C^3 (k) me C^2 aut W^2 (l) suam K^1 K^2 W^1 W^2 C^2 C^3 (m) sentencia W^1 W^2 communia K^2 C^2 C^3 (n) *deest* C^3 (o) incidentaliter C^2 (p) adiudicata K^1 K^2 C^2 C^3 (q) interfuerit C^3 (r) *desunt* K^1 (s) inde C^3 (t) nullus W^2 ullus C^3

Articulus 108 (a)

[*108*] (b) Hoc est illud iudicium et illud iuramentum, cum quo aut per quod Iudeus iurare sive evadere debet(c) Christianum, quod scriptum est in iure inperatorum. (dIpse debet verti contra solem seorsum, stare nudipes(e) debet(f) super sedem unam, (g) indutus (h) clamide (iesse debeti) et pilleum Iudaicum(j) habere debet(k) super caput.d) Si lapsus fuerit ter(l), totidem (m) fertonem ⟨solidorum⟩(n) ammittit. Et si quarto (o) manet in causa reus (p). Tunc dicit illi(q), qui sibi predicit iuramentum: “Ego te moneo, S(r), Iudee(s), per has tres litteras (t) et per hanc legem, quam Dominus(u) dedit Moÿsi(v) in tabula lapidea (w) in monte Sÿnaÿ(x), quod liber iste aut hoc(y) rodale verum (z) sit, ac(aa) tu(bb), Iudee, iurare debes huic viro Christiano(cc), I(dd), (ee) pro tali (ffculpa siveff) (gg) pro qua te hic(hh) ad iudicium(ii) deduxit.” Extunc sic iurare debet, (jj(kket sic sibi(ll) predicceturjj) (mm), (nnut sequitur huicnn)kk) capitulo(oo).

Articulus 109 (pp)

[*109*] ⟨sic iuravit Iudeus⟩(qq) (rr“Quod turr) in hac causa reus non(ss) sis, ⟨pro⟩(tt)
166r qua | te hic idem(uu) vir(vv) Christianus inculpet, quod(ww) ⟨ita⟩(xx) te Deus(yy) adiuvet. Idem Deus, qui (zz) celum et terram creavit(aaa), aerem et rorem, montes cum(bbb) vallibus, frondes, flores ac gramina (ccc). Et si sis reus, quod terra te(ddd) absorbeat, que Datan(eee) et Abÿran(fff) absorbuit, et si(ggg) reus

(a) S^1 S^4 S^5 S^6 *Art. 108* S^2 K^3 *Art. 111* S^3 *Art. 116* S^8 *Art. 107* S^9 *Art. 114 pars 1* S^{10} *Art. 106* K^4 *Art. 113* K^5 *Art. 115 pars 1* (b) ⟨de Iudeorum iuramento⟩ K^2 ⟨Et Iudeis [s] iuramentum⟩ K^4 (c) *deest* S^4 (d) *desunt* S^4 S^5 (e) indipes [*s*] K^5 (f) *deest* S^2 K^3 K^4 (g) nudipes S^{10} (h) palio aut S^2 (i) *desunt* S^2 K^4 (j) inductum K^5 (k) *deest* S^8 K^5 (l) *deest* K^3 K^5 (m) unum K^4 (n) *probabiliter manus B* S^6 (o) cadet extunc K^4 (p) erit K^5 (q) ille K^5 (r) Helya S^2 ·I· K^5 (s) iudice S^2 *deest* S^4 S^5 (t) quas scripsit Dominus digitto suo K^5 (u) Deus S^2 *deest* K^5 (v) Moysi K^5 (w) quam scripsit Dominus digitto suo K^5 (x) Sinaÿ K^5 (y) *deest* S^{10} (z) ac iustum S^1 S^2 S^3 S^5 S^8 S^9 S^{10} K^3 K^4 K^5 hac iustum S^4 (aa) super quem aut S^1 S^4 S^5 K^3 super quod S^2 S^9 super quem et S^3 super quem S^8 K^5 super quem autem S^{10} quod super quem K^4 (bb) ├aut┤ ⟨tu⟩ S^8 (cc) *deest* S^4 S^5 (dd) .P. K^5 (ee) tali nomine K^4 (ff) *desunt* S^9 (gg) causa S^2 S^3 S^4 S^5 S^8 S^9 K^4 tam K^5 (hh) *deest* S^4 S^5 S^8 (ii) responsionem iure K^4 (jj) *desunt* S^5 (kk) *desunt* K^4 (ll) *deest* S^{10} (mm) iuramentum S^2 (nn) *desunt* K^3 K^5 ⟨De iuramentum Iudeorum supra Christianum⟩ K^3 (oo) *deest* S^1 S^2 S^3 S^4 S^5 S^8 S^9 S^{10} K^3 K^4 (pp) S^1 S^4 S^5 S^6 *Art. 109* S^2 K^3 *Art. 112* S^3 *Art. 117* S^8 S^{10} *Art. 107* S^9 *Art. 114 pars 2* K^4 *Art. 114* (qq) *manus A* S^6 (rr) Sequitur S^{10} (ss) *deest* S^4 S^5 (tt) *probabiliter manus B* S^6 pro S^2 S^9 K^3 in K^5 (uu) *deest* S^{10} (vv) *deest* S^2 K^4 K^5 (ww) ut S^2 sic S^3 (xx) *probabiliter manus B* S^6 (yy) *deest* S^2 (zz) fecit S^9 (aaa) fecit S^2 K^4 (bbb) *deest* K^4 (ccc) perfecit K^5 (ddd) *deest* S^5 (eee) Dathan K^5 (fff) Abiron K^5 (ggg) *deest* S^4

Articulus 113 pars 1 (a)

[*113 pars 1*] | ⟨Iuramentum Iudeorum⟩(b) Hoc est illud (c iudicium et c) iuramentum, per quod vel cum quo Iudeus iurare debet sive evadere debet Christianum, quod scriptum est in iure imperatoris. Ipse debet (d) verti contra solem seorsum(e) et stare nudipes super unam sedem, pallio indutus et pilleum Iudaicum(f) habere debet super caput. Et si lapsus ter(g) fuerit, totidem(h) unum fertonem amittit. Et si quarto cadet(i), extunc reus manet in causa. Tunc dicit ille(j): "Ego te moneo, N., Iudee, per has tres litteras et per hanc legem, quam Dominus dedit Moÿsi in tabula lapidea in monte Synai, quod iste (k liber aut (l) rodale k) verum et iustum sit, super (m) quod tu (n) N. tali nomine pro tali causa (o sive culpa o) pro qua te (p huc ad p) responsionem iure(q) deduxit." Extunc(r) debet sic iurare (s): 55rb

Articulus 113 pars 2 (t)

[*113 pars 2*] "Quod tu(u) in hac causa reus non sis, (v) qua te(w) hic idem Cristianus inculpat(x), quod te Deus (y) adiuvet. Idem Deus(z), qui fecit celum et terram, aerem et rorem, montes(aa) et valles, frondes, gramina et flores (bb). Et si reus sis, quod (cc terra te absorbeat, que Dathan et Abyron absorbuit,

(a) K^1 C^3 *Art. 109 pars 1* K^2 *Art. 108 pars 1* W^1 *Art. 105 pars 1* W^2 *Art. 107 pars 1* C^1 *Art. 113 pars 1* C^2 *Art. 121 pars 1* (b) *manus C* C^1 (c) Iudaicum C^3 (d) se C^3 (e) dorsum K^1 K^2 (f) iudicatum [*s*] K^1 K^2 (g) tribus vicibus C^3 (h) tociens C^3 (i) adderit K^1 K^2 (j) iste, qui sibi predicit iuramentum: K^1 K^2 W^1 W^2 C^2 C^3 (k) libellus C^3 (l) hoc K^1 K^2 W^1 W^2 (m) hoc W^1 (n) Iudee iurare debes huic Christiano, W^1 W^2 (o) *desunt* C^3 (p) *desunt* C^2 (q) iurare W^1 *deest* C^2 (r) Et tunc C^3 (s) dicens K^2 K^1 C^2 et sic dicet W^1 W^2 (t) K^1 C^3 *Art. 109 pars 2* K^2 *Art. 108 pars 2* C^1 *Art. 113 pars 2* W^1 *Art. 105 pars 2* C^2 *Art. 121 pars 2* W^2 *Art. 107 pars 2* (u) *deest* K^1 K^2 (v) pro C^2 quod C^3 (w) *deest* K^1 K^2 (x) inculpet C^1 (y) sic C^2 (z) *deest* K^1 K^2 (aa) *deest* W^1 W^2 (bb) quod prius non fuerat W^1 W^2 (cc) *desunt* K^1 K^2

fueris(a), quod te(b) venenum ac gutta(c) ac lepra invadat, que precibus Helÿseÿ(d) Naaman Sÿrum(e) dimisit(f) et Ÿezi(g) invasit. (hEt si(i) reus fueris(j), quod te ignis conburret celestis et caducus (k) invadat morbus, et sanguinis invadat(l) fluxus,h) (met si reus fueris, quod tu pereas in tua anima et in tuo corpore et in tuis rebus.m) (nEt si reus es, quod ad sinum Abrahe(o) nunquam pervenies n) et (p) tibi(q) accidet (r), ut uxori Loth (s), que transmutata (tfuit (u) int) effigiem(v) salis, dum Sodoma periit et Gomorra(w). (xEt si(y) reus es, quod ad(z) (aasinum Abrahe nunquam(bb) pervenies, et(cc) eciamx) nunquamaa) ad resureccionem pervenies, ubi Christiani(dd) et Iudei et (ee) gentiles ante(ff) Creatorem omium rerum(gg) resurgent. Et si (hh)reus fueris, quod te lex deleat, quam Dominus dedit Moÿsÿ(ii) in monte Sÿnaÿ(jj), quam Deus solus(kk) suo scripsit digitto supra lapideam tabulam, et te confundat omnis scriptura, que scripta est in Quinque Libris Moÿsÿ(ll). Et si(mm) tuum iuramentum non(nn) iustum (oonec(pp) mundumoo) (qq) fuerit, quod te deleat Adonaÿ et sua deitatis potencia. Amen(rr)." ⟨et sue divinitatis in secula seculorum amen⟩(ss)

Articulus 110 (tt)

166v [*110*] | {a} Nunc placeat audire et intelligere, quod presens scriptum informat ex(uu) relacione veridica(vv). Primo de inperio et quomodo(ww) terre Saxonie ius suum ab inicio statutum(xx) fuerit et confirmatum (yy) in suo iure, sicut ab antiquo tempore Babillonia tenebat. (zz) Ibi stetit inperium et regnabat potencialiter per omnia regna, quia Nemroth gentilis rex primo Babiloniam edificavit et circu[m]cinxit (aaa) civitatem nimia amplitudine, (bbbet

---

(a) ⟨si⟩ K4 (b) *deest* S4 S5 (c) iquinaria [*s*] S2 (d) Helisen K5 (e) Sẏrum K5 (f) divisit [*s*] K5 (g) Ẏesÿ K5 (h) *desunt* K5 (i) *deest* S4 (j) ⟨sis⟩ K4 (k) te S2 K4 (l) *deest* S2 K4 (m) *desunt* S2 K4 (n) *desunt* S2 S3 S4 S5 S8 K4 (o) Habrae K5 (p) quod K4 ut K5 (q) ⟨tibi⟩ K4 *deest* S10 (r) ⟨at⟩ K4 (s) accidit K5 (t) cum S5 (u) in statuam sive S4 (v) statuam S2 S3 S9 K4 (w) Gomora K5 (x) Et si reus fueris, quod te ignis comburat celestis et caducus invadat morbus et sanguinis fluxus invadat. Et si reus es, quod K5 (y) *deest* S4 (z) *deest* S4 (aa) *desunt* K3 (bb) non S2 K4 (cc) nec S2 (dd) Cristiani K5 (ee) omnes S2 (ff) *deest* K5 (gg) *deest* S2 S3 (hh) tu S10 (ii) Moẏsi K5 *deest* S4 S5 (jj) Synai K5 (kk) *deest* K5 (ll) Moẏsi K5 (mm) *deest* K4 (nn) *deest* S5 (oo) *desunt* S3 (pp) et S3 non S9 (qq) sit seu S10 K4 (rr) *deest* S2 S4 S5 K4 K5 ⊢Amen⊣ S1 (ss) *manus commentatoris* S6 Nunc omnes dicite Amen. S8 K4 (tt) S1 S6 *Art. 110* S3 *Art. 118* S8 *Art. 109 manus commentatoris* S10 *Art. 108* K3 *Art. 113* K4 *Art. 115* K5 *Art. 116* (uu) et S10 (vv) vindica S10 (ww) quo K5 (xx) constitutum K4 (yy) cum arbitrio S3 K5 (zz) Ubi vel S8 (aaa) vel circulum cinxit S8 (bbb) *desunt* K5

{a} ⟨O mieÿskiem prawie⟩ *ad rubricam* K5

et si reus sis, quod te (avenenum, gutta et lepra invadet, que precibus Elysei Naaman Sirum dimisit et Yesi invasit. Et si(b) reus sis, quod tea) ignis celestis conburet et caducus te invadet morbus, et sangui[ni]s | fluxus, et (c) tibi accidet, ut uxori Loth, que transmutata fuit in statuam salis, dum Sodoma periit et Gomorra. Et si reus sis, quodcc) tu pereas in tua anima et in tuo(d) corpore et (e) tuis rebus. Et si reus sis, quod ad sinum Abrahe non pervenies, (fet eciam ad resurreccionem nunquam pervenies,f) ubi Christiani, Iudei et gentiles ante Creatorem omnium(g) resurgent. Et si reus sis, quod te lex deleat(h), quam Deus(i) dedit Moysi in monte Synai, quam Deus solus scripsit digitto (j) suo super tabulam lapideam, et eciam te confundat omnis scriptura, que scripta(k) est in Quinque Libris Moisi. Et si tuum iuramentum non fuerit iustum et mundum, quod te deleat Adonaÿ et sua deitatis potencia. Amen(l)." Nunc omnes dicite: amen, amen(m). 55va

Articulus 114 pars 1 (n)

[*114 pars 1*] Nunc placeat audire (oet intelligereo), quomodo (ppresens scriptum informat(q) ex relacione veridica. Primop) de(r) imperio (s) et quomodo terre Saxonie(t) ius(u) suum(v) ab inicio (w) fuerit (x) constitutum et confirmatum in suo iure (y), sicut ab(z) antiquo tempore(aa) in(bb) Babilonia tenebat. Ibi(cc) stetit imperium (dd) et regnabat potenter per omnia regna, quia (ee) Nemroth gentilis(ff) rex primo Babiloniam edificavit et circumcinxit civitatem nimia amplitudine, et edificavit in ea multas et altas municiones(gg),

(a) *desunt* C3 (b) *deest* W1 (c) quod W1 W2 C3 (d) *deest* K1 K2 (e) in K1 K2 W1 W2 C2 C3 (f) *desunt* C3 (g) DominumW1 (h) pereat K1 K2 (i) Dominus C3 (j) sancto C2 (k) *deest* C2 (l) *deest* C3 (m) *deest* C3 (n) K1 C3 *Art. 110 pars 1* K2 *Art. 109 pars 1* W1 *Art. 106 pars 1* W2 *Art. 108 pars 1* C1 *Art. 114 pars 1* C2 *Art. 122 pars 1* (o) *desunt* C3 (p) tunc informacio ipso C3 (q) *deest* W1 W2 (r) *deest* W1 (s) ⟨quid ius habet ortum municipale⟩ C3 (t) Saxoniensis K1 K2 (u) *deest* K1 K2 (v) *deest* W1 W2 (w) mundi C2 (x) ortum et C3 (y) et municipali vel arbitratorio C3 (z) *deest* K1 K2 (aa) *deest* C3 (bb) *deest* K1 K2 W1 W2 C3 (cc) *in ms.* Ibit [*s*] C1 Nam in Babilonia C3 (dd) et regnum C3 (ee) nemo W1 (ff) *deest* K2 (gg) turres contra inimicos K1 K2 edificavit [(a]in ea[a)], innumerabiles [(b)] ac altas municiones[bbb)] [(c)], unde [(d)] usque in presens ius municipale nuncupatur[(e)]. Et ibi erat[(f)] manens idem rex Nemroth ac duces multi[(g)] et ceteri viri famosi, qui [(h)] nunc mercatores vocantur, [(i]et omnes uno utebantur[i)] iure[(j)], quod municipale ius [(k)] appellabatur, ut bene in libro presenti patebit. Unde [(l)] nomen sorciebatur absque qualibet transmutacione.

Articulus 111 [(m)]

[*111*] ⟨de imperio quamdiu steterit⟩[(n)] [(o]Nunc dicetur quamdiu inperium steterit [(p)] potencialiter absque[(q)] permutacione usque [(r)] Greciam a tempore Darii[(s)] Secundi, aut[(t)] ultimi, quem[(u)] rex Allexander maximis ac sediciosis devicit bellis. Tunc transmutatum fuit inperium a Babilonia et stetit in Constantinopolim usque ad illud tempus, quod [*s*] se Roma de inperio intromisit, et potencialiter[(v)] obtinuit usque ad presens tempus ex parte beati Petri, qui caput est[(w)] Christianitatis. Cum Inperium Romanum fuisset versum,
167r ibi stetit, ut patet in premissis, [(x)] tunc Christiani[(y)] absque | iure [(z)] fuerint; idcirco quivis [(aa]pro sua[aa)] in terris faciebat voluntate, aut quid facere[(bb)] poterat aut[(cc)] perficere, et hoc absque querela permansit et per iudicium nullum[(dd)], quia nullum fuit ius, ubi quis iudicium[(ee)] consequi posset, et hac[(ff)] usque ad illud tempus perseveravit, quod[(gg)] Roma[(hh)] de inperio se intromisit. Et ipsi ibi[(ii)] venerunt et iusticiam consecuti[(jj)] fuerunt, et ibi exhibuerunt manus, unde manu pacem obtinuimus usque in[(kk)] presens[(ll)]. Tunc Romani[(mm)] convenerunt et decreverunt deliberando, quomodo regna sibi subiugare possent. [(nn]Et omnes unanimi[(oo)] consensu et pari consilio concordaverunt, quod edificarent castra in terris, unde terras sibi subiugare possent.[nn)] Et cum hoc fecissent, tunc arbitrati sunt, [(pp)] quomodo

---

(a) *desunt* S^{3} (b) turres S^{3} (c) contra inimicos S^{8} (d) huc K^{4} (e) nominatur K^{4} (f) *deest* S^{10} (g) milites S^{8} (h) vero K^{4} (i) *desunt* S^{10} (j) *deest* K^{5} (k) nunccupatur vel S^{8} (l) ├nc┤ S^{6} (m) S^{1} S^{6} *Art. 111* S^{3} *Art. 119–120* S^{4} S^{5} *Art. 110* S^{10} *Art. 109–111* K^{3} *Art. 114 pars 1* K^{4} *Art. 116* K^{5} *Art. 117, 118, 119* (n) *manus commentatoris* S^{6} (o) *desunt* S^{4} S^{5} (p) in potencia S^{1} (q) *deest* S^{10} (r) ad K^{4} (s) Gradani [*s*] K^{5} (t) et K^{5} (u) quam S^{10} quod K^{5} Maximus S^{10} K^{5} (v) potenter K^{4} (w) deest S^{10} (x) ⟨Anno Iudaeo 4748, que fuit causa, quod leges sunt condite ante C[h]risti Nativitatem ⟦Cristi⟧ LXI⟩ K^{5} (y) Romani K^{5} (z) steterunt aut K^{3} (aa) *desunt* S^{10} (bb) *deest* S^{3} (cc) et K^{4} *deest* S^{3} (dd) inultum S^{1} S^{3} K^{3} K^{4} K^{5} multa [*s*] S^{10} (ee) iusticiam K^{4} *deest* K^{3} (ff) *deest* S^{1} K^{3} K^{4} (gg) quo S^{1} S^{10} K^{3} K^{4} K^{5} (hh) racio [*s*] K^{5} (ii) *deest* K^{4} (jj) assecuti K^{5} (kk) ad S^{10} K^{4} K^{5} (ll) presentis tempus S^{10} tempus K^{5} (mm) racioni [*s*] K^{5} (nn) *desunt* S^{3} (oo) una manu K^{3} (pp) sibi K^{4}

und[e](a) usque (b in presens(c) b) municipale (d). Et ibi erat manens idem rex Nemroth ac duces multi (e et ceteri (f) viri e) famosi, qui vero(g) nunc mercatores vocantur, et omnes uno utebantur iure, quod(h) municipale ius appellatur, ut(i) und[e](j) in libro presenti patebit. (k Und[e] nomen sorciebatur absque cuiuslibet transmutacione. k)

Articuli 114 pars 2, 115–116 (l)

[*114 pars 2*] | (m) De imperio (n) quamdiu stetit et de eius potencia. Nunc(o) 56rb
dicetur quamdiu stetit imperium(p) et potenter absque permutacione usque xxx
ad(q) Greciam (r) a tempore Darii Secundi, (s aut ultimi, s) quem rex Allexander maximis (t et sediciosis t) devicit bellis. Tunc transmutatum fuit (u) imperium (v a(w) Babilonia v) et stetit in Constantinopolÿm usque ad illud tempus, quo se Roma de imperio intromisit, et potenter tenuit(x) usque ad presens tempus ex parte beati Petri, qui caput est Cristianitatis. Cum imperium Roma[m] versum fuisset, (y ibi stetit, ut(z) patet in premissis y), tunc (aa) Cristiani absque iure fuerunt; idcirco quivis pro sua in terris faciebant voluntate, (bb aut quid bb) facere poterat(cc) et perficere, et(dd) hoc absque querela permansit et per iudicium inultum, quia nullum [ius] fuit, ubi quis iusticia consequi posset, et usque (ee) tempus perseveraverit (ff). Et ipsi(gg) ibi(hh) venerunt et (ii iusticiam (jj) consecuti fuerunt, eciam(kk) ibi ii) exhibuerunt manus, und[e](ll) manu potestate(mm) obtinuimus usque in(nn) presens (oo). Tunc Roma[ni] conven[erun]t et decreverunt deliberando, quomodo sibi regna subiugare possent. Ac omnes unanimi consensu et pari consilio(pp) concordaverunt, quod edificarent castra in terris, und[e] sibi terras possent subiugare. (qq Et cum hoc fecissent, qq) tunc arbitrati sunt sibi(rr), quomodo

---

(a) ergo racione istius C^3 (b) *desunt* C^3 (c) primis W^1 (d) nominatur K^1 K^2 W^1 W^2 nuncupatur C^2 vocatur C^3 (e) *desunt* K^1 K^2 (f) nobiles et C^3 (g) *deest* K^1 K^2 C^3 viri W^1 W^2 (h) *deest* K^1 K^2 (i) unde W^1 (j) bene K^1 K^2 W^1 W^2 C^2 C^3 (k) Et se postquam municipale debet audire. C^3 (l) K^1 *Art. 110 pars 2 Art. 111–112* K^2 *Art. 109 pars 2 Art. 110–111* W^1 *Art. 106 pars 2 Art. 107–108* W^2 *Art. 108 pars 2 Art. 109–110* C^1 *Art. 114 pars 2 Art. 115–116* C^2 *Art. 122 pars 2 Art. 123–124* C^3 *Art. 110 pars 2 Art. 111–112* (m) Pro eo nota. C^3 (n) eius C^3 (o) *deest* C^3 (p) *deest* C^3 (q) *deest* C^3 (r) ibi cepit potencialiter et hoc C^3 (s) *desunt* C^3 (t) *desunt* C^3 (u) illud C^3 (v) Babiloniam K^2 (w) *deest* C^2 (x) obtinuit K^1 K^2 W^1 W^2 (y) ut iam dictum est C^3 (z) videlicet W^1 W^2 (aa) temporis C^3 (bb) quidquid C^3 (cc) *deest* K^1 K^2 (dd) in C^2 (ee) ad illud K^1 K^2 W^1 W^2 C^3 (ff) quo se Roma de imperio intromisit K^1 K^2 W^1 W^2 C^2 C^3 (gg) *deest* C^3 (hh) *deest* K^1 K^2 (ii) et petebant C^3 (jj) ibi W^1 W^2 (kk) et W^1 W^2 (ll) quod C^3 (mm) potenter K^2 pacem W^1 W^2 C^2 (nn) ad W^1 W^2 ad hoc C^2 (oo) tempus W^2 (pp) concordia C^3 (qq) *desunt* K^1 K^2 (rr) *deest* C^2

castra confortarent, ut ipsis esset in iuvamen. Et illos acceperunt, qui nomen militale habuerunt, et eos super castra locaverunt cum tali iure, ut(a) hucusque (b) ius castrense tenet in castrensi feodo. (cEt tuncc) deliberaverunt, (dqualia(e) statuta iurisd)(f) terris constituere vellent, et terris tale ius constituerunt, quale ad[h]uc terra Saxonie protestatur (g). (h) Nunc audire et intelligere potestis (i) principibus (jac baronibusj), et (k) aliis omnibus, qui nomen militale digne sorciuntur(l), quomodo ipsi cum Romanis sint arbitrati, quod scire vellent, (mquo iurem) inperium(n) deberet permanere. Et statuerint regi(o) ius cum consilio, quod(p) ipse sedem regiam Rome(q) regere(r)
167v debeat ex parte beati Petri cum gladio | temporali(s), unde ad[h]uc advocatus Romanus(t) appellatur. (u) Idcirco (v) vitam (w) demereri non potest, nec in suo honore(x) debilitari(y), nisi tribus de causis, que patebunt in sequentibus. Quorum primum est, si Romanam sedem destruere vellet. Secundum est(z), si (aa) contra fidem faceret(bb) Katholicam (cc). Tercium est(dd), si(ee) legitimam sine criminali(ff) causa dimitteret (gg) uxorem. Quorum (hh) horum trium, (iide iure(jj)ii) convictus (kk) fuerit, (llquod absit,ll) extunc deberet iudicari, (mm) (nncaput sibi nn)deberet amputari(oo) cum aureo dolabro, ⟨ora securis⟩(pp) (qqpropterea(rr) quia ipse est(ss) rector gladii temporalis, cum quo habet iudicare omnes hosqq), qui noxam (tt) fecerint, aut qui caput demerentur. (uu) Et insuper omnibus commisit, qui iudicis nomine censentur, cum eo protegere viduas et pupillos, (vvet domos Dei,vv) et omnes iniurias humiliare et iusticias confortare. Insuper iudicium commisit omnibus

(a) et K^{5} (b) in hodiernem tempus K^{3} (c) Extunc K^{5} (d) qualia iura K^{4} (e) *in ms.* qualis [*s*] S^{6} (f) et ius K^{3} (g) per imperatorem Constantinum et per imperatorem Carolum S^{1} S^{3} S^{4} S^{5} S^{10} K^{3} K^{4} per imperatorem Carolum K^{5} (h) *rubrica:* Quare et unde hoc sit quod imperator vocatur advocatus Romanus. K^{5} (i) pro S^{1} S^{3} K^{3} S^{10} K^{5} quod K^{4} (j) *desunt* K^{5} (k) de S^{3} (l) conserunt S^{10} (m) quomodo S^{10} (n) principium K^{3} (o) regni S^{10} (p) cum S^{3} (q) Romane S^{3} *deest* K^{3} Romanam K^{5} (r) *deest* S^{10} (s) seculari S^{3} *deest* K^{5} (t) *deest* S^{10} (u) ⟨In quibus casibus imperator vitam demeretur⟩ K^{5} (v) si K^{5} (w) suam S^{3} K^{4} (x) iure S^{10} (y) *in ms.* debilitatis [*s*] S^{6} (z) *deest* S^{3} (aa) aliquis K^{5} (bb) hesitaverit K^{5} (cc) staret S^{10} vellet facere K^{4} (dd) *deest* S^{1} S^{3} S^{4} S^{5} S^{10} K^{3} (ee) *deest* K^{5} (ff) reali S^{1} S^{3} K^{3} K^{5} legali K^{4} regali S^{10} (gg) suam K^{4} (hh) unum K^{3} K^{5} (ii) *desunt* S^{3} (jj) uno S^{1} S^{10} K^{3} K^{4} K^{5} (kk) si K^{5} (ll) *desunt* K^{5} (mm) *subrubrica:* Qualiter et cumque sibi caput amputatur. ⟨de gladio temporali⟩ K^{5} (nn) nam K^{4} (oo) decolari K^{4} (pp) *manus commentatoris* S^{6} (qq) ideo quod secularem gladium habeat iudicandi super hos omnes K^{4} (rr) *deest* S^{3} (ss) *deest* S^{10} (tt) et iusticiam K^{4} (uu) ⟨Quid imperator commisit iudicibus⟩ K^{5} (vv) *desunt* K^{5}

castra confortarent, ut ipsis esset in iuvamine. (a) Et illos(b) acce|perunt(c), qui nomen militale habuerunt, et eos super castra locaverunt cum tali iure, et(d) usque castrense ius tenet(e) in castrensi feodo. Extunc deliberaverunt(f), qualia (g iuris statuta g) terris (h constitu[e]re(i) vellent h). (j) In(k) terris (l) tale ius(m) constituerunt(n), quale adhuc (o) terra Saxonie (p) protestatur, per Constantinum (q imperatorem et per(r) q) Cawlum cesarem(s). 56va

[*115*] | Nunc (t) audire et intelligere potestis, quod principibus ac baronibus, et hiis omnibus, qui digne nomen sorciuntur, (u quomodo ipsi u) cum Romanis sunt arbitrati, (v (w quod scire w) vellent, quo iure v) imperium debet (x) permanere. (y) Et(z) statuerunt regi(aa) ius cum (bb) consilio, quod ipse sedem (cc Rome regnum(dd) cc) regere deberet(ee) ex parte beati Petri cum gladio seculari, und[e] adhuc Romanus (ff) advocatus appellatur {a}. Idcirco vitam suam non potest demereri, nec in suo (gg) honore(hh) debilitari, nisi(ii) tribus causis(jj), (kk que in sequentibus patebunt kk). Quarum prima (ll est illa ll), si sedem(mm) Romanam destruere vellet. Secunda est(nn), si sedem(oo) contra(pp) Catholicam (qq facere vellet qq). Tercia est(rr), (ss) si[ne] causa legali vellet suam legittimam dimittere uxorem. Quorum (tt) trium(uu) (vv de una vv), si(ww) (xx quod absit (yy), xx) fuerit convictus(zz), extunc debet iudicare, (aaa) hos omnes, qui noxam et iniustam(bbb) fecerunt, aut qui caput demerentur. Et (ccc) insuper omnibus (ddd) commisit, (eee quod iudicis nomen censentur eee), | cum (fff) protegere viduas et pupillos, et domos Dei(ggg), et omnes iniurias humiliare (hhh et iusticiam confortare hhh). Insuper(iii) iudicium commisit (jjj) 57ra XXXI 57rb

---

(a) ⟨Castrense ius vocatur [*unum verbum difficile*] feudum⟩ C^3 (b) illi K^1 K^2 (c) *deest* C^3 (d) ut W^1 W^2 *deest* K^1 K^2 (e) habent et tenent C^3 (f) liberaverunt K^1 K^2 (g) iura C^3 (h) statuerent demum laudum C^3 (i) statuere K^2 (j) et tunc C^3 (k) et W^1 W^2 (l) mundi C^3 (m) *deest* K^1 K^2 (n) statuerunt C^3 (o) in W^1 W^2 (p) servat et C^3 (q) et C^3 (r) *deest* K^1 K^2 (s) imperatores C^3 (t) ulterius C^3 (u) *desunt* C^3 (v) et C^3 (w) quid facere W^1 W^2 (x) Romanum C^3 (y) ⟨de gladio⟩ C^3 (z) Ideo C^3 (aa) imperatori C^3 (bb) ex C^2 (cc) Romanorum regiam K^1 Romane [*s*] regiam K^2 Romani Regni W^1 W^2 Rome regiam C^2 Rome C^3 (dd) *in ms.* regna [*s*] C^1 (ee) ⟨deberet⟩ C^3 (ff) rex C^3 (gg) ⊢iure⊣ C^1 (hh) iure K^1 (ii) exceptis C^3 (jj) casibus K^1 K^2 (kk) *deest* C^3 (ll) *deest* C^2 (mm) fidem K^1 K^2 W^1 W^2 (nn) *deest* C^3 (oo) fidem C^3 (pp) *deest* C^2 (qq) ut hereticus C^3 (rr) *deest* C^3 (ss) si K^1 K^2 C^3 (tt) horum K^1 K^2 W^2 C^2 (uu) *deest* C^2 (vv) unum W^1 W^2 (ww) *deest* K^1 K^2 W^1 W^2 (xx) *desunt* C^3 (yy) voluerit K^1 (zz) devictus C^2 (aaa) caput sibi debet amputari cum aureo delabro. Propterea quia ipse est rector gladii temporalis, cum habet iudicare W^1 W^2 nam decollari debeat cum aureo dolabro. Ideo quod secularem gladium habeat super C^3 secundum C^2 (bbb) iniusticiam K^1 K^2 W^2 C^2 C^3 iusticiam [*s*] W^1 (ccc) si W^1 (ddd) ⟨militibus dicit⟩ C^3 (eee) *desunt* C^3 (fff) eo K^1 K^2 W^1 W^2 C^3 (ggg) *deest* W^1 W^2 (hhh) allis C^3 (iii) Et eciam ideo C^3 (jjj) seculare C^3

{a} ipse woÿt. ⟨woyt⟩ C^3

iudicibus temporalibus, sive secularibus(a), (bcum eob) iudicare super omnes hos, qui (c) in maleficiis deprehensi fuerint in facto manifesto, ad iudicium (d) deducti (eet convictie) fuerint, ut ius dictaverit. Ubi omnes iudices soli(f) iudicare debent, vel(g) preco ipsorum loco. Eodemmodo ut(h) iudices habent temporalem(i) gladium a rege, eodem modo sacerdotes spiritualem gladium habent ab Apostolico.o) (j) Nunc attendatis(k), quis inperatorem(l) iudicare debeat, si ex hiis tribus premissis in aliquo(m) convictus fuerit. (n) Hoc facere debet Sacri Inperii Renensis palati[n]us, qui (oinperatorio) ac(p) inperio ex arbitrio positus fuerat. (qSimili(r) modo, utq) palatinus inperatorem debet
168r iudicare, eodemmodo iudicet burgravius marchionem | pro suo excessu, et scultetus burgravium.

Articulus 112 (s)

[*112*] Extunc mercatores dicebant (tad inperatoremt), quod libenter(u) scire vellent, in quo (v) permanere possent. Tunc indicavit ipsos inperator cum consilio Romanorum ad aquas navipotentes, quod edificarent ibi(w) civitates(x) firmas cum muris(y) et turribus(z). Tunc plus dicebant inperatori, quod libenter(aa) scire vellent, quod(bb) iure stare deberent. Extunc inperator dedit ipsis tale ius, quale cottidie in sua curia habere solebat. Et hoc confirmavit eis cum consilio Romanorum et cum veridicis(cc) signis. Et suam manum exhibuit, (ddquam apprehendit quidam mercator, et dexteram cirotecam(ee) (ff) de manu sibi deposuit, super quo pax beati Petri ipsis formata(gg) fuit. Quod hucusque manet in exemplum, ubi nove civitates edificantur aut fora(hh), quod ibi crux ponitur super forum(ii). In eo probatur et apparet, quod de voluntate regis factum sit, cum(jj) municipale ius ab antiquo tempore(kk)

(a) scolaribus K^5 (b) *desunt* K^4 (c) noxam faciunt aut qui S^3 (d) capti seu K^4 (e) *desunt* S^{10} (f) sibi K^4 S^{10} *deest* K^3 (g) et K^5 (h) et K^5 (i) *deest* K^5 (j) *rubrica:* Quis iudicat imperatorem. K^5 (k) intendo vobis revelare K^4 (l) regem aut cesarem K^4 (m) uno K^4 (n) 〈De imperatore iudicando〉 K^3 (o) ab imperatore S^{10} (p) aut K^4 (q) Similis est K^5 (r) Tali S^{10} K^4 (s) S^1 S^6 S^{10} *Art. 112* S^3 *Art. 121* S^4 S^5 *Art. 111* K^3 *Art. 114 pars 2* K^4 *Art. 117* (t) *desunt* K^3 (u) libere K^5 (v) iure K^5 (w) sibi K^4 K^5 (x) *deest* K^3 (y) iuris S^{10} (z) terris K^5 (aa) *deest* S^3 (bb) quo S^1 S^3 S^4 S^5 S^{10} K^4 K^5 in quo K^3 (cc) vindicis S^{10} (dd) *desunt* S^4 S^5 (ee) *deest* S^3 (ff) sibi S^1 K^4 (gg) firmata S^1 S^3 S^{10} K^3 K^4 confirmata K^5 (hh) forma K^5 (ii) *deest* S^3 (jj) sic ex quo S^1 K^4 (kk) *deest* S^1 K^4 K^5

omnibus iudicibus temporalibus cum eo iudicare super omnes(a) , qui in maleficiis fuerint deprehensi(b) in(c) facto manifesto, et ad iudicium capti, deducti et fuerint convicti, ut ius dictaverit. Ibi(d) omnes iudices soli debent(e) iudicare, (f) vel preco ipsorum loco. Eodem modo(g) ut(h) iudices (i) habent temporalem gladium a rege (j), eodem modo sacerdotes habent spiritualem gladium ab Apostolico.

[*116*] | (k) Nunc attendatis, quis (l) cesarem iudicare debet, si ex hiis tribus 57va
premisis (min unom) fuerit convictus. (n) Hoc facere debet(o) Sacri Imperii
Renensis palatinus, | qui imperatori ac Imperio fuerat ex(p) arbitrio posi- 57vb
tus. Simili modo(q), ut(r) palatinus imperatorem debet iudicare, eodem modo iudicat burgravius marchionem (s) pro sua culpa, et (tburgravium scultetust).

Articulus 117 (u)

[*117*] Extunc mercatores dicebant ad cesarem, quod libenter scire vellent, in quo (v) permanere possent. Tunc indicavit ipsos(w) imperator(x) cum consilio Romanorum ad aquas navipotentes(y), quod (z) edificarent (aa) civitates firmas cum turribus(bb). Tunc (ccplus dixerunt adcc) imperatorem, quod libenter scirent, (dd) quo iure stare(ee) deberent. Extunc(ff) imperator dedit ipsis tale ius, quale cottidie in sua curia(gg) solebat habere. Et hoc confirmavit eis
cum consilio Romanorum et (hh) veridicis signis. Et suam manum ex|hibeat, 58ra
quam apprehendit quidam mercator, et dextram cirothecam sibi de manu XXXII
traxit(ii), super quo pax beati Petri fuit confirmata (jj). Quod hucusque permanet in exemplum, (kk) ubi nove civitates edificantur (llet fora(mm), quod ibi crux ponitur super forumll). In eo probatur et apparet, quod cum voluntate

(a) omnes hos K^1 K^2 W^1 W^2 hos C^3 (b) comprehensi K^1 K^2 (c) *deest* W^1 W^2 (d) Ideo C^3 (e) dicunt W^2 (f) in capita sentenciare C^3 (g) *deest* W^2 (h) sicut C^3 (i) seculares C^3 (j) Romanorum C^3 (k) ⟨de Cesare⟩ C^3 (l) regem Romanorum C^3 (m) *desunt* C^3 (n) Respondere quod C^3 (o) *deest* K^1 K^2 (p) *deest* W^1 W^2 (q) *deest* W^2 (r) sicut C^3 (s) marggraven C^3 (t) burgravius scultetum W^1 W^2 (u) K^1 C^3 *Art. 113* K^2 *Art. 112* W^1 *Art. 109* W^2 *Art. 111* C^1 *Art. 117* C^2 *Art. 125–126* (v) iure W^1 W^2 ⟨loco⟩ C^3 (w) ipsis C^3 (x) *deest* C^2 (y) potentes K^1 K^2 manu [*s*] potentes W^1 (z) ibi sibi C^3 (aa) sibi K^1 K^2 W^1 W^2 (bb) muris et turribus K^1 K^2 W^1 W^2 muris et municipiis C^3 (cc) ulterius quesierit C^3 (dd) in K^1 K^2 (ee) uti C^3 (ff) Tunc C^3 (gg) *deest* C^3 (hh) cum K^1 K^2 W^1 W^2 C^2 C^3 (ii) detraxit C^2 (jj) quasi cruce W^1 W^2 (kk) nam C^3 (ll) aut fora C^3 (mm) aut confirmantur K^1 K^2

hucusque permansit et confirmatum ab inperio[(a)], et nomen obtinuit usque in [(b)] presentem diem[dd)]. [(c)]

Articulus 113 [(d)]

[*113*] Nunc attendatis de civitate Meÿdeburg[(e)]. Cum primo Meÿdeburg[(f)] locatum seu fundatum fuerit inperatoris Ottonis[(g)] Magni consilio, et [(h]cum terre arbitrio, et[h)] stabilitum fuit in suo [(i]iure, sicut nunc tenet [(j]in[i)] [(k)] iure[j)]
168v municipali secundum consuetudinem antiquorum, [(l]et Hallis[(m)] civitas [(n)] | ex ea fundata est[l)], idcirco utraque uno utitur iure. Eapropter omnes de Polonia ac de[(o)] Bohemia, [(p)] qui sub iure locati sunt Teutunico[(q)], et de marchia [(r]et de[(s)] Mÿssenensi provincia, [(t]et de marchia Luziciensi[t)], hii omnes ius suum in Hallis recipere debent, et de civitatibus, que in hiis districtibus locati sunt. Et si sentenciam ignoraverint aut defectum [(u)] habuerint in una sentencia, hanc opportet in Meÿdeburg querere. Idcirco, quia omne municipale [(v)] protegit, quod iure terrestri fieri non potest, quod cum reprobata sentencia de marchia[r)] ad[(w)] comitatum trahi possit, [(x)] quia marchio secundum suum[(y)] [(z)] arbitrium aut propriam[(aa)] graciam iudicat [(bb)] sub banno regio. Hoc idem[(cc)] fit[(dd)] in omnibus civitatibus, ubi bannum est regium, quod [(ee)] vir demeretur tria talenta iudici[(ff)] feodato[(gg)] sub banno regio. Sin autem iudicatur sub banno regio, tunc sculteto demerentur octo solidi [(hh]de iudicio[hh)] cum sentenciis scabinorum. Idem fit burgravio. Scabini undecim esse debent et scultetus sit duodecimus, quia burgravio[(ii)] [(jj]primam sentenciam diffinire debet[jj)]. Quia burgravius [(kk)] bannitum iudicium absque sculteto habere potest, nec[(ll)] scultetus absque[(mm)] hiis undecim scabinis [(nn]in vero loco iudiciali[nn)].

(a) ipso S[1] K[4] (b) hodiernum et S[10] (c) Si infra terminos homicidium contingerit, et si alicui culpa homicidii inponitur, sola manu se expurgabit. Eciam si alicui culpa inponitur, quod eum inter aliquos homicidium contingit, et quod tunc ille daret consilium seu subsidium aliquod, sicut lanceam vel aliam siccam, et si querulatur de ipso coram iudice, extunc ille se mettercius expurgabit cum tamen suum consilium seu subsidium nulli est manifestum etc. S[3] (d) S[1] S[6] *Art. 113* S[4] S[5] *Art. 112* K[3] *Art. 115* K[4] *Art. 118* K[5] Art. 121 (e) Meÿdburgensi K[5] (f) Meydburg K[5] (g) Othonis K[5] (h) *desunt* K[4] (i) *desunt* K[5] (j) *desunt* S[4] S[5] (k) suo K[4] (l) *desunt* S[4] S[5] (m) Halis K[5] (n) ⟨de Halis civitate⟩ K[5] (o) *deest* S[5] (p) ⟨Que terre locate sunt sub iure Theutunnico⟩ K[5] (q) Theutunico K[5] (r) *desunt* K[5] (s) *deest* S[4] S[5] (t) *desunt* S[4] S[5] (u) in ea K[4] (v) ius K[4] (w) *deest* S[4] S[5] (x) ⟨de iudiciis [s]ub banno regio⟩ K[5] (y) *deest* K[5] (z) proprium S[5] (aa) personam S[5] (bb) quod comes non facit, sed iudicat S[1] S[4] S[5] K[3] K[4] (cc) non K[4] (dd) *deest* K[5] (ee) ibi K[5] (ff) iudicio K[3] K[5] (gg) feodat K[5] (hh) deinde K[5] (ii) burgravius S[4] S[5] (jj) diffinitiva prima debet sentencia K[5] (kk) nullum S[1] S[5] K[3] K[4] K[5] ultimum S[4] (ll) *deest* K[3] (mm) ab S[4] S[5] (nn) *desunt* S[4] S[5]

regis est factum. Sic ex[(a)] quo [(b]municipale ius ab antiquo[b)] hucusque permansit et ab imperio confirmatum et nomen obtinuit usque ad diem presentem.

Articulus 118 [(c)]

[*118*] | Nunc attendatis de civitate Maÿdeburg. Cum primo Maydeburg locata fuerit seu fundata imperatoris Octonis Magni consilio, et cum terre arbitrio, et [(d)] fuit stabilita in suo iure, sicut nunc tenet in suo iure municipali secundum consuetudinem antiquorum, et Hallis civitas ex ea est fundata, idcirco uno utraque utitur iure. Eapropter omnes de Polonia et [(e)] Bohemia, qui sub iure Tewtwnico sunt locati[(f)], et de[(g)] marchia et de[(h)] Mÿsnensi provincia, et de marchia Luzinensi, hii omnes in Hallis ius suum recipere debent, et de civitatibus[(i)], que in hiis strictibus[(j)] sunt locate. Et si sentenciam ignoraverint aut defectum in ea habuerint, hanc[(k)] oportet querere in Maydeburg. Idcirco, quia omne municipale ius protegit, quod iure terrestri fieri non potest, quod cum sentencia reprobata de marchia ad comitatum | trahi possit, quia marchio secundum suum arbitrium aut propriam graciam iudicat, quod comes non facit, sed iudicat sub banno regio. Hoc idem fit in omnibus civitatibus, ubi est bannum regium, ubi vir demeretur tria talenta iudici feodato sub regio banno. Si autem iudicatur sub banno regio, tunc sculteto octo solidi demerentur de iudicio sentenciis scabinorum. Idem fit burgravio. Scabini XI debent esse et scultetus sit duodecimus, quia burgravius primam sentenciam debet diffinire. Quia burgravius nullum iudicium absque sculteto bannitum potest habere, nec scultetus absque[(l)] hiis XI[(m)] scabinis in[(n)] vero loco iudiciali.

58rb 58va

(a) *deest* K^1 K^2 (b) *desunt* K^1 K^2 (c) K^1 *Art. 114* K^2 *Art. 113* W^1 *Art. 110* W^2 *Art. 112* C^1 *Art. 118* C^2 *Art. 127–128* C^3 *Art. 114 textus Latinus deest* (d) cum K^2 (e) de K^1 W^1 W^2 (f) *in ms.* locata [*s*] C^1 (g) *deest* W^2 (h) *deest* C^2 (i) civibus K^1 K^2 (j) statutis W^1 W^2 districtibus C^2 (k) *deest* C^2 (l) *deest* K^1 K^2 (m) XII K^1 (n) *deest* K^1 K^2

Articulus 114 (a)

[*114*] Nunc attendatis (b de hiis b) de Hallis, ubi (c reprobatam sentenciam recipere(d) c) debeant, si (e) ignoraverint, aut si (f) sentencia reprobata fuerit. Hanc in Meÿdeburg(g) recipere(h) debent et Meÿdeburgenses(i) ipsis dare debent
169r ante quat[t]uor scampna(j) | et (k scabinis ipsorum ius dari debet(l) k), quia in posterum opportet ipsos esse testes, si necesse fuerit, quod sentencia rite ac racionabiliter sit data absque qualibet contradiccione. Et ibi nuncii presentes esse debent, ubi sentencia diffinitur, ex utraque parte, ubi sentencia fuit reprobata, qui audierunt et viderunt, quod utrique (m) iusticia fiat. Et iudex ipsos(n) in expensis procurare debet [in] eundo et redeundo. (o) Si sentencia sub banno regio reprobata fuerit, tunc debet reportari infra (p decem et p) octo ebdomadas(q). Sin autem (r) sub comitis banno reprobata fuerit, tunc reportari debet infra duas ebdomadas; quia scultetus habet bannum a comite et sculteciam a domino terre. Idem (s) vero habet burgravius bannum a rege et iudicium a domino terre.

Articulus 115 (t)

[*115*] (u) Nunc attendendum est, si in Meÿdeburg(v) reprobaretur sentencia, (w quo aut w) ubi eam querere aut(x) invenire deberent. Ipsi debent (y se trahere y) in Scartow(z) ultra Helle(aa) et ibi accipiunt(bb) quat[t]uor seniores viros, quos ibi(cc) invenire poterint. (dd) Hoc idcirco, quia diucius stetit quam Meÿdeburg(ee) et cezar Otto(ff) a tempore diuturno non(gg) ducatum ex eo constituit, et omnes uno(hh) eodem iure constricti sunt. Tunc trahunt cum eisdem quatuor senibus(ii), quos de Scartow(jj) (kk) duxerunt(ll) et invenerunt(mm), redeunt(nn) in(oo) Meÿdeburg ante(pp) palaciam(qq) (rr) ad curiam,
169v que inperatoris Ottonis(ss) Ruffi fuerat, qui palaciam(tt) | ipsis formaverat(uu)

(a) S^1 S^6 *Art. 114* K^4 *Art. 119* K^5 *Art. 122* (b) *desunt* K^4 (c) ius suum querere K^4 (d) reprobare K^5 (e) ipsum K^4 (f) ipsis K^4 (g) Meÿdburg K^5 (h) querere K^4 (i) Meÿdburgenses K^5 (j) scabinos K^5 (k) scabini ipsorum ius dare debent K^5 (l) *in ms.* debent [*s*] S^6 (m) parti K^5 (n) ipsis K^4 (o) *subrubrica:* Quando sentencia reprobate reportatur. K^5 (p) *desunt* K^5 (q) septimanas K^5 (r) sub comitibus vel K^4 (s) quod K^4 (t) S^1 S^6 S^{10} *Art. 115* S^4 S^5 *Art. 113* K^4 *Art. 120* K^5 *Art. 123* (u) ⟨Quis ibi dat sentencias⟩ K^5 (v) Meÿdburg K^5 (w) quomodo autem S^{10} (x) et S^4 S^5 (y) *desunt* S^{10} (z) Scarthow K^5 (aa) Elbe S^1 K^4 Albe S^{10} esse [*s*] S^4 S^5 Velle K^5 (bb) reprimit S^{10} (cc) *deest* K^4 (dd) Ibi K^4 K^5 (ee) Meÿdburg K^5 (ff) *deest* S^4 S^5 Otho K^5 (gg) *deest* S^1 S^4 S^5 S^{10} K^4 K^5 (hh) *deest* S^{10} ville et K^5 (ii) senioribus K^5 (jj) Meÿdburg K^5 (kk) traxerunt seu K^5 (ll) afferebant K^4 (mm) *deest* K^4 (nn) redemit S^4 (oo) *deest* K^4 (pp) aut ad S^{10} (qq) palacium K^5 (rr) aut S^{10} (ss) Othonis K^5 (tt) palacium K^5 (uu) firmaverunt K^5

Articulus 119 (a)

[*119*] | Nunc attendatis de Hallis, ubi ius suum(b) querere debet, si ipsum ignorant, quia(c) si ipsis sentencia(d) fuerit reprobata. Hanc in Maydeburg querere (edebe[n]t et Maÿdeburgenses(f) ipsis daree) debent ante quat[t]uor scampna et scabinis ipsorum ius dari debet, quia in posterum oportet eos esse testes, si fuerit necesse, quod sua(g) sentencia rite et racionabiliter sit (h) data absque qualibet contradiccione. Et ubi nuncii presentes esse debent, ubi(i) sentencia diffinitur, ex utraque parte, ubi sentencia reprobata fuerit, qui audierunt et viderunt, quod utrique iusticia fiet. Et iudex ipsos in expensis debet procurare ineundo(j) et redeundo. Si sentencia in banno regio fuerit reprobata, (ktunc debet (lreprobarik)(m) infra (n) XVIII ebdomadasl). Si autem sub comitis (obanno fuerit reprobata, tunc debet reprobario) infra duas septimanas; quia scultetus bannum habet a comite et sculteciam a domino terre. (p) Idemque vero habet burgravius bannum a rege et iudicium a domino terre.

59ra XXIII

Articulus 120 (q)

[*120*] | (rNunc attendendum est(s), si (tin Maydeburgt) (u) reprobaretur, quo(v) aut ubi eam | querere vel invenire deberent. Ipsi se trahere(w) debent ultra Scracaw(x) ultra Elbe(y) et ibi accipiunt quat[t]uor seniores viros, quos (z) ibi poterint invenire. Hoc idcirco, quia diucius stetit quam Maydeburg et scilicet(aa) cesar Octo a tempore diuturno (bbex eobb) constituit ducatum, et omnes uno(cc) eodem iure sunt constricti(dd). Tunc trahunt cum eisdem quat[t]uor senioribus, quos de Scracaw(ee) afferebant et redeunt(ff) in Maydeburg ante pallaciam ad(gg) curiam, que imperatoris Octonis Ruffi fuerat,

59rb 59va

(a) K^1 C^3 *Art. 115* K^2 *Art. 114* C^1 *Art. 119* W^1 *Art. 111* C^2 *Art. 129* W^2 *Art. 113* (b) *deest* C^3 (c) aut K1 K2 W1 W2 C^3 (d) *deest* C^2 (e) *desunt* K^1 K^2 (f) ipsi C^3 (g) *deest* K^1 K^2 W^1 W^2 C^3 (h) eis C^3 (i) *deest* W^1 W^2 (j) exeundo K^1 K^2 W^1 W^2 C^3 (k) *desunt* C^2 (l) ipsa in Meydeburg formari 18 septimanis C^3 (m) reportari W^1 W^2 (n) ⊢duas septimanas, quia scultetus bannum habet a comite et sculteciam a domino terre. Idemque vero habet burgra⊣ C^1 (o) debet formari ⟨18 septimanis. Si sub comite debet formari⟩ C^3 (p) Hoc C^3 (q) K^1 C^3 *Art. 116* K^2 *Art. 115* C^1 *Art. 120* W^1 *Art. 112* C^2 *Art. 130* W^2 *Art. 114* (r) Ante pallacium et curiam, que imperatoris Ottonis fuerat, qui pallacium ipsis fecerat, in fine summi templi. C^3 (s) *deest* W^1 W^2 (t) *desunt* K^1 K^2 (u) sentencia K^1 K^2 W^2 C^2 (v) quomodo W^1W^2 (w) *deest* W^1 (x) Schartow K^1 Scharchow K^2 Scharthowo alias Starkow W^1 Scharthow alias in Starchow W^2 Schracow C^2 (y) Elbiam W^1 Albiam W^2 (z) cum K^1 K^2 (aa) *deest* K^1 K^2 W^1 W^2 C^2 C^3 (bb) *deest* W^1 W^2 (cc) *deest* K^1 K^2 (dd) constituti W^1 W^2 (ee) Schartow K^1 Scharcow K^2 Starkow W^1 W^2 Schracow C^2 (ff) *w rkp.* redenut C^1 (gg) et W^1 W^2

et in (a) summi (bfine templib), ut in premissis patet et in sequentibus apparebit, quia continue pro (c) reprobata sentencia ad inperium (dse trahere non potueruntd).

Articulus 116 (e)

[*116*] Nunc attendatis (f) per quem modum ipse palaciam fecerit. Vocavit eosdem quat[t]uor(g) senes(h) de Scartow(i) et quat[t]uor canonicos, qui prelaturas habent in summo: primus prepositus, secundus decanus, tercius episcopi vicarius, quartus cellarius. Insuper recepit quat[t]uor barones ecclesie maioris feodales in Meÿdeburg(j): unus fuit marschalcus(k), secundus dapifer, tercius pincerna, quartus camerarius. Insuper recepit undecim(l) scabinos (m) et scultetum duodecimum(n). Insuper recepit(o) tres duces laicos, qui primi sunt in eleccione inperiali, (pet quartusp), quem accepit, supremus fuit advocatus ecclesie maioris in Meÿdeburg, hoc est burgravius. Tunc inperator accepit eosdem viginti octo viros (qprenominatos acq) prenotatos(r) et super sedes ipsos locavit palacie, et dedit eis potestatem ex parte sui, quecumque sentencia in Meÿdeburg(s) diffiniri non posset, aut reprobaretur, ibi deberet recipi, (tet quidquid daretur t), rite(u) ac racionabiliter pro iure municipali teneri deberet. (v) Et cum sentencia ante palaciam data(w) fuerit, tunc debet dari in signum hiis viginti octo (x), cuilibet [eorum], solidum aureo-
170r rum, et | (y) quivis solidus(z) debet valere duodecim solidos talis pecunie aut talium denariorum, cum quibus ibidem (aa) consuetudo(bb) fuerit forisare(cc). Tunc hiis quat[t]uor dantur quat[t]uor marce (dd), quod(ee) quevis marca (ff) debet duodecim marcas argenteas valere. Hoc datur (gghiis viginti octogg). Hoc illi dare tenentur, quibus sentencia ad (hhprofectum vel [ad]hh) utilitatem (iidiffinita etii) inventa fuerit. (jj)

(a) fine S^4 K^5 sive S^5 (b) sive cornua S^5 sive templi K^5 (c) una K^4 (d) vide tibi utrum S^4 *deest* S^5 (e) S^1 S^6 *Art. 116* S^{10} *Art. 114* K^3 *Art. 118* K^4 *Art. 121* K^5 *Art. 124, 125* (f) de pallacia K^4 (g) *deest* K^4 (h) seni[o]res K^5 (i) Scathow K^5 (j) Meÿdburg K^5 (k) marscelonus K^5 (l) quatuor S^{10} (m) de civitate K^4 (n) *deest* S^{10} (o) *deest* K^5 (p) *desunt* S^{10} (q) *desunt* S^1 S^{10} K^3 K^4 K^5 (r) provocatos S^{10} (s) Meÿdburg K^5 (t) hoc K^4 (u) *deest* S^{10} (v) *rubrica:* Quid datur iudicibus pallacie cum sente[n]cia reprobatur. K^5 (w) *deest* S^{10} (x) viris K^4 (y) ⟦et⟧ S^6 (z) solus K^5 (aa) talis K^4 (bb) *deest* K^5 (cc) *deest* S^{10} (dd) auree K^4 (ee) et K^4 (ff) aurea K^4 (gg) *desunt* K^3 (hh) perfectam K^5 (ii) *desunt* K^5 (jj) Sed iste, qui in sentencia defecerit, solvere debet expensas. Si autem ille in sentencia defecerit, qui eam reprobaverit, extunc solvere tenetur, quam ille, cui sentencia data fuerit ad perfectum. K^4

qui pallaciam ipsis[a] formaverat in fine summi, ut in premissis patebit et [b]in subsequentibus[b] patet, quia continue pro una sentencia reprobata ad imperium se trahere non potuerunt.[r]

Articuli 121–122 [c]

[*121*] | Nunc attendatis de pallacia, per quem modum [d]ipse pallaciam[d] fecit. 59vb
Recipit[e] eosdem quat[t]uor seniores de Scracaw[f] et quat[t]uor canonicos, qui habent prelaturas [g]in summo[g]: primus [h] prepositus, secundus decanus, tercius episcopi vicarius, quartus cellarius[i]. Insuper recipit [j] innatos ministeriales ecclesie maioris in[k] Maÿdeburg: unus[l] fuit marschalcus, secundus dapifer, tercius pincerna, quartus camerarius. Insuper recepit XI scabinos de civitate et scultetum duodecimum. Insuper[m] recepit tres duces laicos, qui primi sunt in eleccione imperiali[n], et quartus, quem accepit[o], supremus fuit advocatus ecclesie maioris[p] [q] Maydeburg, hoc[r] [s] burgravius. Tunc[t] imperator [u]recepit hos[u] XXVIII viros prenominatos[v] et super[w] sedes eos[x] locavit pallacie, et dedit eis potestatem ex sui parte,
quecumque[y] sentencia in Maydeburg diffiniri | non posset[z], aut[aa] repro- 60ra
baretur, hec [bb]ibi deberet recipi, et [cc]quidquid[bb] ibi[cc] daretur, [dd] rite XXXIII
hoc[ee] et racionabiliter pro iure municipali deberet teneri.

[*122*] | Et cum sentencia ante pallaciam fuerit data, tunc[ff] debet dari in 60rb
signum [gg] XXVIII viris cuilibet[hh] unum solidum aureum, et quivis solidus debet VII[ii] valere solidos[jj] talis pecunie aut talium denariorum, cum quibus ibidem consuetudo fuerit forisandi. Tunc[kk] hiis quattuor [ll] dantur quattuor[mm] marce auree[nn], et quevis marca [oo] VII[pp] debet [qq] argenteas valere[rr]. Hoc dare tenetur hiis XVIII[ss] [tt]. Hoc illi dare tenentur [uu], quibus sentencia ad profectum[vv] fuerit [ww]inventa et[ww] diffinita[xx]. Sed [yy] qui

---

(a) ipsius K^1 K^2 (b) sub in sequentibus K^2 in sequentibus C^2 (c) K^1 C^3 *Art. 117–118* K^2 *Art. 116–117* W^1 *Art. 113–114* W^2 *Art. 115–116* C^1 *Art. 121–122* C^2 *Art. 131–132* (d) cum C^3 (e) recipere C^1 (f) Schartavia C^3 (g) *desunt* C^3 (h) fuerit C^3 (i) celerarius K^1 K^2 W^1 W^2 C^3 cancellarius C^2 (j) quattuor K^1 K^2 W^1 W^2 C^3 (k) *deest* C^2 (l) primus K^1 K^2 C^3 (m) Deinde K^1 K^2 (n) municipali K^1 K^2 (o) recepit W^1 W^2 (p) *deest* C^3 (q) in K^1 K^2 W^1 W^2 C^2 C^3 (r) idem C^2 (s) est W^1 W^2 C^3 (t) Postea C^3 (u) accepit C^3 (v) prenotatos, eciam K^1 K^2 predictos seu pretactos C^2 (w) insuper W^1 (x) *deest* K^1 K^2 (y) quod quacumque K^2 (z) *deest* K^1 (aa) ut W^1 W^2 et C^3 (bb) *desunt* K^2 (cc) *desunt* C^3 (dd) et tunc C^3 (ee) *deest* C^3 (ff) *deest* C^3 (gg) istis C^3 (hh) *deest* C^2 (ii) XII K^1 K^2 W^1 W^2 C^2 C^3 (jj) *deest* C^3 (kk) Et sic post quod C^3 (ll) viris C^3 (mm) *deest* K^2 (nn) *deest* K^2 (oo) aurea K^1 C^2 C^3 (pp) XII W^2 C^2 C^3 (qq) marcas C^3 (rr) habere K^1 K^2 (ss) XXVIII K^1 K^2 C^3 XXIV W^1 W^2 (tt) viris W^1 W^2 C^2 (uu) hanc pecuniam C^3 (vv) factum C^2 (ww) *desunt* C^3 (xx) finita K^1 K^2 *deest* W^1 W^2 (yy) iste, K^1 K^2 W^1 W^2 C^3

Articulus 117 (a)

[*117*] ⟨Nota⟩ ⟨Nota⟩(b) Nunc attendatis, quantum plus dare opportet. (c) Dare tenetur illi scabino suam emendam, cuius sentenciam reprobavit, (d quam diffinierat(e)(f), si iuste(g) inventa(h) fuerat d), et iudici suam penam. (i Sin autem ante(j) consensum aliorum(k) scabinorum sentencia reprobata fuerit, tunc cuilibet scabino datur emenda et iudici pena, et quod fuerint emende, tot erunt(l) et pene. i) (m)

[*articulus deest*](n)

[*articulus deest*](o)

(a) S^{1} S^{6} *Art. 117* K^{3} *Art. 119* K^{4} *Art. 122 pars 1* S^{10} *Art. 115* (b) *manus commentatoris* S^{6} (c) aut S^{10} Ipse K^{4} (d) *desunt* S^{10} (e) diffinicionis K^{5} (f) invenit K^{4} (g) iniuste K^{5} (h) diffinita K^{4} (i) *desunt* K^{4} (j) *deest* S^{10} (k) maiorem K^{5} (l) *deest* K^{5} (m) De eo. Utrum iurati et scabini scientes aliquem iuraturum coram ipsis false et iniuste. Utrum iurati et scabini scientes aliquem iuraturum coram ipsis false et iniuste, debeant tale iuramentum admittere in foro iudiciali, et quid facere debeant, dum talis ad iuramentum venerit et dicit: "Domine, permittatis me circa ius meum diffinitum a vobis, quia iurare volo." Respondeo. Si scabini ibi sunt, ut persone publice quevis reddere debent et non possunt eum revocare a suo proposito sive scandalo, eum admittere possunt. Si autem private, tunc non possunt eum admittere nec debent. *articulus distinctus* S^{10} K^{4} (n) K^{4} *in versioni Cracoviensi* (o) K^{4} *in versioni Cracoviensi*

[(a]in sentencia defecerit, solvere[(b)] debet expensas. Si autem ille[a)] in sentencia defecerit, qui eam reprobavit, extunc magis[(c)] [(d)] solvere tenetur[(e)], quam ille, cui sentencia data fuit ad profectum[(f)].

Articulus 123 pars 1 [(g)]

[*123 pars 1*] [(h)] [(i]Nunc attendatis, quantum plus dare oportet. Ipse dare tenetur scabino illi suam emendam, cuius sentenciam reprobavit, quam invenit, si iuste fuerat diffinita, et iudici suam penam.[i)] Si autem ante[(j)] consensum aliorum scabinorum fuerit reprobata, tunc cuilibet scabino datur emenda et iudici tociens sua[(k)] pena.

Articulus 123 pars 2 [(l)]

[*123 pars 2*] Si autem ipsa[(m)] in Hallis[(n)] reprobata fuerit et [(o)] Maydeburg invenitur, et [(p)] pariter ibidem reprobabitur, extunc ambe dabuntur emende et pene [(q]in Maydeburg et Hallis[q)]. Hoc facit rex[(r)] [(s)] Octo taliter [(t]pro eo[t)], quod municipale ius staret[(u)], sicut ab antiquo[(v)] tempore[(w)] hucusque stetit, et ibidem fecit ducatum trans Elbiam[(x)].

Articulus 124 [(y)]

[*124*] | Nunc dicere [(z]volo vobis de pallacia, quomodo[z)][(aa)] illa [(bb)] debeat [(cc)] 60[vb]
convenire, et diffinire volo[(dd)] pro[(ee)] rebus[(ff)] istis, ut[(gg)] in precedentibus est predictum[(hh)].

(a) *desunt* K^1 (b) *deest* K^1 (c) parvis C^3 (d) solus C^2 (e) *deest* K^1 (f) utilitatem W^1 W^2 (g) K^1 C^3 *Art. 119 pars 1* K^2 *Art. 118 pars 1* W^1 *Art. 115 pars 1* W^2 *Art. 117 pars 1* C^1 *Art. 123 pars 1* C^2 *Art. 133 pars 1* (h) ⟨Pena scabinorum⟩ C^3 (i) *desunt* C^3 (j) *deest* C^3 (k) *deest* C^3 (l) K^1 C^3 *Art. 119 pars 2* K^2 *Art. 118 pars 2* K^4 *Art. 122 pars 2* W^1 *Art. 115 pars 2* W^2 *Art. 117 pars 2* C^1 *Art. 123 pars 2* C^2 *Art. 133 pars 2* (m) *deest* K^1 K^2 (n) alio C^2 (o) in K^1 K^2 K^4 W^1 W^2 C^2 C^3 (p) qualiter K^1 K^2 (q) *desunt* C^3 (r) *deest* C^3 (s) Ruffus K^1 K^2 K^4 W^1 W^2 C^2 C^3 (t) ideo C^3 (u) staret C^2 permaneret C^3 (v) ante quo W^1 (w) *deest* K^2 (x) Albam K^1 Albiam K^4 C^3 Elbeam C^2 Wram [*s*] W^1 W^2 (y) K^1 C^3 *Art. 120* K^2 *Art. 119* K^4 C^1 *Art. 124* W^1 *Art. 116* W^2 *Art. 118* C^2 *Art. 134* (z) vobis W^1 (aa) quando K^4 (bb) quo W^1 (cc) de pallacia W^1 (dd) *deest* C^3 (ee) de K^1 K^2 (ff) tribus W^1 (gg) non K^1 K^2 (hh) predictum K^4 *deest* C^3

[*articulus deest*]

[*articulus deest*]

Articulus 125 [(a)]

[*125*] | Scultetus de Maydeburg debet recipere litteram civitatis cum sigillo 61ra ipsius pendente. Hanc litteram debet mittere supremo[(b)] advocato maioris XXXIIII ecclesie[(c)], hoc est burgravius in Maydeburg, ad quem suam [(d)] propriam litteram sigillatam debet recipere, [(e]eapropter ipse est advocatus. Et [(f]ad hoc[f)] debet recipere litteram [(g)] episcopi cum suo sigillo, [(h]et [(i)] eciam [(j]ad hoc[j)] debet recipere litteram[e)] regis, et suum sigillum appendens, si ipsum habere possit in Tewtunico.[h)] Has quinque litteras debet recipere burgravius de Maydeburg. Et eas primo debet mittere duci[(k)] Saxonie cum hiis, qui[(l)] cum sentencia traxerunt[(m)], et cum scitu horum XXIIII[(n)] virorum, qui prius sunt nominati[(o)]. Post hoc mittere debet margravio[(p)] de Brandeburg[(q)]. Tertio ipse[(r)] mittere debet palatino Renensi[(s)]. Hii tres primi duces laici sunt in eleccione imperiali[(t)], [(u]cum novus rex eligitur Thewtunica de terra[u)].

Articulus 126 [(v)]

[*126*] Hic[(w)] [(x]audire et[x)] intelligere potestis, quomodo hii omnes[(y)] domini debent[(z)] citari, qui[(aa)] in premissis sunt nominati. Ipsi ad pallaciam ire debent [(bb)] primo, secundo, tertio, semper[(cc)] ad sex ebdomadas. Et si in tercia non conparuerit, [(dd]extunc citacione [(ee)] hii tres laici duces mittunt[dd)]. Tunc regi[(ff)] de qualibet citacione tres marcas aureas demeretur, [(gg)] quelibet [(hh)] aurea[(ii)] XX[(jj)] marcas argenteas | debet valere. Et [(kk]si preter[(ll)] [(mm)] 61va hoc[kk)] ultra sex[(nn)] septimanas [(oo)] conparuerit, [(pp)] se excusare coram rege [(qq)], ubi ipse fuerit. Extunc omnia sentencialiter ecclesie maiori vacabunt, que [(rr]ad[(ss)] ea[rr)] habebat, et regi bannum vacabat[(tt)], et post hoc proscribunt eum[(uu)] in regis illegalitate.

(a) K^1 C^3 *Art. 121* K^2 *Art. 120* K^4 C^1 *Art. 125* W^1 *Art. 117* W^2 *Art. 119* C^2 *Art. 135* (b) summo W^2 (c) *deest* C^2 (d) sentenciam K^1 K^2 (e) *desunt* W^1 (f) adhuc C^3 K^4 (g) regalem C^3 (h) appendenti C^3 (i) tunc K^1 K^2 (j) adhuc K^4 *desunt* K^1 K^2 C^2 (k) *deest* C^3 (l) qui se C^2 *deest* K^4 (m) transierunt K^1 K^2 taxaverunt K^4 (n) XXVIII C^3 (o) prenominati W^1 W^2 (p) burgravio C^3 (q) Meÿdenburg K^1 K^2 (r) *deest* W^1 W^2 (s) de Reÿnensi K^4 (t) imperatoris C^3 (u) *desunt* C^3 (v) K^1 C^3 *Art. 122* K^2 *Art. 121* W^1 *Art. 118* W^2 *Art. 120* C^1 *Art. 126* C^2 *Art. 136* (w) Si K^1 K^2 (x) eciam C^3 (y) *deest* C^3 (z) *deest* W^1 (aa) dum C^2 (bb) et scultetus vel burgravium citare debet K^1 K^2 et scultetus burgravium citare debet W^1 W^2 C^3 (cc) super K^1 K^2 (dd) citacione, ex eorum istis tribus ducibus laicis C^3 (ee) ad eum K^1 K^2 W^1 W^2 C^2 (ff) *in ms.* rege [*s*] C^1 (gg) quarum K^1 K^2 W^1 W^2 C^3 et C^2 (hh) marca K^1 K^2 W^1 W^2 C^2 C^3 (ii) *deest* K^1 K^2 (jj) XII C^1 C^2 C^3 W^2 (kk) post has C^3 (ll) post K^1 K^2 W^1 W^2 C^2 C^3 (mm) ter C^2 (nn) tres C^3 (oo) non K^1 K^2 W^1 W^2 C^2 C^3 (pp) tunc tenetur C^3 (qq) imperatore C^3 (rr) a rege C^3 (ss) ab K^1 K^2 W^1 W^2 (tt) *deest* C^3 (uu) *deest* C^3

[*articulus deest*]

Conclusio(a)

⟨Conclusio⟩(b) (cIste liber finitus et de Teutunico translatus in Latinum per Conradum scriptorem, notarium condam Sandomiriensem ac civem dicte civitatis, ad peticionem viri famosi, domini Nicolai dicti de Paczonow, civis supradicte civitatis, qui fuit causa movens(d), in cuius (e) est inchoatus. In eiusdem vero nomine est(f) finitus, (gcui laus et gloria per infinita seculorum secula. Ameng).

Idem vero(h) Conradus suppliciter exhortatur diligenter quemlibet lectorem petens, ut cum in hoc libro ipsum legere contingerit, quidquid ibi(i) displi-
170v cencie fuerint, ut(j) hoc non inputet sue ruditati. Cum tamen | per inperatores ac cesares idem liber sit constitutus, (k) licet compendiose, ut [per] Constantinum, Iustinianum ac Karolum confirmatus. Ad(l) eorum peticionibus per sanctos patres Apostolicos sit(m) sanctitus, ac sub anatemate prohibitur, ne quis augmentando vel minuendo eundem librum in aliqua sua distinctione(n) vel diffinicione transponere, aut transmutare aliquatenus(o) presummat (p), sed(q) ipsum in suo(r) vigore inviolabiliter permittere(s) permanere [*s*]. Cum eciam per falsam gramaticam mortale peccatum non committatur, (tet ideot), si minus rethorice aliquid in eodem opusculo repertum fuerit, hoc peto non nimium(u) ponderari, nec michi propter hoc inproperari et cetera.

(vIste liber conpletus(w) est (xin Solecz in die sancte Cecilie virginis sub anno Domini millesimo quadringentesimo quinquagesimo quinto [*22 XI 1455*] P.(y) S. de Oppatow etcx).v)c)

(a) S1 S2 S6 S9 S10 K3 (b) *manu commentatoris* S6 (c) Excipit ius municipale anno Domini 1368, dominica Invocavit me [*26 II*]. S2 Excipit liber municipalis feria quinta proxima post die cinerum sub anno Nativitatis Domini Millesimo CCCCLXXIII. S9 (d) inciens S1 (e) nomine S1 S10 K3 (f) *deest* S10 (g) Amen. Laudo Deum quia finem habeo. S10 (h) vir S10 (i) sibi S1 (j) *deest* S1 (k) ac iuris constituciones S1 (l) Ac S10 (m) *deest* S10 (n) institucione S1 (o) aliquantum S10 (p) debet S10 (q) *deest* S10 (r) eo S1 (s) mittere S1 (t) *desunt* S10 (u) *deest* K3 (v) Hec autem pacta sunt sub anno Incarnacionis Domini millesimo trecentesimo quinquagesimo nono, sabbato in vigilia benedicte Trinitatis ac in festo sancti Viti gloriosi martyris [*15 VI*] . Scriptum per manus Nicolai de Thessyn. S1 *deest* K3 (w) finitus S10 (x) per Martinum Zabowszkÿ de Lwowek in vigilia Sancte Crucis [*13 IX*] anno Domini millesimo quingentesimo tredecimo. Cantor. S10 (y) per [*?*] S6

Articulus 127 (a)

[*127*] Eodem modo sicut scultetus citat burgravium, | sic burgravius debet citare hos tres principes sub banno regio. Et si in tercia non conparuerint citacione, (b ut est predictum, b) extunc de qualibet citacione quivis eorum(c) XVIII(d) aureas(e) marcas regi(f) demeretur(g). Etsi non(h) eadem vice conparuerint(i) iusticiam iurare(j) et ius recipere, actamen(k) illi sua sentencia et (l) ius suum dare(m) debet ante pallaciam. 61vb

Conclusio (n)

(o Et sic finis primi libri. o)

(a) K^1 C^3 *Art. 123* K^2 *Art. 122* W^1 *Art. 119* W^2 *Art. 121* C^1 *Art. 127* C^2 *Art. 137* (b) *desunt* C^3 (c) *deest* C^2 (d) XXII W^2 (e) *deest* K^1 K^2 W^1 W^2 (f) *deest* K^1 K^2 (g) quarum quelibet aurea marca valet XII argenteas C^3 (h) *deest* K^1 K^2 W^1 W^2 C^2 (i) venerint C^3 (j) iuvare K^1 K^2 C^2 (k) actum K^1 K^2 quoque haec C^3 (l) ipse C^3 (m) dicere C^2 (n) C^1 K^1 K^2 (o) Explicunt leges Meydenburgenses K^1 Explicit primus liber legum Theuthunicalium civitatis Meÿdenburgensis K^2

[*textus deest*]

Addenda [(a)]

Nota. De latitudine ac longitudine mansi Franconici[1].

Ulnis [(b)] bisseptem fac virgam, iungito pugnum, bissenis latus ex hiis fiat tibi mansus, bis centum longis ac virgis septuaginta et Franconicus mansus per-
fectus sit tibi sensus. [(c]Virgas tibi quinque solum, sibi iugerum | ⟨Iste liber est 62ra
primus⟩[(d)] habebit, iugera[2] tibi sena sunt in manso numerando etc.[c)] XXXVI

[(a)] C[1] C[2] S[10]   [(b)] vero S[10]   [(c)] *desunt* C[2] S[10]   [(d)] *manus α* C[1]

---

1 *mansus Franconicus—ca. 23,9–27,4 ha*
2 *iugerum—ca. 1/4 ha*

Ius Municipale Magdeburgense in: Commune incliti Poloniae Regni privilegium ...

 | DOI:10.1163/9789004735033_006

Ius Municipale Magdeburgense

in

Commune incliti Polonie Regni privilegium constitutionum et indultuum publicitus decretorum approbatorumque cum nonnullis iuribus tam Divinis quam humanis per serenissimum principem et dominum, dominum Alexandrum, Dei gratia Regem Poloniae, Magnum Ducem Lithwanie, Russie Prussieque dominum et heredem etc. Non tamen in illud privilegium, sed motu proprio regio serenitatis sue per adhortationem pro instructione Regnicolarum proque Regni eiusdem, ac iustitie statu feliciter dirigendis eidem privilegio annexis et ascriptis mandanteque sacra eadem Maiestate accuratissime castigatis

***

The General Privilege of the Famous Kingdom of Poland, constitutions and grants officially issued and approved, with numerous rights both Divine and human, by the most illustrious prince and lord, Lord Alexander, by the Grace of God King of Poland, Grand Duke of Lithuania, Ruthenia and Prussia, lord and heir, etc., nevertheless [included] in that privilege not [otherwise], except by the own will of his royal majesty, through admonition for the instruction of the subjects of the Kingdom and for the prosperity of the same Kingdom and for effectively administering justice, in the same privilege were combined and [inserted into it], and by the command of His Majesty most carefully corrected

***

CLXXVI[r]

Prologus in ius Maÿdeburgense.

(a) In nomine Patris et Filii et Spiritus Sancti. Amen. Hoc opus locatum est supra firmum fundamentum, de quo dicit Apostolus: fundamentum nemo aliud ponere potest, preter id, quod positum est, quod est Christus [*1 Cor. 3, 11*]. Ubi enim Christus(b) fundamentum (c) non est, ibi nullius boni operis potest superesse edificium. Ad invocationem (d) summe et individue Trinitatis, exemplum laudabile me compellit et ratio violenta, quia (e) quod a maioribus factum esse dinoscitur, id a minoribus quoque observari debeat. (f) Mos quippe retinendus est fidelissime vetustatis(g); licet enim non exemplis, sed legibus est iudicandum,(h) verumtamen exemplum aliquis potest sequi maxime, ubi recte factum aliquod intuetur ad probandum.(i) Sed quod in quolibet principio a gloria Trinitatis debeat auxilium peti, sola ratio sufficere potest; cuiuslibet enim rei potissima pars est principium, et ex iis, que inordinate inchoata sunt, non potest aliquid ordinate agi. Per se patet, qualiter bene et laudabiliter omnia geruntur, si principium fuerit decens et amabile Deo, (j) nam vix peragantur exitu, que malo inchoata sunt initio. Quibus omnibus luce clarius apparet, qui[a] finis laudabilis a bono dependet principio et tamquam suo maiori subiacet. In quo quidem principio cautius est agendum. Cum enim inceptio omnium est gravissima, ne is, qui se putat stare, in foribus delinquat, ad causam causarum, ut pro auxilio recurrat, necesse est. Ipsa nanque benedicta Trinitas est, in cuius nomine et consilio omnis actus progreditur. Sic enim ad omnipotentis Dei presidium debemus oculos erigere, ut non in armis scientie vel eloquentie iaculis confidamus, sed omnem spem et omne propositum erigamus ad providentiam Trinitatis (k), ipsa enim laborantibus aurem apperit et inclinat, propter quod nos sermo propheticus exhortatur: (l) Apprehendite disciplinam et sapientiam, nequando irascatur Dominus et ne pereatis de via iusta [*Ps 2,12*]. Felix exhortacio, dulce consilium. (m) Qui enim apprehendit Christum, ut verum, fatear, apprehendit summum bonum. Ipse enim est sapientia, iustitia, veritas, fortitudo, sanctitas. Et qui ignorat sapientiam et

---

(a) Jan Zoamas hodiernus [*?*] scr[iba] [*?*] et lone[r] [*?*] etc. [*?*] JL[14] Noblissimi [*unum verbum difficile*] JL[31] Ius municipale JL[36] (b) Fundamentum est omnium rerum Christus JL[41] (c) Super fundamento Christo omne boni operis edificium, *manus A* JL[26] (d) *org.* qo [*s*] (e) Quod a maioribus factum esse dinoscitur, id a minoribus quoque observari debeat, *manus A* JL[26] (f) Mos vetustatis fidelisime retineatur, *manus A* JL[26] (g) Fidelissima vetustas JL[41] (h) Non exemplis, sed legibus est iudicandum JL[7] Exemplis ubi probati JL[7] Non exemplis sed legibus est iudicandum JL[38] (i) Principium a Deo super summum post omnia JL[17] (j) Bono peraguntur [ex]situ JL[7] (k) Effectus Sanctissimae Trinitatis JL[38] (l) Aprehendite disciplinam JL[7] Sermo propheti[cus] JL[41] (m) Christus summum bonum JL[17]

Prologue to the Magdeburg Law.

In the name of the Father, and of the Son, and of the Holy Spirit. Amen. This work is erected on a lasting foundation, of which the Apostle speaks: "For no one can lay any foundation other than the one that has been laid; that foundation is Jesus Christ." [*1 Corinthians 3:11*]. For where Christ is not the foundation, no edifice of any sound work can survive. I am compelled to invoke the highest and undivided Trinity by a laudable example and urgent reason, because that what is known to have been done by the great should be observed by the lesser ones. The oldest custom should of course be most faithfully preserved, yet judgment should be not by examples, but by statutes; nevertheless, an example can be followed to the highest degree, when an act appropriately confirms it. Meanwhile, at every beginning it is necessary to earnestly seek the assistance of the Trinity, as reason alone may suggest; truly, the most important part of anything is the beginning, and from those things that have been begun improperly, nothing orderly can result. Therefore, it becomes apparent how well and gloriously everything will be accomplished, if the beginning is proper and pleasing to God, but with difficulty will good ends be reached by those which have been wrongly begun. In the light of all this, it clearly follows that the glorious end depends on the good beginning and is subordinate to it, as it were. Therefore, it is precisely the beginning that should be undertaken most carefully. Since the beginning of everything is the most difficult, in order for one who thinks he can manage not to err in judgments, it is necessary for him to turn to the cause of causes for help. For it is the Holy Trinity in whose name and with whose assistance every action proceeds. Thus, we should lift our eyes to the all powerful God for help, so that we do not place our trust in the weapon of knowledge or the skill of language, but entrust all hope and all intention to the care of the Trinity, for It opens the ears of those who work and encourages them, as the word of the prophets exhorts us: "Kysse the sonne, lest the LORDE be angrie, and so ye perish from the right waye" [*Psalms 2:12*]. Happy admonition, sweet advice. For whoever gains Christ to confess the truth, shall gain the highest good. He is wisdom, justice, truth, virtue, holiness. And whoever does not know wisdom and Scripture, as Scripture testifies, does not know Christ. Christ is the

Scripturas, Christum ignorare Scripture testimonio perhibetur. (a) Christus etenim Dei virtus est sapientia. Ignorantia autem Scripturarum ignorantia est Christi. Iuxta Apostolum: apprehendite siquidem sapientiam, que insipientiam procul pellit, (b) egressus enim unius alterius operatur ingressum. Cum renunciatur improbitas, nascitur virtus et cum eiicitur superbia, adest humilitas. Et iterum qui sapientiam non apprehendit, improperabi-
CLXXVI[v] tur ei a Domino, et ideo sacerdotio non fungetur (c) | et in tenebris ignorantie latitans, mentis oculis excecatus (d) iustitiam invenire non poterit. Sine qua, etsi ceterarum virtutum in ipso fulgeant radii, pro nihilo tamen reputantur. (e) Ipsa enim iustitia est (f), que inter ceteras virtutes perfectissima dicitur, que iura omnibus distribuit et ea de causa iustitia appellatur. Illius omnes obediant iudicio. (g) Hec est enim illa virtus laudabilis, que diffinitione nobili diffinitur. (h) Iustitia est constans et perpetua voluntas, ius suum cuilibet tribuens [*D. 1.1.10 pr.*], que concupiscentie "conatus sua virtute comprimit"[1] ac desideria refrenat. (i) Cum igitur subiectum libri presentis nullum sit aliud ponere preter ius et iustitiam, felix liber cui tam nobile famulatur subiectum, felix ille vir, (j) inter cuius verba liber iste, sicut mirrhe fasciculus poterit commorari. Merito ergo, qui opus tantum aggreditur, ut librum signatum septem sigillis apperiat, (k) summe Trinitatis auxilium expetet et imploret. Ego siquidem illud scriptum attendens, quod nemo altiorem locum in scholis quibusvis teneat, nisi cui laboris assiduitas et studiorum prolixitas suffragatur, quamvis inter ceteros lectores minimum me reputans et ignorantie mee tenebras non ignorans, excusare me deberem, et cum propheta dicente: A, a, a, Domine Deus, ecce nescio loqui, qui puer ego sum [*Jr 1,6*], quoniam altus est puteus scientie sapientie, et non est cum quo hauriam, quemadmodum mulier Chananea locuta est cum de Dei omnipotentis Filio, qui aquam vivam distribuit et largitur, tamen confisus de misericordia eius, opus presens aggrediar spem gerens firmissimam, quod de fonte gratiarum suarum ad siccitatem meam rivulum derivando, (l) de pane sue consolationis, ne in via deficiam, buccelam mihi porriget. Sed ne prolixitas, que frequenter parit fastidium, sermonem

(a) Christus Dei virtus et sapientia JL[17] (b) Egressus etiam unius, alterius operatur ingressum JL[7] (c) De damno per negli[g]enciam—CCXXI folio [*in Speculo Saxonici in Commune incliti Poloniae Regni privilegium... , fol. CCXXI*[r]*, SSp. II.38*], *manus B* JL[36] (d) Iusticie laus JL[17] (e) Definitio iustitiae JL[17] Iustitia operetur qualiter JL[38] (f) [I]usticia debet esse fortissima inter [omn]es virtutes JL[41] (g) Ius et iustitia JL[11] (h) Iusticia quod JL[17] Definitio iustitiae, *manus B* JL[25] Iustitia quid est JL[38] [I]ustitia quomodo est JL[41] (i) Subiectum in quo JL[7] Annum huius li. JL[17] (j) Laus et vir[t]us, laus huius li. JL[17] (k) Invocatio Sanctae Trinitatis JL[7] (l) bucellam frustulam JL[11]

1 *cf. Bulla Rex pacificus Gregorii papae IX*: iustitia conatus eius sua virtute reprimeret.

wisdom and virtue of God. Therefore, ignorance of Scripture is ignorance of Christ. According to the Apostle: acquire wisdom, which drives folly far away, because the departure of one ensures the arrival of the other. When wickedness is renounced, virtue is born, and after pride is cast off, humility follows. And again, whoever does not acquire wisdom, deserves rebuke from the Lord, and therefore shall not be allowed into the priesthood, and hiding in the darkness of ignorance, blind with the eyes of the mind, cannot administer justice. Without which, although the rays of other virtues may shine in someone, they are not fit for anything. For justice, which among all other virtues is recognized as the most perfect, which grants rights to all and for this reason is called justice. All must obey its judgment. For such is the glorious virtue, which is defined by noble intent. Justice is a constant and eternal will, distributing to everyone what is their due [*D. 1.1.10 pr.*], which subdues desire with its virtue and controls passions. Therefore, since nothing else has been presented as the subject of this book except law and justice, happy is the book that serves such a distinguished subject, happy is the man among whose words the book will dwell like a bouquet of myrrh.

Therefore, whoever undertakes such a work, to open a book marked with seven seals, should await and invoke the help of the One Trinity. When observing what is written, that no one occupies a superior place in any school, unless diligence in work and length of study allow it, although considering myself the least among other readers and not disregarding the darkness of my ignorance, I should justify myself, and saying after the prophet: "Ah, Lord God! Truly I do not know how to speak, for I am only a boy" [*Jeremiah 1:6*], since the well of wisdom is so deep, and there is nothing with which I could draw, how the Canaanite women spoke with the Son of God, who distributed and gave the water of life, yet trusting in His mercy, I undertake the present work with the most enduring hope that the He will bring a stream from the fountain of His grace to my drought, will take a morsel for me from His bread of comfort, so that I do not falter on the way. But lest prolixity, which often arouses aversion, prolong the discourse

protrahat in immensum, brevibus iam orationem meam absolvam, non in armis scientie vel eloquentie iaculis confisus, sed omnem spem, omnem propositum referens ad omnipotentis Dei legis consilium, que [a] lex est omnium naturaliter salus, fundo principium super lapidem angularem, qui est Christus Ihesus, Alpha et Omega, principium et finis.

(a) Lex est salus JL^7

excessively, I shall now conclude my speech with shorter words, not assured in the weapon of knowledge or the skill of speech, but referring all hope, all purpose to the counsel of the law of Almighty God, the law that is the obvious salvation of all, the beginning founded on the cornerstone which is Jesus Christ, Alpha and Omega, the beginning and the end.

[1] De electione, iuramento, officio et autoritate scabinorum et consulum.

(a) Cesar Otto Ruffus(b) fundavit templum in Maÿdemburg et dedit civibus municipale(c) ius secundum eorum arbitrium (d) et secundum consilium(e) seniorum (f). Extunc arbitrati sunt (g), quod eligerent (h) scabinos et consules, scabinos ad diuturnum tempus et consules ad unum annum. Qui tunc iuraverunt et nunc iurant annis singulis, dum eliguntur, (i) ius ac profec-
CLXXVII[r] tum (j) et honorem civitatis custodire et | (k) agere, quanto cautius et melius sciant aut possunt, cum consilio et iuvamine seniorum (l). Et hoc non dimittendo ratione amoris, molestie, ire vel munerum, sicut eos iuvet Deus et sancti eius. (m) Consules exponunt(n) suum conventum(o) secundum suum placitum(p) ac voluntatem cum seniorum consensu. (q) Consules etiam habent potestatem iudicandi super quamlibet vacuam mensuram(r) et pondera iniusta(s), ac ⟨de quo supra folio XLVI⟩ choretos iniustos et cuiuslibet cibi(t) et potus mercimonia. (u) Et quicunque hoc violaverit, demeretur tres Sclavonicas marcas, (v) que faciunt XXXVI solidos (w). Quando consules suum conventum(x) exponunt(y), extunc quicquid ibi statutum fuerit aut compromissum(z) in isto, quod iuri Divino non contradicit, firmum et inviolabiliter debet observari. Et quicunque violaverit(aa), hoc consules habent agere(bb) et iudicare. (cc) Et quicunque ad conventum venire

---

(a) De eadem Raÿm[undus] lib. i. ar. 60 fol. [x]ii [*infra Commune incliti Poloniae Regni privilegium…, Raimundi Summa legum brevis, levis et utilis…, folio XII[v], articulus* Qui debent ad Consilium eligi*; cf. Die Summa legum brevis et utilis des sogenannten Doctor Raymundus von Wiener Neustadt, ed. Alexander Gál (Weimar, 1926), p. 224–225*] JL[1] de iuramento JL[23] P 3.6.1. JL[33] (b) II Primu[s] JL[28] (c) civile JL[28] (d) lauda JL[28] (e) rady [*?*] JL[28] (f) amiquorum JL[28] (g) mandaverunt JL[28] (h) Divisio scabinorum cum consulibus eligentis [*s*] JL[7] (i) Formule iuramenti consulum et scabinorum; Bur [*s*] JL[6] Ad hec consules universi sunt JL[17] czasu przybyezenya JL[28] Iuramentum consulum Magdeburgensium JL[29] (j) utilitatem JL[28] (k) perizoma vestis auxiliatur [*?*] JL[21] Ex iis quae inordinate in inhoatu sunt non possunt aliquid ordinate agi, *manus A, in marg. superiore* JL[26] (l) Rota iuramenti scabinorum JL[7] stary JL[28] (m) Officium consulare, iuramenta JL[1] Que potestas consulum JL[6] Consulum potestas iudicandi JL[7] Choretos JL[11] Officium consulare JL[17] Consulem finis et intentio que [sunt] JL[38] (n) faciunt JL[28] (o) possiady JL[28] (p) zezwolenÿe JL[28] (q) Consulum est facere conventum sive gromode vulgariter JL[6] Officium consulum, *manus B* JL[26] (r) bezprawnemÿ JL[28] (s) ut vacuis ponderis bez mÿan JL[28] (t) pokarm JL[28] (u) Inobiediens invenire neglexerit pena deme[retur] JL[7] (v) Et infra fol. 245 [*Articuli Iuris de Lubek in: Commune incliti Poloniae Regni privilegium…, fol. CCXLV[v]*] JL[1] Sclavonica marcas constet [*s*] solidorum 36 po polske wiardanek JL[38] (w) Grziwny koronne stand vroslÿ secundum cursum pecuniae. JL[1] Pena 36 solidi JL[7] Sentencia promulgata consulum firma esse d[ebet]; nec decet eam alias strofowa[cz] JL[17] Sclavonice ma[rcae] faciunt 36 so[lidi], *manus B* JL[41] (x) szyedzyenÿe JL[28] (y) vlosza JL[28] (z) obyegano firmatam JL[28] (aa) przistapic JL[28] (bb) czinicz [*?*] JL[28] (cc) Pena ad quemcumque non venientis JL[17]

[1] On the election, oath, duties, and authority of the jurors and councillors.

Emperor Otto the Red[1] built a church in Magdeburg and granted the citizens municipal law, according to their discretion and the advice of the elders. From then they decided that they would elect jurors and councillors, jurors for an indefinite period and councillors for one year.[2] They then swore an oath and now, every year when they are elected, they swear to uphold the law and to care for the prosperity and honour of the city, as wisely and as best as they know or are able to, with the advice and assistance of the elders. And they may not deviate from this out of sympathy, trouble, anger, or duties, in which God and His saints support them. Councillors convene their sessions as they wish and with the consent of the elders. Councillors also have the authority to adjudicate in all cases of deficient measures, and unjust weights and bushel, and trade in all kinds of food and drink. And whoever violates this, shall pay three Slavic marks, which are worth 36 shillings. When councillors convene their session, whatever is then decided or agreed upon, which is not contrary to God's law, must be observed permanently and inviolably. And whoever violates this shall be apprehended by and judged by the councillors. And whoever

1 Otto II the Red, King of Germany and Emperor of the Holy Roman Empire (973–983).

2 The system for the election of authorities in the cities of the medieval and early modern Kingdom of Poland was very different—particularly with regard to vote and right to be elected. As a rule, a one-year term of office was retained for councillors, entering the city council as a self-governing body, and the lifetime election of jurors as members of the bench court. The minimum requirement for both, councilors and jurors, was a municipal citizenship.

neglexerit (a), cum signum datur per campanam, demeretur sex denarios. (b) Sin autem conventus sibi pronunciatus fuerit, demeretur quinque solidos.

[2] De penesticis et eorum excessibus puniendis.

(c) Qui penestici(d) vocantur, si in aliquo demerentur(e) vel si in aliquo deli[n]querint(f) contra statuta(g) civitatis, aut consulum decreta violaverint, si in hoc convicti fuerint, demerentur cutem cum crinibus(h) aut tres solidos. Et hoc arbitrio(i) consulum committitur, quod horum recipere voluerint.

(j) Quando vero penesticus(k) consulum aut civitatis statutum(l) infregerit in communi foro, ita quod cutem cum crine demeretur et cum pecunia hoc redimet, (m) hic manet sine iure (n) et non potest amodo aliquod forum(o) comestibilium(p) absque civitatis aut consulum consensu exercere(q). Et si alii homines, qui com[m]ercium seu fraternitatem habent in foro comestibilium, contra huiusmodi decreta (r) consulum seu civitatis excesserint, super hos oportet emendam dare(s) secundum ius et edictum(t) civitatis, et non possunt ulterius aliqua comestibilia(u) vendere, nec communitatem habere seu acquirere absque consensu consulum et civitatis.

[3] De parvis aut iniustis mensuris.

(v) Si metrete aut alie mensure parve seu iniuste fuerint et iniuste pense, hoc consules bene agere(w) possunt secundum honorem civitatis aut cum ⟨De quo supra folio XLVII capitulum ultimum et folio XCV. Item folio

(a) Poena, qui a[d] senatum non veniet JL[29] (b) Pena non venientis tempestive ad signum quesitus JL[6] (c) Penestici dicuntur penenditores JL[7] Penesticus id est revenditor, przekopien JL[8] Penestici JL[11] penestice JL[23] Przekupień JL[26] (d) Przekupniowie JL[12] (e) przevÿnylÿ JL[28] (f) vistupÿli JL[28] (g) ustavamy JL[28] (h) et circa statuta verberacionem et abscessionem auris JL[28] (i) zezwolyenyem JL[28] (j) Pena eorum si modum excesserint JL[7] penestici et con[tra] [trans]gressores statut[orum] JL[29] (k) przekupyen JL[28] (l) uchwala ustava JL[28] (m) aut mercede puniuntur JL[4] iure privati et infames JL[17] (n) ammisit honorem JL[28] (o) targi JL[28] (p) snÿednÿch pozithkow JL[28] (q) sprawowacz JL[28] (r) Spe. Sax. Iure municipium Art. 44 et 19 [Mikołaj Jaskier, *Iuris Municipalis Maideburgensis Liber vulgo Weichbild nuncupatur…, Cracoviae MDXXXV, articuli XIX, XLIIII, fol. XIX[r], XXXVIII[v]*] JL[7] (s) dacz pokup JL[28] (t) ustawÿ JL[28] (u) szadnego yadla JL[28] (v) Mensuras iniustas JL[1] mensure JL[17] mensura bo[na] JL[24] (w) probare JL[28]

neglects to attend a session announced by bell ringing shall pay six *denarii*. However, if the session was personally announced to him, he shall pay five shillings.

[2] On street traders and punishment for their offences.

Those who are called street traders, if they commit an offence against the city statutes or violate the decrees of the councillors, when they are convicted, shall be punished "on skin and hair"[1] or pay a penalty of three shillings. And it remains at the discretion of the councillors which punishment they choose to impose.

However, if a street trader infringes on the statutes of the councillors or the city during a public market, so that they are subject to punishment "on skin and hair", and they redeem themselves from it with money, they shall remain without rights and may not henceforth engage in trade at the food market without the permission of the city, that is, the councillors. And other people who engage in trading or collusion in the food market, if they act against such decrees of the councillors or the city they shall be subject to a penalty according to the law and edict of the city and they may no longer sell any food, nor have or acquire guild membership without the consent of the councillors and the city.

[3] On understated or unjust measures.

If measures or other weights are understated or unjust, the councillors should act appropriately according to the honour of the city or impose a penalty of 36 shillings. Indeed, it is the right of the councillors to manage

---

1 Translated as "flogging" in *The Saxon Mirror: A "Sachsenspiegel" of the Fourteenth Century*, translated by Maria Dobozy (University of Pennsylvania Press, 1999), p. 187 [The Middle Ages Series]. The punishment could also involve pillorying the convicted person, cutting their hair or branding them.

CV.⟩[1] XXXVI solidis emendare(a). (b) Ius enim consulum est civitati sic providere, quod singule emptiones, et in iure mechanici(c), et pauper populus, (d) valeant sufficere ac sustinere, quod ipsi non efficiantur periuri(e).

[*4*] De iudicio bannito magno ter in anno celebrando.

(f) Ille supremus iudex, qui in Maÿdenburg iudicio presidet(g), hoc est castellanus, ⟨De quo supra folio XCVI De iudiciis, quater(h) in anno celebrandis. (i)⟩[2] (j) qui sedet tria iudicia provincialia(k) iudicare in anno: unum iudicium in die sancte Agathe, secundum in die sanctorum Joannis et Pauli(l), tertium in octava beati Martini. Si vero ceciderit aut evenerit aliquot horum
177[v] iudiciorum ad diem celebrem aut feriatum(m), extunc ammisit(n) | suum iudicium. Et si scultetus aut solus castellanus(o) ad iudicium non venerit, quia scultetus castellano primam sententiam(p) debet invenire, et si scultetus non venerit ad castellanum, extunc X talenta demeretur(q), nisi legale (r) impedimentum (s) ipsum impediverit, quod probare poterit, ut ius dictaverit.

Quicquid(t) in criminali cause factum seu commissum fuerit quatuordecim diebus ante suum iudicium, hoc castellanus debet iudicare et nemo alius.

(a) takoz pokupem JL[28] (b) pena iniu[stis] mensuris JL[17] (c) magistres JL[28] (d) Consulum ius puniendi JL[38] (e) krzyvoprzisyescza JL[28] (f) Nota JL[8] art. 45 [Mikołaj Jaskier, *Iuris Municipalis…, articulus XLV, fol. XL*[v]] JL[33] (g) sadovÿ yest przeloszon JL[28] (h) magnis JL[17] (i) Et qui ipse JL[17] (j) de domino loci; de advocato et viceadvocato; Burgrabius et advocatus superius infra fo. 196 co[ntinenter] et a[lia] [*Ius municipale Magdeburgense infra Commune incliti…, fol. CXCVI recto et verso, articulus 127 in eadem editio*] JL[6] (k) ziyemskye JL[28] (l) martirum JL[28] (m) swyathetnÿ JL[28] (n) traczi JL[28] (o) Castellanus intelligitur burgrabius JL[38] (p) ortel JL[28] (q) pokupÿ JL[28] (r) Legale impedimentum JL[11] yeslyby nye wnÿosl rzeczi pomoczney JL[28] (s) ktorey by doswÿathczicz mogl podlug byegu prawa JL[28] (t) czo ma stavyc w rzeczi wside za sigkodneÿ JL[28]

---

1 *Infra Commune incliti…, articulus in Statuto de Cracovia et Warta (1421/1423):* De fraternitatibus civitatum et rebus per palatinum et capitaneum statuendis.

2 *Infra Commune incliti…, articulus in Statuto Johannis Alberti (1493–1501) (constitutio de anno 1496):* Iudicia quater in anno tenenda, et qui illis debeant interesse.

the city in such a way that individual purchases, both in guild law and for the poor people, could suffice and sustain them, so that they [sellers] themselves do not become perjurers.

[*4*] On the grand formally convened court held three times a year.

The highest judge who presides over the court in Magdeburg is the castellan[1], who holds three provincial court assemblies a year: the first on the feast day of Saint Agatha, the second on the east day of Saints John and Paul, and the third on the octave of Saint Martin. If any of these court sessions fall or occur on a solemnity or feast day, then court session shall not be held. And if the *scultetus*[2] or the castellan himself does not attend the court, because the *scultetus* should determine the first sentence for the castellan, and if the *scultetus* does not come to the castellan, then he shall pay ten talents, unless a legal obstacle prevented him, which he should prove, as the law requires.

Every offence committed within fourteen days before the castellan's court session shall be judged solely by the castellan and by no one else.

---

1 In the case of towns founded under the Magdeburg Law in the Kingdom of Poland, "castellan" should be understood as the lord of a town. He exercised this right either personally (not infrequently in the case of noble towns) or through his representative, for example, the captain (*capitaneus*, starosta in Polish) in the case of royal towns.

2 The meaning of the term *scultetus* [Ger. *Schultheiß*] in the Kingdom of Poland differed from that in the *Weichbild*. While in German sources the *Schultheiß* was "a court official and judge appointed by the count" (*The Saxon Mirror: A "Sachsenspiegel"*, p. 197), in Poland he was a representative of the lord of a village, with administrative and judicial functions. Very often the scultetus' task was to found the village and for this he received goods (*scultetia*). In Polish towns and cities, the role of the *scultetus* was played by the *advocatus*. Therefore, the *scultetus* in the *Weichbild* from the Kingdom of Poland should be understood as the *advocatus*. Cf. Art. 52, footnote 2.

[5] De iudicio castellani seu burgrabii et sculteti.

(a) Stuprum(b) et obsidia(c), irruentiam(d) domiciliorum iudicat castellanus seu burgrabius ⟨De quo supra folio XLV⟩[1] et nullus alter. Sed si castellanus presens esse non poterit, extunc cives eligunt unum iudicem loco castellani, pro excessu manifesto(e). (f) Pena(g) ad sex ebdomadas solvi debet, emenda(h) post penam ad XXIIII dies. Recompensa(i) debet solvi ad XII ebdomadas.

Castellani pena et recompensa, que acquisita fuerit in iudicio bannito, debet solvi per VI ebdomadas. Pena castellani scilicet tria talenta, pena sculteti octo solidi.

Quando castellanus surgit et iudicabit(j), tunc iudicium suum expiravit(k) et statim iudicium sculteti disponit(l) a proximo die ad duas septimanas.

[6] De legalibus iudiciis sculteti ter in anno fiendis.

(m) Scultetus etiam habet tria iudicia legalia in anno. Unum in die crastino Epiphanie Domini. Secundum tertia feria post conductum Pasce. Tertium feria tertia post festum Sanctae Trinitatis. Post hec disponit(n) sua iudicia continue ad duas ebdomadas. (o) Si dies iudicialis evenerit ad diem celebrem, bene potest ultra unam diem aut duos post diem (p) celebrem iudicium(q) disponere.

Iudicium sculteti nemo potest indicare, nisi scultetus solus nec preco nec suus famulus.

Quodsi scultetus in domo non fuerit et criminale nephas exortum fuerit, cives statuant unum iudicem pro crimine manifesto. (r) Scultetus etiam

(a) Advocatus JL[6] art. 45 b. 2 [*Mikołaj Jaskier, Iuris Municipalis…, art. XLV, fol. XL[v]*] JL[33] (b) gwalcenÿe pan JL[28] (c) zastapienÿa JL[28] (d) gwalth domow JL[28] (e) czasu goraczey rzeczy JL[28] (f) Emenda datur actori tantum, nec excedit 30 solidos. Recompensa głowna zapłata, verigeldus JL[12] (g) vyna JL[28] (h) pokup JL[28] (i) dosycz uczynyenye stronye JL[28] (j) [iudica]vit JL[28] (k) przeschite JL[28] (l) nastanye JL[28] (m) scultetum, advocatum Saxones vocatur JL[12] art. 47 b. 2 [*Mikołaj Jaskier, Iuris Municipalis…, art. XLV, fol. XL[v]*] JL[33] (n) spravÿa JL[28] (o) pothem zawszdi na przez dvÿe nÿedzÿelÿ spravÿa swoye sadÿ albo w kaszdych dw nyedzyelyach JL[28] (p) po swyecÿe JL[28] (q) iudicem JL[28] (r) Scultetus quod debet habere JL[28]

1 *Infra Commune incliti…, articulus in* Statuto de Cracovia et Warta *(1421/1423):* De terminis particularibus celebrandis.

[5] On the court of the castellan or the burgrave and the *scultetus*.

Rape, highway robbery and house raid shall be judged by the castellan or the burgrave, and by no one else. But if the castellan cannot be present, then the citizens shall elect one judge in place of the castellan, to judge the red-handed deed. The fine must be paid within six weeks, the compensation[1] after the fine within twenty four days. The wergeld[2] must be paid within twelve weeks.

The fine and the wergeld imposed by a formally convened court must be paid to the castellan within six weeks. The fine for the castellan is three talents, and the fine for the scultetus is eight shillings.

When the castellan rises [from the bench] and pronounces his judgment, then his court concludes its session and thereafter the court of the *scultetus* is in session from the following day for a period of two weeks.

[6] On the competent court of the *scultetus* held three times a year.

The *scultetus*, too, holds three competent courts a year. The first session is held on the day following Epiphany. The second on Tuesday after the first Sunday following Easter. The third on Tuesday after Trinity Sunday. After these [days], his court shall continue for two weeks. If a court day falls on a solemnity, the court may rightfully be held on the day or two days after the solemnity.

No one else can announce the dates of the *scultetus*' court, apart from the *scultetus* alone, neither the court bailiff[3] nor his servant.

If the *scultetus* is not at home and a criminal offence has been committed, the citizens shall appoint one judge to adjudicate upon the red-handed

---

1 The term *emenda*, Ger. *Buße* (*Buze* in a manuscript of Jagiellonian Library, Shelfmark 169) has been translated as "compensation".

2 The term "wergeld" is used if it has an equivalent in the German text of the BJ 169 manuscript (*Weregelt*). In other cases, the term "compensation" is used.

3 Ger. *Fronebote* (*Vronebote* in BJ 169, fol. 274^{v}). Cf. Wolfgang Haubrichs, "Wergeld: The Germanic Terminology of Compositio and Its Implementation in the Early Middle Ages", in: *Wergild, Compensation and Penance*, eds. Lukas Bothe, Stefan Esders, Han Nijdam, (Leiden, 2021), p. 102, 109 [Series: Medieval Law and Its Practice, vol: 31].

debet habere legalitatem(a) seu bannum a domino (b) terre et cum eo debet esse infeodatus(c) et verum suum feodum esse debet. (d) Insuper (e) liber esse debet et legittime natus de terra.

[7] De iudicio vulneratorum, clamore vulnera sua protestantium. Et penis vulnerantium.

(f) Si homo vulneratus fuerit et si clamorem proclamaverit(g), et si cepit hunc, qui ipsum vulneraverit, et eum usque ad iudicium deduxerit, et si tunc ipsum cum iis, qui clamorem suum audierint, (h) protestari poterit metseptimus, propior est eum vincere, quam ille possit eum evadere. Pro vulnere manum, pro homicidio collum. (i)

(j) Si vulnus profunditatem unguis et longitudinem membri habuerit, et si acquirit homo duellum (k) pro uno vulnere, et si victor fuerit(l) (m), victo[ri] dabit pro vulnere manum (n), pro homicidio collum.

Sed si quis per fideiussoriam obligat aliquem pro adiutorio ex parte
CLXXVIIIr homi|cidii statuere et eundem non representat, (o) extunc fideiussor tenetur actori seu querulanti dare plenam recompensam, (p) hoc est XIIII talenta et iudici emendam VIII(q) solidorum (r) istorum nummorum, qui in eodem iudicio et districtu sunt currenti communiter et dantur. (s)

[8] Accusatus de conflictu, quomodo evadere debet.

Si contingit criminale nephas aut conflictus nocte vel in die (t) et si probus homo(u) pro eo accusetur, (v) propius est evadere metseptimus (w), quam ille poterit super eum protestari, quia in isto loco conflictus per neminem visus est.

(a) prava mocznoscz JL[28] (b) od dzÿedzicze JL[28] (c) w dzÿedzyczem JL[28] (d) NB JL[38] (e) dobrowolnÿ i dobrze urodzonÿ JL[28] (f) Nota JL[8] vulneratus vir est proinquior vincere ipsum quam reus JL[17] (g) ÿ islybi obvolal JL[28] (h) ÿ mial by go samosiodm przeswÿczicz tez skazi JL[28] (i) Pro vulnere manum, pro homicidio collum. JL[7] pena vulnere abscisione manus JL[37] (j) Estimatio vulnerum. Evictio JL[7] Temporali Lx JL[38] (k) Duellariter provocare, est accusare criminaliter vel poenaliter JL[12] primam proposicionem JL[28] (l) *org.* fugerit (m) fuerit JL[28] (n) duelliter JL[12] (o) In defectu evictionis JL[28] (p) Recompensa [act]ori, emenda iudicii JL[7] (q) XVIII JL[28] (r) Solidus unum facit grossorum 8 JL[5] Solidus quid? JL[12] (s) Solidorum computacio JL[17] (t) Probus homo propior evadere JL[7] (u) fame bone JL[17] (v) Propior est vir fame bone evadere in cause criminali quam testibus quinti JL[17] (w) observatur JL[38]

deed. The *scultetus* should also receive authorization or ban from the lord of the land, and with it he should be enfeoffed, and his fief should be true. Furthermore, he should be free and lawfully born of the land.

[7] On the court for the wounded, protesting about their wound with an outcry. And on punishments for the wounders.

If someone is wounded and if he protests with an outcry, and if he captures the one who wounded him and brings him to court, and if then, with those who heard his outcry, he is able to protest against him with six oath helpers, he [the victim] is closer to prevailing over him than he [the wounder] is to exonerating himself. For a wound, the punishment is cutting off the hand; for homicide, the punishment is death.

If the wound is fingernail deep and of the length of a limb, and if the person is granted a duel over this wound, and if he is the victor, the vanquished shall give the victor a hand for the wound and throat for homicide.

But if someone gives security that the accused will appear in court in a homicide case, but does not represent him, then the surety shall pay the plaintiff, or the complainant, the full wergeld, which is fourteen talents, and the judge a fine[1] of eight shillings in the coins that are commonly in circulation in that court and district, and are used for payment.

[8] Accused of affray, how he should exonerate himself.

If a criminal offence or an affray occurs at night or during the day, and if a worthy person is accused of it, he [the accused] is closer to exonerating himself with six oath helpers than the accuser is to protesting against him, for the affray was not seen by anyone in that place.

1 Here the term *emenda* was used in the meaning of a fine. Cf. Art. 6, footnote.

[9] De iudicio, qualiter hospiti et domestico sit ministrandum. Et quomodo iudicari potest sine testibus.

(a) Nec castellano nec sculteto scabinus, nec civis tenetur (b) aliquam sententiam extra veros dies iudiciales diffinire, nisi factum manifestum (c) aut vulnera mortalia, aut homicidia, aut furta seu alia criminalia (d) fuerint.

(e) Castellanus et scultetus bene possunt omni die iudicare pro debito, pro quo absque testimonio agitur, nisi civis agat contra hospitem vel hospes (f) supra civem pro debito cum testimonio, de quo alter alteri fassus est, hoc bene potest iudicari sine mora. Et si uni adiudicatur debitum, habet solvere sequenti die, quod tenetur.

(g) Sed hospitem oportet iuramento probare, quod sit alienigena et ita remote domicilium habeat, quod una die ad iudicium venire non possit. (h)

(i) Ille debet esse hospes, qui ultra XII miliaria extra iudicium(j) suum domicilium habet. (k) Et si aliquis alienigena (l) datur per manum in modum pignori(m), iudex tenetur eum dare ad observandum tamdiu, quousque se debito expurget iuridice aut illud persolvat(n).

[*10*] De pernoctato vulnere.

Quodsi vir vulneratus fuerit et eodem die iudicium non quesiverit [*s*] et sua querimonia secum pernoctaverit (o) et, qui inculpatur, (p) tunc comparuit, evadet eum metseptimus. (q) Sed si tribus iudiciis non comparet, quarto iudicio proscribitur (r). Ita tamen, si iuste eum cittaverit et super ipsum conquestus (s) fuerit.

(a) Hospiti de domestico qualiter esse debent administrandum iudicium. JL[1] Nota JL[8] Obiectum pro sentencia difinitiva in diebus feriibus [*s*] et aliis extra iudicialiabus [*s*] non faciend[um] JL[39] (b) de modo [*4 verba difficilia*] JL[14] (c) Excipienter certi casus quibus in reum iurabit. JL[38] (d) capitalis excessus JL[28] (e) Cause sine mora iudicandi hospiti JL[7] (f) Ius hospitum JL[6] (g) Hospes quam dicitur JL[7] Alienigena quis? JL[12] (h) na myescze mÿeszkanÿa JL[28] (i) Hospes quis? JL[12] Hospes quis debet in Mey[deburg] JL[17] Hospes quis dicitur JL[38] (j) *org.* iudiciuum (k) nota JL[14] (l) Bylbÿ fantowanÿ JL[28] (m) dan by komu namastho fanthu JL[28] (n) alias si ipsum iuserit sine consensu partis reversi; iudex ad solvendum debiti JL[17] viprawÿl z długu podlug prawa albo i zaplaczÿl JL[28] (o) Negetur JL[38] (p) obvÿnovanÿ JL[28] (q) Contumacia cittacionis racione vulnerum JL[28] (r) Zaczvÿerdzonÿ albo wÿrokmÿ JL[28] (s) obsialovae JL[28]

[9] On the court, how to ensure justice for guest and local. And how to adjudicate when there are no witnesses.

Neither for the castellan nor for the *scultetus* shall a juror or a citizen determine a sentence outside court days unless it concerns a red-handed deed, a mortal wound, homicide, theft, or other crime.

The castellan and the *scultetus* can justly adjudicate every day upon a debt for which there is no testimony, unless a citizen claims a debt against a guest or a guest claims a debt against a citizen with testimony, of which one admitted to the other, then it should be rightly adjudicated without delay. And if a debt is awarded to one, he shall pay it the next day, as he should.

But it shall be allowed for a guest to prove by oath that he is a stranger and resides at such a distance that he cannot appear in court in one day.

He will be considered a guest who resides 12 miles beyond the court.

And if a stranger is delivered into the hands of a creditor as a pledge, the judge shall be obliged to hand him over to be taken into custody until he exonerates himself judicially of the debt allegation or until he pays the debt.

[10] On a wound reported the next day.

If someone is wounded and does not pursue his case in court on the same day and withholds his complaint overnight, and the accused appears in court then, he [the accused] shall be exonerated with six oath helpers. But if he does not appear at three court sessions, he shall be outlawed at the fourth session. However, it shall be so, if he was rightfully cited and complained against.

[*11*] De iudicio violentie et stupri.

⟨Supra folio XLV et folio XCIII De articulis per capitaneos iudicandis⟩[1] Stuprum et obsidium et irruentiam domiciliorum burgrabius iudicat et nemo alter. Si aliquis irruit super alterius domicilium tempore nocturno aut diurno, temeraria violentia [(a)], nulla procedente querimonia, et si in manuali facto deprehensus fuerit cum clamore, et si clamorem cum auditoribus metseptimus suorum vicinorum hoc ostendendo probare poterit secundum iuris exigentiam [(b)], malefactor collum demeretur. [(c)] Si autem manifestum factum non fuerit, extunc propior[(d)] est evadere metseptimus, | quam aliquo testimonio vinci possit.

CLXXVIII[v]

[*12*] De vulnerato multis vulneribus et de evasione coadiutorum. [(e)]

⟨Supra folio XXI capitulum Item si pluries⟩[2] Quicunque vulneratus fuerit, si clamore proclamaverit et ad iudicium pervenerit, de quocunque querulatur, qui presens fuerit, et si habuerit hos, qui clamorem suum audierint, et quot vulnera [(f)] habuerit, tot homines potest inculpare. Si autem hii homines comparuerint, duellum [(g)] in ipsis acquirere potest. Si autem plures iudicialiter infestaverit, quam vulnera habuerit, alii omnes evadent suo iure quilibet [(h)] metseptimus, vel quivis sua sola manu pro adiutorio ratione homicidii vel vulneris duellaris, vel mettertius ad hoc, si pro eo [(i)] cum testibus [(j)] fuerit impulsatus.

[(a)] temeraria violencia JL[11] [(b)] Secundum iuris exigenciam JL[11] [(c)] Nota bene JL[7] Spectat ad actorem, condempnatur, quia ubilibet testimonium sufficiens [*2 verba difficilia*] nisi [*plura verba difficilia*], *manus B* JL[28] Pena violencie et irruencie in domum JL[17] [(d)] reus JL[17] [(e)] art. 81 p 85 a. j. [*Mikołaj Jaskier, Iuris Municipalis…, art.* LXXXV, *fol.* L[v]] JL[33] [(f)] Vulnera quomodo probanda, *manus B* JL[38] [(g)] primam querimoniam JL[28] [(h)] si quis cum metseptimus actor procedat JL[28] [(i)] per actorem JL[28] [(j)] mettercius JL[28]

---

1 *Infra Commune incliti…, articulus in (1421/1423)Statuto de Cracovia et Warta (1421/1423):* De causis quas soli capitanei iudicare possunt; *et articulis de Privilegiis de Nieszawa (1454), confirmatis a Joanne Alberto rege in 1496:* Quattuor articulos capitanei iudicaturi.

2 *Infra Commune incliti…, articulus in Statutis Casimiri Magni:* Si plures de homicidio accusantur. Quis eorum pena homicidii puniendus.

[*11*] On adjudicating upon violence and rape.

Rape, highway robbery and house raid shall be judged by the burgrave and by no one else. If someone perpetrates a raid on someone's else house, whether at night or during the day, with bold aggression, and no complaint has been filed, and if he is caught red-handed with an outcry, and if he can prove the outcry with six oath helpers, his neighbors who heard it, as required by the law, proving this, the perpetrator deserves the death penalty. However, if he [the perpetrator] was not caught red-handed, he is closer to exonerating himself from the accusation with six oath helpers than to being overcome by any testimony.

[*12*] On the one with multiple wounds and on the exoneration of helpers.

Whoever is wounded, if he proclaims [this] with an outcry and comes to court, whatever he complains of, who is present, and if he has those who heard his outcry, he can accuse as many persons as he has wounds. If those people appear, he can be granted a duel against them. However, if he accuses more [persons] than he has wounds, they shall all be exonerated by their right with six oath helpers or each by his own oath of compurgation from aiding in murder or in causing a wound worthy of a duel, or with two oath helpers, if he is accused of it with witnesses.

[*13*] De iudicio rei obligate.

(a) Obligat aliquis mercimonia aut alia bona mobilia pro debito ex parte iudicii (b), et ille pronunciat (c) tribus iudiciis, ut est iuris, et quarto iudicio super eo dominium receperit et appropriatum sibi fuerit, et cognoscentie domini dederit coram iudice et scabinis. Et si iste in posterum ad repetendum sua bona pervenerit (d), possidens propior est suum pignus servare cum scabinis ac iudice, quam ille, qui caret possessione.

(e) Nullus etiam hospes ab alio advena et e contra, indiget pignus recipere pro debito recognito. (f) Si autem ipsum receperit, extunc ipsum acquirere et prosequi prout alter vir iuridice oportebit, nisi aliter fuisset inter eos ordinatum verbotenus in contractu.

[*14*] De dotalitio(g) feminarum et provisione earum post mortem mariti. (h)

Si aliquis ducit uxorem et si vir de hac luce decesserit, uxor nihil habet in suis bonis, (i) nisi (j) dederit sibi pro dotalitio (k) aut vite provisionem pro eius (l) vita in iudicio bannito.(m)

Nulla mulier potest vite provisionem nec dotalitium hereditarie observare. Et cum de hac luce decedit, ad heredes revertitur sui mariti.

(n) Quando autem maritus nihil dederit mulieri in suis bonis, (o) in possessione bonorum sui mariti debet permanere, et pueri sibi necessaria ministrabunt, quousque in vidualitate et sine marito permanere voluerit. ⟨De quo supra folio XXIX et folio XLII⟩[1] (p)

(a) Obligatio mobilium JL[1] De invadiatione rerum mobilium quomodo iure cum ipsis procedendum JL[39] (b) in iudicio JL[28] (c) ad tercium per terminum concitacionem vel si notificacionem JL[28] (d) in iudicium JL[28] (e) Nullus advena sibi [*?*] recipit pignus JL[14] Nota JL[31] (f) *manicula* JL[17] (g) O wyanye JL[17] (h) Mulier nihil aliud habet in bonis mariti pre mortui saltem inscriptum dotalicium et provisionem vitae. [*manicula*] Tamen cum nichil eorum in scriptum habuerit in possessione bonorum mariti sui permanet usque ad alias nuptias alias quod vidua permanet. JL[39] (i) Iuxta plebiscita civitatis observatur JL[38] (j) quod JL[28] (k) wiano JL[28] (l) tempore sue vite JL[28] (m) Hoc ex sequentibus patet quod dotalicium casu paratis pecuniis debet dari, *manus A* JL[27] (n) x JL[2] Cum maritus nihil dederit uxori ipsa in possessione eius remanere debet JL[7] Vidua relicta non debet eici ex possessione mariti, iurare quod vidua est JL[17] (o) Uxor non dotaliciata permanebit in bonis mariti quamdiu vidua fuerit, *manus B* JL[25] (p) *manicula* JL[13]

---

1 *Infra Commune incliti..., articulus in Statutis Casimiri Magni:* De virginum desponsatione et earum donatione*; et articulus in Statuto de Cracovia et Warta (1421/1423):* De uxore in sede viduali.

[*13*] On adjudicating upon pledges.

If someone pledges merchandise or other movable goods as surety for a debt in court, and declares the [pledge] at three court sessions, as the law requires, he shall be granted the ownership at the fourth session and it will be [vested] in him, and he shall pay to the judge and jurors a fee for attesting ownership. And if [the pledger] subsequently comes to claim back his goods, the possessor shall be closer to retaining his pledge with the jurors and the judge than the one who has lost possession.

Moreover, no guest may take a pledge as surety for an acknowledged debt from another stranger and vice versa. However, if he does obtain it, then he shall accept it and demand like any other man under the law, unless there is some other prohibition established between them in an agreement.

[*14*] On the woman's dower[1] and provision of widows after the death of the husband.

If a woman gets married and the husband passes away, the wife shall have nothing from his goods unless he gave it to her as a dower or, the provision for [her] life in a formally convened court.

No woman can inherit either the provision for [her] life or the dower. And when she dies, they shall revert to the heirs of her husband.

However, if the husband gave nothing to his wife from his goods, she should remain in possession of her husband's goods, and her children shall provide for her as long as she chooses to remain a widow without a husband.

1 Konrad of Sandomierz adapted the German provisions to the Polish circumstances. Thus, instead of the *Morgengabe* (morning gift), we will find *dotalitium* (Pol. *wiano*). The *dotalicium* was a part of the husband's estate that the widow could possess until she remarried.

(a) Si vir oves habuerit, has mulier recipiet ad suppellectilem. Et si pueri vellent dotalitium mulieri infringere, servare potest testimonio virorum ac mulierum metseptima, qui tunc presentes fuerint.

(b) Sed deservitum precium et rationabile debitum debeant solvi de bonis mortui viri pre dotalitio, et hoc si mulier fuerit dotata pecuniis in paratis. (c) Si autem dotata fuerit in hereditate propria, tunc suum dotalitium pre aliis debitis iure valeat obtinere. (d) Etiam quivis vir habens mansionem infra ius municipale, ille sue contorali(e) dare potest pro dotalitio(f) suam propriam hereditatem, quam in posse habeat alienandi, et etiam in CLXXIX^r aliis | bonis suis mobilibus, in quantum voluerit.

[*15*] De pueris hereditantibus et exhereditatis. (g)

Si vir pueros habuerit aut mulier, quicunque ex iis exhereditati fuerint, si moritur vir, hii pueri, qui in hereditate patris sunt, recipiunt bona et non hii, qui exhereditati sunt, sed hereditatem vendere non possunt absque coheredum consensu. (h) Hii pueri, qui in potestate patris mortis tempore fuerunt, si ex iis unus moritur (i), istius partem dividant inter se equaliter, tam exhereditati, quam etiam domestici.

[*16*] De infiscatione possessionum.

(j) Quando alicui sua possessio publicata seu infiscata fuerit (k) iuste ac iudicialiter, quotiens exit vel intrat, totiens penam iudici demeretur, ita si publicatio super ipsum rite ac iuste sit acquisita.

(a) Si vir oves habuerit JL[7] (b) Deservitum precium solvere de bonis tene[n]tis JL[7] Ius antiquum, cum [secu]ndum libri essent et [...]nia probarentur tantum [test]imonio omnia circa promissionem dotalitii. JL[20] (c) Dotalicium locum habet pre omnibus debitis JL[7] De dote uxoris post mortem viri; quatenus Craccovie servatur si accipit eum ante creditores JL[17] reformare mulierum vide JL[43] (d) Vir potest de suis mobilibus dari uxori pro dotalicio quod vult JL[17] (e) uxori JL[17] (f) sza wyano JL[17] (g) Raimundus fol. 23 Exhereditatio. [*Raimundi Summa legum brevis, levis et utilis..., in: Commune incliti Poloniae Regni Privilegium..., folio XXIII^v, articulus:* Exheredatio heredum; *cf. Die Summa legum brevis et utilis, pp. 341–342*]; Spec. Sax. lib. I Art. 17, Art. 14 de causis. Divisio fratrum tam eorum qui in hereditate existant quam eorum qui exhereditati. JL[7] De pueris exhereditatibus [*s*] JL[36] heredes quomodo JL[39] (h) Articulus iste est reprobatus Sp. Sax. art. Lii lib. primo. JL[7] Ex[h]er[ed]itatus accipit partem defuncti fratri cum aliis fratribus non ex[h]ereditaris JL[17] Nota JL[31] Notandum JL[38] (i) Nota JL[11] (j) Pena ingredientis possessionem suam infisca[re] JL[17] (k) Nierozumiem tego puncta JL[38]

If the husband had sheep, the woman shall receive them as paraphernalia[1] [Ger. *Gerade*]. And if the children wish to challenge the dower to the wife, she may retain it through the testimony of six men and women who were present then.

However, due payment and justified debt shall be paid from the deceased husband's goods before the dower, and this if the wife is endowed with ready cash. However, if she is endowed in [i.e. from] his own inheritance, then she shall lawfully receive her dower before other debts. Also, if the husband has a dwelling subject to municipal law, he may give his wife as dower his own inheritance, which he has the power to dispose of, as well as his other movable goods, as much as he likes.

[*15*] On children who become heirs and those who are excluded from succession.

If a husband or wife have children, and any of them are excluded from succession, when the husband dies, those children who remain[2] in the father's inheritance shall inherit it, and those who were excluded from succession shall not; however, they cannot sell the inheritance without the consent of their co-heirs. Those children who were under the authority of their father at the time of his death, if any of them dies, they [the survivors] shall divide that one's portion equally among themselves, both those excluded from succession and the household members.

[*16*] On the confiscation of estate.

If someone's estate is lawfully and judicially confiscated, each time he enters or leaves it, he shall pay a fine to the judge, as long as the confiscation was rightfully and justly pronounced.

1 In *The Saxon Mirror: A "Sachsenspiegel"*, p. 200 woman's personal belongings.

2 They are entitled to inheritance.

[*17*] De re possessa per annum et diem iudicialiter.

Quicquid vir dederit sub iudicio bannito et si possessor hoc possedebit pacifice et quiete absque arrestatione et condictione aliqua anno et die (a), hoc propius et melius obtinere potest cum iudice et scabinis, quam aliquis ab ipso possit exbrigare(b) seu alienare.

[*18*] De re possessa per annum et diem iudicialiter. (c)

Quodsi iudex et scabini mortui fuerint, quod tamen bene cum aliis fidedignis ad minus duobus scabinis et quattuor viris probitate probatis testimonio probet (d), et sic bona donata sibi obtinebit.

[*19*] De legationibus seu donis in lecto egritudinis. (e)

(f) Nemo masculus, nec ulla mulier possunt in loco egritudinis (g) de bonis suis alicui ultra tres solidos dare absque heredum consensu seu voluntate, nec mulier sine consensu mariti.

[*20*] De hereditate fratre et sorore carente. (h)

Quodsi hereditas in fratribus et sororibus defectum habuerit, extunc omnes hii, qui se in linea equali consanguineitatis ostendere poterint, in hereditate succedunt equaliter, sive sint masculi sive femine, ex paterna et materna consanguineitate.

(a) Prescriptio possessionis annus et dies JL[7] (b) Exbrigare JL[11] (c) Possidens iudicialiter et pacifice ⊢t⊣ bona per diem et annum non potest postea reici JL[17] (d) Probatio possessionis JL[7] (e) Reprobatus articulus Spe. Sax lib. I ar. Lii. JL[7] Legacio egritudinis JL[18] (f) Notandum diligis JL[8] sine consensu heredum eger non potest quid leg[are] et alienare sine voluntate eorum; maxime inmobilia JL[17] in lecto JL[39] (g) Servatur, *manus B* JL[38] (h) Hereditatem propior in succesione accipit JL[1] x JL[2]

[*17*] On a thing possessed for a year and a day [acquired] through judicial proceedings.

Whatever a man gives in a formally convened court and if the possessor possesses it in peace and without hindrance, without [any attempts at] seizure or demand for return for a year and a day, then he shall be closer and better to acquiring it with the judge and the jurors than anyone to redeeming or alienating it from him.

[*18*] On a thing possessed for a year and a day [acquired] through judicial proceedings.

Should the judge and the jurors die, however, if he rightfully proves by testimony with at least two trustworthy jurors and four men of proven integrity, then he shall acquire the goods granted to him.

[*19*] On bequests or donations on the deathbed.

No man or woman on their deathbed shall give to anyone from their goods more than three shillings without the consent of their heirs, and likewise, a wife without the consent of her husband.

[*20*] On inheritance when there are no brothers and sisters.

If an inheritance lacks brothers or sisters, then all those who can prove that they are related in equal degree shall succeed to the inheritance equally, whether they are male or female, from paternal or maternal line.

[21] Qui sacerdos cum sorore debet dividere suppellectilia. (a)

Qui autem in possessione manserit et si bene sacerdos fuerit, tunc suppellectilia recipit et hoc si nulla puella ibi fuerit. (b) Si autem puella fuerit et etiam sacerdos, suppellectilia tunc inter se dividunt equali forma.

[22] De dono iudicialiter facto.

CLXXIXv Quicquid masculus dat in iudicio bannito coram iudice et scabinis, ibi | recipiens dat unum solidum pro doni recognitione, quem recipiunt scabini pro se.

[23] De debito necessario iure acquisito et debitore. (c)

Quicunque aliquem coram iudicio pro debito impulsaverit, si debitum coacto iure consecutus fuerit, oportet eodem die solvere(d) et iudex in eo suam penam acquisivit.

(e) Si autem querimonia facta fuerit super aliquem pro debito, de quo fatetur, solvere tenetur infra duas ebdomadas, (f) et si tempore statuto debitor non solverit, extunc iudex in eo suam penam acquisivit. Nihilominus solvere mandat ad octo dies, deinde ad tres dies, tandem die sequenti. Quotiens tunc mandatum debitor adimplere neglexerit, totiens penam suam in eo iudex acquisivit.

(g) Si autem iudici et creditori debitum solvere contempserit, (h) extunc fiscatur sua possessio. Per hoc quoque compellitur, quod debitum creditori et pena iudici persolvatur.

(i) Si et possessione caruerit, extunc banno compellitur, potest quoque bene comprehendi (j), ubicunque visus fuerit, pro debito et pena. Et quicunque ipsum ultra hoc tenuerit, pena iudici demeretur.

(a) *aliqua pictura* JL[13] Sacerdos, *manus B* JL[27] (b) Suppellectilia fr[ater] sacerdos dividit cum sororibus JL[17] (c) Nota. Debitum iure acquisitum eodem die solvi debet JL[17] Solutio debiti. Processus in debiti retento de iuris forma, et pre punctum ultimum solutionis. Processus de possessionibus et impossesionibus iure inobedientibus quomodo pre periuria cum illis procedendum sit JL[39] (d) Creditori debitum iure acquisitum JL[17] (e) Debitum quomodo solvendum JL[1] Si querimonia JL[23] (f) Debitum sponte fassum in secundum septimanis solvi debet JL[17] (g) [D]ebitor odarda [*?*] debet conprehendi et per iudicem iuramentum JL[17] Si iudici JL[23] (h) Possessionati bona apprehendentur, inposesionati persona JL[38] (i) Pena debitoris firmantis [*?*] vel defendentis JL[17] Si possessione JL[23] (j) si odarda [*?*] sit JL[17]

[21] Which clergyman should share paraphernalia with a sister.

Whoever remains in the estate and if he is rightfully a clergyman, then he shall receive the paraphernalia, provided there is no girl there. However, if there is a girl as well as a clergyman, then they shall share the paraphernalia equally between them.

[22] On a donation made in court.

Whatever a man donates in a formally convened court before the judge and jurors, the recipient shall give one shilling by way of a recognition of the gift which the jurors shall receive for themselves.

[23] On an enforceable debt awarded by force of law and on the debtor.

Whoever sues someone in court for a debt, if the debt is awarded by the court by force of law, it must be paid on the same day, and the judge shall obtain his fine in this.

However, if a complaint is brought against someone for a debt to which the debtor admits, he must pay it within two weeks, and if he does not pay on time, then the judge shall obtain a fine. Nevertheless, [the judge] shall order [the debtor] to pay within eight days, then within three days, finally on the next day. Whenever the debtor fails to obey the order, the judge shall obtain his fine each time.

If, however, he neglects his duty to pay [the fine] to the judge and [the debt] to the creditor, then his property shall be confiscated. By this he can also be compelled to pay the debt to the creditor and the fine to the judge.

If he has no property, he shall be banished from that moment onward, and he may also be rightfully apprehended wherever he is seen, for the debt and the fine. And whoever detains him beyond this shall pay the judge a fine.

[24] De volente visitare limina sanctorum seu nundinas et impedito.

(a) Si aliquis ad limina sanctorum aut ad nundinas extra provinciam aut extra limites et terminos ire voluerit, et si aliquis pro debito voluerit impedire, hoc fieri non debet, oportet tunc ius suum coram iudice suo recipere. Et si uni testimonium adiudicatum fuerit, hoc est inducere testes, tunc inducias trinas per duas ebdomadas obtinebit aut ad iudicium proximum, quodcunque horum duorum elegerit.

[25] De scabino in iudicio improperato et male tractato. (b)

⟨De quo supra folio XXXII⟩[1] Quicunque scabinum in scamno seu sede iudiciali improperaverit(c) aut turpibus verbis obruerit, (d) scabinus lucratur suam emendam triginta solidos, (e) et iudex suam penam, videlicet octo solidos, acquirit. Obruitur autem scabinus, postquam sua sententia diffinita sit et consensus aliorum scabinorum preterierit, extunc omnes emendas acquirunt et iudex penas, et quot emende fuerint, totidem et pene iudici acquiruntur.

[26] De probatione concordie iudicialiter facte. (f)

Quando concordia aut diuturni fremitus inter discordantes coram iudicio ordinati fuerint, homo protestari potest cum iudice et scabinis. Quodsi scabini mortui fuerint, tunc protestatur cum hominibus fidedignis, qui eiusmodi iudicio affuerint.

Quicquid scabini protestantur et confirmant, hoc et iudex cum ipsis
CLXXX[r] debet protestari, simul et confirmare. Sed ubicunque con|cordia facta et ordinata fuerit extra iudicium (g), hoc facilius potest protestari seu probare vir cum sex testibus solus septimus(h), qui interfuerunt et viderunt concordiam esse factam.

(a) Limina sanctorum visitanti [s] non debent propter debitum impediri JL[17] Legaliter concordia rectius quaerenda [est] JL[38] (b) Cuicunque scabinum in scamna seu sede improperaverit JL[24] (c) Improperare JL[11] (d) Pena scabinum in iudicio improperanti JL[17] (e) Pro reprehensione iudicii pena. JL[38] (f) Probacio concordie JL[23] Concordia facta, *manus A* JL[36] (g) Si fuerit obiectatum, quod concordia non est necesse testes j e d n a c z e. JL[38] (h) metseptimus JL[17]

---

1 *Infra Commune incliti..., articulus in Statutis Casimiri Magni:* De illo qui sententiam iudicis redarguit.

[24] On the one intending to go on a pilgrimage or to a fair, who is hindered.

If someone intends to set out on a pilgrimage or to a fair outside the province or abroad, and if someone else wants to hinder him due to a debt, this should not be allowed; then he [the plaintiff] shall enforce his right before [the traveller's] judge. And if a testimony is granted to him, that is, he is allowed to bring witnesses, then he shall obtain adjournment three times for two weeks each or until the next court session, whichever of the two he chooses.

[25] On the juror insulted in court and treated unjustly.

Whoever insults a juror on the bench or in the courthouse or offends him with abusive words, the juror shall obtain his compensation of 30 shillings, and the judge shall receive his fine, that is, eight shillings. However, if the juror is insulted when his sentence has become final with the consent of other jurors, then all shall obtain compensation and the judge a fine, and as many compensations there are, that many fines shall be obtained by the judge.

[26] About proving a settlement reached in court.

When a settlement is reached or long standing disputes between the parties are resolved in court, a person may attest it before the judge and jurors. Should the jurors die, then it shall be attested with trustworthy persons who were present during the proceedings.

Whatever the jurors attest and confirm, the judge should also attest and confirm with them simultaneously. However, if the settlement is reached and concluded out of court only, then the man can more easily attest to it or prove it with six witnesses, [making it] seven men in total, who were present and saw that the settlement was reached.

[27] De violatione concordie et non impletione satisfactionis. (a)

(b) Ubi autem concordia et fremitus diuturnus coram iudicio confirmati fuerint et si ipsam violat adversa pars et vincetur, ut ius dictaverit, cum iudice et scabinis, pro vulnere manum, pro homicidio collum.

(c) Si autem contigerit, quod alter eam infregerit, hunc emendare cum recompensa oportet, pro vulnere (d) novem talenta, pro homicidio decem et octo talenta, nisi se possit excusare secundum iuris edictum. (e)

[28] De tribus exceptionibus, quibus pater eximit(f) filium criminaliter inculpatum (g).

Et vir quivis filium suum ter potest eximere, quem habet (h) in potestate, coram iudicio pro quolibet crimine capitali(i) tacto sacramento metseptimus secundum ius municipale.

Si autem pater cum filio simul in eodem crimine coram iudicio inculpati fuerint, extunc pater filium eximere non potest, nisi prius se ab eodem crimine se expurgabit (j).

[29] De famulo mercedem suam repetente a domino. (k)

(l) Famulus potest mercedem suam, quam promeruit, quinque solidis probare tacto sacramento mettertius, ita tamen, si dominus voluerit consentire. Si autem dominus velit probare tacto sacramento mettertius, quod sibi solvit, tunc proprior est evadere, quam famulus obtinere.

Si autem famulus suam merdecem super suum dominum obtinuerit coram iudicio, pro eo dominus nullam penam iudici demeretur, (m) sed famulo eandem mercedem eodem die solvere tenetur indilate. (n)

(a) Quis concordiam non fecerit JL[36] (b) Pena violatoris concordiam initam vel compositam JL[17] (c) Si contigerit JL[23] (d) Novem talenta quid se talentum exquantur valent quaerendum. Talentum u Budeusta rozumie się funt złota JL[1] [*Guillaume Budé (1467–1540)*] (e) Ut quid se defendendo fecerit JL[17] (f) et pater JL[17] (g) qui sit in potestate eius JL[17] (h) Negatur JL[38] (i) erunt criminal[i]a JL[17] (j) ymmo si sit convictus et qualiter cum filio suum isto JL[17] (k) Notandum JL[17] (l) An famulus sit propior de non soluta me[r]cede iurare quam dominus consentire [?] negat JL[17] (m) Ad occasum solis demerita merces solvi debet. JL[38] (n) Respondit: y to y to sa slusznemy JL[17]

[27] On the violation of the settlement agreement and the non payment of compensation.

When a settlement and a longstanding dispute before the court have been confirmed, and the other party violates the settlement and is defeated, as the law requires, before the judge and jurors, the punishment shall be the cutting off of the hand for injury, and death for homicide.

However, if someone else violates it [the settlement], he shall make amends for it with compensation, eight talents for injury, eighteen talents for murder, unless he can justify himself as the law requires.

[28] On three exceptions in which a father exonerates his son accused in a criminal case.

And every man may thrice exonerate his son, whom he has under his authority, in court from any capital crime by oath on the relicts with six oath helpers according to the municipal law.

However, if the father and son are simultaneously accused before the court of the same crime, then the father cannot exonerate the son until he has exonerated himself from that crime.

[29] On a servant demanding payment from his master.

A servant may claim five shillings of his wages that he has earned by swearing on the relics with two oath helpers, if the master is willing to grant it. However, if the master wishes to prove by swearing on the relics with two oath helpers that he has paid him, then he is closer to exonerating himself than the servant is to obtaining it.

However, if the servant has been awarded his wages from his master in court, the master shall pay no fine to the judge, but shall pay the servant the wages immediately on the same day.

[*30*] De aliquo pro vino et alio potu inculpato. [a]

Si alter alterum pro vino aut alio potu inculpare voluerit, evadet ut pro alio debito, in quo nullum dominium ostendere poterit aut protestari.

[*31*] De dato dono viro vel mulieri coram iudicio bannito. [b]

Donum, quod viro vel femine coram iudicio bannito datum fuerit, in eo mulier cum sua parte sive dono pro suo arbitrio facere potest [c] absque
CLXXXv omni contradictione quicquid ei placet. Idem potest facere | vir cum parte sui doni, quicquid deliberavit, velut et mulier.

Si moritur femina absque herede, ita quod nullum heredem a marito suo percepit, [d] ipsa heredat sua successoria seu sua prospera fortuna acquisita super suum proximum naturalem successorem, sive sit masculus sive femina, qui sibi sit paris conditionis. Idem faciet vir illi, qui sibi paris fuerit conditionis.

[e] Insuper omne aurum et argentum non formatum, et omnis siligo, et carnes cum cerevisia, et vino, et panis, que vel quod aut quantum post tricesimum[f] permansit, vel permanserunt, totum cedit heredibus viri et non mulieris, exceptis pulmentariis, de quibus mulier recipit mediam partem et heredes viri reliquam mediam tollunt partem. [g]

[*32*] Que et qualia ad hereditatem pertinent. [h]

Ista sunt, que ad hereditatem spectant: [i] omnes aurum et argentum non formatum, omnia vasa argentea, et tela, que non incisa aut formata fuerit, aut muliebria vestimenta, et sartagines[j], que a loco non moventur [k], et dolia, et vasa distillatoria, et omnia caldaria, excepto caldari magno, in quo liquesit cera, quod spectat ad suppellectilem.

---

[a] Testimonium vel iuramentum proprium JL[17] [b] Cum quo agit quidquid vult JL[17] [c] Si mulier fecit libera. JL[38] [d] Uxor sine herede moritus [*s*] JL[17] [e] Infra 30 dies mulier post mortem viri vinis, comestibilibus et aliis in domo pulmentariis JL[17] Liberi fuerint matris concede[ndi] si bona una cum marito mulieris empta per medium tollunt successores JL[38] [f] Quibus ipsa uti debet ante 30 diebus JL[17] [g] [I]sta sub hereditate continentur JL[17] [h] NB. Ad hereditatem oportant. JL[1] pro parte Organisty JL[1] [Notan]dum JL[8] Ad hereditatem pertinentia JL[23] *manicula, manus B* JL[27] [i] Haereditas eorum videlicet JL[38] [j] Panwie JL[12] [k] res mobiles JL[38]

[30] On suing someone about wine or other drink.

If someone wants to sue another for wine or other drink, he shall exonerate himself as for another debt in which he cannot indicate or attest any ownership.

[31] On a donation given to the husband or wife in a formally convened court.

If a donation is given to the husband or wife in a formally convened court, the wife may do as she pleases with her share or the donation without any opposition. Likewise, the husband may do the same with his share of the donation, whatever he decides, as may the wife.

If the woman dies heirless, having not had any heirs with her husband, she shall herself bequeath her inheritance or property acquired through good fortune to her nearest natural heir, whether a man or a woman, who is equal in status to her. Likewise, the husband shall do the same to someone equal in status to him.

Furthermore, all uncoined gold and silver, and all wheat, and meat with beer, and wine, and bread, which provide sustenance for thirty days, shall be ceded in their entirety to the heirs of the husband and not the wife, except for household food, of which half shall belong to the wife, and the other half shall be taken by the heirs of the husband.

[32] What and of what kind is part of inheritance.

These shall be part of inheritance: all uncoined gold and silver, all silver vessels and fabrics that have not been cut or formed, or women's clothing; and pots that cannot be moved from their place, and barrels, and a distilling vessel, and any cauldron, except for a large cauldron used for melting wax, which belongs to paraphernalia.

Omne proprium, quod locando possessum est, et omnia arma et omnes gladii, et eciam omnes olle eree et morsee, et cinguli, bracales, et an[n]uli viri, hec predicta spectant ad hereditatem. Item mense et lavatoria, omnes ciste cum planis cooperimentis et sedilia spectant ad hereditatem. Item pelves cupree et ciste farine, et ciste annonarum, porci, qui in curiis sive in domibus nutriuntur, etiam spectant ad hereditatem. Item omnes porci impinguati spectant ad pulmentaria ubi pulmentaria dantur, et omnis expensa domestica, que in potestate viri est tempore mortis, et omnes vacue cuppe[(a)]. Pulivinaria recipit mariti uxor, et non sua cognata proxima.

[*33*] De prima querela duorum contendentium.

Vulnerat unus alterum vitam suam defendendo super viam publicam, quod ille ipsum percutit aut vulnerat, et si clamore proclamaverit, [(b)] et invasor comparet violenter seu proterve, et conqueritur iudici, et ille non potest nec audet, pre imbecillitate[(c)] sui corporis[(d)] tunc comparare, [(e)] sed in posterum eodem die compareat et conqueratur, iudici et scabinis ostendat, quod [*s*] sua vulnera, et protestatur per hos, qui suum clamorem audierunt, quod initium contentionis sui adversarii fuerit et non suum, et quod ipse se defenderit defendendo vitam suam, ipse acquirit querimoniam primam. Sed si pernoctabit, hoc fieri non potest.

[*34*] De querela non alio idiomate deponenda.

Quodsi duo se vulnerant mutuo in iure municipali, qui ambo processerunt ex stirpe Slavonica et tamen Slavi non sunt, compareatque unus et conqueratur in Slavonico idiomate, alterum non oportet sibi respondere, [(f)] si placet, nisi conqueratur in eo idiomate, quod sibi innatum est per ius municipale.

(a) Łodigÿ JL[12] (b) Nota. Casum in iure intraverint quis actor iure prius esse debet, in causam suam primo agens JL[17] (c) percussione JL[17] (d) vel ex vulnus JL[17] (e) In recenti oportet vulnera iudici presentare. JL[38] (f) Actor debet conqueri et proponere ideo iure nec si reus voluerit JL[17]

All leased property, and all weapons and swords, as well as all brass and copper vessels, belts, trousers, and men's rings, all these are part of the inheritance. Likewise, tables, water vessels, all chests with simple lids, and chairs are included in the inheritance. Likewise, copper bowls and chests for flour, and chests for grain, pigs, which are raised in manors or houses, are also included in the inheritance. Likewise, all slaughtered pigs are part of household food, where household food is given, and all household expenses controlled by the husband at the time of death, and all empty barrels. The bed linen shall belong to the wife, not his closest female relative on the distaff side.

[*33*] On the first complaint of two contenders.

If someone wounds another in defending his life on a public road, because [the assailant] attempted to strike or injure him, and if he announces it with an outcry, and the assailant quickly and audaciously comes and complains to the judge, and if [the victim] cannot or dares not appear at that time due to the infirmity of his body, but later on the same day appears and presents his complaint, showing his wounds to the judge and the jurors, and proclaims through those who heard his outcry that the quarrel was started by his opponent and not by him, and that he resisted while defending his life, he shall be granted the first complaint. However, if he delays through the night, it shall not be so.

[*34*] On a complaint that does not need to be submitted in another language.

If two people injure each other within the jurisdiction of municipal law, both of whom come from a Slavic lineage but are not Slavs themselves, and one appears and files a complaint in a Slavic language, the other shall not be obliged to respond, if he so wishes, unless he is subject to a complaint in the language that is appropriate to him under municipal law.

CLXXXI^{r}

[35] | De querela ex voluntate iudicis et consensu partium per medium arbitrorum concordata amplius iudicialiter non repetenda.

Quodsi duorum virorum querimonie delate fuerint in iudicio bannito coram iudice, de voluntate quoque iudicis et consensu et partium arbitrio utrarunque efficiatur, quod inter ipsas concordia extra iudicium debeat terminari, nec ultra causa ipsa iudicialiter est peragenda, seque arbitri ad hoc electi de causa intromittant concordandi absque iudicio et querimonia amplius iudicialiter non repetenda cum consensu iudicis. Et si alter ex eis suam querimoniam in posterum vellet renovare hanc causam coram iudicio, extunc suus adversarius sibi respondere non tenebitur coram iudicio, (a) si protestari poterit cum iudice et scabinis, quod causa absque iudicio debeat terminari.

[36] De duobus equaliter mutuo vulneratis, quorum unus coram iudice, alter coram scabinis querelam deponit, quis eorum debeat esse actor. (b)

Quodsi se duo vulneraverint equaliter, ex quibus unus vadat ad iudicem in domum suam et querimoniam faciat, alter veniet ad quattuor bancos seu scabinos et conqueratur cum clamore scabinis et iudicio astantibus, et vulnera ostendat, et mittet pro iudice et conqueratur, ipse primam querimoniam obtinebit, si testes habuerit a scabinis aut astantibus iudicio, quod inter quattuor bancos querimoniam fecerit.

[37] De duobus conquerentibus pro vulneribus, quid eorum aliquis demeretur.

Et si duo se mutuo vulneraverint equaliter et querulantur equaliter, quicunque ex eis in alterum duellum acquisierit, tunc eius adversarius manum demeretur. Ita tamen, quod si vulnus monomachale fuerit. Sic(c) quod alter ex eis, antequam duellum acquisitum fuerit, moritur, adversarius collum demeretur (d).

(a) Et maxime sic probaverit, quod per arbitros sit concordata, et de consuetu[dine] vallorum pro iure iuret per tes[tes et] per arbitros ut sentencialiter invenitur JL^{17} (b) Moÿą. Etiam banci intelliguntur scabini JL^{1} art. 84 [*Mikołaj Jaskier, Iuris Municipalis..., art.* LXXXIIII, *fol.* LI^{r}] JL^{33} (c) Si JL^{17} (d) nisi probaverit, quod se defendendo id fecerit JL^{17}

[35] On a complaint settled by the will of the judge and with the consent of the parties through arbitrators, which shall not be adjudicated in the future.

If complaints of two men have been filed in a formally convened court before a judge, it shall be established by the will and consent of the judge as well as the consent of both parties that a settlement between them should be made out of court, and further, that the matter shall not be settled in court, and arbitrators chosen for the purpose shall bring about a settlement out of court, and, furthermore, the complaint shall not be adjudicated again in court with the consent of the judge. If one of them subsequently wishes to file his complaint before the court again, then his opponent is not obligated to respond in court, if he can attest with the judge and the jurors that the matter should be terminated out of court.

[36] If two [people] were equally wounded, and one of them files a complaint before the judge, while the other files his complaint before the jurors, which of them should be the plaintiff.

If two people are equally wounded by each other, and one of them goes to the judge's house and files a complaint, while the other comes to the bench or to the jurors and complains with an outcry to the jurors and those present in court, and shows his wounds, and sends for the judge and complained, he shall be granted the first complaint, if he has witnesses among the jurors or those present in court that he made the complaint to the bench.

[37] On two [people] complaining about wounds, who deserves what.

If two people have wounded each other equally and have filed complaints equally, whichever is granted a duel against the other, then his opponent shall be punished by having his hand cut off. However, this [shall be] if the wound was worthy of a duel. However, if one of them dies before being granted a duel, the opponent shall be punished by death.

[38] De vulnerante aliquem in facto recenti cum clamore capto et ad iudicium deducto.

Si aliquis detinet hunc, qui ipsum vulneravit, in facto recenti et ipsum cum clamore ad iudicium deduxit, qui sic queruletur cum prolocutore: "Domine
CLXXXIv iudex, ego cum querela propono super istum virum, (a) quod ipse | (b) venit intra municipalia vel in strata regia, et in me pacem violavit, et me spoliavit in meo corpore et in meis bonis, meque vulneravit, dum pacem in me confregit. Tunc vidi ego ipsum propria in persona et proclamavi in eum cum clamore, et ipsum captivum huc ad iudicium deduxi, et volo ipsum vincere per eos, qui clamorem meum audierunt, et cum meo testimonio vero, ut ius mihi diffinierit. Et in sententia requiro, quomodo hoc probare debeam et valeam, ita ut proficiam in iure meo." Extunc satisdationem adversarius rectam petat pro hac querimonia, et dicat se de facto innocentem.

(c) Ille autem, qui ipsum captivum in facto manifesto detinuerit, facilius eum vincere potest cum testimonio, quam ipse captivus cum testimonio eum evadere possit. (d) Si, ut iuris est, probaverit testimonio, illi solvet collum, si est homicidium, vel manum, si est vulnus monomachale (e), ex quo ad iudicium ipsum cum (f) manifesto facto deduxerit.

(g) Pro teste potest quivis vir alteri astare, qui in suo iure non possit argui(h), excepto patre(i), fratre, famulo et filio(j) necnon mercenario(k). (l) Etiam ullo precio conventi in aliquibus causis non valent contestari, qui eiici iure possunt.

[39] De duobus, quorum unus gladio, alter cultello mutuo se vulnerant. (m)

Quodsi se duo mutuo vulneraverunt: unus cultello et alter gladio, et si vulnera utriusque fuerint monomachalia(n), ille cum gladio solvet manum,

---

(a) Nota proponent JL[31] (b) Qualiter vulneratus debet conqueri coram iudicio JL[17] (c) Pena vulnerantis manus, pena occidentis est collum, ipso violencie JL[17] Propior est actor in recenti captivum in judicio presentatum ad convicendum quam inculpatus ad evadendum cum testibus convicere debet JL[38] (d) coram quibus clamat JL[17] (e) Vulnus monomachale quod solus soli inflixit JL[11] (f) vulnere et clamore; vinctus JL[17] (g) Pro teste JL[16] Qui testes esse non possunt JL[17] Nota JL[31] Quis potest esse testis JL[40] (h) qui non sunt temerari JL[17] (i) ut impedit JL[17] (j) nec servo JL[17] (k) et ad hoc condemnato JL[17] (l) [Nullo] precio conventus testificare non potest JL[17] (m) *manicula* JL[29] art. 85 [*Mikołaj Jaskier, Iuris Municipalis..., art. LXXXV, fol. LIr*] JL[33] Qui unus gladio, aliter kutello [*s*], *manus A* JL[36] (n) super carne JL[38]

[38] On the perpetrator of an injury caught red-handed with an outcry and brought to court.

If anyone catches the person who injured him red-handed and brings him to court with an outcry, he shall file his complaint with a spokesman saying: "My lord judge, I file a complaint against this man, that he entered the city [jurisdiction] or the royal road and violated my peace, and he robbed me in my body and my goods, and wounded me when he destroyed my peace. Then I saw him personally and cried out against him, and brought him, the one captured here, to court, and I intend to overcome him thanks to those who heard my outcry, and with my true testimony, as provided for me by law. And I demand in the sentence how I should and can prove this, so that I may gain advantage in my right." Then the opponent shall demand proper surety[1] regarding this complaint, and shall say that he is innocent in this matter.

The one who apprehended the culprit red-handed is closer to prevailing with his testimony than the apprehended one is to exonerating himself. If, as the law has it, he proves with testimony, he shall deserve death, if the matter is homicide, or loss of hand, if the wound is worthy of a duel, and this if he brought him to court caught red-handed.

Any man who cannot be accused in his right, except for the father, brother, servant, son, and hired labourer, may stand as a witness for another. In no case shall defendants be called as witnesses, and according to the law, they may be expelled from the court.

[39] On two [people] who have wounded each other, one with a sword and the other with a dagger.

If two persons wounded each other, one with a dagger and the other with a sword, and if the wounds of each are deemed worthy of a duel, the

1 Ger. *Gewere* (BJ 169, fol. 281^{v}) Pol. *gwar*, the plaintiff provided a sum of money as security to ensure that the claim would not have been altered. Cf. *The Saxon Mirror: A "Sachsenspiegel"*, p. 187.

(a) ille cum cultello solvet collum, quia cultellus furtivam infert mortem, et hoc si ambo in recenti actione cum clamore ad iudicium fuerint deducti. (b)

[*40*] De vulneris monomachalis et non monomachalis iudicio. (c)

Etiam si alter alterum vulnerat et causa sua pernoctaverit, sibi debet indici in iudicium proximum. Quodsi vir vulneratus fuerit, vulnus vero non fuerit monomachale, siquidem comparuerit et conquestus fuerit, sibi indici debet ad iudicium proximum. Si autem vulnus monomachale fuerit, tunc incontinenti sibi iudex iudicium facere debet pro facto manifesto.

[*41*] De duobus mutuo vulneratis, quis eorum contra alterum acquirit duellum. (d)

Si duo se vulneraverint et ambo coram iudicio comparent et querimonias proponunt, qui primam querimoniam precellentem protestari poterit, apud suum adversarium duellum acquirit, si ipsum iusto modo salutaverit, siquidem vulnus monomachale fuerit.

CLXXXII^r Si autem ad diem duellum dilatum fuerit et si alter pugilem convenerit super alterum, et si protestari poterit, quia pugil sit mercenarius, extunc iure sibi a duello cedere possit.

[*42*] De occisore cautionato, aliquem in eadem fideiussoria occidente.

(e) Si vulnerat unus vir alterum caucionemque fideiussoriam usque ad iudicium fecerit, iudex quoque ipsis pacem indixerit. (f) Si autem ipsum postea occiderit, et fideiussores posuerit eadem pro causa, sic ipse propior est evadere metseptimus de homicidio, quam contra ipsum aliquis protestari et probare possit.

(a) Vulnera JL[10] Cultello vulnerans collum demeretur respondit JL[17] (b) singularis pugna JL[24] (c) Vulnus monomachale quid zhukem. JL[1] Duellum duorum bellum factum ad probationem veritatis, ita ut quis viverit probasse credatur, et victus in probatione defecisse id est boÿ albo bÿtwhwa dwu ku okasanÿa prawdy, *manus C* JL[36] (d) art. 83 [*Mikołaj Jaskier, Iuris Municipalis…, art.* LXXXIII, *fol.* L^v] JL[33] (e) art. 86 [*Mikołaj Jaskier, Iuris Municipalis…, art.* LXXVI, *fol.* LI^r] JL[33] (f) Distinctionem fecit JL[38]

person with the sword shall be punished by having his hand cut off, while the one with the dagger shall be punished by death. This is because the dagger inflicts death by stealth. This [shall happen] if both are brought to court having been caught red-handed with an outcry.

[*40*] On adjudicating upon wounds worthy and unworthy of a duel.

If someone wounds another and delays his case overnight, a date should be set for him for the nearest court session. If a man is wounded, and the wound is not worthy of a duel, but he appears and files a complaint, a date should be set for him for the nearest court session. However, if the wound is worthy of a duel, then the judge should immediately adjudicate upon the red-handed deed.

[*41*] On two [people] who have wounded each other, which one shall be granted a duel against the other.

If two [people] have wounded each other and both appear before the court and file complaints, the one who can attest his complaint first and as a priority shall be granted a duel against his opponent, if he challenges him in a proper manner, provided the wound is worthy of a duel.

If the duel is postponed for a day and if one hires a champion against the other, and if the other can attest that the champion works for hire, then the other may rightfully withdraw from the duel.

[*42*] On a killer who was vouched for and who killed someone while vouched for.

If one man wounds another and is vouched for until the court session, the judge shall also establish peace between them. However, if he later kills [the wounded one] and places sureties [for himself] in this matter, he is closer to being exonerated from the homicide with six oath helpers than anyone to testifying and proving against him.

[(a)] Si autem coram iudicio comparuerit, et si in iudicio bannito manu pax promissa fuerit coram iudice et scabinis pro primo vulnere, ipsum vero postea occiderit, hoc melius potest super eum protestari, quam ipse evadere possit.

[*43*] De querelis duorum se mutuo vulnerantium, quorum unus moritur, alter superstes manet.

[(b)] Si se duo vulneraverunt pariter et ambo coram iudicio compareant et querulose proponant, et querimonie autem usque ad iudicium dilate fuerint.

Tandem is, qui primo querulatus fuerit, moriatur ab iis vulneribus, mortuus ad iudicium portetur, et alter vulneratus etiam comparuerit, et unus de mortui agnatis loquatur super vulneratum cum testimonio sine duello, quia ipse suum affinem occiderit, et pro eo petat iudicium. Extunc si ipse reus petat satisdationem de iure, ut ostendat innocentiam cum suo testimonio evadendo homicidium. Si hoc, ut iuris est, protestatus fuerit, propior est evadere, quam ille super eum protestari possit, homicidium metseptimus, alias quam protestari et vinci possit. Si autem aliquis agnatus ipsius mortui duellare salutaverit ipsum, tunc pro collo suo respondere oportet. [(c)] Si autem evadere voluerit cum testibus, extunc testimonium sic debet procedere, quod [(d)] initium contentionis illius mortui fuisset et non suum. [(e)] Et si suos testes incontinenti habere non poterit, inducias et terminum trium quindenarum acquiret[(f)], ex iis sibi eligat unam quindenam, quamcunque voluerit, in qua facilius potest evadere homicidium metseptimus, quam ille cum testimonio ipsum vincere possit.

[(a)] art. 87 [*Mikołaj Jaskier, Iuris Municipalis..., art.* LXXXVII, *fol.* LI*r*] JL[33] [(b)] pro homicidio JL[23] art. 88 JL[33] [(c)] Nota JL[31] [(d)] *manicula*; et quod id fecit se defendendo JL[17] Inicium contemtionis iuvat in iur[e] reum JL[40] [(e)] Si occidit in defensione vite cum id ipse probet testibus propior est ad evadendum. JL[38] [(f)] et 6 septimanis JL[15]

If, however, he appears in a formally convened court, and if peace is ensured over the first wound before the judge and the jurors, but later he kills [the wounded one], it is easier to attest against him [the killer] than he [the killer] can exonerate himself.

[*43*] On complaints of two [people] who have wounded each other, one of whom has died, the other has survived.

If two [people] have wounded each other equally and both appear in court, and file complaints and the complaints are postponed until the court session, and eventually the one who filed the first complaint dies from those wounds, his dead body will be brought to court, while the other wounded one will also appear. One of the deceased man's agnate relatives shall say about the wounded man, by testimony [and] without a duel, that he killed his relative, and shall demand a trial for it. Then, if the accused requests a surety[1] according to the law, in order that he can demonstrate his innocence with his testimony, thereby exonerating himself from homicide. If he attested it according to law, he shall be closer to exonerating himself than is someone else to attesting homicide against him with six oath helpers and to defeating him. However, if any agnate relative of the deceased challenges him to a duel, then he shall fight for his life. If he wishes to exonerate himself with witnesses, then he should conduct the testimony in such a way that it proves that the deceased was the attacker, not him. If he cannot have his witnesses immediately, he shall be granted adjournment and a term of three fortnights, from which he shall choose one fortnight that he prefers, when he can more easily exonerate himself with six oath helpers from the charge of homicide than the other can defeat him with testimony.

1 See Art. 38, footnote.

[*44*] De damnis cavendis in venditione equi.

(a) Si mas equum vendit, (b) promittere debet in eo equo (c), quod(d) stabilis non fuerit ita(e), quod a loco tempore se offerente discedere voluerit, item(f) quod apparens videre non sit cecus, item quod non sit arrestatus. (g)

CLXXXII[v]

[*45*] | De impetitione et arrestatione equi.

(h) Si vero aliquis arrestat equum asserens, quod aliquis sibi eum subtraxerit aut subtractus fuerit vel spoliatus, ad hoc se trahere debet, ut iuris est, videlicet ad(i) suum venditorem(j), quem nominare debet et iurare tenetur tacto sacramento, quod ad verum se trahat venditorem. Et quocunque nominaverit, ibi eum sequi oportet, non autem ipsum insequi debet ultra Mare Aquilonis. Et tunc ibi qui se revocat ad venditorem, fideiussoriam cautionem faciat, ut satisfaciat iudici pro pena et pro expensis, quas adversarius suus expendit, diemque nominare debet, quando ibidem pervenire potest. Si autem dixerit, quod in foro communi et libero equum ipsum emerit, extunc suam pecuniam, quam pro eodem dederat, integraliter(k) ammittit, et hoc si non habuerit hospitem, qui mercipotum(l) benedixit.

[*46*] De fure diei et noctis.

(m) Si fur clara diei luce deprehensus fuerit, qui bone fame sit, et furtum non plus quam tres solidos valeat, cutem cum crine demeretur. (n) Sed si furtum ultra tres solidos valeat, reus est patibulo. De hiis denariis tres solidi medium fertonem(o) debent ponderare. (p) Si autem fur tempore noctis deprehensus fuerit cum sex denariis, reus est patibulo sive suspendio.

(a) In venditione equi cautella JL[1] (b) Coram testibus mercipotiis alias lytkupnikÿ JL[17] (c) Hec tria cavenda circa vendicionem equi JL[17] (d) 10 JL[17] (e) declinet JL[17] (f) 20 JL[17] (g) vel furatus: dobrowolnÿ wyikrad JL[17] (h) Qualiter procederi debet dum quis impetraverit [*?*] circa impeticionem equi JL[17] (i) do ysca JL[17] (j) Ad evictorem JL[38] (k) integraliter JL[11] (l) mercipotus JL[11] Mercipotatores JL[38] (m) Fures nocturni et diurni quomodo iudicandi. JL[1] Tres solidi sex grossos valent. JL[7] *manicula* JL[10] solidus in in [*s*] polonos grossos ponderat JL[13] o 6 groszy moze złodzieia uwieszszyć kiedy w noczy ukradnie JL[35] id intelligitur solidus JL[36] [...]cota de furto [...]t eius poena JL[43] (n) Fur de die minus quam de nocte punitur JL[17] (o) Ferto wiardunk. JL[38] (p) quondam non hic est quattuor suspen[si]o JL[17]

[*44*] On losses to beware of when selling a horse.

If a man sells a horse, he shall ensure that it will not be found wanting when time comes to move from its place, likewise, that although it may appear so, it is not blind, and that it cannot be seized.

[*45*] On claiming and seizing a horse.

If someone seizes a horse, claiming that someone took it from him, or that it was taken away or damaged, the buyer shall, according to the law, turn to his seller, whom he shall identify and shall swear on the relics that he has turned to the true seller. And wherever he points, there he shall go, but he should not go after him overseas. Then the one appealing to the seller shall secure for the judge the fine and expenses which his opponent will incur, and he shall specify the day when he can arrive there. However, if he declares that he bought the horse in a common and free market, then he shall lose all his money paid for it, unless he has a host who has celebrated the deal with a customary meal.[1]

[*46*] On a thief by day and by night.

If a thief is apprehended in broad daylight, and is of good repute, and the stolen object is not worth more than three shilling, he shall be punished "on skin and hair". However, if the stolen object is worth more than three shilling, the accused shall deserve the gallows. About these *denarii*, three shillings should weigh half a fierton.[2] If the thief is caught at night with six *denarii*, the accused shall be hanged.

---

1 Customary meal, Lat. *mercipotum*, Pol. *litkup*, one of the ways of ensuring the validity of a legal transaction. It was a rule of Polish customary law, originally absent from the German and Latin texts of the Magdeburg Weichbild and only included in the Weichbild in the *Commune incliti Poloniae Regni privilegium…* of Jan Łaski. Proof of litkup was evidence that a legal act has been performed. See: Stanisław Estreicher, "Freimarkt' i Frymark", *Czasopismo Prawnicze i Ekonomiczne* 25 (1929), pp. 337–355.

2 *Fierton*, Pol. *wiardunek*; 1 *Sclavica marca* = 6 *fertones* = 36 *shillings*, cf. Article 3 and Peter Spufford, *Money and Its Use in Medieval Europe* (Cambridge U.P., 1988), p. 46f.

[*47*] De possessione bonorum hereditariorum ad iudicium delato. [(a)]

Conqueritur vir super alterum pro bonis, quod vera sua hereditas sit, et quod ille teneat cum iniuria, et sua vera sit successio a patre suo vel ab alio suo agnato, aut a suo predecessore, [(b)] et si ille comparet, super quem querela proposita fuerit, et dicit se habere bonorum illorum defensorem, eo[(c)] quod [(d)] bona possederit pacifice et quiete anno et die, contradictione qualibet non obstante et est iuste ac rite meum predium censuale, ipsum oportet suum defensorem[(e)] nominare. [(f)] Si autem sibi defectus fuerit in defensore, actor conservat suam legalem proprietatem in eisdem bonis, quia quivis homo conservat suam innatam hereditatem facilius, quam alter emptam proprietatem aut obligatam, aut predium censuale, cum impossibile est aliquem de naturali[(g)] portione defraudari.

[*48*] De habente bona censualia in bonis spiritualibus.

Si homo habuerit censualia et bona a quodam monasterio aut alio domino, et si dominus aut abbas sibi non fatetur, aut conventus, hic vir potest hoc metseptimus protestari suorum proheredum, quorum quilibet iurabit singulariter, quod iustum et successorium suum sit predium censuale. Et si dominus aut abbas horum septem testimonio stare noluerit aut fateri noluerit, CLXXXIIIr extunc quivis ipsorum metseptimus | suorum coheredum bona sua obtinebit.

[*49*] De testimonio pro hereditate vel debito persoluto[(h)] per septem vel tres viros faciendo.

Si debet vir producere testimonium super proprium alterius metseptimus, aut mettertius, hoc facere debet cum possessionatis hominibus [(i)], qui in suo iure argui non possunt [(j)], et qui iudicio astare solent, et qui domicilia habent in iudicio supradicto.

(a) Nota hic JL[14] NB JL[37] (b) Qualiter quis defendit bona possessa si imperitus JL[17] Nota JL[31] (c) eo JL[32] (d) Possessio bonorum hereditarium quomodo defendendum JL[1] (e) Defensor mellius evictor JL[38] (f) Iustum titulum empcionis vel donacionis probari debet JL[17] (g) iusticia sua JL[17] (h) post mortuam manum JL[17] (i) Probaturus haereditatem testibus possessionatis et fidedignis adesse tenetur JL[38] (j) Testes quales esse dicuntur dum agentur pro hereditate vel pro debito soluto JL[17]

[*47*] On the possession of hereditary goods reported in court.

A man brings a suit against another over goods, claiming it is his true inheritance, and that another holds it unlawfully; he claims it is truly his inheritance from his father or from his agnate relative, or from his ancestor. If the one against whom the suit has been filed appears and states that he has a surety of these goods, that he has held the property in peace and without hindrance for a year and a day, in no way disturbed, and justly and rightfully it is my leasehold, he must appoint his surety. If he lacks a defender, the plaintiff shall retain his legal ownership of the goods because everyone retains their natural inheritance more easily than another retains purchased or pledged property or a leasehold, for it is impossible to deprive anyone of their natural share.

[*48*] On the possession of leasehold in church goods.

If a person holds a leasehold and goods from a monastery or another lord, and if the lord or abbot does not grant it to him, or the convent, then this man may attest to it with his six heirs, each of whom individually swears that his leasehold is legitimate and inheritable. And if the lord or abbot refuses to stand by the testimony of these seven [persons] or refuses to grant it, then each of them should retain his goods with his oath and that of six co-heir.

[*49*] On testimony about inheritance or of a debt paid, given by seven or three men.

If a man is to provide testimony about another's ownership, he should do so with six or two men who hold possession, and who cannot be impugned in their own law, and who are accustomed to appearing in court, and who reside in that judicial district.

Si autem vir debet persoluta debita protestari super proprietatem alterius, etiam debent esse possessionati homines domicilia habentes, si hoc in iudicio non viderunt, nec in iudicio fuerit confirmatum. (a) In nullis etiam causis precio conventi seu empti valeant contestari, qui eiici iure possunt.

Scilicet si aliquis debet persoluta debita probare, protestando pure pro debito, hoc facere debet cum talibus hominibus, qui in suo iure non possunt argui (b).

[50] De privigno(c) noverce succedente in bona patris demortui.

Si vir ducit viduam, que unum filium vel plures pueros habet et ipse nulla bona habuerit nec ipsa, (d) et si vir unum etiam filium habuerit cum prima uxore sua, fortuna tandem arridente per suos labores bona habuerint et proprietatem sive hereditatem emerint(e), aut super bona mobilia sive mercimonia posuerint, (f) in posterum autem vir moritur et uxor, (g) extunc filius viri propior est hereditatem recipere, quam pueri femine, aut pueri sororis sue, vel nepotes seu neptes ex filia sua. Ita tamen, si filius patris sit paris conditionis(h) patri. Proxima cognata(i) uxoris recipit suppellectilia de iure. (j)

[51] De bonis, que extraneis a viro aliquando assignantur, prius vero mulieri et pueris iudicialiter fuerint attributa.

(k) Si vir aliquis dederit pueris suis aliqua bona sua, et sue uxori in iudicio bannito circa vitam suam et bonam rationem, et si sibi pueri paris conditionis fuerint, et si desuper firma pax firmata fuerit, in posterum autem alteri in eisdem bonis aliquid dederit aut heres fuerit aut non, (l) ille, cui prima donatio sit data, bene contradicere potest de iure. Ita tamen, si testimonium iudicis desuper habuerit et scabinorum, quando sibi primum

(a) Precio conventus testis esse non potest, si post iurabit quod non sit condemnatus JL[17] (b) reprobati et qui sunt bone fame JL[17] (c) passÿerb JL[17] (d) Nota JL[31] (e) Ex laboribus sunt JL[17] (f) NB JL[37] (g) observatur; sed plebiscitum nonnullae civitates habent de hoc vegetum [?] JL[38] (h) Si sit legitimus JL[17] (i) vel consanguinea JL[17] (j) Cognata uxoris recipit paraphernalia aut supelectilia JL[36] (k) Pater si uni filio quid coram iudice et testibus dederit et si aliter filius die et anno siluerit extunc deinceps silere debet JL[17] (l) Potioritas eum [s] licet cui prima inscriptio servit. JL[38]

If a man is to attest payment of another's debt on the property of another, it should also be with possessors who are permanent residents, if they did not witness the payment in court, or it was not confirmed in court. In no case shall whose who have been arranged or bribed be summoned [as witnesses], they can be removed [from the court] in accordance with the law.

Of course, if someone is to prove payment of a debt, attesting simply about the debt, he must do so with men such as cannot be impugned in their own law.

[50] On a stepson who succeeds his stepmother in the goods of the deceased father.

If a husband marries a widow who has one son or many children and neither he nor she has any goods, and if the husband has one son from his first wife, and by good fortune they acquired, thanks to their hard work, goods and bought property[1] or inherited property, or they invest in movable goods or merchandise: if the husband later dies and so does the wife, then the son of the husband is closer to receiving the inheritance than the children of the woman, or the children of her sister, or the grandchildren of her daughter. However, this is the case if the son of the husband is equal to him in status. The closest female relative of the wife on the distaff side receives the paraphernalia by law.

[51] On goods that were at some time assigned by the husband to strangers, even though they had previously been ascribed by a court to his wife and children.

If a man gives something from his goods to his children and to his wife during her lifetime in a formally convened court and for a good reason, and if the children are equal in status to him, and if permanent peace is established regarding this, and later he gives something else from this goods to someone else, whether he is heir or not, the one to whom the first gift was given may rightfully oppose it according to the law. However, this shall be the case, if he has testimony from the judge and the jurors that the first gift

1 Here in the sense of real estate (*proprietas*, Ger. *Eigen*; BJ 169, fol. 284^{v}).

donum donatum sit absque contradictione illius, qui ad hoc successor fuerit infra annum et diem. Extunc contradicere non potest, si illi desuper testes habuerint.

CLXXXIII^{v} **[52] | De muliere, que et qualia bona a viro suo poterit habere, etiam contra voluntatem heredum viri.** (a)

Si vir uxori sue sua edificia dederit, que super bona censualia edificata sunt, coram domino proprietatis et coram suis vicinis, tempore sue vite, et inducit eam in possessionem, et si discedit ab hac luce sine prole, sique heres suus super bona sua eadem voluerit loqui post mortem viri, nihil in eis poterit obtinere, si mulier protestata fuerit, quod sibi datum fuerit. (b)

(c) Si autem fundus seu apparatus et edificia viri proprium fuerit, extunc heres mulieri infringere potest, nisi donatio in iudicio bannito fuerit confirmata. (d) Quia nullus suum proprium dare potest, nisi in iudicio bannito (e), vel coram iudice et scabinis, nisi suus heres contradicat.

(f) Si autem hereditaria censualia bona fuerint, extunc sue uxori dare non potest absque heredum consensu, vel absque domini proprietatis consensu, in cuius bonis sunt.

(a) x merk wol auff JL[8] [...] rusticorum lanorum JL[13] Vir sine prole potest sua bona dare uxori et non heredibus JL[17] (b) NB JL[37] (c) Si fundus JL[23] observatur JL[38] (d) Nullus suum proprium dare potest nisi in iudicio bannito et de scitu heredum, qui si non contradicant firmu[m] erit donum JL[17] (e) In bona hereditaria si sit heres vel coheres JL[23] (f) hereditaria JL[23] Reservitur censualis semel in bonis censualibus JL[38]

was given to him without opposition from the one who would become heir within a year and a day. From then on, he may not oppose it, if they have witnesses to this.

[52] On the wife, what and what kinds of goods she may have from her husband, also against the will of her husband's heirs.

If a husband gives his wife his buildings, which were erected on leasehold goods, in the presence of the lord of the estate[1] and his relatives, during his lifetime, and he introduces her into possession, and if he dies without heirs, and if his heir wishes to file a complaint regarding his goods after the husband's death, he shall gain nothing from it, if the wife protests that it was given to her.

However, if the estate, that is the materials and buildings, were owned by the husband, then the heir may challenge the wife, unless the gift was confirmed in a formally convened court. Because no one may give away their property except before a formally convened court, that is before the advocate[2] [Ger. *Vogt*] and jurors, unless his heir protests.

If the goods are hereditary leasehold goods, then he may not give it to his wife without the consent of the heirs or without the consent of the lord of the property in whose goods they are situated.

1 Ger. *Hofe* (BJ 169, fol. 285r).

2 The term *advocatus* appears in the Latin *Weichbild* in a few meanings. [1] Here, the translator of the *Weichbild* from German into Latin, Konrad of Sandomierz, translated the German term *Richter* as *advocatus*. This corresponds to the most common meaning in the medieval and early modern Kingdom of Poland, where the advocatus (Pol. *wójt*, Ger. *Vogt*) was a town administrator on behalf of the town owner (cf. Art. 4, footnote 2). He presided over the bench court. As a rule, he owned considerable property in the town (*advocatia*). Over time, the interests of the advocatus (called hereditary advocatus) and the owner of a town diverged, resulting in ownership transformations. The owner of the town (or the self-governing town represented by the town council) bought out the property of the *advocatus* and the associated judicial functions. In such a situation, the judicial functions began to be performed by the judicial *advocatus* (Pol. *landwójt*). [2] The term *advocatus* exists in the *Weichbild* also in the meaning of spokesman (cf. Art. 59, 61, 102). [3] In *The Saxon Mirror: A "Sachsenspiegel"* (p. 181) we can find a definition: "Advocate. Vogt n.m. A secular judge and magistrate for an ecclesiastical foundation, a monastery, or a bishopric. He presides over a superior court." In this meaning, *advocatus* appears in Art. 53, 111, and 112. In addition, in the Polish legal practice, the advocatus was the superior of a higher court of German law, for example the Higher Court of German Law at the Royal Castle in Cracow. [4] As a governor of the church in Magdeburg (Art. 127, 131).

[a] Si vero vir mercimonia aut alia bona mobilia habuerit, que ex illis bonis, que ex paterna successione ad eum devoluta sunt, emerit, hec sue uxori dare non potest, nisi in iudicio bannito coram iudice et scabinis.

[b] Si autem vir habuerit bona mobilia aut mercimonia, que sibi propriis laboribus [c] aut prospera fortuna accreverunt cum sua uxore, illa potest dare in valitudine vite sue cuicunque placet, cuiuslibet sine contradictione de iure.

[*53*] De bonis, penis et iudicio obnoxii cuiusvis monasterii.

Ubi alicuius monasterii obnoxius suam penam demeretur, hoc est XXX solidi. Obnoxius bene potest sua bona resignare et iterum suscipere et dare cui placet, contradictione qualibet non obstante, que propriis laboribus acquisivit.

Ubi autem obnoxius suo domino suum censum protraxerit, pro eo tria talenta demeretur. Item quicquid[d] obnoxius criminalis cause commiserit, pro eo nullius querat iudicium nisi domini sui advocati.

Quando obnoxius moritur, extunc domino suo advocato oportet dare denarios obnoxietatis et meliorem equum, quem habet. Hoc idem oportet facere sacerdotem suo archipresbitero, dum moritur, tunc sibi oportet dare meliorem equum. [e]

---

[a] mercimonia JL[23] Inter se reg. JL[35] Bona sunt duplici alia successione devoluta alia aquisita JL[38] [b] De propriis laboribus aquisitis concessum est cuilibet dare JL[17] mobilia JL[23] [c] alter est JL[38] [d] Nota JL[17] [e] bannum; Deuteronomii quinto misericordia [*cf. Deut. 5, 10*] JL[22]

If the husband had merchandise or other movable goods purchased with the proceeds from the goods that devolved upon him by paternal succession, he may not give them to his wife unless this is done in a formally convened court before the advocate and jurors.

If the husband has movable goods or merchandise accumulated through his own efforts with his wife or thanks to good fortune, he can give them away during his lifetime to anyone he wishes, lawfully without anyone's objection.

[*53*] On the goods, punishment and judgment of an [servile] subordinate any monastery.

If an [servile] subordinate[1] of any monastery deserves his punishment, it shall be 30 shillings. The [servile] subordinate may rightfully give away his goods and acquire it again for himself and give it to whomever he wishes, unimpeded by any objection, which he had acquired through his own labours.

However, if the [servile] subordinate delays paying his rent to his lord, he shall pay three talents. This [servile] subordinate, if he commits any criminal offense, shall not seek for this [offence] a court of anyone other than his lord advocate.[2]

When the [servile] subordinate dies, it is appropriate to give his lord advocate the *denarii* due from a [servile] subordinate,[3] and a better horse that [the subordinate] has. Likewise, a priest shall do the same to his archpriest, when he dies, then he shall give him a better horse.

1 This is probably a reference to the *laeti* (Pol. *liti*; Ger. *Laz*, BJ 169, fol. 285v): "a separate class of people who occupied a middle ground between the free and the unfree." Karol Modzelewski, *Barbarian Europe* (Frankfurt am Main-Bern-Bruxelles-New York-Oxford-Warszawa-Wien: Peter Lang, 2015), p. 156. I thank Krzysztof Fokt for the help in this clarification.

2 Cf. Art. 52, footnote 2.

3 *Denarius obnoxietatus*—a fee paid by a relative of a deceased [servile] subordinate, entitling him to use the land after the deceased.

[*54*] (a) De filia dotata et exhereditata alicuius mortui viri non habentis heredes, et de filio dicte filie quomodo hereditat.

CLXXXIIII[r] (b) Si moritur vir absque herede et nepotem ex filia habuerit, que est exhereditata circa suam vitam, idem nepos (c) maiori iure(d) recipit bona sui avi mortui, quam iudicium, et hoc si sibi est paris conditionis, sed iudicium recipit arma bellica. (e) Si etiam filius duxerit uxorem tempore vite sui patris, et premoriatur patri indivisus a sua hereditate, (f) extunc ipsius filii hereditatem sui avi recipiunt, equaliter cum suis patruis, et non filii filiarum. Si autem filium a se diviserit, protunc(g) filii filiorum in bonis sui avi equalem recipiunt portionem(h). (i) Sed in hereditatibus avie(j) recipiendis filie filiorum et filiarum iuridice sunt equales.

[*55*] De abtestificatione manus pro falsitate et vulnere.

Si unus alteri manum suam abtestari voluerit pro falso, hoc oportet, quod faciat mettertius cum talibus hominibus, qui in suo iure(k) argui non possunt.

Si autem hoc voluerit facere pro vulnere in facto manifesto, oportet, quod faciat metseptimus, per iustitiam pacis, ita tamen, si manifestum factum cum malefactore ad iudicium deductum fuerit(l).

(a) An nepos accipit partem filie cum patruis JL[17] (b) Divisionem [?] discut[it] xv capitulum. Si pater aut mater u[num] filium aut filiam a se [se]paraverint cum suis [bo]nis, et sive in expe[n]sis separantur sive n[on], et si vellent post [mor]tem patris aut matris hereditariam sortem alloqui frater apud fratres, et marita soror in non ex[do]tata sorore d[um] opportent importa[re], sub ipsorum iuratione hec a[utem] multa bona, quibus fuerint separati et diuisi, demptis suppelectilibus et h[e]c, si fuerint bona mob[ilia] vel peccora; si a[utem] illi sortem hereditariam domesticam [ve]ro se abrenunciant, extunc illam hab[ere] non debent; si hanc abrenunciat[ionem] coram iudicio fecerint, extunc pocius testimonio ii non vincantur. JL[4] De filia dotata JL[23] (c) observatur JL[38] (d) propinquiorum JL[17] (e) et Blasy d[omini] Stanis[lai] filius JL[17] (f) Quod nepotes ex filiis heredita[n]t et non ex filiabus JL[17] (g) nepotes JL[17] (h) sic cum pares JL[17] (i) NB JL[17] (j) sed avi JL[17] (k) nÿe naruszonÿ JL[17] (l) cum clamore JL[17]

[54] On an endowed and an excluded from succession daughter of some deceased man who has no heirs, and on the son of the said daughter, how he inherits.

If a man dies without a heir but has a grandson through his daughter, who received a dowry during his lifetime and has no rights to her father's remaining goods, that grandson shall inherit the estate of his deceased grandfather by a right stronger than the court, provided he is equal in status to him [the grandfather], but the court shall acquire the military equipment.[1] However, if a son marries during his father's lifetime and dies before his father without having received his share of his inheritance, then his sons shall inherit their grandfather's inheritance, equally with their paternal uncles, and not the sons of daughters. If, however, the son has received his share of his goods, at that time the sons of sons shall receive their grandfather's estate in equal parts. But in receiving the inheritances of the grandmother, daughters of the sons and of the daughters are equal in law.

[55] On taking an oath for the benefit of the accused in a case of forgery and injury.

If one person wishes to swear for the benefit of another accused of forgery, he must do so with at least two oath helpers, with men such as cannot be impugned in their own law.

However, if this is intended in a case of red-handed injury, it shall be done with at least six oath helpers, in consideration of the law of peace, but only if the perpetrator has been brought to court having been caught red-handed.

1 Ger. *Hergewete*, Pol. *Szczebrzuch*.

[56] De tutore puerorum, quis esse debeat, et de ratione per eundem tutorem reddenda.

Cum moritur vir, qui pueros habuerit, qui ad annos discretionis [(a)] nondum pervenerunt, proximus [(b)] agnatus debet ipsorum ⟨De quo supra folio xxxiii⟩[1] esse tutor[(c)], quousque ad annos pubertatis et discretionis pervenerint [(d)] et rationem de anno ad annum de bonis pupillorum facere debet vel tenetur.

[57] De iudicio apprehensi in manifesto scelere, presertim vero stuprum et aliam violentiam committentis.

[(e)] Omnes querimonie et testimonia, que cum criminosis violentiis ac cum clamore ad iudicium in facto manifesto deprehensa et deducta fuerint, virum metseptimum oportet ea protestari circa ius pacis, exceptis vulneribus[(f)], que monomachalia non fuerint.

[(g)] Manifestum autem factum ibi esse dicitur, ubi vir captivatur cum furto[(h)] aut spolio, manifesto et deprehensus ducitur ad iudicium cum clamore. Insuper etiam manifestum factum ibi esse dicitur, ubi viro cultellus, sicca, gladius aut alia arma in sua manu deprehensa fuerint, cum quibus pacem[(i)] infregit, aut si in fuga facti deprehensus fuerit et captivus ad iudicium cum clamore ductus fuerit. Hunc actor [(j)] metseptimus vincere debet circa ius pacis. ⟨Supra folio xxxiiii.⟩[2] [(k)] Et si factum manifestum cum viro ad iudicium deductum fuerit, sic est stuprum, obsidium, irruentia domicilii, homicidium, furtum, spolium, tunc homo probare debet protestando metseptimus. [(l)]

[(a)] Proximus agnatus [debet] tutorem pup[illorum] JL[23] [(b)] Quis tutor puerorum esse debet JL[17] [(c)] Tutor JL[38] [(d)] In defectu agnati sit cognatus quod si deficit sic [?] consules tutorem [?] ipsi eligant JL[17] [(e)] Manifestum factum quod victe super libro 2 folio ccxx [*Speculum Saxonum in: Commune incliti Poloniae Regni privilegium…, fol. ccxii^{v}, capitulum: De facto manifesto et de rebus apud aliquem inventis et iure arrestatis, SSp. I.66§1*] JL[8] [(f)] scilicet parvis JL[17] [(g)] et factus; factum manifestum debet qualiter probari JL[17] [(h)] s z l y c z e m JL[17] [(i)] vel arestando vel etc. JL[17] [(j)] *manicula* JL[17] [(k)] Violencie facti manifesti sunt, quam debent probari per metseptimum JL[17] [(l)] vulnera, percussiones, laceracio JL[17]

---

1 *Infra Commune incliti…, articulus in Statutis Casimiri Magni:* De tutoribus puerorum, qui non possunt hereditatem ipsorum vendere.

2 *Infra Commune incliti…, articulus in Statutis Casimiri Magni:* De violationibus virginum et oppressionibus viduarum vel maritarum.

[56] On the guardian of children, who should become one, and on the accounts the guardian should submit.

If a man who had underage sons dies, the closest male relative by blood should become their guardian until they come of age, and the guardian should submit an annual account [of the management] of the wards' goods.

[57] On the court for the perpetrator caught in the act, particularly rape and other acts of violence.

All complaints and testimonies relating to criminal violence and a red-handed deed brought to court shall be attested with six oath helpers according to the law of peace, with the exception of injuries that do not warrant a duel.

A red-handed deed is said to occur when a man is openly caught while committing theft or robbery, and when apprehended, is brought to court with an outcry. A red-handed deed is also said to happen when a man is found holding a knife, dagger, sword, or other weapon, with which he violated the peace, are seized in his hand, or if apprehended while fleeing and brought to court with an outcry. A plaintiff shall prevail over such a man with six oath helpers according to the law of peace. And if a red-handed deed with a man is brought to court, a deed such as rape, highway robbery, house raid, homicide, theft, or robbery, then [the plaintiff] should attest it with six oath helpers.

CLXXXIIII[v] [(a)] Si vero vir de istis conqueritur, utpote de stupro, extunc sua querimonia sic debet procedere: [(b)] "Domine iudex, ego conqueror Deo et vobis, quod hic homo venit intra municipalia et in me pacem violavit, et me stupravit et spoliavit in corpore, rebus et honore muliebri, de quo sufficiens habeo testimonium per eos, qui meum clamorem audierunt, et ostendere volo factum, ut de iure teneor aut debeo, [(c)] et requiro in sententia diffinitiva, quomodo ipsum vincere debeam, ut mihi proficiat in iure meo." Extunc ille petat satisdationem, si vult, quam sibi facere oportet, et dicat se de facto esse innocentem. Tunc tutor mulieris interroget in diffinitiva sententia, si mulier violentiam melius poterit protestari cum his, qui clamorem suum audierunt, quam ille possit evadere, cum ad iudicium sit deductus. Tandem diffinitur iure, quod possit ipsum possibilius vincere cum iis, qui clamorem suum audierunt, quam ille evadere possit. Et si hoc protestabitur, ut iuris est, adversarius collum demerebitur. [(d)] Idem vero iudicium super irruentiam domus iudicatur.

[*58*] [(e)] De documento qualiter querimonia sit formanda pro violentia in via.

[(f)] Hic stat Conradus et conqueritur super Henricum, Deo et vobis, domino nostro, regi aut duci, aut vobis, domine iudex ac toti universitati civitatis, divitibus ac pauperibus, quod ipse inter municipale venerit ad locum talem, ubi Conradus pace et quiete perfrui debuerat et sibi obsidium[(g)] fecit in strata regia, et regia in pace, et in eo municipali pacem infregit ac ipsum vulneravit ac destruxit et spoliavit in corpore et in rebus suis, in eoque talem strepitum perfecit, quem bene probare potest; et cum ipse in eo pacem violavit strepitumque in eo commisit, tunc propria in persona vidit ipsum, et in persona propria ipsum clamore proclamavit. Si hoc fatetur, stet, si autem negabit, ipse eum vincere intendit per hos, qui suum clamorem audierunt [(h)] ac testimonio. Et sicut ipsum captum in manifesto facto deduxit ad iudicium, sic in sententia requirit, quomodo ipsum vincere debeat, ut sibi proficuum sit in suo iure. [(i)]

[(a)] Mulier qualiter pro stupro conqueri debet JL[17] Proposicio pro stupro JL[31] [(b)] Forma accusationis JL[38] [(c)] Mulier stuprata propior est si in facto manifesto metseptima reum vincere, quam reus [met]septimus evadere JL[17] [(d)] Pro stupro collum demeretur. JL[38] [(e)] proposicio JL[31] [(f)] Qualiter querimonia sit formanda, *manus A* JL[25] [(g)] Henricum [*?*] JL[17] [(h)] vide JL[8] [(i)] quod idem metseptimus facien[do] JL[17]

If a man is investigated for these [crimes], namely for rape, the complaint [against him] shall proceed as follows: "My lord judge, I complain to God and to you that this person came within the municipal [jurisdiction], violated my peace, raped me, and defiled in body, things and honour of a woman, for which I have sufficient testimony from those who heard my outcry. I wish to present the incident as I owe or should according to the law, and demand a definitive sentence on how I should prevail over him, to get justice for me." Then the accused may request surety[1], if he wishes, which should be provided, and shall declare his innocence. Then the woman's guardian shall request a definitive sentence on whether the woman might better be able to attest the violence with those who heard her outcry than the accused might defend himself when brought to court. Finally, it shall be decided according to the law that she shall be able to prevail most certainly with those who heard her outcry than the accused could defend himself. And if it is thus attested, as the law stipulates, the accused shall be sentenced to death. The court shall adjudicate upon a house raid in the same manner.

[*58*] On the template for composing a complaint about violence on the road.

Here stands Conrad and complains against Henry to God and to you, our lord, king or duke, or to you, judge, and the whole community of the city, the rich and the poor, that the aforementioned came within the city [jurisdiction] to such a place, where Conrad should have been able to fully enjoy peace and quiet, and he attacked him on the royal road, and in the royal peace, and violated the city's peace in him, and wounded, maimed, and damaged him, and robbed him in body and in his possessions, and caused him such disturbance which can be rightfully proven; and when he violated the peace and caused disturbance, then he [the victim] saw him in person, and in person protested against him with an outcry. If he admits to this, let him stand, but if he denies it, the victim intends to defeat him with those who heard his outcry and with testimony. And just as he brought the aforementioned [man] caught red-handed to court, he shall demand in the sentence how he should defeat him, so that he may benefit in his right.

1 See Art. 38, footnote.

[59] De accusatione viri pro vulnere aut alio crimine manifesto, ad iudicium clamore deducti, quomodo procedendum sit contra eum.

Si vulneratus vir cum clamore ad iudicium decuctus fuerit in facto manifesto, et si ita imbecillis aut debilis fuerit, quod per tutorem ipsum querulari oportet et prolocutorem per sententiam petat, extunc tali modo sua procedat[(a)] querimonia: [(b)] "Domine iudex, si me huic vulnerato dedistis pro
CLXXXV[r] advocato, extunc in sententia requiro, si propter iustitiam insidias | propter aliquem pati debeam, [(c)] quam iure tueri debeam aut sustinere, cum suam causam propter iuris exigentiam teneo." Cui diffinitur, quod non, denique sibi petat correctionem. Cum obtinuerit correctionem, tunc petat colloquium pro consilio. Cum vero habuerit colloquium, tunc requirat, qualiter inchoare debeat per sententiam diffinitivam, ut sibi proficiat in suo iure. Tandem diffinitur sibi cum clamore. Tunc interroget sententialiter, si requiri debeat de ore ad os, a quo suam habeat lesionem. Tunc sibi diffinitur, quod debeat. Extunc emittuntur duo scabini et cum ipsis preco, [(d)] aut duo viri, qui iudicio astare consueverunt, qui ab ipso solo audiant, a quo receperit vel habuerit damna, aut quis in eo pacis federa confregerit. Extunc requiritur sententialiter et requiri debeat circa iuramentum prestitum aut ius civitatis, quid ab eo audierunt. Tunc unus interrogatur ad dicendum, quid ab eo audierint. Audita responsiva, posthac in sententia requiratur, si sibi profecerit, tunc sibi diffinitur, quod sic. Etiam secundus et tertius interrogetur, extunc sibi diffinitur, quod sibi profecerit. Postea querelam incipiat: "Domine iudex, placeat attente audire. Tunc hic N. conqueritur super unum N. et super I., quod ipsi venerunt intra municipale et in eo pacem infregerunt, et ipsum vulneraverunt aut suum affinem proximum trucidaverunt, [(e)] si homicidium fuerit, et ipsum spoliaverunt corpore et rebus, et pro eo iudicium petit." Extunc illi ter vocantur. Quando vocati per clamorem ter fuerint, tunc conqueritur ulterius et nominet malefactores, ut prius querulatum fuit. Idem faciet tertia vice. Extunc inducie dantur per noctem. Si tunc non comparent, inscribantur[(f)]. Si autem comparent, duellum in eis acquiri potest.

(a) pro iuramenciis JL[17] (b) De formando querimonia, *manus A* JL[25] (c) Modus antiquatus JL[38] (d) Modus procedendi contra homicidium pro homicidio propositio JL[31] (e) Quali iure procedendum [est] de affinis alicuius occisis JL[17] (f) proscribuntur JL[17]

[59] On accusing a man of injury or another evident crime, bringing him to court with an outcry, how to proceed against him.

If an injured man is brought to court with an outcry, following a red-handed deed, and if he is so weak or infirm that the complaint must be made through a guardian, and he requests [the appointment] of a spokesman in the sentence, then his complaint shall proceed in this way: "My lord judge, since you have appointed me as the spokesman[1] for this injured man, I demand, in the sentence, if for the sake of justice I am obliged to suffer someone's trap, how should I guard the law or proceed, since I am argued his case in compliance with requirements of the law." If they decide against it, then he shall request correction. When he obtains the correction, then he shall request a consultation for advice. And when he is granted consultation, then he shall seek guidance on how to begin, through a definitive sentence, so that he may be vindicated in his right. Ultimately, it shall be established for him, with an outcry. Then he shall request in the sentence whether he [victim] should be personally interrogated about who caused his injury. It shall then be established that he should. Then two jurors shall be sent with the court bailiff[2], or two men accustomed to appearing in court, who shall hear from him personally who caused him harm or injury, and who thus violated the covenant of peace. Then he shall request in the sentence, and he should request it for the sake of the oath and law of the city, what they heard from him. Then one of them shall be asked to state what he heard from him. Upon hearing the response, then he shall request in the sentence whether it brings benefit to him, then it shall be declared to him that it does. Likewise, the second and third man shall be asked, then it shall be declared to him that it brings benefit to him. Then he shall initiate the complaint: "My lord judge, please, listen carefully. At that time, this N complains against one N and against I, that they came within the city jurisdiction, thereby violating the peace, and they injured him, or killed his closest relative, if it was murder, and they robbed him in body and things, and he demands justice for this." Then they shall be summoned three times. When they are summoned by outcry for the third time, then he shall complain for the last time and identify the malefactors, as he did previously. Likewise, he shall do so for the third time. Then adjournment shall be set for the night. If they do not appear at that time, they shall be considered outlawed. However, if they do appear, he may demand a duel against them.

1 *Advocatus* in the sense of spokesman (Ger. *Vorsprechen*, BJ fol. 287^v), cf. Art. 52, footnote 2.

2 See Art. 6, footnote.

[*60*] De querela super furem captum in recenti crimine et pro spolio contra raptorem.

[a] Quando vir furem aut spoliatorem protestari voluerit, qui cum manifesto facto ad iudicium cum clamore deductus fuerit, qui conqueritur sic: "Domine iudex, ego conqueror Deo et vobis super meum furem, quem cum apparenti furto captivavi et ligatum ad iudicium usque perduxi, quod ipse venit intra meos quattuor angulos et subtraxit mihi mea bona, [b] super quo bonum habeo testimonium ab iis, qui clamorem meum audierunt, et ipsum vincere volo iure meo ac meo testimonio, ut hic mihi ius dictaverit. Et requiro sententialiter sciscitando, quomodo ipsum vincere debeam iure, ut mihi proficiat in iure meo." [c] Et sic diffinitur, quod metseptimus, si furtum presens fuerit. Idem iudicium fiat pro spolio et super raptorem.

[*61*] De vulnerati querela, quomodo per prolocutorem[d] fieri debeat.

CLXXXV[v] [e] Ubi vir alterius verbum loqui debet, ad quod sententiis scabinorum vel iure compellitur in facto manifesto, dicat sic: "Domine iudex, me dedistis illi homini prolocutorem, extunc requiro in sententia, si ab aliquo inimicicias[f] aut timorem habere debeam, quod verbum suum pro iuris loquar exigentia quantum melius possum aut valeo." Quando sibi hoc diffinitum fuerit, tunc sibi diffiniat correctionem, quod si ipsum in aliquo neglexerit, quod se corrigere poterit mecum, aut per me, aut per alterum advocatum. Cum sibi hoc diffinitum fuerit, petat colloquium, si vult, et requirat in sententia, quando querela inchoari debeat, ut sibi proficiat in suo iure. Cum hoc sibi diffinitum fuerit, tunc in sententia interroget, si l[e]sus interrogari debeat, quis in eo pacem infregit, etsi ita fuerit debilis, quod suum malefactorem nominare non possit. Cum igitur hoc diffinitum fuerit et ipsum iudex aut duo scabini aut duo viri, qui iudicio astare solent, viderunt, requirat in sententia, si ipsi causa iustitie dicere debeant circa iuramentum ipsorum et ius civitatis, quod notorium ipsis de hoc facto sit. Cum hoc sibi diffinitur

---

[a] De formanda querimonia, *manus A* JL[25] proposicio JL[31] Fur JL[38] [b] Furtum vel spolium quomodo debet probari contra aliquem ut conveniatur JL[17] [c] Furti metseptimus proba[n]tur JL[38] [d] procuratorem JL[17] [e] De formanda querimonia, *manus A* JL[25] Correctio; Nota pro ultra dedit [*unum verbum illegibile*] JL[31] [f] insidias JL[17]

[*60*] On a complaint against a thief caught red-handed and against a robber for robbery.

If a man wishes to protest against a thief or robber who has been brought to court caught red-handed with an outcry, he shall file the complaint in the following manner: "My lord judge, I complain to God and to you against my thief, whom I caught in the act of theft and brought bound to court, that he came within my four corners and deprived me of my goods, for which I have credible testimony from those who heard my outcry, and I wish to defeat him by my right and my testimony, as the law commands me. And I demand that it should be attested in the sentence how I should defeat him according to the law, so that I may vindicate in my right" And it shall be established by the testimony of seven oath helpers, if the theft was evident. The court shall proceed likewise with a robbery and against the robber.

[*61*] On a complaint of a wounded person, how it should be argued by a spokesman.

If a man is to speake the word on behalf of another, to which he has been obliged by the sentences of jurors or by the law, he shall say: "My lord judge, you have appointed me a spokesman of this person, therefore I demand it be established in the sentence that if I should suffer any enmity or fear on account of complying with the requirement of the law to make statements on his behalf as well as I can and know how." When this is established, then he shall reserve the right to correct, that if he neglects anything, he shall be able to correct it with me, or through me, or through another spokesman.[1] When this is established, he shall request a consultation, if he wishes, and shall demand that it be established in the sentence when he should begin the complaint so that he may benefit in his right. When this is established, then he shall request that it be established in the sentence whether the wounded man should be asked who violated his peace, even if he is so infirm that he cannot name his assailant. Therefore, when this is established, and the judge and two jurors or two men accustomed to appearing in court have seen him, he shall demand that it be established in the sentence whether for the sake of justice they should testify under oath and municipal law what they know about the matter. When this is established

1 *Advocatus* in the sense of spokesman, cf. Art. 52, footnote 2.

ab uno ad secundum et tertium, extunc requirat in sententia, si iam profecerit. Cum sibi hoc diffinitum fuerit et pacis violator per clamorem cittatus fuerit, ut iuris est, tunc dicat sic: (a) "Domine iudex, placeat audire verbum suum. (b) Tunc conqueritur vobis super hunc N., quod ipsum in strata libera(c) infestavit ac intra municipalia in eo pacem infregit, ac ipsum vulneravit et violentiam in eo peregit, quam probando ostendere potest, quod ipsum depredatus est corpore et rebus, et tantum recepit sibi, quod non minus valeat, nisi bene duellum mereatur. Et super eo a vobis iustum petit iudicium." (d) Extunc pacis violator proclamatur primo et secundo et tertio per nominem suum N., et iterum suam querimoniam renovet in hunc modum: "Domine iudex, vobis conqueritur super unum N., quod ipse venit intra municipale in strata regia, in eo Dei pacem infringendo, et ipsum rebus et corpore sanitatis depredatus est ac ipsum vulneravit et in eo strepitum fecit, quem apparenter potest demonstrare." Et pro eo petit iudicium, et sic tertia vice faciat. Tunc ostendet vulnus et interroget in sententia diffinitiva, si suum pacis violatorem in aliquo loco invenerit, si ipsum licite arrestare possit ex parte iudicii. Cum igitur hoc diffinitum fuerit, tunc petat pacem, que sibi indici debet.

[*62*] De salutatione seu concittatione ad duellum.

(e) Qui monomachaliter suum equalem salutare seu alloqui voluerit, hunc iudicem petere oportebit, ut se intromittere possit de uno pacis sue violatore, quem videat in presenti. Cum hoc sibi per sententiam diffinitum fuerit, tunc etiam in sententia requirat, per quem modum se de ipso intro-
CLXXXVI[r] mittere debeat, ut sibi in suo iure proficere possit. | Tunc sibi de iure diffinitur, curialiter per oram vestimenti (f). Et cum se de ipso intromittet, pronunciet sibi causam, pro qua se de ipso intromisit, quod statim potest facere, si vult, aut pro eo habere colloquium. Tunc ipsum inculpare oportebit, quod pacem in eo infregit aut in strata regia, (g) qualitercunque infregerit, eodem modo queruletur super eum. Tunc ipsum iterum inculpet, quod ipsum depredatus est et eam vim in ipso fecerit, quam bene probare poterit. Ibidem vulnus aut vulneris cicatricem demonstret, si vulnus sanatum fuerit. Tunc ultimus conqueratur, quod ipsum spoliavit bonis et

(a) Modus proloquendi JL[38] (b) Qualiter querulatus esse debet qui pars violatoris JL[17] pro JL[31] (c) na dobrowolney drodze JL[17] (d) Alia querela qui vulnerantes JL[17] (e) art. 35 [*Mikołaj Jaskier, Iuris Municipalis..., art. XXXV, fol. XXXIII[v]*] JL[33] (f) Ceremonia minus utilis JL[38] (g) Modus proceden[di] per modum domini N[...] JL[31]

from one to another and to the third, then he shall demand that it be established in the sentence whether he has already gained benefit. When this is established, and the violator of peace is summoned by outcry, as the law demands, then he shall say: "My lord judge, please, listen to his [the victim's] word. Then he complains to you about this N., that on the public road he harassed him and violated his peace within city [jurisdiction], and he injured him and used violence against him, which he can prove by evidence, that he was robbed in body and his things, and so much was taken from him that he rightly deserves no less than a duel. And he asks for a just judgment from you for this." Then the violator of peace shall be summoned by name for the first, second, and third time, and he [spokesman] shall renew his complaint in this manner: "My lord judge, I complain against this N., that he came within the city [jurisdiction] on the royal road, thereby violating the peace of God, and he robbed him in property and bodily health, and he injured him, and he caused the disturbance which he can evidently prove." And on his behalf he requests a judgment, and he shall do so for the third time. Then he shall show the wound and request that it be established in the definitive sentence, if he encounters his violator of peace in any place, whether he may arrest him with the court's permission. Therefore, when this is decided, then he shall request [the establishment of] peace.

[*62*] On the invitation or challenge to a duel.

Anyone who wishes to invite or challenge his equal to a duel must request permission from the judge to apprehend the violator of his peace whom he sees. If granted by the sentence, he must also demand that it be established in the sentence how he should apprehend the violator, so that he may benefit in his right. Then, according to the law, he shall be allowed to do so delicately, by the hem of clothing. When he apprehends the violator, he must inform him why he is apprehended, which he may do immediately, if he so wishes, or he can have a consultation about it. He shall then accuse him of violating the peace either on a public road or in any manner, and a complaint shall be filed against him accordingly. He shall further accuse him of robbery and assault, which he can rightfully prove. He shall show the wound, or scar from the wound, if the wound has healed. Next, he shall accuse him of the last [offence], that he robbed him of his goods and took

de ipsis sibi tanta recepit, quod bene duellum meretur. Hec tria criminalia facta omnia simul conqueratur, de quocunque horum trium, si de uno obliviscatur aut tacuerit, extunc suum duellum ammisit. Et loquitur ulterius: "Tunc ipsum vidi solum, hoc est in persona propria, et ipsum clamore proclamavi. Si fateri voluerit, ego sum contentus, et si non fatebitur, ipsum omni iure vincere volo, ut mihi vulgus iudicaverit, aut scabini, si sub banno regio fuerit." Extunc ille petat satisdationem, quam sibi facere debet.

Tamen vir potest suam querimoniam meliorare ante satisdationem, si voluerit. Facta satisdatione, ille suam exhibeat innocenciam, hoc est iuramentum, quod ipsum iure[(a)] oportet. Et iuramentum monomochale, si ipsum iure[(b)] incitaverit, si ibi fuerit, hoc est si ille iuramentum perficere poterit pre imbecillitate sui corporis. [(c)] Quivis vir potest se a duello excusare illi viro, qui sibi paris conditionis non fuerit. Illi etiam, qui nobilioris nature fuerit, ille preesse non potest, qui deterioris nature fuerit, si ipsum alloquetur. [(d)] A duello etiam cedere potest, qui post meridiem allocutus fuerit, nisi ante meridiem fuisset inchoatum. Iudex etiam debet habere clipeum et gladium illi, super quem allocutum fuerit. A duello etiam homo potest excipere suos affines, si uterque suus affinis et in consanguineitatis linea coniuncti fuerint, quod simul pugnare non poterint. [(e)] Iudex etiam duos nuncios dare debet cuilibet horum, qui pugnare debent, qui videant, ut habeant attinentiam secundum veram consuetudinem. [(f)] Coreum et linea indumenta induere possunt et debent in quantum placet, [(g)] capite et pedibus, in anteriori parte denudati, et in manibus cirotecas habeant. Unum gladium nudum in manu et alio actincti, aut duobus, hoc arbitrio eorum admittitur, et unum clipeum rotundum in sinistra manu, quod non aliud quam ligneum et corio superductum preter umbonem, seu manuum tectorium, quod potest esse ferreum. Unam tunicam absque manicis super preparamenta. [(h)] Etiam iudex, vel preco communis, debet indicere sub pena colli, quod nemo eos impediat circa duellum. Cuilibet ipsorum iudex unum virum dare debet, qui phalangam ferat, qui ipsos in
CLXXXVI[v] nihilo[(i)] impedire debent, nisi unus ceciderit, quod phalangam | interponat, aut si vulneratus fuerit, aut si phalangam desiderat. Hoc idem facere, nisi voluntas iudicis fuerit, non potest. Postquam circulo pax indicta fuerit, ambo debent circulum affectare, quem ipsis iudex licentiare debet de iure. Finalia fer[ri]menta de vaginis gladiorum deponere debent, nisi a iudice

---

[(a)] *org.* iurare [(b)] *org.* iurare [(c)] *manicula;* Nota. Exceptiones a duello prohibentes JL[17] [(d)] Qui a duello excipiuntur JL[38] [(e)] Ad duellum nunciare JL[17] [(f)] Requisita ad duellum JL[38] [(g)] *manicula* JL[17] [(h)] Nota. Preco quid clamans JL[17] [(i)] scilicet nec iuvare JL[17]

so many of them that he rightly deserves a duel. He shall simultaneously bring all these three criminal charges against him; if he forgets or omits any one of those three, he shall lose his duel. He shall then say, "Then I saw him by himself, that is, in his own person, and proclaimed him by an outcry. If he confesses, I am content; if he does not, I wish to defeat him with full law, as the people may judge for me, or the jurors, if this comes under royal ban." At that moment, he [the accused] shall demand a surety[1], which shall be granted.

However, [the plaintiff] may correct his complaint before surety is granted, if he wishes. After surety is granted, the accused must prove his innocence by an oath, which he ought to do by law, swear and a duel, if he has been lawfully challenged, if he [the plaintiff] is there, namely, if is able to fight a duel despite the injury to his body. Any man may excuse himself from a duel with a man who is not of a condition equal to his. However, one of lesser birth may not excuse himself from a duel with one of higher birth, if challenged. A man may also withdraw from a duel, if challenged after noon, unless [the proceedings] began before noon. The judge should also have a round shield and sword for the one who has been challenged. A man may also exclude his relatives from the duel, if both the challenger and the relative are so closely related that they may not fight together. The judge shall assign two deputies to each of those who are to fight, to ensure they are armed according to proper custom. They may wear as much leather and linen as they wish, with heads and feet bare in front, and gloves on their hands. One sword bare in hand and the other belted, or two, as permitted to them by their choice, and one round shield in the left hand, which shall be of wood only and covered with leather, except for an *umbo*, that is, a handguard, which may be made of iron. One sleeveless tunic over the armour. The judge or the common court bailiff[2] should also announce, on pain of death, that no one may interfere with them during the duel. To each of them a judge should assign a man carrying a spear; they must not interfere, unless one [fighter] falls, [then the deputy is] to place the spear between them, or if one is wounded, or if one demands the spear. This may not be done without the judge's permission. After peace is announced in the ring, both parties should enter the ring, upon the judge's permission by law. They shall unfasten the iron tips from their sword sheaths, unless

1 See Art. 38, footnote.

2 See Art. 6, footnote.

licentiam habuerint. [(a)] Ambo ornati debent ire ante iudicem et ambo iurare debent: unus, scilicet actor[(b)], quod causa sit vera, pro qua super ipsum querelam fecit, et respondens[(c)], quod sit innocens. Sic ipsos Deus adiuvet et suum duellum. Sol etiam ipsis dividi debet per medium, quando primo conveniunt. Si vincetur ille, super quem conqueritur, tunc iudicetur sententia capitali. Si autem vicerit, dimittetur cum pena et emenda. [(d)] Actor primo circulum intrabit. Alter si diu tardaverit, iudex debet ipsum per preconem vocare in illa domo, ubi se preparaverit, et duos scabinos seu iuratos cum ipso mittere debet. Sic cittari debet primo, secundo et tertio, et si ad tertiam cittationem non venerit, tunc querulator surgat et se ad duellum exhibeat. Et statim percutiet duos ictus et tertium figat contra ventum, cum eo ipse suum adversarium devicit tali causa sive querela, pro qua ipsum fuerat allocutus. Et iudex sibi iudicare debet, sicut per duellum adversarius suus convictus.

Sic mortuus debet convinci, si in furto aut in rapina, aut in simili crimine occisus fuerit. ⟨Articulus condemnatus. De quo supra folio CLXXIIII arti. XI⟩[1] Si autem mortuus cum septem testibus protestari poterit, extunc ad duellum se non potest exhibere contra ipsum. Si autem ipsum alter agnatus mortui, quiscunque fuerit, loco ipsius ad duellum se exhibuerit, hic extinguet omne testimonium, quia tunc ipsum absque duello vincere non potest, ut superius est expressum. Sic vincitur etiam et ille, qui ad duellum captivatus aut salutatus fuerit, aut promittit aut fideiussorie cautionem fecit, quod debuit comparere et non comparuit ad iustitiam responsivam.

[*63*] De accusatione violatoris pacis cum duello.

Quicunque occisum seu vulneratum virum captivum ad iudicium deduxerit et ipsum pacis violatorem accusaverit, per duellum vel absque duello, si non probaverit secundum iuris exigentiam ipse desuper ipsum, idem iudicium iudicari debeat, quod super illum procedere debuerat, ac si iudicio convictus fuerit, et hoc per iustitiam pacis.

[(e)] Si vulneratus hunc alloquitur, qui ipsum vulneravit, per duellum et si pre debilitate corporis duellum perficere non possit, et si tutorem non

(a) Ceremonia in duello JL[38] (b) p o w o d JL[17] (c) et adversa JL[17] (d) [s]i adversarius intrare circulum noluit quod est iuris JL[17] (e) Loco sui quis aliquem ad duellum sta[t]uere potest dum solus perficere non potest; impedimento ex ante legali autem inducie sibi dande, quoad solus perficere potest JL[17]

1 *Infra Commune incliti…, Articuli reprobati Gregorii* XI *papae.*

the judge does give his permission. Both, furnished, should approach the judge and both should swear: the first, the plaintiff, that the case is true, for which he filed the complaint against the other, and the defendant, that he is innocent. And thus God may help them and their duel. They should be allotted equal time under the sun when they first meet. If the accused is defeated, the penalty of death shall be imposed. However, if he wins, he shall go free with a fine and compensation. The plaintiff shall enter the ring first. If the defendant tarries too long, the judge should summon him through the court bailiff[1] from the house where he was preparing himself, and should send two jurors with him. He should be summoned in this manner for the first, second, and third time, and if he does not arrive at the third summons, then the plaintiff shall rise and present himself for the duel. He shall immediately strike two blows and make a third [thrust] into the air, by which he shall overcome his opponent in the case or complaint for which he challenged him. The judge should rule as if his opponent had been convicted by a duel.

Similarly, a deceased man's offence should be proven, if he was killed in theft, assault, or a similar crime. However, if the deceased man's guilt can be attested with seven witnesses, a duel cannot be offered against him. If, however, another agnate relative of the deceased, whoever they may be, appears in his place for the duel, this nullifies all testimony, as then they cannot be defeated without a duel, as mentioned above. Likewise, the one who was apprehended and challenged to a duel, and promised or provided surety to appear in court but did not come to do justice, shall be defeated in the same way.

[*63*] On accusing the violator of peace with a duel.

Whoever brings a captured slain or wounded man to court and accuses him of violating the peace, with or without a duel, if he fails to prove it as the law requires, the same proceedings should be instigated against him as would be against the first accused, and as if he were convicted in court; and this [is] for the justice of peace.

If the wounded [man] challenges the one who wounded him to a duel, and if due to weakness of the body he is unable to go through with the duel,

1 See Art. 6, footnote.

habuerit, qui pro eo pugnare velit, inducie sibi iudicari et ordinari debent, quousque suum duellum perficere possit.

CLXXXVII[r]

[*64*] | De iure privatis periuris et infamibus.

[a] Qui vitam aut manum pecunia redemerit, quod demeruerit, hic iure suo privetur seu infamis efficitur. [b] Et si tempore vite unius plura bona fuerint, quam quod suo iuramento exactionaliter alias solvendo exactionem comprobasset, et si fatetur eadem [c] bona esse sua, tunc periurus existit perdiditque omne ius suum civile et caret[d] iure[e], propter quod infamis dicitur. Et quidcunque periurus debeat protestari, hoc coram iudicio oportet fieri, ita quod sibi causa nominatur propter quam sit periurus. Et si fateatur vel bona sub ipso valeant promptari, alias cognosci vel inveniri, pro quibus patenter iuravit, extunc periurus est et convictus carensque iure et perdens suum ius civile.

[*65*] De fideiussione sceleratorum[f].

[g] Qui etiam fideiusserit unum virum pro scelere ad statuendum ipsum coram iudicio, et ipsum statuere non poterit, recompensam ipsum solvere oportet, et sibi in suo iure non oberit illi, qui fuerat fideiussor. [h] Et nemo proscribi debet [i], nisi[j] culpa ad collum sive ad manum sibi procedit.

[*66*] De suppellectili, que ad mulieres pertineant. [k]

[l] Si mulier [recipit] suppellectilia, [m] ad que spectant: oves, vascula et capisteria; et omnia cibaria domestica, de quibus vir indiget ad unius anni revolutionem, que in sua possessione inveniuntur, quorum cibariorum medietas ad mulierem pertinet.

---

[a] De infamibus et periuris JL[1] Manum vel vitam pecunia redimens infamis efficitur et ad dignitatem inhabilis JL[17] [b] Exactiones ex bonis non ex toto nec inte[gro] solvens periurus est, honore carens JL[17] [c] periurus infamis JL[31] [d] b e s z e c z n ÿ vel p r z e r z e c z ÿ JL[17] [e] fama bona JL[17] [f] pro ipso [*?*] JL[17] [g] Si quis virum scelestum coram iure non potest s[tatu]ere JL[17] [h] cause proscripcionis JL[17] [i] vel ad honorem vir infamis JL[17] [j] propria JL[17] [k] mulier JL[23] De rebus supelectilibus cui pertinent JL[36] [l] Nota JL[31] [m] Hec suppellec[tilia] donantur JL[17]

and if there is no champion willing to fight for him, he shall be granted and set a postponement until he is able to fight his duel.

[*64*] On perjurers and *infamis*, deprived of [their] rights.

Whoever redeems life or a hand with money, for what he deserved, shall lose his right, that is, he shall become an *infamis*. And if there are more goods in his lifetime than what he proved with his oath by paying taxes, and if he admits that these goods belong to him, then he shall be revealed as a perjurer and shall lose his full civil rights and all his rights, for which reason he shall be called *infamis*. Whatever a perjurer has to attest should be done in court, so that the reason for being a perjurer is made known to him. And if he confesses or goods are discovered on him, or are recognized or found regarding which he openly swore, then he shall become a perjurer and shall be convicted, deprived of his rights, and shall lose his civil rights.

[*65*] On giving a surety for criminals.

Also, whoever gives surety for a man regarding a transgression, that he will appear in court, and cannot produce him, must pay the wergeld, and this shall not damage the rights of the one who was the surety. And no one should be deprived of his rights unless there is a crime worthy of the death penalty or loss of hand.

[*66*] On paraphernalia that belong to women.

If a wife [receives] paraphernalia, they include sheep, pots and vessels; and all household food which the husband needs over the course of up to one year, [and] which are found in his possession, half of this food shall belong to the wife.

(a) Cum viro uxor sua moritur, (b) proxima sua cognata recipit suppellectilia, que debet pro viro suum stratum decorare, ut stetit, cum uxor sua vixit, cum lecto, cussinis, lintiaminibus, culcitra et tectura, sedem etiam suam cum pulvinari, quod singulis diebus desuper iacuit, suam mensam cum mensali et manutergio. Hec eadem cognata nulla recipit pulmentaria.

[67] De armis bellicis, ad quem devolvuntur per successionem. Item de tutore puerorum. (c)

(d) Mulier pro armis bellicis dare debet gladium mariti et suum equum vel dextrarium meliorem sellatum et meliora arma, (e) que habuerit pro corpore unius viri, cum decessit, in sua potestate, deinde dare debet pulvinar bellicale, hoc est lectum et duos cussinos, et duo lintiamina, et unum mensale, et duas pelves, et unum manutergium. Hec sunt universalia arma
CLXXXVII[v] bellica. Sed tamen aliqui | homines diversa apponunt, que ad ea non pertinent. Sed quicquid ex his nominatis mulier non habuerit, ad hoc, quod det, compelli non potest, si iuramento probaverit pro qualibet re per se. (f) Ubi vero ostendere patenter poterit, ibi vir nec mulier per iuramentum evadere possunt. Ubi duo aut tres ad una bellica arma nati fuerint, senior pro se recipit gladium(g) et cetera divident inter se equaliter, (h) ita quod senior dividet et iunior eliget. (i) Ubi etiam duo vel plures unam simul habuerint hereditatem, ibi unus alium ad divisionem iure valeat coartare.

Ubi vero pupilli annos pubertatis(j) nondum attigerunt, eorum senior agnatus(k) recipit arma bellica solus, et in eis est tutor puerorum quousque ad annos discretionis pervenerint; extunc ipsis reddere tenetur et insuper ipsorum omnia bona, nisi eis rationem fecerit, quo ea ad eorum usus seu profectum converterit, aut per spolium aut per apparens infortunium et absque sua voluntate(l) ammiserit. (m) Ipse etiam est vidue tutor, quousque maritum duxerit, qui sibi paris conditionis fuerit.

(a) Suppellectilia d[ebent] post mortem uxo[ri] defuncte heredi sue cederi JL[17] vertendo folium inveniuntur quod spectat a[d] supellectilem, *manus B* JL[31] de mortua uxore JL[36] Plebiscita civitatum alienabuntur in eo passo JL[38] Nota qual[iter] gerada spect[at] et quis illa n[...] accipit JL[43] (b) [*3 verba illegibilia*] herede JL[17] (c) *manicula*; Nota JL[37] T[...] JL[43] (d) De his vide infra in secundo libro fo. CCIIII de relicta [*Speculum Saxonum in: Commune incliti Poloniae Regni privilegium..., fol. CCIIII[v], capitulum: De relicta quod et qualia arma bellica dare tenetur propinquioribus mariti sui, SSp. I.22§4*] JL[15] (e) Arma bell[ica] sunt JL[17] (f) quod hec non habuerit nec post mortem viri receperit JL[17] (g) Imprimis ponere JL[17] (h) Ita quod senior dividet et iunior eliget JL[14] Senior super dividere debet, iunior vero eligere JL[17] (i) Heres unus alium ad divisionem potest compellere heredorum JL[17] (j) discretionis JL[34] (k) propinquior JL[17] (l) culpa JL[17] (m) Nota JL[31]

If the man's wife dies, her closest female relative on the distaff side receives the paraphernalia, she should make her husband his bed, as it was when his wife was alive, with the bed, pillows, sheets, blanket, and cover, also his chair with a headboards, on which he rests every day, his table with a tablecloth and towel. This female relative shall not receive any food supplies.[1]

[67] On military equipment, who inherits it. Also, on the guardian of children.

A wife shall hand over from the military equipment her husband's sword and his horse, that is, a superior warhorse with saddle and superior armour, which [the husband] had for the body of one man, when he died. Then she shall provide a war cot, which includes a bed and two pillows, two sheets, one table, two basins, and one towel. These are common military equipment. However, some people may include other items that do not belong. But whatever of these items the wife does not have, she may not be compelled to give, if she proves each item by oath by herself. If she could clearly prove, no man or woman can exonerate themselves with an oath. Where two or three are born into one set of military equipment, the elder keeps the sword for himself, and the remaining items are divided equally among them in such a way that the elder divides, and the younger chooses. Also, where two or more simultaneously have one inheritance, one may compel another by law to divide it.

If the sons are not yet of age, their elder agnate relative shall receive the military equipment for himself, and in those [items], he shall be the guardian of the children until they come of age; from that moment onward, he must return it to them along with all their goods, unless he can explain to them what he has allocated for their use and benefit, or has lost unwittingly through theft or misfortune. He shall also be the guardian of the widow until she marries a husband who is of a condition equal to hers.

---

1 Ger. *Musteile* (BJ 169, fol. 289^{r}). In monograph M. Mikuła, *Municipal Magdeburg Law* incorrectly: "compulsory portion" (p. 174). I would like to thank Professor Bernd Kannowski for this comment. Cf. Bernd Kannowski, "Mikuła, Maciej, Municipal Magdeburg Law (Ius municipale Magdeburgense) in Late Medieval Poland. A Study on the Evolution and Adaptation of Law (=Medieval Law and Its Practice 30). Brill, Leiden 2021. XX, 472 S., ISBN 978-90-04-45619-8", *Zeitschrift der Savigny Stiftung für Rechtsgeschichte: Germanistische Abteilung* 142/1 (2024), p. 451.

Post arma bellica, mulier vite provisionem recipere potest [(a)] et alia omnia, que ad suppellectilia [(b)] pertinent, [(c)] sicut sunt: omnes oves, anseres, auce, anete et ciste cum elevatis tecturis, omnia strata, pulvinaria, cussini, linthiamina mensalia, pelves, manuteria, lucibula, candelabra, semen lini et linum, et omnia muliebria [(d)] vestimenta, an[n]uli, brachialia et crinilia, psalteria et omnes libri, in quibus mulieres legere consueverunt, qui[(e)] ad Dei cultum pertinent, sedilia ac scrinia, capecia et vela, dorsalia vel tectoria, balneamina et omnia pepla, et alia ornamenta capitis muliebria, hec etiam sunt, que ad suppellectilia femine pertinent. Insuper adhuc diversa sunt clenodia[(f)], que ad suppellectilia pertinent, singulariter non nominata, sicut sunt seticula, pectines, forpices, specula. Sed tela non incisa, argentum et aurum non textum non pertinet ad mulieres, sed quicquid extra prenominata in rebus inventum fuerit, pertinet ad heredes[(g)]. Si aliquid ex iis obligatum fuerit circa vitam viri, qui mortuus est, redimet, si vult, ad quem de iure pertinent[(h)].

[(i)] Sacerdos dividit cum fratre, si non fuerit monachus. [(j)]

[*68*] De his, qui relligioni quam antehac susceperant abrenunciantes, possunt obtinere ius suum, et qui non. [(k)]

[(l)] Si puer infra annos pubertatis relligionem intraverit, bene potest ante annos, si vult, exire ac observare ius feodale et terrestre.

CLXXXVIII[r] Si autem vir, qui dum annos pubertatis implevit, | [(m)] intraverit relligionem, hic se a iure terrestri ac feodali alienavit, et sua feodalia vacant, quia scutum bellicum resignavit. Quod hoc possit protestari per hos, cum quibus similem vitam visus est suscepisse.

(a) Hec ad suppellectile[m] pertinent: grati domowe alias [*?*] sczebrzuchÿ JL[17] Diversae sunt in eo passu opiniones iuristarum JL[38] (b) [Ist]e sunt que ad supellectilia pertinent JL[31] (c) Gerada ceperit fusi alias przeslicze JL[30] (d) Ad vestimenta muliebria pertinentia sunt si ad eius suppellectilem JL[17] (e) *org.* que (f) insignia JL[34] (g) ad hereditatem heredi JL[17] (h) propinquus JL[17] (i) Sacerdos propinquis cum fratre et sorore si non monachus JL[17] sacerdos JL[23] (j) nam hic mortus est aliquando JL[17] (k) Quorum [*?*] is post annos pubertatis sue exierit JL[17] De monachis intrantes [*s*] claustra JL[36] (l) Casus ├simile┤ bonis Leopoli[ensis] per d[ominem] Casper Organski presbiterum [*?*] JL[17] (m) Ibi post professionem remanens; post si se exiret JL[17]

After [handing over] the military equipment, the wife may receive the dower and everything that comprises the paraphernalia, which are for example[1]: all sheep, geese, ducks, and chests with hinged lids, all bed covers, headboards, pillows, tablecloths, bowls, jugs, candlesticks, linen thread and canvas, and all women's garments, rings, bracelets, and headbands[2], psalters, and all books commonly read by women, which pertains to the worship of God, benches and chests, rugs and curtains or covers, bath towels and all outer garments, and other women's head ornaments—all these [goods] also belong to a women's paraphernalia. Moreover, there are various jewels that are part of paraphernalia, not individually named, as are [also] brushes, combs, tweezers, mirrors. However, uncut fabric, uncrafted silver and gold do not belong to women. But whatever beyond the afore-named is found among the items belongs to the heirs. If anything from these is pledged during the lifetime of the husband who has passed away, it shall be redeemed by the one to whom in belongs by right, if he so desires.

A priest divides [property] with his brother, if he is not a monk.

[*68*] On those who renounce the clerical estate which they had previously joined: [who of them] may receive their law, and who [may] not.

If an underage boy joins the clerical estate, he may rightfully, before coming of age, if he wishes, leave it and be subject to feudal and land law.

If a man who is already of age joins the clerical estate, he has renounced land and feudal law, and abandoned his fief, because he has abandoned his knightly shield. This may be declared by those with whom as he was seen to have led a similar life.

1 The Polish edition of 1581 by Paweł Szczerbic varied here from the Latin of 1506, see: Urszula Sowina, "Trousseau according to the Ius municipale Magdeburgense by Paweł Szczerbic and the position of a woman in the craftsman family at the beginning of the early modern time", *Kwartalnik Historii Kultury Materialnej* 68/4 (2020), p. 493–494.

2 In *The Saxon Mirror: A "Sachsenspiegel"* (p. 77) chaplets.

[*69*] De sententia et interlocutione. (a)

De qua sententia vir prius queritur, hec prius debet diffiniri(b). Actor et reus possunt colloquia habere pro qualibet causa tribus vicibus, quousque preco ipsos revocabit.

[*70*] De honestate iudicii. Item de prolocutore et principali.

In omni loco iuris est, ut iudex iudicet cum sententia scabinorum. (c) Aperte vir non loquatur coram iudicio, postquam prolocutorem habuerit, nisi si iudex eum requisierit. Si in verbo consentiat (d) sui prolocutoris seu procuratoris, tunc bene dicere potest, sic vel non sic, aut desuper petere colloquium (e).

[*71*] De pueris mortui fideiussoris. (f)

(g) Si vir pro pecunia aut pro debito fideiussor fuerit et idem vir moritur, sui pueri non tenentur pro eo solvere. (h) Si autem vir fideiussor fuerit pro pecunia, fideiussorem pecuniam solum solvere oportet, aut probare, quod pecunia sit integraliter persoluta.

[*72*] De vulneribus flaveis et fuscis baculo et fustibus illatis. (i)

(j) Si vir fustibus aut baculis percussus fuerit supra dorsum suum aut supra ventrem et verbera fuerint flavea aut fusca et inflata, et si desuper iudicem pro teste habuerit et homines iudicio dignos, qui hoc viderunt et

---

(a) De sententia et interlocutione JL[1] Sententia de quo prius quis conqueritur, prius diffiniri debet JL[17] Nota JL[31] (b) terminari JL[17] (c) Nota. Scabinorum est sentenciam invenire iudicis vero eam promulgare etc. JL[17] (d) Nota JL[31] (e) Collocuium alias n a poradii odstampicz JL[17] (f) De expedicione fideiusoris JL[36] (g) Filii fideiussoris mortui non tenentur ad solvendum debiti etc. JL[17] (h) Pueri fideiussionem patris non tenentur [*?*] solvere JL[19] observatur JL[38] (i) percussio vulneracio JL[23] Machatar, *manus C* JL[28] *cf.* Jan Chrzciciel Machatar of Vyškov (Id: 2016602), in: Corpus Academicum Cracoviense (CAC), URL: http://cac.historia.uj.edu.pl/osoba/2016602_Jan_Chrzciciel_Machatar_z_Vy%C5%A1kov (19.04.2024). (j) Verbera id manifestum verberis cum actor propior est reum vincere quam ipse iure evadere JL[17] Percussus si vulnera officio presentaverit propior ad litem probandam. JL[38]

[*69*] On the sentence and the interlocutory order.

The sentence which a man first requests, shall be given first. The plaintiff and the defendant may have consultations on every case three times, until the court bailiff[1] calls them back.

[*70*] On the dignity of the court. Likewise, on the spokesman and the principal.

In every place the law demands that a judge should judge with the sentence of jurors. A man may not address the court directly when he has a spokesman, unless the judge requires it of him. If he agrees to the word of his spokesman, that is, proctor, then he may rightfully speak, either yes or no, or demand a consultation [with the spokesman] in the matter.

[*71*] On the children of a deceased surety.

If a man was a surety for money or for a debt and died, his children shall not be obliged to pay for him. If, on the other hand, the man was a surety for money, the surety shall pay the money himself or prove that the money has been paid in full.

[*72*] On bruises and dark wounds inflicted by a stick or rod.

If a man is beaten on his back or abdomen with sticks or rods, and the wounds are bruised or darkened[2] and swollen, and if he has as witnesses the judge and people worthy of [presence in] a court who saw and heard it,

1 See Art. 6, footnote.

2 Black and blue injuries.

audierunt, ipse(a) est duellum propior (b) super eum acquirere, quam ille ipsum evadere(c) possit(d) suo iure.

Si autem super caput aut brachia percussus fuerit, quod aliter ostendi(e) (f) non possit, illi homines melius evadere possunt(g), quam ipse super eos protestari seu probare possit suo iure. (h) Si autem fatentur, quivis ammittit emendam et iudex acquirit suam penam. Si vero verbera mortalia fuerint, respondere tenentur cum duello, qui pro eodem iudicialiter fuerint impulsati(i). Si autem mortalia non fuerint, respondebit unus cum duello et alii respondebunt absque duello, quia ipsi evadunt suo iuramento.

[*73*] De hereditate lege caduca ad regiam maiestatem devolvenda. (j)

Si hereditas absque successoribus (k) relinquitur, ita quod nullus se trahat ad eadem infra annum et diem, hoc pertinet ad regiam maiestatem. (l)

CLXXXVIII^v

[*74*] | (m) De viro occiso, pro quo pueris superstitibus actio prohibetur.

(n) Si vir occisus fuerit, qui pueros tres vel plures habuerit, et vir unus pro eo iudicialiter impulsatus fuerit et evaserit, ut ius dictaverit, sibique super eandem querimoniam vera satisdatio facta fuerit, non debet in posterum ab iis pueris pro eodem homicidio infestari. (o)

[*75*] De iuramentis absque pena et de impedimento iurantis.

Si vir alteri iurare debet coram iudicio digne et sine pena, potest bene supraponere et deponere absque licentia iudicis, per hoc nihil ammittit.

(p) Si etiam iuramenta promissa venerint super diem ligatum et feriatum, hec iudex protrahere potest super alium diem iudicialem, qui venerit extra dies ligatos(q).

(a) *signum indefinitum* JL[17] (b) Nota. byli szdrowego pobya ranÿ szdrow JL[17] (c) negare JL[17] (d) iurari JL[17] (e) probari JL[17] (f) Nota JL[31] (g) iurare iura[men]to [*?*] JL[17] (h) Emenda intelligitur poena. JL[38] Emenda triginta solidorum et non dare nisi actori JL[44] (i) con[pulsati] JL[17] (j) Ius caducum JL[1] Lex caduca her[...] JL[17] (k) heredibus JL[17] (l) Mortuus sine propinquis bona eius regi devolvuntur post diem et annum JL[17] (m) Non placetur pro homicidio debeant agere testem unum JL[36] (n) [accu]set ab homicidio iure evadens non debet eo impeti JL[17] (o) Excepto si pueri sint minorennes XII JL[38] (p) Iure iuramenta potest iudex differere JL[17] No[ta] JL[31] (q) prohibitos JL[17]

he is closer to obtaining a duel against the perpetrator than the perpetrator is to releasing himself with his rights.

If the beating is on the head or shoulders, which cannot be proven otherwise, the perpetrators are closer to releasing themselves than the victim is to protesting or asserting his rights against them. If they confess, each shall pay compensation, and the judge shall receive his fine. If the wounds are fatal, those who are judicially compelled to do this, are bound to answer with duel. If they are not fatal, one shall stand trial by combat and the others shall stand trial without combat, as they shall exonerate themselves with an oath.

[*73*] On an inheritance going to the royal majesty by right of escheat.

If an inheritance remains without heirs, such that no one claims it within a year and a day, it belongs to the royal majesty.

[*74*] On a killed man, in the case of whom [action] is forbidden to the surviving children.

If a man is killed, leaving behind three or more children, and one man is accused of this in court and is cleared as the law demands, and a just surety[1] has been provided against this action, he shall not be disturbed in the future over this murder by those children.

[*75*] On oaths without a judicial fine, and [on] the impediment of the swearer.

If a man is to swear to another in court, honourably and without fine, he should rightfully present and express [the oath] without the judge's permission, thereby losing nothing.

However, if the promised oaths were to be sworn on a holiday or feast day, the judge may postpone them to another court day that falls outside holidays.

1 See Art. 38, footnote.

Etiamsi vir balbutiens vel alter, seu testis aliquis fuerit impeditus, ita quod imperfecte suum dixerit iuramentum, ille seipsum emendare valeat, quotiens impeditur et manebit de huiusmodi melioratione sine damno.

[*76*] De repetitione penarum per iudicem.

Quando iudex extorquet suam penam, ulterius nec aliquam aliam super hanc penam potest extorquere. Et si vir bona iudicialiter alloquitur, ut iuris est, aut hereditatem, pro eo non indiget iudici quicquam dare, cum ipse iustitiam tenetur iuvare. Etsi homo suam querelam tenere promiserit, hoc autem interim per bonum pacis medio tempore concordatum fuerit, pro eo non plus ammittit, quam iudex acquirat suam penam.

[*77*] De invita querela ad quam nemo potest coartari.

(a) Si vir vulneratus aut trucidatus fuerit et conqueri noluerit, iudex ipsum nec ad aliquam querimoniam compellere potest ultra suam voluntatem. (b)

[*78*] De bonis proscripti aut ad mortem sententiati.

(c) Si vir proscriptus(d) aut ad sententiam mortis iudicatus seu condemnatus fuerit, nullus sua bona habet recipere, quam sui heredes veri. (e)

[*79*] De bonis mortui ad successores devolvendis. (f)

CLXXXIX[r] (g) Si vir moritur, qui habet pueros et bona habuerit nulli donata, pueri sui sibi succedunt, si equales (h) sibi fuerint in natura (i). Si autem ex his(j)

(a) Quilibet debet concordari JL[36] Iudex in iuramentum ad conquerendum corporalis non potest JL[17] (b) nam sibimet iniuria sit si invite JL[17] (c) Bona proscripti vel sententia [con]demnavit ad heredes pertinent JL[17] (d) bannitus JL[34] (e) nisi id ob crimen lese maiestatis sit factum JL[17] Excepto si sit infamis in certis causis JL[38] (f) Scitu dignum si modo practicatur summum videtur practicanti JL[1] (g) Bona post pueros super matrem heredet JL[1] vide S.S. iure mun[i]cipali ar. LXIII de b[o]nis ex admortuis adventis post mortem illius cui cedunt [*Jaskier Mikołaj, Iuris Municipalis..., articulus LXIII, fol. XLVI[v]*] JL[1] *manicula* JL[13] de bonis mortui JL[23] (h) id est liberum JL[17] (i) Per naturam intellige legitimitatem JL[38] (j) *org.* hic

Even if a man stutters, or another, that is, some witness, is impeded, so that he utters his oath imperfectly, he is to correct himselves as many times as he encounters the impediment, and he shall suffer no harm due to such correction.

[*76*] On the judge's demand of fines.

When a judge compels payment of his fine, he may not impose any more or any other fine beyond it. If a man acquires goods or inheritance in court, in accordance with the law, he is not obligated to give anything to the judge for it, as the judge is bound to administer justice.

Even if someone promises to pursue his complaint, and a settlement has been reached for the sake of peace in the meantime, he shall not lose for that more than what the judge shall gain as his fine.

[*77*] On an unwanted complaint, to which no one can be compelled.

If a man has been injured or maimed and does not wish to file a complaint, the judge may not force him to file any complaint beyond his will.

[*78*] On the goods of someone who has been outlawed or sentenced to death.

If a man is outlawed or sentenced to death, no one shall receive his goods except his rightful heirs.

[*79*] On the devolution of the goods of the deceased to his successors.

If a man dies, leaving behind children and goods, not given to anyone else, his children shall succeed to them, if they are of equal status to him. If one

pueris unus decesserit, mater sibi in parte sua succedit. (a) Et mater (b) cum his bonis nihil facere potest absque suorum heredum consensu aut voluntate. (c) Si vero omnes pueri, patre mortuo, moriuntur, extunc bona sua heredant super suam matrem, et postea, si mater decesserit ab hac luce, tunc eadem omnia bona heredant super mulieris proximiores heredes, sive sint masculi, sive femine, ex paterna et materna consanguineitate. (d) Etiam mulier non potest talem hereditatem vendere nec donare, sed cum rebus mobilibus potest facere quicquid vult. (e) Sed cum hereditate quicunque facere non potest absque consensu heredum.

[*80*] De puero (f) duodecim annorum, qui possit sibi tutorem eligere et pro se in iudicio respondere. (g)

(h) Quando puer est duodecim annorum, tunc potest eligere pro sua voluntate quem voluerit pro tutore. Et qui suus fuerit tutor, hic matri rationem facere habet et adolescenti, quid cum bonis factum fuerit. (i) Cum etiam puer fuerit duodecim annorum, is mundiburdius(j) alias sui potens est factus; et potest in eo iudicium perpetrari et etiam bona sua a se sine tutore alienare. Sed innatam hereditatem et proprium debet dare cum consensu heredum. Etiam iste puer de iure ad responsionem valeat coartari seu compelli.

[*81*] De obiectione illibertatis et probatione libertatis. (k)

Si vir aliquem alloquitur, quod suus sit illiber, si potest suam libertatem protestari et probare, propior est evadere, ⟨De quo supra folio XVI. C.

(a) Nisi reformationem [*?*] habeat in eis JL[38] (b) Mater pueris succedit post mortem in bona p[uerorum], ad quam iure divolvunt JL[17] (c) Nota pro ultra JL[31] observatur JL[38] Mo[...] soror[...] fa[...] JL[43] (d) Impotentia donatoris et venditoris hereditatis a muliere JL[15] Mater cum bonis mobi[libus] ad eam devolutis ag[ere] quidquid vult sed immobilia sine consensu heredum non potest alienare JL[17] (e) bonis immobilibus JL[17] (f) masculo JL[17] (g) *2 maniculae* JL[9] (h) An puer XII annorum possit cum rebus suis disponere eciam et mu[ndiburdium] eligere vide Raymundus huic iuri contraretur d[um] annis perficere puberum [*Raimundi Summa legum brevis, levis et utilis..., in: Commune incliti Poloniae regni privilegium..., folio IIII[v], articulus:* Conditio hominum generalis, Articulus XXI*; cf. Die Summa..., ed. Alexander Gál, p. 158*] JL[17] Nota JL[31] (i) mundiburdius, puer JL[38] (j) mundiburgius [*s*] JL[18] (k) *manicula* JL[1] *manicula* JL[23]

of these children dies, the mother shall succeed to the child's share. And, the mother may not do anything with these without the consent and will of their heirs. If all the children die after the father's death, then his goods shall pass as inheritance upon their mother. And afterwards, if the mother passes away, then all the goods shall pass as inheritance upon the closest heirs of the mother, whether they are male or female, from both the paternal and maternal lines. In addition, the wife may not sell or give away this inheritance although she may do anything she wants with the movables. However, she may not do anything with the inheritance without the consent of the heirs.

[*80*] On a twelve-year-old child[1] who can choose a guardian for themselves, and represent themselves in court.

When a child reaches the age of twelve, they may choose at their own discretion whomever they wish as their guardian. Whoever becomes the guardian shall provide an account to the mother and to the adolescent child of what has been done with the goods. Also, when the child reaches the age of twelve, the guardian, or assistant to the child, shall be appointed, and legal proceedings may be conducted on behalf of the child, and the child's goods may be alienated without a guardian. However, the innate inheritance and property must be transferred with the consent of the heirs. In addition, such a child may by law be coerced or compelled to respond [to a complaint in court].

[*81*] On the accusation of unfreedom and proving freedom.

If a man brings an action against another in court [claiming] that he is his bondman[2], if [the defendant] can assert and prove his freedom, he shall

1 Ger. *Kint* (BJ 169, fol. 295^{r}).

2 Ger. *Eigen* (BJ 169, fol. 295^{r}). Cf. *The Saxon Mirror: A "Sachsenspiegel"*, p. 182.

Nobilitatis⟩[1] quam ille ipsum vincere possit. [a] Libertatem suam vir probare potest cum tribus cognatis et tribus agnatis, [b] sic metseptimus esse debet, sive sint viri sive femine.

[c] Etiam hoc scire quilibet legens debet, quod quando scribitur agnatus, significat proximos ex par[t]e patris et ex parte gladii. Sed ubi scribitur cognatus, ex parte matris et fusi consanguineos significat. [d]

[82] De servo bona domini sui perludentis seu alienantis.

Si servus bona domini perluserit taxillis, aut obligat aut vendit, dominus CLXXXIX[v] bene potest arrestare denuo iure, ut se ad ea bona [e] | trahat, ut iuris sit. Si autem propria bona deluserit [f] aut quocunque modo a se alienaverit sua voluntate, dominus super ea bene [s] alloqui potest, quia servo solvere non tenetur, et sic domino pro bonis servi non est licitum respondere. [g] Si autem servo suus equus vel alia bona furtive aut spoliando recepta fuerint absque servi culpa in domini servicio, hoc oportet dominum solvere servo, et pro eo oportet dominum respondere, si super eum queruletur.

[83] De bonis in deposito [h] alicui commissis [i].

[j] Quicunque alteri bona sua dederit ad servandum aut in deposito posuerit, si sibi subtracta fueri[n]t, aut spoliatus eis fuerit, aut combusta, vel si mortuum fuerit, si equus vel pecora fuerint, non debet aliquod damnum pro eis sustinere, si presumit iurare, quod absque sua culpa ammissum fuerit. Sed quod viro concessum aut obligatum fuerit, hoc in destructum

---

[a] Propior est quis libertatem suam probare quam co[ntra] JL[17] [b] Agnati, cognati qui sunt JL[17] [c] De quo infra fol. 199 [*Speculum Saxonum in: Commune incliti Poloniae Regni privilegium, fol. CXCIX[v], articulus* De differentia agnationis et cognationis*; SSp. III.15§4*] JL[1] Agnatus Cognatus JL[18] Agnatus et cognatus quis sit, *manus D* JL[36] Agnatus respectu patris proximiores [s] Cognatus respectu matris JL[38] [d] Z c z t e r y b a b y m o g ą probare nobilitatem JL[1] [e] Servus non potest domini bona perludere vel alienare JL[17] [f] Venditionem aut donationem JL[17] [g] [S]i equus servo mortuus [ve]l furatus in servicio [domi]ni fuerit quod iuris JL[17] Certum est si in operis servitio aliquid perdit JL[38] [h] Bona in depositum comissa alieni in ff. infra de eodem fol. 227 [*Speculum Saxonum in: Commune incliti Poloniae Regni privilegium…, fol. CCXXVII[r], capitulum:* De rebus per venditorem et dantem iterum repetendis, *SSp. III.6*] JL[1] depositis; si fideiussus JL[17] [i] vel concessis JL[17] [j] *manicula* JL[9] Res deposita si casum amissa vel corrupta sit JL[17] […]er continetur quomodo de[p]ositum est re[sti]tuendum JL[31]

---

1 *Infra Commune incliti…, articulus in Statutis Casimiri Magni:* De nobilitate inculpata.

be closer to exonerating himself than [the plaintiff] is to prevailing against him. A man can prove his freedom with three relatives on the paternal side and three on the maternal side, making a total of six persons, whether they are men or women.

Also, everyone should know this when reading: when "agnate" is written, it refers to the closest relatives on the father's and paternal side. But when "cognate" is written, it refers to relatives on the mother's side, and refers to those relatives on the distaff side.

[*82*] On the servant who loses or alienates of his master's goods.

If a servant loses his master's goods in a game of dice, pawns it, or sells it, the master may rightfully attach[1] it in order to claim it, in accordance with the law. However, if the servant loses his own goods or alienates them in whatever way, by his will, the master may [*s*] rightfully assert his claims on this property, as he is not obligated to pay the servant, and so it is not appropriate for the master to be responsible for the servant's goods. However, if the servant loses, through no fault of his own, his horse or other goods as a result of theft or robbery while in the service of his master, the master ought to compesate the servant for this, and he ought to be responsible for this, if [the servant] brings a complaint against him.

[*83*] About goods deposited with someone.

Whoever gives his goods to another for safekeeping or deposits them, if they are taken from him [i.e. the depositary], stolen, burned, or if they die, in the case of horses or cattle, depositary shall not suffer any loss, if he swears that the loss occurred through no fault of his own. However, whatever was entrusted or pawned to a man must be returned intact or paid for

1 Cf. *The Saxon Mirror: A "Sachsenspiegel"*, p. 181.

reddere tenetur aut secundum suum valorem solvere. [(a)] Si autem moritur equus aut vel pecus infra obligationem absque illius culpa, cui obligatum fuerat, si hoc probaverit, et si iuramentum super eo prestare presumpserit, quod sine sua culpa decesserit, non solvit, sed suam recompensam ammittit, in qua sibi fuerat obligatum.

[*84*] De debito in ludo taxillorum contracto. [(b)]

Si aliquis conqueritur super aliquem pro debito aut pecunia ludo aut taxillis acquisita et detasserata, pro eo sibi non habet respondere. [(c)] Si aliquis etiam conqueritur super alium pro cibariis preparatis, hic propior est obtinere iuramento, quam ille ipsum evadere possit suo iuramento.

[*85*] De cassatione inscriptionis iudicialiter facte.

Qui se extraxerit a descriptione, etsi solutus iudicatus fuerit, iudex tamen in eo obtinet suam penam. Et si sibi iudex fateri voluerit [*s*], ipse eum potest deponere per unum, qui eodem interfuit iudicio, quia nec captivus apparuit, nec proclamatus. Si autem iudex ipsum in posterum obiurare voluerit, ipsum in nullo ulterius obiurare potest, quam ad suam penam, si super eo testes habuerit, quod se extra descriptionem obiuravit.

(a) Res concessa si amissa sit quod iuris JL[17] Nota, *manus B* JL[31] (b) *manicula* JL[23] (c) Pro cibariis propior actor probare quam cittatus evictore JL[38]

according to its value. If, however, a horse or another beast dies while held in pledge with no fault of the one to whom it was pawned, if proves this and swears an oath that it died with no fault of his own, he shall not pay, but forfeit his compensation for which it was pawned.

[*84*] On a debt incurred by the game of dice.

If someone brings a complaint against another for a debt or money acquired through gambling with dice or cards, for that, [the debtor] does not have to respond. Likewise, if someone complains against another for the food prepared, [the plaintiff] is closer to obtaining a judgment by oath than [the defendant] could be to exonerating themselves with his own oath.

[*85*] On judicial erasure of an entry from court records.[1]

Whoever removes an entry from court records[2], even though [he is] released through judgment, the judge nevertheless shall obtain his fine from him. And if the judge [does not][3] do this, he may swear [an oath] through the one who was present in the same court, because he did not appear either as a captive or as a defendant. However, should the judge want to demand [anything] from him in the future, he may not obligate him to anything more than to [pay] his fine, if he has witnesses that he has already sworn an oath on the entry in court records.[4]

---

1 The author of the rubrica did not understand the original meaning of the provision; he used *inscriptio* (an entry in court records) as a synonym of *descriptio*. Yet the right meaning of descriptio should be *proscriptio* (this term exists expressis verbis in W^2, C^2, with a failure *prescriptio* in W^1). In the German text (manuscript of Jagiellonian Library, Shelfmark 169, fol. 295^v) the term used is *Vorvestung*—limited outlawry (cf. "Limited, or regional, outlawry because it was limited to the jurisdiction of the specific court that outlawed a person.", in: *The Saxon Mirror: A "Sachsenspiegel"*, p. 194). This is an example of the evolution of meaning through the translation of a legal provision and its adaptation to local needs.

2 Alternative translation (close to the German wording and to W^1, W^2, C^2): "Whoever release himself from limited outlawry."

3 A failure—positive sentence—in a few Latin texts (S^4, S^5, S^{10}, K^5, C^2), negative sentence in German text (a manuscript of Jagiellonian Library, Shelfmark 169, fol. 295^v) and other Latin texts.

4 Alternative translation (close to the German wording and to W^1, W^2, C^2): "limited outlawry".

[*86*] De salario deservito per dominum servo suo eodem die solvendo.

Si servus deservitum precium super suum dominum (a) obiurgaverit coram
cxc[r] iudicio, pro eo dominus ullam iudici demeretur penam et | dominus servo hoc tenetur eodem die solvere. (b)

[*87*] De debitorum probatione. (c)

Si vir conqueritur super alterum pro suo debito cum testibus coram iudicio, hoc bene potest obtinere cum viris fidedignis, (d) qui in suo iure reprobari non possunt. Ita tamen, si ille dixerit se innocentem. (e) Si autem reus hoc debitum dixerit se persolvisse, (f) extunc impedit sibi suum testimonium. Hoc bene probare potest cum viris fidedignis mettertius tacto sacramento.

[*88*] De satisdatione facienda.

Si super virum conquestum fuerit et satisdationem (g) pecierit, alter sibi eam denegare non potest, quin eam sibi faciat (h), si ipsum per sententiam ad hoc compulerit. Si autem satisdationem fecerit sibi, ad suum ius non nocet, nec iste plus lucratur cum satisdatione, qui eam petit, nisi quod nullus alter amicorum suorum ipsum amodo pro hac causa valeat impedire.

(i) Satisdatione facta nullus suam querelam meliorare (j) potest. (k)

[*89*] De querelis in factis manifestis et probatione earum.

Omnis querela, que ad iudicium pro capitali crimine in facto manifesto deducta fuerit, debet conqueri cum clamore propter factum manifestum, quod ostendi debet.

(a) conquesta fuerit JL[17] (b) Si iuramento id probaverit, ius negavit JL[17] (c) debitorum probatione JL[1] (d) Nota JL[17] (e) Si cittatus agat se solvisse debitum propior est actor comprobare 2 testibus si allegat se persolvisse. JL[38] (f) Qualiter quis debitum solutum probari debet JL[17] (g) alias gwar scilicet regendo debitum pellitur usque ad unum litem JL[17] (h) actor; id est gwiiarzy JL[17] (i) effectus sa[tis]dacionis JL[31] (j) nec audere JL[17] (k) Effectus satisdacionis JL[17] Nota, *manus B* JL[31]

[*86*] On earned wages to be paid by the master to the servant on the same day.

If a servant demands his earned wages from his master in court, for that the judge shall not impose any fine on the master, and the master must pay the servant on the same day.

[*87*] On proving debts.

If a man brings a complaint in court against another for his debt with witnesses, he shall rightfully obtain [a sentence] with trustworthy men who may not be reproached in their right; however, this is the case, if the defendant says that he is innocent. However, if the defendant says that he has paid the debt, then his testimony stands in the way of the plaintiff; the defendant may rightfully prove this with two trustworthy men by swearing an oath on the relics.

[*88*] About providing surety.

If a complaint has been filed against a man and he demands surety[1], the other party cannot refuse him; rather, he [the plaintiff] shall provide it, if it is imposed on him by a sentence. However, if the defendant provides surety, it does not harm his right, nor does the one who demands it gain more from the surety, except that no one else among his relatives may henceforth hinder [the plaintiff] in this matter.

Once surety has been provided, no one may correct their complaint.

[*89*] On complaints [in cases] of red-handed deeds and their proof.

Any complaint brought to court about a red-handed deed punishable by death should be brought with an outcry because of the red-handed deed, which should be demostrated.

1 See Art. 38, footnote.

Manifestum [a] factum ibi est, ubi[b] vir cum furto[c] aut preda captivus[d] ad iudicium deductus fuerit cum clamore.

Etiam factum manifestum est ibi, ubi apud unum gladius aut cultellus aut sicca, aut alia defendicula in [e] manu sua [f] deprehensa fuerint, cum quibus pacem violavit, aut si in fuga [g] facti captus fuerit et captivus ad iudicium ductus fuerit cum clamore. Hunc actor metseptimus vincere debet circa ius pacis, si manifestum[h] factum cum reo ad iudicium deductum fuerit.

[*90*] De actione debitorum in iudicio burgrabii.

In iudicio burgrabii Maÿdemburgensis potest vir pro debito bene querulari, actorem autem oportet ab uno iudicio burgrabii ad aliud iudicium suam sequi querelam, ita quod super suo adversario denunciet.

Si autem super virum querimonia cum [i] testimonio facta fuerit in eodem iudicio pro debito, et si dicit, quod persolverit, hoc potius probabit per homines fidedignos [j], quam ille ipsum vincere possit, quod facere potest [k] incontinenti, si vult, aut per sex ebdomadas in iudicio sculteti. Si autem vir iuramentum unica manu [l] prestare debet, hoc in eodem iudicio facere oportet.

[*91*] De iudicio iudicis et loco iudicandi ac solutione recompense et emende.

CXC^v [m] Iudex debet iudicium exercere et de eo temptare quottidie [n] in vero loco iudiciali, excepto quod vir absque testibus voluerit[o] querulari, hoc ubilibet potest iudicare sine mora. Iudex etiam iudicium coordinare debet, quando iudicare debet, et non actor nec reus.

[p] Recompensa et emenda et pena iudicis solvi debent ad diem, ut fuerit diffinita, cum talibus denariis, prout tunc in eodem iudicio sunt transeuntes et daturi, recompensam et emendam actori, iudici vero penam.

(a) factum manifestum*;* Et qualiter probandum est vel eciam qualiter convincendum JL[17] Crimen manifestum quomodo intelligitur. JL[38] (b) fur JL[17] (c) s z l y c z e m JL[17] (d) vel violencia JL[17] (e) inventa [*?*] JL[17] (f) s z l y c z e m JL[17] (g) quomodo facit etc. JL[17] (h) l i c z e JL[17] (i) Nota quilibet probuisse debitum solutum JL[17] (j) mettertius JL[17] (k) g d y w s a n d z y e n y e c h c z e b y c z JL[17] (l) metsolus JL[17] (m) *manicula* JL[1] Quando iudex extra loco iudicii iudicare potest JL[17] (n) ubi opus fuerit, *manus B* JL[17] (o) *org.* noluerit (p) Recompensa actori et pena iudici quomodo debet solvi JL[17]

A red-handed deed is when a man is apprehended with a stolen thing or loot and is brought to court with an outcry.

Similarly, a red-handed deed occurs when a sword, knife, dagger, or other weapon that violates the peace is taken from a man's hand, or if he is captured while fleeing and brought to court with an outcry. The plaintiff should prevail over such a person with six oath helpers for the sake of the law of the peace, if the accused was brought to court having been caught red-handed.

[*90*] On the action for debt in the burgrave's court.

In the court of the burgrave of Magdeburg, a man may rightfully file a complaint for debt. The plaintiff should pursue his claim from one court of the burgrave to another court in such a way that he declares against his opponent.

However, if a suit with testimony about the debt is brought against the man in the same court, and if he says he has paid, he shall prove it sooner with trustworthy persons than the plaintiff can defeat him. He can do this immediately, if he wishes, or within six weeks in the court of the *scultetus*. And if the man ought to declare on oath by a single hand [i.e., by himself], he should do so in the same court.

[*91*] On the court of judge, and the place of judgment, and the payment of wergeld and the compensation.

The judge shall hold court, and ensure this daily, at the appropriate place of judgment, except when a man wishes to bring a suit without witnesses, in which case he may hold court wherever he deems fit without delay.

The judge shall also set the date for the court session, not the plaintiff or the defendant.

The wergeld, compensation, and judge's fine should be paid by [that] day, as may be determined, in the currency commonly used and provided in that judicial district, the wergeld and compensation to the plaintiff, and the fine to the judge.

[92] De publicatione et infiscatione bonorum occasione debiti.

(a) Si vero aliqua bona fuerint publicata seu fiscata, sive predicta bona possidet ille, qui hoc deduxerit in fiscationem cum fiscatione tribus diebus et tribus noctibus. (b) Insuper ibidem debet comedere et bibere, simul et dormire cum fiscatione. (c) Deinde debet coram iudicio pronunciare diebus tribus, tribus vicibus semper ad duas ebdomadas, et ad quartum iudicium iudex sibi pacem desuper debet formare, et sibi ap[p]ropriare per sententiam scabinorum. Et tunc bene potest vendere eadem bona cum scitu hominum probum. (d) Si autem aliquid ultra suum debitum superfuerit, hoc illi debet reddere, cuius fuit hereditas. Sed si defecerit, extunc agat ulterius repetendo id, quod deficit.

[93] De arrestatione quorumvis bonorum et equorum. (e)

Si vir alloquitur aliqua bona, ut pannos aut quicquam suarum rerum fuerit, quod sibi subtractum aut raptum fuerit, ad hoc se unica manu trahere debet et iurare debet tacto sacramento, quod tunc suum fuit et nunc suum sit, cum sibi subtractum seu raptum fuerat.

Si autem equus fuerit, quem vir alloquitur, quod sibi subtractus aut eo spoliatus sit, ad hoc se trahere debet: cum dextro suo pede calcare (f) debet equum supra suum pedem anteriorem sinistrum, et sinistra manu equum per dextram aurem capere, et petere debet reliquias et prolocutorem. Et iurabit supra caput equi tacto sacramento, quod tunc suus fuerit et nunc suus sit, cum sibi subtractus aut eo depredatus fuerit. Extunc ille se trahere debet ad suum tutorem seu venditorem et iurare debet tacto sacramento, quod equum trahat ad verum tutorem, ad quem ille ipsum iure sequi debet, non autem ultra Mare Aquilonis. Si autem dixerit, quod equum emerit in foro libero et venditorem habere non possit, extunc equum suum ammittet et argentum suum, quod pro eo dedit, et non perdet pro eo aliquam penam.

(a) De bonis pro debito acquirendis JL[12] *manicula* JL[14] Infiscacio bonorum JL[23] (b) Nota JL[31] (c) observatur JL[38] (d) tum JL[31] (e) Arestatio bonorum et equi etc. JL[1] (f) Ceremonia ista abolenda JL[38]

[92] On the confiscation of goods due to debts.

If, indeed, any goods are confiscated, the said goods shall be possessed by the person who has brought about the confiscation for three days and three nights. Moreover, during that time, he should eat, drink, and sleep there as part of the confiscation. Next, before the court, three days shall be announced, three court sessions always a fortnight apart, and at the fourth session, the judge should ensure him a peace [regarding] the above, and place him in ownership through a sentence of the jurors. Then he may rightfully sell the goods with the knowledge of worthy people. If there is anything left [from the sale] after paying off his debt, he shall return it to whoever owned the inheritance. But if there is a shortfall, then he shall continue [the proceedings] to recover the missing amount.

[93] On the seizure of any kind of goods and horses.

If a man brings a claim for any goods like cloth or any of his belongings because they were taken or forcibly seized from him, he shall proceed with his own oath and swear on the relics that they were his at that time, and are his now, even though they were taken, or forcibly seized, from him.

If it is a horse for which a man brings a claim, that it was taken or pillaged from him, he should proceed as follows: he should touch the horse with his right foot above its hind left hoof and grab the horse by the right ear with his left hand, and ask for relics and a spokesman. And he shall swear on the relics over the head of the horse that it was his then, and is his now, when it was taken from him, or when he was deprived of it. Next, the possessor shall turn to his guardian or seller, and swear on the relics that he will bring the horse to the true guardian whom he himself should follow according to the law, but not overseas. If he says that he bought the horse in a free market[place] and cannot identify the seller, then he shall lose his horse and the silver he gave for it, without incurring any penalty for it.

[*94*] De querimonia pro debito post mortuam manum. (a)

cxci[r] (b) Si vir conqueritur super virum pro pecunia post mortuam manum (c), et ipsum de hoc, ut iuris est, voluerit informare, (d) hoc facere potest unica manu tacto sacramento, (e) et hoc si ille sibi voluerit consentire. (f) Si autem ille dixerit, super quem querimonia fuerit prolata, se de debito esse ignorantem, aut quod ille persolverit ex parte, cuius fuerit inculpatus, hoc oportet iurare metseptimus tacto sacramento. (g) Si autem dixerit, quod solus illi debitum hoc persolvisset, hoc iurare debet(h) mettertius tacto sacramento cum hominibus fidedignis.

[*95*] De antequerelis.

(i) Si vir cum scitu contra alium ad iustitiam se exhibuerit, et alter noluerit et spreverit, et vulneret alium non querulando absque iure, et ille vulneratus veniet ad defensionem et vulneret illum mutuo, et hic, qui primo vulneraverit suum adversarium, prius ad iudicium veniet et conqueratur, (j) tandem alter, in quo pax sit violata, etiam postea veniet circa lucem diei et dicat, quod initium illius fuerit et non suum. Si hoc, ut iuris est, metseptimus protestabitur cum probis hominibus, qui viderunt et audierunt, vel qui presentes fuerunt, ipse acquirit primam querelam.

[*96*] De filio, quem pater potest proprio iuramento iudicio eximere.

Vir potest filium suum unica manu eximere, qui est in pane suo non uxoratus, tacto(k) sacramento sic, quod filius suus reus non sit. Si autem pater

(a) Advertem JL[8] (b) *manicula;* Debitum post mortuam manum quomodo probare JL[1] Simile folio 193 [*Ius municipale Magdeburgense infra Commune incliti…, fol.* cxciii[v], *articulus 116 in eadem editio*] JL[3] (c) Hic habere actoribus nusquam in iure Magdeburgensi JL[34] (d) Nota JL[17] (e) De debito p[ost] mortuam ma[num] se reus confirm[at] unica man[u] [*unum verbum difficile*] JL[42] (f) Debitum solutum qualiter quis probar[i] et post mortuam manum qualiter JL[17] Cittatus pro debito post de mortuam manum propior evadere testibus quam pacto lege JL[38] (g) si pars secunda dicit ⊢pre⊣ persolvisset, iuramentum metseptimus, si solus solv[it] mettertius iurabit JL[42] (h) actor JL[4] Actor proponit post mortuam m[a]num, quod pater ignoratur [*?*] decem marcas; reus si velit negare [*?*], dum constat alias czeka [*?*], t[unc] actor eodem judicio metseptimus jura[t], quia, qui vult nunciare, debet esse [confir]matus. JL[4] (i) De duobus se vulneratis quis eorum actor sit JL[17] (j) Si mutuo sese vulnerent, qui dedit eorum litis casum, de ratione est. JL[38] (k) *org.* facto

[*94*] On a complaint about a dead man's debt.

If a man complains against another man about a deceased man's debt, and in this, as it is in the law, he would like to instruct him, he may do so by his own oath on the relics, and this is the case if the [relative of the deceased] is willing to grant him [the debt]. If, however, the one who is the subject of the complaint says that he knows nothing about the debt, or that he has paid the portion for which he is being sued, this ought to be proven by an oath on the relics with six oath helpers. If he says that he himself has paid the debt to him, then it must be proven by an oath on the relics with two trustworthy persons.

[*95*] On priority in filing a complaint.

If a man deliberately seeks justice against another and the latter refuses and rejects the demand, and injures the man unlawfully without filing a complaint, and the injured man begins to defend himself and injures the first man in return, and the one who first injures his opponent shall come first to court and lodge a complaint [about the injuries], eventually, the second man, whose peace was violated, shall also arrive later in the light of day and declare that the beginning was caused by the other man, not by him. If, as it is in the law, he declares this with six worthy persons who saw and heard, or who were present, this man shall acquire the first complaint.

[*96*] On the son whom the father can exonerate with his own oath in court.

A man may clear his unmarried son who is under his dependent with his own oath on the relics, so that his son shall not be a defendant. However,

et filius ambo pro uno facto fuerint impulsati, extunc patrem oportet se primo de facto veridice expurgare.

[*97*] De mulieris manifesto facto utpote homicidio.

Si femina fuerit deprehensa in facto manifesto pro homicidio aut vulneribus duellaribus seu duello dignis, hanc vir propior est vincere metseptimus cum hominibus fidedignis, quam innocens fieri possit. Extunc iudicium ipsam pati oportet. (a) Si autem vir querulatur pro homicidio aut vulneribus super feminam, quod eodem die factum sit aut visum, et si femina cautionem fideiussoriam fecerit supra ius, de quo femina propior est evadere metseptima cum hominibus fidedignis, quam aliquis ea vincere possit. (b) Si autem mulier inculpatur de querimoniis pernoctatis, hoc propior est evadere femina unica manu tacto sacramento, quam eam aliquis vincere possit, aut aliquid contrarii in posterum pati.

[*98*] De successione duplicium puerorum alicuius viri.

(c) Si vir duplices pueros habuerit et primos antea eradicaverit(d) exponendo, et si postea aliquid dederit aliis pueris in suis bonis, et moriatur
CXCI[v] idem vir, hoc secundi pueri antetollunt. Extunc quicquid | superfluum fuerit, hoc equaliter inter se dividunt, cum omnes equales sibi fuerint in natura.

[*99*] De scabini vituperatione et dilatione sententie. (e)

(f) Si vir scabinum in scamno indecenter in iudicio bannito increpaverit, si hoc probaverit per suos consodales, qui audierunt, illum oportet emendam dare scabino et iudici penam.

(a) Femina qualiter pro homicidio inculpa[ta] se expurgabit JL[17] (b) *manicula;* Mulier quomodo evadere debet de querimoniis pernoctatis JL[1] (c) x JL[1] De pueris ex pluribus uxoribus natis quomodo succedunt bonis JL[17] (d) odprawyl JL[17] (e) Notandum. Homo jure municipali; vir liber juris Theuthonici Meydburgensis dicitur, quo utatur, quia suum jus est habile et [h]ii ex Lipczko et [Ha]lle [et] alis civita[tibu]s et jure cezareo cum consi[li]o sapientium et jure [cez]aris et ex voluntate municipalis juris [*unum verbum illegibile*] civilis, quod [*unum verbum difficile*] [...]ini non dividunt sediminis [*?*] patris [*?*] [...]t quarta distinctio x capituli. JL[4] (f) De scabini vituperacione JL[36]

if both the father and the son are sued in the same case, then the father should exonerate himself by oath truthfully.

[*97*] On a red-handed deed, namely homicide, [committed by] a woman.

If a woman is apprehended red-handed in the act of murder or in the act of inflicting wounds worthy of a duel, a man is more likely to defeat her with six trustworthy oath helpers than she can prove her innocence. In such a case, a trial against her should be allowed. However, if a man accuses a woman of murder or injuries committed and witnessed on the same day, and the woman provides surety according to the law, she is closer to exonerating herself with six trustworthy oath helpers than anyone is to prevailing over her. If the woman is accused on the next day, she is closer to exonerating herself with an oath on the relics, by a single hand, than anyone is to prevailing over her or suffering otherwise in the future.

[*98*] On succession from a man by two sets of children.

If a man has two sets of children, and has already rooted out the first [ones] by an offer [of a gift, or of a succession], and if afterwards he gives something from his goods to the other children, and this man dies, the second children shall redeem that first. From then on, whatever remains in excess, they shall divide equally among themselves, if they are all of equal birth.

[*99*] On insulting a juror, and an adjournment of the sentence.

If a man indecently insults a juror on the bench in a formally convened court, and the juror proves this with his companions who heard it, the man should pay compensation to the juror and a fine to the judge.

[a] Scabini si non fuerint in una sententia unanimes vel eam ignorantes, [b] extunc eandem ad secundum et tertium iudicium valebunt differre, et tunc eam inferre debent ⟨De quo supra folio CXXI capitulum: Item cum iudex⟩[1], vel eam mittere, ferre illuc quo competit, si nequeant invenire et non diutius prolongare.

[*100*] De proscriptione alicuius occasione non comparationis in iudicio pro homicidio. Et de extensione fideiussionis.

[c] Si super virum querimonia facta fuerit pro homicidio aut pro vulneribus, et ipse se accommodaverit circa suam hereditatem ad comparendum, et si non comparuerit, et profugus factus fuerit, tunc debet vocari cum clamore, ut iuris est. Et si non compareat in iudicio eodem die, tunc debet proscribi et recompensa in sua hereditate iudicatur, et iudici sua pena. Et etiam nullus altius cogi potest cautionem facere fideiussoriam, quam se sua extendit recompensa, nisi sit pro debito, quod maius sit.

[*101*] De contentione et inculpatione diurnali vel nocturnali pro homicidio vel vulneribus.

[d] Si casu contentio oritur clara die, si probus vir pro eo accusaretur, qui ibi visus non fuerat, de quo propior est evadere metseptimus cum hominibus fidedignis, qui presentes fuerunt, quam in eo duellum acquirere possit. [e] Si autem super virum idoneum circa noctis tempestatem querimonia facta fuerit pro homicidio aut vulneribus duello dignis, que tempore noctis facta sunt, de quo propior evadet metseptimus cum hominibus bonitate probatis, [f] circa quos tunc fuit, cum hoc factum perpetratum fuerit, ita quod sit de facto innocens.

---

[a] Deliberare possunt rationabiliter [*?*] JL[38]   [b] Dilacio sentencie per scabinos potest fieri JL[17]   [c] Ob homicidium non comparens proscibitur [*or.* proscibitso] JL[17]   [d] Vir fama bona inculpatus de homicidio metseptimus propior est evadere quam convinci JL[17]   [e] Servatur JL[38]   [f] Casus Leopoli[iensis] ex parte dampni si tunc non est convictus [*?*] ob depilacionem JL[17]

---

1 *Infra Commune incliti…, articulus in Consuetudines terre Cracoviensis:* De tempore ad interrogandum in iudiciis servando et de interrogatione per partes non audienda.

If the jurors are not unanimous in their sentence or do not know [the resolution], they may adjourn it to the second and third court sessions. Next, they should either deliver it or refer the case to where it should be brought if they are unable to reach the verdict or further adjourn it.

[*100*] On depriving someone of their rights for failing to appear in court in a homicide case. And on the provision of surety.

If a complaint of homicide or injury is brought against a man, and he remains available at his estate for appearance, but fails to appear and becomes a fugitive, then he shall be summoned with an outcry, as the law demands. If he fails to appear in court on that day, then he should be deprived of his rights, and the wergeld shall be awarded from his estate, and his fine [goes] to the judge. And also no one can be compelled to provide surety higher than their wergeld, unless it is for a debt that is larger.

[*101*] On a dispute and an accusation during the day or at night, regarding homicide or injury.

If a dispute happens to arise during the full day, and a worthy man, who was not seen there, is accused in it, he shall be closer to exonerating himself with six trustworthy persons who were present, than his [opponent is] to obtaining a duel. However, if a complaint is brought against a trustworthy man during the night, for homicide or serious injuries worthy of a duel, which were committed during the night, he shall be closer to exonerating himself with six persons of confirmed goodness, with whom he was present when the deed was committed, so that he is effectively innocent.

[*102*] De petitione prolocutoris.

⟨De quo supra folio x.⟩[1] (a) Quem vir pro advocato seu prolocutore rogaverit, hunc causam et verbum suum loqui oportet iure, nisi se excusaverit cum pena.

[*103*] De bonis ad suppellectilem dominarum mortuo marito pertinentibus.

CXCIIr (b) Et si quando moritur vir, tunc (c) uxori oves dari et presentari debent ad suppellectilia, ubicunque ierint. Anete, colcidre, vela, tecture currum(d), olle picte etiam ad suppellectilem pertinent.

[*104*] De probatione incolatus. (e)

(f) Nemo potest nec pro homicidio aut vulneribus seu pro aliquo debito suo iuramento probare incolatum. (g)

[*105*] De cive, qui exactionem non secundum iuramentum solvit.

(h) Consules si iuramentum unius viri recipient, quod iuste secundum civitatis statuta et consuetudinem exactionem dedisset, tandem vero post mortem illius iurantis plura bona sub ipsius possessione fuerint inventa, quam per[ex]actionata fuissent, (i) illa bona consules non habent recipere, sed ipsius defuncti heredes, nisi aliquis heredum eadem denegata bona coram iudicio vel sedenti consilio recipere abrenunciasset, et tunc ipsa bona consulibus pro utilitate civitatis permanerent, quemadmodum arbitratur et laudum civitatis disponit.

(a) Advocatus causam non agens penam iudici meretur JL[17] (b) Ad suppellectilem pertinent JL[17] (c) Gierada vocatur de qua inferius JL[38] (d) *org.* curuum (e) Post mensualem inhabitationem JL[4] (f) Hic tangit omnem in mu[nici]pio, que diferi[t] iure provinciali JL[4] (g) Quia reo datur evasio JL[4] (h) Nota. [...]dinum aut si a[...] *folia abscisa* JL[17] (i) Et ex hoc aliqua infamia periurii aquiritur JL[17] Non est in usu JL[38]

---

1 *Infra Commune incliti..., articulus in Statutis Casimiri Magni:* De advocatis, procuratoribus et proloquutoribus in iudiciis habendis cui expedit.

[*102*] On requesting a spokesman.

Whom[ever] a man requests as his advocate[1] or spokesman, that one ought to speak his case and his word in accordance with the law, unless he excuses himself, with a penalty.

[*103*] On goods belonging to the paraphernalia of women after the death of a husband.

And when the husband dies, to the wife should be given and presented, as part of the paraphernalia, sheep, wherever they graze. Ducks, blankets, curtains, cart covers, decorated pots also belong the paraphernalia.

[*104*] On proving resident status.

No one can prove with their own oath their status as a resident in cases of homicide, injury, or any debt.

[*105*] On the citizen who paid the tax contrary to the oath.

If the councillors reçeive an oath from a man who says that he has paid taxes in accordance with the law, statutes, and custom of the city, but after the death of this oath-giver, more goods are found in his possession than would have been taxed, the councillors shall not receive those goods, but they shall belong to the heirs of the deceased, unless one of the heirs renounces those [undeclared] goods before the court or the seated council, and then those goods shall remain with the councillors for the benefit of the city, according to the decision and resolution of the city.

1 *Advocatus* in the sense of spokesman, the translation "attorney" as a synonym of "spokesman". Cf. Art. 52, footnote 2.

[*106*] De iuramento iudicialiter ad prestandum premisso. (a)

Ubi vir iuramentum promiserit coram iudicio pro enormibus verbis aut depilatione, vel verberibus, vel sanguinis effusione, (b) de quo solutus dimitti non potest, nisi voluntas iudicis fuerit aut consensus. Actor etiam si reum pro iuramentis premissis causa Dei vel petitionis hominum proborum mittere absolutum voluerit, extunc iudici etiam competit ad hoc dare suam voluntatem. Et si suum consensum (c) noluerit adhibere, tunc actorem iuramenta recipere oportebit vel iudici demeretur in pena octo solidorum et non plus pro causis singulis specialiter.

[*107*] De pueris nondum annos discretionis habentibus et tutore carentibus.

(d) Quando pupilli suum verum tutorem habere non poterint, (e) tunc nullus ipsos ad aliquam iudicialem responsivam deducere potest, (f) nisi prius ad annos discretionis seu pubertatis pervenerint.

[*108*]. De eo, qui in alterius hereditate aliquid edificaverit.

(g) Si vir super alterum conqueritur, quod sibi aliquid edificaverit de suis bonis aut hereditate, hoc ille possibilius obtinet, qui habet in possessione unica manu, nisi ipsum cum testimonio allocutus fuerit. Extunc possessor cum testibus servat, si voluerit.

[*109*] De non evocatione civium de iure civili ad quodcunquem ius alienum.

CXCII[v] (h) Quousque et quamdiu cives Meydenburgenses veram actionem aut responsivam tenuerint et se coram suo domino episcopo aut burgrabio aut

(a) *manicula* JL[1] (b) Pars iuramentum parti non potest dimintere [*s*] sine consensu iudicis JL[17] Nota JL[31] (c) *manicula* JL[17] (d) Pueri sin[e] tutore nil agant nec [ali]cui respond[eant] ante annos p[u]bertatis JL[17] (e) Magistratus tutores dare tenetur iuxta jura Regni. JL[38] (f) Nota JL[31] (g) Casus Leopoli[ensis] in filiis Fraibork puerulis et Stayslavs [*?*] JL[17] (h) Nemo debet evocari reum extra suum forum. JL[38]

[106] On the oath taken in court for evidentiary purposes.

When a man has expressed assurance on oath before a court regarding outrageous words, or shearing [someone's] hair, or beatings, or shedding of blood, he shall not be released from that unless such is the judge's will or consent. Similarly, if the plaintiff wishes to release the defendant from the aforesaid oaths because of God or by petition of worthy persons, from that moment on, the judge shall have the authority to grant consent to this. And if the judge refuses to give his consent, then the plaintiff should withdraw the oaths, or the judge is owed as a fine eight shillings, and no more, separately for each individual case.

[107] On underage children who are without a guardian.

When underage persons have no proper guardian, no one can hold them accountable in court until they come of age or reach puberty.

[108] On one who has built something in the inheritance of another.

If a man complains against another that he has built something on his goods or his inheritance, the one who is in sole possession [of the land] shall more easily prevail with his own oath, unless [the other man] presents counterclaims against him with witnesses. In that case, the possessor with witnesses will retain [the possession] if he chooses to.

[109] On not summoning citizens from civil law to any kind of other law.

As long as the citizens of Magdeburg proceed and seek justice in their rightful complaint or response before their lord bishop or burgrave, or *scultetus*

sculteto ad iustitiam exhibueri[n]t circa ius civitatis, (a) tunc nemo eos extra civitatem in alio iure convenire et occupare seu contra eos agere potest in iudicio alieno.

[*110*] De impedimento coram iudicio non fiendo.

(b) Nullus alterum impedire debet coram iudicio, postquam iudicium bannitum fuerit, cum iniuria talibus impedimentis, que ipsum impedire possint in sua querela, sicut clamore aut turpiloquiis, aut ceteris insolentiis. (c) Si hoc contra iustitiam fecerit, et si patiens ipsum protestari poterit cum iudice et duobus scabinis, extunc suam acquirit emendam et iudex acquirit suam penam. (d) Si contigerit in iudicio castellani, tunc tria talenta demeretur, et in iudicio sculteti octo solidos. Nam ubi actor suam emendam acquirit, ibi iudex suam penam acquirit.

[*111*] De pena sculteti nolentis alicui iustitiam ministrare nec querelas audire volentis.

Nunc attendatis super eo, si scultetus aliquem impedierit in sua querela et sibi iustitiam non fecerit, et hoc sibi iniuste recusat, si pro eo coram castellano aut advocato impulsatus fuerit cum testibus, extunc ipsum cum testibus evadere oportet.

(e) Cum qualicunque testimonio super iudicem querulatum fuerit, tali ipsum iudicem testimonio evadere oportebit, sive sint scabini aut alii astantes iudicio. Si autem hoc coram iudicio bannito actum fuerit, tunc melius vinci potest testibus iure, quam ipse cum testibus evadere possit. Si autem vir cedere voluerit testimonio et ipsum inculpare pro suo scitu, de hoc (f) unica manu evadere possit.

(g) Quando querimonia coram advocato super aliquem facta fuerit, pro hac causa respondere tenetur sine mora, ita quod ibi sit iudicium bannitum, quia ipsum (h) oportet ibi esse presentem, nisi legale (i) impedi-

(a) Nota Actor sequitur forum re[i] JL[17] (b) Nullus pro iudicio debet impediri alias penam demeretur JL[17] (c) Quando pars acquirit emendam iudex eciam penam, *manus B* JL[17] Nota JL[31] (d) Castellani iudicium. JL[38] (e) Si quis contra iudicem conqueratur JL[17] De iusticia derelicta, *manus B* JL[17] (f) iam ipse [*?*] JL[17] (g) Legali excepto impedimento cittatus respondere debet JL[38] (h) reum JL[17] (i) legitimum JL[17]

under the law of the city, no one may summon or compel them to another law beyond the city, or proceed against them in a foreign court.

[*110*] On an impediment not to be inflicted before a court.

No one shall obstruct another before a court, especially in a formally convened court, with unlawful impediments that could harm their complaint, such as an outcry, indecent words, or other kinds of insolence. If someone does this against justice, and if the victim can prove this with the judge and two jurors, then the victim shall receive compensation and the judge shall receive his fine. If this occurs in the court of the castellan, then three talents are due, and in the court of the *scultetus*, eight shillings. Indeed, when the plaintiff receives his compensation, then the judge shall receive the fine.

[*111*] On the penalty imposed on a *scultetus* who refuses to administer justice, or does not wish to hear complaints.

If a *scultetus* obstructs someone in their complaint and unjustly does not give him [i.e., the complainant] justice, and unjustly denies it to him: if he is summoned for this before the castellan or the advocate[1], with witnesses, then he must exonerate himself with witnesses.

If anyone testifies against a judge with any kind of testimony, that judge should exonerate himself with such testimony, whether they are jurors or others present in court. If this were to occur in a formally convened court, then it may be easier to lawfully prevail over the judge with witnesses, than he can exonerate himself single-handedly with witnesses. However, if anyone wishes to withdraw the testimony and accuse him on the basis of his knowledge, he [the judge] may exonerate himself with an oath.

When a complaint is filed against someone before the advocate, he must respond promptly, this is because there is a fully convened court, because [the *scultetus*] must be present there, unless a legal impediment prevents

1 Cf. Art. 52, footnote 2.

mentum ipsum occupaverit, [a] quod impedimentum statim probare oportet. Si hoc non ostenderit et non nominaverit, et hoc per iustitiam facere denegaverit, se excusare de sua iniuria, quam exercuit, et se ad iustitiam exhibere, extunc condemnatur advocato in decem talentis idem scultetus et illi suum debitum, de quo negavit facere iustitiam; et medio quo ille non solvit solus, aut se iure excusaverit iudicio proximo, tunc amplius iudex esse non potest, nisi se ex hac culpa exemerit, secundum hoc ut est premissum.

Si autem pro facto criminali, pro quo iudicium facere recusavit, sicut pro homicidio aut vulneribus, [b] aut furto, aut spolio, aut ecclesie violentia, aut incendio, aut pro his similibus, que crimina capitalia tangunt, idem [c] | CXCIII^r iudicium super eundem ire debet, quod super illum ire debuerat, pro eo nec recompensa, nec aliquid fieri potest, si in his vincitur [d], ut iuris est.

[e] Si autem unus vir pro debito in captivitatem publicam presentatus fuerit ad tenendum iure, [f] si ipsum [g] ammiserit aut si evaserit absque sua culpa aut negligentia pro crimine, quod transit ad collum, pro eo solvet integram recompensam et hoc ipsum iuramento probare oportet tacto sacramento, si sibi parcere noluerit, quod ipsum absque omni sua culpa ammiserit.

Integra autem recompensa facit decem et octo talenta, media recompensa facit novem talenta.

[*112*] De iniusto iudicio advocati et de pena eius quomodoque proinde iudicari debeat.

[h] Nunc attendatur de advocato, si non iuste iudicaverit, cum sibi querulatur, et hoc propter amorem aut munera, aut ob aliquam causam dimittit, vel si solus noxam fecerit iniustam, quam de iure facere non debuit: postquam ad iudicem electus sit ius confortare aut iniurias suffocare seu debilitare. Si querela super ipsum in suo iudicio facta fuerit, [i] tunc scultetus iudex esse debet super advocatum seu super burgrabium, et per hoc cogitur cum sententiis, quod ante ipsum oportet respondere, ut in posterum

---

[a] impeditur absentencialiter JL[17] [b] Facta criminalia nota, *manus B* JL[17] [c] Iudex si in causa criminalia [s] iusticiam denegaverit quis iuris, *manus B* JL[17] [d] iudex JL[17] [e] Si quis ex captivi[tate] aliquam inserit JL[17] [f] Notandum*;* Si judex reum ad publicum arestum arestaverit quid licet vide. JL[38] [g] iudex vel scultetus JL[17] [h] Iniustum iudicium advocati scultetus iudicat JL[1] Modus procedendi et agendi quando advocat[um] vel iudicem mal[um] iudicantem et iurista[m] JL[17] [i] Advocatum quis iudicare debet ex officio eius JL[38]

him, which should be proven immediately. If he fails to prove and explain this, and refuses to do so according to justice, justify his injustice and failure to come to justice, then the *scultetus* shall be fined ten talents by the advocate, plus the debt owed to the one to whom he denied justice; and until he pays or justifies himself as the law demands at the next court session, he may no longer be a judge, unless he exonerated himself from this fault as mentioned earlier.

If, however, for a criminal deed, regarding which he has refused to preside, for example, homicide, assault, theft, robbery, violence against the church, arson, or for similar offences punishable by death, court proceedings shall be conducted against him as should be done against the perpetrator, for which he may not pay the wergeld nor anything else, if proven, as the law demands.

If a man has been committed to public prison for debt to be held according to the law, if he escapes or is released without the fault or negligence of [the judge], for a crime punishable by death, [the judge] shall pay the wergeld and should prove with an oath on the relics that he did not intend to spare him and that he released him entirely without his fault.

The full wergeld amounts to eighteen talents, half of the wergeld is nine talents.

[*112*] On an unjust judgment of the advocate[1] and his punishment, and how he should be judged because of it.

Now, let us consider the advocate: if he judged unfairly when someone brought a complaint to him, out of favouritism or bribery, or for any reason dismissed the case, or if he himself committed unlawful harm, which he should not do according to the law; [this is because] once he was elected a judge, [he is] to uphold the law to suppress and weaken injuries. If a complaint is brought against him in his court, then the *scultetus* should be the judge over the advocate or the burgrave, and he shall be compelled in sentences to answer before him for this reason, in the following

1 Cf. Art. 52, footnote 2.

patebit. Petatque advocatum seu burgrabium surgere per sententiam, quod super ipsum habeat querulari et sententialiter petat, ut alium ponat iudicem loco sui, quod ipsum facere oportet. Et tunc locet scultetum, qui sibi debet iudicare. Simili modo scultetus iudicet advocatum seu burgrabium. Idcirco(a) advocatus bannitum iudicium absque sculteto facere non potest, quia coram eo ad ius se debet exhibere, si super ipsum aliquis querulatur. Si hoc contra iustitiam anno et die recusaverit, extunc domino terre iudicium vacat, quod ab eo habuit, et regi bannum, si prosecutus fuerit cum veris sententiis.

[*113*] De iudicio et probatione stupri et violentiarum.

(b) Insidias, stupra et domorum irruentiam burgravius iudicat et nullus alter nec etiam scultetus. Si domorum irruentia probabitur, potest ostendi cum vulneribus et edificio vulnerato; si super hoc iudicem et homines, qui clamorem audierunt, in testimonium habere poterit, extunc ille sibi propior (c) cum duello debet respondere, quam suo possit evadere iuramento.

[*114*] De captis in facinore manifesto, qua pena sunt puniendi.

CXCIII[v] (d) Si aliquis alteri fecerit domorum irruentiam die ac nocte, et si ipse il|lum detinuerit in facto manifesto, et ipsum captivum cum clamore ad iudicium perduxerit, si super hoc clamatores habere poterit metseptimus suorum vicinorum, et si factum ostendi potest, ut iuris sit, (e) illi ad collum transit. Si autem factum manifestum ostendi non potest, extunc iste propi[us] metseptimus(f), quam per eum vinci possit.

(a) *org.* iccirco (b) Quam facientem violenciam JL[17] (c) blissi go powod swÿetkÿ pokonacz JL[17] (d) Pena cuiuslibet convi[ctio]nis quis pro violencia in facto manifesto JL[17] (e) Violator si in recenti capietur in facto manifesto decollatur. JL[38] (f) *commentator delens* metseptimus, *explanavit:* [pro]pior est evadere JL[11]

manner: And he shall request the advocate, that is the burgrave, to arise in the course of the sentence that is sought from him, and shall request that, by [an interlocutory] sentence, another judge be placed in his stead—which it is right for him [the advocate or burgrave] to do. Then, he shall seat the *scultetus*, who should adjudicate the matter against him. Similarly, the *scultetus* judges the advocate or the burgrave. For this reason, the advocate may not administer justice in a formally convened court without the *scultetus* because one should turn to him [the *scultetus*] for justice, if someone complains against him [the advocate]. If he [the advocate] resists this proceeding for a year and a day against justice, then the jurisdiction shall pass to the lord of the land, from whom he received it, and the ban to the king[1], if there are rightful sentences against him.

[*113*] On the trial and proof of rape and violence.

Ambushes on the road, rape, and a house raid shall be judged by the burgrave and no one else, not even the *scultetus*. If a house raid is to be proven, [then] it may be demonstrated by wounds and by damage to the building; if [the plaintiff] can have testimony about this from the judge and the people who heard the outcry, then [the defendant] shall be closer to answering him in a duel than he can be to exonerating himself with his oath.

[*114*] On those caught red-handed, what punishment they will be subjected to.

If someone carries out against another a house raid during the day or at night, and if the victim captures him red-handed and brings him to court with an outcry, if, as [proof] of this, he has co-participants in the outcry, who include himself and six of his neighbours, and if he can prove the deed, as it is in the law, that [defendant] shall be sentenced to death. If [the plaintiff] cannot clearly demonstrate the deed, then [the defendant] shall be closer [to exonerating himself] with six oath helpers than to being overcome by him [the plaintiff].

1 Cf. "Royal judicial authority (Ban)" in *The Saxon Mirror: A "Sachsenspiegel"*, p. 196.

[*115*] De pena occasione concordie post querelam inite.

(a) Etsi vir suam querelam tenere promiserit, tandem vero tempore medio concordia facta fuerit, extunc pro eo non plus (b) [a]mittit, nisi iudici dat suam penam.

[*116*] De repetendo et probando debito post mortuam manum. (c)

(d) Si vir querulatur super alterum, quod pro suo patre teneatur, ipse debet super eo, ut iuris est, informari. Si autem voluerit iurare, quod pater suus hoc debitum persolvisset, hoc ipsum facere oportet metseptimus, (e) post mortuam manum. Si autem dixerit, quod hoc debitum solus persolverit, hoc mettertius iurabit heres. (f) Si vero debitum sui patris recognoscit, hoc solvere debet, in quantum recepta hereditas se extendit. Et si solvere noluerit vel heres hoc consentire recusat, tunc sibi hereditas sua vel proprium potest iudicio possideri pro isto debito et acquiri, aliter ille non potest constringi ad vendendam hereditatem et proprium suum.

[*117*] De cane et quovis alio animali damnum faciente. (g)

Si aliquis habuerit equum vel canem aut aliud pecus quodcunque sit, quod loquela caret, si quoque hoc(h) damnum et noxam fecerit, ipse vero cuius est eiusmodi animal dicit suum non (i) esse damno perpetrato, istud sibi in suo iure non nocebit. (j)

(a) Pena concordie facit post querelam absque voluntate iudicii JL[17] (b) *org. error:* amor est evadere*; commentator delevit propter errorem* JL[11] (c) Mortua manus JL[1] Nota JL[8] Ibi quis post mortuam manum et qualiter debitum probari JL[17] (d) Quomodo debitum probatur post mortuam manum esse persolutum JL[1] Simile folio 191 [*Ius municipale Magdeburgense infra Commune incliti…, fol. cxci^r, articulus 94 in eadem editio*] JL[3] *manicula* JL[16] (e) Metseptimus evadit post demortuam manum. JL[38] (f) debita JL[16] (g) de damno JL[23] De equo vel cane [d]apnum faciente JL[29] (h) *org.* hoct (i) Ipsum expellendo nec fovendo JL[17] (j) Servus si presens fuerit precustodius per vicinos JL[17]

[*115*] On the fine owed from a composition reached after [filing] a complaint.

If a man promises to pursue his complaint, but ultimately a composition has reached in the meantime, then he shall not lose anything more for it, except that he shall pay his fine to the judge.

[*116*] On claiming and proving a debt after a person's death.

If one man accuses another of having an obligation from his father, he shall be instructed about that according to the law. If he wishes to swear that his [deceased] father paid the debt, he must do so with six oath helpers. If he says that he has paid the debt himself, the heir shall swear with two oath helpers. If he acknowledges his father's debt, he should pay it from the inheritance. If he refuses to pay, or if the heir refuses to agree to this, then his inheritance or property may be seized and taken by the court for the settlement of that debt. Otherwise, he may not be forced to sell his inheritance or property.

[*117*] On a dog and any other animal causing damage.

If someone has a horse or a dog or any other beast incapable of speech, and if it causes harm and damage, the one to whom the animal belongs shall declare that it is not his, after the damage has been done, and the animal shall not harm him in his rights thereafter.

[*118*] De spoliatore concivium.

(a) Si aliquis spoliaverit cives suos, qui proprium aut feodum aut hereditatem intra municipale habeat et si hoc faciat non prehabita ante dominum terre vel ante suum iudicem querela, illi sua edificia abiudicari debent super suam curiam et secari, et illa edificia erunt communia et omnibus hominibus publicantur. Si autem edificia iudicialiter fuerint abiudicata, ita quod ibi puella aut femina fuerit stuprata intra illud edificium, etiam debet resecari et abinde nullas [*s*] deduci.

[*119*] De iuramento Iudeorum contra Christianos. (b)

Hoc est illud iudicium et illud iuramentum, cum quo aut per quod Iudeus iurare sive evadere debet Christianum, quod scriptum est in iure imperatorum. ⟨De quo supra folio CLXIII⟩[1] Ipse debet verti contra solem seorsum
CXCIIII^r et stare nudipes super unam sedem, clamide indutus et pile|um Iudaicum habere debet super caput. Et si lapsus ter fuerit, totidem unum fertonem ammittit. Et si quarto cadet, extunc manet reus in causa. (c) Tunc dicit ille, qui sibi predicit iuramentum: "Ego te moneo, N., Iudee, per has tres litteras et per hanc legem, quam Dominus dedit Moysi in tabula lapidea in monte Synai, quod iste liber aut hoc rodale verum sit et iustum, super quem tu N. tali nomine pro tali causa sive culpa pro qua te huc ad responsionem iure deduxit." Et tunc debet sic iurare, et sic sibi predicetur: "Quod tu in hac causa reus non sis, qua te hic Cristianus inculpat, quod te Deus adiuvet. Idem Deus, qui fecit celum et terram, aerem et rorem, montes, valles, frondes, gramina et flores. Et si reus sis, quod te terra absorbeat, que Dathan et Abyron absorbuit, et si reus sis, quod te venenum, gutta, paralisis et lepra invadat, que precibus Elisei Naaman Syrum dimisit et Jesy invasit. Et si reus sis, quod te ignis comburet celestis et caducus morbus te invadat, et sanguinis fluxus. Et quod tibi accidat, ut uxori Loth, que transmutata fuit in

---

(a) De stupratore vel violatore cuius edificia in forma debent esse communia hominibus JL[17]
(b) Juden aid, *manus B* JL[8] *manicula* JL[23] Judeorum iuramentum Nota Bene JL[35] De iuramento Iudeorum, *manus A* JL[36] Rodale dicitur hoc iuramentum JL[38] (c) Forma iuramenti Iudeorum quomodo se expurgare debent JL[17]

---

1 *Infra Commune incliti…, Iuramentorum variorum forme, iuramentum:* Iudeorum iuramentum contra Christianos.

[*118*] On a robber of fellow citizens.

If anyone, who has property[1], fief, or inheritance within the municipal [jurisdiction], robs his fellow citizens, without having earlier made a complaint before the lord of the land or his judge, these buildings of his should be judicially confiscated and cut off from his estate, and these buildings shall become common and made accessible to all. If the buildings are judicially confiscated because a girl or a woman was raped inside such a building, it shall also be razed, and nothing [shall] be removed from there.

[*119*] On the oath by Jews against Christians.

This is the [course of] trial, and that oath with which, or by which, a Jew swears against, or absolves himself from, a Christian, as is written in imperial law. He should turn his back to the sun and stand barefoot on one chair, dressed in a cloak, with a Jewish hat on his head. And if he makes a mistake three times, he forfeits one fierton each time. And if he errs for the fourth time, he shall be deemed guilty in the matter. Then the one who first utters [the words of] the oath to him says: "I admonish you, N., Jew, by these three letters and by this law, which the Lord gave to Moses on the stone tablets on Mount Sinai, that this book or scroll is true and just, on which you, N., are to swear on which [the Christian] has brought you here, N. of such [and such] a name, by law, to give a response, for such cause or fault." And then he shall swear in this manner, and it shall first be uttered to him, thus: "If in this cause you are not guilty of what this Christian accuses you, may God assist you in this matter. This God, who created heaven and earth, the air and mist, mountains, valleys, bushes, grass, and flowers. And if you are guilty, may the earth swallow you up, as it swallowed up Dathan[2] and Abiram[3]; and if you are guilty, may you be overcome by poison, a blotch, paralysis, and leprosy, which, through the pleas of Elisha, left Naaman the Syrian and afflicted Gehazi.[4] And if you are guilty, may the fire of heaven consume you, and debilitating disease and haemorrhage afflict you. And may what

1 The enumeration may suggest that the term *proprium*, Ger. *Eigen* (BJ 169, fol. 302v), may mean allod here.

2 See Book of Numbers 16.

3 See Book of Numbers 16.

4 See 2 Kings 5.

statuam salis, dum Sodoma periit et Gomora. Et si reus sis, quod tu pereas in tua anima et in tuo corpore et in tuis rebus, et si tu reus sis, quod ad sinum Abrahe non pervenias, et etiam ad resurrectionem nunquam pervenies, ubi Cristiani, Iudei et gentiles ante Creatorem omnium rerum resurgent. Et si tu reus sis, quod te lex deleat, quam Deus dedit Moysi in monte Synai, quam Deus scripsit digito suo supra tabulam lapideam, et etiam te confundat omnis scriptura, que scripta est in Quinque Libris Moysi. Et si tuum iuramentum non iustum nec mundum fuerit, quod te deleat Adonai et sue deitatis potentia." Nunc omnes dicite: amen.

[*120*] De origine iuris municipalis et Saxonie. (a)

Nunc placeat audire et intelligere, quomodo presens scriptum informat ex relatione veridica. Primo de imperio, quomodo terre Saxonie ius suum ab initio fuerit constitutum et confirmatum in suo iure, sicut ab antiquo tempore Babilonia tenebat. Ibi stetit (b) imperium et regnabat potenter per omnia regna, quia Nemrot(c) gentilis rex primo Babiloniam edificavit in eaque innumerabiles ac altas munitiones posuit, unde hucusque in presens ius municipale nominatur. Et ibi erant manentes idem rex Nemroth (d) ac duces multi et ceteri viri famosi, qui vero nunc mercatores nominantur, et omnes uno utebantur iure, quod municipale ius appellatur, ut bene in libro presenti (epatebit. Undee) nomen sortiebatur absque qualibet transmutatione.

(f) Nunc dicetur quamdiu stetit imperium potentialiter absque permu-
CXCIIII[v] tatione usque ad Gretiam a tempore | Darii Secundi, aut ultimi, quem rex Alexander maximis et seditiosis devicit bellis, tunc transmutatum fuit imperium a Babilonia et stetit in Constantinopoli usque ad illud tempus, quo se Roma de imperio intromisit, et potenter obtinuit usque ad presens tempus ex parte beati Petri, (g) qui caput est totius Christianitatis. Cum imperium Romam versum non fuisset, ibi stetit, ut patet in premissis, tunc Cristiani absque iure fuerunt; idcirco(h) quivis pro sua in terris faciebat voluntate aut quid facere poterat et perficere, et hoc absque querela permansit et per iudicium inultum(i), quia nullum ius fuit, ubi quis

(a) Origo iuris municipalis et Saxonis [*s*] JL[1] Qualiter Saxonie ius sit ab iudicio constitutum JL[17] *manicula* JL[23] Weichbild, *manus C* JL[27] art. 6 [*Mikołaj Jaskier, Iuris Municipalis…, art. VI, fol. VI[v]*] JL[33] (b) Primo in Babilonia JL[17] (c) Nemrot Babiloniam edificavit JL[38] (d) Ius mercatorum est ius municipale JL[17] (e) *org.* patebit unde (f) art. 7 [*Mikołaj Jaskier, Iuris Municipalis…, art. VII, fol. VII[r]*] JL[33] (g) B. Petrus caput totius Christianitatis JL[38] (h) *org.* iccirco (i) impunitum JL[34]

happened to Lot's wife, who was turned into a pillar of salt[1] when Sodom and Gomorrah perished, happen to you. And if you are guilty, may you perish in your soul, body, and things; and if you are guilty, may you never come to Abraham's bosom, nor attain resurrection, when Christians, Jews, and pagans rise before the Creator of all things. And if you are guilty, may you be swallowed by the law that God gave to Moses on Mount Sinai, which God wrote with His finger on the stone tablet, and may the entire Scripture, which is written in the Five Books of Moses, confound you. And if your oath is neither just nor honest, may Adonai and His Divine power erase you." Then everyone shall say: Amen.

[*120*] On the beginning of municipal law and the law of Saxony.

Now please listen and understand, for this document conveys a true account. First, about the highest public power, how from the beginning the Saxon land was established and confirmed in its law, just as it had been observed since antiquity in Babylon. There arose monarchy and ruled strongly in all lands, for Nimrod[2], a gentile king, first built Babylon and set up countless and high city walls, and henceforth, even to the present day, the law has been called municipal. There resided King Nimrod and numerous princes, and other illustrious men, who are indeed now called merchants, and all are governed by one law, which is called municipal law, as shall be well shown in this book. That is why the name was adopted without any alteration.

Now it shall be told for how long the monarchy lasted in strenght without change, until Greece from the times of Darius the Second[3], or the last, whom King Alexander[4] defeated in great and tumultuous wars. Then it was transferred from Babylon, and endured in Constantinople until the time when Rome took over the monarchy, and has effectively ruled up to the present on behalf of Saint Peter, who is the head of all Christianity. When the monarchy were not yet transferred to Rome, where it lasted, as is evident from the above, at that time Christians were without law; therefore, everyone acted according to their will across the lands, or whatever they could do and achieve, and this remained without complaint and

1 See Genesis 19: 15–26.

2 See Genesis 10: 8–10.

3 Darius II, King of Persia and pharaoh of Egypt (423–404 B.C.).

4 Alexander III of Macedon, King of Macedonia (336–323 B.C.).

iustitiam consequi posset, quid usque ad illud tempus perseverabat[(a)], quo se Roma de imperio intromisit. Et ipsi subvenerunt et iustitiam consecuti fuerunt, et ibi exhibuerunt manus, unde pacem manu obtinuimus usque ad presens. Tunc Romani convenerunt et decreverunt deliberando, quomodo sibi regna subiugare possent. Et omnes unanimi consensu et pari concilio concordaverunt, quod edificarent ⟨De origine iuris castrensis [(b)]⟩ castra in terris, unde sibi terras possent subiugare. Et cum hoc fecissent, tunc arbitrati sunt, quomodo castra confortarent, ut ipsis essent in iuvamen. Et illos acceperunt, qui nomen militare habuerunt, et eos supra castra locaverunt cum tali iure, ut hucusque castrense ius tenet in castrensi feodo. Tunc quoque deliberaverunt, qualia iura terris statuerent et statuerunt tale ius in terris, quale adhuc terra Saxonie protestatur, per Constantinum et Karolum imperatores.

[*121*] De autoritate imperatoris et iudicio eius, et ex quibus causis debet puniri, et quod omnium secularium iudicum ab eo potestas equ[al]e ac sacerdotum ab [(c)] Apostolico dependeat.

[(d)] Nunc audire et intelligere potestis de principibus ac baronibus, et hiis omnibus, qui digne nomen militare sortiuntur, [(e)] quomodo ipsi cum Romanis sunt arbitrati, quod scire vellent, quo iure imperium deberet permanere. [(f)] Et statuerunt regi ius cum consilio, quod ipse sedem regiam Rome regere deberet ex parte beati Petri cum gladio seculari[(g)], unde adhuc Romanus advocatus appellatur. [(h)] Idcirco[(i)] vitam suam non potest demereri, nec in suo honore debilitari, nisi tribus de causis, que patebunt in sequentibus. [(j)] Quarum prima est illa, si sedem Romanam destruere vellet. Secunda est, si contra fidem Katholicam vellet facere. Tertia est, si sine causa legali vellet suam dimittere legittimam uxorem. Quorum trium de
CXCV[r] una, | si quod absit, fuerit convictus, extunc debet iudicari, nam decol[l]ari [(k)] debeat [(l)] cum aureo dolabro ideo, quod secularem gladium habeat

---

[(a)] durabat JL[34] [(b)] Romanorum JL[17] [(c)] Omnia potestas a Domino Deo in omnes alios JL[17] [(d)] art. 8 [*Mikołaj Jaskier, Iuris Municipalis…, art.* VIII, *fol.* VIII[v]] JL[33] [(e)] Advocatus Romanorum imperator JL[17] [(f)] Tribus causis rex debet iudicari JL[23] [(g)] seculari [*unum verbum difficile*] JL[28] [(h)] Qualier et quare imperator primus JL[17] [(i)] *org.* iccirco [(j)] art. reprobatus y [*?*] p. in 174 art. 2 [*articulus 2 Articuli reprobati papae Gregorii* XI, *in: Commune incliti Poloniae Regni privilegium, fol.* CLXXIIII[r]] JL[33] Imperator quibus de causis potest debilitare suum imperium et ipso privari JL[38] [(k)] Imperator quali gladio et quare decollates JL[17] [(l)] M i t e i n e r g ů l d e n e n M a r k e n W e i c h b i l d a r t . 8 . [*Mikołaj Jaskier, Iuris Municipalis…, articulus* VIII, *fol.* VIII[v]], *manus C* JL[27]

unpunished by the court, because there was no law for anyone to obtain justice, which lasted until the time when Rome took the highest public power. And those who came with help administered justice, and there they made a sign with the hand, for which reason we have expressed peace with the sign of the hand until the present. Then the Romans gathered and, having considered the matter, decided how they could subjugate kingdoms to themselves. And they all agreed, by unanimous consent and equal counsel, to build castles in the lands, in such a way that they could subjugate the lands to themselves. And when they did this, then they decided how to strengthen the castles so that they would serve them. And they accepted those who had military rank, and settled them in the castles under such law that to this day *ius castrense* is observed in the castle fief. Then they also deliberated about what earthly laws to establish, and they established such law in the lands as the land of Saxony still upholds, by Constantine[1] and Charlemagne[2], the emperors.

[*121*] On the authority of the emperor and his court, and for what reasons he should be punished, and that the power of all secular judges depends on him, as that of the priests depends on the pope.

Now you can hear and understand about princes and barons, and all those who hold military rank honourably, and how they debated with the Romans, because they wanted to know under what law the state should remain. They established a law for the king, following the counsel that he should rule on the royal throne in Rome on behalf of Saint Peter with a secular sword, which is why he is called the defender of Rome to this day. Therefore, he shall not lose his life or suffer damage to his honour, except for three reasons, that shall be revealed as follows. The first of these is if he should wish to destroy the Roman See. The second is if he wishes to act against the Catholic faith. The third is if he wishes to dismiss his lawful wife without a legal cause. Of these three, if he were found guilty of one, may it never happen, then he should be judged, namely he shall be beheaded with a golden axe because he wielded a secular sword to judge

1 Constantine the Great, Roman Emperor (306–337).

2 Charlemagne, King of Franks (768–814), Emperor of the (Holy) Roman Empire (800–814).

iudicandi super hos omnes, qui noxam et iniustitiam fecerunt, aut qui caput demerentur. (a) Et insuper omnibus commisit, qui iudicis nomine censentur, protegere viduas, pupillos, et domos Dei, et omnes iniurias humiliare et iustitiam confortare. Insuper iudicium commisit omnibus iudicibus temporalibus, sive secularibus, cum eo iudicare super omnes hos, qui in maleficiis deprehensi fuerint in facto manifesto, ad iudicium capti seu deducti fuerint et convicti, ut ius dictaverit. (b) Ibi omnes iudices soli iudicare debent, vel preco loco ipsorum. Eodemmodo ut iudices habent temporalem gladium a rege, eodemmodo sacerdotes habent spiritualem gladium ab Apostolico.

[*122*] De eo quis imperatorem iudicare debeat.

(c) Nunc intendo vobis revelare, quis regem aut cesarem iudicare debeat, si ex hiis tribus premissis in uno fuerit convictus. Hoc facere debet (d) Sacri Imperii Rhenensis palatinus, qui imperatori ac Imperio ex arbitrio et laudo positus fuerit. Tali modo, ut palatinus imperatorem debet iudicare, eodemmodo iudicet burgravius marchionem pro suo excessu et scultetus burgravium.

[*123*] De iurisdi[c]tione et iure per cesarem civitatibus et mercatoribus dato.

(e) Tunc mercatores dicebant ad imperatorem, quod libenter scire vellent, in quo iure permanere possent. Et iudicavit ipsis imperator cum consilio Romanorum ad aquas navipotentes(f), quod edificarent sibi civitates firmas cum muris et turribus. Tunc populus dicebat ad imperatorem, quod libenter scire vellent, quo iure stare (g deberent. Extunc g) imperator dedit ipsis tale ius ⟨Hoc ius civile est imperiale ius.⟩ (h), quale cottidie in sua curia solebat habere. Et hoc confirmavit eis cum consilio Romanorum et cum veridicis (i signis. Et i) suam manum exhibuit, quam apprehendit quidam mercator, et dexteram cirothecam sibi de manu deposuit, super quo pax

(a) Ad imperatoris spectantia sunt JL[17] NB JL[38] (b) Sacerdotes JL[23] (c) Imperatorem quis iudicare debeat ostendit JL[1] Quis imperatorem iudicat JL[17] art. 9 [*Mikołaj Jaskier, Iuris Municipalis..., art. IX, fol. IX^v*] JL[33] (d) Palatinus Renensis iudicat imperatorem JL[38] (e) art. 9 [*Mikołaj Jaskier, Iuris Municipalis..., art. IX, fol. IX^v*] JL[33] (f) aquae navipotentes JL[11] (g) *org.* deberent extunc (h) vel municipale JL[17] (i) *org.* signis et

with him all those who commit crimes and injustice, or who deserve the death penalty. And in addition, he instructed all those designated as judges to protect widows, orphans, and houses of God, to weaken all lawlessness, and strengthen justice. In addition, he entrusted judicial authority to all temporal, that is secular, judges, to judge all those who were caught red-handed committing a crime, brought to court, and sentenced, as the law commands. There, all the judges should judge by themselves, or the court bailiff[1] [should judge] in their stead. Just as judges have the earthly sword from the king, in the same way priests have the spiritual sword from the pope.

[*122*] On the one who should judge the emperor.

Now I intend to reveal to you who may judge the king or emperor, if he is convicted of one of these three aforesaid [offences]. This should be done by the Palatine of the Rhine of the Holy Roman Empire, who is appointed judge to the emperor and the empire by will and resolution. Just as the palatine should judge the emperor, in the same way the burgrave shall judge the margrave for his offense, and *scultetus* the burgrave.

[*123*] On the judicial authority and law granted by the emperor to cities and merchants.

At that time the merchants turned to the emperor, expressing their eagerness to know under what law they could abide. Upon the advice of the Romans, the emperor decreed that they should build cities with walls and towers along navigable waters. Then, the people turned to the emperor, expressing their eagerness to know by what law they should be governed. From then onward, the emperor granted them the same law which was in daily use at his court. And he confirmed this for them by the counsel of the Romans, and with his truthful signs [of his seal]. He extended his hand, which a certain merchant noticed, and removed the right glove from his

1 See Art. 6, footnote.

beati Petri ipsis confirmata fuit. Quod hucusque permanet in exemplum, ubi nove civitates edificantur aut fora, quod ibi crux ponitur super forum. In eo probatur et apparet, quod cum voluntate regis est factum. Sic ex quo municipale ius ab antiquo usque huc permansit et ab imperio confirmatum nomen obtinuit usque ad diem presentem.

[*124*] De fundatione Maydenburg et Hallisch. Et quod ad ipsas civitates in dubiis sententiis ex certis provinciis recurritur.

CXCV^v^ [(a)] Nunc attendatis de civitate Meydemburgensi. Cum enim primo Maydemburg locata et fundata fuit imperatoris Ottonis Magni consilio, et cum terre arbitrio, et fuit stabilita in suo iure, sicut nunc tenet in suo iure municipali secundum consuetudinem antiquorum, et [(b)] Hallis civitas ex ea est fundata, idcirco utraque uno utitur iure. Eapropter omnes [(c)] de Polonia et de Bohemia, qui sub iure Theutonico sunt locati, et de marchia, de Misnensi provincia, et de marchia Lauziciensi, hii omnes ius suum Hallis recipere debent, et de civitatibus, que in hiis districtibus locate sunt. Et si sententiam ignoraverint aut defectum in ea habuerint, hanc oportet querere in Maydemburg. Idcirco[(d)], quia Maydemburg omne municipale ius protegit, quod iure terrestri fieri non potest, qui cum sententia reprobata de marchia ad comitatum trahi potest, quia marchia secundum suum arbitrium aut propriam gratiam iudicat, quod comes non facit, sed iudicat sub banno regio. Hoc idem fit in omnibus civitatibus, ubi bannum est regium, quod vir demeretur tria talenta iudici feodato sub banno regio. Si autem iudicatur sub banno regio, tunc sculteto demerentur octo solidi de iudicio cum sententiis scabinorum. Idem fit burgravio. Scabini undecim esse debent et scultetus sit duodecimus, quia burgravio primam sententiam diffinire debet. Quia burgravius nullum bannitum iudicium absque sculteto potest habere, nec scultetus absque hiis undecim scabinis in vero loco iudiciali.

[(a)] De appellacione in Hallis post eandem in Maydemburk JL[17] art. 10 [*Mikołaj Jaskier, Iuris Municipalis..., art. x, fol. xi*[r]] JL[33] [(b)] Hallis civitas JL[38] [(c)] Hoc ante recipiebatur [*?*], non nunc JL[17] [(d)] *org.* iccirco

hand, upon which [act] Saint Peter's peace was confirmed for them. This tradition has persisted to this day, where new cities or markets are established, with a cross placed above the market square, demonstrating and proving that it was done by the will of the king. Thus, this municipal law endures from ancient times until now, and receives its name, as confirmed by the empire, until the present day.

[*124*] On the foundation of Magdeburg and Halle. And that in doubtful sentences, recourse is made to those cities from certain provinces.

Now, consider the city of Magdeburg. Specifically, when Magdeburg was first established, or founded, on the counsel of Emperor Otto the Great, with the agreement of the land, and was established in its law, just as it now holds itself in its municipal law, according to the custom of the oldest. Similarly, the city of Halle was founded under the same principles, thus both cities are governed by the same law. For this reason, all from Poland and Bohemia who have been settled under German law, as well as those from the Marches, the Meissen province[1], the Lusatian March[2], all these shall receive their law in Halle, and from the cities founded in these districts. And if they do not know [the meaning of] a sentence, or if they discern a flaw in it, in that event they should inquire in Magdeburg. This is because Magdeburg shields all municipal law—[an effect] that cannot be achieved on the basis of the land law, where, after a sentence rejected by the [court of the] march [the case] may not be brought to the [court of the] county—because the march adjudicates according to its decision or its own grace, which the count does not do, but adjudicates under the royal ban. The same applies in all cities where there is the royal ban, so that a man owes the feudal judge three talents under the royal ban. If a judgment is rendered under the royal ban, then, with the sentence of the jurors, the *scultetus* is entitled to eight shillings. The same is done for the burgrave. There should be eleven jurors, and the *scultetus* should be the twelfth, as he should deliver the first sentence to the burgrave. Indeed, the burgrave may not hold any formally convened court without the *scultetus*, nor the *scultetus* without these eleven jurors in the proper judicial venue.

1 The March of Meissen (Ger. *Mark Meißen*, Upper Lusatia) was established by Emperor Otto I in 965 after the death of Gero, Margrave of the Eastern March. Its capital city was Meissen, also the seat of a bishop.

2 The March of Lusatia (Ger. *Mark Lausitz*, Lower Lusatia), was created as a result of the division of the Eastern March in 965, encompassing its northern part.

[*125*] De ortilegiis civitatis Hallis in Maydemburg querendis.

(a) Nunc attendatis de Hallis, ubi ius suum querere debent, si ipsum ignorant, aut si ipsis sententia fuerit reprobata. Hanc in Maydenburg querere debent et Maydemburgenses ipsis dare debent ante quattuor scamna et scabinis ipsorum ius dari debet, quia in posterum ipsos oportet esse testes, si necesse fuerit, quod sententia rite ac rationabiliter sit data absque qualibet contradictione. Et ibi nuncii presentes esse debent, ubi sententia diffinitur, ex utraque parte, ubi sententia fuit reprobata, qui audierunt et viderunt, quod utrique iustitia fiat. (b) Et iudex ipsis in expensis debet procurare
CXCVI[r] exeundo et redeundo. Si sententia sub banno regio fuerit reprobata, | tunc debet reportari infra decem et octo hebdomadas. Si autem sub comitibus vel sub comitis banno reprobata fuerit, tunc reportari debet infra duas hebdomadas; quia scultetus habet bannum a comite et sculteciam a domino terre. Idem vero habet burgravius bannum a rege et iudicium a domino.

[*126*] De inquisitione ortilegii et sententie civium Maydemburgensium.

(c) Nunc attendendum est, si in Maydemburg reprobaretur sententia, quo aut ubi eam querere aut invenire deberent. (d) Ipsi se debent trahere in Schartaviam ultra Elbe et ibi recipiunt quattuor seniores viros, quos poterint invenire ibi. Et hoc idcirco(e), quia diutius stetit quam Maydemburg et cesar Otto a tempore diuturno ex eo constituit ducatum, et omnes uno et eodem iure sunt constricti. Tunc se trahunt cum eisdem quattuor

(a) Hallis cives in Maydeburg apellant et ius queruntur JL[17] art. 11 [*Mikołaj Jaskier, Iuris Municipalis..., art. XI, fol. XII[v]*] JL[33] (b) Vide expensa in iure JL[38] (c) art. 12 [*Mikołaj Jaskier, Iuris Municipalis..., art. XII, fol. XII[v]*] JL[33] (d) De pallacia in Scharthania ultra Elbe, ubi Maydeburk appellare p[otest] JL[17] (e) *org.* iccirco

[*125*] On the instructions sought by the city of Halle in Magdeburg.

Now, pay attention to Halle, where they should inquire [about] their law if they do not know it, or if their sentence is contested. About that, they should inquire in Magdeburg, and the citizens of Magdeburg should give [the answer] before the bench, and their jurors should be given the law, as they are to serve as witnesses in the future, if necessary, so that the sentence is delivered justly and reasonably without any opposition. Representatives from both sides, where the sentence was delivered and where the sentence was rejected, should be present, having heard and seen that justice was done to both [parties]. The judge shall cover their travel expenses to and from there. If a sentence is rejected under the royal ban, it must be reported within eighteen weeks. However, if it is rejected under the counts, or under the ban of a count[1], then it should be reported within a fortnight, because the *scultetus* has the ban from the count, and [his] *scultetia*[2] from the lord of the land. Similarly, the burgrave has the ban from the king, and the court from the lord.

[*126*] On the inquiry the instruction and sentence by the citizens of Magdeburg.

Now, it is to be noted: If a sentence is contested in Magdeburg, from whom or where they should seek or find it [i.e., the correct sentence]. They should go to Schartau[3] beyond the Elbe and there recruit four old men whom they are able to find there. This is because [Schartau] has existed longer than Magdeburg, and Emperor Otto[4] long ago established a duchy for this reason, and all are bound by one and the same law. Then they shall go with

---

1 *Comitatus* in the sense of a count's jurisdiction. Cf. Paweł Szczerbic, *Ius Municipale, to jest prawo miejskie majdeburskie nowo z łacińskiego i z niemieckiego na polski język z pilnością i wiernie przełożone* [Ius Municipale, or the Magdeburg Municipal Law: A New and Meticulously Accurate Translation from the Latin and the German], ed. Grzegorz M. Kowalski, (Bibliotheca Iagellonica. Fontes et Studia) 20 (Kraków, 2011), p. 70, footnote 129.

2 *Scultetia*, the property and the rights of the *scultetus*.

3 Schartau—appearing in the "Treaty on the Constitution of Magdeburg" and subsequently in the Magdeburg *Weichbild*, the name of the Saxon duchy encompassing the area around Magdeburg.

4 Otto I the Great, King of Germany 936–973, Emperor of the Holy Roman Empire 962–973.

senioribus, quos de Schartavia afferebant et redeunt Meydemburg ante pallatiam[a] ad curiam, que imperatoris Ruffi Ottonis fuerat, qui pallatiam[b] ipsis formaverat in fine summi templi, ut in premissis patet et in sequentibus patebit, quia continue pro una sententia reprobata ad imperium se trahere non potuerunt.

[*127*] De pallatia, per quem modum ab imperatore Ottone in Schartavia fuerit constituta.

[c] Nunc attendatis de pallatia, per quem modum ipse pallatiam fecerit. Vocavit eosdem quattuor seniores de Schartavia et quattuor canonicos, qui habuerunt prelaturas in summo: primus prepositus, secundus decanus, [d] tertius episcopi vicarius, quartus cancellarius. Insuper recepit quattuor barones et innatos ministeriales ecclesie maioris feodalis et Maydembur-
CXCVIv gensis: primus fuit marschalcus, secundus da|pifer, tertius pincerna, quartus camerarius. Insuper recepit undecim scabinos de civitate et scultetum duodecimum. Item recepit tres duces laicos, qui primi sunt in electione imperiali, et quartus, quem accepit, supremus fuit advocatus ecclesie maioris in Maydemburg, hoc est burgravius. [e] Tunc imperator accepit eosdem viginti et octo viros prenotatos et super sedes ipsos locavit pallatie, et dedit eis potestatem ex parte sui, quecunque sententia in Maydemburg diffiniri non posset, aut reprobaretur, hec ibi deberet recipi [f], et quicquid ibi daretur, [g] hoc rite ac rationabiliter pro iure municipali teneri debet.

[*128*] De precio dando in iudicio pallatie pro sententia diffinitiva.

[h] Et cum sententia ante pallatiam data fuerit, tunc debet dari in signum his viginti octo viris cuilibet unum solidum aureum, et quivis solidus debet valere duodecim solidos talis pecunie aut talium denariorum, cum quibus ibidem tali consuetudo fuerit forisare. Tunc hiis quattuor dantur IIII marce auree, et quivis marca[i] aurea duodecim marcas argenteas debet valere. Hoc datur hiis viginti octo viris. Hoc illi dare tenentur, quibus sententia ad

---

[a] *org.* pallatium [b] *org.* pallatium [c] art. 13 [*Mikołaj Jaskier, Iuris Municipalis..., art. XIII, fol. XIIv*] JL[33] [d] Ordo officialium JL[38] [e] Nota bene JL[17] [f] et decidi diffinite JL[17] [g] inveniuntur, *manus B* JL[17] [h] art. 13 [*Mikołaj Jaskier, Iuris Municipalis..., art. XIII, fol. XIIv*] JL[33] [i] *org.* merca

these four elders, who originate from Schartau, and return to Magdeburg before the *pallatia*[1] to the palace of Emperor Otto the Red; he placed the *pallatia* at the end of the highest church, as is apparent from the above, and will be apparent from the following, because they cannot continuously turn to royal power regarding a single contested sentence.

[*127*] On the *pallatia*, how it was established by emperor Otto [the Red] in Schartau.

Now consider about the *pallatia*, how he established the *pallatia*. He summoned the same four elders from Schartau and four canons who held the highest prelatures: first, the provost; second, the dean; third, the bishop's vicar; fourth, the chancellor. Moreover, he added four barons and ministerials[2] by birth of the greater feudal church of Magdeburg: the first was the marshal, the second the steward, the third the butler, the fourth the chamberlain. Furthermore, he added eleven jurors from the city, and the *scultetus* as the twelfth. Similarly, he added three secular princes who are foremost in imperial elections, and the fourth, whom he added, was the highest advocate[3] of the greater church in Magdeburg, namely the burgrave. Then the emperor received those twenty eight men and seated them in the *pallatia*, and gave them his power, so that if any sentence could not be delivered in Magdeburg, or was contested, it should be received there, and whatever [sentence] is issued there, should be duly and wisely observed as municipal law.

[*128*] On the payment due in the court of the *pallatia* for a definitive sentence.

And when the sentence is delivered before the *pallatia*, then as a sign, to those twenty eight men, one gold shilling should be given to each, and each shilling shall be worth twelve shillings of such money or such *denarii* as are customarily used there. Then, to those four, four gold marks shall be given, and each gold mark shall be worth twelve silver marks. This shall be given to those twenty eight men. Those to whom the sentence was devised

1 *Pallatia* (Ger. *Pfallencze*) in the sense of a judiciary body.

2 Cf. *The Saxon Mirror: A "Sachsenspiegel"*, p. 193.

3 Cf. Art. 52 footnote 2.

profectum vel utilitatem fuerit inventa vel diffinita. (a) Sed iste, qui in sententia diffinitiva defecerit, solvere debet expensas. Si autem ille in sententia defecerit, qui eam reprobaverat, extunc solvere tenetur plusquam ille, cui sententia data fuerit ad profectum.

[*129*] De eo quem plus dare oportet pro reprobatione sententie.

(b) Nunc attendatur, quem plus dare oportet. Ipse dare tenetur illi scabino emendam suam, cuius sententiam reprobavit, quam invenit, si iuste fuerit diffinita, et iudici suam penam. Si autem ante consensum aliorum scabinorum fuerit reprobata sententia, tunc cuilibet scabino datur emenda et iudici totiens sua pena. Si autem ipsa in Hallis fuerit reprobata et in Maydenburg invenitur, et pariter ibidem reprobabitur, extunc ambo(c) dabuntur emende et pene in Maydenburg et(d) Hallis. Hoc fecit Ruffus rex Otto taliter pro eo, quod municipale ius sisteret, sicut ab antiquo tempore hucusque stetit, et ibidem fecit ducatum trans Albiam.

[*130*] De pallatia, quomodo convenire debet.

(e) Nunc dicere vobis volo de pallatia, quomodo quando illa debeat convenire, et diffinire volo pro rebus istis, ut in precedentibus est predictum.

CXCVIIr

[*131*] | De cit[t]atione pallatie, quomodo fieri debeat.

(f) Scultetus de Maydemburg debet recipere litteram civitatis cum sigillo ipsius pendente. Hanc litteram debet mittere supremo advocato maioris ecclesie, hoc est burgravio in Maydenburg, ad quem suam propriam litteram sigillatam debet recipere, eapropter quod ipse est advocatus. (g) Et adhuc debet recipere litteram episcopi cum suo sigillo, et etiam adhuc debet recipere litteram regis, et suum sigillum appendens, si ipsum habere possit in Theutonico [*s*]. Has quinque litteras debet recipere burgravius de Maydenburg. Et eas primo mittere debet duci Saxonie cum iis, qui se

---

(a) Qui defecit in sententia difinitiva debet solvere expensas JL38 (b) art. 13 [*Mikołaj Jaskier, Iuris Municipalis..., art. XIII, fol. XIIv*] JL33 Intelligendum [est] de appellatione retractata JL38 (c) *org.* ambe (d) *org.* ex (e) art. 14 [*Mikołaj Jaskier, Iuris Municipalis..., art. XIIII, fol. XIIIv*] JL33 (f) art. 14 [*Mikołaj Jaskier, Iuris Municipalis..., art. XIIII, fol. XIIIv*] JL33 (g) Modus eligendi regis novi JL38

or issued in favor or for their use shall provide this. However, the one who loses in the definitive sentence, should pay the expenses. But if the one who had contested [a sentence] loses in the definitive sentence, in that case he is obliged to pay more than the one to whom the sentence was delivered in favour.

[*129*] On who should give more for a contestation of a sentence.

Now, let it be noted who should be given more. The one who had contested a sentence is obliged to give, to that juror whose sentence he contested—which was determined justly—his compensation; and to the judge his fine. If, however, the sentence is contested prior to [the expression of] consent by the other jurors, then compensation is to be given to each juror, and to the judge his fine, that same number of times. If it [i.e., the sentence] is contested in Halle, and [subsequently] noted in Magdeburg, and likewise contested there, at that point both shall pay compensation and fine in both Magdeburg and Halle. King Otto the Red has established this in this way, in order for municipal law to be upheld, as it has been upheld from ancient times until now, and there he established the duchy beyond the Elbe.

[*130*] On the *pallatia*, how it should be convened.

Now I want to tell you about the *pallatia*, how and when it should be convened, and I want to settle these matters, as previously mentioned.

[*131*] The summons to the *pallatia* should be conducted as follows.

The *scultetus* of Magdeburg should receive a document from the city with its seal attached. He should forward the document to the highest advocate of the greater church, that is, the burgrave of Magdeburg, to which he should attach his own sealed document, for the reason that he is the advocate. Additionally, he should receive a document from the bishop with his seal, and he should also obtain a document from the king, with his seal attached, if he is able to have him in German [*s*]. These five documents should be received by the burgrave of Magdeburg. Firstly, he should send [them] to the Duke of Saxony, along with those who contested the

cum sententia traxerunt, et cum scitu horum XXVIII virorum, qui prius sunt (anominati. Posta) hoc mittere debet margravio de Brandenburg. Tertio ipse mittere debet palatino Renensi. Hii tres primi duces laici sunt in electione imperiali, cum novus rex eligitur Theutonica de terra.

[*132*] De hiis, qui cittati non comparent coram pallatia, quid demerentur.

(b) Hic intelligere et audire potestis, quomodo hii omnes domini debent cittari, qui in premissis sunt nominati. Ipsi ad pallatiam ire debent et scultetus burgravium cittare debet primo, secundo, tertio, semper ad sex hebdomadas. Et si in tertia non comparuerit cittatione, extunc tres laici duces mittunt. (c) Tunc regi de qualibet cittatione tres marcas aureas demeretur, quarum quelibet marca aurea XII marcas argenteas debet valere. Et si post has ultra sex septimanas non comparuerit, se coram rege excusare, ubi ipse fuerit. Extunc omnia sententialiter ecclesie maiori vacabunt, que ab eo habebat, et regi bannum vacabat, et post hoc proscribunt eum in regis illegalitatem.

[*133*] De tribus ducibus Imperii Romani electoribus, quomodo cittari debeant ad pallatiam.

(d) Eodemmodo sicut scultetus cittat burgravium, sic burgravius cittare debet hos tres principes sub banno regio. Et si in tertia cittatione non comparuerint, ut est predictum, extunc quivis eorum de qualibet cittatione decem et octo marcas(e) aureas regi demeretur, quarum quelibet marca(f) aurea (g) XII marcas(h) argenteas debet valere. Etsi non eadem vice comparuerint iustitiam iuvare et ius recipere, attamen illi sua sententia diffinire debet et ipse suum ius dare debet ante pallatiam.

Finis primi libri. (i)

(a) *org.* nominati post (b) art. 15 [*Mikołaj Jaskier, Iuris Municipalis..., art. XV, fol. XV*[r]] JL[33]
(c) Nostra est ad primam; marcas JL[38] (d) art. 15 [*Mikołaj Jaskier, Iuris Municipalis..., art. XV, fol. XV*[r]] JL[33] (e) *org.* mercas (f) *org.* merca (g) Marcae auri JL[3] (h) *org.* mercas
(i) Mandeburg et municipale, *manus A* JL[36]

sentence, and with the knowledge of the aforementioned twenty-eight men. Next, he should send [them] to the Margrave of Brandenburg. Thirdly, he should send them to the Palatine of the Rhine. These three secular princes are foremost in the imperial elections when a new king of the German lands is chosen.

[132] On those who, when summoned, fail to appear before the *pallatia*, this is what they deserve.

Now you can understand and listen to how all those previously mentioned lords should be summoned. They shall proceed to the *pallatia*, and the *scultetus* should summon the burgrave for the first time, the second time, the third time, always within six weeks. And if he does not appear at the third summons, then the three secular princes shall send [a messenger]. For each summons, the king shall be entitled to three gold marks, each gold mark being worth twelve silver marks. And if he fails to appear after these six weeks, he must justify himself before the king as to his whereabouts. Thenceforth, in the sentence, everything shall fall to the greater church [in Magdeburg], which he had from it, and the ban shall remain with the king, and then he shall be proscribed, outlawed by the king.

[133] On the three prince electors of the Holy Roman Empire, in what manner they should be summoned to the *pallatia*.

In the same manner as the *scultetus* summons the burgrave, so the burgrave shall summon those three princes under royal ban. And if they fail to appear at the third summons, as has been said, then from each of them the king shall be entitled to eighteen gold marks for each summons, each gold mark being worth twelve silver marks. Although they may not appear simultaneously, in order to administer justice and uphold the law, nonetheless [the burgrave] should deliver his sentence to him [the party] and [the burgrave] should grant his right before the *pallatia*.

End of Book One.

Bibliography

Sources

Archival sources

Cracow

Jagiellonian Library in Cracow, Shelfmarks 168, 169, 170a, 4405

Częstochowa

Library and Archives of the Pauline Monastery in Częstochowa, Shelfmark AJG II-3

Gniezno

Archdiocesan Archives of Gniezno, Shelfmark 104

Kielce

Library of the Diocesan Seminary in Kielce, Shelfmark RK 45/28

Kórnik

Kórnik Library of the Polish Academy of Sciences, Shelfmarks 800, 801

Leipzig

University Library in Leipzig "Albertina", Shelfmark 951b

Sankt-Florian Monastery

Sankt-Florian Monastery Library in Austria, Shelfmark 551/II

St. Petersburg

Library of the Russian Academy of Sciences in St. Petersburg, Shelfmark F 143

National Library of Russia in St. Petersburg, Shelfmark Lat. Q II 157

Przemyśl

State Archive in Przemyśl, Archives of the City of Przemyśl, Shelfmark 428

Warsaw

National Library in Warsaw, Shelfmarks 3068 III, 12600 III, 12607 III, BOZ 90

University of Warsaw Library, Shelfmark 5

Wrocław

Ossoliński National Institute, Shelfmark 832/I

Wrocław University Library, Shelfmarks II F 8, II Q 4

Commune incliti Poloniae Regni privilegium constitutionum et indultuum publicitus decretorum approbatorumque …, [ed. Jan Łaski] (Cracoviae, MDVI):

Berlin

Staatsbibliothek zu Berlin, Shelfmark 4" Ho 15050

Bonn

Universitäts- und Landesbibliothek Bonn, Shelfmark Sav 4' 152

Bydgoszcz

Kazimierz Wielki University Library in Bydgoszcz, Shelfmark S 104

Cieszyn

Książnica Cieszyńska in Cieszyn, Shelfmark CL 1212 III

Cracow

Czartoryski Library in Cracow (branch of the National Museum in Cracow), Shelfmarks Cim. 13 III, Cim. 30 III, Cim. 1239 III

Emeryk Hutten-Czapski Museum (branch of the National Museum in Cracow), Shelfmarks MNK VIII-XVI.134, MNK VIII-XVI.190, MNK VIII-XVI.1308, 4022

Jagiellonian Library in Cracow, Shelfmarks St. Dr. Cim. 8002–8003, 8004–8005, 8006–8007, 8008–8009, 8470, 51

Scientific Library of the Polish Academy of Art and Science and the Polish Academy of Science in Cracow, Shelfmark St.Dr. 4017 (= 4483W VIIII.-1), 4022

Gdańsk

Gdańsk Library Polish Academy of Science, Shelfmarks In 20146 4°, Uph. F. 1393

Gniezno

Archdiocesan Archives of Gniezno, Shelfmarks PL 346, PL 388, PL 398

Kalisz

Adam Asnyk City Public Library in Kalisz, Shelfmark ST 000020 zb. spec.

Katowice

Silesian Library in Katowice, Shelfmark ZS III 224111

Kaunas

Central Library of the Kaunas University of Technology, Shelfmark KTUB Es 72

Kielce

Witold Gombrowicz Provincial Public Library in Kielce, Shelfmark Pol. 1522

Kórnik

Kórnik Library of the Polish Academy of Sciences, Shelfmarks Cim.F.4117, Cim.F.4118, Cim.F.4119, Cim.F.4139, Cim.F.4240

London

British Museum, Shelfmark C.107.g.14

Lublin

Hieronim Łopaciński Provincial Public Library in Lublin, Shelmarks P-16-f-26, P-16-f-61

The John Paul II Catholic University of Lublin, University Library, Shelfmarks XVI. 1738, XVI.1760, XVI.1741, XVI.1820, XVI.1874

Łódź

Library of University of Łódź, Shelfmark 1022575

New Haven

Yale University, Beinecke Rare Book and Manuscript Library, Shelfmark P4-5 R9 +506

Newtown

Harvard Library Hollis Houghton Library, Shelmark f type 556.06.706

Nieborów

Nieborów and Arcadia Musem (branch of the National Museum in Warsaw), Shelfmark I/62

Olomouc

Olomouc Research Library, Shelfmark II 7.937

Olsztyn

University Library University of Warmia and Mazury in Olsztyn, Shelfmarks SD BGST.30, ZZ102516

Paris

Polish Library, Sehlfmark FA 38439 III

Płock

Płock Scientific Society, Shelfmarks XVI.184, XVI.185

Poznań

Adam Mickiewicz University Library in Poznań, Shelfmarks SD 188 III, SD 372 III, SD 1994 III, SD 9017 III

Poznań Society for the Advancement of Arts and Sciences, Shelfmarks 11495 III, 14989 III

Raczyńscy Library in Poznań, Shelfmarks 194.III, 246.III, III.J.a.6, IV.G.a.8

Praha

National Library of the Czech Republic, Shelfmark P 009015

Riga

National Library of Latvia in Riga, Shelfmark Rare books RW3S/179

Szczecin

Książnica Pomorska in Szczecin, Shelfmark ST7511 (XVI.491.II)

Tarnów

Juliusz Słowacki Public Library in Tarnów, Shelfmark SD 173

Toronto

Toronto Thomas Fisher Rare Book Library Rare Book Collection, Shelfmark hutt f 00004

Toruń

Książnica Kopernikańska in Toruń, Shelfmark Gzw 101788

Nicolaus Copernicus University Library in Toruń, Shelfmark Pol. 6.III.106

Uppsala

Uppsala University Library, Shelfmark Sv. Rar. fol. 10:31

Vatican

Vatican Apostolic Library, Shelfmark Barberini FF.IV.8

Vilnius

Martyno Mažvydo National Library of Lithuania, Shelfmark Clot.1/506/155672

Vilnius University Library, Shelfmarks BAV.I.12b, II-2223-224

Warsaw

The Central Archives of Historical Records in Warsaw, Shelfmarks dok. perg. no. 5632, SD.III.50

Library of the Higher Metropolitan Seminary of the Archdiocese of Warsaw, Shelfmark D.17.D15.(50935)

Library of the Royal Castle in Warsaw, Shelfmark 43

National Library in Warsaw, Shelfmarks SD XVI.F.9, SD XVI.F.57, SD.XVI.F.88, SD.XVI.F.211, SD.XVI.F.335, SD XVI.F.337, SD.XVI.F.350, SD.XVI.F.432, SD.XVI.F.735

National Museum in Warsaw, Shelfmark SD 348

University of Warsaw Library, Shelfmarks Sd.612.523, Sd.612.540, Sd.612.545, Sd.612.553

Warsaw Public Library, Shelfmark XVI. F. 74

Wrocław

Ossoliński National Institute in Wrocław, Shelfmarks XVI.F.4088, XVI.F.4089, XVI.F.4092, XVI.F.4320, XVI.F.4654

Wrocław University Library, Shelfmark St. Dr. 401097

Zielona Góra

Provincial and Municipal Public Library in Zielona Góra, Shelfmark S III 260

Jaskier Mikołaj *Jaskier, Iuris Municipalis Maideburgensis Liber vulgo Weichbild nuncupatur...* (Cracoviae MDXXXV)

Printed sources

[Eike von Repkow], *Sachsenspiegel. Landrecht*, ed. Karl August Eckhart, 2. Bearb. (Göttingen, 1955) [Monumenta Germaniae Historica—Leges, Nova series, 1,1].

Maisel Witold, "Prawo magdeburskie miasta Pleszewa" [Magdeburg Law of the City of Pleszew], *Studia i Materiały do Dziejów Wielkopolski i Pomorza* 9/1 (1963), pp. 67–82.

Polskie statuty ziemskie w redakcji najstarszych druków (Syntagmata) [Polish land statutes in the redaction of the oldest printed copies (Syntagmata)], eds. Ludwik Łysiak, Stanisław Roman (Wrocław, 1958) [Starodawne Prawa Polskiego Pomniki, seria II, Pomniki Prawa Polskiego, dział I: Prawo ziemskie, t. 2].

Statuty Kazimierza Wielkiego. [Cz. 1] [Statutes of Casimir the Great. [Part 1]], ed. Oswald Balzer, from a posthumous manuscript published by Zdzisław Kaczmarczyk, Michał Sczaniecki, Stefan Weyman (Poznań: Poznańskie Towarzystwo Przyjaciół Nauk, 1947).

Statuty Kazimierza Wielkiego. Cz. 2, *Statuty wielkopolskie* [Statutes of Casimir the Great. Part 2, Statutes of Wielkopolska], ed. Ludwik Łysiak (Poznańskie Towarzystwo Przyjaciół Nauk, Warszawa: PWN, 1982).

The Saxon Mirror: A "Sachsenspiegel" of the Fourteenth Century, translated by Maria Dobozy (University of Pennsylvania Press, 1999) [The Middle Ages Series].

Die Summa legum brevis et utilis des sogenannten Doctor Raymundus von Wiener Neustadt, ed. Alexander Gál (Weimar, 1926).

Szczerbic Paweł, *Ius Municipale, to jest prawo miejskie majdeburskie nowo z łacińskiego i z niemieckiego na polski język z pilnością i wiernie przełożone* [Ius Municipale, or the Magdeburg Municipal Law: A New and Meticulously Accurate Translation from the Latin and the German], ed. Grzegorz M. Kowalski (Kraków, 2011) [Bibliotheca Iagellonica. Fontes et Studia, 20].

Monographs and articles

Carls Wieland, "Rechtsquellen Sächsisch- magdeburgischen Rechts im Untersuchungsgebiet", in: Wieland Carls, Inge Bily, Marija Lazar, and Katalin Gönczi, *Sächsisch-magdeburgisches Recht in Tschechien und in der Slowakei. Untersuchungen zur Geschichte des Rechts und seiner Sprache* (Berlin, 2021), pp. 99–126 [Ivs Saxonico-Maidebvrgense in Oriente, 5].

Carls Wieland, "Rechtsquellen Sächsisch-magdeburgischen Rechts", in: Inge Bily, Wieland Carls, and Katalin Gönczi, *Sächsisch-magdeburgisches Recht in Polen. Untersuchungen zur Geschichte des Rechts und seiner Sprache* (Berlin, 2011), pp. 69–109 [Ivs Saxonico-Maidebvrgense in Oriente, 2].

Cytowska Maria, *Bibliografia druków urzędowych XVI wieku* [Bibliography of 16th Century Legal and Government Documents] (Wrocław, 1961).

Estreicher Stanisław, "Freimarkt' i Frymark", *Czasopismo Prawnicze i Ekonomiczne* 25 (1929), pp. 337–355.

Gönczi Katalin, "Städte des Magdeburger Rechts in Osteuropa", in: *Städtische Räume im Mittelalter*, eds. Susanne Ehrich and Jörg Oberste (Regensburg, 2009), pp. 181–193.

Graś Wojciech, "Rozważania nad problemem nakładu Statutu Jana Łaskiego" [Some considerations on the question of the volume of copies of the Statute by Jan Łaski], *BIBLIOTEKA* 26/35 (2022), pp. 122–133.

Haubrichs Wolfgang, "Wergeld: The Germanic Terminology of Compositio and Its Implementation in the Early Middle Ages", in: *Wergild, Compensation and Penance*, eds. Lukas Bothe, Stefan Esders, Han Nijdam, (Leiden, 2021), pp. 92–112 [Series: Medieval Law and Its Practice, vol: 31]

Heiner Lück, "Sachsenspiegel und Magdeburger Recht. Grundlagen für Europa", *Denkströme. Journal der Sächsischen Akademie der Wissenschaften zu Leipzig* 4 (2010), pp. 81–104 (http://www.denkstroeme.de/heft-4/s_81-104_lueck, accessed April 28, 2023).

"Jan Chrzciciel Machatar z Vyškov" (Id: 2016602), in: Corpus Academicum Cracoviense (CAC), URL: http://cac.historia.uj.edu.pl/osoba/2016602_Jan_Chrzciciel_Machatar_z_Vy%C5%A1kov (19.04.2024).

Janicka Danuta "Wkład polskich historyków prawa w badania nad prawem magdeburskim w XX w. (1945–2010)" [The contribution of Polish law historians to the study of Magdeburg Law in the 20th century (1945–2010], *Studia Iuridica Toruniensia* 10 (2013), pp. 46–75.

Janicka Danuta, "Neuere Rechtsgeschichte in Polen in den Jahren 2002–2014", *Zeitschrift für Neuere Rechtsgeschichte* 37 (2015), pp. 130–142.

Kannowski Bernd, "Mikuła, Maciej, Municipal Magdeburg Law (Ius municipale Magdeburgense) in Late Medieval Poland. A Study on the Evolution and Adaptation of Law (=Medieval Law and Its Practice 30). Brill, Leiden 2021. XX, 472 S., ISBN 978-90-04-45619-8", *Zeitschrift der Savigny Stiftung für Rechtsgeschichte: Germanistische Abteilung* 142/1 (2024), pp. 447–452.

Koprukowniak Albin, *Biblioteka Włodzimierza księcia Światopełka-Czetwertyńskiego w Milanowie* [Library of Vladimir Prince Światopełk-Czetwertyński in Milanów], in: Drogą historii. Studia ofiarowane prof. Józefowi Szymańskiemu w 70. rocznicę urodzin, eds. Piotr Dymmel, Krzysztof Skupieński, Beata Trelińska (Lublin, 2001).

Kutrzeba Stanisław, *Historia źródeł dawnego prawa polskiego* [History of the Sources of Old Polish Law], 2 (Lwów–Warszawa–Kraków, [1926]).

Lück Heiner, "Das sächsich-magdeburgische Recht als kulturelles Bindeglied zwischen den Rechtsordnungen Ost- und Mitteleuropa", in: *Rechts- und Sprachtransfer in Mittel- und Osteuropa. Sachsenspiegel und Magdeburger Recht. Internationale und interdisziplinäre Konferenz in Leipzig vom 31. Oktober bis 2. November 2003*, eds. Ernst Eichler, Heiner Lück, and Wieland Carls (Berlin, 2008) [Ivs Saxonico-Maidebvrgense in Oriente, 1].

Lück Heiner, "Die Verbreitung des Sachsenspiegels und des Magdeburger Rechts in Osteuropa", in: *Der sassen speyghel. Sachsenspiegel—Recht—Alltag*, Vol. 2: *Aus dem Leben gegriffen—ein Rechtsbuch spiegelt seine Zeit. Beiträge u. Katalog zur Ausstellung 'Aus dem Leben gegriffen—ein Rechtsbuch spiegelt seine Zeit'*, ed. Mamoun Fansa, 2nd ed. (Oldenburg, 1996), pp. 37–49 [Archäologische Mitteilungen aus Nordwestdeutschland, 10].

Lück Heiner, "Prawo magdeburskie jako czynnik identyfikacji europejskiej rodziny miast" [Magdeburg Law as a Factor in the Identification of a European Family of Cities,] in: *Europejskie miasta prawa magdeburskiego: tradycja, dziedzictwo, identyfikacja. Sesja komparatystyczna Kraków, 13–15 października 2006. Materiały konferencyjne*, eds. Anna Biedrzycka and Agnieszka Kutylak-Hapanowicz (Kraków, 2007).

Lück Heiner, *Sachsenspiegel und Magdeburger Recht. Europäische Dimensionen zweier mitteldeutscher Rechtsquellen* (Hamburg, 1998) [Adiuvat in itinere, 5].

Malicki Marian, Zwinogrodzka Ewa, eds., Malicki Marian, Gołuszka Małgorzata, Ptak-Korbiel Wanda, Wawrykiewicz Zofia, Zwinogrodzka Ewa, coop., *Katalog poloników XVI wieku Biblioteki Jagiellońskiej* [Catalogue of Polonica from 16th Century in Jagiellonian Library], 1: A–Ł (Kraków, 1992).

Mikuła Maciej, "Das Magdeburger Weichbildrecht in seiner schlesisch-kleinpolnischen

Fassung. Anmerkungen zur Autorschaft und Textevolution", in: *Kulturelle Vernetzung in Europa. Das Magdeburger Recht und seine Städte. Wissenschaftlicher Begleitband zur Ausstellung 'Faszination Stadt'*, eds. Gabriele Köster, Christina Link, Heiner Lück (Sandstein Kommunikation, 2018), pp. 147–165.

Mikuła Maciej, "Das sächsisch-magdeburgische Recht in den Manuskripten der Bibliothek des Priestseminars in Kielce, Signatur RK 45/28—Ergänzung zu Deutsche Rechtsbücher des Mittelalters", *Zeitschrift der Savigny-Stiftung für Rechtsgeschichte: Germanistische Abteilung* 137/1 (2020), pp. 505–510.

Mikuła Maciej, *Municipal Magdeburg Law (Ius municipale Magdeburgense) in Late Medieval Poland. A Study on the Evolution and Adaptation of Law* (Leiden-Boston: BRILL, 2021) [Series: Medieval Law and Its Practice, vol: 30].

Modzelewski Karol, *Barbarian Europe* (Frankfurt am Main-Bern-Bruxelles-New York-Oxford-Warszawa-Wien: Peter Lang, 2015).

Polonia Typographica Saeculi Sedecimi, z. IV: *Jan Haller Kraków 1505–1525*, introduction, list of printed copies, ed. Helena Kapełuś, ed. by Alodia Kawecka-Gryczowa (Wrocław–Warszawa–Kraków, 1962).

Potkowski Edward, *Książka rękopiśmienna w kulturze Polski średniowiecznej* [The Handwritten Book in the Culture of Medieval Poland] (Warszawa, 1984).

Rymaszewski Zygfryd, *Łacińskie teksty Landrechtu Zwierciadła Saskiego w Polsce. Versio Vratislaviensis, versio Sandomiriensis, Łask*i [Latin Texts of the Landrecht of the Sachsenspiegel in Poland: Versio Vratislaviensis, versio Sandomiriensis, Łaski] (Łódź, 1975).

Rymaszewski Zygfryd, *Łacińskie teksty Landrechtu Zwierciadła Saskiego w Polsce. Jaskier—tekst główny i noty marginesowe* [Latin texts of the Sachsenspiegel Landrecht in Poland: Jaskier—the main text and the marginal glosses] (Łódź, 1985).

Sowina Urszula, "Trousseau according to the *Ius municipale Magdeburgense* by Paweł Szczerbic and the position of a woman in the craftsman family at the beginning of the early modern time", *Kwartalnik Historii Kultury Materialnej* 68/4 (2020), p. 493–506.

Spufford Peter, *Money and Its Use in Medieval Europe* (Cambridge U.P., 1988).

Tafiłowski Piotr, *Jan Łaski (1456–1531) kanclerz koronny i prymas polski* [Jan Łaski (1456–1531): Grand Chancellor of Poland and Primate of Poland] (Warszawa, 2007).

Uruszczak Wacław, "'Commune incliti Poloniae Regni privilegium constitutionum et indultuum': O tytule i mocy prawnej Statutu Łaskiego z 1506 roku" ['Commune incliti Poloniae Regni privilegium constitutionum et indultuum': The title and legal validity of Łaski's Statutes (1506)], in: *Prace poświęcone pamięci Adama Uruszczaka*, eds. Jan Halberda, Michał Hosowicz, and Anna. Karabowicz (Zakamycze, 2006) [Prace Instytutu Prawa Własności Intelektualnej UJ, 96].

Wolff Adam, "Projekt instrukcji wydawniczej dla pisanych źródeł historycznych do połowy XVI wieku" [Draft Publishing Instructions for Written Historical Sources up to the Middle of the 16th Century], *Studia Źródłoznawcze* 1 (1957), pp. 155–181.

Index of Persons and Geographical Names

Italics – authors; capitals – places; regular font – historical persons. Abbreviation bibl. – biblical.

Index of Cited Works

Index of Polish Phrases

Index of German Phrases

Index of Subjects (Latin)

Items in the index are generally given in classic Latin. In brackets are significant spelling deviations (apart from those typical of medieval Latin, such as c/t and ae/e), or other indexed forms of the given word. Explanations of meaning are given in square brackets, for example: collum [poena], liber [book], liber [child].

Index of Subjects (English)

www.ingramcontent.com/pod-product-compliance
Lightning Source LLC
Chambersburg PA
CBHW071335230926
51849CB00002B/406
* 9 7 8 9 0 0 4 7 3 0 1 2 0 *